FROM **TOUSSAINT** TO **TUPAC**

FROM TOUSSAINT

TO **TUPAC**

The Black International since the Age of Revolution

EDITED BY

MICHAEL O. WEST, WILLIAM G. MARTIN,
& FANON CHE WILKINS

The University of North Carolina Press *Chapel Hill*

Marc D. Perry's essay appeared previously in different form as "Global Black Self-Fashionings: Hip Hop as Diasporic Space," Identities 15, no. 6 (December 2008) (http://www.informaworld .com), and is reprinted here with permission.

Designed by Rebecca Evans
Set in Arno Pro and Seria Sans by Rebecca Evans
Manufactured in the United States of America

The paper in this book meets the guidelines for permanence and durability of the Committee on Production Guidelines for Book Longevity of the Council on Library Resources.

The University of North Carolina Press has been a member of the Green Press Initiative since 2003.

Library of Congress Cataloging-in-Publication Data
From Toussaint to Tupac : the Black international since the age of revolution / edited by Michael O. West, William G. Martin, and Fanon Che Wilkins.—1st ed.
    p. cm.
Includes bibliographical references and index.
ISBN 978-0-8078-3309-4 (cloth : alk. paper)
ISBN 978-0-8078-5972-8 (pbk. : alk. paper)
ISBN 978-0-8078-9872-7 (ebook)
1. African diaspora. 2. Blacks—Politics and government.
3. Internationalism—History. 4. Blacks—Intellectual life.
5. Black power—History. I. West, Michael O. (Michael Oliver)
II. Martin, William G., 1952– III. Wilkins, Fanon Che.
DT16.5.F766 2009
320.54'6—dc22
2009003100

FOR **THE NEXT GENERATION OF STUDENTS OF GLOBAL AFRICA**

CONTENTS

ILLUSTRATIONS

This project has its origins in a search for something we could not find: a single volume that offers a broad overview of the black international in time and space—from the late 1700s, the Age of Revolution, to the present, and on both banks of the Atlantic, west and east, from the Americas to Africa and points in between. The envisaged text would be grounded in the most recent and relevant sources, secondary and primary, and would at once attract the attention of scholars, teachers, students, and engaged intellectuals. Furthermore, the text would cohere around the central theme of black internationalism from the outset, that is, struggle. To qualify as black internationalist, those struggles, although situated mainly in specific localities, would have to be connected in some conscious way to an overarching notion of black liberation beyond any individual nation-state or colonial territory. That is to say, at the core of black internationalism is the ideal of universal emancipation, unbounded by national, imperial, continental, or oceanic boundaries—or even by racial ones. Such are the aims of this volume. They make for an ambitious goal. Our readers will have to determine how much, or little, success we have had.

Epistemically, the volume makes no claim to novelty. Its subject, the story of the black international, is as old as the black international itself. This narrative, as told by scholars, became more intellectually sophisticated and ideologically diverse in the early decades of the twentieth century. Black internationalism fared less well in the Western (or, for that matter, the African, Caribbean, or Latin American) academy in the post–World War II era, when regional area studies emerged as an intellectual handmaiden to the Cold War. Still, a hardy band of scholars, some within the academy (often in black studies and related ethnic studies programs) and others outside, continued to produce scholarship on black internationalism during this period. The end of the Cold War, and with it a loosening of the hegemony of area studies, along with concomitant efforts to demarginalize ethnic studies, opened new prospects for scholarship on black internationalism. The resulting output, often presented under the label of African Diaspora or Black Atlantic studies, attests to the renaissance in the black international narrative. This is not the place to offer an accounting of this fine body of work. Perusal of the volume's endnotes will, however, reveal our debt to the previous literature, the old as well as the new.

What, then, is the rationale for this book? To begin, and as already noted, it tells, in a single volume, major aspects of the story of the black international, from the beginning to the present, that is, over a period spanning four different centuries (the eighteenth to the twenty-first). But that is just a beginning, albeit an important one.

The volume is organized into three parts, plus an expansive introduction that ranges far beyond a summary of the individual chapters and offers an interpretive overview of black internationalism as a whole. The first part breaks new ground, recentering the U.S. and Haitian revolutions as epochal and foundational events in the making of the black international. Especially curious here is the Haitian case. Strange as it may seem, the black internationalist dimensions of the Haitian Revolution, so self-evident to contemporaries, has been woefully neglected by scholars (with a few notable exceptions), particularly in works produced since the end of World War II, including the most recent output.

In the second part of the volume, we move forward in time more than a century, to the years following the end of World War I. By this point, the black international had expanded in space to include the African continent, an unintended consequence of the European conquests of the late nineteenth century. (Previously, only relatively small coastal areas of Africa, some of them populated by scions of returnees from the diaspora in the Americas and Europe, partook of black internationalism.) Among other things, the chapters in Part 2 highlight two well-known groups, the Garvey movement and the Communist International (the Comintern), which competed furiously to articulate and channel black grievances and aspirations on both banks of the Atlantic. Some of the material here presented is new, from both the geographical (world areas covered) and documentary (archival sources) standpoints. Additionally the two movements, Garveyism and the Comintern, are seen to interface in unusual ways, and thus new interpretive vistas are opened.

The main subject of Part 3 is Black Power, which is to say the rebirth of black internationalism in the 1960s, following the post–World War II struggles against colonialism and legalized racism on both banks of the Atlantic, the battle for decolonization and desegregation. As with many other black internationalist struggles, so also with Black Power: too often it is presented, whether implicitly or explicitly, as a singular movement, specific to this or that nation-state. The chapters in Part 3, on the contrary, show not just the wide spatial range of Black Power but also the global interlocution it set in train. This section includes, too, discussions of Black Power's transnational and transracial antecedents, and of hip hop, a movement that, at least in its origins, claims ideological descent from Black Power.

Such, we contend, are the claims and achievements of this volume. It is offered as an installment in the ongoing narrative of the black international, in the hope that it will stimulate further discussion, research, and production.

ACKNOWLEDGMENTS

As editors, our greatest debt is to our contributing authors, who have waited entirely too long for this project to come to fruition. In some small way, we hope, their patience and forbearance have been rewarded. As editors and authors, we could not have asked for more diligent and searching manuscript reviewers than those chosen by the press. Their thorough and thought-provoking reports pinpointed omissions, uncovered errors of both fact and interpretation, and forced us to rethink many of our assumptions. The reviewers, later revealed to be Lisa Brock and Komozi Woodard, helped to make this a better volume. We remain in their debt. Indeed, Professor Woodard went so far as to convene a workshop, "The Black International: The Haitian Revolution to the Black Consciousness Movement." Held at his institution, Sarah Lawrence College, the workshop was inspired by this volume. Greater solidarity hath few in the academy. We are grateful, too, to our editor, David Perry. From our first substantive encounter, at a meeting of the Southern Historical Association in Birmingham, Alabama, David posed a series of critical questions that helped to frame the volume. David's assistant, Zachary Read, has proven to be a wonderful conduit and invaluable resource in his own right. We also give thanks to Stephanie Wenzel for splendid work as project editor, to Margie Towery for indexing, to Mary Caviness for proofreading, and to Ravi Palat for moral and material support.

For their many and random acts of kindness, friendship, and solidarity, intellectual and personal, we wish to thank Ibrahim Abdullah, Mark Beittel, Merle Bowen, Joye Bowman, Horace Campbell, Jacques Depelchin, John Higginson, Savi Horne, Lashanda Ingram, David Johnson, Robin D. G. Kelley, Ricardo Laremont, Marcus Rediker, Marjorie Thomas, Nigel Westmaas, and Coltrane and Irie Zerai-Che, along with Harpur College, Binghamton University; the Graduate School of American Studies at Doshisha University; the Department of African-American Studies and the Research Program and Department of History at the University of Illinois at Urbana-Champaign; and the Black Atlantic/African Diaspora Seminar at the Rutgers Center for Historical Analysis.

FROM **TOUSSAINT** TO **TUPAC**

Queen Mother Moore (1898–1997) in an undated photograph. Queen Mother Moore was a legendary freedom fighter throughout the twentieth century, across Garveyite, communist, black nationalist, and pan-Africanist organizations. ("Queen Mother Moore" from Brian Lanker, I Dream a World: Portraits of Black Women Who Changed America [1989]; courtesy of Brian Lanker Photography)

Contours of the Black International

From Toussaint to Tupac

MICHAEL O. WEST & WILLIAM G. MARTIN

This volume is an act of recuperation. It seeks to reclaim and advance an old, but largely unheralded, story of black struggles worldwide. The subject, in brief, is black internationalism. The black international, we argue, has a single defining characteristic: struggle. Yet struggle, resistance to oppression by black folk, did not mechanically produce black internationalism. Rather, black internationalism is a product of consciousness, that is, the conscious interconnection and interlocution of black struggles across man-made and natural boundaries—including the boundaries of nations, empires, continents, oceans, and seas. From the outset, black internationalism envisioned a circle of universal emancipation, unbroken in space and time.[1] It is a vision personified, respectively, by the Haitian revolutionary Toussaint Louverture and the U.S. rap impresario Tupac Shakur, the one illustrating the struggles against slavery and the other signifying contemporary cultural insurgencies.

Our collection examines a variety of events and movements that manifest the multilayered and interconnected character of black internationalism. First, the essays show the emergence of black traditions of struggle and resistance in particular localities. Second, the contributions demonstrate how local struggles intersected with one another across diverse boundaries to form, loosely and informally, a black international that was greater than the sum total of its constituent parts. Third, the black international, in its turn, variously quickened, inspired, and stimulated local struggles. These essays chart aspects of that black internationalist resistance, from the onset of modern capitalism to the current postmodern era, in sum, since the Age of Revolution.[2]

Historical scholarship, including most of the writings on black experiences, has not been kind to black internationalism. Two dominant scholarly traditions, the metanarrative and the national narrative, have intellectually marginalized the black international. The metanarrative, despite its vaunted claim to universality, pays scant attention to most of humanity outside the white Atlantic, while the national narrative, with its singular focus on the nation-state, is largely oblivious to transnational concerns.[3] Caught between these two hegemons—the Eurocentric metanarrative and the exclusivist national narrative—the discourse of black internationalism, although never fully silenced, has been much muted.

The recuperation we attempt in this volume necessarily runs counter to the dominant master narrative, whether in the form of the metanarrative or of the national narrative. Contrary to the existing literature on social movements and revolutions,[4] we argue that black movements have been a leading force in the search for emancipation since at least the second half of the eighteenth century. In contrast to those who celebrate globalization as a new phenomenon,[5] we maintain that black movements have long imagined and operated on a world scale. Against the master narrative, we posit that successive waves of black international struggles have countered, shaped, and at times destroyed central pillars of capital and empire, racial as well as political. In short, the story of the black international requires nothing less than a rethinking of received wisdom about life under capitalism over the long *durée*—and the possibility of alternative social worlds in the past and the future.

Our project, as noted, is more reclamation than innovation. Black activists, scholars, and movements have long made many of the claims we sketch here, in broad outline if not in specific detail.[6] But the master narrative, as produced especially in the historically white academy, has steadily and effectively effaced the black internationalist counternarrative. Thus we have been told of an "Age of Revolution" with little, if any, mention of the Haitian Revolution. Repeatedly, we hear stories of twentieth-century revolutions that conveniently elide black internationalism. Incessantly, we are regaled with praise poems about the good, nonviolent 1960s and the new social movements it spawned, with scant reference to their black internationalist antecedents.

In our own time, the erasure of global black histories, which is to say the story of the black international, may be attributed primarily to the remaking of the Western academy, and especially the U.S. academy, after World War II. The demands of the Cold War, as determined by the national security state, gave rise to a new Orientalist-style branch of knowledge, area studies, of which African studies was a component part. African studies, as we have argued elsewhere,[7] separated and isolated continental Africa from black North America, and both from the Caribbean and Latin America. Thus did an iron curtain, to appropriate a formulation made famous elsewhere, descend over the study of African peoples. With the possible exception of Atlantic slavery, the resulting intellectual segregation generally precluded investigation of shared black or African experiences, much less shared black struggles for emancipation across nations and empires, continents and oceans. Accordingly, black studies in North America, which emerged out of later struggles in the 1960s and 1970s,[8] were increasingly confined to a narrower, national locale. Likewise, black British studies remained separate from African studies in the British academy, just as African American studies and African studies were distinct areas of inquiry in the leading U.S. universities.[9] Taking the nation-state as the unit of analysis, and utilizing a comparative method that required isolated cases, the Cold War academy effectively ruled out the notion of a black international that cohered the freedom struggles of African peoples globally.

But no condition, it has been noted, is permanent. More recent scholarship, driven by forces as diverse as the Afrocentric protests of the 1980s and the end of the Cold War, has challenged the master narrative, including the African studies one.[10] By the beginning of the new millennium, more and more scholars and activists were being drawn to the connections, old and new, between peoples and movements across the globe. As area studies and African studies receded, along with the Cold War, insurgent forces within and without the academy forged new ties between the previously discrete fields of African, African American, Caribbean, Latin American, and Black European studies. These trends resulted in the appearance of new journals (e.g., *Contours*, *Diaspora*, and *Black Renaissance*), new Ph.D. programs in diaspora and Africana studies, and new conferences and associations dedicated to the black world (e.g., the Association for the Study of the Worldwide African Diaspora). The resulting synergy has, among other things, sparked renewed interest in the forces—ideological, cultural, and organizational—that have long linked black life and activity in various parts of the globe.[11]

The studies brought together in this volume represent some of the first fruit of the most recent labor. Collectively, they demonstrate the multiple and complex ways in which local black struggles and revolts have been conjoined to larger processes and movements among black folk here and there,[12] such that one can credibly speak of globally connected waves of struggles by African peoples over the past two and half centuries. These struggles, and their cumulative effect, are fundamental to a full accounting of the early formation and transformation of capitalism in the Atlantic world, specifically, and more generally to the story of humankind in the modern world.

Such a project, furthermore, recovers a past within the world of activist scholarship. Already at the turn of the twentieth century, circles of movements and bodies of scholarship had emerged with a common mission: to challenge scientific racism worldwide, to contest colonialism and its reputed civilizing mission in Africa and the Caribbean, and to confront new forms of racial oppression in postemancipation societies such as the United States, Brazil, and Cuba.[13] These antinomian expressions, in turn, were built on still older traditions of common resistance, traditions that date back to the second half of the eighteenth century. In that era of ferment throughout the Atlantic world, local struggles for emancipation, although expressing a wide range of lived experiences in specific societies, began to link together in a broad insurgency against imperial and racial orders.[14] The linkages were forged amid the iconic movements of the modern North Atlantic, notably the Enlightenment, the Evangelical Revival, and the U.S., French, and Haitian revolutions. These were not just European and European-settler phenomena but, rather, world-historical events that were fundamentally shaped by the African agency and the African presence, literal and figurative. Such lines of inquiry, however, were largely foreclosed by the post–World War II rise of U.S. hegemony and, more specifically, by what it wrought: area and African studies. Exiled from the mainstream academy, black counternarratives were literally driven underground.

Reclaiming and advancing that intellectual tradition is a huge task, one that will have to be collaborative and can only be achieved over the long haul. We certainly make no pretense here of offering anything approximating a comprehensive accounting of the emergence and evolution of black internationalism. What we attempt, rather, is a rough outline of such a project and its promise. Our volume unearths moments when struggles against a racially ordered world system coalesced, creating black international moments of considerable—and often violent—force. In so doing, we claim uniformity of neither conditions, identities, nor movements; just the contrary, racial identities and forms of protest varied over space and time. The notion of black or African remained in constant flux, changing over time. At certain moments, however, racial struggles and identities cohered across vast masses of land and bodies of water, challenging and changing dominant modes of white supremacy. The volume focuses on three such moments of black internationalism—and their legacy.

The foundational moment of black internationalism occurred in the second half of the eighteenth century. In that Age of Revolution, the black international began to coalesce around opposition to the central fact of black life on the west bank of the Atlantic: racial slavery. This is not, most assuredly, to argue that resistance to slavery began in the Age of Revolution. Clearly that was not so. From the very beginning of their involuntary sojourn in the Americas, enslaved Africans resisted racial bondage in multiple ways, overt and covert, violent and nonviolent.[15] It is to say, however, that black antislavery increasingly became more interconnected, ideologically and organizationally, in the Age of Revolution.

A key event in this evolution of black struggles was the rise of a significant and articulate free black community on the North American mainland, consequent on the U.S. Revolution.[16] No less significant, from the black internationalist standpoint, were the newly freed black people who escaped the United States in the wake of the patriot victory, "fleeing the founding fathers," as one writer has termed it.[17] The free North American black community, along with its diaspora, whose members settled on both banks of the Atlantic, east and west, powerfully shaped an emerging discourse about the possibilities of universal emancipation.[18] The idea of universal emancipation, in turn, would become the foundational core of black internationalism.

If the first principle of black internationalism was universal emancipation, then its foundational language often had a biblical accent.[19] That particular inflection derived from the Evangelical Revival, better known in the United States as the Great Awakening, an important episode in the making of the black international. A major reformation within Protestant Christianity, the Evangelical Revival was a transatlantic phenomenon, spreading from England to its American colonies in the second half of the eighteenth century.[20] Although it did not target them exclusively, the Evangelical Revival succeeded in converting large numbers of enslaved Africans, one of its main achievements. The ensuing Afro-Christianity was the first of its kind in the Anglo-American world.[21] This was quite unlike the situation in the Catholic-dominated areas of the Americas, where church, state, and masters collectively had long embraced mass conversion, or at least mass baptism, for the enslaved Africans.[22] British Protestant slaveholders, by contrast, initially equated Christianity with freedom, assuming manumission would necessarily follow conversion. Even after laws were passed explicitly rejecting any such connection, most Anglo-

American slaveholders remained averse to the conversion of their human chattel. Then came the Evangelical Revival, which began the mass Christianization of slaves in British lands, a task that would be completed by black preachers and evangelists, slave and free. In time the Evangelical Revival, originally no friend of slavery, morphed into the institutional church of the slaveholders, notably in the United States. On the North American mainland, at least, white evangelicalism had parted company with black liberation. The blacks, on the contrary, kept faith with the nascent liberationist theology of their conversion, encapsulated in the notion that God is no respecter of races or nationalities, having "made of one blood all nations of men for to dwell on the face of the earth."[23] This biblical passage appeared repeatedly in the earliest black internationalist narratives and had special resonance for slaves.[24] Thus the Evangelical Revival helped to create an intellectual scaffolding for the black international, or at least a particular expression of black internationalism.

The U.S. Revolution, coming hard on the heels of the Evangelical Revival, opened up new possibilities for black liberation. Seizing the moment, a small but important minority of the enslaved people in British North America defiantly claimed freedom. It was the first such assertion of the black agency in the Age of Revolution, but it would not be the last, or even the most significant. Notably, the rise of a free African American community was not part of the blueprint of the U.S. Revolutionary leadership, in which the slaveholders were well represented, if not hegemonic. Of the three institutions—colonialism, slavery, and white supremacy—on which European rule in the Americas had been constructed since the advent of the Columbian era, the U.S. Revolution challenged just one, colonialism. The other two institutions, slavery and white supremacy, most of the leading U.S. patriots were content, if not eager, to keep.

As Sylvia Frey's chapter demonstrates, the enslaved people upset such plans. Striking a blow against slavery and white supremacy amid the chaos of war, they ran away, enlisted for military service in return for freedom (especially but not exclusively on the loyalist or British side), waged guerrilla warfare, and petitioned for manumission, among other acts of self-emancipation.[25] Enslaved Africans, too, would claim the rights and freedoms enunciated in the Declaration of Independence, despite its attack on them and on the Native Americans.[26] This was not, however, solely an American story. As Frey narrates, African Americans, drawing upon both evangelical and Revolutionary traditions, played a foundational role in the development and transnational dispersion of a diasporic consciousness and of pan-Africanism.

The consequences of these developments emerged as the U.S. Revolution approached its denouement and cataclysm struck the French colony of Saint Domingue, announcing the advent of that canon-busting event of that era, the Haitian Revolution. For the second time in less than a generation, political upheaval among the oppressors, this time the revolution in France, opened up self-emancipatory possibilities for enslaved Africans, this time on Saint Domingue. Originating in the most magisterial of slave revolts, the Haitian Revolution would decisively determine the contours of the emerging black international.

Our chapter on the Haitian Revolution charts how Haitian revolutionaries—in sharp contrast to the dithering of those who led the U.S. and French revolutions—demolished the unholy trinity of slavery, white supremacy, and colonialism.[27] Curiously, however, the centrality of the Haitian Revolution in the rise of black internationalism is largely unacknowledged in the literature on black revolts. That literature, which even in its more recent diasporic and Black Atlantic variations displays a consistent Afro-Saxon bias,[28] relegates the Haitian Revolution to the status of a nonevent, to use Michel-Rolph Trouillot's felicitous phrasing.[29] Contemporaries of the Haitian Revolution knew better. In turning the world that was Saint Domingue upside down, the Haitian Revolution electrified the enslaved and oppressed far and wide, firing their enthusiasm and broadening their horizons. A common wind, as one historian has acclaimed it,[30] appropriating the words of the poet William Wordsworth in his sonnet to Toussaint Louverture,[31] swept through the greater Caribbean and the Atlantic world more generally. The ideological current consisted of underground networks of sailors and other maritime workers, runaways, and itinerant traders, individuals who collectively linked the city and the sea, the port and the plantation.

Thus were hopes of liberation fueled well beyond the shores of Saint Domingue. Indeed, as our chapter recounts, summarizing the work of others, the Haitian Revolution marked the apex in a long series of revolts across the Atlantic that both preceded and followed it. Among other things, the Haitian Revolution drew on the legacy of the evangelical revivalist tradition that so forcefully propelled the black internationalism that emanated from the U.S. Revolution. At the same time, the Haitian Revolution lent a powerful impetus to a second tradition in black internationalism, namely, the revolutionary tradition, as discussed in both Frey's chapter and ours. It was heady stuff, this wind of change, and the Haitian Revolution stood as the powerful exemplar of its potential. Nor did it matter that, for the most part, the leaders of independent Haiti made little attempt to export revolution and, fearful of retaliation by neighboring powers, even disavowed the idea. The Haitian example was enough of an incitement: it provided the spark that fired a new and revolutionary black internationalism.

Part 2: The Great War and the Black Internationalist Revival

The second moment of black internationalism that the volume takes up coincided with World War I, known to contemporaries as the Great War, and its aftermath. Here, the chapters examine the elaboration and refinement of the black international in response to the transformation wrought by the war. In this second moment, the black international moved from the realm of ideological coherence to actual political organization. Not only was this latest wave of resistance and revolts better coordinated than ever, but it also encompassed a much wider geographical area. By the era of the Great War, the African continent, now under the colonial yoke, had become a full and integral part of the black international, which previously had been confined to the west bank of the Atlantic and a few outposts along the Atlantic coast of Africa, areas settled disproportionately by freed people from the west bank and their descendants.[32] The widening circle of the black international revealed, once again, how particular struggles in different locales came to a common appreciation of the global nature of the racialized systems of oppression that everywhere diminished the lives of black folk, making a mockery of their aspirations for full emancipation.

African peoples were centrally involved in the Great War. More than 2 million continental Africans served in the war, many of them forcibly recruited. Organized mainly in labor brigades, they worked under horrific conditions and had a higher mortality rate than non-Africans. Even more Africans than went to the military theater were mobilized for the war on the home front, in many cases also involuntarily. The result was a massive increase in mining, agricultural, forestry, and industrial production, along with an expanded infrastructure (roads, railroads, and harbors) to move the increased production to Europe.[33] Africans of the diaspora, too, played their part in the war. The British and French recruited tens of thousands of soldiers from their Caribbean possessions, while the United States, which finally joined the fray in 1917, some three years after hostilities began, conscripted African Americans in disproportionate numbers, around 400,000.[34]

On both banks of the Atlantic, the wartime demand for industrial and related labor on the home front led to a vast upsurge in black urbanization. Although global in scope, the migration of black folk to the city was most conspicuous in the United States, which witnessed a "Great Migration" (so called after the Great War) of African Americans from the rural South to the urban North.[35] Actually, the Great Migration occurred in two waves: a bigger one from the U.S. South and a smaller one from the Caribbean and Central America, which also sent tens of thousands of African-descended people to the United States, mainly to the northern cities, New York above all.[36] All told, the Great War set in motion a massive movement of black folk (and many others, too). Everywhere, African peoples were crossing boundaries—regional and provincial, national and imperial, continental and oceanic—on a scale unseen since the end of the Atlantic slave trade.

The upsurge in migration and urbanization was matched by an upsurge in consciousness. There was a rise in expectations among peoples of African descent everywhere. Pronouncements by the leaders of the Allied powers, most notably U.S. president Woodrow Wilson's Fourteen Points—a document that seemed to advocate global peace, democracy, and self-determination—encouraged hopes for a better postwar deal.[37]

In fact, African peoples were not repaid for their contributions to the Great War, and the global black revolution in expectations would be frustrated. Instead of getting better, in many respects black life became worse after the war. The formal postwar settlement, contained in the Treaty of Versailles, offered black folk nothing. In Africa, state repression of waged workers, the proletariat, which had grown in both numbers and consciousness, intensified after the war. Repression also increased in the diaspora, most notably in the United States, where the government set out to crush radicalism, including black radicalism, while the mob unleashed its fury on entire black communities, most deadly in the "Red Summer" of 1919.[38] Nor were violent attacks on the physical presence and political assertiveness of African peoples limited to the United States: there were similar manifestations against black folk and other colonial subjects in Britain and France.[39]

As Lara Putnam demonstrates so vividly in her chapter, virulent white supremacy in the Central American states in the 1920s and 1930s led to increased oppression of black folk, many of whom were from the British Caribbean.[40] Indeed, and as Putnam further charts, a British Caribbean–centered, black transnational network had already emerged in the opening decades of the twentieth century, a migratory community that stretched from northern Venezuela to southern Harlem. Bound together by church and culture, voluntary and formal organizations, this world developed a "race consciousness" as it came under increasing attacks. The results included explicit black internationalist critiques of imperial and colonial orders.

The phenomena Putnam describes were part of a larger renaissance across the black world, a reaction to the hopes and dreams so brutally repudiated by the reemergent global white Thermidor. At the core of the rebirth stood the Universal Negro Improvement Association (UNIA). Officially, the UNIA was founded in 1914 in Jamaica under the leadership of Marcus Garvey, back on the island from an odyssey that included a stint among the Caribbean diaspora in Central America and an extended stay in England. In reality, the UNIA that meteorically rose to the forefront of black internationalism after the war had only a faint likeness to its original incarnation. Now headquartered in the United States, the reconstituted UNIA was a product of wartime developments far beyond Jamaica—namely, the Great Migration, both the southern U.S. and Caribbean waves, including Garvey himself, who arrived in New York in 1916; the broader global African urbanization; the growth of the urban and industrial black proletariat globally; and the violent repression, after the war, of the revolution in expectations on both banks of the Atlantic.[41]

Garveyism gave black internationalism, for the first time, a return address. From its headquarters in Harlem, New York, newly transformed into a pan-African metropolis, the UNIA, with its secretariat, entered into sustained communication with movements and individuals throughout global Africa. Most significantly, the message of Garveyism was carried far and wide by its official organ, the *Negro World*, published mainly in English but with Spanish and French supplements. Colonial and national powers waged war against the paper, banning and interdicting it, even imprisoning readers. An underground distribution network, at the center of which were black sailors, proved equal to the challenge, and despite the attempts to suppress it, the *Negro World* continued to circulate worldwide.

Garveyism, like the Haitian Revolution more than a century earlier, engendered fear and alarm among the guardians of empire, territorial and racial. The hostility of white imperial powers and white-dominated nation-states to the UNIA was even more widespread than in the case of the Haitian Revolution, although not as intense; the attacks on Garveyism extended from the west to the east bank of the Atlantic. What made Garveyism dangerous was not just its demand for a modern black nationality in Africa in the face of colonialism, but that it was making the demand in the changed circumstances of the postwar era and then mobilizing a mass constituency behind it. "Africa for the Africans, at home and abroad," Garvey cried out, reducing his program to a slogan. From the centers of power, the power of existing states and empires, came a uniform denunciation of the agitation and a determination to suppress it.

Suppression was no easy task because Garveyism, despite its formal structure and hierarchy, mirrored the historic informality and looseness of the black international. In its day, Garveyism was the pan-African potter's clay: it could be molded any which way. Globally, Garveyism was more metaphor than movement—a rhetorical, stylistic, and organizational model easily replicated. Black folk everywhere with grievances against the system could find in Garveyism an archetype for seeking redress, as indeed many did, from dockworkers in South Africa to sharecroppers in the United States, from cocoa farmers in Ghana to intellectuals in Nigeria, from ethnic mobilizers in Zimbabwe to activists in Cuba, from the Anglophone to the Francophone black world.[42] Outside the United States, perhaps even outside New York, Garveyism was a hydra with multiple heads,[43] more inspirer than executor. In global Africa as a whole, Garveyism, in the inspirational sense, remained independent of Garvey and the UNIA.

Garveyism, as both inspirer and executor, was on full display in South Africa, as Robert Vinson's chapter recounts. South African Garveyism blended two strands of a long-standing interconnection between black South Africans and "American Negroes" (a category that included West Indians as well as African Americans). The first of these was the nineteenth-century notion of Providential Design, which was an outgrowth of the revivalist tradition in black internationalism and which promoted the "redemption" of Africa through Christianity and commerce, a project that would be spearheaded by Africans of the diaspora. This was the black version of the "civilizing mission," and it was allied with emigration, or the "return" of diaspora blacks to the African continent.[44] The most noted exponents of Providential Design were the West Indian Edward Wilmot Blyden and the African American Alexander Crummell, both of whom resettled to Africa, although Crummell eventually returned to the United States.[45] In addition to Providential Design, South African Garveyism drew on a tradition of black South African celebration of African Americans as agents of modernity and models in the quest for a modern, regenerated Africa. South Africa and neighboring territories would become key centers of Garveyism in Africa, its transmitters including not just sailors, preachers, and newspapers, the usual vectors, but also migrant workers.

Women were a key part of the new Garveyite mass constituency. Women were seen, and heard, in the UNIA to a degree without precedence in black internationalism. Those women included such high-profile figures as Henrietta Vinton Davis, Laura Kofey, Amy Ashwood Garvey, and Amy Jacques Garvey, the latter two wives of Marcus Garvey. Every UNIA branch had a "lady president," complementing the (male) president. Rank-and-file Garveyite women were organized into the Black Cross Nurses and the Motor Corp, the female branches of the uniformed services.

Despite the visibility of women in the movement, Garveyism would not have been confused with feminism. The ideal Garveyite woman was the helpmeet. Official UNIA propaganda extolled the roles of mother and housewife, emphasizing women's reproductive as well as productive work in the domestic realm. Marcus Garvey, now assuming the role of poet, celebrated the queenly black woman, an object of worship and an arbiter of (Victorian) morality. Such images bore little relationship to the lived experiences of most Garveyite women, who belonged to the working class. It is another anomaly of the UNIA that despite the formal reverence for bourgeois domesticity, practical Garveyism required women not in the private realm of the home but in the public arena. They were drawn there by, among others, the Black Cross Nurses and the Motor Corp, whose missions centered on social work, health care, and manufacturing. Meanwhile, Garvey continued to indulge his poetical imagination, obliviously composing panegyrics to motherhood and to home and hearth.[46] A group of women in New Orleans, where female (and working-class) leadership in the local UNIA was especially strong, offered an all-encompassing assessment of the movement. The UNIA, they averred, "is our church, our clubhouse, our theatre, our fraternal order and our school, and we will never forsake it while we live; neither will our men forsake it."[47]

True to its reputation for being all things to all black folk,[48] Garveyism doubled as a religious movement—of the big-tent, Christian ecumenical sort. The UNIA had an official religious head, the chaplain-general, while branch meetings could often be mistaken for Sunday morning services, complete with hymns and prayers. Garveyism also inspired the creation of the African Orthodox Church, a pan-Africanist denomination whose founder, the former Anglican clergyman George Alexander McGuire, previously served as the UNIA's chaplain-general. Despite a temporary tiff between Garvey and McGuire, everywhere in global Africa the UNIA and the African Orthodox Church became fellow travelers, the one movement helping to promote the other, including through their respective publications, the *Negro World* and the *African Churchman*.[49]

More fascinating, perhaps, is Laura Kofey's African Universal Church and

Commercial League, a riff on the Garvey movement's full name, the Universal Negro Improvement Association and African Communities League. A charismatic personality, preacher, and organizer, Kofey deployed her considerable talents in the service of the UNIA in Florida and elsewhere. In time, she became a victim of her own success. Her star, having already surpassed that of many of the movement's male leaders, seemingly began to rival Marcus Garvey's, at least in her particular sphere of influence. Garvey, who in happier times had received the UNIA's "female John the Baptist" in his prison cell in Atlanta, publicly repudiated Kofey. Excommunicated from the UNIA, Kofey turned to inspirational Garveyism. Her vehicle for preaching Garveyism without Garvey was the African Universal Church and Commercial League, which, rather like the UNIA, elided the boundaries between religion and politics. Kofey's career as an independent operator was short lived; she was soon assassinated—not the first ex-Garveyite to suffer that fate.[50]

Kofey's African Universal Church, along with the African Orthodox Church, was a direct offspring of the UNIA. But it was not just executive Garveyism that spawned religious progeny; so, too, did inspirational Garveyism. New manifestations of spiritualism, stimulated by the Garvey phenomenon to varying degrees, appeared in a number of places. Although assuming different forms, these groups were invariably syncretic: they fused multiple traditions—sacred and secular, old and new, eastern and western.

In the United States, for instance, a highly unorthodox form of Islam emerged, one decisively determined by black nationalist discourses and practices. The first group to organize on such principles was the Moorish Science Temple of America, but black-nationalist-determined Islam eventually found its most enduring redoubt in the Nation of Islam. Both groups were greatly influenced by Garveyism, although the Moorish Science Temple had been founded on the eve of World War I, before the postwar black renaissance.[51] Islam, with its deep roots in the Western black diasporic past, was never fully erased by the slavery and postslavery experiences but became ensconced in the deep recesses of African American culture and consciousness.[52] More overtly, the African American "rediscovery" of Islam coincided with the postwar renaissance, or the second moment of black internationalism. The engagement with Islam was promoted from various quarters; some of these were missionary efforts from outside the United States, while others were more indigenous.[53] Scholars have largely ignored the fact that the latter included groups like the African Blood Brotherhood (ABB), the Harlem-based black radical formation that initially, though critically, supported the UNIA.[54] A staunchly secular movement, the ABB commended the Muslim religion to black folk purely on political grounds, arguing that Islam, in sharp contrast to Christianity, opposed colonialism and supported racial equality. Christianity and Islam, ran a typical broadside in the ABB's official organ, "have an exactly opposite reaction upon the mind of the Negro convert. One as clearly induces to a servile state of mind and slavish acquiescence in white tutelage on the part of the Negro convert as the other inspires self-respect and love of liberty."[55] It is a cry that would later be taken up by representatives of the Nation of Islam, most famously by a second generation of converts led by Malcolm X, a descendant of Garveyism two times over—by religious-political choice and by family heritage, his parents having been ardent Garveyites.

Concurrent with the evolving black-nationalist-determined Islam in the United States, another variant of the new religious-cum-political movement emerged in Garvey's native Jamaica. Rastafari, even more so than the Moorish Science Temple and the Nation of Islam, was a testament to the impact of inspirational Garveyism and its ideological antecedents. Similarly Rastafari, like black-nationalist-determined Islam, appealed largely to the weaker segments of the working classes and the *Lumpenproletariat*. Both movements were steeped in a biblicism descended from the revivalist tradition in black internationalism, the founders of black-nationalist-determined Islam having much greater familiarity with the Bible than with the Koran. But Rastafari, hewing closer to the biblical line, eventually arrived at a novel theological conclusion. Its founders determined that Ras Tafari, the prince who in 1928 ascended the Ethiopian throne as Emperor Haile Selassie, was really the messiah.[56] A decisive factor in sealing Selassie's divinity in Rastafarian theology was the 1935 Italian invasion of Ethiopia, by far the single most important event in black internationalism in the years between the two world wars, and one that outraged African peoples everywhere.[57] If Selassie was the God of Rastafari, then Garvey was his noted forerunner—one who came, in the style of the biblical John the Baptist, to make straight the way of the Lord. Significantly, Garvey was assigned a similar role in the holy book of the Moorish Science Temple, the Holy Koran (not to be confused with the Koran of orthodox Islam), where he became the advance man for the Moorish leader Noble Drew Ali.[58]

Garveyism, in both its executive and inspirational incarnations, may have ruled the roost of black internationalism in the period following the Great War, but its reign was not uncontested. One important contestant was the Pan-African Congress under the leadership of the African American intellectual W. E. B. Du Bois. Four sessions of the Pan-African Congress were held between 1919 and 1927.[59] The inaugural session was convened in Paris in 1919 to coincide with the conference that produced the Treaty of Versailles, which the first Pan-African Congress, like the UNIA, tried but failed to influence.

The UNIA and the Pan-African Congress represented opposing tendencies in the black international. Initially, at least, the split was grounded in real programmatic and ideological differences. The UNIA, with its mass base, stood for transformation, while the Pan-African Congress, with its elite constituency, advocated accommodation. Whereas postwar Garveyism was founded on anticolonialism, the first two Pan-African Congresses called for reforming rather than ending colonialism. Indeed, the second Pan-African Congress, which officially condemned Garveyism, stood out for its decidedly procolonial rhetoric, especially by the Francophone delegates.

Yet by 1923, the year of the third Pan-African Congress, there was something of a seesaw change in the black international. Although a puny affair, even compared with the first two congresses, which were hardly mass events, the third Pan-African Congress heralded an important ideological revision, Du Bois having now rid himself of the procolonial Francophone contingent. The fourth Pan-African Congress of 1927 confirmed and deepened the critique of colonialism and global black oppression begun at the previous session. As Du Bois and the Pan-African Congress moved to the left, executive Garveyism headed in the opposite direction, since Garvey had drifted rightward in response to a number of political and personal challenges.[60] Meanwhile, though, the personal animus and bitter polemic between Garvey and Du Bois,[61] each more bullheaded and egotistical than the other, had come to overshadow the substantive differences, and similarities, of the movements they represented.

Among the many resolutions passed by the fourth Pan-African Congress was one commending the Soviet Union for its "liberal attitude toward the colored races."[62] The nod to Soviet racial policy represented a marked departure from the first two congresses, which were no more hospitable to Bolshevik communism than to Garveyism. The fourth Pan-African Congress, held in New York (the previous three convened in Europe), broke new ground in another, related manner: the delegates included black members of the U.S. Communist Party and black fellow travelers.

The communist presence at the fourth Pan-African Congress highlighted another important tendency in black internationalism in the period after the Great War, namely, Black Bolshevism.[63] Black Bolshevism battled with Garveyism and the Pan-African Congress for leadership of the black international—that is, in articulating and mobilizing the grievances and aspirations of black folk globally.

Black Bolshevism resulted from the interface of the black international and the more formally organized communist international, the Comintern. After the triumph of the Bolshevik Revolution in 1917, the leaders of Soviet Russia declared for worldwide revolution, motivated by idealism and "internationalist duty" as well as by enlightened self-interest. Rejecting "socialism in one country," an idea Joseph Stalin would later embrace, the "old" Bolsheviks, facing global capitalist hostility, even outright aggression, argued that the survival of Soviet Russia depended on successful revolutions in other parts of the world, especially in western Europe. The result was the Moscow-based Comintern, formed in 1919 and charged with promoting world revolution, the Bolsheviks having decided to throw down the gauntlet to the capitalists or, rather, to pick up the gauntlet the capitalists had thrown down.[64]

Two items on the Comintern's agenda commanded the attention of exponents of black internationalism: colonialism and racism. Bolshevism's "liberal attitude toward the colored races," as the fourth Pan-African Congress would style it, was the starting point of the black engagement with the international communist movement.

Hakim Adi's chapter demonstrates the Comintern's reach in the black world, extending from the United States to South Africa, from the Caribbean to Europe, from French-ruled to British-ruled Africa. In contrast to its competitors, the Garvey movement and the Pan-African Congress, the Comintern was an ideologically and organizationally coherent network, and it proclaimed the "Negro Question" a central part of the coming world revolution. The boldness of this assertion, together with the strength of its network, underpins Adi's conclusion that the Comintern was, "perhaps, the era's sole international white-led movement to adopt an avowedly antiracist platform, and certainly the only one formally dedicated to a revolutionary transformation of the global political *and* racial order."

The Comintern's great contribution to pan-Africanism, then, was its role in internationalizing, beyond global Africa, the black liberation struggle. In declaring the Negro Question integral to the world revolution it sought to promote, the Comintern broke new ground. For the first time, an organized body of white revolutionaries officially and unequivocally made nonracialism, even antiracism, part of a global struggle for social transformation.

The Haitian Revolution had arrived at a similar global antiracist posture nearly a century and a half previously, during an earlier age of revolution. In making this ideological breakthrough, the Haitian revolutionaries practically stood alone. Their contemporaries, the French revolutionaries, granted equality to the free people of color, but only to cement the backing of Saint Domingue's mulattos, many of whom were slaveholders, in the campaign against the slave rebellion. Then, under military threat from Britain and Spain, each desiring to seize Saint Domingue, revolutionary France abolished slavery, aiming to retain control of the colony by wooing the slave revolutionaries to its side. Yet even these decisions, which were driven by expediency rather than principle, eventually would be reversed. The third great political transformation of that era, the U.S. Revolution, fared even worse on black liberation. Whereas the foundational French Revolutionary document, the Rights of Man and Citizen, passed over African slavery in silence, its U.S. equivalent, the Declaration of Independence, did the same and then hypocritically lambasted black folk as potential British allies. The other major document that came out of the U.S. Revolution, the Constitution of 1787, went further and explicitly endorsed slavery.

In seeking to make the Negro Question part of the world revolution, therefore, the Comintern broke decisively with the revolutionary tradition of the white Atlantic. Yet even in the international communist movement, white supremacy died hard. Indeed, as Adi shows, the Comintern often encountered obstacles from unexpected quarters: its own affiliates, the national communist parties. The communist parties of the United States and South Africa, along with those of Britain and France, were the most important so far as the Negro Question was concerned. White-minority-ruled South Africa was to Africa what the United States was to the world: its top industrial power. Each country had relatively large numbers of black industrial workers, the class the Comintern considered the linchpin of the revolution. Britain and France, for their part, were the major colonizers of black folk, ruling over far-flung empires in Africa and the Caribbean, among other places. Together, the four nations—the United States, South Africa, Britain, and France—controlled the greater part of global Africa, including its most economically dynamic sections. The communist parties of the same four nations frequently were uncooperative on the Negro Question; in many cases, they refused outright to implement the Comintern's antiracist and anticolonial policies.

Behind the Comintern's struggle with its national affiliates on the Negro Question stood the Black Bolsheviks. Whether in South Africa, the United States, France, Britain, or Cuba, Black Bolsheviks had little faith in the national communist parties and their predominantly white leaders, who often pandered to nationalist, racist, and colonialist sentiments. On racial and colonial issues, black party members everywhere turned to Moscow for redress. From the national parties they expected little—except neglect, and perhaps worse. Accordingly, Black Bolsheviks looked to the Comintern to enforce its writ on the Negro Question and to impose the correct antiracist and anticolonial Bolshevik line on the national parties.

Those expectations would be fulfilled only in part, and then just for a season. Soon after its formation, the Comintern promised to hold a special Negro Congress, a conclave that would showcase its commitment to black liberation. Meanwhile, and as part of the disillusionment with the national parties, several Comintern congresses created Negro commissions. The idea was straightforward enough: a Negro commission, funded by the Comintern, staffed largely by Black Bolsheviks, and authoritatively backed by an extraordinary Negro Congress, would bypass the national parties and directly engage black struggles and strugglers globally. However, the proposed Negro Congress never materialized, while the various Negro commissions hardly functioned, explaining why successive congresses had to form new ones.

Finally, in 1930 the Comintern, in its most important *organizational* foray into black liberation ever, formed yet another Negro commission: the International Trade Union Committee of Negro Workers. The acronym-unfriendly Committee of Negro Workers descended lineally from the Comintern's watershed sixth congress of 1928, which ratified, on the stage of international communism, the new Soviet dispensation. Following the death of Vladimir Lenin, the chief architect of the Bolshevik Revolution, Stalin variously eliminated and sidelined his rivals in a brutal succession struggle, before emerging triumphant. In the Comintern, as in the Soviet Union, Stalinism meant increased centralization of power. As originally constituted, the Comintern was a clearinghouse of revolution, organizing congresses and seeking to enforce their decisions. Real power over the national parties, however, the Comintern never had, as evidenced by its inability to impose its will on the Negro Question. Stalinist centralization inaugurated unprecedented Soviet dominance over the Comintern and its affiliates. Still, some affiliates remained defiant, including on the Negro Question, demonstrating that Soviet control of international communism, even in the Stalinist era, was never as complete as the anticommunist school of communist studies has claimed.[65]

Stalinism intensified confrontation within and without the communist movement. The sixth Comintern congress, consequently, declared war on the noncommunist Left worldwide. For black internationalism, this meant doing battle with "Negro reformism," as Adi shows. According to the Comintern, Negro reformist organizations and leaders, or rather, "misleaders," abounded on both banks of the Atlantic. The Comintern's chief black target, however, was Garveyism. By the time the campaign against Negro reformism began, the UNIA, or executive Garveyism, was in terminal decline, a mere shadow of its former self. Yet the Comintern's battle with Garveyism was no phantom war. The UNIA's collapse as an organized body did not unduly affect Garveyism's life as metaphor. In sum, the Comintern had taken up arms against the UNIA's greatest legacy: inspirational Garveyism. The Trinidadian-born George Padmore, later to emerge as the most conspicuous combatant against Negro reformism, admitted as much. Although celebrating the disintegration of the UNIA, which he considered "the most reactionary expression in Negro bourgeois nationalism," Padmore bewailed that Garveyism, as an inspiration, "continues to exert some influence among *certain* sections of the Negro masses."[66]

Soon after it was established, Padmore became head of the International Trade Union Committee of Negro Workers. Although it held the occasional meeting, the committee's most important work was carried out through its official organ, the *Negro Worker*. Edited by Padmore during its most febrile phase, the *Negro Worker* was a monthly journal published from 1931 to 1937, initially in Hamburg, Germany. It was the Comintern's answer to the *Negro World*, the now defunct Garveyite organ. Tendentious and polemical, the *Negro Worker* emphatically set Black Bolshevism apart from its black internationalist rivals, the Pan-African Congress and, especially, Garveyism. The *Negro Worker* focused on two broad, and related, themes. First, the *Negro Worker* argued that the black toilers, not the black middle classes—the despised reformists and petit bourgeois Negro misleaders—were the vanguard of black liberation globally. Second, and in accordance with the Comintern's founding claims, the *Negro Worker* advanced the view that black liberation was inextricably linked to the global proletarian revolution.

But then the global proletarian revolution, as defined by the Stalinist Comintern, began to backpedal on black liberation. The rise of fascism in Europe led the Soviet Union to abandon its overt antagonism to the noncommunist Left, and even to the nonfascist colonial powers, meaning concretely Britain and France. Presently, communists everywhere received orders from on high to tone down the campaign against the "democratic imperialists," Britain and France, and to focus instead on the "fascist imperialists," Germany and Italy, which posed a more immediate threat to the Soviet Union. Ever the nationalist champion of socialism in one country, Stalin now determined on a course he believed to be best for the Soviet Union. It was not, however, a policy consistent with black liberation. With the exception of certain individuals and organizations that supported Japan as a champion of the "darker races,"[67] black internationalism broadly agreed on the dangers of fascism to African peoples. Seeing fascism and colonialism as two sides of the same coin, however, most black internationalists rejected the notion of privileging antifascism above anticolonialism. After all, the "democratic imperialists," Britain and France, were the preeminent colonizers of black folk. By contrast, fascist Italy was a minor colonial power in Africa, despite its brutal invasion of Ethiopia in 1935. Previously, the Treaty of Versailles had punished Germany by, among other things, dismantling its African empire and turning most of it over to Britain and France.

Black Bolshevism now faced a dilemma that was felt most acutely in the Comintern's leading organs on the Negro Question globally, the International Trade Union Committee of Negro Workers and its mouthpiece, the *Negro Worker*. Deciding they could not support the most recent directive from Moscow, two of the committee's leading lights bolted. The first to go was Tiemoko Kouyaté of French West Africa, the Comintern's most prominent black Francophone. An organizer of black and other colonial sailors and allied workers in France, Kouyaté had long been a thorn in the side of the French Communist Party on account of his championship of the Negro Question. Following his close ally Kouyaté, George Padmore then resigned his positions as head of the Committee of Negro Workers and editor of the *Negro Worker*.[68] Short on forbearance and long on denunciation, as always, the Comintern retaliated by formally expelling both men, charging them with the same offense Padmore had so often leveled against others: Negro petit bourgeois nationalism. The *Negro Worker* survived intermittently for some time longer. For all practical purposes, though, the Comintern had abandoned its founding commitment and called off the engagement with the black international. For sure, individual communist parties, especially in the United States and South Africa, continued to engage black toilers and intellectuals, but mostly as part of a national rather than an international strategy.[69]

Black women, a small but determined band among the Black Bolsheviks, were more consistent. In the United States, where they were most prominent, women were present at the founding of Black Bolshevism, and they would remain a crucial bloc in that tendency of black internationalism in the decades to come. The first outstanding female leader of Black Bolshevism was Grace Campbell. A charter member of the radical and black internationalist ABB,

Campbell pioneered a kind of Black Bolshevik feminism. She did not write much, but her ideology may be inferred from her actions, notably her keen interest in the "Woman Question." Hers was a socialism attuned to the imperatives of women's liberation, in and out of the workplace, including the particular gendered and racialized oppression of black women. Campbell remained with the ABB when it made its great metamorphosis, even as she retained her commitment to women's liberation. The ABB, previously an uneasy ally of the UNIA, supporting as well as critiquing it, formally broke with executive Garveyism in 1921 and melded into the emerging U.S. communist movement.[70]

The generation of female Black Bolsheviks that came after Campbell built on her work. Most of these women had proletarian backgrounds, but a few came from the ranks of the black middle classes; a number had Caribbean roots. Some—like Hermina Huiswoud, Maude White, Louise Thompson, Claudia Jones, and Esther Cooper—became political activists upon joining the U.S. Communist Party. Others—most signally Audley Moore, later Queen Mother Moore, who began her political career as a Garveyite—migrated to communism from black nationalism. To varying degrees all of these women, along with other black comrade sisters, were committed to the fusion of socialism, black internationalism, and women's liberation initiated by Grace Campbell. Theirs was often an uphill struggle. They fought not just against male chauvinism in the party, including on the part of black male members, but also against the party's ideology, which emphasized class unity above all other considerations, including those centered on gender and race.[71] On the Woman Question, at least, the fight of female Black Bolsheviks, like that of their Garveyite sisters, was at once external and internal.

Part 3: The Long Black Sixties

The second wave of black internationalism was followed, in the post–World War II era, by the rise and improbable success of independence movements in the colonies and civil rights struggles in the United States. As Vijay Prashad traces in his chapter on the "Black Gandhi," many of these struggles drew upon strategies and leaders forged in the black international cauldron of the interwar years. Certainly this was the case with Gandhi, whose philosophy and movement developed first in South Africa, matured in British colonial India, and later inspired movements around the world, including in South Africa, the Gold Coast (later Ghana), and most famously in the United States.[72] Yet this postwar order, even as it resulted in independence for scores of African, Asian, and Caribbean states and civil rights gains for African Americans in the United States, was inimical to black internationalism. As self-determination became equated with state sovereignty, black identities increasingly assumed a national, even nationalist, form.

Black internationalism, however, witnessed a remarkable reversal of fortunes in what we call the long black Sixties, which is the subject of Part 3 of the volume. This moment in black internationalism was a reaction to the unfinished struggles of the previous two centuries, and especially the previous generation. The movements and activists that made up the long black Sixties were driven into combat by the unfulfilled dreams and broken promises of abolition, decolonization, and desegregation. The two decades before the onset of the long black Sixties were a period of heady changes in global Africa. World War II, which came at the end of the revival in black internationalism that followed the previous global war, introduced a new order in international politics, as the fifth Pan-African Congress of 1945 readily noted.[73] The subsequent contest between the United States and the Soviet Union for global hegemony, the Cold War, opened up new opportunities as well as posed new challenges for black liberation.[74] For global Africa as a whole, the major accomplishments of the Cold War era were juridical independence and formal racial equality—that is, the termination of colonial rule in most of Africa and parts of the diaspora, notably the Anglophone Caribbean, and the end of legalized racism and state-sponsored segregation, most significantly in the United States.

Decolonization and desegregation were far-reaching and costly achievements, wrenched from the claws of oppression, even terror, and paid for in blood, sweat, and tears. In the end, however, decolonization and desegregation failed to deliver on their major promise: a better life for the masses of black people. Kwame Nkrumah, who in 1957 led Ghana to independence, the first country in sub-Saharan Africa to achieve that status, had argued that the better life could be achieved by ending European rule and transferring political power to the colonized. "Seek ye first the political kingdom," Nkrumah, a sometime former preacher, exhorted in a riff on the King James Bible, "and all other things shall be added unto you."[75] In many cases the addition amounted to little, if there was any addition at all.

The result was the onset of a new black internationalist wave. The long black Sixties lacked the organizational coherence of the preceding wave, devoid as it was of any umbrella movement with the global reach and influence of the UNIA, or even the Comintern or the Pan-African Congress. Ideologically, however, the third wave of black internationalism was more cohesive than the second one. Unlike the previous two waves—which culminated in abolition and decolonization, respectively—the movements and activists of the third wave did not succeed in their avowed aims. Their success lay elsewhere, in undermining the postwar liberal order and U.S. hegemony, while showing the way to postliberal identities, alliances, and movements.

Signs of a new wave appeared in the early 1960s, when radical protest began to erupt in widely disparate locales across the black world. Among the most notable on the African continent was Patrice Lumumba's outburst at independence day celebrations in the Belgian Congo (presently the Democratic Republic of the Congo). Affronted by King Baudouin's speech celebrating Belgium's reputed civilizing mission in Africa, Lumumba, the incoming Congolese prime minister, seized the podium and denounced the whole colonial enterprise:

> We have known ironies, insults, blows that we endured morning, noon, and evening, because we are niggers. . . . We have seen our lands seized. . . . We have seen that the law was not the same for a white and for a black, accommodating for the first, cruel and inhuman for the other. . . . We have seen that in the towns there were magnificent houses for the whites and crumbling shanties for the blacks, that a black was not admitted in the motion-picture houses, in the restaurants, in the stores of the Europeans. Who will ever forget the massacres where so many of our brothers perished, the cells into which those who refused to submit to a regime of oppression and exploitation were thrown? [applause].[76]

There was to be no replay in the Congo of Nkrumah's long and felicitous transition to power in Ghana (1951–57). An incensed Baudouin fled from the stage and returned to Belgium before independence came at midnight. Lumumba simultaneously became a marked man. Within months he would be dead, the victim of neocolonial intrigues emanating from Belgium and the United States.[77]

The confrontation at Congo's independence celebration was not an isolated event: Baudouin and Lumumba were well aware that a new wave of radical nationalism had broken out to the north and south as well as to the east and west of where they were standing. To the north, the armed revolt against French rule in Algeria was peaking amidst white settler and French army mutinies.[78] To the east, a state of emergency remained in effect in Kenya after the brutal suppression of the Land and Freedom Army, the armed resistance movement the British colonialists called Mau Mau.[79] To the west and south, nonviolent nationalist movements were giving way to armed struggles, especially in the Portuguese colonies of Guinea-Bissau, Angola, and Mozambique.[80] In apartheid South Africa, the police shot down scores of unarmed demonstrators in March 1960 in the town of Sharpeville. Following the Sharpeville Massacre, the apartheid regime declared a state of emergency and banned the Pan-Africanist Congress and the African National Congress, South Africa's leading liberation movements. Both movements, in turn, declared armed struggle against the apartheid state.[81]

Each of these developments rejected, implicitly or explicitly, previous nationalist struggles, their strategies, and the statehouses their leaders increasingly came to inhabit. Most prophetic was Frantz Fanon, the Caribbean-born theorist who made his name in the Algerian Revolution. Speaking on the "pitfalls of national consciousness," Fanon warned of the predatory nature of the African middle class, the group that would inherit the colonial administrative apparatus and corrupt the postcolonial state, turning it into a handmaiden of neocolonialism.[82] Armed struggle, and the support it required from peasants and the urban *Lumpenproletariat*, led to new analyses of popular participation and the racial and class bases of colonial rule. Amilcar Cabral, the leader of the struggle in Guinea-Bissau, became renowned for working through these problems on the ground. In Cabral's view, there would be no greater obstacle to emancipation than the postcolonial state.[83]

Similar eruptions and explorations were taking place on the other side of the Atlantic. In the United States, younger activists in the civil rights movement became increasingly impatient as white southerners countermobilized against any substantive dismantling of white power, wealth, and privilege. Meanwhile nonviolent, multiracial protest and an increasing number of elected black politicians failed to change de facto segregation in the North.[84] It was in this context that Malcolm X's voice found such a receptive audience, from his calls for the renewal of the tradition of self-defense and the necessity of independent black organizations, through his rejection of nonviolence and assimilation, to his emphasis on a common white enemy and international black action for *human*—as opposed to *civil* (state)—rights.[85] Central to this vision was a relinking of African American and African identities and struggles, a project facilitated by Malcolm's own trips across Africa. As the draft program of his Organization of Afro-American Unity stressed, "The time is past due for us to internationalize the problems of Afro-Americans. We have been too slow in recognizing the link in the fate of Africans with the fate of Afro-Americans."[86]

Members of the Student Non-Violent Coordinating Committee (SNCC) were reaching similar conclusions. By the mid-1960s nonviolence training sessions were being abandoned and attention increasingly turned to African affairs and armed movements worldwide. When SNCC chairman Stokely Carmichael (later Kwame Ture) famously raised the cry of "Black Power" at a gathering in Mississippi in 1966, he found an immediate, explosive response.[87] In Oakland, California, the cry for Black Power found organizational expression in the formation in 1966 of the Black Panther Party for Self-Defense, which would eventually draw in so many stars of the young black movement. Thirty chapters quickly sprung up around the United States, and the Black Panther Party at one time or another worked with almost every radical U.S. organization of the day, including women's and gay movements.

These developments gave rise to debate over sexuality and women's participation within the wider black nationalist movement and the Black Panther Party in particular. As the paths of Elaine Brown, Kathleen Cleaver, and Angela Davis (to mention only the most celebrated) attest, a few women rose to prominent positions within the party, notwithstanding its masculinist character. Still, the Panthers were light years ahead of more openly patriarchal organizations, such as the Nation of Islam and Maulana Karenga's U.S. organization.[88] By the early 1970s the Black Panther Party was publicly calling for alliances with the Women's and Gay Liberation movements, reflecting internal gender struggles within the party and the Panthers' public engagement with gay and feminist activists.[89] In contrast to women involved in the white New Left, fewer black women left black nationalist organizations to join feminist groups. And when they did, the continuing racism and class privilege within the emerging white feminist movement led them to launch new organizations, such as Third World Women's Alliance, formed by Frances Beal and other SNCC women in 1968.[90] As the emphasis on "Third World" suggests, black feminists remained linked to an anti-imperialist and pan-Africanist vision.

As the chapter by Robyn Spencer traces, the Black Panther Party created an organizational network and a consciousness that were radically internationalist, weaving into a single tapestry a critique of U.S. imperialism abroad and capitalism at home. No longer was it possible to imagine national solutions to black international problems. Global solidarity links rapidly expanded, propelled in part by Panther leaders who had been driven into exile. This led inexorably to calls for a new black identity that was not wedded to U.S. citizenship but was based on international black alliances. Huey Newton, the top Panther leader, put it in words that Malcolm X (assassinated in 1965) would have appreciated:

"We cannot be nationalists when our country is not a nation but an empire."[91] Newton offered instead an alternative vision of a world of independent and allied communities, what he called "revolutionary intercommunalism."

As Spencer demonstrates, the theory of intercommunalism was a long way indeed from the ideological and programmatic beliefs of the Old Left, the civil rights movement, liberal social democrats, and the white student movement. It even marked out new ground in relation to Stokely Carmichael's and Charles V. Hamilton's influential 1967 book *Black Power: The Politics of Liberation*, which paved the way not only by rejecting essentialized notions of race but by recasting liberal "race relations" as a colonial relationship between global white supremacy and the "black nation within the nation." The future, Newton proclaimed, was one of linking oppressed communities worldwide in opposition to a common enemy.

By the late 1960s, local eruptions had given way to international networks operating across the Americas, Africa, and Asia and beyond. Leaders of national liberation movements in Africa, such as Amilcar Cabral and Eduardo Mondlane of Mozambique, visited the United States, while U.S. movement leaders and personalities—including Muhammad Ali, Malcolm X, Stokely Carmichael, Eldridge Cleaver, Kathleen Cleaver, and Robert Williams, among others—traveled widely in Europe, the Caribbean (especially Cuba), and Asia, spreading the message of black revolt.[92] African and Caribbean students resident in Europe and North America did likewise, protesting in support of various causes at home and elsewhere. In this way, a common language of black liberation gained worldwide prominence and currency.

Even old imperial centers were shaken. In Britain, West Indians and Asians in the early 1960s coalesced to oppose racism and increasing attacks on their basic rights, most notably by lobbying against the key 1962 Commonwealth Immigrants Bill. These efforts failed, and the incumbent Labour Party subsequently moved against immigrants, particularly after losing seats in 1964 to Tory candidates who campaigned on the slogan "If you want a nigger neighbour, vote Liberal or Labour."[93] In this climate the stirrings of Black Power, disseminated in part by visits by Malcolm X in 1965 and Stokely Carmichael in 1967, met a ready response among a new generation of British-born and -educated young people of African and Asian descent. As black militancy rose, older organizations pursuing integrationism and a legislative strategy, such as the National Committee against Racial Discrimination, collapsed. In their place arose new organizations espousing black consciousness and black control of black communities.

In Britain, 1967 was to prove a breakthrough year, marked by the founding of the Universal Coloured People's Association (UCPA), led by Obi Egbuna (who had traveled to the United States in 1966);[94] the banning of Stokely Carmichael; and the arrest of a major Black Power figure for "stirring up hatred."[95] More than fifty other radical black organizations joined the UCPA to create a broad Black Power movement. By 1969 the Home Office's Special Branch estimated that there were 2,000 active Black Power militants in Britain.[96]

As elsewhere in the black world, Black Power organizations in Britain expressed local concerns. Yet these concerns were now no longer directed toward state-sponsored amelioration of the condition of new immigrants but were placed within global black networks, consciousness, and demands. As Sivanandan, a key activist of the time, recalls,

> We related to both the struggles back at home and the struggles here, the struggles then and the struggles now, the struggles of Gandhi and Nehru, of Nkrumah and Nyerere, of James and Williams, of Du Bois and Garvey and the ongoing struggles in Vietnam and "Portuguese Africa"—Guinea Bissau and Cape Verde—and the struggles for Black Power in the United States of America. . . . And *black* was a political colour.[97]

The language of Black Power was even heard in places without direct diasporic or African slave histories, such as Australia, where an avowed Black Power movement, formed in 1972, directly confronted the government. Australian black activists, like their counterparts elsewhere, deployed the term "black" to reject state-imposed classifications and to express solidarity with racially oppressed peoples everywhere. In the words of Bobbi Sykes, "In an effort to elevate the broad struggle being undertaken here [in Australia] to a Third World level, use of the word 'black' becomes highly desirable."[98]

Back on the west bank of the Atlantic, the new black assertiveness sprouted forth from roots in Brazil's favelas, nightclubs, and schools, as military rule in that country became increasingly unpopular. Buoyed by the examples of national liberation movements in Portugal's African colonies and by growing ties to Black Power and soul culture in North America, black activists in Brazil charted new paths. Exposing the myth that Brazil was a "racial democracy," they unearthed local racial inequalities and practices, reclaimed ties to Africa and global black resistance, and began to redefine "black" to encompass both "preto" (literally, black) and "pardo" (roughly, mulatto or mestizo).[99] By 1978 this cultural and political renaissance led to the formation of a national organization, Movimento Negro Unificado (Unified Black Movement).[100]

Symbolically, and significantly, the Unified Black Movement rejected May 13, the traditional day for celebrating nationally the abolition of slavery in 1888. Instead, black activists created a National Black Consciousness Day, November 20, to mark the anniversary of the death of Zumbi, renowned leader of the Republic of Palmares, which was created by runaway slaves in the seventeenth century. As links with activists and movements in the Americas and continental Africa deepened, participants argued quite boldly, "Perhaps the most important contemporary phenomenon in the African world is the emergence and re-assertion of the African people of South and Central America within the context of Pan-Africanism. A new militancy and black consciousness has burst in Latin America."[101]

Black Power arose, too, amidst the horrors of apartheid. This was no isolated affair, peculiar to South Africa. As one chronicler of the movement there charted, "Waves generated by African independence lapped at American shores, slogans shouted in American ghettoes echoed in Africa."[102] In South Africa, the interlocution was most evident in the rise of Black Consciousness, the local name for Black Power. Inspired by radical movements and writings elsewhere in Africa, black students led by Steve Biko and the South African Students' Organisation (SASO) found SNCC's rejection of white liberalism and Fanon's rejection of Europe especially apt as they struggled as subordinates within multiracial organizations.[103] SASO training meetings, for example, involved close study of SNCC's work and its struggles with U.S. white liberals. In South Africa, again as elsewhere, the term "black" was radically recast along political lines, in this case to encompass all oppressed peoples defined as "nonwhite" by the apartheid state. Thus Indians, "Coloureds," and Africans were all included under a single flexible category, namely, black. As the SASO constitution stated, "We define Black people as those who are by law or tradition, politically, economically, and socially discriminated against as a group in the South African society, and identifying themselves as a unit in the struggle."[104] This redefinition marked a radical departure from South African norms, including those of the African National Congress, which had operated through links among racially distinct organizations.

Black international crosscurrents fused in the events of 1968 and its immediate aftermath. In the United States, the assassination of Martin Luther King was followed by a nationwide rebellion: revolts erupted on the streets of more than 100 cities, with scores killed, thousands injured, and tens of thousands of troops called out across the country to restore order. In Mexico City, coming on the heels of the Mexican government's slaughter of hundreds of protesting students, U.S. athletes Tommie Smith and John Carlos raised the Black Power salute on the Olympic reviewing stand. They were immediately expelled from the U.S. team, banished from the Olympic village, and sent back to the United States, where they were greeted with death threats.[105] In Detroit, a wildcat strike by the recently formed Dodge Revolutionary Union Movement shut down the Dodge Main auto plant.[106] The year 1968 also saw Huey Newton on trial for his life, while the Panthers came under murderous police attacks in California and Chicago. Again in 1968, FBI director J. Edgar Hoover announced that the Black Panther Party was the greatest threat to U.S. internal security.

In Africa, student protests against corrupt governments and neocolonial domination exploded in 1968 and later. In the Congo, student agitators declared that "the deep discontent from which we suffer is the colonialist spirit.... The [university] is an enclave of Belgium in the Congo."[107] Next door in Tanzania, students at the University of Dar es Salaam marched in 1969 against the "American" curriculum. In the same year, but on the other side of the continent, Guinean students protested "an anti-Guinean plot hatched by French imperialism,"[108] even as their counterparts in Burkina Faso (then Upper Volta) denounced "the politic-bureaucratic opportunist bourgeoisie" and attacked the U.S. Peace Corps as a "nest of spies."[109] Still in West Africa, similar sentiments at Senegal's University of Dakar propelled a rolling confrontation with the state in 1968–69 that eventually led to a strike supported by unions, the closure of the university, and the arrest of hundreds of students. Back in East Africa, student protests in 1968–69 in Kenya and Ethiopia followed similar trajectories.[110] All across the continent, meanwhile, students demanded action against the rebel white regime in Rhodesia (later Zimbabwe).[111]

The global ideological commerce that was Black Power, and the attendant political protest, also crisscrossed the Caribbean.[112] As Brian Meeks states in the opening line of his chapter, "In 1968, Black Power swept across the Caribbean." During the next three years, Black Power demonstrations, strikes, and riots would erupt in, among other places, Curaçao, Bermuda, the Bahamas, Aruba, Anguilla, Jamaica, and Trinidad, where a civil uprising/army mutiny threatened to topple the government.

The most visible trigger for the Black Power cascade across the Caribbean was the banning from Jamaica in 1968 of Walter Rodney. A Guyanese national and Black Power activist, Rodney taught at the Jamaican campus of the University of the West Indies. Even then, he was emerging as a key theorist of the drive to unite poor communities of African and Indian (South Asian) descent behind an international Black Power program—as revealed in his 1969 book,

The Groundings with My Brothers. University students marching in protest of Rodney's banning were joined by urban youths; the result was a virtual uprising.[113] Nothing of the sort had been seen in Jamaica since the colonial era, in the 1930s.

The "Rodney riots" highlighted the interchange between Black Power in the Caribbean and on the North American mainland. The emergence of black nationalist groupings in Canada, particularly among West Indian students, provided a critical focal point for Caribbean intellectuals as well as a link to more prominent movements in the United States.[114] Caribbean governments moved to cut those ties, including banning the works of U.S.-based black radicals, along with the radicals themselves. But the genie could not be returned to the bottle: protests continued, including by Caribbean students in North America, most notably in Canada.[115] Indeed, protests in Canada would powerfully influence events in Trinidad, where things came to a head in 1970. Eric Williams—prime minister of Trinidad and Tobago, noted historian, and erstwhile anticolonial bête noire—had little patience for Black Power. Its advocates, Williams announced, were "hooligans." Challenged by a Black Power movement reaching out to ever-expanding segments of society, Williams declared a state of emergency and arrested Black Power leaders. When the regime called on the army to enforce the state of emergency, however, a unit headed by junior officers mutinied, refusing to move against fellow "black brothers." The government appeared close to collapse.[116]

But then the wily Williams opened negotiations with the mutineers, agreeing to some of their demands, only to arrest them once they laid down their arms. Williams had been emboldened by the hemisphere's forces of order, which rushed to his support: Venezuelan gunboats appeared on the horizon, the British navy went on alert, U.S. warships set sail at high speed from Puerto Rico, and a U.S. airlift delivered fresh supplies of arms to Williams's government. Bereft of leadership, and unprepared to seize power, as a Leninist party might have done, the insurgency collapsed in the face of the countermobilization by Williams and his allies. Soon the island was still, the regime secured.

Trinidad's "aborted revolution" of 1970 would prove to be the apex of Caribbean Black Power, as Meeks argues in his chapter. Subsequent Black Power–inflected or –inspired attempts at mobilization receded or collapsed entirely, despite some initial successes. These include attempts at armed struggle, as in Trinidad in 1972–74;[117] Indian and African working people's comity, as in the work of Walter Rodney (assassinated in 1980) and the Working People's Alliance in Guyana in the mid- to late 1970s;[118] Black Power mobilization, as in

South Africa leading up to the 1976 Soweto rebellion;[119] and Leninist vanguard politics, as in the Grenada revolution of 1979–83.[120] In the United States, Brazil, and elsewhere, once-vibrant black movements also declined.

An attempt in 1974 to create an international network, through the sixth Pan-African Congress, achieved little success, in no small measure because of the pitfall Amilcar Cabral had warned against: the unreformed postcolonial state. The state sponsors of the sixth Pan-African Congress, held in Tanzania, insisted on respect of the Organization of African Unity's principle of non-interference in the internal affairs of sovereign states. This decision excluded opposition activists not only from Africa but from the Americas and else-where as well. Pan-Africanism, as conceived by the sixth Pan-African Con-gress, would be an affair of states, standing firmly against civil society and black internationalists outside the state sector. The conference's plenary ses-sions naturally descended into "the self-adulation of governments as diverse as Cuba and Mobutu Sese Seko's Zaire." Amidst the hubbub, there she was, the ubiquitous and always resplendent Queen Mother Moore, appearing alongside the equally redoubtable Ras Makonnen, the longtime clearinghouse of black internationalism and chef extraordinaire of pan-Africanism.[121]

The demise of Black Power globally remains a puzzle for its analysts and exponents alike. As Meeks deftly charts in his chapter, by the late 1970s, Black Power in the Caribbean, as in the United States and elsewhere, had become a shadow of its former self, increasingly isolated from its social base, particularly the working classes, and supplanted by Marxist-Leninist, vanguard party prin-ciples. Explanations for this rapid descent vary. Like the movements that came after it, Black Power's emphasis on identity and its rejection of bureaucratic state power posed a fundamental and unresolved dilemma. For some analysts, Black Power thus failed to appreciate the need to overthrow the postcolonial and post–civil rights orders and instead became rooted in community work, emphasizing race over class and rejecting vanguard revolutionary parties. In Trinidad, for example, it is argued that Black Power organizations could have seized power in 1970 but, at the critical moment, lacked the necessary ideo-logical and organizational maturity.[122] C. L. R. James's posthumous critique of Rodney's political practice in Guyana argued along similar lines.[123]

Others point to the patriarchal and masculinist limitations of Black Power,[124] and to the emergence of alternate identities and new social movements for which Black Power could not provide a home. In the United States, the pre-dominance of cultural black nationalism, often expressing the interests of a rising black petite bourgeoisie and political elite, is often cited for the inability of black nationalists to construct broad-based political organizations.[125] In South Africa, the resurgence of the African National Congress after the 1976 Soweto rebellion is similarly attributed to its bureaucratic capacity to absorb the thousands of activists who fled the country in the wake of the repression that followed the rebellion.[126] This was so despite the fact that the Soweto rebellion was rooted in Black Consciousness, an ideology that explicitly rejected the form of political mobilization the African National Congress had pursued before it was banned in 1960. Organization, it seemed, had trumped ideology.

In addition to its own internal weaknesses, organizational and ideological, Black Power's demise was due to another major consideration: the sheer weight of the counterrevolution directed against it globally. The Thermidor, white and black, expressed itself most immediately in violent repression, as charted in the chapters by Meeks and Spencer. National liberation and Black Power leaders were everywhere imprisoned, exiled, and, assassinated—including Malcolm X, Amilcar Cabral, Steve Biko, Fred Hampton, George Jackson, Eduardo Mondlane, Samora Machel, and Walter Rodney. In the United States, Africa, and the Caribbean, state repression resulted in death, exile, and imprisonment for thousands of lesser-known activists, even as their organizations were disrupted, infiltrated, and banned. In Africa, student activists were often arrested and impressed into the army. And although COINTELPRO, the U.S. intelligence operations against Black Power and other radicals, has received the most attention, it was hardly the only such undertaking.[127] Spymasters worldwide linked up to pursue black radicals, as seen in the cooperation of Jamaican, Guyanese, and U.S. (and apparently British) intelligence services in tracking the activities of Walter Rodney.[128]

By the early 1980s, a more formative response, less dependent on overt repression, had emerged. Faced with unruly populations at home and abroad, powerful states and some of their leading intellectuals conceded key pillars of the postwar liberal order. The quest for integration was abandoned, the hubris of equality and progress was jettisoned, and national development planning, so extensively promoted by theorists of modernization in the preceding decades, was cast aside as the detritus of a bygone era. In their wake arose a new program, neoliberalism, which dictated the end of the welfare and social democratic state in the global North and the developmental state in the global South.[129] Simultaneously, the language of assimilation and equality was replaced with the discourse of a neoracist "multiculturalism," whereby difference could be accepted and celebrated even as racial and ethnic inequality accelerated.[130] These innovations went hand in hand with increasing racial and social controls, marked most vividly by the criminalization and incarceration of black communities in the Americas and Europe and the erection of new barriers to protect white communities.[131]

This time around, as before, the white Thermidor provoked a black countermovement. Drawn from and appealing to communities increasingly marginalized by state design, a younger generation began to forge new forms of protest rooted in cultural, as distinct from organizational, politics. This reflected, in turn, the legacy of the long black Sixties, from which cultural nationalists emerged relatively unscathed and were thus well placed to seize the opportunities of a new stirring of black internationalism. A common thread connected the efforts of cultural nationalists across global Africa, from Afrocentrists in North America to promoters of Ubuntu in southern Africa. They all denounced the traducers of black folk and celebrated a common African humanity.

The channels of communication were global, coursing most notably through today's black telegraph, namely, the world-embracing black music community. One of its iconic figures, Tupac Amaru Shakur, was quite literally the product of the long black Sixties: his Black Panther mother, Afeni Shakur, was pregnant with him while in jail on bombing charges. Tupac, like many others, was inspired by the revolutionary chants of early rap that called for a return to a radical, African consciousness.[132] Even those artists who became commercially visible—such as KRS-One, Public Enemy, and NWA—revived the historic black internationalist chant against the forces of Babylon and sang for those who were, increasingly, assigned to social death in the growing U.S. prison archipelago.[133]

This miniwave in black mobilization reached its peak in the United States with the Million Man and Million Woman marches, apparently the largest black public political events ever in the United States.[134] Led and organized by neither black politicians nor civil rights organizations, the 1995 Million Man March marked a startling affirmation of a black nationalism that had been growing throughout the new neoliberal, neoracist era. It also marked the flourishing of cultural nationalism, but not yet any organized, political black nationalism. Thus it was left to cultural nationalist Maulana Ron Karenga to compose the founding statement of the Million Man March, while Louis Farrakhan, committed to both patriarchy and black capitalism, emerged as its most prominent figure. None of this prevented the now legendary Queen Mother Moore—one of the most redoubtable freedom fighters of the twentieth century, having made the journey from Garveyite black nationalism to communism and then back to black nationalism—from making her last major public appearance at the Million Man March. She would die less than two years later, just shy of her ninety-ninth birthday.

The Million Woman March, held in 1997, offered a far more trenchant critique of the new world order than did the Million Man March. Indeed the second march, which attracted nearly as many participants, was a counterpoint to the first. The Million Woman March singled out the U.S. state, attacking its social retrenchment at home and imperial ambitions abroad. Unlike the Million Man March, whose leading lights saw much virtue in the fact that they made no demands on the state, the Million Woman March advanced a twelve-point program and excoriated U.S. policy at all levels. Going well beyond the Million Man March's mantra of personal redemption, the Million Woman March rejected the rule of capital and called for protection of the environment.

Sentimentally, the Million Woman March set the stage for the Black Radical Congress (BRC). Organized in 1998, the BRC's goal was to give organizational coherence to the insurgent ideas that had surfaced and spread in this period.[135] It was a bold attempt to mobilize the political consciousness that the two marches had so vividly displayed, but with an explicit rejection of the "end-of-politics" tendency associated with the Million Man March. Espousing a program that was proletarian, feminist, and internationalist, the BRC sought to be a big tent for all self-identified black radicals. Its inaugural meeting in Chicago was the most significant gathering of the African American Left since the Gary Convention of 1972, which attempted a similar undertaking in black radical coalition building.[136] The BRC, which soon became inactive, would prove to be no more enduring than the Gary Convention.

The consciousness that the BRC set out to cohere was hardly confined to the United States. Already in 1994, black activists from various parts of the world had gathered in Kampala, Uganda, seeking to stimulate black mobilization globally. Convened in a region that had just witnessed the Rwanda genocide, and one close to the center of the AIDS pandemic that has wreaked such death and destruction on global Africa, the seventh Pan-African Congress illustrated the revival of civil society in black internationalism. Accordingly, the state actors that had so thoroughly dominated the sixth Pan-African Congress of 1974 were conspicuous by their absence at the seventh Pan-African Congress.[137]

These organizational efforts have yet to bear full fruit in the new millennium. What has formed a new, international black consciousness of surprising and continuing strength is hip hop culture, which has blossomed through music, dance, fashion, video, television, and advertising. Infused by rhythms from beyond the shores of the United States, and infusing them in turn, hip hop emerged out of and brought together very diffuse youth cultures and music genres. As Marc Perry's chapter demonstrates, the growing global space of hip hop has also mobilized new black struggles that have at times contested and attempted to transcend nationally imposed racial identities and the neoliberal era's marginalization of black youth. Perry shows that this is a worldwide phenomenon rooted in local contexts, struggles, and identities. In Cuba, *raperos* have opened new black spaces and identities as the dollarization of the economy has exacerbated social and racial inequalities; in Brazil, rappers target racist police violence and government corruption; in South Africa, rap has expressed the struggle to forge postapartheid black identities from within apartheid's Coloured and African townships; in France, rappers from the elder statesman MC Solaar to younger artists like Disiz le Peste have challenged the neoliberal state and racism.[138] If the lyrics everywhere express locality, they also everywhere chant against the global processes seeking to control, marginalize, and racialize youth.

This global communicative process, involving movement back and forth across continents, is highly conflicted. On one hand, it has resuscitated an oppositional and transnational black identity attractive to black communities. On the other hand, hip hop's movement from creative play in the streets of poor neighborhoods to global success has channeled hip hop into the commercial service of a few global firms. Indeed, a central tension in hip hop everywhere is the battle between the culture's roots in oppressed communities and the currently dominant forces, propelled by corporate capital, that celebrate money, material things, and masculinity.[139] Lament at the loss of artistic grounding due to success is an old refrain and can be widely heard in today's hip hop.[140] However, its hip hop counterpoint is singular, highlighting the power of rapacious white corporations to control and profit from stereotypes of black men and women.[141] The commodification and marketing of black youth culture is now very much in ascendance.

This speaks a common truth: both the political and cultural initiatives of the latest countermovement have yet to be carried forward to a new wave of black internationalism. Is the current moment a replication of the early 1960s, redolent of a latent sensibility that seeks to redefine the black and international agenda? We do not know. Of one thing, however, we can be certain: the struggle for black liberation in all its changing hues and places is now, as ever, an international one.

1. The writings of some of the foundational figures of black internationalism are contained in various anthologies. See, for example, Potkay and Burr, *Black Atlantic Writers*, and Brooks and Saillant, *"Face Zion Forward."*

2. The point here is that black internationalism is a product of exile, and that it emerged among the Western diaspora (in the Americas and Europe) as opposed to the Eastern diaspora (in West Asia, the Mediterranean, and the Indian subcontinent). Although considerably older than the one in the West, the Eastern African Diaspora, for all its achievements, including any number of writers, soldiers, and leaders, never developed the transcendent sense of African consciousness that produced black internationalism. See, for example, Harris, *African Presence in Asia*; Hunwick and Powell, *African Diaspora in the Mediterranean*; Catlin-Jairazbhoy and Alpers, *Sidis and Scholars*; and Alpers, "Recollecting Africa."

3. The neglect of black experiences in the traditional Western metanarrative is discussed below. In the case of the national narrative, even studies that go against the grain of the standard storyline of "The Rise of the West," as in the best social history from below, remain burdened by Western universalism–national historicism. See, for example, the otherwise admirable text produced by the American Social History Project, *Who Built America?*

4. See, for example, across a very wide literature and number of perspectives, such works as Tilly, *Social Movements*; Sanderson, *Revolutions*; and McAdam, McCarthy, and Zald, *Comparative Perspectives on Social Movements*.

5. Among a wide range of highly cited works, see, for example, Appadurai, "Disjuncture and Difference"; Castells, *Information Age*; and Hardt and Negri, *Empire*.

6. Representative samples from the early twentieth century include Du Bois, *The Negro*; Padmore, *Life and Struggles*; and James, *History*. Subsequent scholarship in this vein includes Shepperson and Price, *Independent African*; Harris, *Global Dimensions*; Robinson, *Black Marxism*; Walters, *Pan Africanism*; Lemelle and Kelley, *Imagining Home*; Okpewho, Davies, and Mazrui, *African Diaspora*; and Zachernuk, *Colonial Subjects*. Then there is Appiah, *In My Father's House*, which denies the existence of an African world.

7. West and Martin, "Introduction: The Rival Africas"; Martin and West, "Ascent, Triumph, and Disintegration." On the history and crises of African studies, see also Guyer, *African Studies*, and Zeleza, *Manufacturing African Studies*.

8. Huggins, *Afro-American Studies*; Hall, *In the Vineyard*; Rojas, *From Black Power to Black Studies*; Grady-Willis, *Challenging US Apartheid*, 143–68; Joseph, "Black Studies."

9. On the isolation and the decline of the British African studies establishment, see Bundy, "Continuing a Conversation"; Fyfe, "Emergence and Evolution of African Studies"; Hodder-Williams, "African Studies"; and McCracken, "African History in British Universities."

10. See, for example, Asante, *Afrocentric Idea*. Asante was widely attacked in the culture wars of the 1990s, as in Howe, *Afrocentrism*. Bernal was also targeted for his criticism of European classicists' treatment of Africa in his *Black Athena*. For Bernal's critics, see Lefkowitz and Rogers, *Black Athena Revisited*, along with Bernal's response in Moore, *Black Athena Writes Back*.

11. On the revival and extension of the key term "diaspora," see Brock, "African [Diaspora] Studies"; Palmer, "Defining and Studying"; Patterson and Kelley, "Unfinished Migrations"; Manning, "Africa and the African Diaspora"; Harris, "Expanding the Scope"; Alpers, "Recollecting Africa"; Akyeampong, "Africans in the Diaspora"; and Zeleza, "Rewriting the African Diaspora."

12. The phrase is borrowed from St. Clair Drake, who in turn partly riffs on Du Bois. See Drake, *Black Folk Here and There*, and Du Bois, *Black Folk*.

13. The critique began at the Pan-African Conference of 1900 and continued in other forums in the years leading up to World War I, including the Universal Races Congress. See Mathurin, *Henry Sylvester Williams*; Geiss, *Pan-African Movement*; and the *Radical History Review* special issue on the First Universal Races Congress of 1911.

14. Scott, "Common Wind"; Santiago-Valles, "World-Historical Ties."

15. See, for example, Aptheker, *American Negro Slave Revolts*; Craton, *Testing the Chains*; and Price, *Maroon Societies*.

16. Quarles, *The Negro*; Frey, *Water from the Rock*; Rael, *Black Identity*; Nash, *Forgotten Fifth*; Egerton, *Death or Liberty*.

17. Pybus, *Epic Journeys of Freedom*, 57–72.

18. Sanneh, *Abolitionists Abroad*; Pybus, *Epic Journeys of Freedom*; Rael, *Black Identity*; Byrd, *Captives and Voyagers*.

19. Callahan, *Talking Book*; Wimbush, *African Americans and the Bible*; Kidd, *Forging of Races*, 247–70.

20. Bebbington, *Evangelicalism*; Ditchfield, *Evangelical Revival*; Hempton, *Methodism*; Kidd, *Great Awakening*.

21. Raboteau, *Slave Religion*; Frey and Wood, *Come Shouting to Zion*. The Evangelical Revival was not the first serious attempt to convert enslaved Africans to Protestant Christianity. A previous revival in the Danish Caribbean, one in which the black missionary Rebecca was centrally involved, proved quite successful. But, in contrast to the black internationalism that would become associated with the Evangelical Revival, "Rebecca's revival" developed no sustained critique of black oppression or offered any vision of black liberation. See Sensbach, *Rebecca's Revival*.

22. Rout, *African Experience*; Palmer, *Slaves of the White God*; Thornton, *Africa and Africans*; Sweet, *Recreating Africa*.

23. Acts 17:26.

24. It is cited, for instance, in Cugoano, "Thoughts and Sentiments," 140, and Equiano, "Interesting Narrative," 178.

25. See also Frey, *Water from the Rock*.

26. The Declaration of Independence denounced the British monarch because, among other reasons, he "excited domestic insurrections amongst us, and has endeavoured to bring on the inhabitants of our frontiers, the merciless Indian Savages, whose known rule of warfare, is an undistinguished destruction of all ages, sexes and conditions." The reference to "domestic insurrections" recalled the proclamation of Lord Dunmore, the royal governor of Virginia, who offered slaves freedom in return for joining the British army.

27. In addition to our chapter below, for the broad scholarly treatment of the Haitian

Revolution, see, most notably, James, *Black Jacobins*; Fick, *Making of Haiti*; Geggus, *Haitian Revolutionary Studies*; and Dubois, *Avengers*.

28. See, most famously, Gilroy, *Black Atlantic*. But see, too, Edwards, *Practice of Diaspora*, which artfully bridges the Anglophone/Francophone divide.

29. Trouillot, *Silencing the Past*, 70–101.

30. Scott, "Common Wind."

31. The sonnet is titled "To Toussaint Louverture." See <http://thelouvertureproject .org/index.php?title=To_Toussaint_Louverture_-_poem_by_Wordsworth>.

TOUSSAINT, the most unhappy man of men!
Whether the whistling Rustic tend his plough
Within thy hearing, or thy head be now
Pillowed in some deep dungeon's earless den;
O miserable Chieftain! where and when
Wilt thou find patience? Yet die not; do thou
Wear rather in thy bonds a cheerful brow:
Though fallen thyself, never to rise again,
Live, and take comfort. Thou hast left behind
Powers that will work for thee; air, earth, and skies;
There's not a breathing of the common wind
That will forget thee; thou hast great allies;
Thy friends are exultations, agonies,
And love, and man's unconquerable mind.

32. Fyfe, *History of Sierra Leone*; Shick, *Behold the Promised Land*; Zachernuk, *Colonial Subjects*.

33. Farwell, *Great War*; Strachan, *First World War*; *Journal of African History*, special issue; Echenberg, *Colonial Conscripts*; Page, *Chiwaya War*.

34. Howe, *Race, War, and Nationalism*; Sweeney, *History of the American Negro*; Barbeau and Henri, *Unknown Soldiers*.

35. Trotter, *Great Migration*; Harrison, *Black Exodus*.

36. Watkins-Owens, *Blood Relations*; James, *Holding aloft the Banner*.

37. Ferrell, *Woodrow Wilson*.

38. Kornweibel, *"Seeing Red"*; Schneider, *We Return Fighting*.

39. May and Cohen, "Interaction"; Jenkinson, "Glasgow Race"; Stovall, "Colour Blind France?"; Wilson, "Britain's Red Summer."

40. See also Putnam, *Company They Kept*.

41. The standard works on Garveyism include Vincent, *Black Power*; Martin, *Race First*; Hill, *Marcus Garvey*; Stein, *World*; and Lewis and Bryan, *Garvey*. Recent specialized studies include Rolinson, *Grassroots Garveyism*, and Harold, *Rise and Fall*. There is also Colin Grant's recent biography, which, although offering few new revelations, is highly readable and engaging, if satirical at points. See Grant, *Negro with a Hat*.

42. Hill and Pirio, "'Africa for the Africans'"; Rolinson, *Grassroots Garveyism*; Okonkwo, "Garvey Movement"; Williams, "Garveyism"; West, "Seeds Are Sown"; Robaina, "Marcus Garvey in Cuba"; Baba Kake, "L'influence"; Garcia Dominguez, "Garvey and Cuba."

43. The metaphor has been popularized of late in Linebaugh and Rediker, *Many-Headed Hydra*.

44. Adeleke, *UnAfrican Americans*, accuses African American supporters of Providential Design of complicity in European colonialism and of even being its advance guards. The censure of Providential Design is fair enough, if a tad ahistorical, but the African Americans had nothing like the power and influence Adeleke ascribes to them. The critique further fails to note that many among the first generation of Western-missionary-educated continental Africans, notably in the British colonies, also subscribed to Providential Design, albeit with an emphasis on the indigenous rather than the external black agency. Hence its currency with black South Africans, among others. See, for example, Willan, *Sol Platjee*, and Zachernuk, *Colonial Subjects*.

45. Crummell, *Future of Africa*; Moses, *Alexander Crummell*; Blyden, *Christianity, Islam, and the Negro Race*; Lynch, *Edward Wilmot Blyden*.

46. Taylor, *Veiled Garvey*; Martin, *Amy Ashwood Garvey*; Bair, "'Ethiopia Shall Stretch Forth'"; Satter, "Marcus Garvey"; Martin, "Women in the Garvey Movement"; Ford-Smith, "Women and the Garvey Movement in Jamaica"; McDuffie, "Black Women"; Martin, *Poetical Works*.

47. Quoted in Harold, *Rise and Fall*, 45.

48. This includes the black underworld, most notably Casper Holstein. The top "numbers" man in Harlem, Holstein was also patron of the arts; defender of his native Virgin Islands against the United States, which had recently acquired the islands from the Dutch; supporter of the UNIA; and frequent contributor to the *Negro World*, largely on the Virgin Islands question. See Grant, *Negro with a Hat*, 235–36.

49. Burkett, *Garveyism as a Religious Movement*; Terry-Thompson, *History*; Newman, "Origins." On the African Orthodox Church in Africa, see Natsoulas, "Patriarch McGuire"; Johnson, *Archbishop Daniel William Alexander*; Wentink, "Orthodox Church"; and West, "Ethiopianism and Colonialism."

50. Bair, "'Ethiopia Shall Stretch Forth.'"

51. Essien-Udom, *Black Nationalism*; Lincoln, *Black Muslims*; Clegg, *Original Man*; Turner, *Islam in the African American Experience*; Gomez, *Black Crescent*; Curtis, *Black Muslim Religion*.

52. Gomez, *Black Crescent*, 128–275.

53. Turner, *Islam in the African American Experience*, 47–67, 109–46.

54. On the ABB, see Makalani, "For the Liberation."

55. Valentine, "Two Religions." "C. Valentine" was a pseudonym for the ABB leader and *Crusader* editor Cyril Briggs. Other black radicals, such as the learned Hubert Harrison, also evinced a keen interest in and knowledge of Islam. See, for example, Perry, *Hubert Harrison Reader*, 310–19. See also Jeffrey Perry's biography, *Hubert Harrison*.

56. Post, "Bible as Ideology"; Hill, "Dread History"; Barrett, *Rastafarians*; Campbell, *Rasta and Resistance*; Murrell, Spencer, and McFarlane, *Chanting Down Babylon*; Zips, *Rastafari*.

57. Asante, *Pan-African Protest*; Scott, *Sons of Sheba's Race*; Harris, *African-American Reactions*. The assault on Ethiopia, which for the black internationalists marked the onset of World War II, would have a profound effect on black politics in various localities. As is often the case, the literature on the United States is richest; see, for example, Plummer,

Rising Wind; Von Eschen, *Race against Empire*; and Meriwether, *Proudly We Can Be Africans*.

58. Ali, *Holy Koran*.

59. Geiss, *Pan-African Movement*, 229–62; Langley, *Pan-Africanism and Nationalism*, 58–88; Esedebe, *Pan-Africanism*, 80–94; Lewis, *W. E. B. Du Bois*, 37–84.

60. On this point see, most authoritatively, Hill, "Introduction."

61. See, for example, Garvey, "Exposé of the Caste System," and Du Bois, "Back to Africa."

62. *Daily Worker*, August 30, 1927.

63. The term, apparently an old one, appears in Haywood, *Black Bolshevik*.

64. On the Comintern, see Degras, *Communist International*.

65. See, for example, Draper, *American Communism and Soviet Russia*, and Klehr, Haynes, and Anderson, *Soviet World of American Communism*.

66. Padmore, *Life and Struggles*, 125–26 (emphasis in original).

67. See, for example, Gallicchio, *African American Encounter*.

68. On Padmore, see Hooker, *Black Revolutionary*. On Padmore, Kouyaté, black internationalism, and communism, see Edwards, *Practice of Diaspora*, 241–305.

69. Naison, *Communists in Harlem*; Kelley, *Hammer and Hoe*; Solomon, *Cry Was Unity*; Maxwell, *New Negro, Old Left*; Mullen and Smethurst, *Left of the Color Line*; Ellis and Sechaba, *Comrades against Apartheid*; Drew, *South Africa's Radical Tradition*; Davidson, Filatova, Gorodnov, and Johns, *South Africa and the Communist International*.

70. James, *Holding aloft the Banner*, 155–84; Solomon, *Cry Was Unity*, 3–21.

71. McDuffie, "Long Journeys" and "Black Women Radicals"; Turner, *Caribbean Crusaders and the Harlem Renaissance*; Sherwood, *Claudia Jones*; Davies, *Left of Karl Marx*.

72. The connection between Gandhism and black internationalism is well exemplified in the life and labor of the African American Bill Sutherland, who expatriated to Ghana in the 1950s and moved on to Tanzania in the 1960s, working for both governments in the process. He was also engaged with anticolonial and peace (including nuclear proliferation) struggles and activists in Africa, the United States, and Europe. See Sutherland and Meyer, *Guns and Gandhi in Africa*; Sutherland, "Bill Sutherland"; and Gaines, *American Africans in Ghana*. On Gandhi and South Africa, see Brown and Prozesky, *Gandhi and South Africa*, and Swan, *Gandhi*.

73. Geiss, *Pan-African Movement*, 385–408; Padmore, *Pan-Africanism or Communism?*, 152–70; Adi and Sherwood, *1945 Manchester Pan-African Congress*.

74. Among the challenges were Cold War–inspired, anticommunist attacks on movements and individuals most committed to radical change and black solidarity across national boundaries, including blacklistings, expulsions, deportations, and, in the case of British Guiana (Guyana), the termination of self-rule under colonial tutelage. Such attacks were carried out both by colonial and national powers and by nationalist movements fearful of being red-baited. See, variously, Padmore, *Pan-Africanism or Communism?*; Morgenthau, *Political Parties*; Anderson, *Eyes off the Prize*; Horne, *Black and Red* and *Red Seas*; Duberman, *Paul Robeson*; Smith, *Becoming Something*; and Rabe, *U.S. Intervention in British Guiana*.

75. Matthew 6:33: "But seek ye first the kingdom of God, and his righteousness; and all

these things shall be added unto you." For Nkrumah's own account of the rise of Ghana, see his *Ghana*. The standard scholarly treatment is Austin, *Politics in Ghana*.

76. Lumumba, "Independence Day Speech."

77. De Witte, *Assassination of Lumumba*.

78. See, among others, Horne, *Savage War of Peace*; Quandt, *Revolution and Political Leadership*; Amrane and Djamila, *Femmes en combat*.

79. Anderson, *Histories of the Hanged*; Elkins, *Imperial Reckoning*; Presley, *Kikuyu Women*.

80. Birmingham and Ranger, "Settlers and Liberators in the South"; Davidson, *People's Cause*.

81. Lodge, *Black Politics in South Africa*, 231–60.

82. Fanon, *Wretched of the Earth*, 148–205.

83. Cabral, *Revolution in Guinea* and *Return to the Source*.

84. Van Deburg, *New Day in Babylon*.

85. Malcolm X, *Malcolm X Speaks*.

86. Malcolm X et al., "Program of the Organization of Afro-American Unity," 2.

87. On the radicalization of SNCC, see Carson, *In Struggle*; Payne, *I've Got the Light of Freedom*; and Carmichael with Thelwell, *Ready for the Revolution*. For a guide to the growing literature on Black Power (still largely on the United States), see the historiographical surveys by Joseph, "Introduction," and Self, "Black Panther Party." As these surveys note, many of the hallmark elements of the radical black 1960s, such as armed self-defense and the critique of state power, predated the mid-1960s (on this last point, see also Wendt, "Protection or Path?"). For internationalist perspectives on the period, see Edmondson, "Internationalization of Black Power"; Singh, "Black Panthers"; Kelley, "Stormy Weather"; Wilkins, "Making of Black Internationalists" and "'In the Belly'"; and Johnson, *Revolutionaries*, 131–72.

88. The party's misogyny and homophobia are cast wide in Wallace, *Black Macho and the Myth*. See, by contrast, the perspective of former Panther Party chair Elaine Brown, *Taste of Power*; Cleaver, "Women, Power, and Revolution"; and more broadly, contrasting the United States and the party, Matthews, "'No One Ever Asks,'" and Brown, *Fighting for US*.

89. Newton, "Women's Liberation and Gay Liberation Movements."

90. On black and other feminisms of the period, see Collier-Thomas and Franklin, *Sisters in the Struggle*; Matthews, "'No One Ever Asks'"; Ward, "Third World Women's Alliance"; Springer, *Living for the Revolution*; and Roth, *Separate Roads to Feminism*. For an overview that places gender at the center of the movement, see Grady-Willis, *Challenging US Apartheid*.

91. Newton, "Message to the Vietnamese," 595.

92. The international connections of the Black Panther Party are summarized in Clemons and Jones, "Global Solidarity," and Cleaver, "Back to Africa." See also Carmichael with Thelwell, *Ready for the Revolution*; Marquese, *Redemption Song*; Tyson, *Radio Free Dixie*; and Woodard, *Nation within a Nation*.

93. Hiro, *Black British*, 44; James and Harris, *Inside Babylon*.

94. See Obi Egbuna's biography, *Destroy This Temple*.

95. Shukra, *Changing Pattern of Black Politics*, 24–25.

96. Hiro, *Black British*, 64.

97. Sivanandan, *Communities of Resistance*, 66 (emphasis in original).

98. Sykes, "Opening Statement," 11–12.

99. Hanchard, *Orpheus and Power*; Leal, "Fárígá/Ifaradá"; Mitchell, "Blacks and the Abertura Democrática"; Fontaine, "Transnational Relations and Racial Mobilization."

100. Gonzalez, "Unified Black Movement." For the postemancipation backdrop to these developments, see Butler, *Freedoms Given*.

101. Nascimento, *Pan-Africanism and South America*, 1.

102. Gerhart, *Black Power in South Africa*, 273.

103. Biko, *I Write What I Like*, especially the chapter "White Racism and Black Consciousness," 61–72.

104. South African Students' Organization, "South African Students' Organization Amended Constitution," C210.

105. Hartmann, *Race, Culture, and the Revolt of the Black Athlete*.

106. Georgakas and Surkin, *Detroit, I Do Mind Dying*; Geschwender, "Marxist-Leninist Organization."

107. Hanna and Hanna, "Cynical Nationalists," 54–55.

108. Cited in Hanna, "Student Protest in Independent Africa," 180; for an overview, see Legum, "Year of the Students."

109. Legum, "Year of the Students," A9.

110. Hanna, Hanna, and Sauer, "Active Minority," esp. 71–78; Dirlik, "Third World in 1968."

111. Hanna and Hanna, "Cynical Nationalists," 53; Legum, "Year of the Students," A12, A14, A26.

112. See, among others, Meeks, *Radical Caribbean*; Oxaal, *Black Intellectuals*; Nettleford, *Identity, Race, and Protest*; and Thomas, *Modern Blackness*.

113. On Rodney, see Alpers and Fontaine, *Walter Rodney*; Bogues, *Black Heretics*, 125–50; Lewis, *Walter Rodney's Intellectual and Political Thought*; and Rohlehr, *Transgression*, 338–73.

114. Austin, "All Roads Led to Montreal."

115. Ibid.; Forsythe, *Let the Niggers Burn!*

116. Meeks, "1970 Revolution."

117. Millette, "Guerrilla War in Trinidad."

118. Abraham, "Exceptional Victories"; Lewis, *Walter Rodney's Intellectual and Political Thought*, 202–53; Westmaas, "Resisting Orthodoxy."

119. Gerhart, *Black Power in South Africa*, 257–316.

120. Meeks, *Caribbean Revolutions and Revolutionary Theory*, 129–86.

121. Nascimento, *Pan-Africanism and South America*, 137. On the sixth Pan-African Congress, see also Rodney, "Towards the Sixth Pan-African Congress," and Fuller, "Notes." Born George Griffith in Guyana, Makonnen eventually made his way to England, where he came to prominence during the 1935 Italian invasion of Ethiopia, when he assumed the persona of an Ethiopian prince (*ras*), changing his name to Ras Makonnen. His restaurants served the dual function of meeting places and eating houses for pan-Africanists in England during the interwar years. Unlike Queen Mother Moore,

Makonnen left a published testament of his personal and political peregrinations. See his *Pan-Africanism from Within*.

122. Meeks discusses such views in "1970 Revolution."

123. James, "Walter Rodney"; Bogues, *Black Heretics*, 143–46.

124. See Wallace, *Black Macho and the Myth*; Brown, *Taste of Power*; and for Africa, Campbell, *Reclaiming Zimbabwe*.

125. This reflects the long-standing classification, based on the writings of Harold Cruse, dividing the integrationist tradition from the nationalist tradition and, subsequently, cultural nationalists from political nationalists. See Cruse, *Crisis of the Negro Intellectual*; see also Van Deburg, *New Day in Babylon*, 292–308, and Bush, *We Are Not What We Seem*, 194–213.

126. Marx, *Lessons of Struggle*, 91–105; Lodge, *Black Politics in South Africa*, 321–62.

127. Grady-Willis, "Black Panther Party"; Churchill, "'To Disrupt, Discredit, and Destroy'"; Churchill and Vander Wall, *COINTELPRO Papers*.

128. West, "Walter Rodney and Black Power."

129. Harvey, *Brief History of Neoliberalism*.

130. Balibar, "Is There a 'Neo-Racism'?"

131. The literature is diffuse and expanding. See, for example, Garland, *Culture of Control*; Sudbury, *Global Lockdown*; and Wacquant, *Deadly Symbiosis*.

132. See Dyson, *Holler If You Hear Me*; Keeling, "'Homegrown Revolutionary'?"; Cobb, *To the Break of Dawn*; and as memoir, Bastfield, *Back in the Day*.

133. Allen, "Making the Strong Survive"; Rose, *Black Noise*, 99–125; Kelley, "Kickin' Reality"; Chang, *Can't Stop, Won't Stop*; Neal, *What The Music Said*, 134–35; Basu and Lemelle, *Vinyl Ain't Final*. For a discussion of the broader cultural context in which hip hop emerged, see Cheney, *Brothers Gonna Work It Out*.

134. Madhubuti and Karenga, *Million Man March/Day of Absence*; West, "Like a River."

135. Cha-Jua, "Black Radical Congress"; Zerai and Campbell, "Black Radical Congress."

136. Woodard, "Amiri Baraka."

137. Abdul-Raheem, *Pan-Africanism*; Bankie, *Globalising Africans*.

138. In addition to Marc Perry's chapter, on these and related instances, see the essays in Basu and Lemelle, *Vinyl Ain't Final*; Durand, *Black, Blanc, Beur* (France); West-Durán, "Rap's Diasporic Dialogues" (Cuba); and Condry, *Hip-Hop Japan*.

139. Compare, for example, the interpretation of Kelley's "Kickin' Reality," which celebrates and defends black youth culture, with Queely's more critical stance in "Hip Hop"; see also Lipsitz, *Dangerous Crossroads*.

140. See, for example, the Black Eyed Peas, "Going Gone."

141. As in this sample from the Pete Rock and Black Ice collaboration, "Truth Is":

So the business feed you all the weed and ecstasy
and a little bit of paper to provide some pacification
from all the bullshit frustration they serve you
Meanwhile they corrupt your perception of what the real is
See they takin' all our businessmen, and givin' 'em the mindsets of drug dealers

Took all our messengers, made 'em rappers
just flappin' they jaws afraid to admit their treason
Took all our soldiers for the cause, made 'em killers for no reason. . . .
I just know what the truth is
Been intertwined in this puddin' for 'bout a year now so I know where the proof is
See, it lines these midtown Manhattan skyscrapers
where former hustlers like myself sign papers
and pull off fucked capers like, 16 infamous stars of the time
They got us choppin' and baggin' and
servin' that shit to niggaz 16 bars at a time now . . . .

44

PART **1**

General Toussaint Louverture (1743–1803), as conceived by Jacob Lawrence. Leader of the Haitian Revolution, Toussaint Louverture was born into slavery but led African armies that defeated French, British, and Spanish forces and abolished slavery in Haiti and Santo Domingo. He was eventually captured and shipped to a cold and damp prison fortress in France, where he died in solitary confinement. (Jacob Lawrence, "General Toussaint L'Ouverture" [1986], ©2009 The Jacob and Gwendolyn Lawrence Foundation, Seattle/Artists Rights Society [ARS], New York)

The American Revolution and the Creation of a Global African World

SYLVIA FREY

The second half of the eighteenth century was a period of breathtaking historical change. It was an era in which peoples and ideas, commodities and cultures, crossed and recrossed regional and national boundaries from multiple corners of the world, transforming global demographics, building new Atlantic economies, and making connections in a variety of arenas—economic, political, linguistic, and religious. Africa was among the key points of circulation in this emerging world order, and African peoples made up a disproportionately large share of the human cargoes that traversed global waters. The African continent and its inhabitants were centrally involved in a vast process with overlapping and interacting parts, some of which were engaged in struggles against slavery and the expansion of capitalist modes of production. Within those transnational circuits lay the foundations of black internationalism, or pan-Africanism.

In this essay I argue that the era of the American Revolution played a seminal role in the development and spread of pan-Africanism. By contrast, North American historiography usually locates the origins of pan-Africanism in the nineteenth century, with the rise of emigration and colonization movements. An even more constricted temporal approach marks pan-Africanism as a twentieth-century phenomenon, associating it with W. E. B. Du Bois and the five Pan-African Congresses (1919, 1921, 1923, 1927, and 1945), along with Marcus Garvey and the Universal Negro Improvement Association.[1] In fact, African Americans of the American Revolutionary era played a significant part in the foundational wave of pan-Africanism: they helped to create and spread a diasporic consciousness unified by a collective memory of a lost homeland.

Definitional problems bedevil the subject of pan-Africanism. I use the term in the sense suggested by George Shepperson, who distinguished *Pan-*

Africanism as a "clearly recognized movement associated with the five Pan-African Congresses" from *pan*-Africanism as "a group of movements, many very ephemeral," in which cultural elements often predominate.[2] My conceptual boundaries are the Black Atlantic created by the Atlantic slave trade, as distinct from the African Diaspora, a term that refers to the worldwide migration of African peoples, which began some 1,500 years before the emergence of the Atlantic diaspora.[3]

The phenomenon of pan-Africanism did not sprout by happenstance but was driven by ideological forces with truly complex origins. Its lineage can be traced to three main sources: evangelical Protestantism, whose affirmation of a millenarian future was a source of inspiration and promise; the era of the American Revolution, when the messianic destiny seemed to be at hand; and the black writers whose living memories of Africa served as a cultural anchor for exiled African peoples. An essential first step in the development of pan-Africanism was the emergence of a corporate African or racial identity in place of numerous ethnic identities. This occurred at different rates in different places, developed in multiple centers and institutional structures, and drew from diverse sources, the threads of which twisted into a knot during the tumultuous era of the American Revolution. For generations of enslaved men and women born in Africa, memory of the homeland remained strong and vital. Such memory was not just visibly present in architecture and dance but was also preserved aurally in language and music. African consciousness faded more quickly in slave societies that ceased to import slaves directly from Africa early, such as Virginia and Barbados. As direct imports slowed and the slave trade gradually ended, firsthand knowledge of Africa faded. Africa, however, lingered in the collective memory secretly passed down through the generations, whispered as the home of the ancestors and a place of freedom, once upon a time. Indeed, it seemed that the greater the distance in time, and the more removed from its physical reality, the more compelling Africa became as a symbol for people exiled from their homelands.

Evangelical Pan-Africanism, Black Seafaring, and the New Black Identity

A preliminary step in the rise of pan-Africanism began in the eighteenth century, with the forging of a spiritual community within autonomous black churches that sprung up throughout the Caribbean and North America under black leadership during the period of international revivalism.[4] Evangelical revivalism was black and white, slave and free, more female than male, and unfolded within wide regional and transatlantic networks. At just about the time that John Wesley launched the Methodist movement in England, the Moravians, a pietistic offshoot of the Lutheran Church, inaugurated a revolutionary system of evangelization known as itinerancy. One of the pioneers of that system was a Dutch-speaking former slave named Rebecca Protten. Born in the Caribbean, Rebecca was in the vanguard of the first phase of a transatlantic black evangelical movement that had its genesis in white evangelical Protestantism but developed its own distinctive theology and ritual practices and provided some of the core beliefs of the black Atlantic revolutionary tradition. Decades before such better-known black evangelists as Olaudah Equiano, John Marrant, John Jea, George Liele, and David George began their worldwide itinerancy, Rebecca had traveled thousands of miles over two continents and several islands, broadcasting the evangelical message of divine deliverance from the bonds of sin.[5]

Rebecca is unique, but her story is not. David Margate was almost certainly the only black British missionary to work in the American colonies and quite possibly the first to articulate in unequivocal terms the biblical story of Exodus as both a spiritual pilgrimage and literal freedom from captivity, an idea that became a crucial motif in black diasporic discourse. "David the African" arrived in Charleston, South Carolina, in 1775. Claiming he was a second Moses "called to deliver his people from slavery," David "not only severely reflected against the laws of the Province respecting slaves but even against the thing itself; he also compared their state to that of the Israelites during their Egyptian Bondade [sic]." David preached in South Carolina only seven months before he had to be spirited out of the colony to escape a lynch mob. But he had planted the seed of African consciousness and antislavery that continued to flower in all kinds of ways and in a variety of different contexts.[6] The journey from international evangelical revivalism to evangelical pan-Africanism had begun.

One of the forces driving the change was the black seafaring tradition. It is impossible to exaggerate the importance of black sailors in the creation of a diasporic consciousness. Black seafaring men were broadcasters of news, creators of a black literary tradition, and prime movers of rebellion. By the middle of the eighteenth century, the maritime industry employed a significant percentage of the Atlantic male slave populations as sailors, wharf workers, or fishermen.[7] Sailing vessels functioned as global conveyor belts circulating around ocean basins, connecting Caribbean island communities to the great metropolitan ports of Europe, the docks of Atlantic North America, and the village markets and forts of Atlantic Africa. There were remarkable men among the black crews, pioneers in the antislavery movement and architects of a new diasporic consciousness formed around a remembrance of Africa.

Olaudah Equiano, John Jea, John Marrant, and others were not just sailors but, equally important, Christian ministers. In their professional identities as sailors, merchant mariners, fishermen, and preachers, they circulated through what Paul Gilroy calls "the black Atlantic world."[8] Men like Jea, who signed on as a ship's cook, were as much part of the transnational circuit of evangelical preachers as John Wesley and George Whitefield, who launched the international movement known as the Great Awakening. Sailors wrote the first six autobiographies of blacks published in English before 1800. They included celebrated figures like Equiano, Marrant, Jea, Briton Hammon, Quobna Ottobah Cugoano, James Albert Ukawsaw Gronniosaw, and Paul Cuffe. Their writings speak of a new sense of energy and power derived for the most part from a variety of religious and secular ideas, and they collectively contributed in major ways to shifting consciousness away from ethnicity and toward a collective psyche.[9]

Equiano embodied that experience, and his memoir served as a fascinating chapter in the development of a black diasporic consciousness. His ethnic or national identity was fluid. Whereas Jea and Cugoano identified closely with their native land, Equiano was not really from any single place, but an international figure. His Interesting Narrative related his personal journey from his birth in 1745 in Benin, Africa, to his kidnapping at age eleven. Subsequently he became, like so many other pan-African pioneers, a sort of vagabond, moving from country to country as an enslaved sailor, his name changing with the same frequency as he changed owners and crossed cultural and geographic boundaries—from Michael to Jacob to Gustavus Vassa, the last the name he came to use most often.[10]

Equiano's writings are an extraterritorial mirror on pan-Africanism, more a state of mind than a specific place. Like Briton Hammon, Equiano demonstrated no unified sense of racial identity; if anything, he came to view himself as both African and European, an Afro-Briton perhaps.[11] In describing his native country and his fellow Ibos, Equiano used personal pronouns to characterize a certain "collective belonging," which referred to his identity either or both a European and as an African. Gradually, however, as his travels as a mariner took him through the Caribbean islands, he came to experience a sense of solidarity with the sufferings of enslaved people and to assign to them a collective identity as "Africans." By the time he published his autobiography in 1789, Equiano had finally come to understand himself as African and to return to the use of his Ibo name, Olaudah Equiano.

As Equiano's case demonstrates, the appropriation of Christianity by slaves and free black men and women did not obliterate their African identity. Rather, Christianity helped them to forge a new pan-African identity out of disparate and often antagonistic ethnic identities. Cugoano probably spoke for many Africans of the diaspora who asserted themselves as Christians. Kidnapped from his birthplace in the Fanti region of modern-day Ghana in 1770 and enslaved in the Caribbean for two years, Cugoano was brought to England in 1772, at age fifteen. A year later he was baptized. Cugoano accepted the Christian name of John Stewart as part of his ritual incorporation into the church but insisted it did not alter his ethnic identity: "Christianity does not require that we should be deprived of our personal name, or the name of our ancestors, but it may very fitly add another name unto us, Christian, or one anointed."[12] The same cultural past that was so crucial to Cugoano's sense of personal identity also centrally determined a collective sense of historical identity for diasporan Africans as a whole. The naming of black institutions offers a window onto that collective identity. It is impossible to say exactly when black churches in the United States began to assume racially specific designations, but with such names as the First African Baptist Church of Savannah, Georgia, in 1775, African Americans celebrated both an African heritage and a Christian identity.[13]

For enslaved people, becoming Christian was more than simply a metaphorical escape from the bonds of sin into the land of spiritual freedom. Little by little, the connection between religion and politics emerged, and religious identity began to meld with a national, African American one. The American Revolutionary era was a key moment in that transformation. The congruence of an evangelical idiom with secular republican ideology dramatically shifted the intellectual basis and the actual grounds for the construction of pan-Africanism. Petitions, sermons, and the writings of the emerging black leadership reflected that process. In them are found the historical antecedents for what Marcus Garvey and various nineteenth- and twentieth-century black intellectuals would preach: race pride, African redemption, and the return to Africa, in some cases in spiritual form, in others physical.

Some of the embryonic pan-African tendencies are apparent in slave petitions of the American Revolutionary era. All of them tentatively contemplated an unfamiliar possibility, a return of freedom. Some contained seemingly modest notions of what freedom meant and what to do with it. Most made it clear that enslaved people were cognizant of the antislavery principles articulated by churchmen and Revolutionary leaders, on one hand, and of British policies, on the other. The petitions marked the first phase in the development of an abolitionist movement. Black protests against slavery moved in tandem with white antislavery arguments, the two mutually influencing each other. In affirming the natural right of enslaved people to freedom, the petitions universalized the Revolutionary principles of liberty and equality. Some of the documents defined behavioral and moral values different from those practiced by white Americans; in many cases, they implied that white Americans had corrupted Christian teaching. This sense of spiritual superiority foreshadowed race pride and race memory and anticipated the politicization of spiritual salvation.

The back-to-Africa movement is clearly evident in a 1773 petition to the legislature of Massachusetts by four Boston slaves, Peter Bestes, Sambo Freeman, Chester Joie, and Felix Holbrook. The petitioners identified themselves as "*Africans*," suggesting that they saw Africa as their historic homeland and a place to which they wished to return after years in exile. Their request for permission to work one day a week for themselves to "procure money to transport ourselves to some part of the coast of Africa, where we propose a settlement," made them the ideological forebears of Prince Hall, Paul Cuffe, and Marcus Garvey.[14] Though embryonic in form, this search for justice and representation in a racially hierarchical society would, over the course of the next decade, become the mission and motivation of emerging black politics in the Atlantic.

The American Revolution, Revolutionary Pan-Africanism, and Emigrants of Revolution

Eighteenth-century African consciousness was not limited to inchoate expressions in petitions and sermons. Side by side with the development of a cultural and essentially nonviolent diasporic consciousness emerged a tradition of armed resistance; thus a double heritage was created. Both traditions—the nonviolent and the revolutionary—drew from Christian theology, even though the two were quite at odds with each other in important ways.

No single event of the American Revolutionary era was more important in constructing a consciousness of kind, and in laying the basis for revolutionary pan-Africanism, than the organization of the Ethiopian Regiment by Virginia's colonial governor, Lord Dunmore, who offered freedom to slaves who joined the fight on the British side. Dunmore's designation of his black volunteers as "Ethiopian" represented a defining moment in the history of the black diaspora's response to Africa. Since ancient times, the word "Ethiopian" referred to all of Africa and all Africans, not simply those from northeast Africa. Biblical references to Ethiopia in Psalm 68:31 proclaim that "Princes shall come out of Egypt, and Ethiopia shall soon stretch forth her hands unto God." Whether Dunmore consciously used the term to imply that enslaved Africans would soon be free is, of course, purely conjectural. Regardless, the Ethiopian Regiment of armed black men fearlessly demanding "Liberty to Slaves" was visual language that needed no translation. It asserted a common heritage shared by all peoples of African descent and explicitly linked New World blacks to Africa. As such, the Ethiopian Regiment was a key factor in both the development of an African American diasporic consciousness and the history of pan-Africanism.[15]

The organization of the Ethiopian Regiment, furthermore, was an archetypal event in the history of a black revolutionary tradition. It marked the incorporation of the Exodus story into a militant self-liberation ideology that projected an image of the enslaved man as a latter-day Moses and, more broadly, proclaimed black people as agents of their own fate, responsible for the fulfillment of the biblical promise of deliverance.[16] That historical development not only heightened African American participation in the Revolutionary War; it also foreshadowed a succession of formidable rebellions in the Caribbean and the United States in the nineteenth century.

Dunmore's Ethiopian Regiment was eventually defeated, but its remnants independently kept alive the tradition of armed resistance. One of the most distinguished of those independent fighters, Colonel Tye, formerly Titus, fled his Quaker owner in New Jersey when the revolution began. On joining Dunmore's regiment, he changed his name to Colonel Tye, thereby signifying his personal transformation from slave to warrior-soldier. After Dunmore's defeat at Norfolk, Virginia, in 1776, Colonel Tye retreated to Staten Island, New York, with about 100 men, "the remains of the Aetheopian Regiment." Tye and twenty-four black former British soldiers continued their military service as members of the Black Brigade. In 1779 they joined the Queen's Rangers and waged guerrilla warfare in New York and New Jersey, until Tye's death from a gunshot wound.[17]

For some, like the African-born Thomas Peters, Dunmore's offer of freedom in return for military service opened an actual path back to Africa. A member of the Yoruba ethnic group, Peters was captured in what is now Nigeria around 1760 and enslaved on a sugar plantation in French Louisiana. Beaten, branded, and shackled, he was later sold into North Carolina, where he was working as a millwright when news of Dunmore's proclamation broke. He escaped and joined the Black Guides and Pioneers, small companies of about thirty each that were assigned to various noncombatant duties, thus beginning a protracted personal struggle that would culminate in the 1790s in his African homeland. At the end of the war, Peters was evacuated to Nova Scotia along with thousands of other black loyalists, as the black supporters of the British cause were called. In Nova Scotia he became the principal spokesman for black emigrants dissatisfied with their land allotments and the discrimination they encountered at every turn. In 1791 he went to England to plead their case. There he met Granville Sharp, the noted British abolitionist, who put him in touch with the company that had founded the Sierra Leone colony as a haven for free blacks from the British Empire. Peters ended up serving as an intermediary for the resettlement of black loyalists from Nova Scotia to Sierra Leone.[18]

Thomas Peters was an acknowledged leader of the movement to Sierra Leone, but the task of articulating the biblical, theological, and historical meaning of the journey was left to John Marrant. In roughly a hundred sermons between 1785 and 1790, Marrant argued that African Americans, including the black loyalists who had fled the United States, were "a chosen generation," "an holy nation, a peculiar people" with a divine ordination to restore Zion, God's holy city. His call to face "zion forward" struck a chord of racial consciousness among black loyalists in Nova Scotia, coming as it did at the moment when their dream of racial utopia had become a nightmare under the combined weight of white intimidation, violence, and fraud.[19] A similar process was unfolding in England, where London's black community was also expanding on account of the global black dispersal in the wake of the American Revolution.

The result was the creation of Sierra Leone as the first permanent resettlement community in Africa for blacks from the diaspora. Its capital city, significantly, was named Freetown. Sierra Leone, and Freetown in particular, became a physical anchor for a variety of nineteenth-century pan-African projects designed by members of the black revolutionary generation. These included a trading society established by Paul Cuffe, the black nationalist and sea captain, to create economic opportunities for "my scattered brethren and fellowmen"; the West African Methodist Church, founded by Daniel Coker, cofounder with Richard Allen of the African Methodist Episcopal Church; and the American Baptist mission movement, led by Lott Carey.

In a significant variation on the same institutional-building theme, Prince Hall, a strong advocate of African colonization, "domesticated" the Freetown ideal in the United States. He appropriated the history and ritual of Freemasonry as African history, the rightful legacy of Africans worldwide. In 1775, Hall, a Barbadian by birth, and fourteen other free black men joined a Masonic lodge attached to the British army in Boston. Rejected by segregated, pro-slavery white Masonry in the postrevolutionary era, the black Masons struck out on their own. Under Hall's leadership, they secured a full warrant from the Grand Lodge in London for their African Lodge, becoming a separate branch of Freemasonry in the United States.[20] As grand master of the African Lodge, Hall subsequently organized and chartered a network of black Masonic lodges in Boston, Philadelphia, and Providence.[21] Hall also established a direct linkage between black churches and black Freemasonry, a nexus that became the primary institutional vehicle for disseminating ideas of race pride and race unity among ordinary black men and women.

African American Freemasonry, furthermore, promoted pan-African consciousness. At Hall's request, John Marrant, fresh from his itinerancy in Nova Scotia, delivered *A Sermon to the African Lodge*, in which he used sophisticated biblical arguments to reconnect historical Africa with African Americans. In an appeal to race pride, Marrant reminded his listeners that they, too, were descendants of the builders of Solomon's Temple. The development of a theology of social action was the logical and inevitable next step. The resulting pan-African civil religion, a fusion of the social and the spiritual, came into clear focus in Hall's *Charge to the Brethren of the African Lodge*, which elaborated on the theme of Ethiopianism while emphasizing a political mission of racial uplift. One of the duties of Masons, Hall told his audience, was to "help and assist all his fellow-men in distress, let them be of what colour or nation they may, yea even our enemies, much more a brother Mason."[22] Marrant's *Sermon* and Hall's *Charge* can, in fact, be read as two parts of a single text. Together they contain all of the elements later associated with modern black liberation, black nationalism, and Afrocentric thought.[23]

The Black Literary Tradition and the Articulation of Evangelical and Revolutionary Pan-Africanism

The link between pan-African consciousness and pan-African practice was mediated by the black literary tradition. Here, the discourses of John Marrant and Prince Hall, along with Richard Allen and Absalom Jones's 1794 *Narrative of the Proceedings of the Black People during the Late Epidemic in Philadelphia*, represent "the first black texts that publicly expressed a corporate consciousness."[24] The emergence of a black print tradition in the late eighteenth century was an important factor in shaping and articulating certain global themes and in broadening the geographic scope of pan-Africanism, evangelical and revolutionary.

The official separation of the thirteen colonies from Britain in 1783 marked a new era in the development of an African diasporic consciousness. The chaos of the Revolutionary War years created, for the first time, an opportunity for people to choose a national identity. Tens of thousands of people of African descent who fled to British lines chose to identify themselves as Afro-Britons. So, too, did a number of black writers, such as Equiano and Gronniosaw. Others opted for a new political identity as African Americans.[25]

Regardless of national identity, black writers of the generation after the American Revolution spoke with one voice in constructing an intellectual genealogy of an African cultural unity, which was based on two principal biblical themes: Ethiopianism and the exodus from Egypt. Although modern critics of the New York slave poet Jupiter Hammon and the African-born Phillis Wheatley have complained about their failure to explicitly address issues of slavery and race, both affirmed black affinity.[26] Despite Hammon's seeming preoccupation with Christian salvation over social action and Wheatley's apparent preference for Christian America over Africa, their poetry and prose represent the biblical beginnings of not only African American literature but also a pan-African intellectual tradition linked to a new black global culture. One finds in Hammond and Wheatley an awareness that the Bible had been used as a tool for the historical oppression of African peoples.

Hammon's writings set out the major narrative skeins of the evolving black thought. The first black writer to describe enslaved people as a separate corporate nation, he repeatedly referred to his "brethren" as "African," "Ethiopian," and "African by nation" and as "a poor despised nation." His distinctive reading of sacred texts reenvisioned the landscape of the biblical world and populated it with Africans, whose "ancient" history and culture were older than those of their masters. Hammon was also the first black writer to establish the connection between Israel's bondage and African slavery. His admonition to black people to "stand still and see the salvation of God" recalled Moses' speech to the Israelites when he parted the Red Sea: "Fear ye not, stand still, and see the salvation of the Lord, which he will show to you to day: for the Egyptians who ye have seen today, ye shall see them again no more for ever" (Exodus 14:13).[27]

Hammon and Wheatley appropriated the Bible abstractly. Some of their black contemporaries went further, mining biblical scriptures, along with natural rights philosophy, for their liberatory potentials. Writers who belonged to this category included John Marrant, Prince Hall, Richard Allen, Absalom Jones, Boston King, David George, George Liele, Olaudah Equiano, and Quobna Ottobah Cugoano. Collectively, their prose and sermons brought into clear focus a pan-African Christianity with race unity at its core. One skein linking all such voices is the idea of an ancient black history rooted in Africa as a source of common identity. Black Christian mariners like Equiano were acutely conscious of their relationship to the global African presence. Without surrendering their adoptive national identities, they embraced Africa as their special domain. Like Wheatley, who described her native Senegal as "the sable land of error's darkest night," Equiano was often torn by a contradictory desire to defend Africa from its detractors and to "redeem" it from "paganism." But like Hammon, he stressed its biblical origins and traced the "pedigree of the Africans from Afer and Afra, the descendants of Abraham by Keturah his wife and concubine."[28] In his sermon to the black Masonic lodge in Boston, Marrant suggested that paradise might have been in "African Ethiopia." He also elaborated on Hammon's efforts to ennoble the African origins of enslaved people: "If you study the holy book of God, you will find that you stand on a level . . . with the greatest kings on the earth, as Men and as Masons. . . . Ancient history will produce some of the Africans who were truly good, wise, and learned men, and as eloquent as any other nation whatever, though at present many of them in slavery."[29]

Consciousness of common African roots paved the way for an international network of descendant Africans. By the end of the American Revolutionary War, evangelical itinerancy and maritime slavery had produced a cadre of black leaders whose lives intersected at various points. The result was a transnational black network, which in turn was tied to the larger fabric of international revivalism and Atlantic revolutions. In terms of origins, the members of this network were a diverse lot. George Leile, a pioneer in the black foreign missionary movement, was a native Virginian; David George, Liele's disciple, was the son of African parents; John Marrant was born into a free black family in New York; Ukawsaw Gronniosaw hailed from modern-day Nigeria; Ottobah Cugoano was a member of the Fanti ethnic group in what is now Ghana; Olaudah Equiano was born in Nigeria's Iboland region. Although ethnically diverse, the emerging black leaders were drawn together into a self-defined network of *Africans* by their common experiences in slavery, as Christians, and often as Masons.

Members of the black evangelical network had achieved an international presence by the turn of the nineteenth century, even if their presence is largely ignored in the grand narrative of revivalism. The American Revolution was followed by the largest migration of free blacks in the Atlantic world up to that point. In this way, the rolling waves of the Atlantic Ocean carried black forms of Protestantism outward in a continuously moving flow of ideas and people—across the Caribbean to Jamaica, north to Nova Scotia, and east to Sierra Leone. Each current had its own characteristics, but all overlapped and intersected at various points to form a global process that forged spiritual linkages between Africa, Europe, and the Americas.

Consider some individual cases of the black evangelical network. George Liele, a Baptist who began his itinerant ministry in Georgia, launched African American foreign missionary work with the founding of Jamaica's first Baptist church, out of which sprang the island's Native Baptist movement. David George's mission to Sierra Leone preceded the first West Indian Church Association missionaries to Africa by three-quarters of a century.[30] John Jea preached to large crowds in Methodist, Baptist, and Presbyterian churches in Liverpool and Manchester as well as in Lancashire and Yorkshire. Jea's travels took him to Ireland, where he preached in country villages from Limerick to Cork, then moved on from there to Amsterdam and Rotterdam. On returning to the United States from Europe, Jea traveled overland, enjoying success everywhere but in New Orleans, where, he complained, "the people were like those of Sodom and Gomorrah."[31]

The pan-African pioneers embraced a variety of evangelical creeds. Collectively, their spiritual lives reflected the cosmopolitanism of the emerging black leadership as well as the remarkable degree of interracial harmony that characterized eighteenth-century evangelicalism. Linked in dynamic relationships among themselves, the blacks were enmeshed in the larger Atlantic evangelical culture through personal relationships with one another and with the white leadership of the international revival movement. For instance, Gronniosaw was enslaved in New York by the evangelical Dutch Reformed pastor Theodous Frelinghuysen. Baptized in England by the Baptist theologian Andrew Gifford, Gronniosaw was befriended by the Methodist founder Whitefield, whom he claimed as his "dear friend." Whitefield prayed daily with Marrant as the latter struggled through the throes of conversion. Marrant, a Huntingdonian Methodist, who may have learned of the Countess of Huntingdon's Connexion from David Margate, the first black British missionary in North America, was later ordained a minister in the countess's chapel in Bath.[32] White evangelicals like Whitefield and Frelinghuysen influenced black evangelicals and were, in turn, influenced by them.

Brought into close contact with one another through their peripatetic lives, the members of the black evangelical network skillfully navigated multiple connections, all the while maintaining close contacts with white abolitionists. The pan-African bond is explicit in Cugoano's pointed references to details in the lives and writings of Gronniosaw and Marrant.[33] As friends and "countrymen," the blacks provided the avenues through which British abolitionists like Granville Sharp and William Wilberforce were directly exposed to the consequences of slavery and to Afro-Atlantic cultures. In 1783, Equiano persuaded Sharp to intervene in the Zong case, in which slave traders dumped scores of their human cargoes at sea; through Cugoano's intervention, Sharp managed to free Harry Demane, who had been seized in London and put on a slave ship bound for the Caribbean.[34] John Wesley was one of the subscribers of Equiano's *Narrative* and was moved enough by it to write to Wilberforce, who was leading the antislavery fight in Parliament. Organized as the Sons of Africa, a name that might have been inspired by the American Revolutionary Sons of Liberty, twenty-four black men, including Equiano and Cugoano, petitioned Sharp and members of Parliament. Together, the black and white antislavery advocates created the abolitionist movement in England and America, establishing an immediate point of departure for liberationist struggles in the United States, Britain, Saint Domingue, and Jamaica.

The convergence of black theology and republican ideas that flourished at the grassroots level crystallized in the 1780s and 1790s in the globalization of the struggle against slavery and racism, with the aim of mobilizing black communities and transforming Atlantic societies. Although Christian salvation remained a constant, increasingly the emphasis came to center on temporal freedom and an end to racism. The geographic scope and intellectual reach of the black freedom struggle is nowhere more apparent than in the antislavery writings of the Afro-Britons Equiano and Cugoano. From England, both men tapped into the growing interest in the Atlantic slave trade and the less restrictive racial climate of Britain, writing powerful antislavery essays.

Although deploying conventional biblical and moral arguments, Equiano and Cugoano also displayed a "secularized consciousness" that reflected the growing influence of natural rights philosophy. In his *Thoughts and Sentiments*, Cugoano appealed to "the light of nature" and the "dictates of reason" to argue "that no man ought to enslave another." Slavery was, he contended, "the grossest perversion of reason," while its defense was an "inconsistent and diabolical use of the sacred writing." Equiano's *Narrative* likewise charged that slavery "violates that first natural right of mankind, equality and independency, and gives one man a dominion over his fellows which God could never intend."[35]

While Equiano's firsthand account of the physical and moral abominations of slavery is rightly considered by some to be "the most important single literary contribution to the campaign for abolition,"[36] it was the slave trade, not the institution of slavery, that his 1788 antislavery petition to Queen Charlotte addressed.[37] Despite Cugoano's bold demand that "a total abolition of slavery should be made and proclaimed; and that an universal emancipation of slavery should begin," like most eighteenth-century abolitionists, black and white, he proposed a gradual form of emancipation.[38]

Conservative though they might seem in retrospect, the early black narratives of liberty disseminated ideas of racial unity, rebellion, and resistance in all directions, intensifying pan-Africanism even while leaving its meaning open to interpretation in different contexts. Although they did not propose a course of action, and indeed seemed to postpone action to a later date, the narratives brought the plight of suffering slaves to public attention and, in so doing, advanced the moment of action. But eighteenth-century black writers did more than that. In the face of violent racial injustice, they implicitly invoked the inalienable right of revolution espoused by white revolutionaries and so established two distinct processes of racial construction, one nonviolent and the other revolutionary. Noting the "artless tale" told him by a black creole in Montserrat who had his catch of fish repeatedly seized by whites, Equiano raised the possibility of violent action through his expression of sympathy for Moses as the slayer of an Egyptian (Exodus 7.1–25): "I could not help feeling the just cause Moses had in redressing his brother against the Egyptian."[39] The threat of violence also hung heavily over Prince Hall's lecture to black Masons in Boston. Reflecting on the frequent insults and injuries suffered by black people, Hall expressed admiration for the violent means of self-liberation pursued by Haitians, with whom, he emphasized, black Bostonians were united through common experience. "Let us remember what a dark day it was with our African brethren six years ago in the West Indies, but blessed be God, the scene is changed," Hall noted, before invoking the Ethiopianist trope. "Thus does Ethiopia begin to stretch forth her hand, from a sink of slavery to freedom and equality."[40]

The American Revolution and the Spread of Revolutionary Pan-Africanism

One of the principal mediums for the transoceanic voyage of pan-Africanism was the dispersal of black war veterans at the end of the American Revolution.

The postrevolutionary migration scattered thousands of black Americans to islands throughout the Caribbean and Europe and halfway across the world to Tasmania.[41] It is impossible to argue with any degree of certainty that revolutionary ideology inspired them. It is probably safe to say that, at the very least, their military experience in British regiments and the example of Dunmore's Ethiopian soldiers and the Black Carolina Corps, raised among ex-slaves and free blacks, were part of their political transformation.[42] The black veterans carried their political experiences throughout the Atlantic world and beyond. Over time, the notion of military service as a political strategy became reconfigured, charged with new meaning in different social and racial settings.

Black veterans of the American Revolutionary War took to heart the idea that service to the king entitled them to freedom. The 1787 rebellion in the Bahamas clearly shows that connection. Transported from New York and Florida, the ex-slave soldiers claimed freedom by virtue of loyal military service. Instead, on arrival in the Bahamas many were reduced to a form of apprenticeship, or even outright bondage. Predictably, they resisted, fleeing to the bush. White militias rounded up some, but the rest continued to create havoc.[43] While there is no direct evidence of a connection between the Ethiopian Regiment and the 1787 Bahamas rebellion, the two were symbolically linked in the person of Dunmore, who was governor of the Bahamas from 1787 to 1796. Dunmore set up a court to hear black claims for freedom. Believed by whites to be a "friend of the Negroes," Dunmore's court ruled against the black claimants in all but one case.[44]

The 1787 Bahamas rebellion marked the beginning of black soldiers' long march across multiple cultural frontiers that ended in West Africa, completing for many a geographic return to ancestral homelands and a journey from slavery back to freedom. During the turbulent decade of the 1790s, something profound began to change in politics and philosophy. Different ideas about humanity were emerging, some encouraged by the growing power of the antislavery movement, others by the 1791 slave revolution in Saint Domingue that eventually dismantled the old colonial hierarchies, and still others by the insatiable need of the European powers for soldiers during the long wars of the French Revolution. The Black Carolina Corps, like the Ethiopian Regiment, was both a model and a catalyst for a profound reorientation of black political culture based on an expansion of the meaning of military service as the prerogative of free, white propertied men to a new definition that included the enslaved. Following the British surrender in 1783, veterans of the corps were scattered throughout Europe and the Caribbean. The experience of one veteran, Richard Durant, was perhaps not so much typical as generic, and it suggests how the personal decisions of hundreds, indeed thousands, of anonymous individuals affected the course of Atlantic history. Durant was born in America, and at the end of the war he shipped to Martinique, where he enlisted in the British army. By age thirty-eight he had sixteen years of military experience in British operations in the long wars of the French Revolution.

Roughly 300 of Durant's fellow soldiers from the Black Carolina Corps ended up on the neighboring island of Grenada, where they were reconstituted into a new military unit.[45] Ostensibly loyal to Britain, black veterans in Grenada and Tobago, in what can be considered a first step in the transition from slave-soldier to citizen-soldier, revolted against British authority on learning of the French Revolutionary decree of 1794 abolishing slavery. Already heavily dependent on black combat troops in the long and costly wars of the French Revolution, the British responded by creating a new system of Caribbean defense based on permanent black regiments.[46] The policy proved a success. The regiments, recruited mainly from slave ships, came to make up a third of all British forces in the Caribbean. In 1807, almost 10,000 members of the British West India regiments were freed, one of the largest single acts of manumission prior to the abolition of slavery in the British Empire.[47] After the War of 1812, several hundred freed American black veterans were settled in Trinidad, where they founded the famous "company towns." However, the majority of discharged soldiers and their families ended up in military communities in Sierra Leone, finally closing the Atlantic circle.[48] Taken together, these events permanently established a connection between military service and abolition, providing continuity between the revolutionary movements of the late eighteenth century.

Pan-Africanism and the American, French, and Haitian Revolutions

The logical consequences of the developments set in motion by the American Revolutionary War were fully revealed in the French Caribbean. The tendency of Anglo-American historians to examine the American Revolution through the narrow lens of Anglo-American history obscures the links between black history on mainland North America and in the Caribbean. Recent studies suggest that the American Revolution significantly influenced black popular politics in the French Caribbean. Ideas of liberty and equality penetrated the Caribbean during the Revolutionary War, when American corsairs and merchant ships used some of the islands as strategic bases. Contraband trade was so extensive that the islands became, in the words of one historian citing a governor, "le principal theatre de la guerre d'Amerique," where "aux idees de liberte et d'egalite, que tout de monde a la bouche."[49] This contraband trade, in ideas as well as goods, constituted a Caribbean backdrop to the French and Haitian revolutions.

American Revolutionary War veterans formed human links in a chain that flowed from the American Revolution through the French Revolution and the Haitian Revolution and back around to mainland North America. The emerging scholarship on black resistance in the French Caribbean reveals deep connections between the islands and to the French and Haitian revolutions, including links in leadership and the circulation of words, symbols, and slogans. The story began with the American Revolution. Under the Franco-American alliance of 1778, France dispatched a force of about 4,000 to fight on the American side. The French forces consisted of regular French troops and units of Saint Domingue's all-white militias, along with free black and mulatto volunteers from Saint Domingue, Guadeloupe, and Martinique.[50] Almost a thousand men of color responded to the call for service and were deployed with the rest of the French forces to Savannah, Georgia, in 1779. Among the volunteers of color were such future leaders of the Haitian Revolution as Andre Rigaud, Henri Christophe, Jean Baptiste Villatte, Louis-Jacques Beauvais, and Christophe and Martial Besse.[51]

Only a small number of the colored troops returned immediately to Saint Domingue at the conclusion of the Savannah campaign. More than a third were sent to Grenada and remained there for more than two years. Several detachments initially went to France, only later returning to Saint Domingue.[52] The French interlude, occurring as it did amid an emerging discourse on notions of citizenship, identity, and equality, offered the men of color an opportunity to broaden their education in revolutionary politics. As early as the 1760s and 1770s, French writers like Rousseau, Montesquieu, Voltaire, Raynal, and Diderot were using African slavery to criticize the monarchy and advocate radical equality. More than a decade before the formation of the Amis des Noirs, the French abolitionist group, French lawyers were developing arguments against slavery. In pleading the case of a Louisiana slave before a Paris naval court, one lawyer condemned the entire institution of slavery.[53] At just about the same time, the islands received news about the abolition of slavery in the northern states of the United States and the formation of the Amis des Noirs.[54] The convergence of events, exacerbated by the French Revolution, precipitated a series of slave plots and revolts, beginning with the Martinique rebellion of August 1789.

Although largely a response to local issues, slave rebellions in French Martinique and Guadeloupe occurred in a broader context that included the circulation of Revolutionary news during and after the American Revolution. Moreover, individuals with ties to the American Revolution frequently appeared as leaders of rebellions and conspiracies. Martinican veterans of the siege of Savannah had witnessed the Revolutionary ferment firsthand, had been exposed to the new ideas of liberty and equality, and carried those experiences back home with them. An event in August 1789, two weeks before the news of the storming of the Bastille and the advent of the French Revolution reached the French Caribbean, reveals the evolution of a radical vision of emancipation to which Dunmore's Ethiopian Regiment had given practical meaning. A group of enslaved Martinicans sent two anonymous letters to the governor and the military commander of Martinique, signing them "us blacks." The immediate inspiration for this action might well have been the publications of the Amis des Noirs, which were read to slaves in the main towns, except that the letters departed radically from the standard abolitionist advocacy of gradual emancipation and embraced violent self-liberation instead. "Remember that we the Negroes . . . are ready to die for this freedom, for we want to and will obtain it at any price, even with the help of mortars, canons, and rifles," the letters boldly announced. The repeated reference to "the entire Nation of the Black Slaves," even if used, as David Geggus suggests, in "a local, particularist" sense of ethnic consciousness rather than the "universalist outlook" of revolutionary France, showed how far notions of racial solidarity had progressed.[55]

Geggus calls the subsequent 1789 St. Pierre rebellion in Martinique "a strikingly novel departure in Afro-American resistance." It represented, he asserts, a new type of rebellion based on false rumors of a royal emancipation decree allegedly blocked by local slaveowners and local authorities.[56] In fact, this strategy was part of a historical process that began as early as 1730 in Virginia, emerged again in South Carolina during the American Revolution, and came to full maturity during the turbulent revolutionary years in the French Caribbean. It was a rumor that "there was a great War coming soon to help the poor Negroes" that convinced the South Carolina slave Jeremiah that change was possible and that the time was right for enslaved people to seize their freedom through organized rebellions.[57] This same logic became generalized in the wave of revolts that spread through the French Caribbean between 1789 and 1791.[58] Conscious that "the whole nature of political rights and institutions was being redefined and discussed,"[59] black people throughout the French Caribbean used rumors of expanded rights to demand the extension of rumored rights, as Laurent Dubois puts it.[60]

Black politics in the French Caribbean navigated between two tendencies, one pressing for equality within the dominant white society and the other demanding an end to slavery. In the complex world of island politics, free colored and slave populations formed two distinct social and juridical groups. The free coloreds generally owned modest amounts of property, including one or more slaves, but were subject to various legal restrictions and social and economic limitations.[61] Gabriel Gruel was typical of this group, which in 1789 began to agitate for political rights. The Gruel family exemplified what Anne Perotin-Dumon calls the integrationist faction of Guadeloupe's free black population, those who formed an uneasy alliance with the "petits blancs" against the overwhelming black majority. In August 1791, Gabriel Gruel was chosen by a group of free people of color to present their request for full citizenship rights. Significantly, the petitioners emphasized that Gruel had served ten years in the colonial militia and had fought with the French forces in the American Revolution.[62] Although framed in deferential language, the proud record of military service represented the political vitae of the free people of color. In the context of the 1789 French Revolutionary Declaration of the Rights of Man and Citizen, the coloreds, however moderate their tone, were demanding full citizenship rights by virtue of demonstrated loyalty to *la patria*.[63]

The 1793 Trois Riviere rebellion in Guadeloupe also stood on the geographic path between the American Revolution and black resistance in the French Caribbean. Although not directed against slavery, the rebellion inspired slaves to assert their rights. The Trois Riviere rebellion began on the plantation of Jacques Coquille Dugommier, a veteran of the American Revolution and the leading republican in Guadeloupe. Dugommier acted after the local authorities refused to supply troops under his command with wine to celebrate the feast of Saint-Louis. For days, Dugommier's soldiers paraded through the streets, loudly proclaiming the republican ideals of equality and liberty. No one was quicker to perceive the connection between the rhetoric of freedom and the reality of slavery than slaves themselves. Led by Jean-Baptiste, a manager on Dugommier's plantation, the enslaved people arose, mobilizing the language of republicanism to formulate their own notion of rights and defend their actions.[64]

Again in 1793, and in the same Trois Riviere area of Guadeloupe where the Dugommier rebellion occurred, a remarkable transference of revolutionary symbols, mediated by the American and French revolutions, reportedly helped to inspire a slave insurrection in which some twenty whites were killed. The event is said to have been triggered by "an unknown individual . . . walking around, saying that since a liberty tree had been planted, there would be no more slaves."[65] The notion of the tree as a symbol of liberty and fraternity had ancient roots, but its use as a political metaphor became associated with the American Revolutionary tradition and was used after 1765 to protest British policies. The liberty tree later emerged as a staple of the French Revolution.[66] Its appropriation by black insurgents in Guadeloupe was a compelling link to both the American and French revolutions, but of a radically different sort. The circulation of rumors that "the liberty tree had been planted for all" apparently emboldened the insurgents, who transformed the symbol into a demand to end chattel slavery.[67]

Nowhere did the liberty tree, as defined by the enslaved, sink deeper roots than in Saint Domingue, where the slave revolt of 1791 opened a new chapter in Atlantic revolutionary history. The Haitian Revolution regrouped descendant Africans in the Atlantic world around a revolutionary ideal and a newfound sense of African ethnicity, and so reconnected through a human chain the histories of Africa, North America, and the Caribbean. The mostly unforeseen revolt required a new ideology, one that transcended the muted abolitionism of the period. The revolution occurred in a region swept by powerful currents emanating from the American and French revolutions. But that was not all. European ideological currents gained force and energy from the new political tide of black self-liberation initially sparked by Dunmore's recruiting of fugitive slaves as soldiers, a process amplified by radical black theology and by rebellions in Martinique and Guadeloupe.

Ideas and peoples of the black Atlantic united in a new way in Saint Domingue to produce what Michel-Rolph Trouillot has called "the most radical revolution of that age."[68] If some of its leaders were mulattos with military experience in European armies, the revolution itself had genealogical links that reached back to Africa. The majority of enslaved men who fought in the ranks were born in Africa. Many of them may have served in African armies. Their military skills, as John Thornton has argued, contributed greatly to the success of the revolution in Saint Domingue.[69] Haiti, in throwing off the shackles of slavery and becoming an independent nation, also became a birthing ground for self-liberation movements around the Atlantic. The revolutionary violence from which Haiti emerged may have confirmed white opinion that blacks were a separate and degraded people, incapable of participating in civil society, but people of African descent everywhere in the Atlantic drew inspiration for their own struggles for freedom and equality and recognized the black republic as "their spiritual fatherland."[70]

The violent conflict in Saint Domingue sent thousands of black and white refugees into permanent exile. After wandering in search of safe havens, some members of this diasporic community settled in American cities from Philadelphia to New Orleans. There, displaced black Haitians made transnational connections based on common experiences of oppression with other black communities, such as African, Afro-Louisianan, and Afro-Virginian. In Virginia, the migration from Saint Domingue greatly accelerated a shift in consciousness. On one hand, the refugees helped to create a common identity based on skin color. On the other hand, their presence increased black cultural distinctiveness, between the largely Baptist, native-born, English-speaking Afro-Virginians and the French-speaking black Catholics from Saint Domingue.[71]

The success of the Haitian Revolution encouraged revolutionary undertakings in other slave societies. Although not a "race" war, the 1795 Pointe Coupee Conspiracy in Louisiana was inspired by both the Haitian Revolution and Revolutionary developments in France. Well-organized, the Coupee Conspiracy was linked to an anticipated French invasion of Louisiana and was one of a series of actual or planned insurrections that swept the Atlantic world in the revolutionary era.[72] The slave revolt in Saint Domingue was also a source of inspiration for Gabriel Prosser's Revolt in Virginia in 1800, although Gabriel's plan to march on Richmond, Virginia, under the banner of "Death or Liberty" was a deliberate reference to Dunmore's Regiment as well as a paraphrase of an iconic slogan from the American Revolution: Patrick Henry's demand for "liberty or death."[73] Haiti's revolution also helped to inspire the aborted slave revolt in Charleston, South Carolina, in 1822 under the leadership of Denmark Vesey. The biblical story of Exodus provided the basis for Vesey's liberation theology, while Haiti was the promised land to which he expected to lead his followers out of slavery.[74]

Conclusion

In sum, pan-Africanism has a complex genealogy. It emerged from an interweaving of revolutionary principles of liberty and religious notions of spiritual equality, on one hand, and the wartime experiences of enslaved people, on the other. Black evangelicalism helped to transform the religious and political landscape of the Atlantic world. Transported abroad during the postrevolutionary exodus, black evangelicals left as their legacy black forms of Protestantism in Nova Scotia, Sierra Leone, Liberia, Jamaica, and other Caribbean islands. Not coincidentally, their nonviolent struggles for the expansion of human rights coincided with the great Atlantic revolutions and the burgeoning antislavery movement of the late eighteenth and early nineteenth centuries.[75] The Exodus story that lay at the heart of evangelical expectations for the coming of the divinely appointed millennium melded easily with the impatient dreams of those who sought to hasten the day of deliverance. The impatient ones offered another historical model from which Afro-Atlantic peoples drew inspiration. Thus did the two traditions in early pan-Africanism emerge: the evangelical and the revolutionary.

The revolutionary tradition would incubate in curious places. Whatever Dunmore's intention, the Ethiopian Regiment he organized initiated rebellion aimed at changing the system of slavery. The words "Liberty to Slaves," emblazoned on the soldiers' uniforms, had a message that could not be missed. Dunmore may not have succeeded in suppressing the American Revolution, but the legend of the Ethiopian Regiment lived on. It was of paramount importance as an inspiration for other revolts throughout the Atlantic world, creating a tradition of resistance that grew in size and intensity and culminated in the revolution in Saint Domingue. Indeed, one could argue that the Haitian Revolution began not in Le Cap Francais in 1791, but onboard the *William*, near Norfolk, Virginia, in 1775, when Dunmore issued his famous proclamation. By the same token, one could say that the revolts in the United States led by Gabriel Prosser and Denmark Vesey began not in Richmond in 1800 or in Charleston in 1822, but in Le Cap Francais in 1791. Put another way, the cluster of rebellions and conspiracies that began with the American Revolutionary War and culminated in the Haitian Revolution must be viewed in a transnational and transcultural context. Only then will it be possible to appreciate the cumulative power of revolutionary pan-Africanism.

NOTES

1. The literature is vast. Some representative samples include Martin, *Race First*; Stuckey, *Ideological Origins*; Ullman, *Martin L. Delany*; Griffith, *African Dream*; Miller, *Search for a Black Nationality*; Walters, *Pan Africanism*; Lemelle and Kelley, *Imagining Home*; and Moses, *Classical Black Nationalism*.

2. Shepperson, "Pan-Africanism."

3. My definition follows that of Nelson, *Black Atlantic Politics*, 3–4.

4. Wilder, *In the Company of Black Men*, 36, 37, points out that the founding of African voluntary associations "preceded the establishment of the black church" in New York and served as a "prerequisite of the African church."

5. Sensbach, *Rebecca's Revival*.

6. Frey and Wood, *Come Shouting to Zion*, 112–14.

7. The seminal work on the subject of black seamen is Scott, "Common Wind." An important work that portrays seamen as central to the formation of black America is Bolster, *Black Jacks*, 18–20, 36. See Linebaugh and Rediker, *Many-Headed Hydra*.

8. Gilroy, *Black Atlantic*.

9. Bolster, *Black Jacks*, 37.

10. Carretta, in *Unchained Voices*, 16 n. 13, writes, "I accept Equiano's assertion of his African identity" but notes that it is possible that Equiano "invented an African identity for rhetorical and/or marketing ends." Carretta's argument is based on baptismal and naval records, which give Equiano's birthplace as South Carolina. See also Carretta, "Olaudah Equiano or Gustavus Vassa?" and *Equiano, the African*. The most recent contribution to the question of Equiano's identity is Byrd, "Eboe, Country, Nation." Byrd concludes, contrary to Carretta, that "the ethnographic language of his [Equiano's] memoir supplies good internal evidence that the origins of *The Interesting Narrative* lie decidedly in the Biafran interior and were profoundly African" (125).

11. Bolster, *Black Jacks*, 35.

12. Quoted in Potkay and Burr, *Black Atlantic Writers*, 3, 126, 149.

13. Frey and Wood, *Come Shouting to Zion*, 114–17. Scholars do not agree on the meaning of the use of the term "African." Stuckey, *Slave Culture*, 199–200, argues that "direct African cultural influence" was a primary factor in institutional naming by people of African descent in the northern United States. Melish, *Disowning Slavery*, 248–49, maintains that terms such as "black" and "Negro" were used indiscriminately, sometimes in the same document. Melish traces the preference for "African" to Absalom Jones and Richard Allen's establishment of the Free African Society in Philadelphia in 1787. Although Sobel makes no specific claim for when the name "African" became common usage, her chronological listing of early black churches implies that, at least in the South, the practice developed much earlier. See Sobel, *Trabelin' On*. See also Mitchell, *Black Church Beginnings*, 62–66.

14. Aptheker, *Documentary History*, 1:7–8.

15. For a very important discussion of the significance of Dunmore's Ethiopian Regiment for racial identity, see Sidbury, *Ploughshares into Swords*, 32–34. Tony Martin also points to the centrality of Ethiopia to the Garvey movement. See his *Pan-African Connection*, 20–24. See also Schmeisser, "'Ethiopia Shall Soon Stretch Forth Her Hands,'" 265–67. At the climax of his conversion Equiano exclaimed, "Now the Ethiopian was willing to be saved by Jesus Christ." See Equiano, *Interesting Narrative*, 144.

16. See, for example, the story of Yellow Peter, who escaped in 1775 or 1776 and was seen "in Governor Dunmore's regiment with a musquet on his back and a sword by his side." Significantly, Yellow Peter changed his name to Captain Peter. See Holton, *Forced Founders*, 156.

17. Hodges, *Root and Branch*, 144, 152.

18. Nash, "Thomas Peters."

19. See Marrant, "Journal," and Saillant, "Origins of African American Biblical Hermeneutics."

20. Davis, "Documents Relating to Negro Masonry in America."

21. Wilder, *In the Company of Black Men*, 115–16.

22. Hall, "Charge," 192.

23. Brooks and Saillant, *"Face Zion Forward,"* 17–18.

24. Brooks, "Early American Public Sphere," 82.

25. Carretta, *Unchained Voices*, 1.

26. For favorable assessments of Hammond, see O'Neale, *Jupiter Hammon*, and Gilyard, "Bible and African American Poetry," 209; for Wheatley, see Grimstead, "Anglo-American Racism." For a less sympathetic rendering, see Wilder, *In the Company of Black Men*, 64–71.

27. O'Neale, *Jupiter Hammon*, 84, 86, 102, 103, 151, 152, 231.

28. Equiano, *Interesting Narrative*, 31. For Cugoano's defense of Africa, see Cugoano, "Thoughts and Sentiments."

29. Marrant, "Sermon," 88–89.

30. Jacobs, *Black Americans and the Missionary Movement*, 17.

31. Hodges, *Black Itinerants of the Gospel*, 123–27, 136–37, 141–44, 149.

32. Potkay and Burr, *Black Atlantic Writers*, 24, 40, 43, 45, 47, 78, 90.

33. Carretta, *Unchained Voices*, 154.

34. Potkay and Burr, *Black Atlantic Writers*, 127, 165.

35. Wimbush, *African Americans and the Bible*, 156, 221, 227.

36. Linebaugh and Rediker, *Many-Headed Hydra*, 337.

37. The petition is reproduced in Equiano, *Interesting Narrative*, 156, 221, 227; see also 286–88.

38. Carretta, *Unchained Voices*, 171.

39. Ibid., xxv, 226.

40. Brooks and Saillant, *"Face Zion Forward,"* 204.

41. Pybus, *Epic Journeys of Freedom*, 123–38.

42. Military service increased political consciousness among black solders in Continental service as well. In her essay on Lemuel Haynes, Roberts points out that Haynes's political awareness "increased while he was engaged in protecting the freedom of others." His "progression of thought from identification with colonists to identification with slaves" developed during his military activity in 1775 and 1776 and is apparent in two documents, "The Ballard of Lexington" and his antislavery essay "Liberty Further Extended: Or Free Thoughts on the Illegality of Slave-Keeping." See Roberts, "Patriotism and Political Criticism," 570–71.

43. Craton and Saunders, "Seeking a Life of Their Own," 2–3.

44. Craton and Saunders, *Islanders in the Stream*, 184, 200.

45. Buckley, *Slaves in Red Coats*, 4, 20–22. Two of the leading proponents of the use of black soldiers, Earl Balcarres, governor of Jamaica, and General Sir John Vaughan, were veterans of the American Revolutionary War. See ibid., 12, 43.

46. Ibid., 78–79.

47. Buckley, *British Army in the West Indies*, 201.

48. Buckley, *Slaves in Red Coats*, 136–37; see also Buckley, *British Army in the West Indies*, 270–77.

49. Perotin-Dumon, *Etre patriote sous les tropiques*, 86, 106.

50. Rhodes, "Haitian Contributions to American History," 79–80.

51. Haitian historiography tends to regard service in the American Revolutionary War as a major catalyst for the future leaders of the Haitian Revolution. See, for example, Laurent, *Haiti et l'independance americaine*, and Fick, *Making of Haiti*. For American history, see Steward, "How the Black St. Domingue Legion Saved the Patriot Army"; Frey, *Water from the Rock*, 192; and Garrigus, "Catalyst or Catastrophe?"

52. Garrigus, "Catalyst or Catastrophe?," 119.

53. Peabody, *"There Are No Slaves in France,"* 96–97, 101.

54. Geggus, "Haitian Revolution," 25–26.

55. In his analysis of the letters, Geggus discounts the influence of the French Revolution and concludes that the discourse in the letters was probably due more to the antislavery movement. See Geggus, "Slaves and Free Coloreds of Martinique," 286–88, and Reinhardt, "French Caribbean Slaves Forge Their Own Ideal of Liberty," 26–27, 29.

56. Geggus, "Slaves and Free Coloreds of Martinique," 288.

57. Geggus, *Haitian Revolutionary Studies*, 62; Frey, *Water from the Rock*, 58.

58. Benot, "La chaine des insurrections d'esclaves," 179–86. See also Dubois, *Les esclaves de la Republique*, 73–75, and Perotin-Dumon, "Emergence of Politics among Free-Coloureds," 128.

59. Perotin-Dumon, "Emergence of Politics among Free-Coloureds," 128.

60. Dubois, *Les esclaves de la Republique*, 135.

61. Perotin-Dumon, "Emergence of Politics among Free-Coloureds," 104–6.

62. Perotin-Dumon, *Etre patriote sous les tropiques*, 274–76.

63. Garrigus, "Catalyst or Catastrophe?," 116, 124.

64. Dubois, *Les esclaves de la Republique*, 82–83, 114–15.

65. Perotin-Dumon, "Emergence of Politics among Free-Coloureds," 118–19.

66. Ozouf, *Festivals and the French Revolution*, 245–46, 286 n. 18.

67. Perotin-Dumon, *Etre patriote sous les tropiques*, 118–19.

68. Trouillot, "From Planters' Journals to Academia," 93.

69. Thornton, "African Soldiers in the Haitian Revolution."

70. Hunt, *Haiti's Influence on Antebellum America*, 99.

71. Sidbury, *Ploughshares into Swords*, 35–37, 40–41, 44, 47.

72. Hall, *Africans in Colonial Louisiana*, 236–74.

73. Egerton, *Gabriel's Rebellion*, 42–47, 49, 51.

74. Egerton, *He Shall Go Out Free*, 114, 136–38.

75. Frey, "Cultural Migrations," 91–98.

Haiti, I'm Sorry

The Haitian Revolution and the Forging of the
Black International

MICHAEL O. WEST & WILLIAM G. MARTIN

Haiti I'm sorry we misunderstood you. But one day we'll turn around
and look inside you. Haiti I'm so sorry. But one day we'll turn our heads,
restore your glory.—DAVID RUDDER, "Haiti," calypso song, 1988

Revolution came to the French slaveholding colony of Saint Domingue in 1791.
When the upheaval finally ran its course more than a decade later, in 1804, the
landscape had been completely remade. In one fell swoop, the Haitian Revolution banished slavery, colonialism, and white supremacy, the three foundational institutions of the post-Columbian dispensation in the Americas. It was
a historical novelty, including a novel shock to the rising consumer culture of
the Western world, now deprived of its foremost sugar bowl and coffee pot.
The thoroughgoing transformation in Saint Domingue ended slavery in an
entire society, the first such act of general emancipation in the annals of the
human experience. And although it did not eliminate human bondage, meaning concretely African bondage, from the hemisphere as a whole, the Haitian
Revolution left a deep imprint on slavery in the Americas, for masters and
slaves alike. Neither would be quite the same again. More broadly, the Haitian Revolution powerfully influenced major changes in the Atlantic political
economy, and thereby in the course of world history. The slave revolt turned
revolution in Saint Domingue was, quite simply, the single most cataclysmic
and transfiguring event of its time, the Age of Revolution, a historical verity
recklessly omitted from the literature on that era.

For the black international, the events in Saint Domingue were iconic. The
Haitian Revolution represented a culmination of decades of armed struggle

by enslaved Africans in the Atlantic world, even as it heralded exciting new developments in the black quest for universal emancipation. Like no other event before or since, the Haitian Revolution electrified African-descended people all over the Americas, the enslaved majority along with the nominally free minority. Haiti became the bellwether of black freedom in the Atlantic world, albeit one that would not be replicated, although not for want of trying. Haiti's symbolic value to black internationalism was a primary reason for the hostility and isolation it faced from slaveholders and white powers everywhere. To its great shame, however, the dominant historical narrative of the black international has largely neglected the Haitian Revolution, effectively reproducing the scholarly silence of those who write about the Age of Revolution. Actually, the Haitian Revolution was a central moment in the evolution of the black international, forcefully demarcating the two major paradigms in black internationalism that emerged in the Age of Revolution: the revolutionary and revivalist traditions. The one tradition had its origins in the long series of slave revolts that reached its zenith in the Haitian Revolution, while the other derived from the evangelical revival movement of the latter part of the eighteenth century. In time, the two black international traditions, the revolutionary and the revivalist, often merged. On the terrain of black international theory and practice, the Haitian Revolution continued to reverberate into the twentieth century, becoming both a cultural trope and a spark for activist politics in various parts of global Africa following the U.S. invasion of Haiti in 1915.

The Haitian Revolution Outlined

The event that inaugurated the Haitian Revolution was but the latest example, and, it turned out, the most dramatic and successful one, of slaves seizing the moment. Enslaved Africans had a long history of taking advantage of the misfortunes of their enslavers to seek freedom. So it had been since the onset of racial bondage in the Americas, and so it was with the slave revolt in Saint Domingue in 1791. When the French Revolution began two years earlier, in 1789, another group in Saint Domingue saw the potential for advancing its corporate interests and acted accordingly. The free people of color, consisting mostly, although not exclusively, of mulattos—that is, persons of African and European ancestry—had long felt the sting of white supremacy. In the Caribbean, even in the wider Atlantic world, Saint Domingue's mulattos occupied a peculiar place. As a group, they were unusually wealthy, owning a fourth of the colony's slaves and an equal proportion of its land. Yet the mulattos remained pariahs in the larger white-dominated society, their low social and political status belying their economic prowess. In the mulatto struggle for equality with the whites, the upheaval in France came as a godsend. The most fervent partisans of the French Revolution in Saint Domingue were mulattos, their ideological armor its touchstone document, the Rights of Man and Citizen. Most of the colony's whites, unmoved by revolutionary idealism and unconvinced of the mulattos' humanity, disdainfully rejected their demands for full citizenship rights. The ensuing confrontation worsened, and soon white and mulatto militias were at war.[1]

It was then that the slaves made their move, determined to extract freedom from chaos. The chief obstacle to this attempt at self-liberation was the French Revolution. Mindful that Saint Domingue's slave-produced sugar and coffee accounted for the greater part of their country's foreign trade, the French revolutionaries concluded that the Rights of Man and Citizen did not apply to enslaved Africans. High-sounding rhetoric about the universality of liberty could scarcely be allowed to trump the business of the nation. After all, the French revolutionaries, no less than the monarch they had replaced, were duty bound to protect the national interests. Accordingly, the French revolutionaries declared war on their putative ideological equivalents in Saint Domingue, the revolting slaves. Eager to bring the insurgent bondsmen and bondswomen to heel, the French revolutionaries struck on two fronts, military and political. In addition to sending troops to Saint Domingue, they moved to impose a class alliance on the colony's warring white and mulatto slaveholders, acting on the theory that the whites' love of property exceeded their hatred of mulattos. Thus did the French Revolution grant the mulattos their long-sought wish: equality with the whites, which is not to be confused with full racial equality, since the shift left slavery intact; indeed, its whole purpose was to protect African bondage. Legalized racism, insofar as it applied to mulattos, would be sacrificed on the altar of slavery, now designated by the French revolutionaries as a nonracial gathering point for Saint Domingue's diverse men of property.[2]

As a strategy for defeating the slave revolt, the granting of equality to the mulattos failed. Despite serious setbacks, the black servile revolution continued, now supported by the Spanish in the neighboring colony of Santo Domingo (the Dominican Republic). Appalled by the overthrow of a fellow monarch in France, the king of Spain, like his counterparts everywhere in Europe, pledged implacable enmity to the French Revolution. Supporting the slave rebellion in Saint Domingue was part of that policy. Subsequently Spain and

Britain, at war with revolutionary France and coveting the rebellious colony, prepared to invade Saint Domingue.

For the second time, the French revolutionaries faced a momentous colonial crisis. On the first occasion, they had officially abandoned racism against the mulattos in order to save slavery, to no avail. Indeed, the failure to check the slave rebellion had created an opening for France's enemies, Spain and Britain, to invade Saint Domingue, causing a second colonial crisis. This time around, it was not just slavery but also colonialism—French rule over Saint Domingue—that was at stake. The French obviously could not have slavery without colonialism, and yet they could not have both. Having already disavowed racism, partly, in a futile attempt to safeguard slavery, France was now being forced to forsake slavery to preserve colonialism. Emancipation thus became a French political and military imperative, and suppressing the slave revolt was not just impossible but in the new circumstances also undesirable. The rulers of haughty France were reduced to supplicants before erstwhile chattels. To hold Saint Domingue, the French would have to persuade the black revolutionaries to renounce their alliance with Spain and, what is more, turn their guns on the foreign invaders, the Spanish and the British alike. Official acknowledgment of the freedom the blacks had seized by force of arms was the price for winning them over to the French side. Notably the Spanish, who continued to practice slavery, had made no such abolitionist commitment, having backed the Saint Domingue rising out of sheer expediency, as part of the campaign against the French Revolution. France, realizing it would have to make the black revolutionaries a better offer, countered by abolishing slavery, or, to be precise, by ratifying the self-liberation of the enslaved.[3]

France having made an about-face and committed itself to emancipation, the black revolutionaries responded in kind. Now commanded by the exslave and brilliant strategist Toussaint Louverture, they too reversed course, coolly abandoned Spain, and declared for French liberty, equality, and fraternity. It was an independent black revolutionary movement that allied with the French Revolution. The black revolutionaries, although receiving French support, were no more beholden to France than they had been to Spain, their late underwriter. As if to underscore the point, Toussaint, in his new role as the undisputed strongman of Saint Domingue, expelled a number of meddling French representatives, even as his army drove out the Spanish and British invaders.[4]

By 1798, peace had returned to the colony. The new order could not have been more different from the one obtained on the eve of the revolution seven years earlier. Slavery had ended, the plantations lay in ruins, most of the whites had fled, and blacks were in charge. The world of Saint Domingue had been turned upside down. It was independent in all but name; Toussaint refrained from making an official declaration of sovereign nationhood, apparently because he thought the French connection useful, politically and economically. However, as he turned to the issue of reconstruction, in the wake of the ruinous years of war, Toussaint paid scant attention to France. Ever the authoritarian, he ordered a constitution that designated him ruler for life, and even beyond, since the constitution also allowed him to name a successor. On the economic front, Toussaint proposed a longer tenure still for the plantation system. Instead of redistributing the land to the freed people, as they evidently desired, he resurrected the plantations. The workers, although now paid, were bound to the worksite, as in the days of slavery. This was hardly the freedom the ex-slaves envisioned, and they resisted the new regime, as they had the old one, including violent resistance. Toussaint put down such uprisings. For good measure, he executed the official most closely associated with the opposition to the plantation model of reconstruction, the military commander Moise, who was also his adopted nephew.[5] Toussaint the liberator, it now seemed, was metastasizing into Toussaint the liquidator.

Toussaint could ill afford to alienate the masses of the freed people at this historical juncture, for a mortal threat to the revolution in Saint Domingue was brewing. Back in France, Napoleon Bonaparte had staged a military takeover, unofficially ending the French Revolution. Napoleon believed one dictator was enough for the whole French empire, if not the world, and could find no more suitable candidate for the post than himself. He certainly had no intention of sharing the stage with an upstart ex-slave in Saint Domingue. His hatred of black folk every bit the equal of his vainglory, Napoleon intended to reestablish the old regime in the colonies, beginning with Saint Domingue, where the freed people would be put back in chains and the mulattos returned to social and political helotry. As for the black consul, Toussaint, he would be retired, to a cold prison cell in the French Alps.

So important was suppressing the Saint Domingue revolution to Napoleon that he entrusted the task to his brother-in-law, dispatching him to the colony with an appropriate army in tow. On arrival, the French concealed their true intention. Nonetheless Toussaint, unconvinced they were on a fact-finding mission, attempted to mobilize against them. He failed. His base of support had fallen away. In opting for the plantation model, he had given the masses nothing to fight for. After initially resisting the invaders, Toussaint's army also seemed to lose the will to fight. One by one his military commanders, lulled by French reassurance of the safety of their positions and perquisites, defected to France. Increasingly isolated, Toussaint's government fell. He retired to his plantations, but not for long. The French soon put him in chains and bundled him off to the alternate retirement home they had prepared.[6] There he would die a cruel death. This was, perhaps, the nadir of the Haitian Revolution. Whatever his flaws and failings, and they were numerous and serious, Toussaint had guided the struggle from near collapse to its greatest triumphs. With his strong and determined hand, he became the great helmsman of the revolution. Now he was gone. No single person, however, was indispensable, not even Toussaint Louverture. There was more leadership material where he came from, as he avowed in a parting note of revolutionary humility. In taking him, he assured his French captors, they had cut down "only the trunk of the tree of the liberty of the blacks; it will grow back from the roots, because they are deep and numerous."[7]

With Toussaint out of the way, the French revealed their mailed fist and ferociously set out to re-create the old order. Concluding that the freed people, hardened in battle, were no longer fit for slavery, the French determined on a genocidal solution to the Saint Domingue problem. Sparing only those who had not yet reached their teenage years, they would exterminate the population and restock the colony with fresh supplies of human cargo from Africa. It was an astonishing blueprint for mass murder, even by the dastardly standards of European colonialism in the Americas, and the French began actually to implement it. Their weapons included live burnings, crucifixions, and imported killer dogs specially trained to tear black people apart.[8]

The people of Saint Domingue now had something to fight for: their liberty, indeed, their very lives. Urgently recalled to revolutionary struggle, they proved equal to the atrocious French challenge.[9] Their new leader was Jean-Jacques Dessalines, who had a reputation as the most fearsome officer in the revolutionary army. Dessalines's background was notably different from that of Toussaint, his former commander in chief. Toussaint had obtained his freedom before the revolution began; even as a slave, however, he was relatively privileged, serving as a coachman. Dessalines, by contrast, never became more than a field hand in his career as a slave and only tasted freedom with the revolt of 1791. Perhaps more than any other top official, he was a product of the revolution. On joining the struggle, he rose rapidly through the military ranks to become Toussaint's top deputy. As a commander, Dessalines was partial to scorched earth and left little in his wake. Toussaint, always fond of the arborist metaphor, once reprimanded him for overzealousness, noting he had been ordered to prune the tree, not to chop it down. Dessalines, with his blunt ax and avid demeanor, was ill-suited for the precision of pruning, demolition being his forte. The slaveholder's lash still vivid in his memory, reputedly even engraved on his body, he vowed never again. For ruthlessness and cunning, Napoleon had nothing on him. The French had met their match.

Dessalines may have been at its head, but the final campaign of the Haitian Revolution was not of his making. The bloody path to his ascendance, rather, was the handiwork of others. Indeed, he was complicit in the shedding of some of that blood. Dessalines, it turned out, was among the commanders who went over to the side of the French invaders, even if his defection was tactical and temporary. As he contemplated defecting, Dessalines, speaking in the third person, told soldiers under his command, "If Dessalines surrenders to them [the French] a hundred times, he will betray them a hundred times. . . . Then I will make you independent. There will be no more whites amongst us."[10] He would prove to be as good as his word, but only because of the steadfastness of various guerrilla groups, which kept up the resistance, even as Dessalines, in the service of France, deployed his fierce military skills against them.[11] Yet it was that very resistance that made it possible for Dessalines to fulfill his promise to betray France and to return to the revolutionary fold. Rallying under a single banner the whole nation, the freed blacks and the mulattos alike, Dessalines ultimately proved his mettle, presiding over the fiercest struggles of the Haitian Revolution. In victory, he made good on the rest of his promise, declaring independence and getting rid of the whites, expelling or killing the ones who remained. "I have given the French cannibals blood for blood," he exulted triumphantly.[12]

The Haitian Revolution, of course, was far bigger than the colony of Saint Domingue. It was not just imperial powers and slaveholders, however, who staked out claims on revolutionary Haiti. Enslaved and oppressed people throughout the Atlantic world also became stakeholders, political and emotional, in the unfolding drama. By its very nature and its impact on world history, the Haitian Revolution had major black internationalist implications, among others. Independent Haiti's first constitution, commissioned by Dessalines in his capacity as head of state, acknowledged as much. It defined Haiti as a "black" nation and offered citizenship to anyone of African or Native American descent. Symbolically as well as substantively, the Haitian Revolution reshaped the Age of Revolution in ways European and North American policymakers and image-shapers would not understand or appreciate, and indeed still refuse to do.

The World-Historical Impact of the Haitian Revolution

In the grand narrative of Western scholarship, the Age of Revolution ushered in the modern world. From the United States and France, it is said, came modern democracy, while an industrial revolution in Britain changed the world of work forever. If, however, revolutions are defined by mass participation and social and political transformation, then the most substantial revolution of the Age of Revolution did not take place in Europe or North America. Rather, that revolution, forged in a black internationalist cauldron, happened in Saint Domingue.

Haiti's pride of place in the Age of Revolution is absent from the historical accounts of that era, which stress the achievements and continuing legacy of the U.S., French, and British revolutions. None of the classic works on either the period or revolutions generally—such as those by Crane Brinton, Eric Hobsbawm, Barrington Moore, and Theda Skocpol—makes more than passing mention of Haiti, if that.[13] With few exceptions,[14] more recent work equally fails to address the Haitian Revolution, whether the subject is the past and future of revolutions[15] or specific studies on the 200th anniversary of the French Revolution.[16] Yet by comparison to the revolutions of the white Atlantic, the revolution in Saint Domingue effected far greater political, social, and economic change. In Britain an industrial revolution proceeded during a period of political stability, while in the United States and France radical political changes brought little transformation in either the world of work or class and racial hierarchies. Haiti, by contrast, would experience not only the violent overthrow of an old political regime, but the thoroughgoing destruction of the ruling class (the white slaveholders) and the economic system (plantation slavery). Indeed the drive to replace Haiti's slave plantations, which had produced half the coffee and sugar consumed in Europe and the Americas,[17] led to the expansion of slavery elsewhere, most notably in the United States, Cuba, and Brazil.[18] Attempts to circumvent the implications of the Haitian Revolution over the long run would also lead to innovative forms of labor, race, and empire, as the world economy extended from the Americas to Africa, Asia, and the Pacific.

In the Americas, there is much evidence of Haiti's contribution to the demise of colonial empires and, more broadly, in shaping the balance of power among the great powers of Europe. British, Spanish, and French forces suffered staggering losses in defending their colonies and in invading Saint Domingue. Britain's attempt to secure its Caribbean colonies and defeat the Saint Domingue rebels cost the lives of tens of thousands of British troops and untold millions of pounds. Spain would eventually lose its American colonies, with direct Haitian support. Haiti assisted movements to overthrow Spanish rule in Venezuela (1806) and Mexico (1816) and, most notably, Simon Bolivar's expeditions in Venezuela (1816).

For France, the Haitian Revolution meant the loss of its greatest source of colonial products, trade, and profits; Saint Domingue alone had accounted for two-fifths of France's overseas trade.[19] Millions of jobs in port cities like Bordeaux depended on the slave trade, of which Saint Domingue was the center, while state revenues were highly dependent on the slave and colonial trades. Napoleon's attempt to reconquer Saint Domingue and reimpose slavery—with the blessing this time of the United States and Britain—led to the greatest losses of all, almost the entire French expeditionary force of 80,000. In the continuing war between France and Britain for global hegemony, the French struggled with fewer and fewer colonial resources after being defeated in Haiti. In desperation, France pulled out of the North American mainland altogether, selling those colonial possessions to the United States in the Louisiana Purchase in 1803.[20]

In the realm of human consciousness, the Haitian Revolution was the single most important event in bringing about that epoch-making shift of the Age of Revolution: the demise of the legitimacy of slavery in the Western world.[21] This did not translate into equality: freedom for slaves over the course of the nineteenth century moved hand in hand with the rise of new ideologies of domination, most notably scientific racism.[22] At the same time, the major European powers set out to create a new international division of labor that would be less dependent on chattel slavery and less vulnerable to slave revolts. Accordingly, vast new pools of coerced labor were opened up, with Asia coming to replace Africa. By the mid-nineteenth century, coerced labor from China and South Asia was flowing into the Americas, other parts of Asia, the Pacific, and even Africa.[23] Furthermore, the obstacles to colonial accumulation imposed by the abolition of slavery and decolonization in the Americas, of which Haiti remained the most dreaded example, led the Europeans to turn to Asia and Africa for raw materials and precious metals.[24] In this sense, the Haitian Revolution sealed off the history of Atlantic slavery:

the new British-dominated world economy that emerged in the nineteenth century was explicitly constructed to be less vulnerable to black revolt.

The Haitian revolutionaries were not unmindful of the world-historical drama they had wrought. Dessalines, at the moment of final victory, paid homage to the past: he dedicated the Haitian Revolution to the vanquished Native Americans, in whose honor the country was also named, Haiti reputedly meaning "rugged, mountainous" in the Taino Arawak language. Personalizing the tribute at that foundational and inebriating moment of nationhood, Dessalines famously asserted, "I have avenged America."[25] This was the autobiographical rendition of the Haitian Revolution, a transgression for which the remarkable field slave turned head of state may be forgiven. Of course, Dessalines had many coauthors. In fact, it was the Haitian masses who paid dearest of all for victory; half of Haiti's population, some 250,000 souls, died during the course of the revolutionary upheavals. The imperial "we" would have better served the emperor, a title Dessalines assumed at the time of independence in 1804.

The Haitian Revolution, Black Struggle, and Black Internationalism

The violent course of the Haitian Revolution, as charted in C. L. R. James's magisterial *The Black Jacobins* and subsequent monographs, involved shifting alliances among competing world powers, local white colonists, free people of color, and slaves.[26] Most accounts tightly contain the revolution within the boundaries of Saint Domingue, admitting only the determinant influence of the French Revolution. Few scholars dare to broach the broader lessons of the Haitian Revolution and its potential for replay in other slave societies. Noted slavery historian Seymour Dresher is typical. Citing David Geggus, the most widely published current chronicler of the Haitian Revolution, Dresher pronounced, "The one successful slave revolution was the outcome of a unique combination of circumstances. Haiti was both unforgettable and unrepeatable."[27]

That the Haitian Revolution was unforgettable is beyond doubt. It was not, however, the unique and isolated event that Dresher's assertion of unrepeatability implies. Whatever the ex post facto judgment of modern historians, it was not at all self-evident to the ruling and governing classes of the day that Saint Domingue–like events could not happen elsewhere. How else to explain the vast expansion in the regime of control instituted in the other slave societies of the Americas in the wake of the Saint Domingue rising, or the severe repression visited on anything smacking of attempts at another Haiti? Further, the unrelenting hostility to the Haitian Revolution, including major military campaigns against it by the three leading Atlantic powers—France, Spain, and Britain—was driven by more than just a desire to return Saint Domingue to its former status as the crown jewel of Caribbean slave colonies. Political leaders and slaveholders everywhere in the Americas, fearing the contagion of revolutionary slave insurrection, also wanted to create a military cordon sanitaire around Haiti and isolate it from the rest of the hemisphere.

The issue of the Haitian Revolution and its potential for replication turns on conception. It is a matter of imagining black resistance and political organization outside territorial boundaries and Euro–North American categories (the institutionalized, nonviolent social movement; the modernizing state-centered revolution; and the modernizing national identity).[28] Africans in the eighteenth and nineteenth centuries were unencumbered by such Enlightenment classifications. The freedom struggles of enslaved Africans throughout the Americas showed little of the modern historian's deference to imperial and national sovereignty; slave insurrectionists, on the contrary, were blithely oblivious to established political boundaries. Interrogating the hemisphere-wide African quest for emancipation on its own terms makes it possible to chart the interlocution between events in disparate localities and, in so doing, uncover a formative phase in black internationalism.

The starting point of such a project is a recognition that the Haitian Revolution, for all its majesty and iconoclasm, did not emerge in a historical void. It had a prehistory in black resistance. A long series of revolts throughout the Atlantic preceded the Haitian Revolution, revealing a widespread antislavery surge. This trend, paradoxically, was not apparent in prerevolutionary Haiti, with the possible exception of the Makandal poison conspiracy of 1757. Elsewhere in the Americas, however, slave revolts and conspiracies advanced steadily from the 1730s onward, notably in North America, the Caribbean, South America, and even Atlantic West Africa.[29] Jamaica's massive Tacky's Revolt of 1760 rounded out more than a generation of violent antislavery resistance.[30] With the Haitian Revolution standing at the apex, another round of revolts began in the 1790s, including uprisings in Saint Lucia (1795–97), Grenada and Saint Vincent (1795–96), and Guadeloupe (1802) and wars against maroons in Surinam (1789–93) and Jamaica (1795–96).[31] These events emerged from lived experiences in a highly racialized Atlantic political economy and, as such, defy portrayals that cast them as atavistic and isolated.

Indeed, a transnational slavery underground was alive and well throughout the eighteenth century, if not before, and various individuals, acting as itinerant revolutionaries, personally linked multiple revolts in different territories. As a group, these revolts were bound together by a common rejection of plantation slavery, the most fundamental pillar of mass production and accumulation in the capitalist world. In this sense, even apparently disconnected revolts, by their very character and synchronicity, reveal a transnational African response to capital and the political masters of the capitalist world.

The claim for a nascent black international before the advent of the Haitian Revolution runs counter to a scholarly tradition that stresses the difficulty of even local coordination among Africans, in view of the linguistic and cultural differences that separated them. Such divisions, to be sure, were real enough. Moreover, the massive mortality rate among the enslaved everywhere in the hemisphere (with the exception of North America, and then only after the late eighteenth century), and the attendant need to continuously introduce new slaves reinforced the diversity of the various slave societies.[32] Yet, as Tacky's Revolt and, even more emphatically, the Haitian Revolution demonstrate, internal divisions among enslaved Africans was no impassable barrier to mass antislavery insurrections. Revolutionary activity by the enslaved did not require homogeneity—linguistic, cultural, or religious.

In their majestic work *The Many-Headed Hydra*, Peter Linebaugh and Marcus Rediker show how the construction of Anglo-Atlantic capitalism gave rise to an unruly, multiethnic, "motley crew" of coerced workers, slaves, and seamen on all sides of the Atlantic. Impressed seamen, working under extremely oppressive conditions, carried ideas and tactics of resistance throughout the Americas, with black seaman playing a central role. Julius Scott's equally magnificent work on black resistance in the greater Caribbean in the era of the Haitian Revolution offers detailed evidence of the "common wind" that propelled resistance, showing how sailors, including enslaved ones, carried news of revolts and revolutions and rumors of freedom to come.[33] Nor were seamen the only traveling vectors of revolution and discontent. Uprisings in British Honduras drew on the hundreds of rebels exiled there after Tacky's Revolt, while veterans of the French brigade that fought for the U.S. Revolution later emerged as leaders of the Haitian Revolution (e.g., Henri Christophe and André Rigaud).

The Haitian Revolution electrified the nascent black international circuits, which irrupted with news of emancipation, of slave armies defeating great white powers, and of the emergence of a mighty black republic. Slaves everywhere celebrated Haiti, from Philadelphia to Trinidad, from Havana to Cu-raçao. In Kingston, Jamaica, captives yearning for freedom composed a hymn to the anticipated new order, singing, "black, white, brown, all the same."[34] Surveying the political landscape, slaveholders feared ruin for themselves and a dim future for their scions. Thomas Jefferson, ever the spokesman for his class, summed up the apprehension. "The revolutionary storm now sweeping the globe," he allowed, "will [soon] be upon us."[35] The prediction was not unfounded. Veterans of the Haitian campaigns, or witnesses to them, could be found in the vanguard of revolts in other territories. Some of the seeds of insurrection were unwittingly sown by masters who fled Saint Domingue with their human chattel; at the new destinations, a number of slaves so transported promptly took to the revolutionary path, as in Curaçao, Venezuela, and most notably, Louisiana.[36] In some cases, slave revolutionary leaders looked to Haiti for inspiration, even direct assistance, or else falsely created the impression of such assistance, apparently as a way to gain and solidify support among the enslaved. Thus Denmark Vesey, head of the 1822 conspiracy in Charleston, South Carolina, told his followers Haitian help would arrive to support the capture of the city.[37] Aponte had done pretty much the same in Havana, Cuba, in 1812, using portraits of Toussaint, Dessalines, and Christophe to solicit sup-port and to inspire fellow rebels.[38] These connections, forged by Julius Scott's common wind, point to the existence of vast antislavery efforts among the enslaved across imperial and national boundaries, *in fine*, to a nascent black international.

Black internationalism in the Atlantic world was defined by the emergence of a common black identity rooted in the struggle against slavery and, despite the efforts of some revolutionaries to counter such trends, the polarization of racial identities. Notably, the racial and territorial contours of the black international rested not on biology nor on a single ancient culture, but on com-mon experiences, that is, actual struggles against white world supremacy.[39] The black international, then, only emerged with racial slavery and Atlantic capital-ism and altered, waxed, and waned with successive emancipatory struggles. Such dynamics can be seen in the great struggles of the late eighteenth and early nineteenth centuries, when racial as well as class conflicts accelerated, driven by black insurrections and the ensuing counterrevolution of the white Thermidor.

The juxtaposition of black revolution and white reaction throws into sharp relief a major achievement of the black international in its formative stages: common visions of life outside the bounds of capitalism, and the active pursuit of those visions. Such a reading flies in the face of accounts that portray black revolts and uprisings as premodern, backward-looking, and seeking only to return to a precapitalist mode of production. In this interpretation, it was the bourgeois-democratic revolution, and specifically its French incarnation, that opened the door to the modern black pursuit of freedom, beginning with the Haitian Revolution.[40] Actually, neither the French nor the U.S. republic facilitated, much less promoted, slave emancipation, a fact stubbornly ignored in French Revolutionary studies, especially.[41] Rather, it was black rebels who opened the door to freedom. Only black resistance and black revolution consistently stood for liberty without regard to race, class, or condition of servitude. Black struggles, culminating in the Haitian Revolution, did not just expand but redefined notions of freedom.

Negating the Black International:
Haiti and the White Thermidor

The white Thermidor, full of fear and loathing for the black internationalism Haiti had come to symbolize, was brutal to the newly independent state. Faced with rebellious slaves and natives, white planters, merchants, and imperial powers coalesced to enforce white power. If the Haitian Revolution could not be rolled back, it would certainly be contained. Having won the war, the Haitians would be denied the fruits of victory: they would be made to lose the peace. The cost of throwing off the shackles of colonialism, slavery, and white supremacy would be very high, even crippling. European powers and white-run states variously isolated Haiti, embargoed its goods, demanded reparations, and barred from their shores its dangerous achievements and citizens. Everywhere in the Americas, the authorities circumscribed and repressed suspected black middle classes—free blacks and mulattos—further cementing racial polarization and identities. Meanwhile, scientific racism as a mode of securing postabolition global racial hierarchies flourished, initially and not accidentally, in post-Napoleonic France, most notably in the writings of Count Gobineau, "the father of racist ideology."[42] The multiracial motley crew that formed in the previous era of revolution, and about which Linebaugh and Rediker write with such feeling, could not survive the pressure and dissolved into separate racial and class components.[43] This was irony of a large order: through counterrevolution, the struggle for emancipation from racial slavery would result in a sharper and wider racial order than had existed in the eighteenth-century Atlantic world.

Faced with the new order in Haiti and its possibilities, white revolutionaries made an abrupt about-face. The case of the Jeffersonian republicans in the United States is instructive. The self-proclaimed keepers of the U.S. revolutionary flame, Jefferson and his acolytes recoiled in horror at the events in Haiti and attempts to reproduce them in the United States, most conspicuously in the Gabriel Prosser conspiracy of 1800.[44] Accordingly, the Jeffersonians forsook the notion of global and permanent revolution, a notion they had previously affirmed. In their minds, the pursuit of liberty and happiness was no longer the exclusive preserve of orderly white men of property and scions of the European Enlightenment, since enslaved Africans and other lesser breeds had taken up the cry.[45] In yet another irony, however, it was the Haitian Revolution that made possible Jefferson's most enduring legacy as U.S. president: the humiliating defeat in Haiti forced France to abandon its imperial ambitions on the North American mainland. The resulting Louisiana Purchase, under Jefferson's presidency, opened the door for the emergence of the United States as a "slave country."[46]

Naturally, the legacy of the Haitian Revolution was anathema to the United States in its capacity as both slaveholding power and emerging hegemon of the Americas. Accordingly, a letter from the Haitian government requesting diplomatic ties between the two countries elicited scorn; U.S. president John Quincy Adams (1825–29) penned in the margins, "Not to be answered."[47] U.S. senator Thomas Hart Benton of Missouri, a slaveholding state, explained why:

> Because the peace of eleven states in this Union will not permit the fruits of a successful negro insurrection to be exhibited among us. It will not permit black Consuls and Ambassadors to establish themselves in our cities, and to parade through our country, and give their fellow blacks in the United States, proof in hand of the honors that await them, for a like successful effort on their part. It will not permit the fact to be seen, and told, that for the murder of their masters and mistresses, they are to find *friends* among the white People of these United States.[48]

The resulting embargo on Haiti ran the gamut from the political to the economic and the discursive. Haiti was the only independent state excluded from the pioneering Pan-American Conference of 1826.[49] Writers of various stripes, scholarly and popular, joined the blockade. As Michel-Rolph Trouillot has so eloquently chronicled, Western scholarship declared a blackout of the events that unfolded in Saint Domingue from 1791 through 1804. Haiti was both censured and censored: the country having become a nonentity, its revolution became, in Trouillot's formulation, a "nonevent."[50] Yet this intellectual embargo, which few dare to breach,[51] was only imposed after the fact. Many Western observers and commentators, including slaveholders who had fled Haiti, wrote and published about the revolution while it was still in progress.[52] The whiting out, which came after Haiti became independent, negated, at the level of written historical memory, not just the Haitian Revolution but also the black internationalism it had come to symbolize. The one as well as the other would be suppressed, whether by omission or commission.

The Haitian Revolution and the Narrative of the Black International

To contemporary friends and foes alike, the Haitian Revolution was an event of momentous black international import. Yet, incredibly, published accounts of the black international largely ignore the Haitian Revolution. Inspection of the literature reveals little about the Haitian revolutionary antecedents of black internationalism. There are two notable exceptions, standing two generations apart. The first is C. L. R. James's little gem of 1938, *A History of Negro Revolt*, which began with the Haitian Revolution and used it as a yardstick for judging a number of subsequent pan-African struggles.[53] Julius Scott's 1986 Ph.D. dissertation, which, alas, remains unpublished, greatly expanded on the black internationalism of the Haitian Revolution in its own era, using as an organizing principle the vast underground intelligence networks that circulated a common wind of revolutionary possibilities between Haiti and the greater Caribbean.[54] The pioneering and exceptional work of James and Scott aside, the pan-African narrative has been most unkind to the Haitian Revolution. The silence relegates the epochal and black internationalist transformation in Saint Domingue to the status of a nonevent, to use Trouillot's felicitous term for the burial of the Haitian Revolution in Western scholarship.

It need not have turned out that way. Some of the first chronicles of the struggling black international offered visions of a historiography much different from the one that became dominant, a narrative that would have centered, rather than silenced, the Haitian Revolution. One such pioneering text, a key if often forgotten one, is *The Life and Struggles of Negro Toilers*, published in 1931.[55] Its author, George Padmore, was himself an outstanding toiler in the realm of pan-African liberation in the twentieth century.[56] *Life and Struggles* charted the struggles of black workers and peasants—Negro toilers—in Africa, the

United States, the Caribbean, and Latin America. Such resistance—revolts, strikes, and other forms of discontent—demonstrated, the 126-page booklet concluded, "the tremendous revolutionary potentialities of the Negro toiling masses."[57]

Where Padmore led, his fellow Trinidadian and boyhood friend, C. L. R. James, followed. Making his maiden appearance on the stage of black international scholarship, James came out with *A History of Negro Revolt* in 1938, the same year he published his magnum opus, *The Black Jacobins*. The beauty and grace of the Haitian revolutionary book, at once a great work of history and literature, quickly overshadowed the comparatively puny ninety-seven-page booklet on the struggling black international. Yet *A History of Negro Revolt* made manifest a point that was only implied in *The Black Jacobins*. *A History of Negro Revolt* demonstrated the impact and relevance of the Haitian Revolution for black internationalism, in its own era and later.

Unlike *A History of Negro Revolt*, Padmore's *Life and Struggles* neglected the Haitian Revolution, although it had a section on the plight of the Haitian toilers "under the yoke of Yankee imperialism," that is, during the U.S. occupation of 1915–34.[58] Yet despite differences in emphasis, style, and interpretation, Padmore and James began their narration from a common foundation: both works privileged the toilers—slaves, peasants, and workers. The contrast with later narratives of the black international could not be greater.

After *A History of Negro Revolt*, the black masses lost their position at the forefront of pan-African intellectual inquiry, dethroned in favor of the elite. Henceforth, the major narratives of the black international would highlight the activities of the transatlantic black petite bourgeoisie, especially the intelligentsia. Not incidentally, the turn away from the toilers was also a turn away from the Haitian Revolution.

The first installment on the new narrative of the black international appeared in 1956. Authored by no less a personage than Padmore, the volte-face came with a stark and provocative title: *Pan-Africanism or Communism? The Coming Struggle for Africa*.[59] This was, above all, a Cold War text. Since writing *Life and Struggles*, Padmore had made a grueling political odyssey, from the pan-Africanism of the international communist movement to an anticommunist pan-Africanism. As such, his chief concern in *Pan-Africanism or Communism* was to demonstrate that the anticolonial revolt then sweeping Africa in no way owed its inspiration to communism, as alleged by the defenders of empire and their consorts, political and intellectual.

In the process of cleansing pan-Africanism of the communist taint, Padmore repudiated his 1931 work, albeit without actually saying so. All the essential premises of *Life and Struggles*, epistemic and organizational, were abandoned in *Pan-Africanism or Communism*. Gone was the expansive definition of pan-Africanism. Where *Life and Struggles* focused on three continents—Africa and the Americas—the much longer *Pan-Africanism or Communism* singled out one: Africa, and then with a predominant emphasis on the British territories. In his later work, Padmore also narrowed the social foundations of the black international. If *Life and Struggles* placed the emphasis on the toilers as a class, then *Pan-Africanism or Communism* privileged particular individuals. The masses and their movements had given way to the thoughts and actions of great men. One of those men was W. E. B. Du Bois, whom Padmore had thrashed in *Life and Struggles* as a petit bourgeois reformist misleader but rehabilitated in *Pan-Africanism or Communism*, where he was elevated to the lofty status of "Father of Pan-Africanism." According to this rendition, pan-Africanism "came of age" in the immediate post–World War II era, when Padmore himself succeeded Du Bois at the helm. In a final changing of the guard, Padmore in turn gave way to his star student, the Gold Coast nationalist and future Ghanaian president, Kwame Nkrumah, the two men having jointly organized the pivotal fifth Pan-African Congress of 1945. In Padmore's estimation, Nkrumah embodied all the virtues of pan-Africanism as conceived by Du Bois and refined at the 1945 congress. In sum, Du Bois had planted, Padmore had watered, and Nkrumah was bringing forth the increase. The pan-African triumvirate, or rather, trinity, stood triumphant.

With such Whiggish tales of the heights that great men reached and kept, *Pan-Africanism or Communism* scarcely had a word to spare for the Haitian Revolution, even for such presumably towering figures as Toussaint and Dessalines. But the die was cast. The framework of *Pan-Africanism or Communism* would prove enduring. Imported into the academy, the Padmorian teleology exercised a determining influence on the narrative of the black international for the remainder of the Cold War and, indeed, continues to do so down to the present time.[60]

Even Imanuel Geiss's *The Pan-African Movement: A History of Pan-Africanism in America, Europe, and Africa*, a work widely considered the standard text on the subject, failed to break with Padmore's framework, and indeed duplicated it.[61] Although offered as a corrective to Padmore's rendition of the black international, *The Pan-African Movement* accepted the major assumptions of *Pan-*

Africanism or Communism. Geiss merely transposed Padmore's interpretations, casting as irrational many of the ideas, actions, and events that were celebrated in *Pan-Africanism or Communism*—but without questioning its basic structure or the validity of its narrative line. On the great slave revolt turned revolution in Saint Domingue, Geiss was not quite as silent as Padmore. Still, the various references to the Haitian Revolution in *The Pan-African Movement* remained peripheral and were never systematically developed.[62]

The rise in the post–Cold War era of African Diaspora studies in the Anglo-American academy and beyond has hardly disrupted the dominant narrative of the black international. The reigning teleology, so fundamentally shaped by *Pan-Africanism or Communism*, remains ascendant in its main features. Thus the text that would become the touchstone of the revived African Diaspora studies, as well as a virtual canon of postmodern and cultural studies black internationalism, reproduced in important ways the narrative line of *Pan-Africanism or Communism.* That text, of course, is Paul Gilroy's *The Black Atlantic: Double Consciousness and Modernity*, with its quintessentially Du Boisian subtitle.[63]

The Black Atlantic, despite mentioning Padmore only in passing,[64] has much in common with *Pan-Africanism or Communism.* For one, the authors share an Afro-Saxon bias: Padmore for the east bank of the black Atlantic and Gilroy for the west. In substance, if not in tone, Gilroy is no less fulsome than Padmore in celebrating the great pan-African man, most tellingly Du Bois and his fellow African American Richard Wright, a communist apostate like Padmore and the contributor of a laudatory foreword to *Pan-Africanism or Communism.* The corollary snubbing of masses and mass movements explains, to a large extent, the virtual silence of both texts on the Haitian Revolution. Yet Gilroy could well have accommodated the Haitian Revolution within his own paradigm, even if not as a mass movement. Few figures in black internationalism, surely, exemplify the ordeal of modernity and double consciousness more poignantly than Toussaint—who, in the event, does not even merit a single reference in *The Black Atlantic.*[65] Despite such limitations, Gilroy's book skillfully deploys certain tropes, most notably the ship, that offer the possibility for a different kind of narrative of the black international—one that would reserve a rightful place for the Haitian Revolution. Seven years before *The Black Atlantic* appeared, Julius Scott had done just that, deepening the pioneering insights offered by James in *A History of Negro Revolt.* Gilroy's influential work, on the contrary, took the well-trodden path on the Haitian Revolution, thereby perpetuating a serious lacuna in pan-African scholarship.

Emergent Black International Traditions:
Revolutionary and Revivalist

Beginning in the Age of Revolution, the black international evolved into two traditions, which we will call revolutionary and revivalist. The Haitian Revolution, which capped a long line of violent antislavery resistance, even as it qualitatively altered the nature of that resistance, became an emblem of the revolutionary tradition. Evolving alongside the revolutionary tradition, and serving as both its counterpart and its counterpoint, was the revivalist tradition, with its center in the Anglo-American world and its origins in the Evangelical Revival. The dominant narrative of the black international is derived largely from the revivalist tradition and its permutations.

The two traditions in black internationalism, the revolutionary and the revivalist, emerged under different conditions, the one grounded in armed struggle and the other formally, although not always actually, committed to nonviolent resistance. Frequently, if not in all instances, epistemic distinctions further set the two traditions apart. Scholars of the Haitian Revolution, a defining event in the revolutionary tradition, are broadly agreed that it originally cohered around vodun, the dominant slave religion of Saint Domingue.[66] Boukman Dutty, the first leader of the Haitian Revolution, was a noted practitioner of vodun. Of syncreticism, a term that would later be used to describe the melding of African and European (and often Native American) cultures, Boukman was disdainful, at least in the realm of religion. At the Bois Caiman ceremony, simultaneously the inaugural moment of the Haitian Revolution and the most iconic of vodun events, Boukman categorically rejected Christianity. "The God of the white man calls him to commit crimes," he informed the assembled vanguard of the coming revolution, in what amounted to the keynote address at Bois Caiman, whereas "our God asks only good works of us." But a good God demanded justice, even vengeance. "This God who is so good," Boukman continued, "orders revenge! He will direct our hands; he will aid us." He then concluded, no doubt on a note of high drama and perhaps even to acclamation, "Throw away the image of the God of the whites who thirsts for our tears, and listen to the voice of liberty that speaks in the hearts of all of us."[67]

The adherents of the black international revivalist tradition also listened to the voice of liberty, even as they rejected Boukman's binary religious categories. The revivalists did not so much discard the God of the whites as to make him anew, transforming him into the God of the blacks, all the while preserving his universality. It was a deft maneuver, ideologically speaking, and it began with the Evangelical Revival.

Before the Evangelical Revival, enslaved Africans in the British colonies, whether on the North American mainland or in the Caribbean, had little real contact with Christianity. The Evangelical Revival inaugurated the meeting of African spiritualities and Protestant Christianity.[68] A movement that came out of the Church of England, or the Anglican Church, the Evangelical Revival was, in part, a reaction to the European Enlightenment, then nearing its end. Rejecting Christianity as part of the dark past best consigned to the dustbin of history, the Enlightenment proposed to replace faith with reason, tradition with progress, and contentment with happiness. The Evangelical Revival came to defend faith and to affirm the truth of revealed religion. In the process, the Evangelical Revival launched a critique of the established church, insisting on a more vibrant, engaged, and relevant Christianity. The Enlightenment argued that Western society, which it assumed to be the human norm, was excessively religious. On the contrary, the Evangelical Revival countered, the problem was not too much religion but not enough of it.[69]

In the colonies, if not in the center of the empire, the message of the Evangelical Revival appealed most to the disinherited and the dispossessed. In British North America, where it would become known as the Great Awakening, the outstanding organizing mechanism of the Evangelical Revival was the camp meeting. Spiritual conversion, not familiarity with the catechism or mastery of the minutiae of Christian doctrine, the evangelists insisted, constituted evidence of salvation. The Holy Spirit, they continued, was readily and freely available to all, irrespective of class, servile status, race, or gender. It was simply a matter of heeding the revelation, that is, the revelation of the Holy Spirit. To the enslaved Africans and their descendants who flocked to the camp meetings, the concept of revelation would have been quite familiar; it was an established feature of most African religions. The correspondence facilitated conversion, allowing the slaves to accept the new without rejecting the old.[70] Thus began the mass conversion of Africans in British lands, and with it the origins of the black international revivalist tradition.

The U.S. Revolution would prove to be a boon to the revivalist tradition. Out of the free black community that emerged from the U.S. Revolution would come some of the notable exponents of that tradition.[71] Then there were the black refugees from the U.S. Revolution, a diaspora within a diaspora. Armed with the gospel of the Evangelical Revival, sometimes combined with the founding ideals of the U.S. Revolution, these refugees would have a profound effect on the societies in which they resettled. Scholars are still pursuing their footprints in places as diverse as the Bahamas, Bermuda, Jamaica, Sierra Leone, Canada, and England, among others.[72] In this way, the U.S. Revolution unwittingly produced vectors of black internationalism, in its revivalist guise, on both banks of the Atlantic.

It was not just the revivalist tradition, however, that benefited from the U.S. Revolution. As Sylvia Frey so incisively shows in her essay, some among the enslaved seized the opportunity offered by the war for U.S. independence to launch armed struggles of their own making against racial bondage. A number of these self-organized freedom fighters previously belonged to the black units of the British army, and some were steeped in evangelical Christianity. The result was a merger of the revivalist and revolutionary traditions in black internationalism, or what Frey calls, respectively, "evangelical pan-Africanism" and "revolutionary pan-Africanism." In the main, though, the revivalist tradition was more closely linked to the U.S. Revolution and its black internationalist consequences than was the revolutionary tradition.

Pioneers of the revivalist tradition produced an important body of literature, part of it destined to be incorporated into later chronicles of the black international. These founding texts, which began to emerge in the late eighteenth century, consisted of poetry, sermons, autobiographical accounts, and philosophical musings by ex-slaves, some of whom had personally experienced the transatlantic journey of the Middle Passage.[73] Part of the Western canon, even as they challenged that canon, such works mirrored the position of black folk in the white-dominated Atlantic world. The founding texts thus occupied a peculiar intellectual and political space, precariously perched between the Evangelical Revival and its ideological nemesis, the Enlightenment. From an uneasy synthesis of the two—the Revival and the Enlightenment, the sacred and the profane—arose abolitionism, which became the first great organizing principle of the revivalist tradition.

Abolitionism, then, was not the exclusive product of the white imagination, as the Eurocentric master narrative would have it.[74] For one, the black founding narrators of the revivalist tradition powerfully mediated abolitionism, as only they *experientially* could do. In any case, abolitionism was hardly an intellectual abstraction. Whether as an idea or as a movement, it emerged in concert with slave resistance, especially slave revolts.[75] The violent attempts

at self-liberation spurred the literary and organizational exertions of the abolitionists, whose campaign, it bears remembering, initially targeted not slavery
but the slave trade. It remained for the enslaved themselves, in the midst of
their essays in self-liberation, to formulate the "genius of universal emancipation," to borrow the title of an early-nineteenth-century African American
publication. In sum, the *plan* to end slavery as a form of social organization
was conceived not in the heads of the abolitionists, black or white, but in slave
revolts, culminating in the Haitian Revolution, which decisively shifted the
locus of abolitionism from the slave trade to slavery. The official termination of
the slave trade by Britain in 1807, and by the United States the following year,
confirmed that shift. In both cases, but especially that of the United States, a
major consideration in abandoning the commerce in human cargoes was the
fear of slave revolts, behind which stood the greatest specter of all, the Haitian
Revolution.[76]

The boost to abolitionism was also a boost to the revivalist tradition in
black internationalism, its ideological helpmeet. Broadly, the revivalist tradition shared the goals of the revolutionary tradition—namely, antislavery,
antiracism, and more equivocally, anticolonialism. Unlike the revolutionary
tradition, though, the revivalist tradition was constrained by its alliance with
white abolitionism. With few exceptions, white abolitionists throughout the
Atlantic were committed to a pacific, and often gradual, approach to emancipation. Generally, white abolitionists saw the Haitian Revolution as unhelpful,
even as a setback to their cause.[77] Some revivalists rejected that depiction,
extolling the emancipationist glory of the Haitian Revolution. Already in 1797,
seven years before Haiti officially became independent, Prince Hall rejoiced
in the outcome of the revolt there. A staunch revivalist and pioneer of African American masonry, Hall asserted that events in Saint Domingue had
shown that "God hath no respect of persons," paraphrasing a biblical passage
(Acts 10:34) much beloved by the founders of the revivalist tradition. Invoking another scripture (Psalms 68:31) that would gain even greater popularity,
becoming a rallying cry in black internationalist circles down to the Garvey
movement, Hall concluded of the Saint Domingue revolt, "Thus doth Ethiopia
begin to stretch forth her hand, from a sink of slavery to freedom and equality."[78] Not all revivalists, however, followed Hall's lead. Others, more closely
allied with white abolition, remained mum on the Haitian Revolution. Thus
publicly, at any rate, the founding generation of revivalists was not of one mind
on the subject of Haiti.

The heirs to the revivalist tradition would help to keep alive memory of the Haitian Revolution outside Haiti. One such individual was James Theodore Holly, the African American clergyman and staunch supporter of the emigration of free blacks to Haiti in the years leading up to the U.S. Civil War. A sectarian Protestant, like so many of his generation of black international revivalists, Holly's enthusiasm for Haiti was tempered only by his disdain for its official religion, Catholicism (he largely ignored vodun, the faith of most Haitians). Holly proposed to replace Catholicism, which he apparently considered effete, among other errors, with a "manly" Protestantism. Otherwise, Holly's fervor for Haiti seemed boundless. In his view, the Haitian Revolution was an epochal event, "vindicating" as it did the capacity of black folk for "self-government and civilized progress," in short, to attain modernity and rise in the scale of white bourgeois culture.[79]

The black masses were equally buoyant on Haiti. In various parts of the Caribbean and South America, enslaved people and free people of color incorporated tropes of the Haitian Revolution into their culture—music, dance, visual art, and folkways.[80] Meanwhile, free African Americans also embraced the Haitian revolutionary legacy, turning January 1, Haiti's independence day, into a popular, if unofficial, public holiday. The embrace of Haiti was facilitated by the exclusion of black people, often by violent means, from U.S. independence celebrations.[81]

David Walker had a keen appreciation of the legacy of the Haitian Revolution, at both the intellectual and popular levels. His iconic pamphlet hailed Haiti as "the glory of the blacks and the terror of tyrants,"[82] even as he helped to organize Haitian independence celebrations in Boston, his adopted hometown. Walker came a generation before his fellow African American James Theodore Holly, for whom he may as well have been a model, balancing enthusiasm for Haiti with a Protestant chauvinist aversion to its official religion, Catholicism, "that scourge of nations," all the while displaying a vibrant black internationalism. Walker linked the fate of African Americans, slave and free, to the liberation of black folk globally, a pan-African connection evident in the title of his deeply biblical and black text, *David Walker's Appeal to the Coloured Citizens of the World*. Walker wrote in the urgent tone of the prophetic tradition—the tradition of speaking truth to power, damn the consequences.[83] In his vacillation between the pacific tendencies of abolitionism, on one hand, and armed struggle, on the other, he stood athwart the two traditions in black internationalism: the revivalist and the revolutionary. Similarly, Walker's epistle was situated between a biblically based teleology of emancipation and a Christian theology of liberation—the one founded on providential predetermination and the other appealing to the agency of the oppressed.

Two years after Walker wrote, the two conceptions—the hand of God and the human hand—found a synthesis in revolutionary praxis. The year of reckoning was 1831, when the Nat Turner Revolt in Virginia and the Christmas Rising in Jamaica, two attempts at self-emancipation, occurred just four months apart. Whatever their other connections (and Julius Scott's common wind, although calmed by repression, had hardly faded away), the two rebellions were related, ideologically, through a common adherence to the Baptist faith. Turner was a Baptist preacher, while the Jamaican insurrection is also known as the Baptist War, black Baptist refugees from the U.S. Revolution, among others, having brought their faith to the island.[84] With the Turner Revolt and the Christmas Rising/Baptist War, black Christianity had given rise to a liberation theology based on armed struggle, much more explicitly than the independent black revolutionary activities attendant on the U.S. Revolution. For the first time since the Haitian Revolution, the revivalist and revolutionary traditions in black internationalism had merged on the field of battle, if ever so briefly. It was a meeting, finally, of Boukman and the Baptists.

It was only partially, however, a rendezvous of victory.[85] The revolutionary antislavery crusades of 1831, the Turner Revolt and the Christmas Rising, had quite different historical outcomes. In yet another demonstration of the dialectical interrelationship between slave revolts and abolitionism, the Christmas Rising served as an important and final impetus for emancipation in the British Empire. Relative to its economic value in the emerging British industrial order, the cost of slavery had become prohibitively high.[86] Moreover, suppressing revolts and maintaining armies in the slave colonies were burdens the British treasury had grown tired of bearing. Given the frequency and ferocity of such uprisings, Britain seemed to face two choices: risk another Haiti or decree abolition from above. With the Abolition of Slavery Act, which was passed in 1833 and became effective the following year, the British authorities chose the safer option.[87]

The situation was quite different in the United States, where slavery had become more important than ever, centering increasingly on the production of cotton, primarily for the British textile industry. Accordingly, the U.S. slaveholders and the state, over which they exercised ever more dominance, responded to the Turner Revolt with even more repression. The revolutionary tradition negated, there would be no more major slave insurrections in the United States. Yet, the tradition of black self-organization, everywhere the foundation of antislavery revolutionary activities, remained alive and well among African American slaves, in their cultural and religious institutions and practices. The "sable arm," recalled to martial duty by a repentant state more than three decades after the Turner Revolt, during the U.S. Civil War, would play a major role in bringing about emancipation.[88] For many of its black participants, the Civil War effectively constituted a synthesis of the revolutionary and revivalist traditions in black internationalism. All they needed was President Abraham Lincoln's Emancipation Proclamation, which actually freed not a single slave but, rather, appealed to the agency of the enslaved and incited them to rebellion. Thus unchained, the sable arm would become its own liberator.[89] The Emancipation Proclamation, then, was the equivalent of the Bois Caiman ceremony in the Haitian Revolution—not a bestowal of freedom but a clarion call for the enslaved to revolt against bondage and make real the promise of liberty.

The connection between the two emancipation campaigns—the Haitian Revolution and the U.S. Civil War—was deeper still.[90] Matthew Clavin has recently shown how the transformation of black men, free and slave, into soldiers during the Civil War at once deepened and brought to light hidden identification among African Americans with the Haitian Revolution, and especially with Toussaint Louverture. For many African American soldiers and their boosters, "Toussaint and the men who followed him into battle affirmed the redemptive quality of violence to prove black manhood."[91] This black international legacy, in the form of memory of the Haitian Revolution, was transmitted through both the literary and oral traditions—that is, the writings of the free blacks and the word of mouth of the slaves, including a handful of old bondsmen who claimed to have seen action in Toussaint's army. The resulting consciousness and cultural tropes deeply inspired African Americans in the theater of war and beyond, as revealed in matters ranging from martial music to naming practices, including the names of military units, places, and individuals.[92] Here, indeed, was an affirmation of the unbroken circle of emancipation envisioned at the foundational moment of black internationalism, a vision most readily symbolized by the Haitian Revolution and its legacy.

Coda

Since assuming more definite form in the latter part of the eighteenth century, the black international had ebbed and flowed. The revolutionary tradition, on becoming associated with the Haitian Revolution, caused much excitement and helped to fuel insurrectionary activities among the enslaved throughout the Americas. But the vigilance and repression of colonial and slaveholding powers, not some preordained historical force, ensured that despite repeated attempts, the revolutionary tradition would not gain any real traction outside Haiti after the revolution there. Meanwhile, the other paradigm in black internationalism, the revivalist tradition, adopted as its guiding principle universal emancipation, a principle first proclaimed *and* put into practice by adherents of the revolutionary tradition. Later, champions of the revivalist tradition would draw inspiration from the Haitian Revolution and defend Haitian sovereignty. At certain moments, the two traditions merged, as in the black guerrilla warfare on the sidelines of the U.S. Revolution, in the Turner Revolt and the Christmas Rising, and rather more tentatively, among the black contingent in the U.S. Civil War. In the main, though, the revivalist tradition remained dominant in black internationalism in the post–Haitian Revolution era, certainly in Anglo-American lands. In the United States, meanwhile, some among the free blacks advocated leaving the country in search of real liberty, and Haiti was one of the suggested destinations for potential African American emigrants in the period leading up to the Civil War.

Then, in the early twentieth century, Haiti and the legacy of the Haitian Revolution dramatically reappeared in black internationalism. The cause was the U.S. invasion of Haiti in 1915, followed by a generation-long military occupation lasting until 1934.[93] Historically and symbolically, this violent repudiation of Haitian sovereignty constituted a payback for the revolution against slavery, white supremacy, and colonialism over a century earlier. As such, it amounted to Jefferson's revenge. Accordingly, Haiti and the Haitian Revolution became an important, if not fully appreciated, trope in the black international renaissance, political and cultural, that followed World War I.

Since the aggression emanated from the United States, the cause of "bleeding Haiti" became especially dear to African Americans.[94] Black folk in the United States were all the more outraged because the invasion of Haiti came just weeks after the premiering of the film *Birth of a Nation*, a vilely racist attack on African American political rights and a vindication of the violent white-supremacist overthrow of Reconstruction, the brief but remarkable experiment in nonracial democracy that had followed the Civil War.[95] In the circumstances, African American activists, writers, and artists swung into action, protesting the occupation of Haiti in multiple forms, including demonstrations, commissions of investigations, essays, books, paintings, plays, and poems. "Black Majesty," an ode by Countee Cullen, among the most equivocal of the African American poets of that era, his racial eulogy frequently tinged with apologia, was typical of the outbreak of celebration of Haitian revolutionary figures:

These men were kings, albeit they were black,
Christophe and Dessalines and L'Overture;
Their majesty has made me turn my back
Upon a plaint I once shaped to endure. . . .
Stifle your agony; let grief be drowned;
We know joy had a day once and a clime.

Still in verse, the lesser-known Ben Burrell, in one of the radical, U.S.-based pan-African journals, went beyond celebration of the past and issued a call to arms against the U.S. occupation. Listen to Burrell's "Haiti, Awake!":

Haiti, Awake! A hundred years
Of toil is marked upon thy brow. . . .
Oh, brethren, for your fathers brave
Assert your free and ancient rights. . . .
The Haitian nation never dies. . . .
Great champion of the Indies West,
Arise! The world shall guard your fame. . . .
The memory of thy dead endure;
The Dessalinos of faith sublime.
The noble knight; L'Overture.[96]

In fact, the U.S. occupation did produce vigorous martial resistance in Haiti, guerrilla warfare, along with a cultural resurgence.[97] Interestingly, a central figure in the Haitian cultural rebirth was the physician and man of letters Jean Price-Mars, a scion of the nineteenth-century African American emigration to Haiti.[98] Concurrently, Haiti and its revolutionary inheritance also attracted the attention of the apostles of Negritude, the cultural movement produced on French soil by colonial subjects from Africa and the Caribbean, in dialogue with the Haitian and African American renaissances, among others.[99] Indeed, Price-Mars was a founder of Negritude, albeit an oft-neglected one.[100] Aimé Césaire, in his long prose-poem, the single most famous work of Negritude, lauded "Haiti, where negritude stood up for the first time and swore by its humanity."[101] The great irony is that the historical narrators of the black international, who began to emerge around the same time, failed to take a cue from the literary figures. As is often the case in telling the story of African-descended peoples, "fiction" turned out to be truer than "fact," imaginative productions offering a more accurate portrayal of lived experiences than historical accounts.[102] Accordingly, the greater body of pan-African historical scholarship would pass over in silence an epic moment in the making of the black international. It remains for the reconstituted field of African Diaspora studies to correct the record and affirm the black international majesty that was the Haitian Revolution, sparing others from having to wail, like the calypso singer David Rudder, "Haiti, I'm sorry."

NOTES

1. For the broad scholarly treatment of the Haitian Revolution, see, most notably, James, *Black Jacobins*; Fick, *Making of Haiti*; Geggus, *Haitian Revolutionary Studies*; and Dubois, *Avengers*. See also, most recently, Bell, *Toussaint Louverture*, which credits the claim, rejected by almost all modern historians, that the revolution began as a royalist conspiracy.

2. James, *Black Jacobins*, 163–98; Geggus, *Haitian Revolutionary Studies*, 157–70; Fick, "French Revolution."

3. Geggus, *Slavery, War, and Revolution* and *Haitian Revolutionary Studies*, 171–78; Dubois, *Avengers*, 152–70.

4. James, *Black Jacobins*, 199–240; Geggus, *Haitian Revolutionary Studies*, 119–36.

5. James, *Black Jacobins*, 241–68; Fick, *Making of Haiti*, 157–203.

6. James, *Black Jacobins*, 269–321.

7. Quoted in Dubois, *Avengers*, 278.

8. Ibid., 290–93.

9. Fick, *Making of Haiti*, 204–36.

10. Quoted in ibid., 211–12.

11. Long an autonomous force within the revolution, these guerrillas were heavily African-born, compared to the leadership of the mainline revolutionary army, which consisted mainly of Creoles (individuals born in the Americas), men like Toussaint and Dessalines. For a portrait of Sans Souci, whose career illustrates the African-born/Creole divide, see Trouillot, *Silencing the Past*, 31–69.

12. Quoted in Geggus, *Haitian Revolutionary Studies*, 27.

13. Brinton, *Anatomy*; Hobsbawm, *Age of Revolution*; Moore, *Social Origins*; Skocpol, *States*.

14. The most notable exception is perhaps Langley, *Americas*, which discusses the experiences of the United States ("the revolution from above"), Haiti ("the revolution from below"), and Spanish America ("the revolution denied"). See also Blackburn, *Overthrow*, 161–211; Benot, *La révolution française*; and from the side of Haitian studies, Fick, "French Revolution."

15. See, for example, Defronzo, *Revolutions*; Foran, *Future*; and Goldstone, *Revolutions*.

16. See, for example, the special issue of *Social Research*, 56, no. 1 (Spring 1989), and the summary of bicentennial debates in Doyle, *French Revolution*, 98–108.

17. Geggus, "Haitian Revolution," 402–20 (citation from 402).

18. Berlin, *Generations of Captivity*; Knight, *Slave Society*; Stein, *Vassouras*.

19. Geggus, "Haitian Revolution," 402.

20. While most historians attribute this to European balance of power politics, the loss of Haiti had a key role; see Paquette, "Revolutionary Saint Domingue," and Hunt, *Haiti's Influence*.

21. See, especially, the following works by David Brion Davis: *Problem of Slavery in Western Culture, Problem of Slavery in the Age of Revolution, Slavery and Human Progress,* and *Inhuman Bondage*.

22. Drescher, "Ending of the Slave Trade"; Fields, "Slavery, Race, and Ideology."

23. Northrup, *Indentured Labor*; Jung, *Coolies and Cane*; Yun, *Coolie Speaks*.

24. See Lewis, *Growth and Fluctuations*; Wallerstein, *Modern World-System III*, 127–89; and Wolf, *Europe and the People*, 310–53.

25. Geggus, *Haitian Revolutionary Studies*, 27, 207; Dubois, *Avengers*.

26. See, most notably, Fick, *Making of Haiti*; Geggus, *Haitian Revolutionary Studies*; and Dubois, *Avengers*.

27. Drescher, "Limits of Example," 13.

28. Beckles, "Caribbean Anti-Slavery"; Trouillot, *Silencing the Past*.

29. Santiago-Valles, "World-Historical Ties."

30. Linebaugh and Rediker, *Many-Headed Hydra*, 221–24.

31. See the list of rebellions and conspiracies in Geggus, "Slavery, War, and Revolution," 46–49.

32. Klein, *African Slavery*; Berlin, *Generations of Captivity*.

33. Scott, "Common Wind."

34. Geggus, "Slavery, War, and Revolution," 14; Childs, "'Black French General'"; Branson and Patrick, "Étrangers dans un pays étrange."

35. Quoted in Newman, "American Political Culture," 79.

36. LaChance, "Repercussions"; Dessens, *From Saint-Domingue*.

37. Robertson, *Denmark Vesey*, 51–53; Starobin, *Denmark Vesey*.

38. Childs, "'Black French General.'"

39. Robinson, *Black Marxism*.

40. This argument is most clearly articulated in Genovese, *From Rebellion to Revolution*.

41. Trouillot, *Silencing the Past*; Fick, "French Revolution."

42. Biddiss, *Father of Racist Ideology*.

43. Linebaugh and Rediker, *Many-Headed Hydra*, 33–34.

44. Egerton, *Gabriel's Rebellion*.

45. Newman, "American Political Culture."

46. Rothman, *Slave Country*; Hunt, *Haiti's Influence*.

47. Quoted in Fischer, *Modernity Disavowed*, 4.

48. *Century of Lawmaking*, col. 330 (emphasis in original). See also Logan, *Diplomatic Relations*.

49. Fischer, *Modernity Disavowed*, 4.

50. Trouillot, *Silencing the Past*.

51. Among the most curious exceptions at the turn of the twentieth century was the white-supremacist ideologue Lothrop Stoddard, whose work on the Haitian Revolution studiously avoided that term, underlining Trouillot's point. Stoddard considered the "French Revolution in San Domingo," as he called it, "the first great shock between the ideals of white supremacy and race equality, which erased the finest of European colonies from the map of the white world and initiated that most noted attempt at negro self-government, the black republic of Haiti." See Stoddard, *French Revolution*, vii.

52. Popkin, *Facing Racial Revolution*.

53. James, *History of Negro Revolt*; this text was refurbished and published anew in 1969 as *A History of Pan-African Revolt*.

54. Scott, "Common Wind."

55. Padmore, *Life and Struggles*.

56. On Padmore's life and politics, see Hooker, *Black Revolutionary*, and Edwards, *Practice of Diaspora*, 241–305.

57. Padmore, *Life and Struggles*, 78.

58. Ibid., 64–68.

59. Padmore, *Pan-Africanism or Communism?* This book reappeared in 1972 under a new, more politically anodyne title, simply, *Pan-Africanism or Communism*, without the question mark and the subtitle.

60. See, for example, such otherwise admirable works as Langley, *Pan-Africanism and Nationalism*; Esedebe, *Pan-Africanism*; and Zachernuk, *Colonial Subjects*.

61. Geiss, *Pan-African Movement*.

62. Ibid., 37, 80, 127–28.

63. Gilroy, *Black Atlantic*.

64. Ibid., 13, 18.

65. For a discussion of Toussaint and modernity, see Scott, *Conscripts of Modernity*, 132–69.

66. James, *Black Jacobins*, 86; Fick, *Making of Haiti*, 104–5; Dubois, *Avengers*, 101.

67. Some scholars of the Haitian Revolution have questioned whether the Bois Caiman ceremony really happened. The weight of opinion, however, supports its authenticity. See, most authoritatively, Geggus, *Haitian Revolutionary Studies*, 81–92.

68. Raboteau, *Slave Religion*; Frey and Wood, *Come Shouting to Zion*.

69. Bebbington, *Evangelicalism*; Ditchfield, *Evangelical Revival*; Hempton, *Methodism*; Kidd, *Great Awakening*.

70. Thornton, *Africa and Africans*, 235–71.

71. On blacks and the U.S. Revolution and the resulting free black community, see Quarles, *The Negro*; Frey, *Water from the Rock*; Rael, *Black Identity*; and Nash, *Forgotten Fifth*.

72. Fyfe, *History of Sierra Leone*; Walker, *Black Loyalists*; Sanneh, *Abolitionists Abroad*; Pulis, *Moving On*; Whitfield, *Blacks on the Border*; Pybus, *Epic Journeys of Freedom*; Byrd, *Captives and Voyagers*.

73. Such figures include James Gronniosaw, John Marrant, Quobna Ottobah Cugoano, Olaudah Equiano, Phillis Wheatley, and John Jea. A number of anthologies contain

their writings, in whole or in part. See, for example, Potkay and Burr, *Black Atlantic Writers*; Gates and McKay, *Norton Anthology*; and Gates and Andrews, *Pioneers*. Marcus Rediker has discoursed incisively on the impact of the Middle Passage on the ideas of some of these figures, most notably Equiano. See Rediker, *Slave Ship*.

74. The standard statement in this regard is Coupland, *British Anti-Slavery Movement*. For more recent, and nuanced, recapitulations, see Brown, *Moral Capital*, and Schama, *Rough Crossings*.

75. Linebaugh and Rediker, *Many-Headed Hydra*, 211–47.

76. Rothman, *Slave Country*, 19; James, *Black Jacobins*.

77. Geggus, *Haitian Revolutionary Studies*, 2.

78. Hall, "Charge," 204.

79. Holly, *Vindication*.

80. Geggus, *Impact*; Fischer, *Modernity Disavowed*; Geggus, "Influence."

81. Sweet, "Fourth of July"; Rael, *Black Identity*, 223–26. See also White, "'It Was a Proud Day.'"

82. Walker, *David Walker's Appeal*, 23.

83. On the black prophetic tradition internationally, see Bogues, *Black Heretics*. On the same phenomenon in the United States more specifically, see Howard-Pitney, *Afro-American Jeremiad*.

84. Rugemer, *Problem of Emancipation*; Greenberg, *Nat Turner*; French, *Rebellious Slave*; Turner, *Slaves and Missionaries*, 148–78; Craton, *Testing the Chains*, 291–321; Pulis, "Bridging Troubled Waters."

85. The expression is borrowed from Césaire, *Notebook of a Return*, 140.

86. The classic statement on this subject is Williams, *Capitalism and Slavery*.

87. As J. R. Kerr-Ritchie has so ably shown, British emancipation would have considerable impact on African Americans, notably the free blacks, including those who took refuge in Canada, especially after the U.S. Congress passed the Fugitive Slave Act of 1850. See Kerr-Ritchie, *Rites of August First*. In the same connection, see also Rugemer, *Problem of Emancipation*.

88. Cornish, *Sable Arm*.

89. Du Bois, *Black Reconstruction*.

90. British emancipation, along with the Haitian Revolution, had provided an important template for the struggle between the defenders and opponents of slavery in the decades leading up to the U.S. Civil War. See Rugemer, *Problem of Emancipation*.

91. Clavin, "American Toussaints," 89.

92. Ibid., 87–113.

93. Schmidt, *United States Occupation*; Plummer, *Haiti and the Great Powers*.

94. Plummer, "Afro-American Response"; Pamphile, "NAACP and the American Occupation"; Suggs, "Response."

95. Boston Branch, *Fighting a Vicious Film*.

96. *Crusader*, May 1920, 11.

97. For an effective roundup of the Haitian experience, from colonial times to the Duvaliers, including the impact of the U.S. occupation, see Dupuy, *Haiti in the World Economy*.

98. Shannon, *Jean Price-Mars*.

99. Irele, *African Experience*; Fabre, *From Harlem to Paris*; Ellis, "Nicolas Guillen and Langston Hughes."

100. See, however, Geiss, *Pan-African Movement*, 305–21, which places Price-Mars at the center of Negritude's origin.

101. Césaire, *Notebook of a Return*, 66. Césaire would later write a play about Christopher, Dessalines's successor, in addition to a biography of Toussaint.

102. On this point, see Depelchin, *Silences in African History*.

PART 2

Isaac Theophilus Akunna Wallace-Johnson (1894–1965). Born in Sierra Leone, Wallace-Johnson was an anticolonial activist, founder of the West African Youth League, a political prisoner during World War II, and a pan-Africanist. (Courtesy of Hakim Adi)

Nothing Matters but Color

Transnational Circuits, the Interwar Caribbean,
and the Black International

LARA PUTNAM

In the first decades of the twentieth century, sojourners from the British West Indies created a migratory sphere that stretched from northern Venezuela to southern Harlem. Not only did individual lives and family units cross national boundaries, but so, too, did social networks, formal institutions, and cultural consumption. Marcus Garvey's Universal Negro Improvement Association (UNIA) had chapters across the region, and the UNIA's newspaper, *Negro World*, everywhere read, published news and letters from correspondents in Cuba, Panama, Jamaica, Barbados, and beyond. The Anglican and Wesleyan Methodist churches, the Salvation Army, and other Christian missions had a similar spread and helped members of distant chapters keep in touch. Records and radios let sounds circulate even faster than singers, shaping a musical tradition in which calypso, mento, plena, son, and jazz acquired echoes of mutual influence.[1]

Local newspapers played an important role in uniting distant settlements into a single social world. British West Indian–owned newspapers published in Kingston (Jamaica), Port Limón (Costa Rica), Panama City (Panama), and Port of Spain (Trinidad) circulated far and wide, as did the UNIA's New York–based *Negro World*. News articles, social notes, and obituaries were commonly picked up and reprinted among these papers.[2] Unusually high rates of literacy among British West Indian emigrants in these years assured a wide readership.[3] The *Negro World*, the Kingston *Daily Gleaner*, the Limón *Searchlight* and *Atlantic Voice*, the Bocas del Toro *Central American Express*, the *Panama Tribune*, and the "West Indian News" page of the *Panama Star and Herald* bridged elite and popular culture within their sites of publication even as they linked these sites together. The frequency of steamer traffic also facilitated private correspondence. As early as 1883–84 (the heyday of Jamaican migration to the French Panama canal project), more than 82,000 letters were dispatched from Jamaica to Colombia in the space of twelve months.[4] Oral, epistolary, and print lines of communication together cycled rumors, ideas, and news around the region.[5]

At the height of migration in the late 1920s, British West Indian immigrants and their children made up roughly 16 percent of the population of Panama, 3.8 percent of that of Costa Rica, 1.2 percent of that of Cuba, and almost one-quarter of that of Harlem.[6] Smaller but significant communities resided in the Dominican Republic, Honduras, Guatemala, Nicaragua, Colombia, and Venezuela. Put another way, by 1930, at least 150,000 first- or second-generation British West Indians lived in the Spanish-speaking circum-Caribbean, while 145,000 more resided in the United States.[7] Nearly 300,000-strong, then, the British West Indian diaspora was almost twice as large as the population of Barbados and fully six times that of Belize. Yet because these men, women, and children did not reside in a single nation, scholars have rarely seen them for the interrelated whole they were. True, the transnational world they created did not endure. Economic crisis and racist immigration laws cut short the circulation of migrants in the 1930s, and post–World War II political and economic shifts redirected migratory circuits toward the North Atlantic. Yet the legacy of that early British West Indian diaspora is extraordinary and marks black internationalism to this day.

Scholars have long recognized the disproportionate number of foundational pan-African thinkers that came from the Caribbean, among them Marcus Garvey, Amy Jacques Garvey, Cyril V. Briggs, Richard B. Moore, Claude McKay, George Padmore, C. L. R. James, and Eric Williams. Winston James has argued that the migration experience itself was a key factor in their radicalization.[8] I would go further to note that they were not just products of one particular migratory system; they were also products of a particular moment in its history. All stepped on the public stage in the interwar years, a critical juncture for British West Indians abroad. Most importantly, these leaders were not unique. In this same era, voices across the Caribbean public sphere were speaking out about the common experiences of African peoples around the globe, about their common suffering and common aspirations, and about the need for collective action to make shared dreams a united reality.

Such a vision of brotherhood and sisterhood among African-descended peoples on all sides of the Atlantic was built both against something and out of something. It was built against something: the racially defined nationalism of Latin American states, which across the region imposed race-based exclusions (often for the first time) in the late 1920s and 1930s. It was also built in opposition to the racist imperialism of U.S. military interventions, most especially in Panama, Cuba, and Haiti. But it was at the same time built out of something: a diverse yet interdependent array of voluntary associations, evangelical movements, and moral reform movements, all of which reinforced and in turn were reinforced by British West Indian newspapers that combined international circulation with detailed local commentary. Many of these moral reform movements and voluntary associations were of British origin (such as the Salvation Army and the Boy Scouts); others were originally British but reached the Caribbean via African American adaptations in the United States (such as the Independent Benevolent Order of Elks and the Oddfellows). With striking consistency, the lodges, churches, scouts, and newspapers preached a doctrine of racial uplift through individual self-improvement and collective brotherhood.

This essay presents a three-part argument. First, that migration and migrants' activities created a West Indian–centered black internationalist world in the first decades of the twentieth century; second, that this world came under attack as a result of the rise of narrow, racially defined nationalisms and imperial closures in the interwar years; and third, that the attacks reinforced "race consciousness" among migrants, spurring increasingly explicit black internationalist critiques of imperial and neocolonial power. The story unfolds in many places, at sites distant in space yet closely linked by individual travels, institutional ties, and the flow of news of shared concerns. It is a history made in places like the Methodist Episcopal church of Guachipali, Panama, where returned veterans of the British West Indies Regiment, barely out of adolescence themselves, gathered boys and girls into troops, drilled them in marches, and instilled the gospel of a scout's loyalty to fellow scouts.[9] It was made, too, on docksides at ports across the Caribbean, where black merchant seamen surreptitiously passed along copies of the *Negro World* in the years when employers and officials did everything they could to block its circulation.[10] It was made, as well, in the slums of West Kingston, where migrants returning from Cuba in the 1930s gathered in crowded yards to hear about the divinity of an Ethiopian monarch named Ras Tafari.[11] The saga here presented was made, yet again, on railroad sidings like the one in Ciego de Avila, Cuba, where one hot afternoon in 1925 a mother stood with her three children, looking in vain for the husband she had traveled all the way from Barbados to rejoin. Another man walked by. She stared. "Joseph Goodridge, that's you? Joseph, Joseph, Joseph." "Ms. Greaves? Wait, what you doing here?" They had known each other years before in the cities of Panama, and now they met by chance at a crossroads amid the canefields of Cuba. A Barbadian bar owner and his Jamaican wife fed the family that day, Mrs. Greaves's son Earl would recall some seventy years later, while another gentleman went to tell Earl's father his family had arrived two months ahead of schedule. "And when Mr. Greaves was coming up to us mama says 'Look at your father coming there.' And he says 'Oh Lord, look at my children. Look at my children.' And he start to cry."[12] Such repeat encounters, open doors, and long-awaited reunions wove distant sites into a single social world that stretched across the interwar Caribbean.

Self-Help, Salvation, and Solidarity:
Overseas West Indian Civic Activism

A UNIA Mass Meeting Hymnal printed in Panama in 1948 lies today under glass in the tiny Museo Afroantillano (Afro-Caribbean Museum) in Panama City. "Blessed be the tie that binds / Our hearts in Christian love. / The fellowship of kindred minds / is like to that above," read the lyrics labeled "Introduction Hymn." The Ethiopian National Hymn follows. Christian conviction suffused fraternal rituals in the early-twentieth-century Caribbean, and in this regard Garveyism was no different. Its collective affirmation of black brotherhood built upon familiar models. One elderly Jamaican, interviewed in 1973, described how UNIA meetings in eastern Cuba in the 1920s always began with a "political song and a church song. . . . You see we get up and we sing and after we sing, we talk about how the whites have us trampling and how they treat us."[13]

Like this man, countless Garveyites first encountered the movement while far from home.[14] The UNIA was very much a phenomenon of the British West Indian diaspora. While the association had chapters in forty-two countries by 1926, 45 percent of all non-U.S. chapters were located in just three countries: Cuba, Panama, and Costa Rica. The importance of the UNIA to British West Indian migrants—and the migrants to the UNIA—is evident when one compares membership statistics from sending and receiving societies. The association had four times as many chapters in Panama as it did in Jamaica.[15] And the Garveyites were not the only black organization whose membership spanned the Caribbean in these years. Nor were the Garveyites the first to make black pride and racial solidarity the cornerstone of their philosophy. To give just one example, the Mosaic Templars of America was an African American fraternal society founded in Little Rock, Arkansas, in 1882 that provided death, burial, and loan benefits to its members. By the 1920s, the Mosaic Templars had chapters totaling tens of thousands of members worldwide.[16] Advertisements in Port Limón's English-language press in 1911 read, "Join the people's fraternity. No discrimination because of your color, no privileges debarred. A Templar in Costa Rica is welcomed in the U.S. or elsewhere. A Policy by a member here is paid equally as in the U.S. We aim at the protection of our race and people as members of one family. If you deem yourself worthy of the name and claim, then be a member of our order."[17]

Within the Canal Zone in Panama, the U.S. authorities maintained strict Jim Crow segregation, affecting everything from pay scales (labeled gold and silver, after the different coinage that had been used for white and black employees at the start of canal construction) to drinking fountains. White U.S. citizens, who drew their pay from the "Gold Roll," enjoyed superior facilities in YMCA clubhouses, while the Jamaican, Barbadian, and other Afro-Caribbean immigrants on the "Silver Roll" were relegated to the "Colored" clubhouses. Yet, even in such circumstances of economic and social apartheid, West Indian workers created an extraordinarily vibrant civic life in the "Silver Y's," Anglican and Methodist churches, and UNIA halls in and around the Canal Zone. Among groups meeting in one month in 1920 were the West Indian Democratic Club, the Chorillo Dominoe Team, the Boys Brigade, the Anti-Cussing Club for Boys, a half-dozen cricket teams, a like number of literary societies, multiple UNIA and Black Cross Nurse chapters, and dozens of local lodges of the Independent Benevolent Order of Elks, the Independent United Order of Mechanics, the Loyal Order of Ancient Shepherds, the Lebanon Foresters, and the Grand United Order of Odd Fellows (GUOOF).[18] Memberships necessarily overlapped. Obituaries listed the highest offices the deceased held in each of the lodges to which he or she belonged, then specified the order in which those lodges were to march in the funeral procession.[19] Island-specific friendly and benevolent societies, with primarily mutual aid and banking functions, made up an additional layer of associational life.[20]

Fraternal lodges blanketed overseas West Indian communities, literally one atop the other: in 1916, in the tiny town of Guácimo, Costa Rica, the "Beacon Lodge" of the Independent United Order of Mechanics rented hall space to the Mosaic Templars, the Good Samaritans, and the Star of Bethlehem Lodge.[21] Providing sickness, injury, and burial benefits; in some cases widows' pensions; and a host of informal support from job referrals to help hiding from the law, the lodges cushioned the risks and the sorrows of peripatetic lives. Printed "Traveling Cards" or "Clearance Cards" ensured that lodge brothers and sisters would be recognized as such wherever they went.[22] The promise of welcome was no mere formalism. Lodge meeting minutes from Limón from the second decade of the twentieth century record constant arrivals of new brothers presenting credentials from Panamanian lodges.[23] Over the decades, emigrating Barbadian members of Court Western Star of the Ancient Order of Foresters (AOF)—which had been founded in 1846 and included men and women of color from 1847 onward—set up AOF lodges in St. Vincent, the United States, British Guiana, Grenada, St. Lucia, Panama, and British Honduras.[24] The British West Indian migrants who moved north to Harlem from Panama or from the islands in the interwar years joined African American fraternal orders, but they also established U.S. branches of orders that had been exclusively British and British Caribbean until then, including the Ancient Order of Shepherds and the Mechanics. Men who had joined the Lebanon Foresters in Panama found themselves obliged to found a new incarnation of that body in New York after all-white local chapters refused to recognize black immigrants as lodge brothers.[25]

If the lodges most immediately linked members to other black lodges within the West Indian migratory sphere, they also tied members to a broader African American civic world. These were transnational voluntary associations, and the flow of paperwork they entailed meant no one could forget it. In the second decade of the twentieth century, the Limón Lodge of the GUOOF received quarterly circulars from the Sub-Committee of Management in Philadelphia and filled out annual reports to send to the same. The circulars included the names and addresses of lodge officers from Thelma, North Carolina, to Ponce, Puerto Rico.[26] The "Ritual of the Juvenile Society of the Grand United Order of Odd Fellows" followed in Port Limón had been "Prepared by Sister Tillie M. Brooks, of Household of Ruth No. 48, Paducah, Ky., and Sister Rhoda A. Moore, of the Household of Ruth No. 197, Houston, Tex."; the juvenile society's founding, readers of the printed ritual learned on page 15, had been proposed by the Grand Household in St. Louis, reaffirmed by the Grand Household in Chicago, and approved by the General Meeting of the Order at Indianapolis.[27] This expansive geography of fraternal action stretched lodge members' sphere of belonging beyond their own potential destinations to encompass the New World African Diaspora more broadly.

Enterprises from life insurance to evangelical missions followed the fraternal template in the British West Indian diaspora. For instance, the Salvation

Army, founded in London in 1878, began missionary work in the West Indies in 1892. By 1912 it had twenty-nine local "Corps and Outposts," carrying out spiritual "rescue missions" and social work in Jamaica, Panama, Costa Rica, British Honduras, Barbados, Trinidad, British Guiana, and the Leeward Islands.[28] This evangelical mission functioned much like the fraternal lodges described above, speeding the flow of information within the migratory system through interpersonal networks and publications, creating ready-made communities for incoming immigrants, and innovating social services.[29] The Salvation Army's regional newspaper, the *West Indies War Cry*, began publication in Kingston in 1905 and was sold by "boomers" on street corners and in ports across the Caribbean. By 1913, the paper had a monthly circulation of 10,000.[30] Readers used the *War Cry* to reach across the political boundaries their own lives crossed so routinely. The "Enquiry Department" published notes like the following, from 1906: "News Wanted of Marcus Solomon Samson, native of Suriname, Dutch Guiana, who about twenty years ago left there for Brazil, Panama, or Colón. Age about 60. Any information will be thankfully received by his daughter."[31]

It is not coincidental that the *War Cry* sold best in the same places where Garvey's UNIA was most popular. Both the Salvation Army and the UNIA benefited from the heyday of Christian civic enthusiasm and "joining" that swept the British West Indian diaspora as it did North America.[32] Migrants used the UNIA and the Salvation Army, as they did the far more numerous fraternal societies, to cushion the risks and loneliness of an economic system built on extreme mobility. Remittances from Panama fueled an explosion of friendly societies in Barbados during canal construction; migrants returning to the Leeward Islands from Central America and the United States led the burgeoning friendly society movement there in the same years.[33] The lodges, the friendly societies, the UNIA, and the Salvation Army each linked members to broader circum-Caribbean or transatlantic social movements that promised collective uplift though clean living, Christian prayer, and brotherly love.

The enthusiasm for communal uplift through civic participation spawned another set of transatlantic associations in the interwar period, as enterprising young men founded "scout" troops across the western Caribbean. A generation after preachers William and Catherine Booth had founded the Salvation Army to transform London's slum dwellers into stalwart Christian soldiers, Robert Baden-Powell, a former British regimental officer, decided to renew the vigor of the empire by providing a quasi-military outdoor experience for England's youth. His foundational essay, *Scouting for Boys*, was published in 1908. By 1909 there were more than 130,000 "Baden-Powell boy scouts" enrolled in troops in Great Britain, and affiliated troops were being founded rapidly across the British Empire. Soon other international movements created youth brigades with similar aims and activities. Youth scouting found eager adherents in Colón, Bocas del Toro, and Port Limón, destinations of the first generation of British West Indian emigrants and places that, by the post–World War I years, had sizable numbers of locally born youths. Repeatedly, we find boys' groups founded by returning veterans of the British West Indies Regiment (BWIR), which had served in Europe, Egypt, and East Africa during World War I.

Black men had demanded the right to serve in a spirit of proud imperial patriotism.[34] Volunteers came from overseas West Indian communities as well as the islands. An open letter to "His Majesty's Recruiting Agent for the Republic of Panama" in the *Central America Express* in 1917 applauded the "rush to the colors" in Panama and Colón and noted that some eager volunteers from Bocas del Toro had gone so far as to pay their own way to Jamaica in order to enlist. "As Britishers we demand our share of the privilege of having you here in your official capacity."[35] In the end the regiment's volunteers totaled more than 15,000 men, including more than 2,000 from Panama alone.[36] Those who survived returned home deeply disillusioned by the open racism and discriminatory treatment they had endured. After BWIR troops rioted in Italy in 1918, colonial authorities feared violent uprisings would accompany their return to the Caribbean. In fact, returnees did lead violent protests in British Honduras and fueled a strike by longshoremen in Trinidad.[37] Ultimately, though, few veterans led riots back home. Yet the war had changed all. New loyalties had been forged, new strategies learned, new possibilities revealed. In the western Caribbean, at least, wartime experiences seem to have fed renewed community activism with a view to the future of "the race."

In 1920, David Watson founded the Colón Boys Institute. A "native of Jamaica, and ex-corporal in the British West India Regiment," Watson, "while a soldier at the front ... formed his idea to help the unfortunate youths of the city of Colón, should he return."[38] That same year, the "West Indian News" page of the *Panama Star and Herald* announced the founding of a "Boys' Brigade ... under the auspices of Grace Church, Methodist Episcopal, at Guachipali. The Staff of officers in command consists of ex-soldiers of the Ninth Battalion, West Indian Regiment.... The primary object of the brigade is to assist in the physical and moral training of our boys and girls and keep them out of mischief."[39] Significantly, and perhaps not coincidentally, it was this very same unit, the Ninth Battalion, that had rioted in Italy during the war. In the weeks after the riot, fifty to sixty sergeants from the Ninth Battalion formed a "Caribbean League," arguing that the black man "should have freedom to govern himself in the West Indies" and that "force must be used, and if necessary bloodshed to obtain that object."[40]

Some veterans seem to have brought this same vision to their work as scout leaders. Like their counterparts elsewhere in the region, in 1922 former BWIR servicemen in Bocas del Toro organized a scout troop, this one loosely tied to the UNIA. As they led the boys in drills with wooden rifles, the scout leaders reputedly declared that they were training to seize control from "the white people." In response, the Panamanian authorities arrested twenty-seven men, who were then blacklisted by the United Fruit Company, the region's chief employer.[41] Why such fear over a group of boys with sticks? The authorities knew imperial experience, race consciousness, and local grievance to be an explosive mix. Three years earlier in Bocas, labor leaders had summoned United Fruit workers to a violent strike precisely by recalling the rhetoric of rights that had accompanied BWIR recruiting. "Do you remember what the white man told us during the war that we were fighting for democracy, equality and therefore to become free subjects? . . . If we could have given a good account of ourselves in the bloody war, why not here too. Why must we be afraid of the few white parasites around here, we will teach them a lesson for life."[42] In arresting scout leaders in 1922, bosses may have been overreacting to a mocking joke. Or the scout leaders may indeed have been planning revolution. They certainly were not alone in pairing civic activism and racial allegiance. In the interwar years, West Indian community leaders of diverse class positions and ideologies came to a common conclusion: only by putting race first could people of African descent attain collective uplift in a modern, racist world.

Mestizo Nationalism, Antiblack Legislation, and the Impact of Returnees

Across Latin America in the 1920s and 1930s, faith in scientific racism was ceding to a new nationalism that celebrated *mestizaje*—racial and cultural mixing—in each nation's distant past.[43] But when global market crises devastated the export-based economies of the Caribbean basin, black immigrants and their children became nationalist politicians' favorite scapegoat. Left- as well as right-wing leaders embraced xenophobia even as they insisted their opposition to black—and only black—immigration was based on culture, and thus not racist.[44] In 1927, a typical editorial asked, "Is Cuba Being Africanized?"

"The term *Africanization* is used, as all of the Cuban authors who have turned their attention to our ethnic problems have used it, in the sense of undesirable immigration, not because it is African, but rather because it is less civilized, weaker, and more easily exploited by foreign capitalism, more easily enslaved by it."[45]

Nationalist intellectuals' diagnoses were strikingly similar across the region. A pamphlet titled *The Antillean Menace in Central America (Defending the Race)* went through multiple printings in Panama in the early 1920s.[46] An influential newspaper there wrote in 1924, "The *antillanos* [Afro-Caribbeans] who abound in our terminal cities lower our standards of living and with their alien customs imprint upon Panama, Colón, and Bocas de Toro the appearance of African cities; they constitute one of the most serious problems that this country must solve."[47] Meanwhile in Costa Rica, "the black race" found itself lumped together with the "vice-ridden Chinese" in official rhetoric and immigration law alike for the first time.[48] In a 1934 interview on the occasion of El Día de la Raza (Columbus Day; literally, "The Day of the Race"), Limón's school superintendent accused Costa Rican celebrants of hypocrisy. "Have we indeed conserved the purity of the Spanish race?" he asked. "Haven't we instead darkened it a bit, or given it a yellowish tint?" He called for "the imposition of drastic measures which will impede the crossing of our pure Spanish blood with other races, which we consider inferior, so that the gentility and grace of our ancestors may be reborn and we can take pleasure in celebrating with real pride the festival of the race."[49] "Drastic measures" were in fact being implemented even as he spoke. The same issue of the newspaper announced the expulsion of undocumented Chinese residents. Two months later, Costa Rica's congress passed a law forbidding the employment of "colored" workers on the United Fruit Company's new Pacific coast plantations, devastating the country's long-settled British West Indian community, who with their seniority and expertise had dominated skilled employment in United Fruit's operations on the Caribbean coast.[50]

Doors slammed shut across the region in the 1920s and 1930s. The United States, which had become the single most important destination for West Indian migrants in the postwar years, passed race-based restrictions in 1924 that cut annual black immigration by 95 percent in a single year.[51] Panamanian legislators incrementally restricted access to employment and citizenship by "foreign" blacks in 1926, 1928, and 1941.[52] Honduras limited foreign black employment in 1923 and 1926 and entry in 1929 and 1934; Venezuela prohibited black immigration in 1929; and the Dominican Republic limited seasonal migration by British West Indian workers in the same year.[53] (Eight years later, the regionwide pattern of official scapegoating of black migrants reached a grotesque extreme with the massacre of some 15,000 ethnic Haitians by Dominican troops.)[54] More than 100,000 British West Indian and Haitian migrants had flocked to Cuba during the immediate postwar sugar boom; but as exports collapsed, scores of thousands of Haitians were deported between 1933 and 1939, while hunger and lack of work pushed tens of thousands of British West Indians out, in some cases back to islands where their parents or grandparents had been born but which they themselves had never known.[55]

With each large-scale wave of returnees, the islands witnessed new labor activism and political agitation by their disenfranchised black majorities. This, in part, reflected the fact that hard times spurred both return migration and popular unrest. Economic crises hit hard across the region, given that island and rimland economies alike depended on the same export crops (prominently sugar, bananas, and cacao), the same sources of capital, and the same North Atlantic markets. Lean years triply impacted the sending societies. Island economies contracted, remittances dropped, and emigrants (or, in the dire years of the 1930s, the children and grandchildren of previous generations of emigrants) returned to join the ranks of the unemployed. But the link between the returnees' arrival and political and labor agitation seems to go beyond shared structural causes. Again and again, we find returnees playing leadership roles in island agitation. In a typical example among many, in 1918 a St. Kitts police inspector warned the colonial secretary that the leaders of that island's Universal Benevolent Association had apparently "associated in America with men of their own colour embued [sic] with racial hatred of the white man and, perhaps also with extreme labour movement views of a physical force type."[56] The mix was unmistakable. Calls for black loyalty and white comeuppance rang out in every labor upheaval led by returnees in the interwar era.

A few examples must suffice to illustrate the trend.[57] In Barbados, British West India Regiment veteran Clennell Wickham edited the *Barbados Herald* from 1919 to 1930, providing the first sustained forum for working-class criticism of planter hegemony.[58] In Jamaica, where labor organizing surged in the 1920s and 1930s, the most prominent leaders, from Marcus Garvey to Alexander Bustamante, were veterans of the Caribbean migratory system. "The radical group of young, racially conscious, black labour leaders" of the Jamaica Workers and Tradesmen Union in 1936 included L. E. Barnett, who had become a UNIA and union leader in Costa Rica, and Hugh Buchanan, whose years in Cuba had brought him into contact with both Garveyite and Communist

organizing.[59] Other returnees preached an even more radical rejection of colonial rule, hailing Ras Tafari, who had become Haile Selassie on being crowned
emperor of Ethiopia in 1928, as the divine "King of Kings" and rejecting the
legitimacy of imperial authorities. Indeed, all three initiators of what would
become known as Rastafari were former emigrants who returned to Kingston
in the 1930s from Cuba, Costa Rica, and Panama.[60] Deprivation and hunger,
together with the ever-more-explicit denunciations of the racist colonial order
as the underlying problem, culminated at the end of the decade in a wave of
"labour rebellions" across the British colonies. Returnees abounded among
leaders and rank and file alike.[61]

In contrast to the labor activism and open insurgencies led by veterans of
the British West Indian migratory sphere in the sending societies of the Greater
Caribbean, their cousins, nieces, and nephews who remained in the receiving
societies may at first glance appear to have been absent from the public stage
in the 1930s. The West Indian communities of Panama, Costa Rica, and Cuba
in the lean years of the 1920s and 1930s have been described as isolated, defensive, and dependent; yet I would suggest that this judgment rests on a falsely
truncated view of those communities' boundaries. Yes, times were hard and
xenophobic slander was common. Demography and employment patterns,
combined with cultural divides and racist suspicions, largely kept these first-
and second-generation immigrants outside the expanding labor movement
in each country.[62] Yet such local isolation should not obscure the fact that
the immigrants were connected, vitally so, to something much bigger. They
were becoming "race enthusiasts"; they were speaking of, and speaking to, the
"Negro World" the Atlantic system had wrought. To the extent that nations
are imagined communities, these West Indian emigrants were creating a new
nation.[63]

Racial Uplift and the Overseas
British West Indian Press

Sidney Young founded the *Panama Tribune* in 1928 in the wake of a new constitutional amendment withholding citizenship from locally born West Indians
until their twenty-first birthday. Young and others had mobilized unsuccessfully
against the proposed amendment. The *Tribune* was Young's vehicle to carry on
the same battle by other means and to strengthen the West Indian community
through civic participation and racial solidarity. Its masthead drawing was a
radiant book with the inscription, "Let the people have light and they shall find

their way." Young's highest praise was reserved for "race enthusiasts"—men and women who chose to speak to and for the Negro race.[64]

> This is the creed of the West Indian, to be exacting and hard with his own people and to be as meek as the lowly worm in his dealings with others of a different race and color, particularly those who do not give as much as the well known tinker's damn about him. . . . We need a new sort of education. Unfortunately we have never developed either a fierce spirit of nationalism or a deep pride of race. . . . What we need, friends and countrymen, is a little more holding together, a little more toughness where other people are concerned and a little more softness, understanding and cooperation where we ourselves are concerned.[65]

The *Panama Tribune* would become an enduring community institution, in large part because Young and George Westerman, his protégé and the paper's onetime sports writer, were extraordinary leaders.[66] Yet Young's articulation of the crises facing the West Indian diaspora in the 1930s was hardly unique. Up the coast in Costa Rica, British West Indian–run newspapers like the Limón *Searchlight* offered similar diagnoses and remedies. Like Young, the editors of the *Searchlight* insisted "cooperation" was the first step toward surviving antiblack racism.

> In these Latin countries there is the tendency among the more ig-norant, the unwashed to feel that because one is a Jamaican he is inferior to him; the most abject depraved wretch will be ignorant enough to feel that he is superior to you because you happen to be a Jamaican, be your intellectual abilities and moral standing in the Community ever so much appreciated by the best blood of the coun-try. It is now necessary therefore that we ought to cooperate and put away trivial objections to the contrary, and strive to support any-thing that will tend towards the improvement of the Negro Race.[67]

A similar letter published in the *Searchlight* in 1931 under the heading, "De-plores Lack of Racial Sentiment," called for unity in the face of hostility. "One of our black men," a public employee, had called a Jamaican teen "Nigger Girl." "Well now, if this is the attitude our black men hold toward their black girls, what can we expect our white brothers to hold for us? . . . We should protect our women, especially those who try to lead righteous lives." The young woman in question, the writer explained, sang in the Anglican church choir and was a founding member of a local civic club.[68] "Therefore now is the time for us to cultivate a better opinion of the race, and steer to national recognition and equal rights. Let us have a greater respect for our women, whether they be nearer white, or ebony black [they are all Negritos]."[69]

In the midst of calls for color-blind racial solidarity, the phrase "especially those who try to lead righteous lives" should give us pause. It was not atypical. The West Indian businessmen who published these papers and the men and women of the black middle class who wrote for them often promoted criteria of respectability that highlighted their distance from those they sought to uplift. Elite West Indian authors, like the one quoted above, indignantly complained that "ignorant . . . unwashed" Latins denied them the public respect that their "intellectual abilities" and "moral standing" merited. They also employed the identical criteria—"intellectual abilities" and "moral standing"—to distinguish among black people. The same correspondent quoted above demanding "greater respect for our women" frequently castigated the locally born generation of "our Negro community" for their lack of ambition and disinterest in education. "These people are contented to remain a dark race all the days of their lives," he sneered.[70]

Class tensions were real, as were elite notions of culture that denigrated the African in Afro-Caribbean popular culture. Yet equally real was the call for pan-African unity as the best form of communal defense in a hostile age.

> The Negro who does not desire a betterment of his condition is today a dead man—one who is but an obstacle in the path of progress. Allow me to ask this pertinent question. "Can we attain our ends without a united resistance against the forces that are keeping us down?" . . . Instead of limiting our efforts to our own island groups, let us cultivate the tendency to devise plans for the Universal Coloured Brotherhood. When we have developed ourselves to that stage where we can sincerely say "brother, I am from Demerara, and because you are my own, as you hail from Dominica, whatever hurts you hurts me also," we will have entered a broader field where the opportunities for racial success will be unlimited.[71]

That success also depended on the appropriate union of male and female efforts. The *Tribune*'s editors hoped that "women of our community will avail themselves of the opportunity to contribute articles that will help to uplift their sisters and thereby uplift our race. For is not the mother the one in whose hand the prosperity and the future of our race depends, and on whose shoulders the future advancement lies?"[72] A follow-up letter from a female correspondent underlined the Victorian morality of the message. "It is said a people cannot

rise higher than its women and so the responsibility hangs on us fellow West
Indian women to raise the standard by aiming high and living clean lives. . . .
God first, business next, pleasure last, we must succeed."[73]

This language of gendered virtue and racial solidarity, with its implicit disdain for the bawdier elements of lower-class culture, has far more in common
with Baden-Powell's mission of imperial renewal and with Latin American
mestizo populism than with earlier expressions of African identities in the
Caribbean. For centuries poor black Caribbeans had created and sustained
cultural practices (in religion, song, dance, sport, speech, and collective action)
whose signal elements and underlying aesthetics were manifestly African in
origin.[74] Far from embracing these expressions of Africa in the Americas, the
same community leaders and newspaper editors who praised Garveyism and
denounced white racism disparaged or even attacked Revivalism, Pocomia,
and other popular religions with African associations.[75] The black internationalism articulated by British West Indian migrants in the interwar years
was not a revival of tradition but a particular vision of the future, developed in
dialogue and in step with the other nationalisms that defined North Atlantic
modernity.[76]

Unlike many of its interlocutors, though, black internationalism could be
amply inclusive. Perhaps reflecting the experiences of West Indian troops in
British colonial domains in World War I, or perhaps reflecting the frequency
with which Chinese and South Asian migration was restricted alongside black
migration to circum-Caribbean destinations, some authors stretched the notion of racial solidarity to incorporate not only those of African origin but all
"colored races." In 1930, the British West Indian press in Port Limón reported
frequently on Gandhi's anticolonial struggle on the Indian subcontinent, re-
printing sympathetic articles to demonstrate, the editors wrote, "how intrigues
by religion, and other diplomatic propaganda, are brought to divide the solidarity of any subjected races."[77] That same year the editors used the occasion of
Empire Day to denounce the British government's "indifference to these what
she calls inferior races which in reality are only inferior in 'opportunities.' . . .
For after all what is it worth to be a British subject in foreign parts, especially
to the Negro, the Chinese, or Hindu? Nothing but indignities by depreciation
and discrimination against in trade, in labour, in social equality."[78]

These were not radical activists speaking, but the most upright of businessmen. Ultimately, the print circuits of the western Caribbean reinforced antiracism and anti-imperialism as essential components of an expansive sense of
Afro-Caribbean commonality shared across class lines. While this was most

explicit in the pages of the UNIA's *Negro World,* all the West Indian–run papers of the region contributed to the process. The *Panama Tribune* frequently criticized U.S. racism abroad, including atrocities committed by "Yankee Marines" against "the Haitian People," and, in 1929, denounced the violent arrests of editors of *Le Petit Impartial* in Port-au-Prince "for protesting against the vile policy and race prejudice of U.S. imperialism."[79] The editors insisted that the "inability of the American occupation to regard the Haitians in any other way except as 'niggers' is responsible for the recent outbreaks on the island." The English-language press in Port Limón reprinted these and similar articles from the *Panama Tribune* at length.[80] The *Tribune,* in turn, offered its readers a panoramic view of the African Diaspora by reproducing articles from black papers around the globe, including the *Chicago Defender,* the *Pittsburgh Courier,* and *La Depeche Africaine* (identified for readers as "a Negro newspaper published in Paris").[81]

This was a world peopled by outsized heroes, from Marcus Garvey to Ras Tafari to boxer "Kid Chocolate, the Cuban 'buzz-saw,'" to the first "Bantu" to obtain a bachelor of divinity degree at London University.[82] It was also a world in which allies were not always black. Thus the editors of the *Tribune* could identify Clarence Darrow simply as the "hero of the celebrated Sweet case." They apparently trusted *Tribune* readers in Panama to remember that Darrow, a white lawyer, had won acquittal in 1926 for Dr. Ossian Sweet, a black man charged with firing on a threatening white mob. On that occasion, Darrow had acclaimed the right of blacks to "fight even to the death for their home, for each other, for their people, for their race, for their rights."[83] Now the *Tribune* reprinted the text of a speech by Darrow under the headline "Nothing Matters but Color." "The tariff, the labor question, the power question, even religious liberty, is of no consequence compared with the question of the right of the colored man to have an equal opportunity in the world with the white."[84]

Conclusion

Barbara J. Fields once wrote that while Euro-Americans invented the fiction that defined Afro-Americans as a race, "Afro-Americans invented themselves, not as a race, but as a nation. They were not troubled, as modern scholars often are, by the use of racial vocabulary to express their sense of nationality."[85] In the interwar Caribbean, West Indian migrants increasingly used racial vocabulary to capture a sense of belonging that went beyond the borders of any single nation. As they traveled from the commissaries of the Canal Zone to the army tents of northern Africa, as they read dispatches from Paris and Ethiopia and Bridgetown and Detroit mixed among their local news, they recognized a commonality of experience in the present even more than a unity of origins in the past. Like other working- and middle-class men and women of the turn-of-the-century Atlantic world, British West Indian emigrants sought self-improvement and collective betterment through fraternal "combination" and Christian faith. Like others, they founded lodges and chapters, and missions and publications, and they sought to organize and guide a young generation they perceived as menaced by the deceptive pleasures of modern life. But there are key particularities here. Buying burial insurance and paying lodge dues, and singing "Onward Christian Soldiers" in Salvation Army halls and at UNIA assemblies, British West Indian emigrants partook of a civic world that had international membership and universal moral claims—and a pervasively black public face.

Global commodity crises in the 1920s made anti-immigrant xenophobia an irresistible alibi for Hispanic nationalist politicians, and a wave of immigration restrictions truncated the travels on which the West Indian migratory sphere depended. Antiblack racism rang out in politicians' oratory and scraped the soul in a thousand daily insults. Given the transatlantic frame of reference West Indian migrants had acquired, they had a panoramic vision of *who* was under attack: the members of the Negro Race, wherever they lived, whatever their citizenship or allegiance, whatever their claims to "intellectual abilities" and "moral standing," and whatever the shade of their skin. If we think of ideology as "the descriptive vocabulary of day-to-day existence, through which people make rough sense of the social reality that they live and create from day to day,"[86] we see clearly why black internationalist ideology achieved such wide currency throughout the British Caribbean in these years. It expressed a reality lived daily not only by well-known figures like Marcus Garvey, George Padmore, or C. L. R. James, but by their neighbors and classmates and bunkmates and kin: anonymous, indispensable interlocutors of the thinkers whose words we read to this day.

Recognizing the vast participation in the making of their black internationalist vision requires acknowledging the synergy between early-twentieth-century moral reform movements and voluntary associations, often of British origin, and the emerging "race consciousness" that insisted "nothing matters but color." The former have generally been seen as British imperial impositions—and, as such, the essence of accommodation—while the latter has been seen as the vanguard of post–World War II anticolonialism and, as such, the essence of radical resistance.[87] Yet for "race enthusiasts" like Sidney Young, or for the Ninth Battalion veterans who drilled Boy Scouts week after week, or for the loyal matrons of the Household of Ruth, collective civic engagement and political and economic empowerment, far from being mutually exclusive, constituted a single, indivisible mission.

NOTES

I am grateful to Rina Cáceres, William Martin, Rebecca Scott, Ronny Viales, Michael West, and the members of the Programa de Estudios de Diáspora of the Centro de Investigaciones Históricas de América Central of the Universidad de Costa Rica for comments on earlier drafts of this material. The research reflected here began under the auspices of the David Rockefeller Center for Latin American Studies at Harvard University and was financed by the Vicerrectoría de Investigación of the Universidad de Costa Rica as part of Proyecto No. 806-A2-047. An earlier version of this paper was presented to the Segundo Congreso NOL@N [Network of Latin American Studies in Nordic Countries], Ibero-American Center, Renvall Institute, University of Helsinki, Finland, May 13–14, 2004.

1. See Monestel, "El calypso en Costa Rica," and Hutton, "Cuban Influence on Popular Jamaican Music."

2. Senior, "Colón People," 62.

3. On literacy, see James, "Explaining Afro-Caribbean Social Mobility"; Putnam, *Company They Kept*, 170; Murphy, *Dominican Sugar Plantations*, 43; and McLeod, "Undesirable Aliens."

4. Senior, "Colón People," 70 n. 47. Panama was a province of Colombia at the time.

5. Eloquent examples are provided by the Dowridge-Challenor correspondence excerpted in Watkins-Owens, *Blood Relations*, chap. 2.

6. Conniff, *Black Labor*, 47; Putnam, *Company They Kept*, 64–75; McLeod, "Undesirable Aliens," 4–5; Cuba, Dirección General del Censo, *Informe general del censo de 1943*, 888–89; Foner, "Introduction"; James, *Holding aloft the Banner*, 12.

7. James, "Explaining Afro-Caribbean Social Mobility," 220; James, *Holding aloft the Banner*, 357. The clearest regionwide accounts of the timing and extent of the migratory movements that created overseas British West Indian communities are Thomas-Hope, "Establishment of a Migration Tradition," 66–81; Marshall, "History of West Indian Migrations"; and Richardson, "Caribbean Migrations."

8. James, *Holding aloft the Banner*, esp. 50–100.

9. Cf. "Boys Brigade Organized," *Panama Star and Herald*, December 3, 1920, 3.

10. Elkins, *Black Power in the Caribbean*, 29–45; United Fruit correspondence, Costa Rica Division, 1919, reproduced in Hill, *Marcus Garvey*, vols. 11 and 12.

11. Chevannes, *Rastafari*, 119–44.

12. Marshall, "Nothing in My Hands," 22–23.

13. "Life in Jamaica in the Early Twentieth Century," volume: St. James, Respondent:

64StjMb, 3–4. Local chapters of the UNIA remained active in Costa Rica and Panama long after the movement had collapsed elsewhere. Indeed the "Black Star Line" UNIA meetinghouse in Port Limón was central to Afro–Costa Rican community life there through the 1970s. See Capelli, "Promised Ship."

14. Consider the example of Victor Cohen, who left Jamaica to work in Costa Rica, Bocas del Toro (where he first encountered Garveyism), Cuba, and eventually New York, where he would become associate editor of *African Opinion* magazine. See Lewis, *Marcus Garvey*, 113.

15. Martin, *Race First*, 16; James, *Holding aloft the Banner*, 196–97, 366; Lewis, *Marcus Garvey*, 97–123. A rich range of primary sources on Garvey and the UNIA in Central America and the Caribbean will soon become available in *The Marcus Garvey and Universal Negro Improvement Association Papers*, edited by Robert A. Hill, vols. 11–12, forthcoming.

16. See Smith, "John E. Bush."

17. See *Times* (Limón, Costa Rica), June 2, 1911.

18. *Panama Star and Herald*, November 28–December 31, 1920.

19. E.g., "Old Timer's Lamented Death," *Panama Tribune*, November 18, 1928, 5. Copies of the *Tribune* were consulted in the Museo Afroantillano in Panama City.

20. Cf. Conniff, *Black Labor*, 70–71; Watkins-Owens, *Blood Relations*, 56–74; Westerman, *Los inmigrantes antillanos*, 113–15; Richardson, *Panama Money*, 223–28; Duncan, "El negro antillano"; and Fletcher, "Friendly Societies."

21. *Costa Rica District No. 1, I. U. O. of Mechanics* (Kingston, Jamaica: Educational Supply Company Printers, n.d.), 13–14, Limón Lodge materials, personal collection of Miguel Guzmán Stein, Cartago, Costa Rica (hereafter PCMGS).

22. Clearance card, Costa Rica District No. 1, Independent United Order of Mechanics, PCMGS.

23. See, for instance, bound minutes, Limón Lodge 16 (9180) G.U.O. of O.F., April 23, 1910, through March 6, 1912, PCMGS.

24. *125th Anniversary of the Ancient Order of Foresters, Caribbean and Western Hemisphere, Souvenir Brochure* (n.p., 1971), Barbados Department of Archives, Pamphlet A 806. Apparently one year after the lodge was founded, many of its white elite members left in a dispute over whether persons of other classes and colors would be admitted; they set up an all-white lodge instead. See "Origins of A.O.F. in W.I.," by Sister Enid Harris, in ibid.

25. Watkins-Owens, *Blood Relations*, 72.

26. *Fourth Quarterly Circular, 1915 . . . G.U.O. of O.F., Phila., PA*, 10, PCMGS (printed book, title page lost).

27. *Ritual of the Juvenile Society of the Grand United Order of Odd Fellows . . . Prepared by Sister Tillie M. Brooks, of Household of Ruth No. 48, Paducah, Ky., and Sister Rhoda A. Moore, of the Household of Ruth No. 197, Houston, Tex.* (Philadelphia, 1912), 15, PCMGS.

28. "West Indian Progress," *All The World*, May 1912, 243.

29. These functions are well-illustrated in the pages of the *West Indies War Cry*, a complete run of which is held in the internal archive of the Salvation Army regional headquarters in Kingston, Jamaica.

30. Jamaica, *Blue Book*, 6V.

31. *War Cry*, April 1906, 4. See, similarly, *War Cry*, September 1906, 3.

32. This was the heyday of joining in the United States as well, in a pattern shared across the stark divides of ethnicity, class, and region that fractured the nation. See, for instance, Beito, "To Advance the 'Practice of Thrift And Economy,'" and Gamm and Putnam, "Growth of Voluntary Associations."

33. Richardson, *Panama Money*, 205–12; Richards, "Friendly Societies."

34. The region's black-owned newspapers, in particular T. A. Marryshow's *West Indian*, advocated black military service as a strategic move toward greater political rights. See Howe, *Race, War, and Nationalism*, 16–40, and Phillips, "'Go Ahead, England; Barbados Is Behind You.'"

35. "An Open Letter to Mr. Hitchens," *Central American Express* (Bocas del Toro), June 23, 1917, 4, Hemeroteca, Biblioteca Central Simón Bolívar, Universidad de Panamá, microfilm roll 13. The authors wondered darkly whether "influential pressure [was] being exerted" to prevent direct recruitment in Bocas, presumably by United Fruit Company officials anxious to maintain their workforce.

36. Howe, *Race, War, and Nationalism*; James, *Holding aloft the Banner*, 52–62; Conniff, *Black Labor*, 68.

37. James, *Holding aloft the Banner*, 62–69; Elkins, *Black Power in the Caribbean*, 5–15, 64–76; Bolland, *Politics of Labour*, 216–20.

38. "Colón Boys Institutes Tops All Community Effort," *Panama Tribune*, December 2, 1928, 13.

39. "Boys' Brigade Organized," *Panama Star and Herald*, December 3, 1920, 3. The Boys' Brigade movement, like its more famous rival, Baden-Powell's Boy Scout movement, had been founded in England at the start of the century. See Rosenthal, *Character Factory*.

40. Elkins, *Black Power in the Caribbean*, 9. Richardson quotes a British observer who reported that "most of the men" of the Ninth Battalion had come from Panama; see *Panama Money*, 217.

41. Harpelle, *West Indians of Costa Rica*, 61.

42. Anonymous report from company informer to United Fruit Company manager H. S. Blair, April 16, 1920, reproduced in Bourgois, "One Hundred Years" (quotation on 135).

43. Graham, *Idea of Race in Latin America*; Stepan, *Hour of Eugenics*.

44. Chomsky, "West Indian Workers" and "'Barbados or Canada?'"; Tinker Salas, "Relaciones de poder y raza"; de la Fuente, *Nation for All*, 46–50.

45. Emilio Roig de Leuchsenring, "¿Se está Cuba africanizando?," *Carteles* 10, no. 48 (November 27, 1927): 27, cited in Chomsky, "'Barbados or Canada?,'" 458–59. For similar antiblack declarations by Costa Rican anti-imperialists, see Chomsky, "West Indian Workers."

46. Olmedo Alfaro, "El peligro antillano en la América Central (La Defensa de la Raza)" (1925), quoted in Westerman, *Los inmigrantes antillanos*, 96–97 (author's translation). For a subtle discussion of Panamanian nationalism in this era, see Szok, *La última gaviota*.

47. *Gráfico* (semanario de Panamá), August 30, 1924, quoted in Westerman, *Los inmigrantes antillanos*, 96 (author's translation).

48. On the history of anti-immigrant thought in Costa Rica, including the long tradition of anti-Chinese discrimination, see Quirós, "Inmigración e identidad nacional." On antiblack policies in the 1930s, see Chomsky, "West Indian Workers"; Harpelle, "Racism and Nationalism" and *West Indians of Costa Rica*; and Putnam, *Company They Kept*, 71–75, 165–72.

49. *La Voz del Atlántico* (Limón, Costa Rica), October 13, 1934 (author's translation).

50. Harpelle, "Racism and Nationalism," 29–51; Chomsky, *West Indian Workers*, 235–53.

51. Jacobson, *Whiteness of a Different Color*; King, *Making Americans*.

52. Davis, "West Indian Workers on the Panama Canal," 141–42; Newton, *Silver Men*, 162–63; Conniff, *Black Labor*, 65–66, 80–84, 98–106, 127–30. The retroactive denationalization was reversed in 1945, but exclusions in employment and access to public education persisted. See Westerman, *Los inmigrantes antillanos*, 95–101.

53. Euraque, "Banana Enclave," esp. 152; Proudfoot, *Population Movements*, 15; Tinker Salas, "Relaciones de poder y raza," 95–97; Richardson, "Caribbean Migrations," 211–12, 215; del Castillo, "La inmigración de braceros," 49–54.

54. Turits, "World Destroyed."

55. De la Fuente, *Nation for All*, 104–5, 194–98.

56. Quoted in Richards, "Friendly Societies," 142.

57. The best overall accounts of this era are Bolland, *Politics of Labour*, 155–211, and *On the March*.

58. Beckles, *History of Barbados*, 155; Howe, *Race, War, and Nationalism*, 191.

59. Richards, "Race, Class, and Labour Politics," 358; Post, *Arise Ye Starvelings*, esp. 5, 242.

60. Post, *Arise Ye Starvelings*, 159–95. On the influence of black newspapers from abroad, in particular the *Pittsburgh Courier*, on the developing Rastafarian philosophy in the 1930s, see Chevannes, *Rastafari*, 133–36. Coverage of the Italian invasion of Ethiopia by black-run newspapers in the islands and rimlands alike also contributed importantly to radicalizing black internationalism in this era. See Yelvington, "War in Ethiopia and Trinidad."

61. Think, for instance, of Charles Payne, the Trinidad-born child of Barbadian emigrants, whose speeches and eventual deportation sparked the 1937 riots in Barbados. See Beckles, *History of Barbados*, 154–69, and Richardson, *Panama Money*, 239–47.

62. There were exceptions, and Communist labor leaders in particular were consistently antiracist and pro-inclusion in this era. See Carr, "Identity, Class, and Nation"; Chomsky, "West Indian Workers," 28–31, 35–36; and Euraque, "Banana Enclave," 157.

63. See Anderson, *Imagined Communities*.

64. See, for instance, "Happenings in the Zone Towns," *Panama Tribune*, November 11, 1928, 12.

65. "Sid Says," *Panama Tribune*, January 20, 1929, 8.

66. Westerman's collected papers today form part of the Schomburg Center for Research in Black Culture of the New York Public Library. On Young and the *Tribune*, see Westerman, *Los inmigrantes antillanos*, 123–28, and Conniff, *Black Labor*, 71–72, 80–81.

67. "Cooperate," *Searchlight* (Limón, Costa Rica), January 4, 1930, 2.

68. See Putnam, *Company They Kept*, 169–70.

69. Dolores Joseph, "Deplores Lack of Racial Sentiment," *Searchlight* (Limón, Costa Rica), June 13, 1931 (brackets and bracketed material in original).

70. Dolores Joseph, letter to editor, *Searchlight* (Limón, Costa Rica), June 14, 1930.

71. C. G. Whittingham, "Perils That Confront Our Race," *Panama Tribune*, January 13, 1929, 8.

72. "Hope for a Woman's Page," *Panama Tribune*, December 9, 1928, 16.

73. "A Word to My People," *Panama Tribune*, January 6, 1929, 16.

74. The literature on African culture and identity in the Caribbean is, of course, vast. A helpful point of entry is Bolland, "Creolization and Creole Societies." An interpretive synthesis is Burton, *Afro-Creole*. The risk of describing pan-Africanism as the fruit of a long tradition of Afro-Caribbean "resistance" to white hegemony is that such a perspective can obscure just how *modern* pan-Africanism was. On the fallacy of ascribing Afro-Caribbean cultural creations to the realm of the "traditional" rather than the realm of "modernity," see Palmié, *Wizards and Scientists*.

75. Harpelle, "Ethnicity, Religion, and Repression"; Putnam, *Company They Kept*, 165–72; Bryce-Laporte, "Crisis, Contraculture, and Religion." The Afro-Christian religion known in Jamaica as Pocomania or *pukumina* was known in Limón as Pocomia; see, for instance, Duncan, "Pocomia Rebellion."

76. The early twentieth century has been described as the heyday of "integral nationalism," in which racial/ethnic/language criteria were promoted to strengthen national ties and demote the importance of religion and class. See Alter, *Nationalism*, and Hobsbawm, *Nations and Nationalism*. Baden-Powell, writing about the British Empire, used rhetoric almost identical to the *Tribune* editors': "If our empire is to stand Britain cannot be divided against itself. . . . Remember that whether rich or poor, from castle or from slum, you are all Britons in the first place. . . . If you are divided amongst yourselves then you are doing harm to your country. You must sink your differences" (*Scouting for Boys*, 278). See discussion in Pryke, "Popularity of Nationalism," 317.

77. *Searchlight* (Limón, Costa Rica), August 23, 1930, 1.

78. *Searchlight* (Limón, Costa Rica), May 31, 1930. On the other hand, British West Indian writers could be as negative about Chinese immigrants as the societies around them. When a newspaper in Costa Rica's highland capital published an antiblack caricature, the *Searchlight*'s editors held it up as evidence of how right Garvey was in promoting a "spirit of clannishness and adhesion to the cause of Africa for Africans. . . . We could more understand the cartoonist if he had caught the Chinaman or the habitual drunkard as the subject of his theme, but no, the Negro is unprotected, so anything can be done with him" (*Searchlight* [Limón, Costa Rica], January 18, 1930).

79. "U.S. Charged with Atrocities in Haiti," *Panama Tribune*, February 3, 1929, 3.

80. *Searchlight* (Limón, Costa Rica), May 3, 1930.

81. "Garveyites Warn Editor of Times," *Panama Tribune*, November 18, 1928, 10; "French Officers Back Up Negro Colleague," *Panama Tribune*, December 2, 1928, 4.

82. "Oh for a leader!!," *Panama Tribune*, November 18, 1928, 1; "New Colored Champion Looms," *Panama Tribune*, December 16, 1928, 6; "Bantu Wins Difficult Degree," *Panama Tribune*, November 11, 1928, 14.

83. The passage is from Darrow's closing arguments in Sweet's trial. See Weinberg, *Attorney for the Damned*, 248.

84. "Nothing Matters but Color," *Panama Tribune*, December 2, 1928, 8.

85. Fields, "Slavery, Race, and Ideology," 115.

86. Ibid., 110.

87. But see the nuanced analyses of fraternal and voluntary associations in Downes, "Freemasonry in Barbados" and "Sailing from Colonial into National Waters."

Providential Design

American Negroes and Garveyism in South Africa

ROBERT VINSON

The Universal Negro Improvement Association and African Communities League (UNIA) was the largest and most widespread black movement ever. At its height in the early 1920s, the UNIA had an estimated 2 million members and sympathizers and more than 1,000 chapters in forty-three countries and territories. Founded and led by the Jamaican-born Marcus Garvey, the New York–based UNIA's meteoric rise resulted from an agenda that included shipping lines, corporations, and universities; a Liberian colonization scheme; a resolute desire to reconstitute African independence; and a fierce racial pride. Outside North America and the Caribbean, these aims and ideals—generically called Garveyism—had their greatest impact in South Africa, as reflected in that country's eight official and numerous unofficial UNIA chapters. Garveyism, furthermore, pervaded black South African political, religious, educational, and socioeconomic movements throughout the 1920s and 1930s.[1]

In this essay I make three arguments. First, Garveyism in South Africa was related to notions of "Providential Design" and modernity, which were central to the racial interface between black South Africans and "American Negroes," a category that encompassed black West Indians as well as African Americans. Second, an international black sailing community played a crucial role in transmitting Garveyism from the Americas into South African political culture. Third, in South Africa, as elsewhere in the black world, religion was an important aspect of Garveyism.

The conclusions here offered contrast sharply with interpretations that confine the UNIA to South Africa's national boundaries, only to assert in the end that Garveyism was a "rather remote model" in that country's black freedom struggle.[2] Far from being peripheral, I argue, Garveyism was a central aspect of black South Africa's political culture in the interwar years. Besides charting a transnational dimension of the black South African experience in the twentieth century, I also seek to call attention to the relative neglect of Africa and Africans in African Diaspora studies. In short, I make the case for a "homeland and diaspora" model that bridges the study of Africa and the African Diaspora.[3]

Segregation, Black Modernity, and Providential Design: The Making of a Transnational Relationship

Britain's conquest of various independent African states in the nineteenth century, along with its war against the Afrikaner Republics between 1899 and 1902, culminated in the creation of the Union of South Africa in 1910. The Union of South Africa was part and parcel of a crystallization of segregation, in both thought and legislation, into a race-based political and socioeconomic program that would spur rapid industrial growth. The discovery in the late nineteenth century of gold and diamonds made South Africa the world's largest producer of both commodities, setting the stage for its transformation from a rural, agricultural society to an urban, industrializing one that relied on cheap African labor. Ultimately, segregation aimed to make the agricultural self-sufficiency of many Africans virtually impossible, thus compelling them to sell their labor to white-controlled mines, farms, and industry.[4]

As official government policy, South African segregation was implemented through a coordinated set of racially discriminatory legislation, the most significant of which included the Natives Land Act of 1913 and the Natives (Urban Areas) Act of 1923. The Natives Land Act rendered millions of Africans landless, forcing them to sell their labor cheaply to white-owned mines, farms, and other industries. The architects of South African segregation were hardly bashful about their objectives. Jan Hofmeyr, one of the most prominent among them, stated, "It is inconceivable that the white man should be able completely to dispense with the black man's labor on his farms, in his mines, in his factories; it is just as inconceivable that there should be set aside for the black man's occupation land sufficient to provide for all his needs independent of the white man's wages."[5] The Natives (Urban Areas) Act was the urban equivalent of the Natives Land Act. The Urban Areas Act undergirded a policy that sharply controlled and restricted the movement of Africans from country to town, allowing them into the urban centers only insofar as their labor was necessary to "minister to the white man's needs." Africans were also denied the right to vote, were condemned to the lowest-paying jobs by "color-bar" legislation, and had little judicial recourse against their systematic subordination.

The rise of segregation in South Africa paralleled the emergence of Jim Crow in the United States, and there was a direct relationship between the two systems of racial oppression. In this context Garveyism arrived and flourished in South Africa. Indeed, the black South African encounter with Garveyism merely continued, and deepened, a decades-long transatlantic relationship. Since the late nineteenth century, at least, black South Africans had seen African Americans as quintessential modern black people and as models. African Americans, for their part, engaged black South Africa as part of Providential Design, a divinely ordained mission to forge a decolonized "Africa for Africans." This transnational relationship, which became particularly close during the period of Garveyism, challenged an international color line that denied both groups full citizenship rights in their respective societies and also manifested itself in European colonialism of Africa.

The African American presence in southern Africa began as early as the 1780s, with a trickle of sailors, traders, and adventurers.[6] In 1890 the Virginia Jubilee Singers, an African American theatrical troupe, began a five-year tour of South Africa. This launched a period of intense black South African admiration for African Americans that laid the groundwork for South African Garveyism and a wide array of other transatlantic institutional and personal linkages. Orpheus McAdoo, the leader of the college-educated Virginia Jubilee Singers, had been born into slavery. He often opened performances with a Booker T. Washington–esque "Up from Slavery" recitation of African American history and culture, beginning with the degradation of slavery and ending with an impressive catalog of achievements during the first generation of freedom. Black South African journalist Josiah Semouse typified the rapturous African reaction to the Jubilee Singers: "Hear! Today they have their own schools . . . and also universities. They are run by them without the help of the whites. They have magistrates, judges, lawyers, bishops, ministers, and evangelists, and school masters. Some have learned a craft such as building, etc. When will the day come when the African people will be like the Americans? When will they stop being slaves and become nations with their own government?"[7]

In late-nineteenth- and early-twentieth-century South Africa, the Jubilee Singers and other African American visitors and residents were treated as "honorary whites," exempt from the segregationist legislation that hobbled the lives of black South Africans. Such a status was a tacit admission by the South African authorities that African Americans possessed the supposed characteristics of modern, "civilized" citizens.[8] The concession was important, coming as it did at a time when European colonialism was becoming entrenched in Africa and Asia and South African whites were justifying the denial of citizenship rights to black South Africans on the ground that blacks were an inferior, backward race that lacked the attributes of modern Western civilization. Such attributes included Christianity, Western education, Western dress, English language skills, an industrious work ethic, and an abiding faith in capitalism.

White South Africans further rationalized their dominance over blacks as the culmination of a 2,000-year European ascent from barbarism to a position as the world's most "civilized" race. It was the "White Man's Burden," they claimed, to uplift the lesser race by "civilizing" the Africans. In 1884 James Stewart, South Africa's most famous missionary and educator of the late nineteenth century, responded to African demands for equality by invoking a social Darwinist "racial time," an argument popular among white South African politicians, colonial officials, and scholars: "Starting but as yesterday in the race of nations, do you soberly believe that in the two generations of the very imperfect civilisation you have enjoyed and partially accepted, you can have overtaken those other nations who began that race two thousand years ago, and have been running hard at it for a thousand years at least?"[9] African Americans, including the members of the Virginia Jubilee Singers, debunked such claims because they seemed to possess all of the characteristics that defined modern, "civilized" people, as acknowledged by their "honorary white" status. More importantly, they had "civilized" themselves in *just one generation out of slavery, not two thousand years.* Black South Africans eagerly pointed to African Americans as proof that the attributes of modern civilization, far from being racially exclusive, were a universal human heritage, and that such attributes could be acquired in a relatively short span, even a lifetime. With the acquisition of modernity, particularly Western education, there could be no justification for relegating Africans to the status of hewers of wood and drawers of water. Western-educated Africans, inspired by African Americans, would demand full participation in society and perhaps even seek to regain their lost independence in a modern, regenerated continent of "Africa for Africans."

For African Americans, the engagement with South Africa centered on Providential Design, which assigned diasporic blacks a divinely ordained role in the "redemption" of Africa. Henry McNeal Turner was a leading exponent of Providential Design. A bishop of the African Methodist Episcopal Church, an African American denomination founded in the late eighteenth century, Turner inaugurated his church's mission in South Africa in 1896. In typical

Providential Design fashion, he argued that God had willed the enslavement of diasporic blacks so that they would be taught the "civilizing" traits of Christianity, the Protestant work ethic, thrift, and moral rectitude, qualities they would then return to Africa to promulgate. In other words, diasporic blacks would transmit the "light of civilization" to a slumbering "Dark Continent" that would be regenerated as a modernized, independent Christian Africa resplendent in God's favor. For diasporic blacks, an independent "Africa for Africans" would be a "Promised Land": an emigrationist homeland that would provide historical and cultural grounding and serve as a source of protection.[10]

The claims of Providential Design, along with notions of black modernity, cohered African-descended peoples across a wide spectrum, including many African Americans and black South Africans. In the diaspora, even such political adversaries as Booker T. Washington, W. E. B. Du Bois, and Marcus Garvey were linked by a common belief in various strands of Providential Design and black modernity. In the interwar period, those providential and modernist ideals were most powerfully expressed in Garveyism, which exploded across South Africa's political landscape during those years.

Black Sailors and the Transmission of Garveyism to South Africa

A combination of black sailors, ships, and newspapers—the era's most effective means of pan-African communication—transmitted Garveyism into South Africa. In May 1919, Garvey announced the UNIA's plans to operate the Black Star Line, a steamship corporation.[11] By September 1919, the UNIA had purchased its first ship, the *Yarmouth*, which was promptly renamed the *Frederick Douglass*.[12] Before the commonplace usage of airplanes, ships were quintessential symbols of modernity and nationhood. Black South Africans, relentlessly told by white segregationists that they were outside the realm of modernity, saw the Black Star Line as evidence to the contrary.

Black sailors, particularly from the Caribbean and North America, were especially effective pan-African vectors, disseminating news of Garveyism throughout the black world, including South Africa. In 1920 a Jamaican sailor, identified only as "Ennis," proclaimed, "We all come out to South Africa to free our brothers and sisters out there."[13] Subsequently, the Natal branch of the African National Congress (ANC), black South Africa's leading political movement since its founding in 1912, convened a meeting in Durban that reportedly attracted more than 1,000 people. The highlight of the affair was an unscheduled appearance by an "American Negro" sailor known only as "Moses," who had recently arrived from New York, site of the UNIA headquarters. Moses told his audience that "Marcus Garvey was the man they relied upon, and [that he] would free Africa: that the first vessel of the fleet was named 'Frederick Douglass', and this vessel had been sailing to different places. . . . Africa would be freed . . . by Marcus Garvey."[14] Vectors of Garveyism like Ennis and Moses had an important advantage over resident Garveyites: as sailors they could enter and leave South Africa before the authorities, who were openly hostile to Garveyism, even became aware of their presence.

Garveyism spread quickly in South Africa. In the port city of East London, there were persistent rumors that the "Americans" would arrive in ships with weapons to help Africans kill whites.[15] Kenneth Spooner, a West Indian missionary, joyously proclaimed that "his people were now on the seas coming to South Africa with a view to beating the European people here, and that in about six months time changes would be observed."[16] Addressing a meeting of the Transvaal branch of the ANC, an African known only as "Mgoja" raised the emphatic cry that "America had a black fleet and it is coming."[17] In neighboring Basutoland (now Lesotho), ardent nationalist Josiel Lefela editorialized, "Let us look forward to his Excellency Marcus Garvey the President of Africa, and the Americans, with anxious anticipation."[18] These prophecies were also proclaimed in the Eastern Cape and the Transkei. Gilbert Matshoba, a young African clerk, reported rapturously to his uncle, Enoch Mgijima, the leader of a religious group called the Israelites, that Garvey had predicted that the "blood of all wars is about to arrive" and that the UNIA would soon force European colonizers to leave Africa. "Father, that is the news of our black countrymen. It is published in the newspaper."[19]

West Indian Sailors and Garveyism in Cape Town

As transmitters of Garveyism, black sailors enjoyed a mobility that made it difficult for the authorities to apprehend them. But the peripatetic nature of their work also precluded the sailors from transforming rhetoric into sustained political organization. In South Africa, that task was assumed by, among others, a 200-member "American Negro" community in Cape Town.[20] Actually, most of these "American Negroes" were West Indians, who, beginning in the 1880s, had fled the economically depressed Caribbean for the relatively brighter prospects of South African port cities, especially Cape Town, where they formed distinct communities. According to a 1904 Cape Colony census, there were 298 black West Indians in the region, many of whom worked in the dockyards.[21] The West Indians had a reputation as "tough, hard back-boned Negroes . . . of the he-man type, aggressive and daring," and they displayed pan-African sensibilities, fostering "notions of Combination and Co-operation amongst the disparate ethnic groups" of Africans and mixed-race people called "Coloureds" in the Cape Town dockyards.[22]

The West Indians were especially attracted to Cape Town, the site of South Africa's earliest European settlement, because of its employment prospects, its large English-speaking population, and its racially liberal reputation in relation to the rest of the country. Cape Town, as part of the Cape Province, had a nonracial franchise that accorded voting rights to blacks who met certain property requirements, unlike South Africa's other three provinces, which totally excluded Africans from the political process. By the early twentieth century, Cape Town had developed into an industrial town of approximately 80,000 inhabitants, most of whom were Africans and Coloureds. The Africans lived mainly in segregated townships outside the city, while the majority of black workers were subjected to the industrial color bar, which excluded them from many lines of work.

West Indians in Cape Town, many of whom were Garveyites, were prominent in the leadership of the Industrial and Commercial Workers Union of Africa (ICU), South Africa's first major black trade union, which claimed 100,000 members at its peak in 1927.[23] In January 1920, ICU members elected "out and out Marcus Garvey" West Indians A. James King as president and James Gumbs as vice president.[24] Gumbs, a shipwright and former chemist, would later become an executive officer of the Cape Town UNIA branch. Another Caribbean, Emmanuel Johnson, an agent for the *Negro World*, the UNIA's official organ, and the future organizing president of the Cape Peninsula UNIA branches, also served as an ICU vice president.[25] Clements Kadalie, the ICU founder and general secretary, came from Nyasaland (now Malawi), and he, too, exemplified the movement's cosmopolitan character, including at the leadership level. By his own account, Kadalie's "essential object is to be the great African Marcus Garvey and I don't mind how much I shall pay for that education."[26] These men, along with the mercurial Samuel Bennett Ncwana, suffused Garveyism into the *Black Man*, the ICU's official newspaper, which proclaimed that "we should show our cordial appreciation of the very first step taken by the Hon. Marcus Garvey to show his solidarity with us. . . . Liberty and freedom calls upon . . . Africans to respond."[27]

Cape Town Garveyites established the earliest and largest number of South

Africa's UNIA chapters (five), and they also subscribed to claims of Providential Design.[28] West Indians founded the first two chapters, but the leadership and membership included West Indians, Africans, and Coloureds—a demographic mix quite unusual for segregationist South Africa. The branches generally held weekly Sunday meetings that were an eclectic mix of Christian worship and political exhortation. Branch chaplains and officers led the membership in religious songs and made fiery sermons that cast Garvey as a new Moses, poised to lead his people from the Pharoah's Egypt that was South Africa. William Jackson, the Cape Town UNIA president and a native of Jamaica, appealed to the Providential Design motif that linked blacks in Africa and the diaspora. For Jackson, Africans of the diaspora had been enslaved in the Western Hemisphere as a necessary prelude to acquiring the technological, economic, and educational skills to liberate Africans: "Ethiopia will be taken naked from Egypt to a foreign country, there to be lynched, whipped, gimecrowed (jimcrowed), killed and finally, after experiencing many vicissitudes of torments and misery, will return to Africa and impart the civilization and knowledge obtained in the foreign country to his people."[29] The agents of African liberation, according to Jackson, were the "15,000,000 negroes of America who have to-day reached the highest scientific attainments in the world. Those Negroes are now preparing to come back to the land of their forefathers and impart the knowledge gained in foreign countries to their brethren in Africa. Your slogan must be 'One Aim, One God, and One Destiny.'"[30] UNIA branch meetings were also occasions to collect membership dues, to sell stocks in the Black Star Line, and to promote the *Negro World*.[31]

The religious character of the UNIA in Cape Town was broadly similar to that of the U.S.-based parent body, the religiosity of which remains underappreciated. Clergy constituted one-fifth of the signatories to the UNIA's "Magna Carta," the 1920 "Declaration of Rights of the Negro Peoples of the World."[32] Garvey's speeches, reprinted in the *Negro World*, often employed a sermonic character that utilized biblical references and imageries. In the United States, UNIA Sunday meetings featured processional, recessional, and missionary hymns, sermons, and benedictions, while the organization's official motto was "One God, One Aim, One Destiny." Predictably, Psalms 68:31 ("Princes shall come out of Egypt; Ethiopia shall soon stretch out her hand unto God"), a passage much beloved by the exponents of Providential Design, was also a UNIA favorite. But other biblical verses were popular with the UNIA, too, such as Acts 17:26 ("He created of one blood all nations of men for to dwell on all the face of the earth"), which appeared on the group's stationery.[33] In short, providential religious language suffused the political objectives of the UNIA, and its self-described "missionaries" set out to "convert" unbelieving blacks to the project of African "salvation" and "redemption."[34]

The Cape Town UNIA branches responded to Garvey's 1925 incarceration for alleged mail fraud by inaugurating Garvey Day mass meetings on the first Sunday of each month. These meetings often included processionals through the streets of Cape Town, and members donated monies to their leader's legal defense fund.[35] The UNIA, in conjunction with the ICU and the ANC, also organized against segregationist legislation, low wages, and massacres of blacks by the security forces in Port Elizabeth and Bulhoek, both in South Africa, and in Southwest Africa (now Namibia), the former German colony ceded to South Africa after World War I. Reaching out to other oppressed racial groups in South African society, the UNIA, ICU, and ANC made links with the Cape Indian Council and the Indian nationalist and poet Sarojina Naidoo, who visited South Africa. James Thaele, president of the ANC's Cape Town branch and recipient of two degrees from Lincoln University, an African American institution, was a key player in all of these endeavors. Thaele, along with Jamaican Arthur McKinley, replicated the stepladder speeches that West Indian immigrants like Garvey had made famous in Harlem. Open-air political speeches, Thaele's Garveyite newspaper the *African World*, and the frequent translation of *Negro World* articles into African languages all were instrumental in spreading Garveyism.[36]

The Cape Town UNIA branches also distributed Garveyite literature to other parts of South Africa, creating an internal black communication network beyond the reach of white authorities. In 1920, for example, Cape Town Garveyites placed copies of the UNIA's classic manifesto, the Declaration of Rights of the Negro Peoples of the World, in packages of goods to be shipped to stores in the country's interior. Black workers who opened these packages would remove the documents and further disseminate them. Cape Town Garveyites also sent Garvey's books and pamphlets and copies of the *Negro World* to the diamond-mining town of Kimberley, where Garveyism found fertile ground in the House of Athlyi, a religious organization with internationalist links to the United States and Jamaica.[37]

Garveyism in Kimberley: The House of Athlyi

Joseph Masogha, the founder of the South African branch of the House of Athlyi, was the key disseminator of Garveyism in the diamond-mining town of Kimberley. Masogha distributed UNIA books and pictures, the *Negro World*, and other "American Negro" newspapers throughout South Africa and in his native Basutoland. Educated up to Standard IV (grade five), Masogha's Garvey- ite activities earned him the enmity of government officials, who considered him a "notorious agitator." He was dismissed from his jobs as a postman and a constable for "drunkenness," presumably from the intoxicating ideology of Garveyism.[38] White postal workers regularly pummeled Masogha with "kicks, punches, sneers, [and] insults" as he collected *Negro World* shipments from the Kimberley post office, threatening ominously that he would soon be a "dead nigger."[39] Yet the indefatigable Masogha persevered, telling the UNIA headquarters in New York that he made professional and personal sacrifices to disseminate Garveyism in order to "spread this spirit of the New Negro. I have given my heart as an offering for this land of ours. I quite follow that there must be a sacrifice. I hope the UNIA will guide me."[40]

Masogha's efforts were instrumental in making Kimberley a Garveyite stronghold. South Africa's diamond center, Kimberley was an early model of urban segregation, with its townships, restrictive pass laws, closed compounds, migrant-labor system, and color-bar policies. De Beers Consolidated Mines, the world's largest diamond company, was headquartered in Kimberley, giving it the feel of a "company town." Correspondents to the *Negro World* attested to the paper's extensive circulation in Kimberley, and they railed against the town's segregationist practices; one writer asserted that "the time has arrived for the black races to assert themselves and throw off the white yoke."[41] James Charles Diraath, a Kimberley hospital worker and amateur photographer, noted of the *Negro World* that "every copy is carefully preserved and passed from hand to hand so that as many as possible may hear the truth." He concluded, "Thousands of our native people here . . . are greatly encouraged by the efforts of the Hon. Marcus Garvey and the splendid work of the UNIA."[42]

Such were the circumstances in which Masogha, in 1924, established a branch of the House of Athlyi.[43] Headquartered in Newark, New Jersey, the House of Athlyi was founded by Richard Athlyi Rogers, who hailed from the Caribbean island of Anguilla. Rogers articulated a version of the Providential Design ideal, and he assumed the title of shepherd, watching over his Ethiopian flock. God, he asserted, had commanded him to become a modern-day Moses to lead "Ethiopia's generations from the oppressive feet of the nations" and to transform them into a "nation among nations."[44]

In 1922, after they both addressed a UNIA meeting in Newark, Rogers "anointed" Marcus Garvey as his chief apostle. Impressed by Garvey's message, Rogers proclaimed him "an apostle of the Lord God for the redemption of Ethiopia and her suffering posterities." He commanded his congregation, estimated at 500, to join the UNIA, asserting further that he and Garvey "were anointed and sent forth by the Almighty God to lay the foundation of industry, liberty and justice unto the generations of Ethiopia that they prove themselves a power among the nations and in the glory of their God."[45] Defending Garvey against his detractors, Rogers commanded, "Raise not the weight of your finger on Marcus Garvey, neither speak ye against Him."[46]

Rogers and Garvey agreed on a number of issues, spiritual and material, including a belief that black people should conceive of God in their own image and seek economic empowerment. Garvey believed his program of economic self-reliance, which included the Black Star Line, the Negro Factories Corporation, and the Black Cross and Navigation Company, was a necessary complement to spiritual prophecies of African redemption. Rogers concurred: "For as much as the children of Ethiopia, God's favorite people of old, have turned away from his divine Majesty, neglecting *life economic*, believing they could on spiritual wings fly to the kingdom of God, consequently became a dependent for the welfare of others."[47]

Rogers wrote the *Holy Piby: The Black Man's Bible*, the preeminent sacred book of the House of Athlyi. The *Holy Piby* articulated an aggressive black liberationist theology, and it would later become a foundational text of Jamaica's Rastafarian movement.[48] Rogers's narrative included Twelve Commandments, otherwise known as the doctrine of Athlicanity. These commandments shared the Holy Bible's injunctions to observe thriftiness, cleanliness, and honesty but made several significant departures. The *Holy Piby* interpreted the Battle of Adwa, in which Ethiopia defeated Italy in 1896, as a sign of impending black liberation.[49] Rogers also claimed that blacks could only attain the "Kingdom of God" if they demanded social justice on earth, instead of passively waiting for heavenly rewards.[50] The *Holy Piby* advocated the establishment of a powerful black nationality through unity and self-reliance and forbade blacks from fighting one another. Rogers's text further refuted the "Hamitic Hypothesis," said to be a biblical curse on blacks as the supposed descendants of Ham, a claim long used by white Christians to justify the oppression of African peoples. Rogers warned black Christians to eschew such biblical interpretations: "Woe be unto a race of people who forsake their own and adhere to the doctrine of another. They shall be slaves to the people thereof."[51] Rather, blacks should use the *Holy Piby* as their guiding religious text, as it contained "all worthy prophecies and inspirations endowed by God upon the sons and daughters of Ethiopia."[52]

The House of Athlyi, according to Rogers, had been established to provide "a real religious and material brotherhood among the children of Ethiopia" and to combat the "confusion and hatred" practiced by white Christians. Resorting to the language of Providential Design, Rogers asserted that God would "tear down the walls" of oppression he had "permitted to hold Ethiopia in bondage, that she may know the devil and his unrighteousness." "Now I shall send forth an army of Athlyians who shall redeem my children and deliver them again to my arms."[53] "When the Lord God of Ethiopia is with us in the battle for that to which we are entitled, show me the foe so powerful to set us down? Verily I say unto you there is none."[54]

In South Africa, such doctrines predictably met with strong official reproof. The local authorities in Kimberley denied Masogha land on which to build a church and school, while the national government refused to grant him and his ministers marriage licenses, denying them the right to marry congregants.[55] Considering the movement subversive, the authorities speculated that the term "Gaathly" was a contraction of Garvey and Athlyi, which "proved" that the "notorious Marcus Garvey" was a prime instigator of the House of Athlyi. Somehow, Masogha and his coworkers apparently managed to weather the storm of hostility: the House of Athlyi, or some remnants thereof, is reported to have been in existence as late as the 1980s.

"Dr. Wellington" and the Promise of American Negro Deliverance in the Transkei

Garveyism in South Africa took a particularly fascinating twist in the mid-1920s in the Transkei, when an African named Wellington Butelezi claimed the alternate identity of Dr. Butler Hansford Wellington, an "American Negro" and Garvey disciple. A largely rural area, the Transkei was quite different from Cape Town and Kimberley, the other two major centers of Garveyism in South Africa. Africans in the Transkei (and other rural districts) were subjected to a dizzying array of taxes, restrictions on landholding and cattle, economic exploitation by white traders, and pass laws that controlled their movement.

Wellington became an "American Negro" to legitimate his crusade against oppression in the Transkei and, not coincidentally, to advance his personal interests. Taking advantage of the high esteem in which many Africans held African Americans, he found fertile ground for his millenarian prophecies of imminent liberation, the agents of which would come from the other side of the black Atlantic. Wellington's ingenious, if opportunistic, use of existing

African American liberatory myths created a brief but electrifying Garveyism in the Transkei, a movement that featured millenarian prophecies, churches and schools, and an increased identification with African Americans.

Wellington was an outsider to the Transkei, which is populated largely by Xhosa-speaking Africans. Wellington, by contrast, was a Zulu-speaker from the neighboring province of Natal. The oldest of five children, he was born on January 26, 1899, and named Wellington Elias Butelezi.[56] After attending a Lutheran mission school, he enrolled briefly at Lovedale Institute, a training ground for those aspiring to become members of the small African elite. On leaving Lovedale, Butelezi worked variously as salesman, clerk, teacher, and herbalist.[57]

Then, in 1923, Butelezi took an important step toward becoming an "American Negro." He petitioned the government to "alter or conceal my name as Elias Butelezi and put it for Butler Hansford Wellington," a "Homeopathic Medical Practitioner and Specialist in Pediatric Diseases."[58] The nomenclatorial transformation apparently was associated with an increasing interest in Garveyism. Wellington subsequently became acquainted with the Caribbean-born Ernest Wallace and other "American Negroes," who had established UNIA branches in various parts of South Africa.[59] Soon, Wellington was organizing under his own UNIA banner, but he would achieve his greatest success in the Transkei.

"Dr. Wellington" attracted numerous followers with an intriguing tale. African American troops under the command of "General Garvey," he told transfixed audiences, would descend on South Africa in airplanes. Armed with flaming balls of charcoal—the imageries were drawn from the Book of Revelation—the Americans would destroy the whites, along with those Africans who had refused to join the UNIA, or Wellington's version of it. A modern black state would replace the segregationist regime, ushering in a new dispensation: "You are not going to pay taxes nor dip cattle. . . . Forces are coming, armies coming from America to drive the white people from Africa, to go to their own country. . . . People who did not register their names with him in his book will die together with the white people."[60] The transatlantic black liberators, according to Wellington, were motivated by pan-African racial affinities, by a desire to return to their African homeland, and by a determination to redeem a promise, made by the British during World War I, to cede South Africa to the United States in exchange for military assistance.[61] As if to give credibility to these fantastic assertions, Wellington claimed personally to have been wounded in the war while serving as a general in an exclusively African American army.[62]

Wellington further maintained that the UNIA had sent him to Africa, along with forty other men, to ascertain African interest in African American emigration. Those in favor of the return of transatlantic blacks would take out UNIA membership, which would offer them protection during the coming invasion.[63] The UNIA's shipping line, plus Garvey's stated intention to establish an aerial fleet to liberate Africa, seemed altogether consistent with Wellington's assertions that a "new and powerful race from the sea . . . dreaded by all European nations . . . will end tyranny and wrong."[64]

So as to not be confused with unbelievers, who would perish with the arrival of the Americans, Wellington's followers took steps to distinguish themselves. They sported badges with red, black, and green (the colors of the UNIA), symbolizing a determination to "pull down the British Empire"; painted their houses black; and slaughtered pigs, white goats, and white fowl.[65] Wellington proclaimed the killing of pigs, which he said represented degradation, decay, and death, a necessary precondition for liberation.[66] On his account, the indiscriminate eating habits of the swine and its unsanitary ways made it an ideal carrier of tapeworms, which gave consumers of pork parasitic illnesses. Furthermore, the despised whites had introduced pigs and chickens into the region.[67] For good measure, Wellington announced, the American liberators would set pigs on fire with burning coals, using the animals as conduits to spread the fatal flames to unbelievers and their properties alike.[68] These apocalyptic predictions unnerved some unbelievers, whose public disavowals of Wellington did not prevent them from hiding in the forests to avoid detection by the coming Americans.[69]

Wellington's American persona was crucial to his attempts to establish his legitimacy. He benefited from the fact that few Africans in the comparatively remote Transkei had ever met an "American Negro" and thus had difficulty uncovering his fraudulence. He also took advantage of the image of African Americans as quintessential black moderns, individuals with both the ability and the will to liberate their African fellow blacks. "Dr. Wellington" reinforced his modernist image by speaking only English at his meetings, by changing suits several times a day, and by touring the Transkei in a chauffeur-driven, American-made Dodge sedan. His supposed American medical degree further added to his allure.[70] These modernist means of deliverance seemingly confirmed a widespread belief that African Americans possessed the requisite educational, technological, and military capabilities to overthrow white supremacy in South Africa.

Wellington's success was due, in part, to his ability to weld the unfamiliar with the familiar. Thus he framed his prophecies in ways that resonated with existing religious conceptions of the colonial state, to which many Africans attributed malevolent spiritual qualities. Africans believed Europeans to be "possessed of powerful materials for sorcery.... All *ubuthi* (magical substances) comes from Europeans. They are the real *amagqwira* (witches)."[71] For the colonized Africans, taxation was a primary means by which the government demonstrated its tyrannical power. Payment of hut taxes allowed Africans access to land; poll taxes facilitated the acquisition of the passes needed by prospective migrant workers; and livestock levies allowed one's cattle to graze freely and enabled one to borrow money against the cattle's value.[72] By the same token, nonpayment of taxes could mobilize the state's powerful *ubuthi*, which partly explains why the vast majority of Africans paid the onerous levies that contributed to their material deprivation. This mindset also explains why Africans referred to the poll tax as *impundulu*, the common term for the destructive lightning storms that regularly killed people and livestock and burned homes. Tellingly, an alternate name for the poll tax was *inkosi*, or chief, a term that recognized the state's dominant position.[73]

Wellington, the respected herbalist with reputed magical powers, was now arguing that the *impundulu* of African Americans would overwhelm that of the Europeans. In this context, the fact that the Mpondo, an ethnic group in the southern Transkei, visualized the *impundulu* bird as red, white, and blue, the colors of the U.S. flag, is significant. Wellington beckoned his followers to gaze into a crystal ball that showed American airplanes, ships, and flying automobiles ready to attack, once Africans demonstrated their receptiveness to the plan. His magic mirror, reputedly an American invention, would turn British bullets into water. To alleviate widespread hunger exacerbated by recent droughts, Wellington held out to his followers the prospects of American ships loaded with cornmeal, which bounty could be supplemented by the harvests left by the vanquished unbelievers.[74]

Some of Wellington's lieutenants claimed to have actually seen the Americans and their military fortifications, and they repeatedly promised liberation on a date certain.[75] Forsaking the theme song of the British Empire, "God Save the King," Wellingtonite children's choirs now sang "Nkosi' Sikeleli Afrika," the anthem of African liberation, and other freedom tunes.[76] Other Wellingtonites boldly informed shocked magistrates that they would pay their movement's membership dues instead of state taxes, and they refused to submit to mandated vaccinations.[77] One flabbergasted magistrate exclaimed, "I have never known any man to get such an influence over the natives in such a short time."[78] Another official concurred: "The natives who to some extent resent the increased taxation, firmly believe this man's saying and look to a happy time of release from European rule which the American Government will bring."[79]

Wellington acolytes did not wait passively for the American liberators. They established some 200 churches and nearly as many schools as alternatives to white-controlled religious and educational institutions.[80] These independent churches and schools formed the institutional bedrock of Wellington's movement.[81] The churches allowed members a religious space to articulate a liberationist Christianity and a setting in which to perform such functions as marriage ceremonies, thereby avoiding the onerous fees, burdensome documentation, and other alien requirements demanded by the colonial state and European ministers.[82] Wellington also established a pair of more ambitious educational institutions, which he generously dubbed universities. And while the number of his most ardent adherents is impossible to ascertain, incessant complaints by government officials and other detractors suggest that his churches and schools were relatively, if perhaps fleetingly, well-attended. South African white supremacy ensured as much. As Wellington himself noted, "In schools you are taught to say Boss to any white man young or big all the same. Your names are Jim, John, George, Jack, etc. You go to Church but they won't mix with you."[83]

Wellington's institutions featured a political, religious, and educational content that reaffirmed Garveyite principles and had an overt Africanism. Walter Sisulu, a onetime secretary general of the ANC and mentor to Nelson Mandela, attended one such school. His mother also taught at a Wellington institution. Sisulu remembered that African cultural values infused a curriculum that was otherwise similar to the one approved by the government. At the Wellington schools, for instance, the pupils prayed to "the God of Mtirara, or Langalibalele," precolonial African political figures, not to "the God of Abraham, Isaac and Jacob, because they were white people."[84]

Wellington's schools were subsidized by a portion of the dues paid by the members of his movement. Additional collections were supposed to pay for new schools, textbooks, and teachers from the United States. School fees provided yet another source of income. Most teachers came from the surrounding communities. Few of them, however, were educated above the eighth-grade level or had undergone teaching training. The problem of poorly educated and poorly paid teachers was exacerbated by inadequate facilities and equipment. Some teachers, left without formal school buildings, resorted to scribbling lessons on the walls of huts.[85] Harassment by the state, the missionaries, and other opponents of Wellington constituted another set of challenges. In time,

Wellington's own supporters became increasingly frustrated with his unfulfilled promises, especially of American teachers and textbooks.

Still, many of the Wellingtonite schools and churches persisted for many years, and they contributed greatly to a generalized unrest that characterized much of the Transkei in the late 1920s.[86] The missionary-run educational centers suffered drastic declines in enrollment during this period, as students defected to the Garveyite schools, sometimes in the face of physical attacks by the "Americans," as Wellington's followers called themselves. Government officials who sought to forcibly close the alternate schools were met with "assegais and sticks as though the enemy had approached." Some Wellingtonites even turned the tables, using boycotts and intimidation to force the closure of several white-run schools.

Yet, by the late 1920s, Wellington was under increased scrutiny from both friends and foes. His failure to produce the American liberators and promised American teachers and textbooks caused much disillusionment. Support faded, as "the Americans were said to be coming to Africa and people will not join the movement as they don't see the Americans."[87] Members increasingly resented Wellington's incessant demands for monies, much of which seemed only to line his pocket. External attacks joined the growing internal dissent. In 1927 the South African authorities banned Wellington from the Transkei. Henceforth, followers had to journey to the Cape Colony, a considerable distance for many, to see him.

To add insult to injury, Wellington's claims to be tied to the UNIA were exposed as fraudulent. Garvey himself disavowed the "Doctor," warning in the pages of the *Negro World* that Wellington was not a UNIA officer and had no authorization to collect money or establish chapters on its behalf.[88] Meanwhile, detractors inside South Africa disproved Wellington's other claim to fame, that is, his Americanness. Hecklers mocked Wellington by calling him Butelezi, his Zulu surname.[89] A Zulu headman noted Wellington's "Zulu tribal mark, a cut in the right ear, which he has sewn up."[90] Samuel Bennett Ncwana, formerly an ardent Garveyite, spoke of his personal knowledge of Wellington's Zulu birth.[91] Wellington's own father delivered the coup de grace, affirming his son's Zuluness.[92] Forced to abandon the charade that "nobody knows me in this country,"[93] Wellington fell silent on his origins. He subsequently confined his pronouncements to the familiar themes of white injustice, black institution building, and black liberationist Christianity.

In 1935 Wellington sought to reverse his declining fortune by capitalizing on widespread African revulsion to Italy's threats to, and eventual invasion of,

Ethiopia. Attendance at his meetings increased dramatically. He demanded a South African economic embargo on Italy and urged black South Africans to embark to "East Africa to defend your own people."[94] Despite the popularity of the cause he now espoused, however, Wellington could not live down his past. Considering him untrustworthy, at least where money was concerned, his newfound listeners rebuffed his requests for funds, allegedly to support the Ethiopian resistance.[95]

Throughout the 1930s Wellington repeatedly appealed to the government to reverse its ban and allow him to enter the Transkei and other prohibited areas for "educational and spiritual purposes only" and to visit his wife and child. He disavowed any political intent. The hostility of many white (and some black) churchmen toward him, he argued, was due to jealousy, notably the defection of African parishioners and schoolchildren to Wellingtonite churches and schools. He also invoked America to support his claims, stating that "there are lawful private schools in the U.S.A."[96] The government, however, adamantly rejected his requests. Instead, the authorities jailed Wellington several times between 1937 and 1944 for, among other offenses, entering the Transkei without a pass, nonpayment of taxes, theft, and possession of alcohol.[97]

An increasingly frustrated Wellington saw no end to government persecution and unsuccessfully attempted to leave the country. In the 1940s he resurfaced in various parts of South Africa, including the industrial center of Johannesburg. A somewhat sheepish sister, embarrassed by her brother's infamy, admitted to one researcher that Wellington had visited her in the early 1950s, but she claimed no knowledge of his subsequent whereabouts. Wellington, who had electrified followers and vexed government officials in the 1920s and 1930s, simply disappeared from the public record, with no indication of his final fate.[98]

In the end, however, Garveyism in the Transkei transcended Wellington. Many of the churches and schools established during the heyday of his movement continued to operate after his personal demise. Wellington's decline and fall also opened the door for the emergence of an official Garveyite presence in the Transkei. Paul Gulwa, in direct communication with Garvey, established UNIA chapters in the Transkei, repeatedly donated monies to the international UNIA, and enrolled in Garvey's School of African Philosophy. Furthermore, the prophetic tradition of externally driven liberation, which Wellington had exploited so well, survived him. During World War II, for example, UNIA adherents improbably put out word that the "Americans," in conjunction with, of all forces, Hitler's Germany, would overthrow the South African state.[99] The

Wellington phenomenon may also be seen as representing, at the rural and popular levels, a culmination of the intense reverence black South Africans had for their black American cousins, a feeling that had been in the making for decades, since the time of the Virginia Jubilee Singers, if not before. Most fundamentally, perhaps, the considerable currency given to the mythic promises of "American Negro" liberation reflected the profound alienation of the black South African masses from the segregationist state and their desperation for salvation from white domination.

Conclusion

"American Negroes" as models, metaphors, political icons, and disseminators of political thought were central to black internationalist politics in South Africa between 1890 and 1940. Garveyism was the culmination of this dynamic between the two world wars, and its pan-Africanist race-conscious ideals would remain important to successive African political groupings, such as the ANC Youth League of the 1940s and the Pan-Africanist Congress of the 1950s. The pan-Africanism and self-determination ethos of Garveyism are also reflected in the ideologies of the Black Consciousness Movement in the 1970s and 1980s and, later still, in former president Thabo Mbeki's African Renaissance. Garveyism itself surfaces in eclectic geographical and cultural spaces in postapartheid South Africa. The country's expanding Rastafarian communities are impassioned followers of Garvey, and there is a Rasta squatter settlement named Marcus Garvey near Cape Town's airport. A mural at the University of Cape Town bears Garvey's image, while South African musical icons from Kwaito groups like Bongo Maffin to reggae superstars like the late Lucky Dube articulate Garveyite perspectives. The recently revived Johannesburg-based UNIA has sought to harness this diffused energy in organizational politics. In a state visit to Jamaica, Mbeki took time to lay flowers at Garvey's tombstone.

African Americans, exemplified most prominently by the Council on African Affairs in the 1940s and 1950s and the Congressional Black Caucus and TransAfrica in the 1970s and 1980s, were at the forefront of the antiapartheid movement in the United States. Today, thousands of African American entrepreneurs, corporate employees, diplomats, religious personnel, exiles, and tourists flock to South Africa. African American entertainers are a particularly ubiquitous presence in South African theaters, television and radio programs, and newspapers, thereby complementing the physical presence of American blacks. Though a dwindling number of South African octogenarians remember the Garveyite-dominated interwar years as "the time of the Americans," it is clear that the time of the Americans has not yet passed.

NOTES

1. See Vinson, "In the Time of the Americans" and "'Americans Are Coming.'" See also the important work of Edgar, "Garveyism in Africa," and Hill and Pirio, "'Africa for the Africans.'" A recent article on Garveyism in southern Africa is West, "Seeds Are Sown."

2. Rich, *State Power*, 39, 43. Standard texts on black South African politics include Walshe, *Rise of African Nationalism*; Odendaal, *Black Protest Politics*; and Gerhart, *Black Power in South Africa*.

3. The general lack of focus on Africa in African Diaspora studies is reflected in the "African Diaspora" special issue of *African Studies Review* 43 (2000) and in the recent "transnational black studies" issue of the *Radical History Review* 87 (2003). Manning invokes the term "homeland and diaspora model" in "Africa and the African Diaspora."

4. Beinart and Dubow, *Segregation and Apartheid*.

5. Hofmeyr, *South Africa*, 313–14.

6. Atkins, "Black Atlantic Communication Network," 6–11.

7. *Leselinyana*, October 1, 1890, cited in Erlmann, *African Stars*, 44.

8. After 1902, South African governments became increasingly concerned that "American Negroes" were fomenting political discontent amongst Africans. The popularity of Garveyism contributed greatly to the virtual ban of African Americans from South Africa and was the death knell of their "honorary white" status. The apartheid-era South African government would revive the "honorary white" designation for visiting African Americans, including Max Yergan, Roy Wilkins, Arthur Ashe, and Eartha Kitt. See Vinson, "Citizenship over Race?" On Yergan, who had an especially long and complex history of engagement with South Africa, see Anthony, *Max Yergan*.

9. Cited in Moeti, "Ethiopianism," 155.

10. For the African Methodist Episcopal (AME) Church in South Africa, see Campbell, *Songs of Zion*. For historical context to the notion of Providential Design, see Moses, *Alexander Crummell*, and Blyden, *Christianity, Islam, and the Negro Race*. For Henry McNeal Turner, see Redkey, *Respect Black*.

11. Stein, *World*, 64; Martin, *Race First*, 152. Other essential texts on Garveyism include Garvey, *Philosophy and Opinions*; Hill, *Marcus Garvey*; Lewis and Bryan, *Garvey*; Vincent, *Black Power*; Cronon, *Black Moses*; and Tolbert, *UNIA and Black Los Angeles*.

12. Martin, *Race First*, 153.

13. South African Government Archives (hereafter SAGA), Papers of the Union Department of Native Affairs, Transvaal Archive Depot (hereafter NTS), Interior Department, Reports on Bolshevism 168/74B, vol. 2, file 7/168/74, "Ennis" to Marcus Garvey, May 9, 1920.

14. Ibid., Secretary for Justice to Secretary for the Interior, December 8, 1920.

15. SAGA, Cape Province Depot (hereafter CA), 1/KNT 40 N1/9/2, affidavit of "Golifili" to Kentani Assistant Magistrate, December 14, 1920.

16. SAGA, NTS, Interior Department, Reports on Bolshevism 168/74B, vol. 2, file 7/168/74, Secretary for Justice to Secretary for the Interior, October 18, 1920.

17. Hill and Pirio, "'Africa for the Africans,'" 211.

18. Josiel Lefela, article excerpt, *Naledi*, November 18, 1921, Public Records Office (England), Co 417/665/02597.

19. SAGA, GG 1728, file 51/6670, Gilbert Matshoba to Enoch Mgijima, August 1920. Matshoba was referring to the August 14, 1920, edition of *Umteteli wa Bantu*, which had reported on the 1920 UNIA convention in New York City, which took place that month.

20. The *Cape Argus*, a Cape Town newspaper, estimated the "American Negro" community at somewhat less than 200 persons; see *Cape Argus*, January 29, 1923.

21. "Census of the Colony of the Cape of Good Hope, 1904," cited in Cobley, "Far from Home," 358. For West Indians and black Americans in Port Elizabeth, see Kirk, *Making a Voice*.

22. James Ghazu in the *Negro World*, July 16, 1932. Ghazu was a black South African sailor who eventually became the president of the South African UNIA in the late 1930s. See Page, "Black America in White South Africa," 332.

23. The union's initials were ICU instead of the seemingly correct ICWU because the enunciation of ICU was an ominous threat by blacks to whites; "I see you" connoted the transparency and insecurity of white domination. The phrase has resonated in South Africa's black nationalist circles, being powerfully revived during Nelson Mandela's first speech after his February 1990 release from prison, when he rallied the crowd with the phrase, "I see you."

24. Kadalie, *My Life*, 220–21.

25. Wickins, *Industrial and Commercial Workers' Union*, 85. For Johnson, see *Black Man*, August 1920, and *Workers Herald*, March 27, 1926.

26. Killie Campbell African Library, University of Natal, J. S. Marwick Papers, Clements Kadalie to Samuel Ncwana, May 20, 1920, in Hill and Pirio, "'Africa for the Africans,'" 215.

27. *Black Man*, August 1920.

28. The five branches were in Cape Town proper and in the city's suburbs of Woodstock, Claremont, Goodwood, and West London. The July 24, 1920, meeting of the Goodwood branch is the earliest documented Cape Town UNIA chapter.

29. SAGA, Transvaal Depot, 3/1064/18, Cape ANC meeting, 1923.

30. Ibid., GG 1556, 50/1058, June 3, 1923. Of course, the slogan "One God, One Aim, One Destiny" was a UNIA invention; it was ubiquitous on UNIA printed material like the *Negro World*.

31. *Negro World*, June 20, July 18, 1925, April 24, 1926.

32. Burkett, *Black Redemption*, 5–6, 9–10.

33. Burkett, *Garveyism as a Religious Movement*, 33–34. AME ministers Richard Allen and Absalom Jones made the earliest documented articulation of Psalms 68:31, which AME-affiliated Ethiopianist ministers found so powerful a century later. See Jones and Allen, "Narrative of the Proceedings of the Black People."

34. *Negro World*, February 19, 1921, 4. See also Burkett, *Garveyism as a Religious Movement*, 25.

35. *Negro World*, December 1, 1923, June 20, 1925.

36. *Negro World*, September 12, 1925, April 30, 1927.

37. Vinson, "In the Time of the Americans," 53; *Black Man*, November 1920; Hill, "Dread History"; Hill and Pirio, "'Africa for the Africans,'" 219.

38. SAGA, NTS, 1455 file 128/214, memorandum of A. W. Richards, Divisional Inspector, Eastern Cape Division to District Commandants, South African Police, Eastern Cape Division, June 16, 1928; Superintendent, Native Locations, to the Chairman and Members, Locations Committee, October 3, 1925; Detective Constable J. D. Justus to Divisional Criminal Investigation Officer, Kimberley, May 14, 1928.

39. *Negro World*, April 18, 1925.

40. *Negro World*, September 13, 27, 1924, August 14, 1926.

41. *Negro World*, January 14, 1922.

42. *Negro World*, June 27, 1925, October 18, 1924, January 17, 1925.

43. The *Afro-Athlican Constructive Gaathly Mamatic Church Hymn Book*, published in 1926, listed "the House of Athlyi, World's Headquarters" at 253 Nyembane St., Kimberley, South Africa. See Hill, "Dread History," 34, 62 n. 18. For Masogha's address, see SAGA, NTS, 1455 file 128/214, Joseph Masogha to the Secretary for Native Affairs, June 30, 1925.

44. Rogers, *Holy Piby*, 10.

45. Ibid., 6.

46. Ibid., 54–55.

47. Ibid., 25 (emphasis added).

48. There is virtually no scholarship on Rogers, an undeservedly neglected figure in pan-Africanist historiography. The notable exception is Hill, "Dread History." The *Holy Piby* was published on January 15, 1924. It and the Reverend Fitz Ballentine Pettersburgh's *Royal Parchment Scroll of Black Supremacy* were the foundational texts of the emergent Rastafarian religion in 1930s Jamaica. According to Hill, Leonard Howell's more famous text, *The Promised Key*, plagiarized heavily from the Pettersburgh book, which was reputedly published in 1926. There are few, if any, original copies of this work, though the text can be found online at <http://www.sacred_texts.com/afr/rps> (accessed February 1, 2008).

49. Rogers, *Holy Piby*, 9, 26–27, 30–31, 36–39, 42–46.

50. Ibid., 9–10, 14, 22.

51. Ibid., 45.

52. Ibid., 7–10, 19.

53. Ibid., 64.

54. SAGA, NTS, 1455 file 128/214, Application for Church Site, April 20, 1926.

55. Ibid., Masogha to Secretary for Native Affairs, June 30, 1925; undated letter of R. A. Rogers to Secretary for the Interior; Secretary for Native Affairs to Secretary for the Interior, May 26, 1926; Superintendent, Native Locations, to Joseph Masogha, October 24, 1925; Superintendent, Native Locations, to Native Locations Department, May 20, 1926.

56. Another document gives his birth as January 1, 1899. See SAGA, Department of Native Affairs, 7602 file 25/328, pt. 2, R. D. Lyle, Pietermaritzburg Magistrate, to Natal Chief Native Commissioner, January 30, 1928.

57. Edgar, "African Educational Protest," 184–91 (esp. 184); SAGA, CA, 2/SPT 16 file NI/9/2, undated article by Rev. Allen Lea. In 1919, the Church of Sweden, which had baptized Wellington, excommunicated him for unexplained reasons. See SAGA, NTS, 7603 file 25/328, statement by J. E. Hallendorff, Church of Sweden missionary.

58. Wellington cited religious reasons for the requested name change and did so as part of an unsuccessful attempt to study medicine at Oxford University. See SAGA, CA, 2/SPT v. 16 file N1/9/3, P. Nkala, Secretary to B. H. Wellington, to the Secretary for Native Affairs, July 16, 1926.

59. SAGA, NTS, 7603 file 25/328, Matatiele Magistrate to Secretary for Native Affairs, August 14, 1928. The quote is reprinted from the *Matatiele Mail*, December 23, 1925.

60. *Umteteli wa Bantu*, January 15, 1927 in SAGA, CA, 1/TSO 5/1/19 file 3/16/6.

61. SAGA, NTS, 7602 file 26/328, Rex vs. Albert Rulashe, Umtata, case no. 663/1928, June 11, 1928; Wilson, *Reaction to Conquest*, 371.

62. SAGA, NTS, 7602 file 26/328, undated report of J. Z. Makongolo, court interpreter. The report details events that occurred on June 9, 1927.

63. Ibid., affidavit of Daniel Dabulamanzi Mbebe, May 16, 1926; pt. 2, affidavit of Edgar Lonsdale, Tsolo Magistrate, March 12, 1927.

64. *Umteteli wa Bantu*, October 8, 1927.

65. *Umteteli wa Bantu*, January 8, 1927; SAGA, CA, 1/NKE 58 file N1/9/3, undated correspondence from Enoch Mgushulu to one Mr. Nyembezi; NTS 7602 file 26/328, pts. 2 and 3, R. Fyfe King, Tabankulu Magistrate, to Chief Magistrate, September 13, 1927.

66. SAGA, CA, 1/ECO 6/1/99 file 2/16/12, Engcobo Magistrate W. J. Davidson to Chief Magistrate, December 31, 1927. See also NTS 7603 file 26/328, Mount Ayliff Magistrate W. H. P. Freemantle to Chief Magistrate, September 19, 1927; pt. 4, F. N. Doran, Qumbu Magistrate to Chief Magistrate, September 26, 1927.

67. Bradford, *Taste of Freedom*, 225.

68. SAGA, NTS, 7602 file 26/328, statement by Benson Gcina, Harding Natal, January 12, 1928; Natal Chief Inspector of Locations to Natal Chief Native Commissioner, January 23, 1928.

69. Personal communication with Jeff Peires, August 3, 2000. Wellington's "American Negro" prophecies tapped into similar "outside liberator" mythologies that had circulated in central and southern Africa since the nineteenth century. See Ranger, "Myth of the Afro-American Liberator," and Higginson, "Liberating the Captives."

70. SAGA, NTS, 7603 file 25/328, affidavit of Samuel Nkwali, January 5, 1927; James Coombs, Qumbu Sergeant, to SAP District Commandant, January 18, 1927; statement by Milton Majola, Matatiele CID Detective, December 12, 1928; Allen Lea, "Bantu Leadership: The Escapade of Wellington," *East London Dispatch*, November 29, 1927.

71. Wilson, *Reaction to Conquest*, 316–17.

72. Redding, "Government Witchcraft."

73. Wilson, *Reaction to Conquest*, 302.

74. SAGA, NTS, 7602 file 25/328, James Coombs, Qumbu Sergeant, to District Commandant, January 18, 1927; undated affidavit of Frank Nolan Doran; affidavit of Qumbu constable Robert John Waldeck, March 10, 1927; undated affidavit of Umtata CID Detective Joseph Mho; pt. 2, statement by Constable Obed Sigenu, August 8, 1928. Wellington

later claimed to be "the doctor in Israel that will heal you of your leprosy" (statement by Eliezer Mguni, Umtata, January 31, 1929).

75. Ibid., pt. 4, Frank Brownlee, Butterworth Magistrate, to Chief Magistrate, October 14, 1927; D. W. Semple to Qumbu Magistrate, November 26, 1927; Ngqeleni Sergeant to SAP District Commandant, December 10, 1927; SAGA, CA, 1/NKE 58 N1/9/2, Nqamakwe Magistrate to Chief Magistrate, October 29, 1927. According to these documents, the actual day of apocalypse shifted from several dates in April and May to November 7, December 5, and the vague "before Christmas."

76. SAGA, NTS, 7602 file 25/328, affidavit by Ncanywa Giyose, Nqamakwe, May 27, 1927.

77. Ibid., pt. 4, undated affidavit of Joseph Mho, Umtatata CID Detective; F. N. Doran, Qumbu Magistrate, to Deputy Commissioner of Police, July 5, 1927. In two Qumbu locations known for their strong Wellington allegiance, only 142 of 1,600 Africans submitted to vaccination.

78. SAGA, NTS, 7602 file 26/328, pts. 2 and 3, affidavit of Edgar Lonsdale, Tsolo Magistrate, March 12, 1927.

79. SAGA, CA, 1/TSO 5/1/19, file 3/16/6, statement by Edward Chalmers Bam, March 12, 1927. Bam was an interpreter in the Tsolo court and a perennial Wellington critic.

80. Edgar, "African Educational Protest," 187; SAGA, NTS, 7603 file 26/328, pt. 4, Nqamakwe Magistrate A. L. Barrett to Chief Magistrate, October 6, 1927; NTS, 7602 file 26/328, pt. 4, undated report of N. A. Mazwai.

81. SAGA, CA, 1/MFE 8/1/14, file 2/12/4, SAP Sergeant to SAP District Commandant, December 19, 1927. The sergeant concluded that "it is not the uncivilized native who is keen on joining the organization but the half educated dressed native." However, Wellington did attract some non-Christian, nonliterate Africans.

82. SAGA, NTS, 7602 file 26/328 (A), Umtata Police Report, July 6, 1932; Lady Grey constable to Aliwal North Commandant, January 29, 1929.

83. SAGA, CA, 2/SPT 16, CID Report, August 15, 1928.

84. Interview by Robert Vinson of Walter Sisulu, Cape Town, April 26, 1998; 47th Annual Report of the South African Missionary Society (1928), cited in Edgar, "African Educational Protest," 187.

85. SAGA, NTS, 7602 file 26/328, Magisterial Court documents of Albert Rulashe, June 11, 1928.

86. SAGA, CA, 1/ECO 6/1/99 file 2/16/12, Engcobo district, was but one example of these multiple difficulties. See C. C. Harris to Engcobo Resident Magistrate, November 10, 1927; Engcobo Magistrate to Chief Magistrate, March 27, 1928, and the affidavit of Chief Alex Mgudlwa, May 20, 1929.

87. SAGA, NTS, 7602 file 26/328, statement by Eliezer Mguni, January 31, 1929.

88. Negro World, July 30, 1927. The government, after considerable deliberation, decided not to publicize Garvey's denunciation, not wishing to give free publicity to Garvey himself. See SAGA, NTS, 7602 file 25/328, pt. 4, undated correspondence of the Secretary for Native Affairs to the Chief Magistrate. However, rival organizations like the Cape African National Congress utilized Garvey's denunciation in their efforts to

discredit Wellington. See the article by E. Mdolomba in *Imvo Zabantsundu*, February 14, 1928, reprinted in SAGA, NTS, 7602 file 25/328, pt. 2, February 17, 1928.

89. SAGA, CA, 2/SPT 16 file N1/9/2, Native Constable Sigenu to Herschel Magistrate August 15, 1928; CA, 1/ELN box 86, South African Police Report, January 24, 1929.

90. SAGA, CA, 1/QBU 2/17, Frank Doran, Qumbu Resident Magistrate, to Robert Welsh, Mount Fletcher Resident Magistrate, February 15, 1927.

91. SAGA, CA, 2/SPT 16 file N1/9/2, statement of Samuel Michael Bennett Ncwana, August 23, 1928.

92. Ibid., Tandinyanso, "Concerning Herschel," *Umteteli wa Bantu*, April 21, 1928.

93. Ibid., Native Constable Sigenu to Herschel Magistrate, August 15, 1928.

94. SAGA, NTS, 7603 file 25/328 (A), CID reports of April 6, September 5, December 6, 1935.

95. Ibid., CID report, January 3, 1936.

96. SAGA, NTS, 7602 file 26/328 (A), Wellington to Minister of Native Affairs, November 4, 1936.

97. SAGA, NTS, 7603 file 25/328, pt. 4, Magistrate to the Secretary for Native Affairs, December 4, 1939; B. H. Wellington to Minister of Native Affairs June 23, 1944.

98. Ibid., Secretary for Native Affairs to B. H. H. Wellington, December 8, 1947. The interviewer was Lwandle Kunene, who visited his sister, a nun, in Swaziland during the 1970s.

99. Beinart and Bundy, *Hidden Struggles in Rural South Africa*, 199; SAGA, NTS, 1681 file 2/276, pt. 2, affidavit of Melvin Hlamvana, June 13, 1940. The African American liberation myth also extended beyond Garvey. For example, in 1937 the Transkeian Bunga reported that an unnamed ex-Wellingtonite now followed "the Negro Father Divine, an American about whom there was something in the papers yesterday." See NTS, 7602 file 25/328, Minutes of the 1937 United Transkeian General Council.

The Negro Question

The Communist International and Black Liberation
in the Interwar Years

HAKIM ADI

At its inception in 1919 the Third Communist International,[1] to its great credit, proclaimed its commitment to the liberation of Africa and people of African descent worldwide. In so doing, it became, perhaps, the era's sole international white-led movement to adopt an avowedly antiracist platform, and it was certainly the only one formally dedicated to a revolutionary transformation of the global political *and* racial order. The Third Communist International, popularly called the Comintern, presented the Russian Revolution as an epoch-making event, a harbinger to the emancipation of all peoples, including those of African descent. In the period between the two world wars, people of African descent globally found merit in this claim. They lauded the Soviet model of economic development and the Soviet Union's approach to racism and national oppression within its borders and welcomed its opposition to colonialism and racism internationally. Many black activists became members of communist parties or became closely associated with the Comintern. Indeed, the Communist International would play a pivotal role in a number of key events affecting black people globally during the interwar years.

This essay examines the interaction between the Communist International and the black liberation struggle, particularly in the United States, South Africa, Britain, and Britain's colonies in Africa and the Caribbean. It highlights the Comintern's position on the "Negro Question," as black-related issues were then called, an approach that played a pivotal role in the evolution of pan-Africanism, or black internationalism, in the interwar years.[2] Three broad conclusions emerge from the inquiry. First, black activists were crucial in the development of the Comintern's pan-African approach to the Negro Question.

Second, the Communist International's repeated expressions of support for black liberation empowered black communists on the ground, strengthening their position within various national communist parties. Third, the Communist International, more than any other political movement in the interwar years, emphasized the capacity of black workers for self-organization and for leadership in the struggle for black liberation globally.

The Backdrop

The Comintern's interest in the Negro Question was not entirely without precedent. The nineteenth-century founders of communism recognized the oppression and exploitation of Africa and people of African descent. Karl Marx noted that in addition to the exploitation of America and Asia, the "turning of Africa into a warren for the commercial hunting of black-skins signalized the rosy dawn of the era of capitalist production." The "veiled slavery of the wage-workers in Europe," he continued, "needed for its pedestal, slavery pure and simple in the new world."[3] Friedrich Engels, Marx's close collaborator, condemned the European colonization of Africa as an enterprise designed to benefit the stock exchange.[4] Both Marx and Engels took a keen interest in the antislavery struggle in the United States.[5] Their ideas were developed further by the Russian revolutionary leader V. I. Lenin, who was particularly attentive to the political problems of the imperialist era of the early twentieth century and to national and racial oppression and colonialism. However, a more systematic communist line on the Negro Question only came with the emergence and evolution of the Comintern.

The Comintern was created in the wake of the Russian Revolution in order to build an international communist movement and organize revolution worldwide. Lenin and the founders of the Comintern viewed the anticolonial movement as vital in this struggle against imperialism and therefore called for an alliance between the working-class movement in the advanced capitalist countries and the struggles of the oppressed peoples in the colonies. Accordingly, the *Manifesto of the Communist International to the Proletariat of the Entire World*, the Comintern's foundational document of 1919, stressed global revolutionary solidarity. Asserting that the "emancipation of the colonies is possible only in conjunction with the emancipation of the metropolitan working class," the manifesto called on the "Colonial Slaves of Africa and Asia" to rise up against their oppressors.[6]

The victorious Bolshevik Revolution and the Comintern's call struck a chord throughout the black world. Wilfred Domingo, a U.S.-based radical of Caribbean origin, wrote in 1919,

> The question naturally arises: Will Bolshevism accomplish the full freedom of Africa, colonies in which Negroes are the majority, and promote human tolerance and happiness in the United States by the eradication of the causes of such disgraceful occurrences as the Washington and Chicago race riots? The answer is deducible from the analogy of Soviet Russia, a country in which dozens of racial and lingual types have settled their many differences and found a common meeting ground, a country which no longer oppresses colonies, a country from which the lynch rope is banished and in which racial tolerance and peace now exist.[7]

Domingo was hardly alone in his enthusiasm for Bolshevism. Another Caribbean immigrant to the United States, the writer Claude McKay, called the Russian Revolution "the greatest event in the history of humanity," and he, too, hoped the Communist International would make his adopted country "safe for the Negro."[8] At the organizational level, the Comintern inspired the African Blood Brotherhood, founded in 1919 in New York by Cyril Briggs, yet another Caribbean immigrant. Combining Marxism and Black Nationalism, and claiming a membership of several thousand in the United States and the Caribbean, the brotherhood aimed at the "immediate protection and ultimate liberation of Negroes everywhere."[9] A number of African Blood Brotherhood members would go on to join the U.S. communist party and to play significant roles in the Communist International.[10]

The impact of the Bolshevik Revolution extended to the African continent, too, and it was especially significant among African soldiers who served in the British and French armies during the Great War.[11] A military officer from Senegal reportedly lost his life leading a Red cavalry regiment against counterrevolutionary forces in Russia.[12] The Comintern's influence in Africa was most pronounced in South Africa, where the continent's first communist party emerged in 1921. At its founding, the South African party was almost exclusively white, with just one black member, but it broke decisively with the racial divisions then existing and appealed to all workers "white and black" to join together to overthrow the capitalist system.[13]

The Comintern and the Negro Question

At its second congress in 1920, the Comintern restated its commitment to nonracial proletarian internationalism and adopted statutes that proclaimed, "In its ranks the white, the yellow and the black-skinned peoples—the working people of the world—are fraternally united."[14] The oppression faced by African Americans had already been discussed at the Comintern's first congress in 1919. In 1920 Lenin himself asked for information on "Negroes in America" and specifically demanded "all Communist parties should render direct aid to the revolutionary movements among the dependent and under-privileged nations (for example, Ireland, the American Negroes, etc.) and in the colonies."[15] Although there was continuing debate as to whether African Americans constituted a nation, the congress had made a decision that would have important implications for the nexus between the Comintern and black liberation: the African American struggle had been linked to the anticolonial struggles in Africa and elsewhere. The issue of black liberation came up again the following year, in 1921, at the Comintern's third congress, where the gathering proposed a commission to study "the question about the blacks."[16]

From the standpoint of the Negro Question, however, the fourth congress of 1922 was the most important to date and was a key moment in the development of the Comintern's revolutionary black internationalism. The congress established a Negro Commission and advanced a "Thesis on the Negro Question" that established Comintern policy in regard to Africa and the diaspora. Easily, the most colorful black personality at the fourth congress was Claude McKay, who had so effusively welcomed the Bolshevik Revolution. Although not formally a member of the U.S. communist party, McKay had a "dominant urge" to make the "magic pilgrimage" to the Soviet Union and was invited to Moscow by the white U.S. communist John Reed.[17] At the congress, McKay criticized the U.S. communist party for ignoring African Americans, arguing that the Negro Question was the central factor in the class struggle in the United States. He urged the Comintern to organize a "Negro Congress," claiming it would be "amazed at the fine material for Communist work there is in the Negro Race."[18]

The other black person attending the fourth congress from the United States was Otto Huiswoud. Originally from the Caribbean, like McKay, Huiswoud was an official delegate to the congress, representing the U.S. communist party, which he was the first black person to join. Huiswoud was among the first in the Communist International to argue that African Americans could play a vanguard role in the liberation of black people globally and was subsequently made chairman of the Negro Commission created by the congress.[19]

The creation of the Negro Commission inaugurated a more active pan-African policy on the part of the Communist International. The new approach was outlined in the "Thesis on the Negro Question," approved by the fourth congress, which both Huiswoud and McKay played a key role in drafting. The resolution declared that the colonization of "regions inhabited by black races is becoming the last great problem on the solution of which the further development of capitalism itself depends." The "Negro problem," consequently, had "become a vital question of the world revolution." The Comintern recognized "the international struggle of the Negro Race is a struggle against capitalism and imperialism" and therefore called for "an international organization of the colored people."[20] The Comintern's concern with the Negro Question was also based on the fear that the colonial powers could use African troops to crush revolutionary attempts in Europe, or even to attack the Soviet Union. Several speakers at the fourth congress, including McKay and Soviet War Commissar Leon Trotsky, alluded to such a possibility.[21]

The emergence of the Comintern's pan-African policy coincided with a new awakening among black people globally. The black political revival was epitomized by Marcus Garvey's Universal Negro Improvement Association (UNIA) and by the Pan-African Congresses, organized by W. E. B. Du Bois. The UNIA, with its Black Nationalist ideology and its mass base, made an especially strong impression on black communists in the United States, including the members of the African Blood Brotherhood, which by this time had become closely linked to the U.S. communist party. At the same time, Garvey, although ideologically opposed to Bolshevism, was not unaffected by the revolutionary events in Russia. He welcomed the emergence of Soviet Russia and mourned the death in 1924 of Lenin, calling him "probably the world's greatest man" and sending a telegram to Moscow "expressing the sorrow and condolence of the 400,000,000 Negroes of the world."[22]

The Communist International, for its part, implicitly recognized the importance of Garveyism and attempted both to undermine it and to have some influence on its members. The fourth congress of 1922, therefore, pledged both to organize a "general Negro conference or Congress in Moscow" and to support "every form of Negro movement which tends to undermine or weaken capitalism or imperialism."[23] The Comintern's approach was fully consistent with that of the African Blood Brotherhood, which vied with the UNIA for leadership of the black masses in the United States and tried to organize among

UNIA members. It was also consistent with the approach of the U.S. communist party, which produced its own pan-African-oriented literature. The brotherhood's program also anticipated many of the points in the Communist International's "Thesis on the Negro Question," including an insistence on the vanguard role of African Americans in global black liberation, the view advanced at the fourth congress by Huiswoud, who was also a member of the brotherhood. From its inception, the brotherhood had announced that "Negroes in the United States—both native and foreign born—are destined to play a vital part in a powerful world movement for Negro liberation."[24]

Not all communists, however, agreed that African Americans were best placed to lead the movement for black liberation internationally. David Ivon Jones, a white South African communist who had shown a strong interest in the Negro Question, insisted on the primacy of the African continent. "Negro emancipation," he declared, "is not an American question; it is a question of Africa."[25] But because at that time there were so few black communists in Africa, the Comintern accepted Huiswoud's countervailing argument that "the history of the Negro in America fits him for an important role in the liberation struggle of the entire African race."[26] Accordingly, African American members of the U.S. communist party were sent to the Moscow-based University of the Toilers of the East, an institution that trained revolutionaries from colonial countries and oppressed nations.[27]

As part of its pan-African policy, the Communist International pressed its affiliates in the imperialist countries to encourage the development of "revolutionary movements" in the African colonies. Officially, both the British and French communist parties claimed to do just that. In the early 1920s, the French party became active in Africa, especially in North Africa, establishing branches in Algeria and Tunisia. The Comintern instructed other parties to follow the French example and especially to publish revolutionary literature in African languages, so as "to establish a closer contact with the oppressed colonial masses."[28] The British party, despite its pronouncements to the contrary, showed little real interest in organizing in Britain's African colonies. The French party also was found wanting on the Negro Question. The neglect earned both parties rebukes at the fifth congress of the Communist International in 1924: the French for not doing enough to organize Africans living in France, and the British for not openly demanding independence for the colonies.[29] The fifth congress, consequently, established a Negro Propaganda Commission and again discussed organizing a special Negro Congress.

Yet no such meeting ever took place. Partly this was because there were numerous logistical problems associated with bringing delegates from the colonies to Moscow, where, it had been envisaged, the congress would be held. The European communist parties also did little or nothing to mobilize black delegates. Then the task of organizing such a congress was given to the U.S. communist party, which largely failed to take up its responsibilities. It was hoped that the American Negro Labor Congress, which was organized by the U.S. communist party in Chicago in 1925, would lead the work to convene the World Negro Congress, but it, too, failed to make the necessary breakthrough. An international conference of "Negro workers" was eventually held under the auspices of the Comintern's trade union center, the Red International of Labor Unions, or Profintern, in Hamburg, Germany, in 1930.

The World Anti-Colonial Conference and the League Against Imperialism

Meanwhile, in 1927, the Comintern sponsored an international conference that had important implications for the Negro Question. Held in Brussels, Belgium, the gathering was called the World Anti-Colonial Conference. Its most important outcome was the creation of the League Against Imperialism and for National Independence, a broad-based anticolonial organization, often led by communists, but which worked with all those forces opposed to colonialism and imperialism. Nearly 200 delegates, representing all the world's major colonial regions, attended the World Anti-Colonial Conference. Representatives from the African world included Lamine Senghor, a member of both the French communist party and the Paris-based Comité de Défense de la Race Nègre; Isaac Wallace-Johnson, head of the Sierra Leone Railway Workers Union; Josiah Gumede and James La Guma of the African National Congress of South Africa; and Richard B. Moore, representing the American Negro Labor Congress and the Garvey movement.[30]

The Negro Question featured prominently at the World Anti-Colonial Conference. Moore played a particularly active role in the proceedings, presenting the "Common Resolution on the Negro Question," which demanded "complete freedom of the peoples of Africa and of African origin." Toward this end, the resolution called for "the organization of the economic and political power" of black people and for a global struggle against "imperialist ideology."[31] The conference was an important site for networking, allowing African activists to consult with one another and to learn from the wider experience of the Communist International. La Guma and Gumede, the South African delegates, along with Sierra Leone's Wallace-Johnson, subsequently visited the Soviet Union. On returning to South Africa, Gumede famously proclaimed, "I have seen the new world to come, where it has already begun. I have been to the new Jerusalem."[32] More broadly, La Guma's participation in the World Anti-Colonial Conference, and especially his visit to Moscow, would prove vital to the subsequent development of the South African communist party, in which he became a leading figure.[33]

The Sixth Congress of the Communist International

During the sixth congress of the Comintern, held in 1928, there were important developments in policy on the Negro Question in general and with regard to South Africa and the United States in particular.[34] The sixth congress was held at a time when the Comintern was already in the process of adopting a new political line which emphasized that the world was entering a new period of economic and political crisis in which there would be an increasing likelihood of wars and an intensification of the revolutionary struggle both in the imperialist countries and in the colonies. The Negro Question, affecting as it did large parts of Africa and the Caribbean, became even more important, while in those areas in which communist parties operated, such as the United States and South Africa, the need to "bolshevize" the parties and rid them of any manifestations of "white chauvinism" became even more urgent. The policies adopted during this "Third Period" also called for a less conciliatory approach to rival political ideologies, leaders, and organizations that were often condemned as "reformist," such as Garvey and the UNIA. In part however, the changes in policy that occurred during 1928 had been discussed for some years before and had often been urged by black communists themselves. One of these changes was a much greater emphasis on "Negro workers," which consequently led to the Negro Question becoming a major concern for the Profintern.

The sixth congress adopted two resolutions, or "theses," on black self-determination in the United States and South Africa, respectively. The thesis on the "Black Belt" of the United States, that is, those southern states and parts thereof in which African Americans formed a majority of the population, argued that they constituted a nation, with the right to govern themselves and to demand independence from the rest of the United States if they so wished. The other thesis advocated what was termed a Native or Black Republic in

South Africa, that is, South Africans should strive for what was later termed black majority rule.

That the Comintern played the decisive role in the adoption of the new line there may be little doubt. It was not, however, simply a matter of centralized imposition. Black delegates to the sixth congress actively participated in the debates on the Negro Question and played a leading role in drafting and advocating the two theses, alongside delegates from the U.S., South African, and other communist parties. The more voluble black participants included South Africa's James La Guma[35] and the African Americans James Ford, who later stood as a vice presidential candidate for the U.S. communist party, and Harry Haywood, then a student at the University of the Toilers of the East. Indeed, for some black communists, such as La Guma and Haywood, the theses on self-determination were an empowering tool, forcing as they did the Negro Question to the center of communist policy not just in the United States and South Africa but throughout the international communist movement.

In South Africa, black self-determination meant increased Africanization of the party, the membership as well as the leadership. The Native Republic thesis specifically instructed the South African party to "orientate itself chiefly upon the native toiling masses," noting that "the Party leadership must be developed in the same sense."[36] The Comintern created all the conditions for African ascendancy in the South African communist movement and for a policy that put Africans at the center of the struggle for liberation in that country. Ultimately, however, it was up to the South African communists to Africanize the party.

The Native Republic thesis met considerable resistance from South African communists, showing that the notion of complete Comintern hegemony, or alleged domination by Moscow, is often at variance with the reality. In 1928 many leaders of the South African party still regarded white workers as the major force for change in the society. Other South African communists, white as well as black, rejected the new policy as "Garveyism," despite its critical stance toward that movement, and as endorsing the Garveyite slogan of "Africa for the Africans," a notion they had long opposed. However, supporters of the Native Republic thesis, such as La Guma, enjoyed the strong support of the Communist International. In the deliberations before the sixth congress, Comintern president Nikolai Bukharin had declared that the Comintern "must say very clearly that in the struggle between the Negroes and the whites that it is on the side of the Negroes."[37] Yet such unequivocal endorsement from the top failed to quell the dissent within the South African party, which continued for several years.

The situation in the United States mirrored that in South Africa, with the Black Belt thesis causing as much contentiousness as did the Native Republic thesis. African Americans, the thesis asserted, were not just a racial minority but also a "nation within a nation," a people for whom racism was a "device of national oppression."[38] Within the U.S. communist party, Harry Haywood became the most ardent champion of black self-determination, defending it against its many critics, white and black alike.

Haywood's position had ample precedence in the African American experience. The notion that black people in the United States constituted a "nation within a nation" had been advanced since the nineteenth century by black writers, such as Martin Delany. Well before the Comintern did so, in 1917 Cyril Briggs, the founder of the African Blood Brotherhood, also had demanded self-determination and a "separate political existence" within the United States for African Americans.[39]

The Black Belt thesis, as Mark Solomon has noted, highlighted several key issues: the right of African Americans to decide their own future and the revolutionary potential of the black struggle in the United States. At the same time, the Black Belt thesis provided a new basis for the struggle against racism and for encouraging a new approach and reevaluation of African American history and culture.[40] The result, according to Robin Kelley, was a new chapter in the development of the U.S. communist party: for the first time, communist ideas began to circulate among African Americans in the southern states, precisely the area where the struggle for civil rights later emerged.[41] Hosea Hudson, an African American communist in the South during the 1930s, remembered the discussions about the right to self-determination and how that concept might empower black people to demand "democratic rights" in the United States. "In the present set-up," ran the black collective wisdom, as related by Hudson, "everybody supposed to have the same rights, but we didn't have no rights."[42]

The Native Republic and Black Belt theses were therefore important developments in the Comintern's pan-African program that continued to be based on the perceived "common tie of interest" that linked people of African descent throughout the world. After the sixth congress, the Negro Question became an even more central concern for the international communist movement, with greater concern being expressed regarding the Negro Question in Africa, South America, and Europe. Black communists were in a stronger position, too, and some, like Haywood and Ford, rose to influential positions within the Comintern.

The International Trade Union Committee of Negro Workers

Consistent with the resolutions of the sixth congress, in 1928 the Communist International also created a new body to organize black workers: the International Trade Union Committee of Negro Workers (ITUCNW). This organization was formally part of the Profintern. Led initially by James Ford, the ITUCNW was assigned the "task of drawing Negro workers into the existing trade unions, of further creating new trade unions and of unifying the wide mass of Negro workers on the basis of the class struggle."[43] Toward that end, the committee called a meeting in Hamburg, Germany, in 1930, the First International Conference of Negro Workers. This conference was the closest the Comintern came to organizing a World Negro Congress, and it marked an important landmark in its approach to the Negro Question.

Although colonial governments barred a number of delegates from attending, the First International Conference of Negro Workers featured representatives from the various parts of the black world, including Africa, the United States, and the Caribbean.[44] The relatively large number of delegates from the African continent was especially noteworthy and reflected Comintern concern for a much greater focus on Africa. By contrast, the movements that competed with the Communist International for the allegiance of black people globally, Garveyism and the Du Boisian Pan-African Congresses, were both dominated by Africans of the diaspora. The participants in the First International Conference of Negro Workers included several figures destined to rise to prominence in pan-Africanism and in the anticolonial struggle in Africa, including Isaac Wallace-Johnson of Sierra Leone and Jomo Kenyatta of Kenya, and the conference was, in many ways, the model for the 1945 Pan-African Congress organized by George Padmore. The conference reaffirmed the Comintern's position on the proletarian foundations of black liberation, and it elected a new executive committee "to give concrete aid and assistance to all Negro workers and to help them build up class unions in their countries."[45]

The First International Conference of Negro Workers was also a major event in the career of George Padmore, who afterward was for several years a top official in the Comintern's black internationalist work. From 1930 to 1933, the Trinidadian-born Padmore edited the *Negro Worker*, the official organ of the ITUCNW. Padmore personally wrote many of the articles in the *Negro Worker*, which was distributed globally, often by black seamen, and sometimes disguised as a religious tract.[46] Simultaneously, he authored a number of related pamphlets, most famously *The Life and Struggles of Negro Toilers*.[47]

These and other publications of the ITUCNW chronicled the struggles of black workers in Africa, the United States, the Caribbean, South America, and Europe. They consistently identified the main enemy of the "Negro toilers" as British, French, and U.S. imperialism, while presenting the Soviet Union as the "champion of the oppressed." In this era, the height of the Comintern's Third Period, with its strong opposition to "reformism," readers of the *Negro Worker* also were warned against the dangers posed by a host of "misleaders," among them the British Labour Party, the American Federation of Labor, the National Association for the Advancement of Colored People (NAACP), and the Industrial and Commercial Workers Union of Africa, South Africa's leading black labor group. Garveyism, however, was presented as the most dangerous form of "ideological deceit," guilty of denying the class struggle and the "possibility of the revolutionary struggle of the Negro masses for self-determination."[48] Perhaps most importantly, though, the *Negro Worker* offered practical advice to those directly involved in struggles, suggesting concrete demands around which to rally. In addition to disseminating communist ideology, then, the paper served as something of a collective organizer, helping to foster a sense of unity of struggle throughout Africa and the African Diaspora.[49] It is a tribute to its effectiveness, or perceived effectiveness, that the authorities in various African and Caribbean colonies banned the *Negro Worker*.

The Caribbean

The ITUCNW, along with the *Negro Worker*, took an important interest in the Caribbean. Indeed, the committee's founders included a Guadeloupean and a Cuban,[50] and, partly through Padmore's contacts, it maintained a strong influence in Trinidad.[51] In the Caribbean, the ITUCNW organized among the workers in Jamaica, British Guiana, Grenada, Haiti, Guadeloupe, Puerto Rico, and the Dutch colonies.[52] The *Negro Worker*, too, carried many articles on the region. It was especially attentive to the 1932 visit to Moscow of Vivian Henry and Hubert Critchlow, respectively the leading trade unionists in Trinidad and British Guiana (now Guyana).[53]

Even before the formation of the ITUCNW, the Communist International had paid attention to the Caribbean. In the late 1920s, the U.S. communist party, which had been given responsibility for the region by the Communist International, dispatched Otto Huiswoud and Cyril Briggs to the Caribbean.[54] During the 1930s, the U.S. communist party was able to strengthen its links with workers in Jamaica, the Virgin Islands, and Puerto Rico and with the communist party in Cuba.

The only communist party in the Caribbean was founded in Cuba in 1925 and was initially dominated by European immigrants. Initially there was some reluctance to recruit large numbers of black members to the Cuban communist party, which had a low estimation of the revolutionary potential of immigrant workers from Haiti and Jamaica, who were described as having "a cultural level below that of Cuban workers and no tradition of struggle or organization."[55] However, after 1929 the Cuban communist party, partly under the influence of the Comintern and the U.S. communist party, began to pay much more attention to the recruitment of black members, especially among the sugar workers. By the time of the second congress of the party, in 1934, several black workers had risen to leadership positions. The congress discussed the necessity of winning over the "Negro toilers" to the revolution and attacked any manifestation of "discrimination against Negroes." The congress also discussed the need for "greater clarification of the Negro Question as a national rather than a 'racial' question typified in the slogan for self-determination of the Negroes in the Black Belt of Oriente Province."[56] Although the Cuban communist party evidently had some weaknesses during its early years, even then its influence spread throughout the Caribbean. One of its members was a Jamaican, Cleveland Antonio King, who is reported to have introduced the communist ideology to Jamaica.[57]

Britain and the Negro Welfare Association

Much of the Comintern's work on the Negro Question centered on the British Empire, since Britain was the world's leading imperialist power, with colonies in Africa and the Caribbean, among other places. Yet the British communist party, to the consternation of the Communist International, consistently resisted all entreaties to engage seriously in anticolonial agitation in Africa and the Caribbean or among black people in Britain.[58] The void was filled, to some extent, by the Negro Welfare Association, which was founded in London in 1931. The association was linked to the Communist International through a number of organizations, most importantly the ITUCNW and the League Against Imperialism. With a disinterested British communist party, the Negro

Welfare Association assumed the task of communist organizing among black people in Britain and in some of the British colonies. One of the association's more important constituencies consisted of African and Caribbean seamen in the major British ports, such as London and Cardiff.[59] Black communists, once again, were pivotal to this endeavor, which was spearheaded by individuals like the Barbadians Chris Jones, who led a committee of black seamen in London, and Arnold Ward, who became secretary of the Negro Welfare Association.[60]

Although charged with organizing blacks and effectively a branch of the ITUCNW, the Negro Welfare Association initially was led by white communists. Its goal was unmistakably pan-Africanist: "to work for the complete liberation and independence of all Negroes who are suffering from capitalist exploitation and imperialist domination . . . [and] to analyze, expose and combat capitalist exploitation and oppression in Africa, the West Indies, the other Negro colonies as well as in the USA."[61] Certainly all the leading black communists in Britain were active in the Negro Welfare Association. So, too, were a number of other black activists who would later become key figures in the anticolonial struggle in Africa, such as Jomo Kenyatta and Isaac Wallace-Johnson, both of whom we have already met in association with Communist International–related activities.

The Negro Welfare Association took up a variety of issues, among them racist legislation in South Africa, land alienation in Kenya, and self-determination in the Caribbean. Most significantly, however, the association, together with the League Against Imperialism, championed the anticolonial struggle in West Africa, a focus that was influenced by two of its most important interlocutors: the British-based West African Students' Union and the Sierra Leonean Isaac Wallace-Johnson.[62] The Negro Welfare Association's anticolonial efforts had both a parliamentary and an extra-parliamentary focus. Its allies in Parliament were kept fully briefed on West African and other colonial issues, enabling them to question official policy. Outside Parliament, the association appealed directly to the British working class to support the anticolonial cause, organized among black people throughout Britain, and established important political links and networks among black people globally.

Scottsboro and Ethiopia

Two events were particularly significant to the development of the black international in the 1930s, namely the Scottsboro case in the United States and the invasion of Ethiopia by fascist Italy. The Communist International was centrally involved in both.

In 1931, nine African American youths were arrested in Scottsboro, Alabama, on bogus charges of raping two white women aboard a freight train. Predictably, the ensuing kangaroo trial resulted in the conviction of all nine defendants, with all but one being immediately sentenced to death. The trial was followed by a bitter struggle over the appeals process. The NAACP, which preferred a fight confined to the U.S. judicial system and was initially reluctant to become involved, eventually lost control of the case to the communist-aligned International Labor Defense, with its call for a broad-based global campaign against the oppression of African Americans. The Communist International turned the case of the Scottsboro Boys, as the youths were dubbed, into a metaphor for racial injustice in the United States, and its campaign has been widely credited with saving the lives of the defendants. The campaign, from 1931 to 1937, was a huge international event: "Workers and activists rallied in Latin America, Asia, the Middle East, and Africa, across Europe and the United States, in parts of the British Empire and its dominions, and in the farming collectives of Russia."[63] Ada Wright, mother of two of the Scottsboro Boys, became a symbol of the campaign, both in the United States and in Europe, her speaking tours largely sponsored by the international communist movement.

The campaign on behalf of the Scottsboro Boys offered the Communist International an opportunity to raise other aspects of the global Negro Question. Black communists and their allies, especially, were inclined to link the Scottsboro case to the anticolonial struggle in Africa.[64] Indeed, the Scottsboro campaign helped the Communist International to expand its pan-African work in multiple ways. The International Labor Defense, in particular, benefited from the goodwill created by its defense of the condemned youths. By the time of its first congress in 1932, the Comintern's legal arm had established branches in South Africa and Madagascar, while delegates from Trinidad, British Guiana, South Africa, Nigeria, Kenya, and Liberia addressed the congress.[65]

In 1935, at a time when communists in the United States were finally uniting with the NAACP over the Scottsboro campaign, fascist Italy invaded Ethiopia, the only African country that had successfully defended its independence against European colonial invasion. The attack on a largely defenseless Ethiopia became an even bigger pan-African cause célèbre than the Scottsboro case. Ethiopia, long a symbol of hope for black people throughout the world, now faced national extinction. Black people globally rallied to its defense, a struggle in which communists played a key role.

The Communist International, and especially blacks in the Communist International, vigorously supported the Ethiopian cause. Appearing at the seventh (and last) Comintern congress in 1935, just a couple of months before the invasion began, the African American James Ford strongly condemned Italy's designs on Ethiopia. The clouds of war gathering over Ethiopia, Ford warned, signaled a wider fascist threat to world peace. Consequently, "the international proletariat must regard the struggle of Ethiopia as a just war, as a national defensive war, and support the Ethiopian people."[66]

As Ford spoke, the seventh congress was debating the need for the broadest unity against the growing danger of fascism and war. It approved a new policy advocating a broad alliance of all progressive and democratic forces against the growing threat of fascism, represented most dangerously by Germany, Italy, and Japan but also by elements within the ruling circles in many other countries. In particular the Comintern emphasized the need for the unity of the working class against fascism, and it even appealed to the social-democratic Second (Amsterdam) International, an organization it had previously denounced, to join it in opposing Italian aggression in Ethiopia.[67]

In the United States, African American communists played an active role in the various Ethiopian defense committees, just as they did in the Scottsboro campaign. The campaign in support of Ethiopia, in turn, helped to create the conditions for the emergence, in 1936, of the historic National Negro Congress. Formed on the initiative of the U.S. communist party, the National Negro Congress, which elected A. Philip Randolph as its president, was one of the broadest political bodies in African American history, with more than 500 organizations represented, including the NAACP, the Urban League, and many churches and lodges.[68]

Everywhere in the black world, people rallied in defense of Ethiopia. In Trinidad, the Negro Welfare Cultural and Social Association spearheaded a "Hands off Abyssinia" campaign, just as it had previously organized support for the Scottsboro Boys and for Angelo Herndon, an African American communist convicted of "insurrection" and sentenced to twenty years on a Georgia chain gang for leading a protest.[69]

On the African continent, at a meeting in Kenya organized in the Kikuyu Central Association, Kenyans vowed to "march to Ethiopia to defend their brothers."[70] In West Africa, Wallace-Johnson, then based in the Gold Coast, took part in organizing an Ethiopian Defense Committee. Meanwhile in South Africa, the communist party organized "Hands off Ethiopia" demonstrations, even persuading dockworkers to refuse to load ships with supplies destined for the Italian military.[71]

In Britain, the Negro Welfare Association took up the Ethiopian cause. In a resolution proposed by Jomo Kenyatta, the association emphasized the symbolic importance of Ethiopia's struggle against fascist aggression. "Millions of colonial and semi-colonial people in Africa and throughout the East," the resolution asserted, "are gaining strength from the magnificent fight which is being put up by the Abyssinians to maintain their independence."[72]

Conclusion

Although often overlooked, the Communist International played an important role in the development of black internationalism during the critical interwar period, leaving a legacy for succeeding decades. One important aspect of this legacy, for example, was the influence of communism on major African American writers, such as Richard Wright, Langston Hughes, and Ralph Ellison.[73] As the evidence demonstrates, the Comintern advanced the black struggle globally, both directly and indirectly. The Comintern established two organizations, the League Against Imperialism and for National Independence and the ITUCNW, along with its journal, the *Negro Worker*, that helped to advance the black liberation struggle. Consistently, the Comintern, in which black communists played a key role, took the lead on the Negro Question, variously cajoling and directing the national parties to put the issue of black liberation on their agendas and empowering black communists on the ground. The experience of Hosea Hudson in the U.S. South during the 1930s is instructive. The communist press, he noted, "was always carrying something about the liberation of black people, something about Africa, something about the South, Scottsboro, etc. etc. We would read this paper and this would give us great courage."[74] The post–World War II struggle for civil rights benefited from the fruit of such courage.

In other areas of the black world, the Comintern's black internationalism provided similar inspiration. For example, despite a ban on its organ, the *Negro Worker*, the ITUCNW exercised considerable influence on various Caribbean labor and mass movements. This was especially the case in the British colonies, where large-scale strikes and anticolonial rebellions broke out in the late 1930s. Labor leaders such as Vivian Henry in Trinidad and Hubert Critchlow in British Guiana were closely associated with the ITUCNW, with Critchlow serving as a contributing editor to the *Negro Worker*. In Trinidad, the Negro Welfare and Cultural Association, which was closely linked to the ITUCNW, played a leading role in the labor rebellions of 1937.[75] The leaders of the association included Jim Headley, formerly a member of the youth league of the U.S. communist party, and Rupert Gittens, who had been deported from France on account of his association with the French communist party.[76]

In the British West African colonies, the ITUCNW also influenced the budding labor movements, which would play key roles in the post–World War II political events. West African labor militants like Wallace-Johnson and the Gambian E. F. Small had close links with the Comintern, as did the Gold Coast's Bankole Awoonor-Renner, who was one of the first continental Africans to attend the Communist International's University of the Toilers of the East.

The impact of the Comintern can be seen, too, in various pan-African networks that emerged during the interwar years. Thus although George Padmore broke with the Communist International,[77] he continued to use the contacts and connections he had forged while in the Comintern in his postcommunist, pan-Africanist career, including associations with Jomo Kenyatta and Wallace-Johnson. The Comintern's black internationalist perspective created the conditions for the new Marxist-influenced pan-Africanism that emerged during the 1930s and reached its height with the convening of the 1945 Pan-African Congress by Padmore and others.

While largely unknown in Britain today, the Negro Welfare Association leader Arnold Ward was a significant figure in the network of black communists that stretched across Europe, the Americas, and Africa in the 1930s. It was Ward, apparently, who first interested Paul Robeson, one of the most famous African American communists of the 1930s and beyond, in the Soviet Union and communism.[78]

The networks established by black communists and the Comintern endured for many years. In 1945, for example, a British-based communist, Desmond Buckle of the Gold Coast, drafted a pan-African document to present to the founding conference of the United Nations. The text, *Manifesto on Africa in the Post-War World*, was delivered by a group of British and U.S. pan-Africanists under Padmore's leadership. In that same year, 1945, Buckle also represented the Transvaal Council of Non-European Trade Unions, a major black South African labor group, at the inaugural meeting of the World Federation of Trade Unions.[79]

Most importantly, perhaps, the Communist International powerfully reinforced the internationalist and revolutionary perspectives in the black liberation struggle—perspectives that offered a vision of a world in which working and oppressed people would cast off the yoke of oppression and take control of their own destinies.

NOTES

1. The International Workingmen's Association, or First International, in which Marx and Engels played an important role, was established in 1864 in London. The Second International was formed in Paris in 1889 but was split in two when most of its members refused to condemn the Great War.

2. Edwards, *Practice of Diaspora.*

3. Marx and Engels, *On Colonialism,* 258, 268.

4. Ibid., 273.

5. Marx and Engels, *Civil War in the United States.*

6. Daniels, *Documentary History,* 2:89.

7. Quoted in James, *Holding aloft the Banner,* 165.

8. Quoted in ibid., 166.

9. *Summary of the Program and Aims of the African Blood Brotherhood.* See also Hill, "Cyril Briggs."

10. On Briggs and the African Blood Brotherhood, see James, *Holding aloft the Banner,* 155–84.

11. Gromyko and Kosukhin, *October Revolution and Africa.*

12. Wilson, *Russia and Black Africa,* 95.

13. Johns, *Raising the Red Flag,* 111–27. See also Drew, *Discordant Comrades,* 46–57, and Johns, "Birth of the Communist Party."

14. Quoted in Bunting, introduction.

15. Lenin, *Selected Works,* 3:435.

16. Davidson, Filatova, Gorodnov, and Johns, *South Africa and the Communist International,* 63.

17. McKay, *Long Way,* 153.

18. Solomon, *Cry Was Unity,* 41.

19. Ibid., 42.

20. Wilson, *Russia and Black Africa,* 130.

21. Ibid., 128–29.

22. Quoted in Haywood, *Black Bolshevik,* 105.

23. Kanet, "Comintern," 90.

24. *Summary of the Program and Aims of the African Blood Brotherhood.*

25. Wilson, *Russia and Black Africa,* 131.

26. Ibid., 133.

27. Solomon, *Cry Was Unity,* 42–43. For more on black students at the University of

the Toilers, see McClellan, "Africans and Black Americans." For the experience of a black alumnus, see Haywood, *Black Bolshevik*, 148–76.

28. Quoted in Wilson, *Russia and Black Africa*, 138.

29. Ibid., 140.

30. Geiss, *Pan-African Movement*, 326.

31. "Statement at the Congress of the League Against Imperialism and for National Independence," in Turner, Turner, and Turner, *Richard B. Moore*, 143–46.

32. Quoted in Bunting, *Moses Kotane*, 36.

33. Simons and Simons, *Class and Colour*, 389–90.

34. Wilson, *Russia and Black Africa*, 160–75; Solomon, *Cry Was Unity*, 68–95; Kanet, "Comintern," 102–11; Berland, "Emergence of the Communist Perspective"; Kelley, "Third International"; Haywood, *Black Bolshevik*, 218–81.

35. La Guma and Adhikari, *Jimmy La Guma*; Haywood, *Black Bolshevik*.

36. For the resolution on "The South African Question," see South African Communist Party, *South African Communists Speak*, 91–97.

37. Davidson, Filatova, Gorodnov, and Johns, *South Africa and the Communist International*, 155.

38. Haywood, *Black Bolshevik*, 218.

39. Draper, *American Communism and Soviet Russia*, 323.

40. Solomon, *Cry Was Unity*, 86–87.

41. Kelley, *Hammer and Hoe*, 13.

42. Painter, *Narrative of Hosea Hudson*, 105.

43. International Conference of Negro Workers, *Report of Proceedings and Decisions*, 9.

44. International Conference of Negro Workers, *Report of Proceedings and Decisions*. See also McClellan, "George Padmore and the Hamburg Conference."

45. International Conference of Negro Workers, *Report of Proceedings and Decisions*, 40.

46. On the *Negro Worker*'s disguises, see the introduction by Cohen in Nzula, Potekhin, and Zusmanovich, *Forced Labour*, 14.

47. Padmore, *Life and Struggles*.

48. "Special Resolution on Work among Negroes in the US and the Colonies: Adopted by the 5th Congress of the RILU," *International Negro Workers Review* 1–2 (February 1931): 19.

49. See, for example, Padmore, "The Fight for Bread," *Negro Worker* 6–7 (June–July 1933): 2–4, and "To Our Brothers in Kenya," *Negro Worker* 8–9 (August–September 1933): 19–25.

50. Sherwood, "Comintern and the Colonies," 6.

51. Reddock, *Women, Labour, and Politics*, 108.

52. "Plan of Work of the Negro TU Committee for February–July 1932," Library of Congress, Records of the CPUSA (hereafter LOC), 515/234/3038.

53. "Report of Negro Workers' Leader on Soviet Russia," *Negro Worker* 4–5 (April–May 1933): 28–31.

54. "Meeting of Negro Department," November 22, 1929, LOC, 515/130/1685.

55. Quoted in Carr, "Caribbean Backwater," 238.

56. "Cuban Workers Strengthen their Organisations," *Negro Worker* 4, no. 3 (July 1934), 30. See also Carr, "Caribbean Backwater."

57. Hart, *Rise and Organise*, 18.

58. Sherwood, "The Comintern."

59. Squires, "Communists and the Fight against Racism."

60. Sherwood, "Racism and Resistance." See also O'Connell to the Editor, *Negro Worker* 4–5 (April–May 1933): 24–25, and *Report of the Annual Conference of the NWA*, October 25, 1935, LOC, 515/301/3943.

61. Report of the International Secretariat of LAI, League Against Imperialism, London, 1935, Bridgeman Papers (DBN 25), University of Hull Archives, U.K.

62. On Wallace-Johnson, see Spitzer and Denzer, "I. T. A. Wallace-Johnson and the West African Youth League," pts. 1 and 2.

63. Miller, Pennybacker, and Rosenhaft, "Mother Ada Wright," 388.

64. Squires, "Communists and the Fight against Racism," 15–16.

65. Thomas Jackson, "The International Defence and Negro Peoples," *Negro Worker* 2–3 (February–March 1933): 9.

66. Ford, "Defense of the Ethiopian People," 159–60.

67. Wilson, *Russia and Black Africa*, 259.

68. Haywood, *Black Bolshevik*, 447–62.

69. Reddock, *Women, Labour, and Politics*, 108–10.

70. *Report of Annual Conference of the NWA*, October 20, 1935, LOC, 515/301/3943.

71. South African Communist Party, *South African Communists Speak*, 124–25.

72. *Negro Worker* 5, no. 2 (December 1935): 8.

73. Maxwell, *New Negro, Old Left*, 1–13.

74. Painter, *Narrative of Hosea Hudson*, 102.

75. Lewis, *Labour in the West Indies*, 31.

76. Reddock, *Women, Labour, and Politics*, 135–36.

77. Padmore left the Comintern in 1933. He was formally expelled the following year for "contacts with a provocateur, for contacts with bourgeois organisations on the question of Liberia, for an incorrect attitude to the national question (instead of class unity striving towards race unity)." See "Expulsion of George Padmore from the Revolutionary Movement," *Negro Worker* 4, no. 2 (June 1934): 14. See also "A Betrayer of the Negro Struggle," *Negro Worker* 4, no. 3 (July 1934), and Helen Davis, "The Rise and Fall of George Padmore as a Revolutionary Fighter," *Negro Worker* 4, no. 4 (August 1934): 15. Padmore published his own version of events in "An Open Letter to Earl Browder," *The Crisis*, October 1935, 302, 305. For Browder's response, see "Earl Browder Replies," *The Crisis*, December 1935, 372. It is interesting that for many years afterward Padmore continued to defend the Soviet Union's approach to the "national question." See, for example, his *How Russia Transformed Her Colonial Empire*.

78. Duberman, *Paul Robeson*, 628 n. 59.

79. *World News and Views* 41 (1945): 324–25; Adi and Sherwood, *1945 Manchester Pan-African Congress*, 29 n. 21.

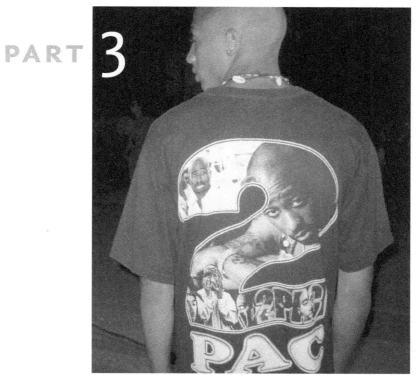

Tupac Shakur (1971–1996). Tupac Amaru Shakur, born in prison to a Black Panther mother, became an icon of resistance to black youth worldwide. He is shown here as lived by a hip hop fan at a *rapero* performance in Havana, Cuba, 2006. (Courtesy of Marc D. Perry)

Waiting for the Black Gandhi

Satyagraha and Black Internationalism

VIJAY PRASHAD

Mohandas Gandhi, the Indian apostle of satyagraha, had the kind of serenity that disarmed even his fiercest opponents. Visitors came away overawed by his presence. His quiet demeanor yet sharp political analysis, while comforting to his allies, drove his enemies to distraction. Gandhi, in his lifetime, came to symbolize a new kind of politics, but his tactics had the weight of history behind them. The elements that distinguished Gandhianism—marches and fasts, disobedience and strikes—had little novelty. What was decidedly new was that Gandhi spoke of peace and compromise even as his people fought an unarmed war, and that at a time when workers' movements were gaining strength and demanding everything. Trade unionism and Bolshevism gained ground and terrified the owners of property and the managers of colonial states. Gandhi, by comparison, seemed serenely safe. In his first years in India, and especially during the Ahmedabad troubles of February–March 1918, he disavowed strikes and workers' organizations, earning the trust of the owners of property and the distrust of the radicals. Workers' groups, the district magistrate wrote, "assailed [Gandhi] bitterly for being a friend of the mill owners, riding in their motorcars, and eating sumptuously with them, while the weavers were starving."[1] Gandhi may not have been unacceptable to the captains of industry, but that does not detract from the sheer force of the movement he engendered, a movement that led him every bit as much as he led it.

In the 1920s and 1930s, as the Indian freedom struggle became synonymous with Gandhi, colonized and oppressed people in the darker nations took notice. From Jamaica, African America, and southern Africa, among other places, came the query, Where is our Black Gandhi? Will our Black Gandhi come?[2] Implicit in such queries was a demand for a replication, across the globe, of the type of anti-imperialist mass movement that Gandhi is believed to have fashioned in India.

Yet Gandhi was no unalloyed radical. Given a choice, the powers would much rather have dealt with him than with Lenin. Both encouraged mass revolt against injustice, both rallied the people for a permanent revolution against imperialism, but something very important set them apart. While Lenin embodied the socialist and communist specter, Marxism and all that it implied in the way of an assault on property, Gandhi symbolized the Orient. The way he dressed, the way he spoke, and the language he used to describe his tactics (some of them quite similar to those of the Bolsheviks) all afforded Gandhi and his movement some legitimacy in certain respectable circles. Instead of being a war on property, his struggle was seen as the spiritual work of an Eastern seer, one more interested in the purification of Indian society than in the radical transformation of the world. That Gandhi made the requisite noises against working-class-led strikes in Ahmedabad in 1918 offered further reassurance that this Oriental seer had more elevated goals than did the Bolsheviks.[3]

Gandhi thus provided many social movements the cover to do just what they might have done anyway, nicely shrouded in the cloak of Eastern pacifism. Nonviolent activism had a very long trajectory, from ancient times onward. However, while most political movements used nonviolent *tactics*, Gandhi raised nonviolence to a moral ethic, to a strategy with a vision for re-creating the world. Other political traditions shared the Gandhian adherence to strikes, fasts, and other nonviolent forms of protest, but without rejecting other tactics, such as sabotage, destruction of property, and militant confrontation with the police. Gandhianism alone affirmed that the end of peace could only be attained through the means of peace. No violent means, according to the Gandhians, could possibly create a nonviolent society. Violence, in this scheme of things, breeds violence.

The black international engaged aspects of Gandhianism that centered on whether it was possible to entirely eschew violence when confronted with an extremely violent colonial or racist regime, such as those in southern Africa and the southern United States. Could nonviolence, as a hard standard, succeed in bringing about popular mobilization when racist violence had shattered the confidence of a people? Would the oppressed not need a violent revolution to restore their sense of self? Despite occasional bouts of violence, the bulk of the population throughout most of the black world came to a simple conclusion: unless forced into guerrilla warfare by a ruthless adversary, it was far better to engage the last ounce of goodness in the enemy through moral nonviolent confrontation. That is the genius of Gandhianism that appealed to many in the black international.

Gandhianism and African America: The Initial Phase

In March 1924, *The Crisis*, the official organ of the National Association for the Advancement of Colored People (NAACP) and a journal edited by W. E. B. Du Bois, published a short, characteristically pungent note from the African American sociologist E. Franklin Frazier. Titled "The Negro and Non-Resistance," Frazier's piece deplored the tendency among "a growing number of colored people" to "repudiate the use of force on the part of their brethren in defending their firesides, on the grounds that it is contrary to the example of non-resistance set by Jesus." Drawing from the biblical injunction to "turn the other cheek" to violence, the Christian critics of violent and direct resistance enjoined the black masses that those who do injustice to them must be met with love. The lynchers, being human, might also grow to love black people. Frazier rejected this argument. "While [those who criticize violence] pretend to emulate the meekness of the Nazarene," he countered, "they conveniently forget to follow his example of unrestrained denunciation of the injustice and hypocrisy of His day and His refusal to make any truce with wrong-doers." Jesus may not have fought oppression with guns, but he did give his life for justice and not for accommodation.[4]

Frazier had good reasons to be frustrated and despondent. Already in the late nineteenth century, lynching had become such a horrifying epidemic that journalist Ida B. Wells-Barnett turned her career over to exposing it.[5] In 1919 the NAACP held a conference on lynching and later published a report documenting more than 3,000 cases of vigilante racist murders between 1889 and 1919.[6] Previously, in 1918, Congressman Leonidas Dyer had introduced antilynching legislation into the House. Then, in 1922, Mary Talbert, Mary Jackson, Helen Curtis, and other women in the NAACP formed the Anti-Lynching Crusaders, but their efforts came to naught in 1923, when the Dyer bill died by a filibuster in the Senate. While the bill languished in Congress, another 200 African Americans fell victim to the lynch mob.[7]

It was in these circumstances that Frazier became disillusioned with non-resistance. His idea of fighting fire also had foundation in African American reality. From the borderlands with Mexico to the Carolinas, African Americans with military experience turned against white supremacy and the lynching regime. During World War I, the government worried about African American,

Mexican, Japanese, and German plots to foment armed strife in the United States (the "Plan of San Diego" of 1916 being the most famous, and the Houston Mutiny of 1917 the most savage response).[8] The authorities were seriously concerned about the loyalty of their second-class citizens. That the disfranchised might take to the gun against white supremacy was not an academic question, especially in the wake of the panic caused by the 1911 Mexican Revolution.[9] The loyalty of African Americans, even though well-demonstrated in the savage campaigns against the Amerindians and in the wars of 1898, could not be vouchsafed in the minds of the elevated citizenry, who feared "Negroes with guns." Frazier's rejection of nonresistance has to be read in this context.[10]

Frazier's position shocked Ellen Winsor, a white Quaker ally of the NAACP and veteran suffragette. She denied that nonviolent protest amounted to passivity and urged Frazier to study the ways of M. K. Gandhi, "who has not one drop of white blood in his veins." Perhaps with the harsh retribution visited upon any retaliation against the lynch mob in mind, Winsor asked, "Has not the Negro learnt to his sorrow that violent methods never win the desired goal?" She concluded, "Who knows but that a Gandhi will arise in this country to lead the people out of their misery and ignorance, not by the old way of brute force which breeds sorrow and wrong, but by the new methods of education based on economic justice leading straight to Freedom."[11]

Du Bois, in his capacity as editor of *The Crisis*, decided not to publish Winsor's response. Instead, he sent her a kind personal note, albeit one with an edgy conclusion: "I am, I must say, compelled to smile at the unanimity with which the great leader, Mr. Gandhi, is received by those people and races who have spilled the most blood."[12]

Du Bois then showed Winsor's letter to Frazier and published his reply in June 1924. The use of violence, Frazier reiterated, anticipating an argument that would be made more famously by Frantz Fanon decades later, was indispensable in self-defense against white supremacist aggression and would gain African Americans self-respect. "A Britisher remarked to me in England a couple of years ago," Frazier continued, "that once in the Far East you could kick a Japanese with impunity, but since the Russo-Japanese war, the Japanese had become so arrogant that they would take you into court for such an offense." Struck by Winsor's call for an American Gandhi, Frazier responded acerbically: "Suppose there should arise a Gandhi to lead Negroes without hate in their hearts to stop tilling the fields of the South under the peonage system; to cease paying taxes to States that keep their children in ignorance; and to ignore the iniquitous disenfranchisement and Jim Crow laws, I fear we would witness an unprecedented massacre of defenseless black men and women in the name of Law and Order and there would scarcely be enough Christian sentiment in America to stay the flood of blood."[13]

Whatever the merits of the debate, neither Frazier nor Winsor really understood Gandhi and the Indian freedom struggle. For them, as for many in the United States, Gandhi had become a mythical figure for whom nonviolence had religious qualities and whose movement had been entirely motivated by an immense faith in him and in his ethical approach. Winsor wanted the black movement to adopt Gandhian pacifism as much as Frazier rejected the purity of that approach. Neither, however, showed an appreciation of the historical Gandhi.

Du Bois came closer to the mark. In July 1929, for the twentieth anniversary issue of *The Crisis*, Du Bois invited Gandhi to submit a message. Gandhi did so, and in the margins Du Bois penned his own thoughts on Gandhian politics: "Agitation, non-violence, refusal to cooperate with the oppressor, became Gandhi's watchword and with it he is leading all India to freedom. Here and today he stretches out his hand in fellowship to his colored friends of the West."[14] The techniques of direct action, the ethos of solidarity, and the refusal to bend to imperialism were far more important to Du Bois than Gandhi's philosophy of ahimsa, life without violence. Individual heroism and self-abnegation meant little to those who suffered the long arm of white supremacy. Even in India Gandhianism was often understood by the masses as the license to rebel violently against authority (as in Chauri Chaura in 1922 and during the mass "Quit India" uprising of 1942). Du Bois recognized the centrality of Gandhi to the rejuvenated mass movement of Indian nationalism, and while he saw Gandhi warts and all, he regarded him as one of the most important figures of his time.

Such a practical approach to Gandhi was rare in the United States, where Gandhi's adherents were prone to depict him as a saint. A popular 1923 account by the University of Michigan's Claude Van Tyne noted, "Millions of Indians believe Gandhi to be a reincarnation of Vishnu."[15] That view irked Gandhi's main Indian interpreter in the United States, Krishnalal Shridharani, who wrote, "Whatever religious and mystical elements there are in the Indian movement, and they are greatly exaggerated by the American journalists and scholars—are there for propaganda and publicity reasons as well as for the personal satisfaction of deeply conscientious men like Gandhi and the members of the Gandhi Seva Sangh." What drew the millions, Shridharani added, was the fact that "the movement has been a weapon to be wielded by masses of men for earthly, tangible and collective aims and to be discarded if it does not work." Shridharani minimized the role of religion in the Indian movement precisely because it was exaggerated in the United States. In fact, religious iconography and ideas did play quite a significant role in Gandhi's attempt to mobilize the population. Nevertheless, Shridharani was right to note that "American pacifism is essentially religious and mystical. West can be more unworldly than East, and the history of the peace movement in the United States is a good illustration of that."[16] In writing these lines, he could very well have had Ellen Winsor, not just her Quaker community, in mind.

The South African Sojourn: How Gandhi Became Mahatma

Gandhi's adoption by American pacifism as an Oriental saint faced a significant contest not only from the diligent analysis by Du Bois but also from Gandhi's own biographical details. Gandhi's history has to be recovered from mythology or else it becomes impossible to understand what attracted him to anti-imperialist movements across the darker nations. Gandhi was not always Gandhi, and the Gandhi that we know only emerged because of his experience in the struggles for justice in southern Africa.

Gandhi arrived in South Africa in 1893 at age twenty-four and left in 1914, aged forty-four. These were his formative years, when the naive man and mediocre lawyer became a major political and moral force in world affairs. How, exactly, did Gandhi become the Mahatma, the Great Soul?

In the 1860s the British imperial project drew people from India as indentured laborers to work in the Natal province of South Africa. There, more than 150,000 Indian laborers worked in a variety of occupations, notably in the coal mines and the sugarcane fields, as well as built railroads. They suffered from the callous indifference of the colonial state, which valued them for their labor power and cared little about their welfare. Women among the indentured lived the harshest lives: all that the colonial state disavowed in the way of social life had to be manufactured with scant material by women within the gendered division of labor.[17]

When their indenture contracts ran out, many "ex-indentured" sought to stay on the land that had become their home. This desire posed a challenge to the colonial state, as did the arrival of a merchant class of Indians who came to sell goods and services to the indentured. The Indian merchants were known to the state as "Passenger Indians" (because they paid their own passage from

India to South Africa) and to themselves as "Arabs" (to differentiate themselves from the indentured laborers). A firm owned by one of these "Arabs" or "Passenger Indians" engaged Gandhi's legal services to resolve one of its internecine disputes. Frustrated by the general lack of dignity accorded the merchants, Gandhi opposed laws that, to his mind, reduced the Indian merchant to a "kaffir" (the stereotypical word used by the white supremacist state to designate black Africans). In 1894 he helped found the Natal Indian Congress, whose goal was to repeal the discriminatory laws that fettered the lives of the Indian merchants. Thus far, actually until 1907, Gandhi had little to say about the oppression of black Africans and working-class Indians. His professional class, caste Hindu, and pro-imperial optic failed to detect them on the political horizon.[18]

From 1894 to 1906, Gandhi and the merchants eschewed mass struggles. According to historian Maureen Swan, the class divide "was a requirement of a colonial situation in which legal distinctions were increasingly being made on a racial basis, and in which the major threat to the merchants' economic interests thus happened to be posed in terms of their being identified as part of a certain group which was placed low in the racial hierarchy."[19] In other words, to preserve their own narrow class advantages, the Indian merchants had to separate themselves from their indentured brethren (although it should also be said that this same class had little confraternity with oppressed castes and exploited classes within India). The Passenger Indians not only feared an alliance or a mass uprising, but they also could not countenance fiscal losses and imprisonment.[20] Even if Gandhi or the merchants had wanted to use the mass power of the indentured laborers, finding common causes on issues would have been difficult. In 1896, when the South African government and press attacked him for his caustic remarks about discrimination against Indians, Gandhi announced, "The lot of the indentured Indian cannot be very unhappy; and Natal is a very good place for such Indians to earn their livelihood."[21] No wonder the Indian indentured did not flock to Gandhi in this period.

In 1906 the South African government introduced a bill to require the registration of all Indians and to control the entry of Indians into the country. The proposed law would have hampered freedom of commerce for the Indian merchants. Incensed, they tried every available tactic: resolutions, petitions to the Colonial Office, requests for meetings with senior officials, and letters and articles in the press. The government remained obdurate, and no compromise seemed possible (unlike in 1894, when 9,000 signatures forced the state to hold back on its attempt to abolish Indian enfranchisement). It is in this context that the merchants acceded to Gandhi's call for "passive resistance" in September 1906.

Amid his call for passive resistance, Gandhi grappled with the failure of the Indian merchants' polite strategy as well as the violent strategy of the 1905 Russian Revolution. "Under British rule," Gandhi wrote, "we draft petition, carry on a struggle through the Press, and seek justice from the King. All this is perfectly proper. It is necessary, and it also brings us some relief. But is there anything else that we should do? And, can we do it?"[22] The "it" referred to the Russian people, notably those whom Gandhi called the anarchists (although they included communists and others), who "kill the officials openly as well as secretly."

Gandhi considered such armed action a mistake, because it kept both rulers and ruled "in a state of constant tension." Nevertheless, the bravery and patriotism of the Russians appealed to him, for these men and women "serve their country selflessly." Indians in South Africa, by contrast, had not attained that level of patriotism. "We are children in political matters. We do not understand the principle that the public good is also one's own good. But the time has now come for us to outgrow this state of mind. We need not, however, resort to violence. Neither need we set out on adventures, risking our lives. We must, however, submit our bodies to pain."[23] Gandhi struggled with the gap between the class interest of the Passenger Indians and the "public good" of the society. This is the first indication of his public disavowal of the narrow class strategy pursued by the Passenger Indians, and of his entry into the broader, messy world of populist, anticolonial nationalism. Indians, he wrote, henceforth should refuse to abase themselves to unjust laws and should, rather, suffer in jail. On September 11, 1906, before a room of merchants, Gandhi pledged to go to jail before submitting to the unjust laws. He asked those in the room to join him. "Imagine that all of us present here numbering 3000 at the most pledge ourselves." But even fewer would suffice: "I can boldly declare, and with certainty, that so long as there is even a handful of men true to their pledge, there can only be one end to the struggle, and that is victory."[24]

Two years later, Gandhi reflected on the 1906 struggle. He noted, "The entire campaign was intended to preserve the status of the well-to-do Indians. . . . It was chiefly a businessmen's campaign."[25] The businessmen, however, did not lead the campaign. It was left to the working class and the small merchants to assume that function. In 1910 Gandhi singled out the hawkers of Transvaal for their important role: "Because of their courage, the campaign has created so fine an impression. It is because hundreds of them went to gaol that it has come to be recognized as a great movement."[26] The strong stand of the workers and small merchants surprised Gandhi, because "questions of self-respect or honour, it was thought so far, could have little meaning for hawkers." But things had changed: "Now, everyone admits that hawkers do care for self-respect and they have risen in the esteem of others."[27]

The masses came forward, mobilized either by class interest (the hawkers, the merchants) or by religious or ethnic fealty (through caste and creed associations, a central player being the Hamidia Islamic Society). Their arrival allowed Gandhi to lay out his theory and to develop his concepts: satyagraha (action on the basis of truth), ahimsa (action without violence), swaraj (self-rule), and sarvodaya (welfare for all). Gandhianism began to be formulated in relationship to the mass upsurge. One crucial element of the revolt and of the theory is that it occurred in the context of widespread deprivation for the indentured and ex-indentured, but also under the heel of a state that, at this point, was more disposed to structural violence than to public and relentless physical violence. Despite the many protests engineered by the merchants and others, the state did not go after the Indian protesters with vehemence. Its rulers played politics with them, which they did not do with the Zulus, who in 1906 rose up in rebellion against colonial rule. The hierarchy of racism and the mediation of an educated, "reasonable" class of adepts provided the Gandhian revolt with a far more genteel state than that experienced by the Zulus and others.

In 1913 the struggle picked up again, when Indians refused to concede to a poll tax and various other indignities. In 1908 Gandhi had signed an agreement with the South African government, but the authorities had only honored it in the breach.[28] In order not to antagonize the merchants, the government deployed measures that disproportionately affected the working class. Gandhi wrote to one of his confidants, "I am resolving in my own mind the idea of doing something for the indentured man."[29] It was in this spirit that Gandhi drafted a strong resolution against the poll tax, and although he called for resistance, he did not draft a program or a plan of action for the campaign. Gandhi wanted to help the indentured, but he made no attempt to organize them. "Gandhi hoped to avoid an attempt to mobilize the underclasses, with whom he had no direct contact," writes historian Maureen Swan, "and he relied on an elite campaign, supported by the threat of mass mobilization which was implicit in the inclusion of the £3 tax question, to put pressure on the government."[30] Gandhi's various ashrams trained fewer than forty satyagrahis, whom he hoped to unleash to conduct moral actions to challenge the government. He did tell the minister of the interior that he would urge a general strike of the indentured, although he had no expectation that this call would amount to much beyond its value as a threat to the government.

Looking back at this event on August 8, 1914, Gandhi marveled at the workers who struck work and held fast. "There were 20,000 strikers who left their tools and work because there was something in the air. People said they did not know why they had struck."[31] Actually, the record shows that the workers struck for a host of reasons: some had heard that a rajah would come from India to liberate them; others, that the rajah would come to decapitate them if they did not stop work; yet others acted against the atrocious conditions in the mines and fields; and some hoped to join a rumored column of Indian troops that would overthrow the government. For Gandhi, the strikers "went out on faith."[32] But the Reverend A. A. Bailie perhaps put it best when he noted that the workers did not have a coherent reason to strike, not because they had no grievances, but because they had so many.[33] The movement, Gandhi wrote, "spread beyond expectations":

I never dreamt that 20,000 poor Indians would arise and make their own and their country's name immortal. . . . South African Indians became the talk of the world. In India, rich and poor, young and old, men and women, kings and labourers, Hindus, Muslims, Parsis, Christians, citizens of Bombay, Madras, Calcutta and Lahore—all were roused, became familiar with our history and came to our assistance. The Government was taken aback. The Viceroy, gauging the mood of the people, took their side. All this is public knowledge. I am stating these facts here in order to show the importance of this struggle.[34]

From these working-class people Gandhi learned an enormous lesson: mass action can paralyze a state and force it, if the action is nonviolent, to its knees. The South African government tried to retaliate with viciousness, with police brutality and murder. But the strike held, and the government lost any moral legitimacy before the people.[35]

Gandhi returned to India in 1916 after being pushed to the fore by this mass movement. He did not start a new movement in India but once again got carried by forces that had almost five decades of organization behind them. The modern Indian nationalist movement began with the resolute struggle of the Indian peasantry, who turned to the leadership of people like Gandhi for a host of reasons. Gandhi represented a class that could stand between the inchoate utterance of mass rebellion and the bureaucratic speech of the state: he was part of the infrastructure of the emergent national bourgeoisie, frustrated into organization as the Indian National Congress (from 1885) but, until his arrival, fairly lackadaisical in its annual meetings. Gandhi adopted the style and idiom of the peasants in an attempt to earn their trust and loyalty.[36] For the peasantry, as for many of the other social classes in British India, Gandhi's power lay in the organization of the congress, the rebelliousness of the oppressed classes, the enthusiasm of the middle-class students, the ideology (nonviolence) that he forged out of his experiences, and the early tactical successes of the mass mobilizations he had provoked (the 1917–18 satyagrahas of Champaran, Kheda, and Ahmedabad).[37]

The Uncrowned King: African America and Gandhi Reprised

In the early 1940s, the pace of black struggles in the United States picked up. The wartime economy opened up some opportunities for blacks. Despite this, whites fiercely maintained their Jim Crow privileges. Tensions grew, particularly in congested spaces where the white and black working class confronted each other; they had less opportunity to segregate themselves into protected spaces. Sociologists Charles Johnson and Howard Odum, among others, wrote at that time of the impending antagonism between whites and blacks, with Odum warning of black soldiers who were "organizing shock troop units all over the country" and putting weapons aside for the inevitable "race war."[38]

With the tempo of struggle being pushed from below, the veteran black activist A. Philip Randolph gave the government an ultimatum to end Jim Crow in wartime industries or else he would lead 10,000 people on a march on Washington on July 4, 1941. Freedom had to be fought for, Randolph wrote, "with our gloves off." Responding to the immense majority of blacks, Randolph readied himself for a stiff confrontation. The government quickly capitulated, and the president issued an executive order meeting Randolph's demand.

Alongside Randolph was Bayard Rustin, who had just broken with the communists to become a leader in the pacifist Fellowship of Reconciliation (FOR). In FOR's magazine, Rustin warned, "Many Negroes see mass violence coming. Having lived in a society in which church, school, and home problems have been handled in a violent way, the majority at this point are unable to conceive of a solution by reconciliation and nonviolence."[39] Bitterness, fear, and frustration governed the imagination of those who had begun to squirrel away arms or else hoped for a Japanese victory because, as one person told Rustin, "it don't matter who you're a slave for."[40] To shift the tenor, Rustin argued that civil rights activists had to "identify" in an organic way with the black masses, by fighting daily for justice. "This demands being so integral a part of the Negro community in its day-to-day struggle, so close to it in similarity of work, so near its standard of living that when problems arise he who stands forth to judge, to plan, to suggest, or to lead is really at one with the Negro masses."[41] But all this talk of nonviolence remained premature.

In 1943, when Randolph began to talk about the need for a nonviolent movement against racism, he faced a great deal of resistance.[42] Du Bois wrote a searing attack on Randolph's desire to adopt Gandhianism.[43] Du Bois conceded that blacks had made some gains from their economic perseverance and from their legal struggles: "Our case in America is not happy, but it is far from desperate."[44] The African American situation, however, was different from India's. Gandhi's struggle thrived in a context where a tiny minority oppressed the vast majority, whereas in the United States blacks comprised a small percentage of the population, and any call for nonviolent resistance "would be playing into the hands of our enemies." Du Bois's major point was that Gandhian tactics were alien to the United States. Fasting, public prayer, and self-sacrifice had been "bred into the very bone of India for more than three thousand years." But African Americans would mock that approach, should the black leadership "blindly copy methods without thought and consideration."[45]

In fact, few Gandhians in the United States advocated or adopted fasting as a method. Shridharani wrote that Gandhianism "should merely point the way," as fasting "may appear ridiculous in America," where it lacked "the same social significance" it had in India.[46] "Other countries," Shridharani wrote in 1939, "are likely to evolve different forms of self-purification, when and if they engage in a Satyagraha."[47] Du Bois's association of Gandhianism with fasting, without engaging the meaning of self-purification in nonviolent resistance, encouraged the view of Gandhi as mystical and Gandhianism as a specifically Indian political philosophy.

Two activists of FOR traveled to India, where they learned of Gandhianism first hand. In 1941 Ralph Templin and Jay Holmes Smith returned to the United States, set up the Harlem ashram in New York City, and translated Gandhian ideas into the theory of Kristagraha, or action on the basis of Christ, an amalgam of Christianity and satyagraha. One of the residents of the ashram was James Farmer, who joined in the creation of the Congress of Racial Equality (CORE) from this base camp.[48] They began to experiment with their version of truth just as ordinary African Americans in southern cities had begun to test the limits of Jim Crow. In Birmingham, Alabama, historian Robin Kelley notes, various organizations (the National Urban League, the Interracial Committee, and the Alabama Christian Movement for Human Rights) spent a decade, from the early 1940s to the early 1950s, trying to harness the everyday frustrations of blacks: a lack of employment, a lack of decent housing, a lack of good schools, and a denial of dignity.[49] Both the minimal demands (better housing, better schools) and the maximum demands (total social transformation) had become clear to the black masses and, to an extent, to the black leadership. What was also clear to the leadership, at the very least, was that the fight had to be nonviolent or else the retribution would be stronger than the people could bear. What had not emerged clearly as yet was the form of struggle, the instrument that would emerge from popular protests. The anarchy of protests, helped along by organized forces, would reveal the tactical form of struggle. The commune, the soviet, the workers' council, and others emerged from the heart of the collision between spontaneous unrest and organization.

In 1955 Rosa Parks's action set in motion a well-organized rebellion against Jim Crow. Thousands had been prepared for action by small forays into nonviolent resistance and by more militant confrontations with the police and white supremacists.[50] Protesters took to the streets, withdrew from the buses, and inaugurated the mass struggle called the civil rights movement. The tactical form was simple: the sit-down strike, the refusal to leave a place where the body was not wanted. Such actions uncovered the essence of Gandhian civil disobedience. For CORE's James Farmer, "It was Martin Luther King, Jr., who established the shrine of Gandhian nonviolence in a southern city in the United States of America, drawing to him, as a magnet, pilgrims and press from all over the world."[51] King's use of Gandhian and Christian imagery, of love and suffering, drew from the decade-long Kristagraha tradition. But in truth, as historian Taylor Branch records, "nonviolence, like the boycott itself, had begun more or less by accident."[52] It is by such accidents that history is propelled.

The civil rights movement, like the freedom movement in India, did not start with its leadership. It began in the acts of the southern black working class, whose refusal to quietly ride at the back of the bus or accept second-class employment in a racist job market was spurred by experience in the world wars and by the legacy of the Congress of Industrial Organization unions. If Gandhi learned his politics among the working class in South Africa and India, King, too, learned to bend to the will of the people while he picked tobacco in the outskirts of Hartford, Connecticut. Protected from the worst of white supremacy by the elite black circles of Atlanta in which he grew up, King did not face the everyday racist trauma as the black working class faced it. With a

few fellow Morehouse College students in the summer of 1944, King worked in the fields of Connecticut with black workers, many from the U.S. South and others from the Caribbean.

While toiling with the workers, King called his mother and told her that he wanted to be a minister; he had found his calling here, among the people who survived to struggle for a better day. King, like Gandhi, was led by the will of the masses, by such stalwarts as high school student Claudette Colvin and seamstress-activist Rosa Parks. The courage of ordinary people drew King into the struggle, and the Gandhian experiences of Farmer, Rustin, and eventually James Lawson served him well. King took the everyday commonsense non-violence of the movement and raised it to philosophy, which, along with his immense charisma, was his contribution to freedom. In 1958 King wrote, "Non-violent resistance had emerged as the technique of the movement, while love stood as the regulating ideal. In other words, Christ furnished the spirit and motivation, while Gandhi furnished the method."[53] King could have added, "The Churches provided the institutional framework, the radicals provided the disciplined leg-work, and the people provided the energy and enthusiasm as well as the resilience." King was pushed by the socialism of his people out of his own narrow class confines into the solidarity of generations.

King's views did not go unchallenged. In the late 1950s Robert Williams, head of the Monroe, North Carolina, branch of the NAACP, had espoused the view that there is no substitute for armed resistance against a recalcitrant and hostile Jim Crow establishment.[54] As the NAACP expelled Williams, King addressed his case in *Liberation*. Williams, King argued, offered two paths of struggle, either "we must be cringing and submissive or take up arms." King disagreed, since the people of Monroe themselves had used "collective com-munity action" to win "significant victory without use of arms or threats of violence." Then King offered his view on the power of nonviolence as he had learned it from Gandhi's example:

There is more power in socially organized masses on the march than there is in guns in the hands of a few desperate men. Our enemies would prefer to deal with a small armed group rather than with a huge, unarmed but resolute mass of people. However it is necessary that the mass-action method be persistent and unyielding. Gandhi said that the Indian people must "never let them rest," referring to the British. He urged them to keep protesting daily and weekly, in a variety of ways. This method inspired and organized the Indian masses and disorganized and demobilized the British. It educates its myriad participants, socially and morally. All history teaches us that like a turbulent ocean beating great cliffs into fragments of rock, the determined movement of people incessantly demanding their rights always disintegrates the old order.[55]

While King knew that the black working class in the South had responded well to the call for nonviolent mass resistance, he also knew that class fissures in the "community" had already prevented the formation of the kind of total resistance he had envisioned. King had read E. Franklin Frazier's *Black Bourgeoisie* (1957), in which the sociologist cataloged the economic powerlessness of the African American middle class, who nonetheless wielded political power over segregated black neighborhoods.[56] In 1958, in *Stride toward Freedom*, King cited Frazier's book, noted that it was unlikely that the middle class would bear the "ordeals and sacrifices" of nonviolence, pointed out that the method "is not dependent on its unanimous acceptance," and then hoped that a few dedicated resisters could "serve as the moral force to awaken the slumbering national conscience."[57]

The American engagement with Gandhi moved from mass protest to individual witness to a combination of the two. But for the struggle against Jim Crow, Gandhi was never a mystical, almost extraterrestrial, Vishnu-like figure, but a shrewd political tactician whose weapons of the weak could, with care, be adopted elsewhere. The Indian Shridharani, Gandhi's chief interpreter in the United States, had called him an "unwilling avatar." Indeed he was. In black working-class and militant African American circles, the Mahatma was transformed into a comrade in arms.

Gandhi and King learned their nonviolence from the masses, whose courage and resilience surprised both of them. It was from these acts of resistance that they developed their theories. Gandhi's Oriental and King's Christian sheen allowed them space to maneuver. Their faith of nonviolence earned them the goodwill of the masses, who were ready to act, and it paralyzed the state, whose response could only turn the population against ruling classes who cannot act without the consent of large sections of the citizenry. Frazier's frustrations with the nonviolent strategy reflected the impatience of those who wanted change to come fast but were not ready to find the organizational form to bring the masses into making that change happen. The real danger, not identified by Frazier, is that whereas Gandhi and King drew their lessons from the masses, and drew the masses into ever-powerful mobilizations, they could just as easily betray the needs and aspirations of those very people.

NOTES

The material for this essay began to accumulate as I researched *Everybody Was Kung Fu Fighting*. What I could not fit into that work I presented as a talk at the symposium in Madison, Wisconsin (2004), to honor the 100th anniversary of Du Bois's *Souls of Black Folk*. Nellie McKay kindly invited me, Robert Warrior and I held it down for the Indians, and Maurice Wallace gave me very useful feedback. A raw version appeared in *Little India*, and for that I thank my editor Achal Mehra. I could not have written this essay without the pioneering work of Sudarshan Kapur's *Raising Up a Prophet* and Richard Fox's "Passage from India." Thanks to Michael West and Bill Martin for their patient encouragement.

1. Brown, *Gandhi's Rise*, 118.

2. For example, in 1933 Leonard Howell, a founder of Rastafari, thought that he might become the Gandhi of Jamaica. See Lee, *Le premier Rasta*, 127.

3. General Jan Smuts had a more caustic view of Gandhi, whose departure in 1914 he welcomed in a letter to Sir Benjamin Robertson: "The saint has left our shores. I sincerely hope for ever" (Brown, *Gandhi's Rise*, 3). Winston Churchill's snide remarks (1931) speak to Gandhi's mobilization of Oriental tropes: "It is alarming and also nauseating to see Mr. Gandhi, a seditious Middle Temple lawyer, now posing as a *fakir* of a type well known in the East, striding half-naked up the steps of the viceregal palace, while he is still organising and conducting a defiant campaign of civil disobedience, to parlay on equal terms with the representative of the King-Emperor." See Churchill, *Never Give In!*, 97.

4. Frazier, "Negro and Non-Resistance" (March 1924), 213.

5. Wells-Barnett, *On Lynching*. For an excellent analysis of lynching and violence, see Feimester, "'Ladies and Lynching.'"

6. NAACP, *Thirty Years of Lynching*.

7. Zangrando, *NAACP Crusade*.

8. All of this is from Horne's highly informed *Black and Brown*, 156–80.

9. Ibid., 92, 110–11.

10. There is always a temptation to read Frazier as impetuous and exaggerated, given the reaction to his *Black Bourgeoisie*.

11. Du Bois, *Correspondence*, 283–84.

12. Ibid., 284.

13. Frazier, "Negro and Non-Resistance" (June 1924), 58–59.

14. Gandhi, "To the American Negro," 225.

15. Van Tyne, *India*, 110.

16. Shridharani, *My India*, 276.

17. Beall, "Women under Indentured Labor."

18. His concentration on Indians is not an indication of a lack of alliance or support, for he worked very closely with the Transvaal Chinese Association and with the Natal Native Congress. On the Chinese, see Harris, "Gandhi, the Chinese, and Passive Resis-

tance." On the Africans (and the Natal Native Congress), see Prashad, *Everybody Was Kung Fu Fighting*, 94–96.

19. Swan, *Gandhi*, 50.

20. I have relied on the outstanding, unpublished dissertation by the former speaker of the South African National Assembly, Frene Ginwala, "Class, Consciousness, and Control," notably 147 onward for this section.

21. Swan, *Gandhi*, 64.

22. Gandhi, "Russia and India," *Indian Opinion*, September 8, 1906, in *Collected Works*, 5:413.

23. Ibid.

24. Gandhi, *Satyagraha in South Africa*, in *Collected Works*, 5:421.

25. Gandhi, "A Brief Explanation," *Indian Opinion*, February 22, 1908, 99–101, in *Collected Works*, 8:100.

26. Gandhi, "Duty of Hawkers," *Indian Opinion*, January 8, 1910, in *Collected Works*, 10:123.

27. Ibid.

28. It was in the context of that agreement that Gandhi wrote, "A satyagrahi bids goodbye to fear. He is therefore never afraid of trusting his opponent. Even if the opponent plays him false twenty times, the satyagrahi is ready to trust him for the twenty-first time, for an implicit trust in human nature is the very essence of his creed" (*Satyagraha in South Africa*, 159).

29. Swan, *Gandhi*, 242.

30. Ibid., 244.

31. Gandhi, "Speech at London Reception," *Indian Opinion*, September 30, 1914, in *Collected Works*, 12:523–24 (quote on 524).

32. Ibid.

33. Swan, *Gandhi*, 252.

34. Gandhi, "The Last Satyagraha Campaign: My Experience," *Indian Opinion*, December 1914, 508–19, in *Collected Works*, 12:509–10.

35. As Jan Smuts put it to Gandhi, "I often wish you took to violence like in English strikes, and then we would know at once how to dispose of you. But you will not injure even the enemy. You desire victory by self-suffering alone and never transgress your self-imposed limits of courtesy and chivalry. And that is what reduces us to sheer helplessness" (Gandhi, *Satyagraha in South Africa*, 325–26).

36. Guha, "Discipline and Mobilise," offers an insightful analysis of Gandhi's relationship to the mass movement that developed around his persona.

37. On Champaran, see Pouchepadass, *Champaran and Gandhi*; on Kheda, see Hardiman, *Peasant Nationalists*.

38. Singh, *Black Is a Country*, 105.

39. Rustin, "Negro and Nonviolence," 8.

40. Ibid., 9.

41. Ibid., 10.

42. Pfeffer, *A. Philip Randolph*, 64.

43. Du Bois, "As the Crow Flies."

44. Ibid., 110.

45. Ibid.

46. Shridharani, *My India*, 281.

47. Shridharani, *War without Violence*, 13.

48. A longer version of this essay will offer more details of the ashram.

49. Kelley, *Race Rebels*, 55–100, esp. 82–85.

50. Ibid.

51. Farmer, *Lay Bare the Heart*, 185.

52. Branch, *Parting the Waters*, 195.

53. King, "Experiment in Love," 17.

54. Robert Williams would eventually put his case in his 1962 *Negroes with Guns*, reprinted in 1998. For the context and Williams's subsequent political career in Cuba and China, see Tyson, *Radio Free Dixie*.

55. King, "Social Organization of Nonviolence," 33.

56. Frazier, *Black Bourgeoisie*.

57. King, *Stride toward Freedom* and *Testament of Hope*, 485–86.

The Rise and Fall of Caribbean Black Power

BRIAN MEEKS

Whatever the objective forces propelling a people towards struggle, resistance and revolution, they would come to that struggle in their own cultural terms.—CEDRIC ROBINSON, Black Marxism

In 1968, Black Power swept across the Caribbean. The immediate trigger was a riot in Jamaica following the banning from the island of Black Power activist and scholar Walter Rodney. Then a lecturer at the Mona campus of the University of the West Indies, the Guyanese-born Rodney was attending a Black Power conference in Canada when the Jamaican government prohibited him from returning to his job.[1] Caribbean Black Power briefly rose to a crescendo in the "1970 Revolution" in Trinidad and Tobago,[2] when a mass movement climaxed in an aborted army mutiny against the government of Eric Williams, the famous historian and erstwhile anticolonial nationalist. The upsurge, however, was short lived: by the middle of the 1970s almost all the important radical Caribbean movements had switched to a Marxist-Leninist ideology,[3] abandoning, at least overtly, the nationalist and populist insights of Caribbean Black Power.

What led to the eclipse of the Black Power movement? Was it the military success of Marxism-Leninism in the Third World? Was it the result of weaknesses and lacunae in the theory and praxis of the nascent Black Power movement? This essay examines these questions as it traces the paths of Caribbean radicalism, paths that led, ultimately, to the ascendancy of the Marxist-Leninist notion of the vanguard party in the Grenadian Revolution and its tragic collapse in 1983.

The name Black Power came from the effervescent struggle for racial justice in the United States, but the Caribbean movement had multiple roots, deriving from a complex interplay of local and international histories. The primary tributary in the twentieth century was Marcus Garvey's Universal Negro Improvement Association (UNIA), which was a significant social and political force in Jamaica, Trinidad, and other Caribbean territories in the 1920s and 1930s.[4] Another powerful local current emerged after the coronation of Haile Selassie as Ethiopian emperor in 1930. The Rastafarian movement, deriving its name from Selassie's original title, Ras (Prince) Tafari, combined millenarianism with militant pan-Africanism and biblical prophecy. Rastafari, diverse and multipronged in its organizational form, gradually developed followers among the Jamaican poor and spread by the early 1960s to other parts of the Caribbean.[5] There is little doubt, however, that the U.S. movement, which was followed with immense interest in the Caribbean, particularly by young people, was the catalyst that brought these nascent trends together. When the civil rights movement made a leftward turn to Black Power in the mid-1960s, radical trends in the Caribbean found a ready-made slogan under which to organize their own deep dissatisfaction with their societies and governments.

Several striking features marked the Caribbean Black Power scene from roughly 1968 to 1973. In Jamaica, as the previous history might suggest, the movement was centrally influenced by powerful Rastafarian currents that stressed the importance of cultural determination in politics and asserted, against the official Jamaican ideology of peaceful multiracial coexistence, the saliency of race as a determining factor in people's lives. By design, Black Power in Jamaica was decentralized, multipolar, and community based. Its ethos was captured in the pages of that essential, radical Caribbean newspaper *Abeng*,[6] which served as a popular forum for expressing a range of conflicting views, rather than as an organ with a single party line.

The various currents of the movement were concentrated around the University of the West Indies at Mona, although they were not exclusively found there. The dominant trends advocated a grassroots/populist notion of the role of intellectuals in the popular movement. In 1967 Garth White expressed such a position at a meeting of the radical intellectual forum, the New World movement.[7] White, then a leading radical student at the University of the West Indies at Mona, attacked the view of Lloyd Best, the noted Trinidadian economist and activist, that intellectuals should focus on research that would provide the movement with feasible options. Rather, White argued, intellectuals should become activists, merging their lives with those of the people: "What about New World? The days of sipping tea and airily contemplating 'high issues' is past. . . . An opportunity for direct political action has been placed in the laps of those desirous to see social change. The possibility exists that existing structures may crumble. They certainly are crumbling. If they crumble the intellectuals will be in no position to move. . . . [We need to mobilize,] . . . actively becoming one of the people and not in any patronizing way."[8]

In Trinidad the 1970 Black Power revolution—by any measure the high point of this period—gave birth to a multiplicity of organizations with competing ideological streams and multiple poles of authority. Black Power groups like the United Movement for the Reconstruction of Black Identity, based in southern Trinidad, competed with Young Power and the island's version of the U.S. Black Panther Party. The trade unions brought to the movement their own spectrum of ideological perspectives, with Marxist trends having significant influence in organizations like Joe Young's Transport and Industrial Workers Union and George Weekes's powerful Oilfield Workers Trade Union. The Tapia House movement, despite being headed by Lloyd Best, one of the most capable Caribbean thinkers of his generation, stood aside from the mass movement and was subsequently marginalized.[9]

It was the National Joint Action Committee (NJAC), a student-led group,[10] that would emerge as the leading force in the marching phase of the movement when young, often unemployed people controlled the streets of Port of Spain and other Trinidadian urban centers. NJAC started from a radically anti-imperialist and Black Nationalist position, as elaborated in the pamphlet *Conventional Politics or Revolution?* "For the people of Tobago, for instance, politics involves the recovery of their land from the white parasites who control the villages, an end to the assault on their dignity by white tourism. . . . For the suffering workers, politics involves freedom from the exploitation in the factories, on the estates, in the offices, on the building sites and the right of control."[11]

On a wider Caribbean level, the goals espoused by NJAC were more famously stated by Walter Rodney in his collected essays, *The Groundings with My Brothers.* Rodney defined Black Power as "(i) The break with imperialism which is historically white racist; (ii) the assumption of power by the black masses in the islands; and (iii) the cultural reconstruction of the society in the image of the blacks."[12] Although radically anti-imperialist and African centered, Rodney's views were far from exclusivist, as we shall see.

NJAC's primary and ultimately fatal weakness was its acceptance and reproduction of Trinidad's reigning political culture and leadership style. This syndrome, epitomized by Eric Williams, stressed reverence and obeisance to the *jefe maximo*. As Winston Suite, a contemporary activist not affiliated with it has suggested, NJAC, as a movement, took an exclusive and monopolistic approach to the struggle: "The leader of NJAC had a sense of messianic mission; he hears a voice from within; he identifies himself with everything as though revolution is not a drama. . . . NJAC behaved as though the movement was its own. . . . They wanted you to do whatever they wanted to be done; they did not want you as an independent entity."[13] NJAC's failure to break with the past eventually resulted in the loss of its leading role in the popular movement. At the same time, the group's adherence to the old political culture and leadership syndrome anticipated the centralist, vanguardist politics that would come to prominence with the ascendancy of Marxism-Leninism.

Similar if distinctive trends emerged on the other islands of the eastern Caribbean. Forum, a nascent Black Power discussion and action movement, emerged autonomously in a number of territories, including Antigua, St. Lucia, and Grenada. Forum's Antigua branch eventually became the Antigua Caribbean Liberation Movement (ACLM), under the leadership of Tim Hector. Although notoriously unsuccessful in electoral politics, Hector's ACLM held together, and through the radical newspaper *Outlet* provided sustained resistance to corruption and venality in Antiguan politics for more than three decades.[14]

The greater focus inevitably has to be placed on Grenada, where the radical movement gained power through revolutionary insurrection. There, the Joint Endeavour for Welfare, Education and Liberation (Jewel) emerged out of Forum and operated as a grassroots, Black Power organization with a broad anti-imperialist, "New Worldist"[15] platform that emphasized direct political action. The other notable Grenadian Black Power formation was the Movement for Assemblies of the People (MAP). As the name implied, MAP was heavily influenced by the notion of popular assemblies as alternative political structures to parliament—a notion associated with C. L. R. James, the celebrated Caribbean scholar and activist. Like Jewel, MAP supported spontaneous, direct action. The two movements eventually found common ground: in 1974 they came together to form the New Jewel Movement (NJM), united in their opposition to the government of Eric Gairy, Grenada's repressive and mercurial prime minister.[16]

From the very beginning, Black Power in the Caribbean connected with popular currents and garnered broad, mass support. In Trinidad, NJAC initially stood at the head of a broad and popular mass movement. The Jamaican movement, always more inchoate, nonetheless generated *Abeng* and acted as the stimulus for a process of popular education and mobilization, the effects of which were not completely felt until the mid- to late 1970s. The 1972 electoral victory of the People's National Party (PNP), now headed by the charismatic Michael Manley, son of the late PNP founder and former prime minister Norman Manley, heralded a peculiarly Jamaican radical movement, albeit one in which anti-imperialism operated within the constraints of the traditional political framework. In Grenada, the two groups that eventually merged to form the NJM were able to organize relatively massive crowds, ranging from the 1972 La Sagesse protest against an English lord's attempt to privatize beaches, to the campaign against Eric Gairy's push for independence from Britain, which was seen as a diversion from the island's social problems.

By the early 1970s, then, Black Power had become a powerful force in various Caribbean societies. A burgeoning movement guided by notions of black nationalism and wedded to an anti-imperialist sense of autonomous Caribbean development, it was accompanied by populist and community-based notions of political participation[17] and mobilization. More to the point, by the early 1970s Caribbean Black Power actually had the ability to influence and mobilize large bodies of people.

1974–1983: The Eclipse of Black Power and Rise of Marxism-Leninism

By the late 1970s, however, the political landscape had changed and Black Power had been eclipsed. With the defeat in April 1970 of the mass movement it had mobilized against the government of Eric Williams, Trinidad's NJAC retreated from the center to the margins, having lost its status as the country's primary revolutionary agency. This was due not only to its approach to leadership but also to a new, overwhelmingly "cultural" orientation, which served to reduce its influence in critical sectors, particularly among the unionized working class.

The Trinidadian movement, after a continued surge during which the radical guerrilla grouping NUFF[18] emerged and militant action increased among students and workers, declined and then practically fell, as the twin-island nation settled into the long quiescence of the oil boom of the mid- to late 1970s. In Jamaica, Black Power divided into two. One section was won to the traditional party system and became the radical cutting edge of Michael Manley's resurgent PNP. The other section was won to Marxism-Leninism, eventually becoming, in 1978, the Workers Party of Jamaica (WPJ). In Grenada, the early NJM strategy of direct action and mass mobilization carried the movement forward to the 1973–74 islandwide general strike and a lockdown against the Gairy regime. Still, the NJM was unable to remove Gairy from power. When, in February 1974, the Grenadian prime minister proceeded to take the country into independence in the face of a strike, and against the wishes of the broad, popular opposition, it was evident that the movement and its chosen approach to politics had suffered a strategic defeat. This led to the important decision by the leadership of the NJM to abandon Black Power as an ideological and organizational strategy and to embrace a local version of Marxism-Leninism.

From 1974, then, with the emergence in Jamaica of the predecessor to the WPJ and the decision of the NJM to change course, we can observe the rise, growth, and partial consolidation of Marxist-Leninist organizations throughout the Anglophone Caribbean. This transformation was accompanied by an adoption of the principles of democratic centralism, hermetic-cell systems, and selective membership. If we take Garth White's notion of the "merging of the intellectual with the people" as a central theme in Caribbean Black Power organizational ethos, then the Leninist philosophy that replaced it saw the party and its members as above the people, patronizingly leading and guiding them. Thus the pamphlet published with the 1978 launching of the WPJ proclaimed, "Whether it is England or America, Angola or Mozambique, capitalism and colonialism prevent the majority of working people from really knowing themselves. . . . The first principle of the real communist working class party therefore is that only the most serious and conscious workers can join. Then it is their job to teach, to guide, to lead, to draw up the rest—not because they have title or position but because the communist workers are the ones who put out more sacrifice, more work and more struggle against oppression than anyone else."[19]

Vanguard party principles did allow for a strong and focused organization. In Grenada, the one place where a classic revolutionary situation emerged, the prior, though very brief existence of a vanguard party laid the basis for an insurrectionary politics leading to the seizure of power in 1979. The WPJ, however, was never able to seriously break into the mainstream of Jamaican politics and never became a truly national force. It garnered only a limited popularity in specific communities where it gave assistance in areas such as security, health care, and legal aid, or in areas where its cadres were particularly well-placed, as in the media. Was this the result, as the party's central committee regularly intimated, of the strength of anticommunism and the absence of a revolutionary situation? While these provide part of the explanation for the party's weakness, it was the WPJ's exclusivist organizational form and the limited appeal of its "proletarian" line that ultimately undermined its popularity.

The Power of an International Paradigm

The failure of Trinidadian Black Power to consolidate as a political movement as well as the inability of the early NJM to remove, or even thwart, Eric Gairy partly explains the waning influence of Black Power in the Caribbean by the mid-1970s. The critical factor in this process, however, was the rise of Marxism-Leninism, which eclipsed Black Power as the dominant, radical paradigm.

Many factors account for the rise of Marxism-Leninism. The Tet Offensive in 1968 seemed to indicate that the Vietnamese had not only survived the U.S. military onslaught but were capable of going on the offensive; this signaled the beginning of a sea change in support for Leninism as a political strategy. That view was further enhanced in the mid-1970s when all the important and successful African liberation movements claimed Marxist-Leninist credentials. In the classic case of Angola in 1975, the non-Leninist movements—Holden Roberto's National Front for the Liberation of Angola and Jonas Savimbi's National Union for the Total Independence of Angola—suffered the opprobrium of being on the same side as the invading South Africans and the United States in opposing the legitimate (and Marxist) Popular Movement for the Liberation of Angola government. In South Africa itself, the apartheid regime was opposed by the militant South African Communist Party (SACP) and the African National Congress, many of whose members either belonged to or were closely allied with the SACP.

In the Caribbean, the Cuban Revolution emerged as a more powerful example than any of these other cases. In addition to Cuba's struggle to survive in its early years (a period of high sugar prices and ample Soviet assistance), the nation's progressive social programs at home and concrete military and civilian assistance abroad, particularly in Africa, served to consolidate the view that if you were radical and anti-imperialist, then it was difficult not to be Marxist and Leninist.

The Marxist-Leninist paradigm of success translated into a number of subtheses. The first centered on the taking of power. Here a hybrid approach based on Bolshevik and Cuban examples emerged. Leninist practices contributed the notion that a small, revolutionary, vanguard party could lead a mass revolution of working people, as so well exemplified in the Russian Revolution. From Third World armed revolts and especially Cuba came the notion of the guerrilla *foco*, as espoused by Regis Debray in his widely circulated book *Revolution in the Revolution?* In Debray's conception the guerrilla *foco*, a small vanguard guerrilla group would provide the model for revolution in rural Third World countries (Debray himself would be captured in 1967 while accompanying Che Guevara's failed guerrilla effort in Bolivia). This combination in essence asserted that it was necessary for a small, committed group of militants to prepare the revolution, which would most likely take the form of an insurrection against the existing state. Allied to the vanguard and *foco* approach was the view that in order to be truly Leninist, one had to work first and foremost among the working classes, as opposed to the "transitional strata" of the unemployed and the petite bourgeoisie.[20]

Second, the political and economic strategy of the postrevolutionary regime was dominated by the notion of a noncapitalist path or socialist orientation. This anchored the new state's development to the false premise that the Soviet Union was willing to and capable of providing military and economic largesse to any successful, Third World, revolutionary government.

The third subthesis captured the ideology of the movement. Here the primary revolutionary literature consisted of the writings not just of Marx but also of Lenin and, occasionally, even Stalin. The works of these writers were easily available from the Soviet publishing house, Progress Publishers; by contrast, literature from other sources was much more difficult to obtain. Up to the early 1970s, the writings of those with the greatest influence on Caribbean Black Power—C. L. R. James, Walter Rodney, Frantz Fanon, Eldridge Cleaver, Malcolm X, and Amilcar Cabral—had been in limited circulation. After 1975, such works became even scarcer, replaced by the Marxist classics and Soviet writers like Karen N. Brutents and Rostislav Ulyanovsky.[21] The rich debates in British Marxism, Antonio Gramsci's powerful work on hegemony, and the published debates surrounding prominent communist George Padmore's and literary star Richard Wright's prior ruptures with international communism were thus largely unknown to the radical movement that emerged after the collapse of Black Power.[22]

The outcome of this Marxist-Leninist turn in the Caribbean radical movement is well known. In Grenada, the decision to adopt Leninist tactics provided the NJM with a tactical flexibility more in tune with the period of "calm" that followed the failed general strike. This approach facilitated the participation of the NJM in the People's Alliance popular front against Gairy in the 1976 elections. In what was generally considered a corrupt exercise, Gairy narrowly won. The NJM became a part of the parliamentary opposition, and as head of the party with the most seats in the alliance, the NJM's Maurice Bishop became Leader of the Opposition. This constitutional position served the party well. Unlike the earlier period when the NJM had no legitimate voice outside Grenada, Bishop now spoke in regional forums as the leader of Grenada's "loyal opposition." Thus when the NJM overthrew the Gairy regime and seized power on March 13, 1979,[23] it was not the work of unknown coup plotters but the action of the very familiar Bishop-led opposition that had been campaigning against Gairy's arbitrary actions for three years. The other critical dimension, of course, was the actual taking of power, which required many years of preparation. In any situation where secrecy is necessarily at a premium—and this was especially the case in tiny Grenada—a clandestine army could only be organized and trained in the context of a political organization with a quasi-military structure, strict compartmentalization, and top-down hierarchy. This was precisely what the vanguard party paradigm provided.

While the vanguard approach made the seizure of power possible, it also became a millstone around the NJM's neck in its four and a half years in power.[24] The party's highly selective criteria for membership severely constricted the number of people who could join it, especially at a moment when it was relatively popular and needed as many members as possible to run the state apparatus. The result was inordinate physical pressure on the few actual party members, which contributed immeasurably to a breakdown of the party in 1983. At the same time, the principle of selectivity served to alienate the NJM from the people. When, for instance, party comrades in September 1983 tried to defend the Central Committee's decision to detain Maurice Bishop, they were often met with the incredulous response, "What is the Central Committee?"

Most analysts argue that the 1983 crisis in the NJM, which led to the death of Bishop and a number of his closest associates, was the result of an ultraleft conspiracy led by Deputy Prime Minister Bernard Coard.[25] My position has been that there is little evidence and even less motive for such a long-standing conspiracy. A more convincing explanation may be found in the vanguardist structures of the party, which led to its alienation from its popular base. As external pressure from the U.S. regime of Ronald Reagan intensified in early 1983 amidst growing economic difficulties, support for the NJM began to ebb even further. The NJM, used to operating in a clandestine, hierarchical fashion, sought in the middle of 1983 to deal with these tests not by bringing the people into the revolution in an unprecedented way but, rather, by juggling with the notion of leadership, as it had done in the past. A top-down solution was sought to a problem that required a massive popular intervention and the democratic reorganization of politics. The subsequent attempt to establish a joint leadership between Bishop and Coard was disastrous, leading to the detention of Bishop after he initially agreed to the measure and then reneged on his agreement. The flawed decision to solve the revolution's political problems from the top was demonstrated in the sequence of events that followed: a popular and successful attempt to release Bishop, the takeover of the fort by Bishop's forces, and then the murder of Bishop and the army's retaking of the captured fort.

The unraveling of the Left in Jamaica followed a different course. After being officially launched as a communist party in 1978, the WPJ grew in a limited but steady fashion over the following two years. In a period when the PNP and its more leftist Youth Organization dominated the anti-imperialist platform, there were clear strictures on the possibility of the growth of the WPJ, imposed first by the fact that in many respects the two parties were saying similar things. There was also the overwhelming popularity of Michael Manley, whose early social programs and "democratic socialist" rhetoric had inspired the poor. Nonetheless, the WPJ was able to establish strongholds in a few areas in Kingston, where its cadres had helped to defend the community against invading gunmen and provided invaluable legal and medical services. The WPJ also had some strength in a number of rural areas where the agricultural working class had long traditions of trade union struggle.[26]

Several events combined to undermine the WPJ. After the electoral defeat of the Manley government in the bloody 1980 elections,[27] it became apparent how much the entire Left had depended on the relatively moderate, "democratic socialist" PNP for its survival. Whereas the PNP could, albeit with significant difficulty, resume its role as a traditional electoral opposition party, the communist WPJ remained in a no-man's-land, caught between a clandestine preparation for imminent insurrection and its attempt to establish itself as a "legitimate" opposition party.[28] This latter objective was fatally undermined after the Grenada events of October 1983. The party, aided by statements from its leaders, was branded in the Jamaican and Caribbean press as part of the regional ultraleft conspiracy against Bishop. Indeed, in the wake of the PNP's defeat, when anticommunist sympathies became widespread in Jamaica, the WPJ was portrayed as the very source of the anti-Bishop conspiracy.

The WPJ was certainly the party with the closest links to the Grenadian leadership. A number of WPJ cadres worked in various capacities in Grenada, and WPJ leader Trevor Munroe consulted regularly with the NJM. It is highly unlikely that the WPJ could have "instructed" the proud NJM leadership to detain Maurice Bishop, but a concurrence with the decision would have been an important ideological green light. Whether this did occur is yet to be proven, but Munroe did not immediately condemn Bishop's murder, leaving a strong impression that the WPJ was implicated in the decision to detain and execute the Grenadian leader. Whatever popularity the WPJ had gained up to this point[29] was lost, never to be regained. The party's failure to win even a single seat in the 1986 local government elections signaled its death knell. By the turn of the decade, the WPJ had dissolved itself, and a phase in radical Jamaican politics had come to an end. Michael Manley was reelected by a landslide in 1989, but with a policy that eschewed the radical nationalism of his earlier regime and accepted the basic tenets of the brave new neoliberal world. The PNP's ability to accomplish this volte-face was no doubt facilitated by the self-dissolution of the WPJ, and thus the absence of a strong popular force demanding more consistent resistance to U.S. and International Monetary Fund demands for a retreat from radicalism. In sum, the program of vanguard elitism weakened, undermined, and in the case of Grenada, the only instance in which an unambiguously leftist movement came to power, destroyed the Caribbean radical movement of the 1970s.

The Matter of Ideology

The failure of elite vanguardism leaves open the question of ideology. Was the adoption of Marxism by Caribbean radical movements a historical error? Or was the error not so much Marxism as an ideology as Leninism, that is, vanguardism, as political tactics?

To attempt to address these questions, I engage with an important intervention by Alex Dupuy, who some years ago wrote an article titled "Race and Class in the Postcolonial Caribbean: The Views of Walter Rodney."[30] Dupuy argues that Rodney went through a transition. In his early work, as captured in *The Groundings with My Brothers*, Rodney is a Black Power advocate. He later travels to Africa, where he writes his classic *How Europe Underdeveloped Africa*,[31] and then returns to Guyana, where he engages in political activity and writes his posthumously published *History of the Guyanese Working People*.[32]

These two periods, Dupuy argues, represented an ideological movement, as Rodney makes the transition to a Marxian mode of analysis. Rodney's Black

Power, Dupuy asserts, is an essentialist discourse, a false consciousness that is exclusivist and therefore fundamentally antidemocratic: "(*Groundings*) . . . remained trapped in the essentialist and racialist categories and language created by . . . imperialism. The ultimate consequence of this racialist discourse is that despite Rodney's claim that the Black Power movement did not aim to create a racially intolerant society, it could not but recreate exclusivist and hence fundamentally antidemocratic practices."[33]

Dupuy develops his reasoning as follows: Rodney recognizes that in the Caribbean there are different racial groups, yet he reduces them to black and white. Such an approach, Dupuy argues, robs distinctive ethnic groups of their cultural and class differences. This applies to both the "black" and "white" groups. For Rodney, Dupuy asserts, class differences among black people are seen not as fundamental social attributes but as aberrant behavior, a distortion of the love that should exist among "black brothers." Black Power, Dupuy further maintains, simultaneously deprives white persons of their social distinctiveness and right to political choice. By fetishizing color, Dupuy argues, Black Power, as proposed by the early Rodney, made all whites exploiters of blacks and made all black exploiters dupes or traitors. Black Power further excluded revolutionary whites from participating in the struggle to overthrow capital.

Dupuy, however, misreads Rodney. While it is possible to find interpretations of Black Power that are indeed racially exclusive and deny the possibility of persons defined as white playing a role in "liberation," this is not Rodney's approach in *Groundings*. In this text Rodney explains at length that Black Power is not concerned with an exclusivist or narrowly racialist agenda. Here he uses an example from the famous Black Panther Party leader and later pan-Africanist Stokely Carmichael (Kwame Ture):

> Cuba is the only country in the West Indies and in this hemisphere that has broken with white power. That is why Stokely Carmichael can visit Cuba but he can't visit Trinidad or Jamaica. That is why Stokely can call Fidel "one of the blackest men in the Americas" and that is why our leaders in contrast qualify as "white." . . . Here I'm not just playing with words—I'm extending the definition of black power by indicating the nature of its opposite—white power—and I'm providing a practical illustration of what black power means in one particular West Indian community where it has already occurred. White power is the power of whites over blacks without any participation of the blacks. White power rules the imperialist world as a whole.[34]

Not only does Dupuy skew his presentation to miss this important emphasis, but he also misses the thrust of Rodney's argument. Rodney is not substituting a racial construction of society as false consciousness in place of a true capitalist construction (requiring a true class consciousness to understand and overcome it); rather, he is arguing that capitalism is inevitably linked to racism. Thus understanding the nature of imperialism as white is not a distraction, but getting to the heart of imperialism and class domination. This is evident in Rodney's definition, cited above, of the program of Black Power in the West Indies: imperialism is the main system of exploitation to be overcome, but in order to do so, it must be combated on the terms of its rule, which is through a racial and cultural system designed to keep black peoples in their place.

One cannot deny Dupuy's assertion that Rodney developed his outlook throughout his long period of travel; it would be hard to imagine that he remained static for a decade. Nor do I wish to suggest that there are not real theoretical problems with a perspective that conflates race as the sole determinant of social and political behavior. Yet Dupuy remains mistaken on the perception of a qualitative transformation in Rodney's outlook. He misses the obvious point that *Groundings* is written in Jamaica with a population overwhelmingly of African decent, a context in which a call to reconstruct the society in the image of black people not only is democratic but also addresses the history of covert denial of an African heritage. *A History of the Guyanese Working People*, by contrast, is written in Guyana, where two racial groups had been in sharp competition for social space and political power. In this context different tactics are required to combat "historically white" imperialism. Rather than a sharp dichotomy between the (flawed) Black Power Rodney and the (correct) Marxist Rodney, what we have instead is a continuum, starting from an approach that is seeking, under quite distinct conditions, to place Marx's insights into capitalist political economy at the service of oppressed Africans and Indians at home and abroad.

If Rodney is not perceived as moving from light to darkness, then perhaps we can see his analyses in *Groundings* and in *History* as part of a single project to grapple with a system of oppression that comes with a racial stamp deeply embedded within it, operating, as it were, as a central feature of its genetic code. Rodney seeks to apply this general insight with different approaches for the specific conditions of Jamaica and Guyana. The outlines of his approach are eloquently expressed in another document lost to the generation of the 1970s: the celebrated poet and playwright Aimé Césaire's famous resignation letter to the French Communist Party. As Césaire declared,

> What I demand of Marxism and Communism is that they serve the
> black peoples, not that the black peoples serve Marxism and Com-
> munism. Philosophies and movements must serve the people, not
> the people the doctrine and the movement. . . . A doctrine is of value
> only if it is conceived by us and for us, and revised through us. . . .
> We consider it our duty to make common cause with all who cher-
> ish truth and justice, in order to form organizations able to sup-
> port effectively the black peoples in their present and future strug-
> gle—their struggle for justice, for culture, for dignity, for liberty. . . .
> Because of this, please accept my resignation from the Party.[35]

Conclusions

The points arising from Dupuy's article are critical for understanding the fate of
the 1970s movements, when the adoption of Leninist tactics also brought with
it the wholesale adoption of a certain approach to Marxism. This approach
brought with it a "clear" class perspective, excluding a popular explanation of
oppression as an interweaving of race and class. It certainly avoided grappling
with Rodney's exploration of the "cultural" dimension of exploitation that
denigrated anything out of Africa. Caribbean Leninism in the 1970s suffered,
therefore, from its inability to construct a "counter-symbolic order"[36] that
could address not only the reality of economic exploitation but also the more
insidious reality of deeply embedded cultural and racial marginalization.

These considerations point to a further, perhaps overdrawn, conclusion,
namely that a movement fully conscious of the political economy of imperialism, but grasping its racialist nature, may have had, in the specific circumstances of this era, a greater potential for mobilizing the population and moving beyond the narrow confines of a partial class theory. This does not deny
that Black Power was always flawed, both organizationally and theoretically.
Indeed, there are very substantial reasons why the Black Power movement
was so rapidly superseded by Marxism-Leninism in the fluid political conditions of the mid-1970s. And yet, Black Power brought with it an openness and
diversity of political forms and politics and, critically, an appreciation of the
importance of countersymbolic and counterhegemonic popular forms. These
features were lost in the transition to Marxism-Leninism. Popular movements
of the future may wish to heed these lessons as they consider the construction
of new organizational and theoretical approaches to resistance.

Assumptions by Caribbean radicals during the 1970s over the nature of state power and its acquisition have a further, final lesson. In this area both Black Power and Marxist movements called for mass uprisings to seize power from corrupt or compromised regimes. The inevitable conclusion was that the Caribbean could eventually be full of little Cubas, each proceeding, with cooperation, on its own path of development. This, as has been suggested, was predicated—at least in its Marxist-Leninist form—on the false assumption that the Soviet Union would provide such regimes with the economic and military aid necessary for surviving and developing on a "path of socialist orientation."

It is worthwhile, admittedly with the corrective lens of hindsight, to consider whether there were alternative strategies. The taking of power meant immediate opposition from imperialism with all the well-known tactics of destabilization, both overt and covert. The example of Nicaragua is only the most egregious illustration. There, the movement, despite adopting commendable democratic forms, including a popularly discussed and ratified constitution, was violently undermined by the Contra war until, physically exhausted and economically prostrate, it was defeated in "free and fair" elections.[37]

Against these outcomes we might well ask, What if movements did not aim, in the short run, at taking power, but sought instead to build up effective communities of resistance, based on self-help, regional and international networks of solidarity, internally generated educational programs, and the like? What would have been the outcome, in other words, if an encircling, counterhegemonic, Gramscian strategy was adopted, as opposed to the tempting shortcut of overthrowing the state? To be sure, this may be entirely wishful thinking. On the night of March 12, when the NJM leadership got wind of Gairy's plans to massacre them, perhaps there was no alternative but, as an act of self-defense, to take power. And state power, of course, may provide the best bulkhead of resources, protection, and legitimacy to enact a counterhegemonic strategy.

But consider for a moment the Rastafarian movement. In 1961 Ronald Henry, under the banner of Rastafari, sought to seize power in Jamaica and failed ignominiously.[38] The Rastafarian movement, complex and quarrelsome in its diversity, nonetheless heeded the failure of this tactic and proceeded on a cultural, multicentered, community-based path. By the late 1970s, the entire Jamaican reggae industry was dominated by Rasta philosophy, and singers were singing, "Everyone join Rasta bandwagon." Then Bob Marley,[39] Peter Tosh, Dennis Brown, and a host of others brought Rastafarian philosophy with tremendous effect to a worldwide audience. And in the twenty-first century, under the banner of Bobo Shanti and other houses, Rastafari and its new chanters like Sizzla, Anthony B, and Buju Banton are enjoying a qualitative revival. Meanwhile the once vibrant radical Left lies dormant, if not extinct. Perhaps there is, after all, virtue in a strategy of encirclement.

NOTES

1. For an assessment of the influence of Black Power on young people in Jamaica in the 1960s, see Lewis, *Walter Rodney's Intellectual and Political Thought*, esp. 85–123.

2. Ryan and Stewart, *Black Power Revolution*; Meeks, "Development."

3. Lewis, "Learning to Blow"; Meeks, *Radical Caribbean*; Mars, *Ideology and Change*.

4. Lewis, *Marcus Garvey* and "Garvey's Perspective."

5. See Campbell, *Rasta and Resistance*.

6. The radical Jamaican newspaper *Abeng* was one of the immediate by-products of the Rodney riots. It was published only from January to October 1969 but served a larger role, in that it brought together key individuals who would play a significant role in the politics of the 1970s. See Lewis, *Walter Rodney's Intellectual and Political Thought*, 121 n. 32.

7. *The New World Quarterly* was a journal published in the 1960s at the University of the West Indies, Mona, and also from Georgetown, Guyana. It was the organ of the New World movement, a group composed primarily of university-based intellectuals that elaborated an extensive Caribbean "dependentista" approach to development.

8. White, "New World," 57, 60.

9. See Meeks, "Lloyd Best."

10. Geddes Granger (who later changed his name to Makandal Daaga), the charismatic leader of NJAC, had been a past president of the Guild of Undergraduates at the St. Augustine campus of the University of the West Indies.

11. National Joint Action Committee, *Conventional Politics*, 1.

12. Rodney, *Groundings*, 28.

13. Suite, "Arrogance."

14. See Henry, "CLR James."

15. The New World movement never elaborated a single program, but there was a dominant approach that stressed the severing of exploitative metropolitan linkages and the fostering of a regional, "bottom-up" economy. For an interesting retrospective and critique, see Green, "Caribbean Dependency Theory."

16. For the early history of the NJM, see Jacobs and Jacobs, *Grenada*, and Meeks, "Social Formation."

17. Not surprisingly, the community-based appeal of Black Power was often seen by aspiring Leninists as an inferior approach to political organization. This view is captured in Rupert Lewis's diary entry of January 24, 1971. Lewis, then an emerging Marxist-Leninist, had just returned from the December meeting of radical Caribbean activists on Rat Island in St. Lucia and noted, in reference to the groups from the eastern Caribbean, "Hardly any of the groups showed any inclination for Leninist theory. . . . None had a clear stand on the working class but all showed a concern for community type groups." See Scott, "Dialectic," 126 fn. 55.

18. Meeks, *Narratives*, esp. 48–74.

19. Munroe, *Workers Party*, 8. It is interesting to note that in Guyana the pattern was somewhat different. The radical trend that consolidated in the 1970s was Marxist, but not Leninist. There, President Forbes Burnham and his People's National Congress (PNC) already occupied, though with a large measure of corruption and authoritarianism, the radical nationalist black platform. Cheddi Jagan's People's Progressive Party (PPP), with its long history of conventional political engagement, occupied the Marxist space. This forced the young, radical opposition in a novel direction, away from PNC's black nationalism and PPP's Marxism-Leninism. It is only here in Guyana, with the Working People's Alliance (WPA) (and debatably, the ACLM in Antigua), that we see the possibility of an organization learning from both the positive and negative experiences of the Black Power movement. But its leader, Walter Rodney, was cut down before the WPA was able to sink deeper political roots. See Lewis, *Walter Rodney's Intellectual and Political Thought*, esp. 202–53, and Mars, *Ideology and Change*, esp. 105–28.

20. This often led to an ironic approach to mass work, with cadres standing, for instance, outside the Kingston industrial estate, waiting for the few workers to emerge from the factories, while thousands of people in nearby communities were often ignored.

21. See, for instance, Brutents, *National Liberation*, and Ulyanovsky, *Socialism*.

22. Padmore, head of the Negro Bureau of the Communist Trade Union International, left the communist party in 1933 in opposition to its colonial policies; see his celebrated book *Pan-Africanism or Communism?* Richard Wright broke with the communist party in 1944 and published "I Tried to Be a Communist," which was shortly and more widely distributed in Crossman, *God That Failed*.

23. Bishop and other leaders argued in the hours and days following the overthrow that Gairy had initiated a plan to arrest and even eliminate the NJM leadership. There was no alternative, they asserted, but to seize power.

24. Meeks, *Caribbean Revolutions and Revolutionary Theory*.

25. See, for instance, Lewis, *Grenada*.

26. A more fulsome history of the WPJ is yet to be written. For an early critique, see Campbell, "Progressive Politics." This reading is appropriately critical of its middle-class leadership but does not sufficiently capture the WPJ's mass work and the basis for its undoubted rootedness in a number of urban and rural communities.

27. The generally used, though largely mythical, figure for the number of people killed in the months before the 1980 election is 800. No serious empirical work has been done to confirm it, though my suspicion is that when it is done, the figure will be significantly greater.

28. Lewis elaborates on this point effectively in Scott's interview, "Dialectic," 159.

29. At perhaps the peak of its popular support, in July 1981, when the PNP had yet to revive from the electoral debacle of 1980, the WPJ could only obtain 3.1 percent support in a national poll of "citizens with a clear party preference." See Stone, *Political Opinions*, 14.

30. Dupuy, "Race and Class."

31. Rodney, *How Europe Underdeveloped Africa*.

32. Rodney, *History*.

33. Dupuy, "Race and Class," 114.

34. Rodney, *Groundings*, 31.

35. Aimé Césaire, quoted in Robinson, *Black Marxism*, 260.

36. The term is taken from Sylvia Wynter. See "Politics of Black Culture," in which she makes the case for the importance in Jamaica of the construction of a counter-symbolic order through Rastafari and other popular forms as an alternative to a middle-class, bureaucratically led movement.

37. For an analysis of the overt and covert attempts to destabilize and overthrow the Sandinista state in Nicaragua, see Sklar, *Washington's War*.

38. Meeks, "Obscure Revolt."

39. See, for example, Bogues, *Black Heretics*, esp. 187–205.

Merely One Link in the Worldwide Revolution

Internationalism, State Repression, and the Black Panther Party, 1966–1972

ROBYN SPENCER

Recent scholarship has combined analytical frameworks from diplomatic and social history to explore the complex relationship between the black freedom struggle in the United States and such events as the Bandung Conference, African decolonization, resurgent pan-Africanism, and guerrilla movements in the Third World.[1] Most importantly, this new literature has revealed the impact on radical black protest of the Cold War, "one of the 'hottest' moments in world history," in the words of Robin D. G. Kelley.[2] On the eve of the Cold War, African Americans all across the political spectrum looked abroad for ideological inspiration, cultural affirmation, and political allies.[3] As the Cold War became ever hotter, the U.S. government also became alive to the international implications of the emerging civil rights movement. The U.S. Justice Department, in its supporting brief to the Supreme Court for the pivotal *Brown v. Board of Education* decision of 1954, declared that the "problem of racial discrimination" had to be viewed "in the context of the present world struggle between freedom and tyranny," noting further that "racial discrimination furnishes grist for the Communist propaganda mills, and it raises doubt even among friendly nations as to the intensity of our devotion to the democratic faith."[4]

As it became more conscious of its image overseas, the U.S. government moved against citizens who raised doubts about its "devotion to the democratic faith," especially if those doubts were shared with international audiences. In this regard, no issue was pricklier than that of racial injustice. As part of its response to the Red threat, the U.S. government sought to rupture the internationalist thrust that had been forged by the black freedom struggle in the decades leading up to the Cold War, persecuting key African American intellectuals and political leaders like W. E. B. Du Bois and Paul Robeson. Flouting the official Cold War line, both Du Bois and Robeson, along with a number of other activists and organizations, continued to link the movement for racial justice in the United States with the worldwide struggle against colonialism and oppression.[5]

The sidelining of Du Bois, Robeson, and others of their ilk did not, to be sure, completely smash the tradition of black internationalism in the United States. Others soon stepped into the gap. Even in the heyday of the Cold War, African American leaders like Robert Williams and Malcolm X and organizations like the Revolutionary Action Movement remained committed to global solidarity among oppressed peoples, and they "flatly rejected unconditional racial unity and developed a nationalism built on a broader concept of revolutionary Third World solidarity."[6] As the civil rights movement developed, even some of the mainstream black leaders who previously had tended to steer clear of internationalist entanglements, in accordance with the wishes of the U.S. government, began to change their tune. Thus in 1960 Fellowship of Reconciliation activist James Lawson expressed the view that "all Africa will be free before the American Negro attains first class citizenship."[7] Similarly Martin Luther King Jr., in his 1963 testament "Letter from a Birmingham Jail," contrasted black Americans, who "creep at horse-and-buggy pace toward gaining a cup of coffee at a lunch counter," with African and Asian nations, who move "with jetlike speed towards gaining political independence."[8] At the 1963 March on Washington, perhaps the iconic event of the civil rights movement, Student Nonviolent Coordinating Committee leader John Lewis proclaimed, "'One man, one vote' is the African cry, it is ours too."[9]

Yet, although not totally obliterated, black internationalism in the United States suffered serious reversals during the heyday of the Cold War, in the 1950s and early 1960s. As a result, an "anti-imperialist and anticapitalist critique of the global political economy" only returned to a central programmatic position in the African American struggle in the mid-1960s, when once again, activists began to conceptualize the black liberation movement in the United States as part of a worldwide struggle for human rights.[10] A number of movements and individuals, including some of those mentioned above, contributed to this ideological renewal. More than any other group, however, it was the Black Panther Party that led the way back to internationalism as a sustained programmatic expression of the black liberation struggle in the United States.[11]

The Black Panther Party, this essay argues, offers provocative new ways to conceptualize the relationships between social movements, international politics, and state repression. The historiography of black internationalism during the Cold War centers largely on presidential politics, State Department policies, international diplomacy, and the activities of leading black intellectuals and middle-class civil rights organizations. Few scholars have taken to heart Mary Dudziak's observation that "an international frame need not eclipse a focus on the grassroots."[12] Much of the existing literature, consequently, takes a top-down approach—relegating to a postscript the Black Power movement's vibrant engagement with international politics. In the latter connection, the Black Panther Party is central. The Panthers fused a radical internationalist posture—anticolonialism, Third World solidarity, and opposition to U.S. imperialism—with an equally radical critique of U.S. society, exposing urban poverty, housing shortages, unequal education, and police brutality.[13]

With more than 5,000 members at its height and one of the country's most popular alternative newspapers, *The Black Panther*, the Panthers combined a mass base with a critique of U.S. foreign policy and a concomitant call for global justice. They argued that at a time when "the people of the world are making their final bid for full and complete freedom," the "American racial problem can no longer be spoken of or solved in isolation."[14] The Panthers' prominence in the effort to heal the breach created by the Cold War in African American political culture was a central factor in the unprecedented state repression that would be unleashed on them. Indeed, the campaign against the Panthers aptly bears out Penny Von Eschen's assertion that "organized state repression" highlighted the enormous stakes involved in the struggle for a "global understanding of economic exploitation and the fight for human rights."[15] At tremendous costs, collective and personal, the Panthers made significant contributions to the practice and theory of internationalizing the black freedom struggle in the United States.

Critiquing Uncle Sam

On a spring evening in 1966, Bobby Seale, who only months later would become one of two cofounders of the Black Panther Party, held forth on a street corner in Berkeley, California. Seale, a resident of the nearby black community of Oakland, was engaged in political theater. He recited a poem titled "Uncle Sammy Called Me Fulla Lucifer,"[16] a witty, irreverent, profanity-laden dialogue between conscript Fearless Fosdick, a newspaper cartoon character, and Uncle Sam, the symbol of U.S. pride and military recruitment. The sheer spectacle of Seale's impromptu performance, coupled with the poem's echo of growing anti–Vietnam War sentiment, attracted a crowd of young people, mostly students from the University of California at Berkeley. The poem recounted a political odyssey in which a naive Fosdick, "schooled . . . to sing red, white, and blue stars and stripes songs," eventually rejected the racialized iconography of the U.S. nation-state, embodied by the pale-skinned, white-haired, star-spangled Uncle Sam. By the end of the poem, Fosdick, having undergone an epiphany, refused "to pledge eternal allegiance to all things blue-true, blue-eyes, blond-blond-haired, white-chalk, white skinned with USA tattooed *all over*." Newly liberated, Fosdick defiantly declared, "I will *not* serve!" The crowd roared. The police, however, were less amused. After a brief scuffle, Seale and his companion, Huey Newton, soon to become cofounder of the Black Panther Party, were arrested for blocking the sidewalk.[17]

This incident is emblematic of the sequence of events that led to the formation, in October 1966, of the Black Panther Party for Self-Defense. Seale, in his autobiography, framed the incident as evidence of early encounters with police authority and as confirmation that Berkeley, one of the epicenters of white student activism, was an important political crossroads for Oakland's grassroots activists.[18] Seale may have added that the poem's satiric disavowal of blind patriotism and military service suggests that the Berkeley incident can also be read as an embryonic articulation of the future Panther policy of not just critiquing U.S. policies, foreign and domestic, but also directly linking them.

Even before founding the Black Panther Party, Newton and Seale had turned to Marxist theoreticians at home and abroad for an explanation of the socioeconomic contradictions they saw around them. In time, the pair made two key conclusions: that capitalism was the root cause of oppression worldwide, and that the African American struggle was inextricably linked with the struggle for Third World liberation. In their studies, Newton and Seale were especially influenced by the ideas of guerrilla warfare and revolutionary violence found in the works of Mao Zedong, Fidel Castro, Frantz Fanon, Malcolm X, and Robert Williams. And although initially founded on a program of combating police brutality, racism, and economic inequality, the Black Panther Party soon evolved into an organizational vehicle for highlighting and critiquing the linkages between U.S. domestic and foreign policies.

The Panthers' ten-point program, their statement of goals and principles, made a direct connection between police brutality in black and Chicano communities, on one hand, and the misdeeds of U.S. troops in Vietnam, on the other.[19] Accordingly, the sixth point demanded that black men be exempt from military service, so they "will not fight and kill other people of color in the world who, like black people, are being victimized by the white racist government of America."[20] Such an analysis resonated in poor communities like Oakland, where African Americans organized more than twenty demonstrations against police violence in 1965 and 1966. The following year, 1967, almost 10,000 antidraft activists protested and engaged in civil disobedience at the U.S. Army induction center in Oakland, as part of a weeklong, nationwide protest called Stop the Draft week.[21] In these circumstances, the Panthers' strong antiwar stance electrified many young people, individuals like Sherwin Forte. An early recruit, Forte mentioned the "riotous atmosphere, the killings, the National Guard, the helicopters, the protest in Berkeley, [and] the anti-draft movement" as events that led him to join the Black Panther Party. "The Vietnam war was happening," he continued, "and I had a choice whether I would go and fight the country's battles in Vietnam or whether I wanted to take my life and use it to redress some wrongs in this country. I didn't see the Vietnamese as the enemy. I saw the enemy as racist America."[22]

The Panther critique, although far more radical than most, emerged at a time when antiwar sentiment was beginning to gain traction nationally. In early 1966, even before the Panthers appeared, the Student Nonviolent Coordinating Committee had come out against the war. When the Johnson administration abolished automatic student deferments for the draft in 1966, thousands flooded into Students for a Democratic Society and other predominantly white, antiwar organizations. Cultural icon Muhammad Ali publicly refused the draft, while antiwar rallies in major cities began to attract thousands. The Fulbright hearings—five televised hearings in 1966 by the Senate Foreign Relations Committee, under its chairman, Senator J. William Fulbright—signaled the mainstreaming of dissent. Then, in early 1967, after a massive buildup of U.S. forces in Vietnam, Martin Luther King condemned the war, a move that garnered international publicity. King did not act solely on moral grounds. The adventure in Vietnam, he objected, was "some demonic destructive suction tube," leading the United States to abandon antipoverty efforts at home, even as the war took a disproportionate toll on the poor, many of whom were being asked to fight for freedom they did not enjoy.[23] The TET offensive of January 1968, complete with graphic news footage and a high casualty rate, increased antiwar sentiment across the land.

The Panthers, however, distinguished themselves from the mainstream antiwar movement. Whereas the latter restricted its demand to "peace" and a withdrawal of U.S. forces from Vietnam, the Panthers went further, calling for solidarity with the Vietnamese resistance and for the defeat of U.S. imperialism. In 1968, deepening their internationalist orientation, the Panthers created the position of international coordinator and appointed Connie Matthews to fill it. Matthews skillfully mobilized a far-flung network of international alliances to provide support for incarcerated Panthers. She promoted the party in Europe, speaking at public events and rallies and making linkages with leftist organizations.[24]

In an interview with Angela Davis, Matthews outlined the Panther internationalist agenda. The party, she declared, sought to educate black people "to the importance of internationalism. To get them to understand that we are in the belly of the whale here and that imperialism, manifested in the U.S., is a monster with tentacles and the other oppressed peoples of the world are trying to cut off the tentacles but that we here have to get the monster from inside."[25] In tandem with Matthews's work, the Panthers reached out to U.S.-based representatives of various liberation movements and sent a delegation to the United Nations to meet with emissaries of "revolutionary countries." The Panthers subsequently issued a press release warning of a civil war in the United States if Huey Newton, who had been jailed for allegedly killing a police officer, was not released. The press release called on "oppressed and colonized" people to demonstrate in front of U.S. embassies worldwide, demanding further that the United Nations station "Observer Teams throughout the cities of America wherein black people are cooped up and concentrated in wretched ghettos."[26]

Solidifying an International Base

In 1968 Eldridge Cleaver, a top Panther leader facing an assault conviction, fled the United States. After some months in Cuba, he moved on to Algeria, which, like Cuba, had no diplomatic ties with the United States. Cleaver's flight opened a new phase in the Panthers' internationalism: he oversaw the creation of the international section of the Black Panther Party, based in Algeria.[27] On a personal level, Cleaver also benefited from the Panthers' global solidarity networks: after he went into exile, activists in four U.S. cities, joined by others in Paris, Rome, London, and Amsterdam, launched the International Committee to Defend Eldridge Cleaver.[28] Shortly after Cleaver relocated to Algiers, a Panther delegation joined representatives from twenty-four countries and six liberation movements there, for the Pan African Cultural Festival. The Panther delegates to the festival included David Hilliard, chief of staff; Raymond "Masai" Hewitt, minister of information; and Emory Douglas, minister of culture. Douglas's bold political drawings had previously received much acclaim internationally, and the Panthers mounted an exhibit of his works at the festival.[29] In Algiers, the Panther leaders discussed areas of potential cooperation with revolutionaries from Angola, Zimbabwe, Mozambique, and Haiti, many of whom considered the Panthers the vanguard of the liberation movement in the United States.[30] Chief of Staff Hilliard recalled that his group's interlocutors in Algiers "were all aware of our problems before we got there. They knew that U.S. imperialism was their problem and that fascism was what Black people in America are faced with."[31]

The Algiers meetings produced a noted expression of moral support for the Panthers. After the festival, representatives of a number of liberation movements sent a strongly worded message to the United Nations. The message read, in part,

> African political organizations are shocked and saddened to learn of the arrests and repressive fascist type crimes perpetrated against the leaders and members of the Black Panther Party on their return to the United States from the First Pan African Cultural Festival by U.S. authorities in flagrant violation of the Universal Human Rights Declaration enshrined in the charter of the United Nations. . . . United Nations would be ignoring its duties should it stand by unconcerned while the principles inshrined [sic] in its Charter are being trampled on at its very doorstep.[32]

The Panthers also received some state support, including from Cuba and Algeria. Cleaver also established a close relationship with the North Korean embassy in Algiers. In 1969 he traveled to Pyongyang, the North Korean capital, to attend the International Conference on Tasks of Journalists of the Whole World in their Fight Against U.S. Imperialist Aggression. In his speech at the conference, Cleaver applauded North Korea and its leader Kim Il Sung for embracing their own brand of Marxism-Leninism, attacked U.S. imperialism, and proclaimed the Panthers' solidarity with the revolutionary peoples of the world.[33]

Deeply influenced by the trip, Cleaver began to promote the writings of Kim Il Sung in The Black Panther.[34] In a related development, the newspaper created an international section with a masthead featuring pictures of Patrice Lumumba, Ho Chi Minh, and Che Guevara, along with a silhouette of a rifle. This section was filled with commentaries and news briefs on the political situation in Vietnam, Palestine, and South Africa, among other places, and with speeches by revolutionary thinkers like Amilcar Cabral, head of the armed anticolonial movement in the Portuguese colonies of Guinea-Bissau and Cape Verde.[35] *The Black Panther*'s international section also chronicled the activities of Panther support committees overseas and carried statements of solidarity from various organizations, such as the Association of Democratic Jurists of Korea and the Committee for Afro-Asian Solidarity of Korea, both based in North Korea.[36]

As their international involvement deepened, the Panthers intensified their critique of the mainstream antiwar movement. In a typical broadside, Panther chief of staff David Hilliard, appearing at the San Francisco Moratorium Demonstration, one of the largest such events of the 1960s, castigated the antiwar movement for focusing on aggression abroad to the exclusion of oppression at home. "We're not going to let you talk about waging a struggle in support of people 10,000 miles from here, when you have problems right here in fascist America," Hilliard lectured his predominantly white audience.[37]

Militant in their insistence on the connection between the domestic and the foreign, the Panthers offered a novel proposal. Incarcerated Panthers, they suggested, could be exchanged for U.S. prisoners of war in Vietnam. *The Black Panther*, accordingly, encouraged readers, "If you have sons, husbands, or friends who are prisoners of war in Vietnam, send us their name, rank and serial numbers. We will forward this information to Eldridge Cleaver, Minister of Information of the Black Panther Party; and attempt to exchange their freedom for the freedom of the Minister of Defense, Huey P. Newton and Chairman Bobby Seale who are political prisoners here in 'fascist Babylon.'"[38] Panthers in Oakland held a rally to popularize the idea.[39] The proposed exchange, needless to say, never materialized. It did, however, powerfully symbolize the Panthers' claim that their incarcerated comrades were political prisoners who deserved the same status and recognition as U.S. prisoners of war in Vietnam.

Huey Newton and Intercommunalism

Huey Newton, the top Panther leader who had become an international cause célèbre during his imprisonment, presided over a deepening of the party's international thrust on being released in August 1970. In an interview with *Sechaba*, the official organ of the African National Congress of South Africa, Newton noted the continuing influence of international revolutionaries on the Black Panther Party and asserted that the Panthers wanted to establish better communications with other liberation movements in order to coordinate their struggles.[40] Having, evidently, sharpened his Marxism during his confinement,

Newton continued, "The bourgeoisie that is based here in America has an international character, because it exploits the world, it controls the wealth of the world; it has stolen, usurped the wealth of the people of the world. . . . We feel that the only way that we can combat an international enemy is through an international strategy, unity of all people who are exploited, who will overthrow the international bourgeoisie, and replace it with a dictatorship by the proletariat, the workers of the world."[41] Subsequently, Newton wrote an open letter offering troops to the Vietnamese National Liberation Front. The offer, he told the Vietnamese, was a "recognition of the fact that your struggle is also our struggle, for we recognize that our common enemy is the American imperialist who is the leader of international bourgeois domination. . . . Therefore our problem is international, and we offer these troops in recognition of the necessity for international alliances to deal with this problem."[42] Nguyen Thi Dinh, a high-ranking commander in the Vietnamese resistance, expressed his gratitude but declined the offer of military assistance. The Panthers' own "persistent and ever-developing struggle [within the United States] is the most active support to our resistance against U.S. aggression for national salvation," he declared.[43]

Some mainstream African American leaders took umbrage to Newton's offer. The NAACP's Roy Wilkins disparaged it, accusing the Panther leader of privileging the Viet Cong over "John Q. Black American." Newton's response underlined what, by then, had become a cornerstone of his party's program. The Panthers, he retorted, were "internationalists because we believe our struggle must proceed on many fronts. While we feed and clothe the poor at home we must meet and attack the oppressor wherever he may be found."[44]

Newton's most significant contribution to Panther internationalism was the theory of revolutionary intercommunalism. U.S. capitalist imperialism, according to this theory, had transformed understandings of sovereignty and self-determination that underlay the concept of nationhood to the point where nations no longer existed, "because of the development of technology, because of the development of the mass media, because of the fire power of the imperialist, because of the fact that the United States is no longer a nation but an empire."[45] Newton's intercommunalism effectively repudiated the old internal colonialism thesis, the idea that African Americans constituted a "nation within a nation" or an "internal colony" within the United States, which previously had been a mainstay of Panther ideology. The new reality, Newton now argued, was a world divided into oppressed and liberated communities, linked by common causes that united them across national boundaries against a common enemy: the U.S. empire.

In this new world order, Newton suggested, race, and even ideology, had declined in importance. The indispensable basis of global solidarity, rather, was common experiences of oppression. He explained: "We see very little difference in what happens to a community here in North America and what happens to a community in Vietnam. We see very little difference in what happens, even culturally, to a Chines [sic] community in San Francisco and a Chinese community in Hong Kong. We see very little difference in what happens to a black community in Harlem and a black community in South Africa, a black community in Angola and Mozambique. We see very little difference."[46] Intercommunalism was a central topic in Newton's college tour after he left prison, and he spoke at length on the same subject at the Panthers' Revolutionary People's Constitutional Convention of 1970. The Panthers, he warned, "cannot make our stand as nationalists, we cannot even make our stand as internationalists, we must place our future hopes on the philosophy of intercommunalism, a philosophy which holds that the rise of imperialism in America transformed all the other nations into oppressed communities."[47] He pointed to Algeria and North Korea as examples of liberated communities and argued for self-determination globally. "Whether on an intercommunal level, a regional level, or on a local level, we hold that all people have the right to proportional representation within the framework of revolutionary intercommunalism and communism," the Panther leader concluded.[48]

Not all Panthers appreciated Newton's latest theoretical pronouncements. Some saw little difference between intercommunalism and the party's long-standing commitment to internationalism. Still, under Newton's prodding, the term was incorporated into the Panther organizational structure.[49] The group's news outlet, the Black Community News Service, was renamed the Intercommunal News Service, while the International chapter became the Intercommunal chapter. Solidarity committees in Sweden, Denmark, Germany, Holland, and England also fell in line, nomenclatorially speaking at least. "Our intercommunal solidarity," they proclaimed in a joint communiqué, "is expressed in our political work to revolutionize our respective communities and to free the third world political prisoners within Germany, England, Holland, Denmark and Sweden."[50]

Political Repression

The Panthers' efforts to build a mass constituency domestically, under a program advocating international revolution, earned them the lasting enmity of the U.S. state, which responded with a campaign of repression. In 1967 the FBI launched COINTELPRO, a program to "expose, disrupt, misdirect, discredit, or otherwise neutralize the activities of black nationalist, hate-type organizations and groupings, their leadership, spokesmen, membership, and supporters and to counter their propensity for violence and civil disorder."[51] The Black Panther Party, although not specifically mentioned in this initial memo, was the chief target of the coming onslaught. The FBI subsequently made that clear. Rectifying the previous omission, a later memo dubbed the Panthers "the most violence-prone organization of all the extremist groups operating in the United States."[52] All but officially designated the principal internal enemy of the U.S. state, the Panthers would bear the brunt of COINTELPRO actions.

The subsequent massive police raids and mass arrests of Panthers went hand in hand with the promised campaign of disinformation to "expose, disrupt, misdirect, discredit, or otherwise neutralize" the party. The repression had the desired effect, exacerbating existing tensions within the organization and pushing it, ideologically speaking, further to the left. State repression also created a wave of political refugees, as Panthers fled overseas to escape the ever-widening dragnet.[53] The fleeing militants joined other party members who had preceded them into exile, most notably Eldridge Cleaver, in giving even greater publicity to the Panther cause on the international stage.

The resulting international networks would prove extremely helpful to the Panthers, offering them both moral and material support. As the raids and arrests began to decimate the organization, activists in Germany, France, Holland, Norway, Denmark, and Sweden, among other places, established solidarity committees, which organized demonstrations and held public hearings to raise awareness of the Panthers' plight.[54] In one notable example of solidarity, the Black Panther Party Solidarity Committee in Sweden organized a march of 300 people to demand the release of Bobby Seale and other political prisoners.[55] After the arrest of twenty-one Panthers in New York, Panther international coordinator Connie Matthews sprung into action, urging the Danish government to use its influence to "convince the American government of the unjustness of their course, and to persuade them to cease immediately the unwarranted harassment of the Black Panther Party and its members."[56] Meanwhile the Danish Socialist Party and allied groups held a demonstration in the course of which speakers highlighted the connections between the Vietnam War, the exploitation of the Danish working class, and the persecution of the Black Panther Party. The event culminated in more than 600 protesters marching on the American embassy in Copenhagen.[57]

The FBI did not fail to note the Panthers' "connections with foreign revolutionaries" and carefully monitored those connections.[58] Chronicling Cleaver's travels in 1970 to North Korea, China, and North Vietnam, the FBI observed that from his base in Algiers, Cleaver "maintains close contact with communist nations and Arab guerilla organizations." On the radio in Hanoi, Cleaver is reputed to have urged African American servicemen "to desert, commit sabotage, and 'rip off' (kill) the United States Commander in South Vietnam."[59]

Indeed, Attorney General John Mitchell justified warrantless electronic telephone surveillance of the Panther headquarters in Oakland by copying the Panthers: he invoked the links between the party's domestic and international activities. Mitchell mentioned the Panthers' strength, along with the threat he considered them to pose, notably, "(1) the large number of Black Panther Party branch organizations in this country; (2) the large number of Black Panther Party members; and (3) the fact that numerous threats of personal attack were being directed by the Black Panther Party against local law enforcement officers."[60] The attorney general feared that the group's allies abroad would finance revolution in the United States. The Panthers, he asserted, had "avenues for channeling foreign funds into this country for the purpose of supporting Black Panther Party revolutionary activities which included the advocacy of the violent overthrow of existing Federal and State government structures."[61] Mitchell based the latter claims on three factors: "(1) the presence of Black Panther Party leader Eldridge Cleaver in Cuba, Algeria and North Korea; (2) contacts in Sweden of Panther members with representatives of the North Vietnamese government; and (3) contacts of Panther members with representatives of communist Cuba."[62] These same foreign connections, the U.S. government maintained, were the source of Panther ideology. As the FBI saw it, the Black Panther Party "relies heavily on foreign Communist ideology to shape its goals," the party's "Marxist" orientation providing a "favorable environment for the support of the Panthers from other Communist countries."[63]

A major result of the crusade against the Black Panther Party was an exacerbation of the differences, ideological and personal, between Huey Newton, its U.S.-based top leader, and the Algerian-based Eldridge Cleaver, the chief Panther spokesman overseas. The FBI's campaign to sow discord between the two men was international in scope, and it involved everything from phony letters to death threats. An FBI memo dated just eight days after Newton's release from prison in 1970 suggested that counterintelligence efforts should aim to "drive a wedge" between Newton and Cleaver.[64] Far from just an attempt to ignite a feud between two leaders, the FBI's maneuverings were an attack on the very foundations of Panther ideology and strategy. In targeting Cleaver, the FBI hoped to undermine the Panthers' international standing and disrupt their attempts to sustain and deepen alliances overseas. If Cleaver was a key element in the Panthers' internationalist thrust, then Newton was their essential helmsman, presiding over the domestic base and standing at the core of the efforts to connect the national and global.

In the wake of the internecine conflict, the party began to decline. The FBI gleefully took the credit, a 1971 report claiming that the "chaotic condition of BPP and the split between BPP leaders Huey P. Newton and Eldridge Cleaver is possibly a direct result of our intensive counterintelligence efforts aimed at causing dissension between Newton and Cleaver and within the Party."[65] This was not the only factor; preexisting tensions within the party also played a major role in its decline. Still, the FBI's crowing was not without merit: its campaign of repression and disinformation contributed mightily to the eventual collapse of the Black Panther Party.

From its foundation in 1966 to its downward spiral in 1972, the Black Panther Party was seen by the U.S. government as a threat to national security. The Panthers' most enduring qualities—their ability to be both crucible and conduit for black internationalist consciousness in the United States, to maneuver on the international stage, and to leverage a global New Left network—made them largely impervious to co-optation. The organized violence of the state, physical and psychological, would have to be brought to bear against them. And it was. As the "greatest threat to the internal security of the United States,"[66] in the words of FBI director J. Edgar Hoover, the Panthers were "savaged by a campaign of political repression that in terms of its sheer viciousness has few parallels in American history."[67] Political repression in the United States was hardly new; it certainly did not begin with the Panthers.[68] However, the repressive apparatus of the U.S. state increased greatly during the Cold War, and the Black Panther Party felt its full sting in the 1960s and 1970s, the peak of the effort to root out subversives and control grassroots protesters at home and abroad.

Conclusion

Although the Panthers no longer maintained missions overseas after 1971, their program and ideology remained internationalist. In September 1971, Newton led a delegation of more than a dozen Panthers to the People's Republic of China, where they met top officials and visited historical and cultural sites.[69]

On returning to the United States, Newton issued a statement declaring that the Panthers had gone to China ahead of U.S. president Richard Nixon, whose subsequent visit to that country constituted a historic Cold War event, "so that we might ask the peace and freedom-loving Chairman Mao Tse-tung to be the chief negotiator . . . for the peace and freedom of the oppressed peoples of the world."[70] Other Panther officials also continued to travel overseas. In 1971 Martin Kenner, a leading member of the Committee to Defend the Panthers, went to Europe to meet representatives of China, North Korea, Cuba, and the Vietnamese resistance. The Vietnamese, Kenner noted in reporting to Newton about the meetings, "were far and away the most outspoken in their desire for more help from us. They requested radio programs, leaflets, and drawings—in short propaganda they can use in Nam—as well as Party propaganda here in the paper about US aggression in S.E. Asia. . . . All of the governments wanted to receive party paper."[71]

At the same time, the Panthers continued to provide material aid to African liberation support organizations, as well as to send medical supplies to liberation movements in the Portuguese colonies of Mozambique, Guinea-Bissau, and Angola.[72] The Panthers also remained a source of inspiration for oppressed groups around the world. In 1972 Australian aborigines independently created a branch of the party and requested official recognition from the Panther headquarters in Oakland, California.[73] Even in decline, then, the Panthers' praxis remained consistent with their ideology. As late as 1972, they issued a revised ten-point platform that, among other things, attributed "the various conflicts which exist around the world" to the "aggressive desires of the U.S. ruling circle and government to force its domination upon the oppressed people of the world."[74] In the throes of death, as in the prime of its life, the Black Panther Party remained committed to a vision of liberation in which the fate of African Americans was inseparable from that of other oppressed and colonized peoples globally.

Robin Kelley has argued that "too often our standards for evaluating social movements pivot around whether or not they 'succeeded' in realizing their visions rather than on the merits or power of the visions themselves."[75] The story of the Black Panther Party, its successes and its failures, is a testament to the merits of this argument. The Panthers both confirmed and tapped into a deep anti-imperialist consciousness that existed at the grass roots of the black community—a consciousness that was separate and apart from African-centered cultural affirmations and engagements with the dominant, white-led antiwar movement. With few resources, the Panthers managed to produce an impressive body of political tracts, along with witty and sarcastic illustrations, cartoons, and poems that connected them to the often-forgotten protest tradition of the African American Left, with its deep commitment to internationalism.[76] As Hilliard affirmed in 1970, the Panthers saw themselves as "merely one link in the worldwide revolution."[76] They boldly operated on the international stage, waging their own version of diplomacy and making linkages with groups representing oppressed peoples in Africa, Asia, and Europe. The Panthers also made important theoretical contributions to the global struggle for freedom. Huey Newton's concept of intercommunalism, although it was not systematically taught or popularized in his lifetime, anticipated much of the present-day critique of globalization. The Panthers may not have achieved the global revolution they envisioned, but their "alternative visions and dreams . . . inspire new generations to continue to struggle for change."[77]

NOTES

1. Dudziak, *Cold War*; Horne, *Black and Red*; Layton, *International Politics*; Meriwether, *Proudly We Can Be Africans*; Plummer, *Rising Wind*; Von Eschen, *Race against Empire*.

2. Kelley, "Stormy Weather," 69.

3. Dudziak, "Little Rock Crisis"; Fraser, "Crossing the Color Line"; Borstelmann, "'Hedging Our Bets.'"

4. Emerson and Kilson, "American Dilemma," 644.

5. See Horne, *Black and Red*, and Plummer, *Rising Wind*.

6. Kelley, "Stormy Weather," 87.

7. Lawson, "We Are Trying," 314.

8. King, *Why We Can't Wait*, 81.

9. Carson, *In Struggle*, 94.

10. Von Eschen, *Race against Empire*, 187.

11. Kelley, "Stormy Weather," 87.

12. Dudziak, *Cold War*, 253.

13. Cleaver, "Back to Africa"; Clemons and Jones, "Global Solidarity." For examples of this frame of analysis in the study of other black nationalist organizations, see Woodard, *Nation within a Nation*, and Kelley, "Stormy Weather."

14. "The Black Man's Stake in Vietnam," *Black Panther*, March 23, 1969, 16.

15. Von Eschen, *Race against Empire*, 187.

16. A poem that began with the line "Uncle Sammy called us full of Lucifer" appeared in the Black Panther Party newspaper under the title "Bobby's poem." The poem appeared in different versions, shaped to fit different critiques of Uncle Sam. See *Black Panther*, October 12, 1968, 9.

17. Seale, *Lonely Rage*, 145–51, and *Seize the Time*, 27–29.

18. Seale, *Lonely Rage*, 145–51.

19. "Black Soldiers as Revolutionaries to Overthrow the Ruling Class," folder: Protest Movements, Black Panther Party Publications, San Francisco African American Historical and Cultural Society Archives, San Francisco, California; *Black Panther*, September 20, 1969, 2.

20. Seale, *Seize the Time*, 67.

21. "Police Brutality, Old Story," *Sun-Reporter*, February 26, 1955, 8; "What's Wrong with Our Police Department," *Sun-Reporter*, June 7, 1958, 6; "New Police Brutality Cases Anger Parents: Ask Police Chief and Mayor 'Stop Brutality,'" *Sun-Reporter*, November 14, 1959, 1; "Victim of Police Brutality?," *Sun-Reporter*, March 4, 1961, 1, 5. See also Lader, *Power on the Left*, 229.

22. Sherwin Forte, interview by author, October 9, 1997, tape recording, Oakland, California.

23. King, *Testament of Hope*, 233.

24. "Interview with Scandinavian Rep. of Black Panther Party: Connie Matthews," *Black Panther*, October 18, 1969, 9.

25. "Interview with Angela Davis," *Black Panther*, November 1, 1969.

26. "Panthers Move Internationally," *Black Panther*, September 14, 1968, 3.

27. Cleaver, "Back to Africa," 216–17.

28. "Project Resistance," 11, box 80, Huey P. Newton Foundation Papers, Special Collections, Green Library, Stanford University, Stanford, California (hereafter HPN Papers). I accessed the HPN Papers at Stanford University in 1996 when the archival recording process was just beginning; box and folder titles, contents, etc., may subsequently have changed.

29. Ibid., 29–30.

30. "Black Panther Discussion with African and Haitian Liberation Fighters," *Black Panther*, August 23, 1969, 16–17.

31. Ibid.

32. "African Liberation Movement," *Black Panther*, October 4, 1969, 11.

33. Eldridge Cleaver, "Solidarity of the People until Victory or Death!," *Black Panther*, October 25, 1969, 12–13.

34. Cleaver, "Back to Africa," 226.

35. For example, see *Black Panther*, September 20, 1969, 16.

36. See various issues of *Black Panther* in October 1969.

37. "Text of Speech of David Hilliard at San Francisco, November 15, 1969," folder: "Hilliard, David. Expert Witness File," box 27, HPN Papers.

38. *Black Panther*, November 21, December 9, 1969.

39. "A Rally Announcing Action," folder: "Oakland, Protests, Demonstrations etc, 1920–1969," Oakland History Room, Oakland Public Library, Oakland, California.

40. Newton, *To Die*, 201–3.

41. Folder: "MSS People's Revolutionary Intercommunalism," 2, HPN Papers.

42. Newton, *To Die*, 178.

43. Ibid., 184.

44. Ibid., 186, 190.

45. "Huey's Message at Boston College, November 18, 1970," 4, box 8, HPN Papers.

46. Ibid., 5.

47. "Revolutionary Peoples Constitutional Convention: Resolutions and Declarations, November 29, 1970, Washington, D.C.," 2, folder: "Re: Revolutionary People's Constitutional Convention," box 15, HPN Papers.

48. Ibid., 4.

49. Newton spoke at New Haven College on February 5, 1971, on "BPP—Ideology" and at Princeton University on February 9, 1971, on "Black Panther Party—New Ideology"; see folder: "Signed Contracts—executed," box 8, HPN Papers.

50. "Joint Communique," folder: "Communication Sheets," box 2, HPN Papers.

51. "August 15, 1967" memo, folder: "Counterintelligence Program Case Histories—FBI files," box 68, HPN Papers.

52. Churchill and Vander Wall, *COINTELPRO Papers*, 124.

53. Cleaver, "Back to Africa," 224.

54. Seale, *Seize the Time*, 34.

55. *Black Panther*, October 25, 1969, 21.

56. "Open Letter to the Danish Foreign Ministry," *Black Panther*, May 11, 1969.

57. "Free Huey Demonstration in Scandinavia," *Black Panther*, June 21, 1969, 18.

58. Churchill and Vander Wall, *COINTELPRO Papers*, 124.

59. "Racial Disorders and law enforcement," folder: "Books to be Written," box 18, HPN Papers.

60. "Sworn statement by John Mitchell dated April 15, 1976," box 80, HPN Papers.

61. Ibid.

62. Ibid.

63. Donner, *Age of Surveillance*, 265.

64. "To SAC SF from Director FBI, 9/9/70," 3, box 80, HPN Papers.

65. Informative note dated 3/4/71, box 80, HPN Papers.

66. Churchill, "'To Disrupt, Discredit, and Destroy,'" 83.

67. Ibid., 78.

68. See Donner, *Age of Surveillance*; Churchill and Vander Wall, *COINTELPRO Papers*; O'Reilly, *Racial Matters*; Schultz and Schultz, *It Did Happen Here*.

69. "Black Panther Party Delegation's Book re: People's Republic of China upon Return," box 46, HPN Papers.

70. Folder: "The Servants Visit to the People's Republic of China," box 44, HPN Papers.

71. Folder: "Rev Rep. in U.S. and Canada, Western Europe, eg. China," box 41, HPN Papers.

72. "Innerparty Memorandum #13," October 25, 1972, 2, box 14, HPN Papers.

73. Folder: "Requests to Start Black Panther Party Centers," box 14, HPN Papers.

74. "The Black Panther Party Program, March 29, 1972, platform," 11, folder: "Misc. Articles," box 41, HPN Papers.

75. Kelley, *Freedom Dreams*, ix.

76. Richard Harwood, "Black Panthers Striving Heartily for Revolution," *Sunday Star-Bulletin & Advertiser* (Honolulu), January 25, 1970, E4, HPN Papers.

77. Kelley, *Freedom Dreams*, ix.

Hip Hop's Diasporic Landscapes of Blackness

MARC D. PERRY

The narrative of hip hop's rise as a global cultural phenomenon has been a rather extraordinary one.[1] I recall in the mid-1970s being dragged to local "street jams" among Manhattan's Lower East Side public housing projects where neighborhood youth, almost exclusively African American and Puerto Rican, gathered summer afternoons to listen and dance to the music of local DJs and their makeshift audio equipment powered via illicit taps into city street lamps. I was clearly unaware at that age that what was going on around me, as was happening throughout New York's inner-city patchwork of public housing projects, would give birth to a cultural movement soon to be celebrated as hip hop. Indeed, I would come into budding self-awareness amidst that formative period of hip hop's early ascendance in New York City during the 1980s. It was during much later travels, however, that I became cognizant of how hip hop, once a collaborative expression of postindustrial cultural improvisation among African American, Puerto Rican, and West Indian inner-city youth, was now being refashioned by other marginalized youth globally to give critical voice to their own subjective experience and sense of selfhood. In the interim, of course, a onetime marginal youth culture encompassing expressive elements of music, verbal lyricism, dance, graffiti art, and fashion had evolved into a multibillion-dollar global industry.

Although hip hop has undergone radical transformation during this movement from street to international marketplace, it has at the same time retained a critical capacity to convey a signifying blackness of representational force and emotive meaning. To underscore this is by no means to suggest that there is something "essentially" black per se about hip hop, but rather it is a recognition of the significant, albeit highly mediated ways hip hop continues to communicate a "black," largely masculine discourse of urban marginality. Hip hop today has emerged globally as the most visible and widely disseminated conduit of

U.S. black popular imagery—commercially mediated not only through music but increasingly through film, television, and corporate merchandising. While the majority of scholarship to date has focused on the cultural politics of hip hop's domestic production and consumption within the United States, there have been more recent moves to examine the sociocultural dynamics involved in the trafficking and spread of rap music and hip hop culture globally.[2]

In this essay I address this second line of inquiry, mapping how the black racial significance of hip hop is received, interpreted, and redeployed transnationally. Rather than a broad survey, this exploration centers on the politics and poetics of hip hop as they find particular expression within the black diasporic world. Beyond simply questions of cultural consumption and reproduction, I argue that hip hop's expanding global reach has enabled the making of new black diasporic subjects in and of themselves. In ways evocative of Benedict Anderson's insights into the role of print media in forging modern national identities,[3] hip hop today has assumed an increasingly significant role in shaping contemporary forms of black diasporic consciousness and subjectivity. Here, African-descendant youth in an array of locales are employing the performative space of hip hop to mobilize notions of black self in ways that simultaneously contest and transcend nationally bound racial framings. Within these contexts understandings of diasporic belonging are often paramount, if not vitally constitutive of such black self-fashioning. Thus, much like print media of a previous moment, hip hop has become a productive technology in the current global mapping and moving of black political subjects via the social workings of diaspora. In pursuing this argument, this essay examines hip hop movements in Brazil, Cuba, and South Africa comparatively as varying examples of how transnationally attuned identities of blackness are marshaled in the making of diasporic subjects through hip hop's performative lens.

When considering the international proliferation of hip hop, one needs to be cognizant of the differing ways hip hop's "black" cultural politics travel as they are engaged by communities beyond the United States. While such diffusion may move along similar global circuits as culturally and geographically divergent as Senegal and Japan, it is clear that hip hop's reception and recontextualization in the formation of local followings can often involve very different kinds of social meaning-making. While hip hop may indeed provide cultural resources in the global shaping of local identities,[4] one must always remain attentive to questions of power and relative positionality. The query, then, becomes one of who is consuming whom, and to what ends.

It is, however, undeniable that hip hop has assumed a wide and particularly marked resonance among more socially marginal communities of youth. This is as much the case for working-class urban youth in Chile as it is for their ethnically marked Basque contemporaries in Spain. In both settings we find examples of how young people appropriate markers of blackness as a means of expressing their own subjective conditions of marginality. Chile's Las Panteras Negras (The Black Panthers) coupled with the Basque nationalist group Negu Gorriak's self-identification as "Afro-Basque" are exemplary of such symbolic deployments.[5] Palestinian hip hop poet Suheir Hammad's evocations of Public Enemy, Amiri Baraka, and Malcolm X in her 1996 collection *Born Palestinian, Born Black* is further illustrative of blackness's global resonance as a hip hop–informed marker of social marginality.[6] Yet while shared understandings of social marginalization may indeed be involved in these examples, such identifications do not in the end constitute these young people in any historical sense as "black" per se. Where lie, then, these practices of black self-making of which I speak?

Within the current literature on hip hop's transnational dimensions there is little scholarship examining the politics of race and racial identification at play globally. In many treatments either African or African-descendant sites are absent from examination, or there is an analytical privileging of cultural or ethnic modes of differentiation vis-à-vis marginalized communities to the exclusion of the racialized processes that often shape the lived experience of these populations. While it is clear, as Tony Mitchell has suggested, that hip hop in a global sense "cannot be viewed simply as an expression of African American culture; it has become a vehicle for global youth affiliations and a tool for reworking local identities all over the world,"[7] this does not mean that race (or blackness) is necessarily erased from the equation.

When assessing hip hop's transnational racial significance, one cannot deny the particular salience of the cultural form within the contemporary Afro-Atlantic world. Whether Haitian immigrants in Montreal, Afro-Colombians in Cali, Colombia, or Afro-Amerindian Garifuna in Honduras, African-descendant youth globally are using the performative space of hip hop as a vital site of critical self-expression. Yet beyond a simple claiming of voice, to what extent might hip hop's "black" cultural framings facilitate new, diasporically attuned identities of blackness themselves? Such a suggestion recalls those diasporic affinities that first gave rise to hip hop via the interchange of African American, Puerto Rican, and West Indian inner-city youth.[8] Cultural agencies of the like found creative expression through the melding of overlapping histories of black diasporic experience coupled with shared conditions of social

marginalization as youth of color in postindustrial urban America. Indeed,
it has been argued that this early period of hip hop's formation engendered
new expressions of black urban subjectivity that found common groundings
through a shared sense of Afrodiasporic belonging.[9]

At this moment, however, hip hop can be seen as an increasingly important conduit for just those kinds of global black identifications and emergent
subjectivities that have historically constituted the African Diaspora as a lived
social formation. The notion of diaspora here is dynamic and ever changing,
one forged through historical plays of power and agency in the continual remaking of diaspora via transnational black identification and communicative
interchange.[10] Such an understanding foregrounds Brent Hayes Edwards's notion of a "mobilized diaspora" in distinguishing between a historically *given*,
"involuntary" sense of diaspora versus a historically *responsive* recognition of
the ways the African, or more appropriately, "black," diaspora is actively employed in the making of globally conscious black subjects and social movements.[11] This framing not only underscores the salience of what Paul Gilroy
has termed the contemporary "routes" of diasporic identification[12] but additionally opens up space for an appreciation of how transnational affinities
of blackness can be fashioned among communities of African descent who
may not necessarily share histories of displacement. Such expansiveness holds
particular currency when considering the vibrant presence of hip hop in Africa
itself, where young people across the continent can be seen asserting their
claim to a globalized space of "modern," postcolonial blackness through hip
hop's diasporic spectrum. Yet while the source of such black self-imaginings
may be initially grounded in the historical specificity of the United States,
subsequent black self-constitutions are neither beholden to nor necessarily
disarticulated from U.S. racial histories. The question, rather, as we shall see,
concerns the complex manner in which such blackness is rearticulated globally
by varying communities of "black" youth.

Brazil

The rise of Brazilian hip hop offers a critically insightful illustration of how
black diasporic identities are currently mobilized through the performative
spectrum of hip hop culture. Articulations of this kind carry added potential given Brazil's location as the most populous concentration of peoples of
African descent outside the African continent—a historical legacy courtesy
of the largest and most enduring slave system in the Americas. While hip

hop's foundations in Brazil were first laid in the 1980s through the circulation of music and images emanating from the United States,[13] Brazilian hip hop's diasporic contours should be understood within a broader recent history of Afro-Brazilian engagement with U.S. black popular culture. Brazil's Black Soul movement of the 1970s represents a particularly notable example of such diasporically informed engagement. Here by way of music, dance, and fashion, young Afro-Brazilians of Rio de Janeiro drew upon the black cultural aesthetics and embodied self-awareness of 1970s U.S. soul music in the voicing of new, transnationally inspired expressions of Afro-Brazilian blackness. During this period parties were organized where young Afro-clad youth donned bell-bottoms and dashikis and gathered to dance to the likes of James Brown and Marvin Gaye.

Transcending questions of simple cultural importation, Michael Hanchard has argued that Black Soul represented an effort to construct alternative forms of self-affirming black identity as oppositional responses to Brazil's historical privileging of whiteness and persistent forms of racial subjugation.[14] Emerging during the repressive era of Brazil's military dictatorship (1964–85), Black Soul events became important venues for the dissemination of information pertaining to the nascent Movimento Negro—a loosely coordinated affiliation of Afro-Brazilian organizations mobilized strategically around black identity claims. Endeavors of this kind, Hanchard suggests, were formative in the early framing of a black identity politics that continue today as an instrumental facet of Afro-Brazilian sociopolitical organizing. Here, politicized assertions of blackness have been central in efforts to contest Brazil's hegemonic claims as a "racial democracy," where race and racism are alleged inconsequential, if not nonexistent, within an ostensibly racially amalgamated national populace with one of the highest levels of social inequality in the world.[15]

The emergence of Brazilian hip hop needs, therefore, to be viewed within this continuum of diasporically engaged Afro-Brazilian identity politics. Young, largely male Afro-Brazilian *favelados*—residents of Brazil's urban shantytowns known as favelas—in and around São Paulo and Rio de Janeiro were the first to take up rap music in the voicing of their own racially informed experiences and concerns. The highly popular São Paulo–based Racionais MC's (Rational MC's) are a prime example of this early movement in Brazilian hip hop. Establishing their reputation in the late 1980s and early 1990s while performing primarily in favelas and the "darker" suburbs on the fringes of São Paulo, the group's aggressive lyrics focused on social themes most pressing in these marginalized communities, such as racism, racially targeted police violence, drug trafficking, and government corruption in the improvised *periferias* (peripheries). The opening salvo to "Capítulo 4 Versículo 3" from the platinum-selling 1998 album *Sobrevivendo No Inferno* (*Surviving in Hell*) stands as a dramatic case in point:

> 60% dos jovens de periferia sem antecedentes criminais já sofreram
> violência policial;
> A cada quatro pessoas mortas pela polícia, três são negras;
> Nas universidades brasileiras, apenas 2% dos alunos são negros;
> A cada quatro horas um jovem negro morre violentamente em São Paulo;
> Aqui quem fala é Primo Preto, mais um sobrevivente[16]

> [60% of youth in the periphery without criminal records have already
> suffered police violence
> In every four people killed by the police, three are black
> In Brazilian Universities, only 2% of students are black
> Every four hours, a young black person dies violently in São Paulo
> Speaking here is "Primo Preto" ("Black Cousin"), another survivor].[17]

As Primo Preto's introduction testifies, blackness and marginality are imbricated realities in many of Brazil's favelas and urban peripheral zones where systemic forms of racialized violence are quotidian. Indeed, Derek Pardue has suggested that São Paulo hip hop artists mediate marginality itself—in both social and geospatial terms—through discourses and practices of negritude in ways that gesture toward diasporic belonging.[18] His discussion of these diasporic dimensions and their articulations vis-à-vis questions of identity, however, remain largely implicit rather than explicitly explored. Alternatively, Jennifer Roth Gordon contends that Brazilian MCs constitute, in effect, "an alternative black consciousness movement" largely through what she sees as their adoption of U.S. racial ideologies via hip hop's transnational lens.[19] My argument is that diasporic rather than U.S. understandings of blackness are in the end instrumental in fashioning critical expressions of black Brazilian self. The emphasis here is on dialogic engagements rather than reductive appropriations of blackness.

Similar mobilizations of blackness can be seen in Rio de Janeiro, where immediately following the infamous Candelaria murders of 1993, in which off-duty police systematically gunned down a group of black street children sleeping aside a Rio Janeiro church, a protest rally was coordinated in the city by a coalition of organizations within the Movimento Negro. Among the speakers and performers condemning the murders and the broader culture of racial violence at the rally were the Rio-based rap duo Consciencia Urbana (Urban Consciousness). At the time of the event, member Big Richard described the political significance of his music this way:

> In the U.S. blacks have a notion that racism exists. Not in Brazil. In Brazil racism is disguised. In Brazil we live in a racial democracy, believe it if you will. Here we have a small number of black youth who fight against racism, while the majority, even as they suffer racism every day like being harassed on the bus by the police, prefer to believe what is shown to them on television and in the media. So what happens is that we present the counterculture to this, and to fight as a counterculture is not easy, especially in Brazil.[20]

In addition to employing rap as a pedagogic device in an effort to inform Afro-Brazilian counterhegemonic sensibilities vis-à-vis dominant Brazilian constructions of racial exceptionalism, Consciencia Urbana's songs evoke black diasporic imagery and identifications as a means of grounding the local within broader histories of black antiracist struggle. In referencing the significance of Malcolm X, for example, Big Richard explains: "We decided to make a rap song about Malcolm X because he was not solely a black American. He lost his Americanness when he fought against racism, for any person who fights against racism anywhere in the world is fighting for blacks, for the survival of black people."[21]

Here the figure of Malcolm X is resignified beyond his U.S. historical specificity in an effort to accommodate a more expansive diasporic reading. Similar moves are echoed in a song by Racionais MC's where baggy-jeaned, baseball-cap-adorned member Mono Brown riffs, "We need a leader with popular credit like Malcolm X as in other times in America, who is black down to the bones—one of us—and reconstructs our pride from ruins."[22] These artists' adoption and rearticulation of Malcolm X's black nationalist imagery within the context of Afro-Brazilian struggle is a cogent example of the ways African-descendant communities draw inspiration transnationally from experiences and cultures of black populations elsewhere. By mobilizing such diasporic resources in this manner, to use Jacqueline Nassy Brown's term, Afro-Brazilian rap artists not only tie their struggles historically to others in the diaspora but, in effect, actively constitute the black diaspora itself as a *lived* social reality.[23] In the case of Malcolm X's imagery, such cultural appropriations were no doubt informed at the time by the revitalization of Malcolm X in the United States by rap artists such as Public Enemy, who along with Spike Lee helped to feed the

"X" fashion trend of the early 1990s. Although these commodified representations of Malcolm's complex legacy were not devoid of their commercially tied contradictions, they nonetheless retained a capacity to transnationally convey and generate meanings of a radical blackness for others.

Rather than simple appropriations, these examples illustrate how U.S. rap music and hip hop–attuned black popular culture serves as a lens through which diasporically informed ideas, messages, and identifications can and are actively fashioned. Such black diasporic processes and understandings are clearly articulated by Big Richard, who elaborates:

> By principle, we think that rap is not a [North] American music. Rap is a music of black people, and black people originated in Africa. In the case of those who are born outside of Africa, we are speaking of the Diaspora. Here in Brazil, it is a regional music, adapted to the Portuguese, to the Brazilian swing where we mix *timbalala* and samba-reggae with rap. We make a connection by joining American music with Brazilian music in creating our own style, but without ever losing the music's roots, because in fact these two roots are sisters—they originated in only one place, Africa.[24]

While emphasizing the African historical "roots" of rap music, Big Richard simultaneously evokes the contemporary routes of rap's black diasporic significance in referencing its aesthetically conveyed blackness as the basis for constructing transnational black "connections" between Brazil and the United States. He suggests that such identifications are made most real not simply through the consumption of hip hop but, rather, through the ways hip hop is proactively transformed in the making of a new, culturally relevant, yet a signifyingly "black" Brazilian music form. Big Richard's reference to "creating our own style" through the fusion of Afro-Brazilian musical elements and the use of Portuguese to indigenize rap further underscores the important interrelationality between style making and identity. On both aesthetic and linguistic levels, then, the creative reworking of hip hop's conveyed blackness not only may give rise to a new Brazilian music genre but might, in fact, serve as an alternative modality for articulating blackness in Brazil altogether. The suggestion here is that hip hop may facilitate black social imaginaries that transcend nationally prescriptive, historically circumscribed fields of Brazilian blackness.

Within the broader space of Brazilian hip hop, style is also key to the ways blackness is performatively marked and bodily exhibited through popular fashion. Glossy hip hop magazines such as *Rap Brasil*, *Hip Hop en Movimiento*, and

Rap Rima that have emerged over the past decade are filled with images of young black and brown, primarily male, Brazilians dressed in U.S.-inspired hip hop attire. The enactive "rocking" of such hip hop fashion is often accompanied by overt body posturing stylistically evocative of that employed by young African American men and male rap artists. Many of Brazil's most established rap groups signify themselves in one form or another through such U.S.-inspired black urban style. As a mode of self-representational practice, style in this way must be understood as "performative" in its own right—performative in the productive sense in which Judith Butler speaks of how individual subjectivities and the social categories that define them are in the end constituted only insomuch as they are enacted or *performed* in everyday life.[25] Indeed, if we consider Stuart Hall's suggestion that "it is only through the ways in which we represent and imagine ourselves that we come to know how we are,"[26] emphasizing the performative nature of black popular style in this way encourages considerations of the active self-representational force of style in its capacity to culturally articulate, more than simply reflect, identities of blackness and ways of being.[27]

Afro-Brazilian rap duo Afro-X and Dexter further illustrate this performative mending of black urban style and the aesthetic production of black selfhood. The duo recorded their first album in 2000 while imprisoned in the infamous São Paulo Carandiru prison complex that first gained international attention in 1992 when 111 inmates were systematically massacred by military police following a prison uprising. Referring to themselves as "509-E" after their prison cell number, Afro-X and Dexter's music assails a corrupt justice system while testifying to the violent realities of being black, male, and poor in contemporary Brazil. In addition to limited performances in prison, the duo recorded a video for MTV Brazil in which they can be seen sporting gold chains and designer sneakers.[28] Their state-regulation beige pants are worn baggy off the hip, stylistically evoking U.S. hip hop–associated fashion practices first coined by young African American males that, ironically, arose out of U.S. prison culture.

As these Brazilian examples suggest, rap music and associated hip hop culture can provide alternative cultural frameworks through which new meanings and identities of blackness can be strategically articulated and performatively mobilized. To the extent that these identifications are forged through transnationally projected black imagery, they are not predicated on linguistic intelligibility. Rather, hip hop's black racial alterity is conveyed most tangibly through its marked blackness of style. Such blackness, in turn, is transformed

through both linguistic and stylistic innovations in the voicing and bodily performance of new kinds of critical black subjectivity that are both products of
and responsive to the particular sociocultural imperatives of contemporary
Brazil. Writing on Afro-Brazilian youth culture in Bahia, Brazil, Livio Sansone
observes that the fashioning of new black-signified youth styles as exemplified in hip hop "offers black people new opportunities for redefining black
difference in Western societies by aestheticizing blackness, in the first place,
through highly visible styles and pop music."[29] Indeed, the adoption of these
transnationally informed youth practices provides young Afro-Brazilians with
means of not only marking their blackness more visibly but actively linking
their struggles to a broader black diasporic experience and transnational frameworks of black antiracism.

Cuba

Much as in Brazil, race and blackness have long been at the center of Cuba's
historical narrative, dating back to the massive importation of enslaved Africans upon whose labor the island's sugar-based plantation economy grew to
the largest in the colonial world by the mid-nineteenth century. Cuba's welding
of race and nation was further deepened in the late nineteenth century during the island's anticolonial wars of independence in which recently liberated
Afro-Cubans comprised the vast majority of the independence movement's
fighting force. Here the struggle to free the island from Spanish colonial control
was inextricably tied to the struggle for black emancipation and correspond-
ing visions for a racially just and equitable Cuban nation.[30] Such expectations
remained largely elusive until after 1959, when the Cuban Revolution took up
socialism and placed racial equality, at least initially, at the center of its declared
program to build a socially egalitarian society. While the extent to which the
Cuban Revolution was able to eliminate racism and hierarchical racial privilege
remains debated,[31] it is unquestionable that many black Cubans did, on the
whole, benefit significantly from the social reforms and programs undertaken
during the early revolutionary period. This did not mean that the deep, historically rooted ideological structures of racism in Cuban society ceased to operate
and to reproduce themselves in everyday life. To speak publicly of racism's persistence, however, became taboo under revolutionary socialism, which by the
mid-1960s had declared racism and racial discrimination officially eradicated
from the island. Assertions to the contrary were ultimately deemed divisive,
counterrevolutionary if not counternational declarations.

The collapse of the Soviet Union and the Eastern Bloc ushered in yet another critical phase of Cuba's racial history. With the 1990 suspension of Soviet subsidies upon which Cuba's economy and the revolutionary project had been largely underwritten, the island fell into a severe economic crisis known as the "special period." In a strategic move to revive the economy, the Cuban state initiated a series of economic reforms in the early 1990s that, in effect, represented a cautious opening of the heretofore-closed Cuban economy to global capital. Possibly the most dramatic consequence of this neoliberal shift has been the dollarization of Cuba's economy and its transformative impacts on everyday life in Cuba.[32] In addition to engendering greater social stratification predicated upon differing levels of access to circulating dollars and other foreign currencies, race (re)emerged as a critical factor affecting who and how one gets such access within Cuba's new economy.[33] Within these workings, new levels, if not racialized modes, of socioeconomic marginalization have surfaced in Cuba today. Under such conditions the ideological claims of a unified, "nonracial" Cuba under revolutionary socialism and the subsequent silencing of race were now laid bare by the everyday lived social consequences of racial difference in Cuba. The critical question to be asked, then, concerns how black and darker-skinned Cubans are currently responding to these new racialized realities and to what extent and in what ways might such efforts be contestatory.

It is no coincidence that the emergence of hip hop in Cuba over the last decade or so has occurred precisely during this current period of rapid social transformation.[34] Though the early roots of rap music in Cuba can be traced back to the mid-1980s, it was not until the economic crisis of the 1990s that hip hop as a cultural movement in Cuba began to take shape. It is significant, moreover, that those who first and most ardently engaged in hip hop were overwhelmingly black and darker-skinned youth. It remained so as interest in rap music spread throughout the greater Havana area. A cultural space, almost exclusively black and young, began to evolve around the transnationally introduced music form. Within a relatively short time, parties began springing up across Havana where young people gathered to listen, dance, and otherwise participate in the collective making of Cuba's nascent hip hop movement.[35] By the mid-1990s these new black spaces had a brief footing in a few state-run cultural centers before garnering the distrust of some Cuban officials who viewed such gatherings with suspicion, ostensibly associating them with capitalist culture and antisocial influences.

Within today's vibrant self-identified Cuban hip hop movement, black youth frequent dance clubs and additional venues throughout the island's urban centers where the latest U.S. hip hop can be heard. Many of these youth, significantly, are drawn from poorer, more socially marginal neighborhoods. As scores of youth dance and sing along with the music—though most do not actually speak English themselves—they don baggy pants, foreign-made athletic shoes, and U.S. baseball caps and team jerseys. These commodified expressions of U.S. black youth culture are tied to the recent opening of the island to transnational flows of people, capital, and cultural influences, as well as a growing culture of consumerism in a once defiantly anticonsumerist Cuba. Yet like their Brazilian peers, these youth mobilize black-signified style as self-constituting practices.

Beyond questions of consumption, however, the cultural meaning-making within Cuban hip hop lies most significantly in the way young Afro-Cubans are critically refashioning rap music and hip hop's black-signified aesthetics into their own idioms of self-expression. With an estimated 500 or more rap groups currently islandwide, there are sites throughout Cuba where local *raperos*, as Cuban MCs are termed, perform original material before packed audiences. While frequently using body posturing and gestures evocative of U.S. rap performances, their lyrics are sung in a distinctly Cuban Spanish vernacular over rhythms often incorporating Afro-Cuban musical elements. At the center of the music, however, is a thematic emphasis on social critique in which many *raperos* evoke their identities as *los negros* (black people) as the basis from which their perspectives are critically voiced. It is important to note that a significant number of *raperos* and their followers who might not necessarily be categorized as "negro" (black) within Cuba's phenotypically graduated system of racial classification self-identify as such. In conversation with some of these individuals, many suggest that it was precisely through their involvement within the Cuban hip hop movement that they came to identify themselves as black. As Randy of the Havana-based duo Los Paisanos explained, "Me? I'm black. Well here in Cuba I'm *jabao*. This is what they tell me here in Cuba, *jabao*. This light brown hair and eyes more or less light, all the same color, and with light brown skin." When asked how long he identified as black (*negro*), Randy replied, "Not very long. It has been a short time, since I began to take seriously the hip hop movement. Hip hop is a thing that frees the mentality, it is freedom. Many people don't understand but for us it is freedom. We have changed our way of thinking and we have completely opened our thinking.

I don't know, it's a powerful weapon. Hip hop is a force, it's life, it's a way of life."[36] As Randy's comments suggest, hip hop can indeed be instrumental in forging new understandings of black selfhood. Rather than simply a question of music, hip hop becomes for Randy a way of life, a transformative, liberating force associated with black self-actualization.

Yet such identities find their most active and politically demonstrative expression through their performance. In addition to everyday concerns, such as struggles for foreign currency and the social impacts of tourism and the related sex trade, *raperos* frequently address manifestations of and struggles against antiblack racism both locally and internationally. In doing so, these youth actively position themselves and their politics within a broader Afrodiasporic context of present-day black struggle. U.S. black radical figures such as Malcolm X, the Black Panthers, and more recently, Mumia Abu-Jamal have become important verbal references among many Cuban MCs. The transnational sites of contact for such black radical iconography stem primarily from two related sources. The first is *raperos'* long-standing engagement with critically oriented African American rap artists from the United States, and the second arises from the influence of African American political exiles, most notably Assata Shakur and Nehanda Abiodun. Abiodun has been particularly active in mentoring capacities within Havana's hip hop community, conferring on her something of a *la madrina*, or godmother, status within the movement.

Another key facilitator of these black radical connections has been the New York–based Black August Collective, which participated in a number of the early Cuban hip hop festivals held annually in Havana. Black August's participation along these lines has been twofold: organizing festival performances of more politically identified African American artists such as Mos Def and Talib Kweli, Common, and Dead Prez, while strengthening bonds with African American political exiles on the island. Largely as a result of these varying engagements, *raperos'* transnationally envisioned notions of social justice are often advanced within overlapping discourses of "revolution"—one rooted in post-1959 Cuban revolutionary society and another informed by U.S. black radical/nationalist traditions and their contemporary struggles.

Yet on another level and resonant with similar examples in other Afrodiasporic sites,[37] such diasporically attuned, self-consciously "modern" expressions of blackness overtly contest Cuba's dominant historical configuration of blackness within the nationally bounded trope of "folklore." Framings of this kind have tended to relegate Afro-Cubans to an ahistorical, unchanging "national" past, effectively freezing blacks within static representations of the "traditional" rather than recognizing the dynamic and ever-changing nature of Afro-Cuban culture, identity, and social agency. The self-affirming, nationally expansive black modernity asserted by Afro-Cuban *raperos* clearly stands in stark juxtaposition to, if not in implicit critique of, such folklorized constraints.

Given the growing marginalization of darker-skinned Cubans from centers of economic activity in an increasingly socially stratified Cuba, *raperos* can be understood as employing the black-identified cultural space of hip hop to articulate and mobilize their racial difference in response to greater levels of racially lived social inequality. Hip hop's black-signified framings offer these youth a racially empowering, yet alternative, nationally transcendent source of black identification. Such diasporically aware blackness, in turn, serves as the basis upon which to act and move politically. Here, *raperos'* musical emphasis on social critique is often aimed at deconstructing the mounting contradictions between the claims of a socially just, racially egalitarian society under revolutionary socialism and the growing realities of class and racial polarization within the island's new neoliberally impacted economy.

Most *raperos*, however, are far from counterrevolutionaries, as some off the island might like to claim. Quite the contrary. The majority of Cuban MCs see their music as critically engaged in one form or another in advancing key principles embodied in the ideals of the Cuban Revolution. As Kokino, a member of Havana's Anónimo Consejo (Anonymous Advice), put it, "Our critique or our protest is constructive. The idea of Anónimo Consejo is not to throw the revolution to the floor. It is rather to make a revolution within the revolution. It is to criticize the things, or to protest the things that are not well within the Cuban revolution. But our objective is not to harass or be destructive, but it is to make a new Cuba for young people."[38] Indeed, these youth represent a generation of socially engaged artists who remain shaped by the socialist-derived notions of egalitarianism embedded and still alive within Cuban society. Implicit critiques of capitalism and its debilitating effects on Cuban society are recurring themes within much of Cuban hip hop. Moreover, vocal challenges to U.S. imperialism—those articulated with Cuban revolutionary discourse as well as more radical voices within U.S. hip hop—hold significant sway among many Cuban MCs. All this said, *raperos'* central object of critique remains Cuban society and its lived contradictions.

MCs Zoandris and Pelón, who comprise the Havana-based duo Hermanos de Causa (Brothers of Cause), are among the most respected and politically outspoken *raperos* on the island. One of their signature tracks from their 2003 album is "Lágrimas Negras" ("Black Tears"). Taking the song's title from a classic Cuban *bolero-son* made famous in the 1930s by the celebrated Cuban composer Miguel Matamoros, Hermanos de Causa's "Lágrimas Negras" presents a lamentable though unabashed denunciation of the prevalence of racism in today's Cuba.

Yo de frente todo el tiempo realista	I in front, all the time a realist
No digas que no hay racismo	Don't say that there isn't racism
donde hay un racista	where there is a racist
siempre y cuando donde quiera	Always, when and where ever I
que me encuentre el prejuicio	find myself, prejudice in one
de una forma o de otra	form or another is always
siempre esta presente	present
[...]	[...]
Siento odio profundo por tu	I feel profound hate for your
racismo	racism
Ya no me confundo con tu ironía	I am no longer confused by your
Ylloro sin que sepas que el llanto	irony
mío	And I cry without you knowing
Tiene lágrimas negras como mi	that my cry has black tears like
vida	my life
[...]	[...]
No me digas que no hay porque	Don't tell me that there isn't any
yo sé, lo he visto	because I know, I have seen it
No me digas que no existe porque	Don't tell me that it doesn't exist
lo he vivido	because I have lived it
No me niegues que hay oculto	Don't deny that there is a hidden
un prejuicio racial que nos	racial prejudice that condemns us
condena y	and
nos valora a todos por igual	values us all the same
No te dejes engañar	Don't be fooled
los ojos de par en par	Eyes wide open
No te dejes engañar ...	Don't be deceived ...

Hermanos de Causa in no uncertain terms seeks to expose the stark incongruities between long-standing revolutionary discourses that deny the workings of racism versus the lived realities and social consequences of racialized existence in Cuba today. Rather than a marker of romantic sorrow as conveyed in the original rendition, in Hermanos de Causa's version of "Lágrimas Negras," the song's title is resignified to foreground a racial positionality at the center of its testimonial critique—in short, a critical black subject, "no longer confused," who refuses to remain silent.

A particularly significant marker of hip hop's Cuban ascendance has been the Cuban state's response to its racially signified cultural politics. In 1999 the Cuban minister of culture organized a meeting with representatives of Havana's hip hop community where he expressed the government's recognition of rap as a legitimate form of Cuban cultural expression. Prior to this moment, as suggested earlier, the Cuban state regarded rap music as an icon of U.S. capitalist culture with implied counterrevolutionary tendencies. Since this shift, however, the state became increasingly involved in the institutionalization of Cuban hip hop within the frame of revolutionary national culture.

The evolution of the annual Cuban Hip Hop Festival serves as a key indicator of the Cuban state's growing interest in, and attempted institutionalization of, the hip hop movement. Initiated in 1995, the festival was founded by a small group of black cultural activists interested in creating a space to showcase Havana's emerging rap talent. With little support from the Cuban government, these individuals ran the festival until 2000, when the cultural branch of the Union of Young Communists stepped in as the event's sole organizer. From this point on, state institutions have played an increasingly active role in making resources and public venues available to rap artists. At the same time, the Cuban state has made consistent efforts to assume a position as a key arbiter and representational face of the movement. The establishment in 2002 of the state-run La Agencia de Rap, or Cuban Rap Agency, represented the most dramatic expression of such incorporative institutionalizing moves. Yet in all its institutional expressions, the Cuban state has conspicuously—though not surprisingly—downplayed, if not completely ignored, the black racial significance of Cuban hip hop in its official dealings with the movement. To acknowledge this racial significance would open the Pandora's box of race and its contemporary dynamics, which the revolutionary leadership remains largely resistant to openly addressing.

Though initial reception on the part of many *raperos* to this new official attention was relatively positive, there was some ambivalence. On one level, the hip hop movement has long fought for recognition and the right to state resources within the context of a socialist society. Therefore, the recent access was much appreciated. Nonetheless, there remained at various levels caution, if not mistrust, on the part of many Cuban MCs regarding the extent to which the state sought to hold the reins. While the Cuban state's recognition of hip hop may have signaled a move toward authorizing it as a valid part of Cuban national culture and thus bestowing upon it just resources, that recognition can also be read as an attempt to incorporate a previously marginalized youth culture — as well as its racial underpinnings — within institutional structures, thereby mitigating its oppositional potential.

While this may certainly be the case, I suggest that such incorporation has simultaneously enabled the development of an alternative space of racial articulation within an otherwise tightly controlled Cuban public landscape. I contend that Cuban hip hop has come to occupy an important site of racially positioned social critique and antiracist advocacy within contemporary Cuba and, in doing so, helps push critical accounts of racial and class dynamics further into realms of public discourse at this critical historical juncture. As such, hip hop can be understood as an increasingly important player in an evolving black public sphere predicated on the assertion of a contemporary black political difference within a previously configured, ostensibly "nonracial" Cuban national imaginary. Within this evolving black counterpublic,[39] Afro-Cuban intellectuals and artists are increasingly engaging *raperos* whose work is seen in vanguardist terms vis-à-vis the island's current spectrum of racial politics. Moreover, courses at the University of Havana are now accessing Cuban rap lyrics as important sources of contemporary social commentary on Cuban society.

The future of Cuban hip hop, as the future of Cuba as a whole at this transformative moment, remains to be seen. Yet the efforts of Afro-Cuban *raperos* illuminate the dialect interplay between shifting regimes of racialized power and emergent forms of race-based social praxis as they are increasingly forged at the intersection of the local and the global. Here, the transnational, black-signified space of hip hop has been instrumental in enabling new forms of diasporically engaged strategies of self-making and self-action in the face of new globally inflected imperatives of race.

South Africa

While traditional scholarship of the African Diaspora has tended to concern itself with populations of African descent that share a common historical experience of dispersion — often involuntary — from an African "homeland," thus privileging the Atlantic as the primary locale of diasporic experience, others have underscored the necessity of (re)centering Africa as a contemporary site in the making and shaping of black diasporic identities and related political expression.[40] When considering the transnational contours of hip hop as a modern-day route of black racial identification, Africa itself has to be reckoned with. The widespread proliferation of rap artists and hip hop culture throughout Africa's urban centers represents an important manifestation of hip hop's global black reach. The rise of vibrant local hip hop movements in Senegal, Ghana, Benin, Kenya, and Cote d'Ivoire—to name just a few—suggests that African youth today are increasingly engaging in the black-signified cultural space of hip hop as a medium of critical self-expression.[41]

The very real, structurally conditioned hardships that much of sub-Saharan Africa continues to live through have no doubt shaped the social commitments and political urgencies found in much of the hip hop produced on the continent. Before Kanye West's anti-"bling" single "Diamonds from Sierra Leone" (2005) helped draw U.S. attention to the economies of violence tied to Africa's diamond trade, Sierra Leonean youth in Freetown had long been active in using hip hop as a medium of social critique in the postwar nation.[42] In East Africa, Swahili-language rap in cities like Dar es Salaam, Tanzania, and Nairobi, Kenya, have similarly become an important vehicle among urban youth for giving critical voice to present-day social concerns such as AIDS, joblessness, and state corruption.[43] For the purposes of this essay, however, the gaze is turned southward toward South Africa—one of the earliest sites of hip hop on the continent—as a poignant example of the ways critically positioned identities of blackness have been mobilized through the transnational lens of hip hop.

South African hip hop has undergone significant development since its emergence during the waning years of apartheid among Cape Town's coloured, or "mixed-race," youth in the late 1980s. Today, Johannesburg has joined Cape Town as one of South Africa's centers of locally produced hip hop, with each reflecting the particular cultural (and racial) dynamics of their regional settings. For one, Johannesburg-based hip hop has had to compete with the rise of kwaito—a frenetic, widely popular dance music out of Johannesburg's black townships that fuses older South African music genres, such as mbaqanga, with Western music styles, including hip hop. Heavily incorporative of the township vernacular isicamtho,[44] kwaito artists have generally tended to gravitate toward festive rather than explicit sociopolitical themes in their lyrics. Some have suggested such orientations reflect a celebratory postapartheid move among many black South African youth away from the more overt political imperatives of the apartheid era.[45] Given the widespread popularity of kwaito among Johannesburg's black township youth—the same demographic fan base from which the region's hip hop traditionally draws—it is not surprising that the music has had a significant impact on the local hip hop scene, leading in some cases to a potential blurring of genres. There are those within Johannesburg's hip hop scene, however, who hold firm to what they see as a clear and necessary artistic distinction between the two genres.[46]

While South Africa's top-selling, Soweto-born hip hop artist Pitch Black Afro may employ blackness satirically as a central performative trope (e.g., his ubiquitous oversized Afro wig), a differing and possibly more politically consequent mobilization of blackness can be found in the context of the genre's birth in Cape Town. Hip hop emerged in South Africa in the late 1980s primarily among coloured youth of Cape Town's sprawling Cape Flats region.[47] Coloureds, as peoples of "mixed race" were legally classified under apartheid's racialized caste system, literally occupied the racial middle ground, historically positioned by the apartheid state as a buffer between the worlds of white and black South Africa. Residentially, educationally, and frequently professionally segregated from both black and white South Africans, coloured communities often developed their own cultural identity, drawing variously upon their African, Indo-Malaysian, and European cultural histories.[48] And unlike black South Africans, coloureds generally spoke either Afrikaans or English as their primary, identifying language, rather than local African vernaculars. Moreover, in accordance with apartheid's divide-and-rule logic, coloureds were allotted limited class privileges over black South Africans. Such efforts contributed to the historical formation of a racialized class of South Africans who generally aspired to and identified more with white South African status, to the detriment of a nonwhite or "black" social identity—a development clearly attuned with the grand designs of apartheid.

As with the rest of South Africa, however, the 1980s were a highly charged time in the Cape Town region with the rise of mass antiapartheid political mobilization. During this period significant numbers of coloured youth were politicized through varying forms of activism. The critical turning point in the antiapartheid struggle culminated in 1990 with the release of Nelson Mandela and the unbanning of the African National Congress (ANC) and the South African Communist Party. It was within this politically charged moment of social transformation that South Africa's self-defined Black Hip Hop Movement first found its footing among Cape Town's coloured youth. Though the movement's followers eventually adopted "African" in the place of "Black" as a self-identifying term, the initial choice was indicative of the movement's early

deployment of blackness as an identity-based social marker.[49] And while the
later shift may have, in part, reflected the broader move in postapartheid South
Africa toward nonracialism as a reconciliatory national project,[50] the use of
"African" as a self-marker by historically configured coloured youth clearly
carried with it additional political significance.

Probably the most influential hip hop group to emerge during this early
period was the Cape Flats–based Prophets of Da City (poc), who are often
celebrated as key pioneers of South African hip hop. Formed in 1990 during
that critical year of political openings, poc was headed by members Ready D,
Shaheen, and Ramone, who drew heavily upon Cape Town's preexisting b-boy
(break-dancing) culture in their performances. From its initiation, the group's
music embraced a strong sociopolitical focus often directed at addressing the
everyday struggles of coloured township life, including those pertaining to
poverty, unemployment, gang violence, and drug abuse.[51] At the center of
these concerns, however, were explicit critiques of apartheid and its various
manifestations of racialized oppression.

Yet a key and defining component of poc's early political voicings was
their use of the term "black" as a self-referential marker. Through their music
and other public engagements, poc's members consistently positioned themselves as both black and African in oppositional stance to their historical classification as coloured under apartheid. This move was particularly significant
when we consider that during this same period, the coloured population of
the greater Cape Town region voted resoundingly for the white Afrikaner-led
National Party—the very architects of apartheid—over Nelson Mandela's
anc in South Africa's first multiracial elections in 1994. poc's assertion of a
black Africanness as coloured youth, in turn, signified a political affront to a
divisive racial paradigm designed to hinder political alliance between people
of "mixed race" and the larger "black" South African majority. Cognizant of
the political stakes of such ideological trappings, poc's track "Black Thing,"
released one year after the national elections, riffs,

The term "coloured" is a desperate case
of how the devil's divided us by calling us a separate race.
They call me "coloured" said my blood isn't pure, but G,
I'm not jakking my insecurity.
So I respond to this and ventilate my mental state with Black
    Consciousness . . . .[52]

Adam Haupt, who among others has chronicled the deployment of racial discourse within Cape Town's hip hop scene of the 1990s, draws attention to POC's allusion to South Africa's Black Consciousness Movement of the 1960 and 1970s as a "unifying narrative" that "provides an alternative to the divisive discourse of apartheid."[53] Indeed, such appeals not only posit a broadened and racially inclusive notion of blackness but also seek to situate POC members within a historical continuum of black political struggle and consciousness in South Africa.

While hip hop proves a performative frame through which such counter-hegemonic assertions of "black" subjectivity can be rooted nationally, it may also facilitate a forging of black self through transnationally expansive understandings of blackness. Black Noise, another key pioneering Cape Town–based hip hop crew comprised of historically situated coloured youth, illustrates this kind of strategic melding of national and transnational frames of blackness. As their name attests, Black Noise placed a self-signifying "black" African identity and social message at the very center of their music and public image. The group's 1994 track "Who Taught You to Hate Yourself?" stands out as a particularly vivid expression of such black political fusions. The song's title is drawn from an oft-cited quote of Malcolm X's in which he rhetorically chides his African American audience about internalized black self-hatred. The track's chorus builds around a sequence of audio samples in which we hear Malcolm X forcibly prompting, "Who taught you to hate yourself? This blue-eyed man," followed by "Don't let the white man speak for you / And don't let the white man fight for you." Embedded within the sequence we hear a South African voice intoning in Afrikaans, *"Kaffirs bly maar kaffirs"* ("Kaffirs (niggers) will remain kaffirs")[54]—or "You remain where you are." Through this intertextual montage a transatlantic dialogue is forged between South African and U.S. historical realities of race. I suggest that it is precisely through such dialogic references that these artists facilitate a nationally transcendent understanding of black political struggle and subjectivity. The outlines of such positioned identity are given active voice by member Emile Jansen, who follows in the track's second verse:

> That's right the whites taught me to hate who I am
> They labeled us as coloured
> But now I know I'm a black man.
> Apartheid's divide and conquer, Made us believe we're a separate race

And who wants to be a creation, of the supremacist pale face,
And if you're not a perpetrator, of white supremacy,
Then ask yourself
Why you're now angry at me
The word coloured implies
That we're genetically 50/50
But the black gene is dominant
And therefore I'm black see
You'll never say, Cause we know about our white past
Making coloureds understand they're black, Is one hell of a task,
Educated with self hatred
Our black past was destroyed . . . .[55]

Such lyrics not only provide a poignant critique of the fragmentizing logics of apartheid's system of racial classification but give narrative form to the political agency of black self-constitution through the performative dimensions of hip hop.

The transnational routes of such black self-makings found further groundings through Black Noise's active participation in the local South African branch of Afrika Bambaataa's Bronx-based Universal Zulu Nation.[56] The extent of these commitments brought Emile Jansen to New York in 1993 as South Africa's representative to the Zulu Nation's twentieth-anniversary celebration.[57] Such affiliations, however, were not without their ambivalences. Jane Battersby has suggested that the African American–derived Afrocentric imagery upon which Bambaataa's Zulu Nation drew was woefully incongruent with the political realities of South Africa's ethno-racial landscape.[58] The use of the expression "Zulu Nation" itself was particularly fraught because it evoked a complex set of politically charged meanings in South Africa, given Zulus' pivotal role in the country's recent history of ethnically manipulated political violence. While such cultural translations clearly had limitations, it would be wholly reductive to dismiss their social significance. The importance of such engagement lies, rather, in the transnational contours of Black Noise's articulations of, if not identifications with, the black-signified cultural symbolism of the Bronx-born Zulu Nation.

Political orientations of these kinds found active social expression through the numerous workshops and speaking engagements both POC and Black Noise have undertaken in South African schools, libraries, and prisons over the years. Such efforts illustrate the creative fusion of the pedagogic tendencies of rap music with social activism as these youth take their message and concerns to a generation of young people throughout the Cape Town region. One noteworthy example of such engagement was the headlining participation in 2000 of POC and Black Noise in a youth AIDS-awareness campaign directed at mobilizing hip hop as a means to promote HIV education among secondary school students.[59] Black Noise member Emile Jansen has been particularly committed to community-based activism, embracing an acutely politicized position vis-à-vis questions of racial identity. Jansen initiated a series of local forums in the Cape Flats area dubbed the T.E.A.A.C.H. Project (The Educational Alternative Awakening Corrupted Heads), intended, as he explained, to "re-educate people to the proud past the black people have and to make them aware that respect for our people by themselves and others will only be attained if we know our past and supply our people with black role models that they can aspire to."[60] Additionally, Jansen founded a school-based touring project titled "Heal the Hood," directed toward promoting what he described as "respect for being African and using these talents responsibly for the benefit of Africa."[61]

As these examples demonstrate, the politics of identity—in particular those embracing a recuperative notion of a black Africanness—stand central to the self-vision and social mission of groups like POC and Black Noise. From performative fashionings to political engagement, these South African youth can be understood not only as constituting new oppositionally positioned identities of blackness through the transnationally attuned space of hip hop, but as strategically deploying them in politically directed ways.

Concluding Thoughts

Reflecting on the political possibilities of global music circuits, George Lipsitz has suggested that transnational music flows can provide resources for "the recognition of new networks and affiliations [while] they become crucibles for complex identities in formation that respond to the imperatives of place at the same time they transcend them."[62] When considering the Afrodiasporic dimensions of present-day hip hop, such multivalent identity formations are decidedly at play. Here my attention has turned to local hip hop followings in Brazil, Cuba, and South Africa as testaments to how African and African-descendant youth employ the space of hip hop to fashion and marshal globally conscious notions of black selves toward liberatory ends. Identity-centered mobilizations of these kinds recall what Leith Mullings has termed "racializations from below" in describing the transnationally inflected ways racially marginalized communities use the language of race itself as the basis to challenge globalized workings of racial subjugation.[63] Such maneuvers are forged through complex interplays of racializing forces, on one hand, and racially grounded social agencies, on the other.

As I have argued, it is precisely through the political framings of diaspora that such contestive self-racializations find their most poignant expression. Nationally transcendent modes of black diasporic identification prove strategic in challenging local conditions of racial oppression while remaining critically responsive to the ways global processes are increasingly reshaping such conditions. In the case of Brazil, hegemonic discourses tied to notions of "racial democracy" are increasingly unhinged as Afro-Brazilian youth utilize the diasporically configured black racial contours of hip hop to construct new identities to critically interrogate the racialized social realities of their everyday lives. Along analogous lines in Cuba, *raperos* are using hip hop to contest long-standing ideologies of Cuban national racelessness, while providing acute public critiques of the racialized workings of neoliberal transformations in a rapidly shifting Cuban social landscape. In South Africa, a new generation of racialized coloured youth have attempted to position themselves amidst shifting racial paradigms of "old" and "new" where current claims to "nonracialism" run counter to the continued lived consequences of hierarchical racial privilege.

Mapping such maneuvers elucidates the social significance of hip hop not simply in terms of its international circulation and consumption but, rather, through the ways it is actively lived and politically employed as a site of racial mobilization and self-formation. Among these black-identified youth, the space of diaspora—through the performative lens of hip hop—operates as a key paradigm of both identity and politics, and as such it has been instrumental in enabling transnationally engaged strategies of black self-fashioning and action in response to new, globally conditioned modes of racialization. In doing so, these young people not only mobilize black selves but ultimately realize the black diaspora as a lived social formation itself. In this way, hip hop can be seen as an active site for the global (re)mapping of black political imaginaries via social dynamics of diaspora. Or, to return to the poetics of Los Paisanos' "El Negro": "¡*Fundamentalmente hip hop quiere decir negro! Corto, pero penetrante*" ("Fundamentally hip hop means black! Concise, but penetrating").

1. In this essay I use the term "hip hop" to refer to the broad set of cultural practices, the stylized aesthetics, and the larger cultural industry associated with, and inclusive of, rap music.

2. See Mitchell, *Global Noise*; Condry, *Hip-Hop Japan*; and Osumare, *Africanist Aesthetic in Global Hip-Hop*.

3. Anderson, *Imagined Communities*.

4. See Appadurai, *Modernity at Large*.

5. Urla, "'We Are All Malcolm X!'"

6. Hartman, "'*Debke* Beat Funky as P.E.'s Riff.'"

7. Mitchell, *Global Noise*, 2.

8. Rose, *Black Noise*; Chang, *Can't Stop, Won't Stop*.

9. Rivera, *New York Ricans from the Hip Hop Zone*.

10. Gilroy, *Black Atlantic*; Gordon and Anderson, "African Diaspora"; Patterson and Kelley, "Unfinished Migrations."

11. Edwards, "Use of Diaspora."

12. Gilroy, *Black Atlantic*.

13. Magaldi, "Adopting Imports."

14. Hanchard, *Orpheus and Power*.

15. For critical discussions of Brazil's "myth of racial democracy" and its impact on black political mobilization beyond Hanchard, see Winant, *Racial Conditions*, and Lilly Caldwell, *Negras in Brazil*.

16. Original Portuguese lyrics accessed September 18, 2007, from <http://www.coquim.hpg.ig.com.br/l1.htm>.

17. Translation drawn from Roth Gordon, "Hip Hop Brasileiro."

18. Pardue, "Putting Mano to Music."

19. Roth Gordon, "Hip Hop Brasileiro."

20. Personal interview, Rio de Janeiro, Brazil, July 27, 1993.

21. Ibid.

22. McDaniels, "Striking Cord with Youths," 7.

23. Brown, "Black Liverpool."

24. Personal interview, Rio de Janeiro, Brazil, July 27, 1993.

25. Butler, *Gender Trouble*.

26. Hall, *What Is This Black?*, 30.

27. Hebdige, *Subculture*.

28. Darlington, *Brazilian Rappers*.

29. Sansone, "New Blacks from Bahia," 461.

30. Helg, *Our Rightful Share*.

31. For a discussion of varying scholarly readings of and the relative effectiveness of the Cuban Revolution's approach to the problematics of race and racism, see Fernández, "Changing Discourse on Race in Contemporary Cuba," and de la Fuente, *Nation for All*.

32. This scenario remained intact until November 2004, when the Cuban state, in an effort to reduce the island's dependency on U.S. dollars, discouraged the flow of dollars

by way of exchange tariffs in favor of other forms of hard foreign currency. While such moves may have contributed to a de-dollarization of the Cuban economy, the fundamental mechanisms of foreign currency dependency continued to function intact, as Cubans remain largely dependent on some form of foreign currency in order to survive in Cuba's new economy.

33. Hammond, "High Cost of Dollars"; de la Fuente, *Nation for All.*

34. My analysis of the Cuban hip hop movement draws primarily from my two and a half years of ethnographic field research conducted in Havana.

35. Fernández, "¿Poesía urbana?"; Pacini Hernández and Garofalo, "Hip Hop in Havana."

36. Personal interview, Havana, Cuba, August 2, 2002.

37. See Thomas, *Modern Blackness,* and Godreau, "Folkloric 'Others.'"

38. Personal interview, Havana, Cuba, December 12, 2001.

39. Dawson, "Black Counterpublic?" Drawing on the work of Fraser, "Rethinking the Public Sphere," Dawson distinguishes an alternative, subalternly positioned black "counterpublic" from that of Habermas's bourgeois concept of the public sphere predicated on formal institutional civic structures such as the media, the academy, and other dominant organizational forms.

40. Diawara, *In Search of Africa;* Echeruo, "African Diaspora."

41. One only needs to glance at the website Africanhiphop.com to get a sense of the remarkable scope and depth to which hip hop has taken root in Africa. Africanhiphop.com is but one of more than 200 websites dedicated to locally produced hip hop in Africa. Networks of these kinds, in turn, provide a once-inconceivable space for communicative interchange among African practitioners and followers of hip hop, while testifying to the technological savviness of those engaged in the production and promotion of hip hop in Africa despite the continent's endemic levels of poverty and resource scarcity.

42. See, for instance, BBC Radio 1's audio documentary *The Beautiful Struggle* (2005).

43. Perullo, "Hooligans and Heroes." Regarding Kenyan hip hop, see the documentary *Hip Hop Colony: The African Hip Hop Explosion* (2005), produced/directed by Michael Wanguhu.

44. *Isicamtho* is derived from a fusion of regional African languages such as Zulu, Tswana, Sesotho, and Afrikaans. In the shifting parlance of the townships, the term has come to replace the expression *tsotsitaal,* or gagster-speak, previously used to refer to the ever-evolving township vernacular.

45. Stephens, "Kwaito"; Boloka, "Cultural Studies and the Transformation of the Music Industry."

46. Interview with Johannesburg-based Skwatta Kamp, one of South Africa's most commercially successful hip hop crews, <http://www.musica.co.za/eMusica/news_article .asp?segmentID=99&GenreID=99&ArticleID=1296> (accessed April 10, 2006).

47. A vast network of townships was erected in the 1960s along Cape Town's sandy floodplains to accommodate large numbers of coloureds forcibly displaced by apartheid's social geography.

48. Significant numbers of enslaved and indentured laborers from what are today Malaysia and Indonesia were brought to the Cape Town region in the late 1600s by Dutch traders. These "Malays" later intermixed with European settlers and indigenous

Africans, resulting in the racial codification of "coloureds" as a population group under apartheid. Large segments of Cape Town's coloured community still practice the Islam first introduced via Malay/Indonesian influences, and the religion continues to be an important component of a distinct cultural identity for many. Within the broader coloured population, both Afrikaans and English are spoken with a distinctive vernacular accent, cadence, and intonation.

49. This observation is drawn from my personal experience in Cape Town in 1991 during the early formation of the region's hip hop movement. At this juncture, youth participating in the scene, the vast majority of whom were coloured, titled themselves as the Black Hip Hop Movement.

50. See Frederikse, *Unbreakable Thread*.

51. Faber, "Cape Town's Hip Hop Scene."

52. Cited in Haupt, "Hip-Hop in the Age of Empire."

53. Ibid., 217. See also Watkins, "'Simunye, We Are Not One,'" and Battersby, "'Sometime It Feels Like I Am Not Black Enough.'"

54. "Kaffir," a word originally derived from Arabic and meaning unbeliever, was used in South Africa by whites to refer to blacks in ways historically resonant with the term "nigger" in the United States.

55. Cited from <http://africasgateway.com/sections-viewarticle-105.html> (accessed September 24, 2007).

56. The Zulu Nation was a social-cultural organization founded in the early 1970s in public housing projects of the South Bronx by Afrika Bambaataa and is credited as a key cradle of early hip hop culture in New York City. The now "Universal" Zulu Nation has its own website (<www.zulunation.com>) containing information ranging from the history of hip hop, to Afrocentric teachings and readings of world events, to black-produced consumer products. The site even provides an online application service for membership, enabling the expansion of what is now the organization's global network of local branches.

57. See <http://www.zulunation.nl/projects/southafrica/introducing_emile_yx .php> (accessed April 12, 2006).

58. Battersby, "'Sometime It Feels Like I Am Not Black Enough.'"

59. See <http://www.africanhiphop.com/update/hivhop.htm>.

60. Mario Pissarra, *Contemporary African Database*, <http://people.africadatabase .org/en/profile/11711.html> (accessed September 24, 2007).

61. Ibid.

62. Lipsitz, *Dangerous Crossroads*, 6.

63. Mullings, "Race and Globalization."

BIBLIOGRAPHY

Abdul-Raheem, Tajudeen, ed. *Pan-Africanism: Politics, Economy, and Social Change in the Twenty-First Century*. New York: New York University Press, 1996.

Abraham, Sara. "Exceptional Victories: Multiracialism in Trinidad and Tobago and Guyana." *Ethnopolitics* 4, no. 4 (2005): 465–80.

Adeleke, Tunde. *UnAfrican Americans: Nineteenth-Century Black Nationalists and the Civilizing Mission*. Lexington: University Press of Kentucky, 1998.

Adi, Hakim, and Marika Sherwood. *The 1945 Manchester Pan-African Congress Revisited*. London: New Beacon Books, 1995.

African Studies Review 43, no. 1 (2000). Special issue on the African Diaspora.

Akyeampong, Emmanuel. "Africans in the Diaspora: The Diaspora and Africa." *African Affairs* 99 (2000): 183–215.

Ali, Noble Drew. *The Holy Koran of the Moorish Science Temple of America*. Chicago: Self-published, 1927.

Allen, Ernest, Jr. "Making the Strong Survive: The Contours and Contradictions of Message Rap." In *Droppin' Science: Critical Essays on Rap Music and Hip Hop Culture*, edited by William Eric Perkins, 159–91. Philadelphia: Temple University Press, 1996.

Alpers, Edward A. "Recollecting Africa: Diasporic Memory in the Indian Ocean World." *African Studies Review* 43, no. 1 (2000): 83–99.

Alpers, Edward A., and Pierre-Michel Fontaine, eds. *Walter Rodney, Revolutionary and Scholar: A Tribute*. Los Angeles: Center for Afro-American Studies and African Studies Center, University of California, 1982.

Alter, Peter. *Nationalism*. London: Edward Arnold, 1994.

American Social History Project. *Who Built America? Working People and the Nation's Economy, Politics, Culture, and Society*. 2 vols. New York: Worth, 2000.

Amrane, Minne, and Deniéle Djamila. *Femmes en combat: La guerre d'Algérie*. Algiers: Éditions Rahma, 1993.

Anderson, Benedict. *Imagined Communities: Reflections on the Origin and Spread of Nationalism*. New York: Verso, 1991.

Anderson, Carol. *Eyes off the Prize: The United Nations and the African American Struggle for Human Rights, 1944–1955*. Cambridge: Cambridge University Press, 2003.

Anderson, David. *Histories of the Hanged: The Dirty War in Kenya and the End of Empire*. New York: Norton, 2005.

Anthony, David Henry, III. *Max Yergan: Race Man, Internationalist, Cold Warrior*. New York: New York University Press, 2006.

Appadurai, Arjun. "Disjuncture and Difference in the Global Cultural Economy." *Public Culture* 2, no. 2 (1990): 1–24.

———. *Modernity at Large: Cultural Dimensions of Globalization*. Minneapolis: University of Minnesota Press, 1996.

Appiah, Kwame Anthony. *In My Father's House: Africa in the Philosophy of Culture*. New York: Oxford University Press, 1992.

Aptheker, Herbert. *American Negro Slave Revolts*. New York: Columbia University Press, 1944.

———. *A Documentary History of the Negro People in the United States*. 3 vols. New York: Citadel Press, 1962.

Asante, Molefi. *The Afrocentric Idea*. Philadelphia: Temple University Press, 1987.

Asante, S. K. B. *Pan-African Protest: West Africa and the Italo-Ethiopian Crisis, 1934–1941*. London: Longman Group, Ltd., 1977.

Atkins, Keletso. "The Black Atlantic Communication Network: African American Sailors and the Cape of Good Hope Connection." *Issue: A Journal of Opinion* 24, no. 2 (1996): 6–11.

Austin, David. "All Roads Led to Montreal: Black Power, the Caribbean, and the Black Radical Tradition in Canada." *Journal of African American History* 92, no. 4 (2007): 516–39.

Austin, Dennis. *Politics in Ghana, 1946–1960*. London: Oxford University Press, 1970.

Baba Kake, Ibrahim. "L'influence des Afro-Américains sur des nationalistes noirs francophones d'Afrique (1919–1945)." *Présence africaine* 112 (1979): 48–65.

Baden-Powell, Sir Robert Stephenson. *Scouting for Boys: A Handbook for Instruction in Good Citizenship*. 4th ed. London: C. Arthur Pearson Ltd., 1911.

Bair, Barbara. "'Ethiopia Shall Stretch Forth Her Hands Unto God': Laura Kofey and the Gendered Vision of Redemption in the Garvey Movement." In *A Mighty Baptism: Race, Gender, and the Creation of American Protestantism*, edited by Susan Juster and Lisa MacFarlane, 38–61. Ithaca: Cornell University Press, 1996.

Balibar, Etienne. "Is There a 'Neo-Racism'?" In *Race, Nation, and Class: Ambiguous Identities*, by Etienne Balibar and Immannuel Wallerstein, 17–28. London: Verso, 1991.

Bankie, B. F., ed. *Globalising Africans: Towards the 7th Pan-African Congress*. Cape Town: Center for Advanced Studies of African Society, 2001.

Barbeau, Arthur E., and Florette Henri. *The Unknown Soldiers: Black American Troops in World War I*. Philadelphia: Temple University Press, 1974.

Barrett, Leonard E. *The Rastafarians: The Dreadlocks of Jamaica*. Kingston: Sangsters Book Stores, 1977.

Bastfield, Darrin. *Back in the Day: My Life and Times with Tupac Shakur*. New York: Da Capo Press, 2003.

Basu, Dipannita, and Sidney Lemelle, eds. *The Vinyl Ain't Final: Hip Hop and the Globalization of Black Popular Culture*. London: Pluto, 2006.

Battersby, Jane. "'Sometime It Feels Like I Am Not Black Enough': Recast(e)ing Coloured through South African Hip Hop as a Postcolonial Text." In *Shifting Selves: Post-Apartheid Essays on Mass Media, Culture, and Identity*, edited by Hermans Wasserman and Sean Jacobs, 109–29. Cape Town: Kwela, 2004.

Beall, Jo. "Women under Indentured Labor in Colonial Natal, 1860–1911." In *Women and Gender in Southern Africa to 1945*, edited by Cheryl Walker, 146–67. Cape Town: David Philip, 1990.

Bebbington, D. W. *Evangelicalism in Modern Britain: A History from the 1730s to the 1980s.* London: Unwin Hyman, 1989.

Beckles, Hilary. "Caribbean Anti-Slavery: The Self-Liberation Ethos of Enslaved Blacks." *Journal of Caribbean History* 22, no. 1–2 (1988): 1–19.

———. *A History of Barbados: From Amerindian Settlement to Nation-State.* Cambridge: Cambridge University Press, 1990.

Beinart, William, and Colin Bundy. *Hidden Struggles in Rural South Africa: Politics and Popular Movements in the Transkei and Eastern Cape, 1890–1930.* Berkeley: University of California Press, 1987.

Beinart, William, and Saul Dubow, eds. *Segregation and Apartheid in Twentieth Century South Africa.* London: Routledge, 1995.

Beito, David T. "To Advance the 'Practice of Thrift And Economy': Fraternal Societies and Social Capital, 1890–1920." *Journal of Interdisciplinary History* 29, no. 4 (1999): 585–612.

Bell, Madison Smartt. *Toussaint Louverture: A Biography.* New York: Pantheon, 2007.

Benot, Yves. "La chaine des insurrections d'esclaves dans les Caraibes de 1789 a 1791." In *Les abolitions de l'esclavage de L. F. Sonthonax a V. Schoelscher, 1793, 1794, 1848,* edited by Marcel Dorigny, 179–86. Saint-Denis, France: Presses universitaires de Vincennes, Paris: UNESCO, 1995.

———. *La révolution française et la fin des colonies: Essai.* Paris: Éditions La Découverte, 1988.

Berland, Oscar. "The Emergence of the Communist Perspective on the 'Negro Question' in America: 1919–1931." Pt. 2. *Science & Society* 64, no. 2 (2000): 194–217.

Berlin, Ira. *Generations of Captivity: A History of African-American Slaves.* Cambridge, Mass.: The Belknap Press of Harvard University Press, 2003.

Bernal, Martin. *Black Athena: The Afroasiatic Roots of Classical Civilization.* New Brunswick: Rutgers University Press, 1987.

Biddiss, Michael D. *Father of Racist Ideology: The Social and Political Thought of Count Gobineau.* New York: Weybright and Talley, 1970.

Biko, Steve. *I Write What I Like.* San Francisco: Harper & Row, 1986.

Birmingham, David, and Terence Ranger. "Settlers and Liberators in the South, 1953–1980." In *History of Central Africa,* vol. 2, edited by David Birmingham and Phyllis M. Martin, 336–82. London: Longman, 1983.

Blackburn, Robin. *The Overthrow of Colonial Slavery.* London: Verso, 1989.

Black Eyed Peas. "Going Gone." *Monkey Business* CD. A&M. June 7, 2005.

Blyden, Edward W. *Christianity, Islam, and the Negro Race.* 1887. Edinburgh: University Press, 1967. Baltimore: Black Classic Press, 1994.

Bogues, Anthony. *Black Heretics, Black Prophets: Radical Black Intellectuals.* New York: Routledge, 2003.

Bolland, O. Nigel. "Creolization and Creole Societies: A Cultural Nationalist View of Caribbean Social History." In *Intellectuals in the Twentieth-Century Caribbean,* vol. 1, *Spectre of the New Class: The Commonwealth Caribbean,* edited by Alistair Hennessy, 50–79. London: Macmillan, 1992.

———. *On the March: Labour Rebellions in the British Caribbean, 1934–39.* Kingston: Ian Randle, 1995.

———. *The Politics of Labour in the British Caribbean: The Social Origins of Authoritarianism and Democracy in the Labour Movement*. Princeton, N.J.: Markus Wiener, 2001.

Boloka, Gibson. "Cultural Studies and the Transformation of the Music Industry: Some Reflections on Kwaito." In *Shifting Selves: Post-Apartheid Essays on Mass Media, Culture, and Identity*, edited by Hermans Wasserman and Sean Jacobs, 97–107. Cape Town: Kwela, 2004.

Bolster, W. Jeffrey. *Black Jacks: African American Seamen in the Age of Sail*. Cambridge, Mass.: Harvard University Press, 1997.

Borstelmann, Thomas. "'Hedging Our Bets and Buying Time': John Kennedy and Racial Revolutions in the American South and Southern Africa." *Diplomatic History* 24, no. 3 (2000): 435–63.

Boston Branch of the National Association for the Advancement of Colored People. *Fighting a Vicious Film: Protest against "The Birth of a Nation."* Boston, 1915.

Bourgois, Philippe. "One Hundred Years of United Fruit Company Letters." In *Banana Wars*, edited by Steve Striffler and Mark Moberg, 103–44. Durham, N.C.: Duke University Press, 2003.

Bradford, Helen. *A Taste of Freedom: The ICU in Rural South Africa, 1924–1930*. New Haven: Yale University Press, 1987.

Branch, Taylor. *Parting the Waters: America in the King Years, 1954–63*. New York: Touchstone, 1988.

Branson, Susan, and Leslie Patrick. "Étrangers dans un pays étrange: Saint-Domingan Refugees of Color in Philadelphia." In *The Impact of the Haitian Revolution in the Atlantic World*, edited by David P. Geggus, 193–208. Columbia: University of South Carolina Press, 2001.

Brinton, Crane. *The Anatomy of Revolution*. New York: Vintage, 1958.

Brock, Lisa, ed. "African [Diaspora] Studies." Special issue of *Issue: A Journal of Opinion* 24, no. 2 (1996).

Brooks, Joanna. "The Early American Public Sphere and the Emergence of a Black Print Counterpublic." *William and Mary Quarterly* 62, no. 1 (2005): 67–92.

Brooks, Joanna, and John Saillant. Introduction to *"Face Zion Forward": First Writers of the Black Atlantic, 1785–1798*, edited by Joanna Brooks and John Saillant, 3–33. Boston: Northeastern University Press, 2002.

———, eds. *"Face Zion Forward": First Writers of the Black Atlantic, 1785–1798*. Boston: Northeastern University Press, 2002.

Brown, Christopher Leslie. *Moral Capital: Foundations of British Abolitionism*. Chapel Hill: University of North Carolina Press, 2006.

Brown, Elaine. *A Taste of Power: A Black Woman's Story*. New York: Anchor Books, 1994.

Brown, Jacqueline Nassy. "Black Liverpool, Black America, and the Gendering of Diasporic Space." *Cultural Anthropology* 13, no. 3 (1998): 291–325.

Brown, Judith. *Gandhi's Rise to Power: Indian Politics, 1915–1922*. Cambridge: Cambridge University Press, 1972.

Brown, Judith M., and Martin Prozesky, eds. *Gandhi and South Africa: Principles and Politics*. Scottsville, South Africa: University of Natal Press, 1999.

Brown, Scot. *Fighting for US: Maulana Karenga, the US Organization, and Black Cultural Nationalism.* New York: New York University Press, 2003.

Brutents, Karen N. *National Liberation Revolutions Today (Some Questions of Theory).* Moscow: Progress Publishers, 1974.

Bryce-Laporte, Roy Simon. "Crisis, Contraculture, and Religion among West Indians in the Panama Canal Zone." In *Blackness in Latin America and the Caribbean,* vol. 1, edited by Norman E. Whitten Jr. and Arlene Torres, 100–118. Bloomington: Indiana University Press, 1998.

Buckley, Roger N. *The British Army in the West Indies: Society and the Military in the Revolutionary Age.* Gainesville: University Press of Florida, 1998.

——. *Slaves in Red Coats: The British West India Regiments, 1795–1815.* New Haven: Yale University Press, 1979.

Bundy, Colin. "Continuing a Conversation: Prospects for African Studies in the 21st Century." *African Affairs* 101 (2002): 61–73.

Bunting, Brian. Introduction to *S. P. Bunting: A Political Biography,* by Edward Roux, 3–34. Bellville, South Africa: Mayibuye Books, 1993.

——. *Moses Kotane: South African Revolutionary.* Bellville, South Africa: Mayibuye Books, 1998.

Burkett, Randall K. *Black Redemption: Churchmen Speak for the Garvey Movement.* Philadelphia: Temple University Press, 1978.

——. *Garveyism as a Religious Movement: The Institutionalization of a Black Civil Religion.* Metuchen, N.J.: Scarecrow Press, 1978.

Burton, Richard D. E. *Afro-Creole: Power, Opposition, and Play in the Caribbean.* Ithaca: Cornell University Press, 1997.

Bush, Rod. *We Are Not What We Seem: Black Nationalism and Class Struggle in the American Century.* New York: New York University Press, 1999.

Butler, Judith. *Gender Trouble: Feminism and the Subversion of Identity.* New York: Routledge, 1990.

Butler, Kim D. *Freedoms Given, Freedoms Won: Afro-Brazilians in Post-Abolition in São Paulo and Salvador.* New Brunswick: Rutgers University Press, 1998.

Byrd, Alexander X. *Captives and Voyagers: Black Migrants across the Eighteenth-Century British Atlantic World.* Baton Rouge: Louisiana State University Press, 2008.

——. "Eboe, Country, Nation, and Gustavus Vassa's Interesting Narrative." *William and Mary Quarterly* 63, no. 1 (2006): 122–47.

Cabral, Amilcar. *Return to the Source.* New York: Monthly Review Press, 1974.

——. *Revolution in Guinea.* New York: Monthly Review Press, 1972.

Callahan, Allen Dwight. *The Talking Book: African Americans and the Bible.* New Haven: Yale University Press, 2006.

Campbell, Horace. "Progressive Politics and the Jamaican Society at Home and Abroad." *Social and Economic Studies* 43, no. 3 (September 1994): 191–205.

——. *Rasta and Resistance: From Marcus Garvey to Walter Rodney.* Trenton, N.J.: Africa World Press, 1987.

——. *Reclaiming Zimbabwe: The Exhaustion of the Patriarchal Model of Liberation.* Trenton, N.J.: Africa World Press, 2003.

Campbell, James T. *Songs of Zion: The African Methodist Episcopal Church in the United States and South Africa.* New York: Oxford University Press, 1995.

Capelli, Luciano, dir. *The Promised Ship.* Rio Nevado Production, 2000.

Carmichael, Stokely, with Ekwueme Michael Thelwell. *Ready for the Revolution: The Life and Struggles of Stokely Carmichael [Kwame Ture].* New York: Scribner, 2003.

Carr, Barry. "From Caribbean Backwater to Revolutionary Opportunity: Cuba's Evolving Relationship with the Comintern, 1925–34." In *International Communism and the Communist International, 1919–43,* edited by Tim Rees and Andrew Thorpe, 234–53. Manchester: Manchester University Press, 1998.

———. "Identity, Class, and Nation: Black Immigrant Workers, Cuban Communism, and the Sugar Insurgency, 1925–1934." *Hispanic American Historical Review* 78, no. 1 (1998): 83–116.

Carretta, Vincent. *Equiano, the African: Biography of a Self-Made Man.* Athens: University of Georgia Press, 2005.

———. "Olaudah Equiano or Gustavus Vassa? New Light on an Eighteenth-Century Question of Identity." *Slavery and Abolition* 20 (1999): 96–105.

———, ed. *Unchained Voices: An Anthology of Black Authors in the English-Speaking World of the Eighteenth Century.* Lexington: University Press of Kentucky, 1996.

Carson, Clayborne. *In Struggle: SNCC and the Black Awakening of the 1960s.* Cambridge, Mass.: Harvard University Press, 1981.

Castells, Manuel. *The Information Age: Economy, Society, and Culture.* 3 vols. Cambridge, Mass.: Blackwell, 1996, 1997, 1998.

Catlin-Jairazbhoy, Amy, and Edward A. Alpers, eds. *Sidis and Scholars: Essays on African Indians.* Trenton, N.J.: Red Sea Press, 2004.

A Century of Lawmaking for a New Nation: U.S. Congressional Documents and Debates, 1774–1875. Register of Debates, 19th Cong., 1st sess.

Césaire, Aimé. *Notebook of a Return to My Native Land.* Paris: Présence Africaine, 1971.

Cha-Jua, Sundiate Keita. "The Black Radical Congress and the Reconstruction of the Black Freedom Movement." *Black Scholar* 28, no. 3–4 (1999): 8–21.

Chang, Jeff. *Can't Stop, Won't Stop: A History of the Hip-Hop Generation.* New York: St. Martin's Press, 2005.

Cheney, Charise L. *Brothers Gonna Work It Out: Sexual Politics in the Golden Age of Rap Nationalism.* New York: New York University Press, 2005.

Chevannes, Barry. *Rastafari: Roots and Ideology.* Syracuse: Syracuse University Press, 1994.

Childs, Matt D. "'A Black French General Arrived to Conquer the Island': Images of the Haitian Revolution in Cuba's 1812 Aponte Rebellion." In *The Impact of the Haitian Revolution in the Atlantic World,* edited by David P. Geggus, 135–56. Columbia: University of South Carolina Press, 2001.

Chomsky, Aviva. "'Barbados or Canada?' Race, Immigration, and Nation in Early-Twentieth-Century Cuba." *Hispanic American Historical Review* 80, no. 3 (2000): 415–62.

———. *West Indian Workers and the United Fruit Company in Costa Rica, 1870–1940.* Baton Rouge: Louisiana State University Press, 1996.

─────. "West Indian Workers in Costa Rican Radical and Nationalist Ideology: 1900–1950." *The Americas* 51, no. 1 (1994): 11–40.

Churchill, Ward. "'To Disrupt, Discredit and Destroy': The FBI's Secret War against the Black Panther Party." In *Liberation, Imagination, and the Black Panther Party: A New Look at the Panthers and Their Legacy,* edited by Kathleen Cleaver and George Katsiaficas, 78–117. New York: Routledge, 2001.

Churchill, Ward, and Jim Vander Wall. *The COINTELPRO Papers: Documents from the FBI's Secret Wars against Domestic Dissent.* Boston: South End Press, 1990.

Churchill, Winston S., ed. *Never Give In! The Best of Winston Churchill's Speeches.* New York: Hyperion, 2004.

Clavin, Matthew J. "American Toussaints: Symbol, Subversion, and the Black Atlantic Tradition in the American Civil War." *Slavery and Abolition* 28, no. 1 (2007): 87–113.

Cleaver, Eldridge. "Solidarity of the People until Victory or Death!" *The Black Panther,* October 25, 1969, 12–13.

Cleaver, Kathleen Neal. "Back to Africa: The Evolution of the International Section of the Black Panther Party (1969–1972)." In *The Black Panther Party [Reconsidered],* edited by Charles E. Jones, 211–54. Baltimore: Black Classic Press, 1998.

─────. "Women, Power, and Revolution." In *Liberation, Imagination, and the Black Panther Party: A New Look at the Panthers and Their Legacy,* edited by Kathleen Cleaver and George Katsiaficas, 123–27. New York: Routledge, 2001.

Clegg, Claude Andrew, III. *An Original Man: The Life and Times of Elijah Muhammad.* New York: St. Martin's Press, 1997.

Clemons, Michael L., and Charles E. Jones. "Global Solidarity: The Black Panther Party in the International Arena." In *Liberation, Imagination, and the Black Panther Party: A New Look at the Panthers and Their Legacy,* edited by Kathleen Cleaver and George Katsiaficas, 20–39. New York: Routledge, 2001.

Cobb, William Jelani. *To the Break of Dawn: A Freestyle on the Hip-Hop Aesthetic.* New York: New York University Press, 2007.

Cobley, Alan Gregor. "Far from Home: The Origins and Significance of the Afro-Caribbean Community in South Africa to 1930." *Journal of South African Studies* 18, no. 2 (1992): 349–70.

Collier-Thomas, Bettye, and V. P. Franklin, eds. *Sisters in the Struggle: African American Women in the Civil Rights–Black Power Movement.* New York: New York University Press, 2001.

Condry, Ian. *Hip-Hop Japan: Rap and the Paths of Cultural Globalization.* Durham, N.C.: Duke University Press, 2006.

Conniff, Michael. *Black Labor on a White Canal: Panama, 1904–1981.* Pittsburgh: University of Pittsburgh Press, 1985.

Cornish, Dudley Taylor. *The Sable Arm: Negro Troops in the Union Army, 1861–1865.* New York: Longmans, Green, 1956.

Coupland, Reginald. *The British Anti-Slavery Movement.* 2nd ed. London: F. Cass, 1964.

Craton, Michael. *Testing the Chains: Resistance to Slavery in the British West Indies.* Ithaca: Cornell University Press, 1982.

Craton, Michael, and D. Gail Saunders. *Islanders in the Stream: A History of the Bahamian People.* 2 vols. Athens: University of Georgia Press, 1992.

———. "Seeking a Life of Their Own: Aspects of Slave Resistance in the Bahamas." *Journal of Caribbean History* 24 (1990): 1–27.

Cronon, Edmund David. *Black Moses: The Story of Marcus Garvey and the Universal Negro Improvement Association.* Madison: University of Wisconsin Press, 1955.

Crossman, Richard, ed. *The God That Failed.* New York: Harper & Brothers, 1949.

Crummell, Alexander. *The Future of Africa.* 1862. Detroit: Negro History Press, 1960.

Cruse, Harold. *The Crisis of the Negro Intellectual.* New York: Morrow, 1967.

Cuba. Dirección General del Censo. *Informe general del censo de 1943.* Havana: P. Fernandéz, 1945.

Cugoano, Quobna Ottobah. "Thoughts and Sentiments on the Evil and Wicked Traffic of the Slavery and Commerce of the Human Species, Humbly Submitted to the Inhabitants of Great Britain, 1787." In *Unchained Voices: An Anthology of Black Authors in the English-Speaking World of the Eighteenth Century,* edited by Vincent Carretta, 154–58. Lexington: University Press of Kentucky, 1996.

———. "Thoughts and Sentiments on the Evil of Slavery." In *Black Atlantic Writers of the Eighteenth Century: Living the New Exodus in England and the Americas,* edited by Adam Potkay and Sandra Burr, 129–56. New York: St. Martin's Press, 1995.

Curtis, Edward E., IV. *Black Muslim Religion in the Nation of Islam, 1960–1975.* Chapel Hill: University of North Carolina Press, 2006.

Daniels, Robert V., ed. *A Documentary History of Communism.* Vol. 2. New York: Vintage, 1960.

Darlington, Shasta. "Brazilian Rappers Speak to the Poor: Popular Duo Launch Recording Career from Notorious San Paulo Prison." *The Globe and Mail* (Toronto), September 5, 2000, A10.

Davidson, Apollon, Irina Filatova, Valentin Gorodnov, and Sheridan Johns, eds. *South Africa and the Communist International: A Documentary History.* 2 vols. London: Frank Cass, 2003.

Davidson, Basil. *The People's Cause: A History of Guerrillas in Africa.* London: Longman, 1981.

Davies, Carole Boyce. *Left of Karl Marx: The Political Life of Black Communist Claudia Jones.* Durham, N.C.: Duke University Press, 2007.

Davis, David Brion. *Inhuman Bondage: The Rise and Fall of Slavery in the New World.* New York: Oxford University Press, 2006.

———. *The Problem of Slavery in the Age of Revolution, 1770–1823.* Ithaca: Cornell University Press, 1966, 1975.

———. *The Problem of Slavery in Western Culture.* Ithaca: Cornell University Press, 1966.

———. *Slavery and Human Progress.* New York: Oxford University Press, 1984.

Davis, Harry E., ed. "Documents Relating to Negro Masonry in America." *Journal of Negro History* 21, no. 4 (1936): 411–32.

Davis, Raymond Allan. "West Indian Workers on the Panama Canal: A Split Labor Market Interpretation." Ph.D. diss., Stanford University, 1981.

Dawson, Michael C. "A Black Counterpublic? Economic Earthquakes, Racial Agenda(s), and Black Politics." In *The Black Public Sphere,* edited by Houston

Baker Jr. and Michael C. Dawson, 199–227. Chicago: University of Chicago Press, 1995.

Debray, Regis. *Revolution in the Revolution?* New York: Monthly Review Press, 1967.

Defronzo, James. *Revolutions and Revolutionary Movements.* Boulder: Westview Press, 1991.

Degras, Jane, ed. *The Communist International, 1919–1943.* 3 vols. London: Oxford University Press, 1956–65.

de la Fuente, Alejandro. *A Nation for All: Race, Inequality, and Politics in Twentieth-Century Cuba.* Chapel Hill: University of North Carolina Press, 2001.

del Castillo, José. "La inmigración de braceros azucareros en la República Dominicana, 1900-1930." *Cuadernos del CENDIA* (Santo Domingo, Universidad Autónoma de Santo Domingo) 262, no. 7 (1978): 49–54.

Depelchin, Jacques. *Silences in African History: Between the Syndromes of Discovery and Abolition.* Dar es Salaam: Mkuki na Nyota Publishers, 2005.

Dessens, Nathalie. *From Saint-Domingue to New Orleans: Migration and Influences.* Gainesville: University Press of Florida, 2007.

de Witte, Ludo. *The Assassination of Lumumba.* London: Verso, 2001.

Diawara, Manthia. *In Search of Africa.* Cambridge, Mass.: Harvard University Press, 1998.

Dirlik, Arif. "The Third World in 1968." In *1968: The World Transformed*, edited by Carole Fink, Philipp Gassert, and Detlef Junker, 295–317. New York: Cambridge University Press, 1998.

Ditchfield, G. M. *The Evangelical Revival.* London: UCL Press, 1998.

Donner, Frank J. *Age of Surveillance: The Aims and Methods of America's Political Intelligence System.* New York: Vintage, 1981.

Downes, Aviston D. "Freemasonry in Barbados before 1914: The Limits of Brotherhood." *Journal of Caribbean History* 36, no. 2 (2002): 285–309.

———. "Sailing from Colonial into National Waters: A History of the Barbados Landship." *Journal of the Barbados Museum and Historical Society* 46 (2000): 93–112.

Doyle, William. *The French Revolution: A Very Short Introduction.* Oxford: Oxford University Press, 2001.

Drake, St. Clair. *Black Folk Here and There: An Essay in History and Anthropology.* 2 vols. Los Angeles: Center for Afro-American Studies, University of California, 1987–90.

Draper, Theodore. *American Communism and Soviet Russia: The Formative Period.* New York: Viking, 1960.

Drescher, Seymour. "The Ending of the Slave Trade and the Evolution of European Scientific Racism." In *The Atlantic Slave Trade: Effects on Economies, Societies, and Peoples in Africa, the Americas, and Europe*, edited by Joseph Inikori and Stanley Engerman, 361–96. Durham, N.C.: Duke University Press, 1992.

———. "The Limits of Example." In *The Impact of the Haitian Revolution in the Atlantic World*, edited by David P. Geggus, 10–14. Columbia: University of South Carolina Press, 2001.

Drew, Allison. *Discordant Comrades: Identities and Loyalties on the South African Left.* Pretoria: University of South Africa Press, 2002.

―――, ed. *South Africa's Radical Tradition: A Documentary History*. 2 vols. Cape Town: Buchu Books, 1996–97.

Duberman, Martin Bauml. *Paul Robeson*. New York: Knopf, 1988. London: Pan Books, 1991.

Dubois, Laurent. *Avengers of the New World: The Story of the Haitian Revolution*. Cambridge, Mass.: The Belknap Press of Harvard University Press, 2004.

―――. *Les esclaves de la Republique: L'histoire oubliee de la premiere emancipation, 1789–1794*. Paris: Calmann-Levy, 1998.

Du Bois, W. E. B. "As the Crow Flies." *New York Amsterdam News*, March 13, 1943, as cited in Sudarshan Kapur, *Raising Up a Prophet: The African-American Encounter with Gandhi* (Boston: Beacon Press, 1992), 109–11.

―――. "Back to Africa." In *Marcus Garvey and the Vision of Africa*, edited by John Henrik Clarke, 105–19. New York: Vintage, 1974.

―――. *Black Folk, Then and Now: An Essay in the History and Sociology of the Negro Race*. New York: H. Holt and Company, 1939.

―――. *Black Reconstruction, 1860–1880*. New York: Harcourt, Brace, 1935.

―――. *The Correspondence of W. E. B. Du Bois*. Vol. 1, *Selections, 1877–1934*. Edited by Herbert Aptheker. Amherst: University of Massachusetts Press, 1973.

―――. *The Negro*. New York: H. Holt, 1915.

Dudziak, Mary L. *Cold War, Civil Rights: Race and the Image of American Democracy*. Princeton, N.J.: Princeton University Press, 2000.

―――. "The Little Rock Crisis and Foreign Affairs: Race, Resistance, and the Image of American Democracy." *Southern California Law Review* 70, no. 6 (1997): 1641–1716.

Duncan, Quince. "El negro antillano." In *El negro en Costa Rica*, 8th ed., edited by Carlos Meléndez Chaverri and Quince Duncan, 120–26. San José: Editorial Costa Rica, 1981.

―――. "The Pocomia Rebellion." In *The Best Short Stories of Quince Duncan/Las mejores historias de Quince Duncan*, comp. Dellita Martin-Ogunsola, 123–34. San José: Editorial Costa Rica, 1995.

Dupuy, Alex. *Haití in the World Economy: Class, Race, and Underdevelopment since 1700*. Boulder: Westview Press, 1989.

―――. "Race and Class in the Postcolonial Caribbean: The Views of Walter Rodney." *Latin American Perspectives* 23, no. 2 (Spring 1996): 107–29.

Durand, Alain-Phillipe, ed. *Black, Blanc, Beur: Rap Music and Hip-Hop Culture in the Francophone World*. Lanham, Md.: Scarecrow Press, 2002.

Dyson, Michael Eric. *Holler If You Hear Me: Searching for Tupac Shakur*. New York: Civitas Books, 2001.

Echenberg, Myron. *Colonial Conscripts: The Tirailleurs Sénégalias in French West Africa, 1857–1960*. Portsmouth, N.H.: Heinemann, 1991.

Echeruo, Michael. "An African Diaspora: The Ontological Project." In *The African Diaspora: African Origins and New World Identities*, edited by Isidore Okpewho, Carole Boyce Davies, and Ali A. Mazrui, 3–18. Bloomington: Indiana University Press, 1999.

Edgar, Robert R. "African Educational Protest in South Africa: The American School

Movement in the Transkei in the 1920s." In *Apartheid and Education: The Education of Black South Africans*, edited by Peter Kallaway, 184–91. Johannesburg: Ravan Press, 1984.

———. "Garveyism in Africa: Dr. Wellington and the American Movement in the Transkei." *Ufahamu* 6 (1976): 31–57.

Edmondson, Locksley. "Black America as a Mobilizing Diaspora: Some International Implications." In *Modern Diasporas in International Politics*, edited by Gabriel Sheffer, 333–49. London: Croom Helm, 1986.

———. "The Internationalization of Black Power: Historical and Contemporary Perspectives." *Mawazo* 4, no. 1 (1968): 16–30.

Edwards, Brent Hayes. *The Practice of Diaspora: Literature, Translation, and the Rise of Black Internationalism*. Cambridge, Mass.: Harvard University Press, 2003.

———. "The Use of Diaspora." *Social Text* 19, no. 1 (2001): 45–73.

Egbuna, Obi. *Destroy This Temple: The Voice of Black Power in Britain*. London: MacGibbon & Kee, 1971.

Egerton, Douglas R. *Death or Liberty: African Americans and Revolutionary America*. New York: Oxford University Pres, 2009.

———. *Gabriel's Rebellion: The Virginia Slave Conspiracies of 1800 and 1802*. Chapel Hill: University of North Carolina Press, 1993.

———. *He Shall Go Out Free: The Lives of Denmark Vesey*. Madison, Wisc.: Madison House, 1999.

Elkins, Caroline. *Imperial Reckoning: The Untold Story of Britain's Gulag in Kenya*. New York: Henry Holt, 2005.

Elkins, W. F. *Black Power in the Caribbean: The Beginnings of the Modern National Movement*. New York: Revisionist Press, 1977.

Ellis, Keith. "Nicolas Guillen and Langston Hughes: Convergences and Divergences." In *Between Race and Empire: African-Americans and Cubans before the Cuban Revolution*, edited by Lisa Brock and Digna Castaneda Fuertes, 129–67. Philadelphia: Temple University Press, 1998.

Ellis, Stephen, and Tsepo Sechaba. *Comrades against Apartheid: The ANC and the South African Communist Party in Exile*. London: James Currey, 1992.

Emerson, Rupert, and Martin Kilson. "The American Dilemma in a Changing World: The Rise of Africa and the Negro American." In *The Negro American*, edited by Talcott Parsons and Kenneth B. Clark, 626–55. Boston: Beacon Press, 1966.

Equiano, Olaudah. "The Interesting Narrative." In *Black Atlantic Writers of the Eighteenth Century: Living the New Exodus in England and the Americas*, edited by Adam Potkay and Sandra Burr, 166–268. New York: St. Martin's Press, 1995.

———. *The Interesting Narrative of the Life of Olaudah Equiano, or Gustavus Vassa, The African, Written by Himself*. Edited by Werner Sollors. New York: Norton, 2001.

Erlmann, Veit. *African Stars: Studies in Black South African Performance*. Chicago: University of Chicago Press, 1991.

Esedebe, P. Olisanwuche. *Pan-Africanism: The Idea and the Movement, 1776–1963*. Washington, D.C.: Howard University Press, 1982.

Essien-Udom, E. U. *Black Nationalism: A Search for an Identity in America*. Chicago: University of Chicago Press, 1962.

Euraque, Darío. "The Banana Enclave, Nationalism, and Mestizaje in Honduras, 1910s–1930s." In *Identity and Struggle at the Margins of the Nation-State: The Laboring Peoples of Central America and the Hispanic Caribbean,* edited by Aviva Chomsky and Aldo Lauria-Santiago, 151–68. Durham, N.C.: Duke University Press, 1998.

Faber, Jörg. "Cape Town's Hip Hop Scene." *Ntama: Journal of African Music and Popular Culture,* Mainz University, Friday, January 23, 2004, <http://ntama.uni-mainz.de/hiphop/faber/>. Accessed September 24, 2007.

Fabre, Michel. *From Harlem to Paris: Black American Writers in France, 1840–1980.* Urbana: University of Illinois Press, 1991.

Fanon, Frantz. *The Wretched of the Earth.* New York: Grove, 1968.

Farmer, James. *Lay Bare the Heart: An Autobiography of the Civil Rights Movement.* New York: Arbor House, 1985.

Farwell, Byron. *The Great War in Africa, 1914–1918.* New York: Norton, 1986.

Feimester, Crystal. "'Ladies and Lynching': The Gendered Discourse of Mob Violence in the New South, 1880–1930." Ph.D. diss., Princeton University, 2000.

Fernández, Ariel. "¿Poesía urbana o la Nueva Trova de los noventa?" *La jiribilla,* 2001, <http://www.lajiribilla.cu/2001/n15_agosto/414_15.html>. Accessed May 4, 2002.

Fernández, Nadine. "The Changing Discourse on Race in Contemporary Cuba." *Qualitative Studies In Education* 14, no. 2 (2001): 117–32.

Ferrell, Robert H. *Woodrow Wilson and World War I, 1917–1921.* New York: Harper & Row, 1985.

Fick, Carolyn E. "The French Revolution in Saint Domingue: A Triumph or a Failure?" In *A Turbulent Time: The French Revolution and the Greater Caribbean,* edited by David Barry Gaspar and David Patrick Geggus, 51–75. Bloomington: Indiana University Press, 1997.

———. *The Making of Haiti: The Saint Domingue Revolution from Below.* Knoxville: University of Tennessee Press, 1990.

Fields, Barbara J. "Slavery, Race, and Ideology in the United States of America." *New Left Review* 181 (1990): 95–118.

Fischer, Sibylle. *Modernity Disavowed: Haiti and the Cultures of Slavery in the Age of Revolution.* Durham, N.C.: Duke University Press, 2004.

Fletcher, Leonard P. "The Friendly Societies in St. Lucia and St. Vincent." *Caribbean Studies* (Puerto Rico) 18, no. 3–4 (1978–79): 89–114.

Foner, Nancy. "Introduction: West Indian Migration to New York. An Overview." In *Islands in the City: West Indian Migration to New York,* edited by Nancy Foner, 1–23. Berkeley: University of California Press, 2001.

Fontaine, Pierre-Michel. "Transnational Relations and Racial Mobilization: Emerging Black Movements in Brazil." In *Ethnic Mobilization in a Transnational World,* edited by John F. Stack, 141–62. Westport, Conn.: Greenwood Press, 1981.

Foran, John, ed. *The Future of Revolutions: Rethinking Radical Change in the Age of Globalization.* New York: Zed Press, 2003.

Ford, James. "Defense of the Ethiopian People." In *The Negro and the Democratic Front,* by James Ford, 159–60. New York: International Publishers, 1938.

Ford-Smith, Honor. "Women and the Garvey Movement in Jamaica." In *Garvey: His Work and Impact,* edited by Rupert Lewis and Patrick Bryan, 73–83. Trenton, N.J.: Africa World Press, 1991.

Forsythe, Dennis, ed. *Let the Niggers Burn! The Sir George Williams University Affair and Its Caribbean Aftermath*. Montreal: Black Rose Book—Our Generation Press, 1971.

Fox, Richard. "Passage from India." In *Between Resistance and Revolution: Cultural Politics and Social Protest*, edited by Richard Fox and Orin Starn, 65–82. New Brunswick: Rutgers University Press, 1997.

Fraser, Cary. "Crossing the Color Line in Little Rock: The Eisenhower Administration and the Dilemma of Race for U.S. Foreign Policy." *Diplomatic History* 24, no. 2 (2000): 233–64.

Fraser, Nancy. "Rethinking the Public Sphere: A Contribution to the Critique of Actually Existing Democracy." In *Habermas and the Public Sphere*, edited by Craig Calhoun, 109–42. Cambridge, Mass.: MIT Press, 1991.

Frazier, E. Franklin. *Black Bourgeoisie*. Glencoe, Ill.: Free Press, 1957.

———. "The Negro and Non-Resistance." *The Crisis* 27, no. 5 (March 1924): 213–14.

———. "The Negro and Non-Resistance." *The Crisis* 28, no. 2 (June 1924): 58–59.

Frederikse, Julie. *The Unbreakable Thread: Non-Racialism in South Africa*. Johannesburg: Ravan Press, 1990.

French, Scot. *The Rebellious Slave: Nat Turner in American Memory*. Boston: Houghton Mifflin, 2004.

Frey, Sylvia. "Cultural Migrations: A Time-&-Space Outline of Black Atlantic Evangelical Protestantism." In *African Diasporas in the New and Old Worlds: Consciousness and Imagination*, edited by Geneviève Fabre and Klaus Benesch, 91–98. New York: Rodopi, 2006.

———. *Water from the Rock: Black Resistance in a Revolutionary Age*. Princeton, N.J.: Princeton University Press, 1991.

Frey, Sylvia R., and Betty Wood. *Come Shouting to Zion: African American Protestantism in the American South and British Caribbean to 1830*. Chapel Hill: University of North Carolina Press, 1998.

Fuller, Hoyt W. "Notes From a Sixth Pan-African Journal." *Black World*, October 1974, 70–81.

Fyfe, Christopher. "The Emergence and Evolution of African Studies in the United Kingdom." In *Out of One, Many Africas: Reconstructing the Study and Meaning of Africa*, edited by William G. Martin and Michael O. West, 54–61. Champaign: University of Illinois Press, 1999.

———. *A History of Sierra Leone*. London: Oxford University Press, 1962.

Gaines, Kevin K. *American Africans in Ghana: Black Expatriates and the Civil Rights Era*. Chapel Hill: University of North Carolina Press, 2006.

Gallicchio, Marc. *The African American Encounter with Japan and China: Black Internationalism in Asia, 1895–1945*. Chapel Hill: University of North Carolina Press, 2000.

Gamm, Gerald, and Robert D. Putnam. "The Growth of Voluntary Associations in America, 1840–1940." *Journal of Interdisciplinary History* 29, no. 4 (1999): 511–57.

Gandhi, M. K. *Collected Works*. Vols. 5, 8, 10, 12. New Delhi: Government of India, 1961, 1962, 1963, 1964.

———. *Satyagraha in South Africa*. Ahmedabad: Navajivan, 1950.

———. "To the American Negro: A Message from Mahatma Gandhi." *The Crisis*, July 1929, 225.

Garcia Dominguez, Bernardo. "Garvey and Cuba." In *Garvey: His Work and Impact*, edited by Rupert Lewis and Patrick Bryan, 299–305. Trenton, N.J.: Africa World Press, 1991.

Garland, David. *The Culture of Control: Crime and Social Order in Contemporary Society*. Chicago: University of Chicago Press, 2001.

Garrigus, John D. "Catalyst or Catastrophe? Saint-Domingue's Free Men of Color and the Battle of Savannah, 1779–1782." *Revista/Review Interamericana* 22 (Spring/Summer 1992): 109–25.

Garvey, Amy Jacques, ed. *The Philosophy and Opinions of Marcus Garvey*. 2 vols. New York: Atheneum, 1969.

Garvey, Marcus. "An Exposé of the Caste System among Negroes." In *Philosophy and Opinions of Marcus Garvey*, vol. 2, edited by Amy Jacques Garvey, 55–61. New York: Atheneum, 1992.

Gates, Henry Louis, Jr., and William L. Andrews, eds. *Pioneers of the Black Atlantic: Five Slave Narratives from the Enlightenment, 1772–1815*. Washington, D.C.: Civitas Counterpoint, 1998.

Gates, Henry Louis, Jr., and Nellie Y. McKay, eds. *The Norton Anthology of African American Literature*. New York: Norton, 1996.

Geggus, David. "The Haitian Revolution." In *Caribbean Slave Society and Economy*, edited by Hilary Beckles and Verene Shepherd, 402–20. New York: New Press, 1991.

———. "The Haitian Revolution." In *The Modern Caribbean*, edited by Franklin W. Knight and Colin A. Palmer, 21–50. Chapel Hill: University of North Carolina Press, 1989.

———. *Haitian Revolutionary Studies*. Bloomington: Indiana University Press, 2002.

———. "The Influence of the Haitian Revolution in Latin America and the Caribbean." In *Blacks, Coloureds, and National Identity in Nineteenth-Century Latin America*, edited by Nancy Priscilla Naro, 38–59. London: Institute of Latin American Studies, 2003.

———. *Slavery, War, and Revolution: The British Occupation of Saint Domingue, 1793–1798*. New York: Oxford University Press, 1982.

———. "The Slaves and Free Coloreds of Martinique during the Age of the French and Haitian Revolutions." In *The Lesser Antilles in the Age of European Expansion*, edited by Robert L. Pacquette and Stanley L. Engerman, 286–88. Gainesville: University Press of Florida, 1996.

———, ed. *The Impact of the Haitian Revolution in the Atlantic World*. Columbia: University of South Carolina Press, 2001.

Geiss, Imanuel. *The Pan-African Movement: A History of Pan-Africanism in America, Europe, and Africa*. Translated by Ann Keep. New York: Africana Publishing, 1974.

Genovese, Eugene. *From Rebellion to Revolution: Afro-American Slave Revolts in the Making of the Modern World*. Baton Rouge: Louisiana State University Press, 1979.

Georgakas, Dan, and Marvin Surkin. *Detroit, I Do Mind Dying: A Study in Urban Revolution*. New York: St. Martin's Press, 1975.

Gerhart, Gail. *Black Power in South Africa: The Evolution of an Ideology*. Berkeley: University of California Press, 1973, 1978.

Geschwender, James A. "Marxist-Leninist Organization: Prognosis among Black Workers." *Journal of Black Studies* 8, no. 3 (1978): 279–98.

Gilroy, Paul. *The Black Atlantic: Modernity and Double Consciousness*. Cambridge, Mass.: Harvard University Press, 1993.

Gilyard, Keith. "The Bible and African American Poetry." In *African Americans and the Bible: Sacred Texts and Social Textures*, edited by Vincent L. Wimbush, 205–20. New York: Continuum, 2000.

Ginwala, Frene. "Class, Consciousness, and Control—Indian South Africans, 1860–1946." Ph.D. diss., Oxford University, 1974.

Godreau, Isar. "Folkloric 'Others': Blanqueamiento and the Celebration of Blackness as an Exception in Puerto Rico." In *Globalization and Race: Transformations in the Cultural Production of Blackness*, edited by Kamari Maxine Clarke and Deborah A. Thomas, 171–87. Durham, N.C.: Duke University Press, 2006.

Goldstone, Jack. *Revolutions: Theoretical, Comparative, and Historical Studies*. Belmont, Calif.: Wadsworth/Thomson Learning, 2003.

Gomez, Michael A. *Black Crescent: The Experience and Legacy of African Muslims in the Americas*. New York: Cambridge University Press, 2005.

Gonzalez, Lélia. "The Unified Black Movement: A New Stage in Black Political Mobilization." In *Race, Class, and Power in Brazil*, edited by Pierre-Michel Fontaine, 120–34. Los Angeles: Center for Afro-American Studies, University of California, 1985.

Gordon, Edmund T., and Mark Anderson. "The African Diaspora: Towards an Ethnography of Diasporic Identification." *Journal of American Folklore* 112, no. 445 (1999): 282–96.

Grady-Willis, Winston. "The Black Panther Party: State Repression and Political Prisoners." In *The Black Panther Party [Reconsidered]*, edited by Charles E. Jones, 363–89. Baltimore: Black Classic Press, 1998.

———. *Challenging US Apartheid: Atlanta and Black Struggles for Human Rights, 1960–1977*. Durham, N.C.: Duke University Press, 2006.

Graham, Richard, ed. *The Idea of Race in Latin America, 1870–1940*. Austin: University of Texas Press, 1990.

Grant, Colin. *Negro with a Hat: The Rise and Fall of Marcus Garvey*. New York: Oxford University Press, 2008.

Green, Cecilia. "Caribbean Dependency Theory of the 1970s: A Historical-Materialist-Feminist Revision." In *New Caribbean Thought: A Reader*, edited by Brian Meeks and Folke Lindahl, 40–72. Mona, Jamaica: University of the West Indies Press, 2001.

Greenberg, Kenneth S., ed. *Nat Turner: A Slave Rebellion in History and Memory*. New York: Oxford University Press, 2003.

Griffith, Cyril. *The African Dream: Martin R. Delany and the Emergence of Pan-Africanist Thought*. University Park: Penn State University Press, 1975.

Grimstead, David. "Anglo-American Racism and Phillis Wheatley's 'Sable Veil,' 'Length'ned Chain,' and 'Knitted Heart.'" In *Women in the Age of the American Revolution*, edited by Ronald Hoffman and Peter J. Albert, 338–444. Charlottesville: Published for the United States Capitol Historical Society by the University Press of Virginia, 1989.

Gromyko, Anatolii A., and Nikolai D. Kosukhin. *The October Revolution and Africa*. Moscow: Progress Publishers, 1983.

Guha, Ranajit. "Discipline and Mobilise." In *Subaltern Studies No. 7*, edited by Partha Chatterjee and Gyan Pandey, 64–120. Delhi: Oxford University Press, 1993.

Guyer, Jane. *African Studies in the United States: A Perspective.* Atlanta: African Studies Association, 1996.

Hall, Gwendolyn Midlo. *Africans in Colonial Louisiana: The Development of Afro-Creole Culture in the Eighteenth Century.* Baton Rouge: Louisiana State University Press, 1992.

Hall, Perry A. *In the Vineyard: Working in African American Studies.* Knoxville: University of Tennessee Press, 1999.

Hall, Prince. "A Charge. Delivered to the African Lodge, June 24, 1797, at Menotomy. By the Right Worshipful Prince Hall (1797)." In *"Face Zion Forward": First Writers of the Black Atlantic, 1785–1798*, edited by Joanna Brooks and John Saillant, 191–208. Boston: Northeastern University Press, 2002.

Hall, Stuart. "What Is This Black in Black Popular Culture?" In *Black Popular Culture*, edited by Gina Dent, 21–33. Seattle: Bay Press, 1992.

Hammond, Jack. "The High Cost of Dollars." *NACLA Report on the Americas* 32, no. 5 (1999): 24–25.

Hanchard, Michael George. *Orpheus and Power: The Movimento Negro of Rio de Janeiro and São Paulo, Brazil, 1945–1988.* Princeton, N.J.: Princeton University Press, 1994.

Hanna, William John. "Student Protest in Independent Black Africa." *Annals of the American Academy of Political and Social Science* 395, no. 1 (May 1971): 171–83.

Hanna, William John, and Judith Lynne Hanna. "The Cynical Nationalists." In *University Students and African Politics*, edited by William John Hanna, 49–70. New York: Africana Publishing, 1975.

Hanna, William John, Judith Lynne Hanna, and Vivian Zeitz Sauer. "The Active Minority." In *University Students and African Politics*, edited by William John Hanna, 71–102. New York: Africana Publishing, 1975.

Hardiman, David. *Peasant Nationalists of Gujarat: Kheda District, 1917–1934.* New Delhi: Oxford University Press, 1981.

Hardt, Michael, and Antonio Negri. *Empire.* Cambridge, Mass.: Harvard University Press, 2000.

Harold, Claudrena N. *The Rise and Fall of the Garvey Movement in the Urban South, 1918–1942.* New York: Routledge, 2007.

Harpelle, Ronald. "Ethnicity, Religion, and Repression: The Denial of African Heritage in Costa Rica." *Canadian Journal of History* 29 (1994): 95–112.

———. "Racism and Nationalism in the Creation of Costa Rica's Pacific Coast Banana Enclave." *The Americas* 56, no. 3 (2000): 29–51.

———. *The West Indians of Costa Rica: Race, Class, and the Integration of an Ethnic Minority.* Montréal: McGill-Queen's University Press, 2001.

Harris, Joseph E. *African-American Reactions to War in Ethiopia, 1936–1941.* Baton Rouge: Louisiana State University Press, 1994.

———. *The African Presence in Asia: Consequences of the East African Slave Trade.* Evanston, Ill.: Northwestern University Press, 1971.

———. "Expanding the Scope of African Diaspora Studies: The Middle East and India, a Research Agenda." *Radical History Review* 87 (2003): 157–68.

———, ed. *Global Dimensions of the African Diaspora*. Washington, D.C.: Howard University Press, 1982.

Harris, Karen L. "Gandhi, the Chinese, and Passive Resistance." In *Gandhi and South Africa: Principles and Politics*, edited by Judith M. Brown and Martin Prozesky, 69–89. Scottsville, South Africa: University of Natal Press, 1999.

Harrison, Alferdteen, ed. *Black Exodus: The Great Migration from the American South*. Jackson: University Press of Mississippi, 1991.

Hart, Richard. *Rise and Organise: The Birth of the Workers and National Movements in Jamaica, 1936–1939*. London: Karia Press, 1989.

Hartman, Michelle. "'A *Debke* Beat Funky as P.E.'s Riff': Hip Hop Poetry and Politics in Suheir Hammad's *Born Palestinian, Born Black*." *Black Arts Quarterly* 7, no. 1 (2002): 6–8.

Hartmann, Douglas. *Race, Culture, and the Revolt of the Black Athlete: The 1968 Olympic Protests and Their Aftermath*. Chicago: University of Chicago Press, 2003.

Harvey, David. *A Brief History of Neoliberalism*. New York: Oxford University Press, 2005.

Haupt, Adam. "Hip-Hop in the Age of Empire: Cape Flats Style." In *Voices of Transition: The Politics, Poetics, and Practices of Social Change in South Africa*, edited by Edgar Pieterse and Frank Meintjies, 215–25. Johannesburg: Heinemann, 2003.

Haywood, Harry. *Black Bolshevik: Autobiography of an Afro-American Communist*. Chicago: Liberator Press, 1978.

———. *Negro Liberation*. New York: International Publishers, 1948.

Hebdige, Dick. *Subculture: The Meaning of Style*. London: Routledge, 1981.

Helg, Aline. *Our Rightful Share: The Afro-Cuban Struggle for Equality, 1886–1912*. Chapel Hill: University of North Carolina Press, 1995.

Hempton, David. *Methodism: Empire of the Spirit*. New Haven: Yale University Press, 2005.

Henry, Paget. "CLR James and the Antiguan Left." In *C. L. R James's Caribbean*, edited by Paget Henry and Paul Buhle, 225–61. London: Macmillan, 1992.

Higginson, John. "Liberating the Captives: Independent Watchtower as an Avatar of Colonial Revolt in Southern Africa and Katanga, 1908–1941." *Journal of Social History* 26, no. 1 (1992): 55–80.

Hill, Robert A. "Cyril Briggs." In *The Marcus Garvey and Universal Negro Improvement Association Papers*, vol. 1, edited by Robert A. Hill, 521–27 (appendix 1). Berkeley: University of California Press, 1983.

———. "Dread History: Leonard P. Howell and Millenarian Visions in Early Rastafari Religion in Jamaica." *Epoche: Journal of the History of Religions at UCLA* 9 (1981): 30–71.

———. "Introduction: Garvey's Gospel, Garvey's Game." In *Philosophy and Opinions of Marcus Garvey*, 2 vols. (in 1), edited by Amy Jacques Garvey, v–lxxix. New York: Atheneum, 1992.

———, ed. *The Marcus Garvey and Universal Negro Improvement Association Papers*. 10 vols. Berkeley: University of California Press, 1983–2006. Vols. 11 and 12 forthcoming.

Hill, Robert A., and Gregory A. Pirio. "'Africa for the Africans': The Garvey Movement in South Africa, 1920–1940." In *The Politics of Race, Class, and Nationalism in Twentieth-Century South Africa*, edited by Shula Marks and Stanley Trapido, 209–53. London: Longman, 1987.

Hiro, Dilip. *Black British, White British: A History of Race Relations in Britain*. London: Grafton Books, 1991.

Hobsbawm, Eric. *The Age of Revolution, 1789–1848*. New York: New American Library, 1962.

———. *Nations and Nationalism since 1780: Programme, Myth, Reality*. 2nd ed. Cambridge: Cambridge University Press, 1992.

Hodder-Williams, Richard. "African Studies: Back to the Future." *African Affairs* 85 (1986): 593–604.

Hodges, Graham Russell. *Root and Branch: African Americans in New York and East Jersey, 1613–1863*. Chapel Hill: University of North Carolina Press, 1999.

———, ed. *Black Itinerants of the Gospel: The Narratives of John Jea and George White*. Madison, Wisc.: Madison House, 1993.

Hofmeyr, Jan. *South Africa*. 2nd ed. New York: McGraw Hill, 1952.

Holly, James Theodore. *A Vindication of the Capacity of the Negro Race for Self-Government and Civilized Progress, as Demonstrated by Historical Events of the Haytian Revolution; and the Subsequent Acts of that People since their National Independence*. New Haven: W. H. Stanley, 1857.

Holton, Woody. *Forced Founders: Indians, Debtors, Slaves, and the Making of the American Revolution in Virginia*. Chapel Hill: University of North Carolina Press for the Omohundro Institute of Early American History and Culture, 1999.

Hooker, James R. *Black Revolutionary: George Padmore's Path from Communism to Pan-Africanism*. New York: Praeger, 1967.

Horne, Alistair. *A Savage War of Peace: Algeria, 1954–1962*. London: Macmillan, 1977.

Horne, Gerald. *Black and Brown: African Americans and the Mexican Revolution, 1910–1920*. New York: New York University Press, 2005.

———. *Black and Red: W. E. B. Du Bois and the Afro-American Response to the Cold War, 1944–1963*. New York: State University of New York Press, 1986.

———. *Red Seas: Ferdinand Smith and Radical Black Sailors in the United States and Jamaica*. New York: New York University Press, 2005.

Howard-Pitney, David. *The Afro-American Jeremiad: Appeals for Justice in America*. Philadelphia: Temple University Press, 1990.

Howe, Glenford D. *Race, War, and Nationalism: A Social History of West Indians in the First World War*. Kingston: Ian Randle, 2002.

Howe, Stephen. *Afrocentrism: Mythical Pasts and Imagined Homes*. London: Verso, 1998.

Huggins, Nathan I. *Afro-American Studies: A Report to the Ford Foundation*. New York: Ford Foundation, 1985.

Hunt, Alfred N. *Haiti's Influence on Antebellum America: Slumbering Volcano in the Caribbean*. Baton Rouge: Louisiana State University Press, 1998.

Hunwick, John, and Eva Troutt Powell. *The African Diaspora in the Mediterranean Lands of Islam*. Princeton, N.J.: Markus Wiener, 2002.

Hutton, Clinton. "The Cuban Influence on Popular Jamaican Music." In *Intra-*

Caribbean Migration: The Cuban Connection (1898-Present), 117–32. Proceedings of seminar held at the University of the West Indies, Mona, Jamaica, June 14–16, 2001.

International Conference of Negro Workers. *A Report of Proceedings and Decisions of the First International Conference of Negro Workers.* Hamburg: International Trade Union, Committee of Negro Workers, 1930.

Irele, Abiola. *The African Experience in Literature and Ideology.* Bloomington: Indiana University Press, 1990.

Jacobs, Richard, and Ian Jacobs, eds. *Grenada: The Route to Revolution.* Havana: Casa de las Americas, 1980.

Jacobs, Sylvia M., ed. *Black Americans and the Missionary Movement in Africa.* Westport, Conn.: Greenwood Press, 1982.

Jacobson, Matthew Frye. *Whiteness of a Different Color: European Immigrants and the Alchemy of Race.* Cambridge, Mass.: Harvard University Press, 1999.

Jamaica. *Blue Book for the Island of Jamaica: 1913–1914.* Kingston: Government Printing Office, 1914.

James, C. L. R. *The Black Jacobins: Toussaint L'Ouverture and the San Domingo Revolution.* New York: Dial Press, 1938; rev. ed., 1963.

———. *A History of Negro Revolt.* London: Fact Ltd., 1938.

———. "Walter Rodney and the Question of Power." In *Walter Rodney, Revolutionary and Scholar: A Tribute,* edited by Edward A. Alpers and Pierre-Michel Fontaine, 133–46. Los Angeles: Center for Afro-American Studies and African Studies Center, University of California, 1982.

James, Winston. "Explaining Afro-Caribbean Social Mobility in the United States: Beyond the Sowell Thesis." *Comparative Studies in Society and History* 44, no. 2 (2002): 218–62.

———. *Holding aloft the Banner of Ethiopia: Caribbean Radicalism in Early Twentieth-Century America.* London: Verso, 1998.

James, Winston, and Clive Harris, eds. *Inside Babylon: The Caribbean Diaspora in Britain.* New York: Verso, 1993.

Jenkinson, Jacqueline. "The Glasgow Race Disturbances of 1919." *Immigrants and Minorities* 4, no. 2 (1985): 43–67.

Johns, Sheridan. "The Birth of the Communist Party of South Africa." *International Journal of African Historical Studies* 9, no. 3 (1976): 371–400.

———. *Raising the Red Flag: The International Socialist League and the Communist Party of South Africa, 1914–1932.* Bellville, South Africa: Mayibuye Books, 1995.

Johnson, Cedric. *Revolutionaries to Race Leaders: Black Power and the Making of African American Politics.* Minneapolis: University of Minnesota Press, 2007.

Johnson, Morris R. *Archbishop Daniel William Alexander and the African Orthodox Church.* Lanham, Md.: International Scholars Publishers, 1999.

Jones, Absalom, and Richard Allen. "A Narrative of the Proceedings of the Black People, During the Late Awful Calamity in Philadelphia, in the Year, 1793." In *Negro Protest Pamphlets,* edited by Dorothy Parker, 1–24. New York: Arno Press, 1969.

Joseph, Peniel E. "Black Studies, Student Activism, and the Black Power Movement." In *The Black Power Movement: Rethinking the Civil Rights–Black Power Era,* edited by Peniel E. Joseph, 251–77. New York: Routledge, 2006.

———. "Introduction: Toward a Historiography of the Black Power Movement." In *The Black Power Movement: Rethinking the Civil Rights–Black Power Era*, edited by Peniel E. Joseph, 1–25. New York: Routledge, 2006.

Journal of African History 19, no. 1 (1978). Special issue on World War I and Africa.

Jung, Moon-Ho. *Coolies and Cane: Race, Labor, and Sugar in the Age of Emancipation.* Baltimore: Johns Hopkins University Press, 2006.

Kadalie, Clements. *My Life and the I.C.U.* London: Cass, 1970.

Kanet, Roger. "The Comintern and the 'Negro Question': Communist Policy in the United States and Africa, 1921–41." *Survey* 19, no. 4 (Autumn 1973): 86–122.

Kapur, Sudarshan. *Raising Up a Prophet: The African-American Encounter with Gandhi.* Boston: Beacon Press, 1992.

Keeling, Kara. "'A Homegrown Revolutionary'? Tupac Shakur and the Legacy of the Black Panther Party." *Black Scholar* 29, no. 2–3 (1999): 59–63.

Kelley, Robin D. G. *Freedom Dreams: The Black Radical Imagination.* Boston: Beacon Press, 2002.

———. *Hammer and Hoe: Alabama Communists during the Great Depression.* Chapel Hill: University of North Carolina Press, 1990.

———. "Kickin' Reality, Kickin' Ballistics: 'Gangsta Rap' and Postindustrial Los Angeles." In *Droppin' Science: Critical Essays on Rap Music and Hip Hop Culture*, edited by William Eric Perkins, 117–58. Philadelphia: Temple University Press, 1996.

———. *Race Rebels: Culture, Politics, and the Black Working Class.* New York: Free Press, 1994.

———. "Stormy Weather: Reconstructing Black (Inter)Nationalism in the Cold War Era." In *Is It Nation Time? Contemporary Essays on Black Power and Black Nationalism*, edited by Eddie S. Glaude Jr., 67–90. Chicago: University of Chicago Press, 2002.

———. "The Third International and the Struggle for National Liberation in South Africa." *Ufahamu* 15, no. 1–2 (1986): 99–120.

Kerr-Ritchie, J. R. *Rites of August First: Emancipation Day in the Black Atlantic World.* Baton Rouge: Louisiana State University Press, 2007.

Keyes, Cheryl. "At the Crossroads: Rap Music and Its African Nexus." *Ethnomusicology* 40 (1996): 223–48.

Kidd, Colin. *The Forging of Races: Race and Scripture in the Protestant Atlantic World, 1600–2000.* Cambridge: Cambridge University Press, 2006.

Kidd, Thomas S. *The Great Awakening: The Roots of Evangelical Christianity in Colonial America.* New Haven: Yale University Press, 2007.

King, Desmond. *Making Americans: Immigration, Race, and the Origins of the Diverse Democracy.* Cambridge, Mass.: Harvard University Press, 2000.

King, Martin Luther, Jr. "An Experiment in Love." In *A Testament of Hope: The Essential Writings and Speeches of Martin Luther King, Jr.*, edited by James Washington, 16–20. San Francisco: Harper, 1986.

———. "The Social Organization of Nonviolence." In *A Testament of Hope: The Essential Writings and Speeches of Martin Luther King, Jr.*, edited by James Washington, 31–35. San Francisco: Harper, 1986.

———. *Stride toward Freedom: The Montgomery Story.* New York: Harper, 1958.

———. *A Testament of Hope: The Essential Writings and Speeches of Martin Luther King, Jr.* Edited by James Washington. San Francisco: Harper, 1986.

———. *Why We Can't Wait.* New York: Penguin Books, 1964.

Kirk, Joyce. *Making a Voice: African Resistance to Segregation in South Africa.* Boulder: Westview Press, 1998.

Klehr, Harvey, John Earl Haynes, and Kryill M. Anderson. *The Soviet World of American Communism.* New Haven: Yale University Press, 1998.

Klein, Herbert S. *African Slavery in Latin America and the Caribbean.* New York: Oxford University Press, 1986.

Knight, Franklin W. *Slave Society in Cuba during the Nineteenth Century.* Madison: University of Wisconsin Press, 1970.

Kornweibel, Theodore, Jr. *"Seeing Red": Federal Campaigns against Black Militancy, 1919–1925.* Bloomington: Indiana University Press, 1998.

LaChance, Paul. "Repercussions of the Haitian Revolution in Louisiana." In *The Impact of the Haitian Revolution in the Atlantic World,* edited by David P. Geggus, 209–30. Columbia: University of South Carolina Press, 2001.

Lader, Lawrence. *Power on the Left: American Radical Movements since 1946.* New York: Norton, 1979.

La Guma, Alex, and Mohamed Adhikari, eds. *Jimmy La Guma—A Biography.* Cape Town: Friends of the South African Library, 1997.

Langley, Ayodele. *Pan-Africanism and Nationalism in West Africa, 1900–1945.* Oxford: Clarendon Press, 1973.

Langley, Lester D. *The Americas in the Age of Revolution, 1750–1850.* New Haven: Yale University Press, 1996.

Laurent, Gerard M. *Haiti et l'independance americaine.* Port-au-Prince: Imprimerie de Seminaire Adventiste, 1976.

Lawson, James M., Jr. "We Are Trying to Raise the Moral Issue." In *Black Protest Thought in the Twentieth Century,* edited by August Meier, Elliott Rudwick, and Francis L. Broderick, 308–15. New York: Bobbs-Merrill, 1971.

Layton, Azza Salama. *International Politics and Civil Rights Policies in the United States, 1941–1960.* Cambridge: Cambridge University Press, 2000.

Leal, Gilberto R. N. "Fárígá/Ifaradá: Black Resistance and Achievement in Brazil." In *African Roots/American Cultures: Africa in the Creation of the Americas,* edited by Sheila S. Walker, 291–300. New York: Rowman & Littlefield, 2001.

Lee, Hélène. *Le premier Rasta.* Paris: Flammarion, 1999.

Lefkowitz, Mary R., and Guy MacLean Rogers, eds. *Black Athena Revisited.* Chapel Hill: University of North Carolina Press, 1996.

Legum, Colin. "The Year of the Students: A Survey of the African University Scene." In *African Contemporary Record,* A3–A30. London: Africana Publishing, 1972.

Lemelle, Sidney, and Robin D. G. Kelley, eds. *Imagining Home: Class, Culture, and Nationalism in the African Diaspora.* London: Verso, 1994.

Lenin, Vladimir Il'ich. *Lenin on the National and Colonial Questions.* Peking: Foreign Languages Press, 1967.

———. *Selected Works.* Vol. 3. Moscow: Progress Publishers, 1971.

Lewis, Arthur. *Growth and Fluctuations, 1870–1913.* Boston: G. Allen & Unwin, 1978.

Lewis, David Levering. *W. E. B. Du Bois: The Fight for Equality and the American Century, 1919–1963*. New York: Henry Holt and Company, 2000.

Lewis, Gordon. *Grenada: The Jewel Despoiled*. Baltimore: Johns Hopkins University Press, 1987.

Lewis, Rupert. "Garvey's Perspective on Jamaica." In *Garvey: His Work and Impact*, edited by Rupert Lewis and Patrick Bryan, 229–42. Trenton, N.J.: Africa World Press, 1994.

———. "Learning to Blow the Abeng: A Critical Look at Anti-Establishment Movements of the 1960s and 1970s." *Small Axe* 1 (March 1997): 5–17.

———. *Marcus Garvey, Anti-Colonial Champion*. Trenton, N.J.: Africa World Press, 1988.

———. *Walter Rodney's Intellectual and Political Thought*. Detroit: Wayne State University Press, 1998; Barbados: The Press, University of the West Indies, 1998.

Lewis, Rupert, and Patrick Bryan, eds. *Garvey: His Work and Impact*. Trenton, N.J.: Africa World Press, 1991.

Lewis, W. Arthur. *Labour in the West Indies*. London: New Beacon Books, 1977.

"Life in Jamaica in the Early Twentieth Century: A Presentation of Ninety Oral Accounts." Unpublished transcripts housed at Institute of Social and Economic Research, University of the West Indies, Mona, Kingston, Jamaica.

Lilly Caldwell, Kia. *Negras in Brazil: Re-envisioning Black Women, Subjectivity, and Citizenship*. Piscataway, N.J.: Rutgers University Press, 2006.

Lincoln, C. Eric. *The Black Muslims in America*. 3rd ed. Trenton, N.J.: Africa World Press, 1994.

Linebaugh, Peter, and Marcus Rediker. *The Many-Headed Hydra: Sailors, Slaves, Commoners, and the Hidden History of the Revolutionary Atlantic*. Boston: Beacon Press, 2000.

Lipsitz, George. *Dangerous Crossroads: Popular Music, Postmodernism, and the Politics of Space*. London: Verso, 1994.

Lodge, Tom. *Black Politics in South Africa since 1945*. London: Longman, 1983.

Logan, Rayford Whittingham. *The Diplomatic Relations of the United States with Haiti, 1776–1891*. Chapel Hill: University of North Carolina Press, 1941.

Lumumba, Patrice. "Independence Day Speech." June 30, 1960. <http://www.africawithin.com/lumumba/independence_speech.htm>. Accessed February 10, 2007.

Lynch, Hollis R. *Edward Wilmot Blyden: Pan-Negro Patriot, 1832–1912*. London: Oxford University Press, 1967.

Madhubuti, Haki R., and Maulana Karenga, eds. *Million Man March/Day of Absence: A Commemorative Anthology*. Chicago: Third World Press, 1996.

Magaldi, Cristina. "Adopting Imports: New Images and Alliances in Brazilian Popular Music of the 1990s." *Popular Music* 18, no. 3 (1999): 309–29.

Makalani, Minkah. "For the Liberation of Black People Everywhere: The African Blood Brotherhood, Black Radicalism, and Pan-African Liberation in the New Negro Movement." Ph.D. diss., University of Illinois at Urbana-Champaign, 2004.

Makonnen, Ras. *Pan-Africanism from Within*. As recorded and edited by Kenneth King. Nairobi: Oxford University Press, 1973.

Malcolm X. *Malcolm X Speaks: Selected Speeches and Statements*. New York: Grove/Atlantic, 1990.

Malcolm X et al. "Program of the Organization of Afro-American Unity." <http://www.themalcolmxmuseum.org/collections/phpweblog/stories.php?story=01/10/13/0732492>. Accessed June 3, 2005.

Manning, Patrick. "Africa and the African Diaspora: New Directions of Study." *Journal of African History* 44 (2003): 487–506.

Marquese, Mike. *Redemption Song: Muhammad Ali and the Spirit of the Sixties*. London: Verso, 1999.

Marrant, John. "A Journal of the Reverend John Marrant, from August the 18th, 1785, to the 16th of March, 1790, [1790]." In *"Face Zion Forward": First Writers of the Black Atlantic, 1785–1798*, edited by Joanna Brooks and John Saillant, 93–160. Boston: Northeastern University Press, 2002.

———. "A Sermon Preached on the 24th Day of June 1789." In *"Face Zion Forward": First Writers of the Black Atlantic, 1785–1798*, edited by Joanna Brooks and John Saillant, 77–92. Boston: Northeastern University Press, 2002.

Mars, Perry. *Ideology and Change: The Transformation of the Caribbean Left*. Barbados: The Press, University of the West Indies, 1998.

Marshall, Dawn. "A History of West Indian Migrations: Overseas Opportunities and 'Safety-Valve' Policies." In *The Caribbean Exodus*, edited by Barry B. Levine, 15–31. New York: Praeger, 1987.

Marshall, Sharon. "Nothing in My Hands: Some Personal Accounts of Migration from Barbados to Cuba." In *Intra-Caribbean Migration: The Cuban Connection (1898–Present)*, 19–28. Proceedings of seminar held at the University of the West Indies, Mona, Jamaica, June 14–16, 2001.

Martin, Tony. *Amy Ashwood Garvey: Pan-Africanist, Feminist, and Mrs. Garvey No. 1, or a Tale of Two Amies*. Dover, Mass.: Majority Press, 2007.

———. *The Pan-African Connection: From Slavery to Garvey and Beyond*. Dover, Mass.: Majority Press, 1983.

———. *Race First: The Organizational and Ideological Struggles of Marcus Garvey and the Universal Negro Improvement Association*. Westport, Conn.: Greenwood Press, 1976.

———. "Women in the Garvey Movement." In *Garvey: His Work and Impact*, edited by Rupert Lewis and Patrick Bryan, 67–72. Trenton, N.J.: Africa World Press, 1991.

———, ed. *The Poetical Works of Marcus Garvey*. Dover, Mass.: Majority Press, 1983.

Martin, William G., and Michael O. West. "The Ascent, Triumph, and Disintegration of the Africanist Enterprise, USA." In *Out of One, Many Africas: Reconstructing the Study and Meaning of Africa*, edited by William G. Martin and Michael O. West, 85–122. Champaign: University of Illinois Press, 1999.

Marx, Anthony. *Lessons of Struggle: South African Internal Opposition, 1960–1990*. New York: Oxford University Press, 1992.

Marx, Karl, and Frederick Engels. *The Civil War in the United States*. New York: International Publishers, 1969.

———. *On Colonialism*. London: Lawrence & Wishart, 1960.

Mathurin, Owen Charles. *Henry Sylvester Williams and the Origins of the Pan-African Movement, 1869–1911*. Westport, Conn.: Greenwood Press, 1976.

Matthews, Tracye. "'No One Ever Asks, What a Man's Place in the Revolution Is': Gender and the Politics of the Black Panther Party, 1966–1971." In *The Black Panther Party [Reconsidered]*, edited by Charles E. Jones, 267–304. Baltimore: Black Classic Press, 1998.

Maxwell, William J. *New Negro, Old Left: African-American Writing and Communism between the Wars*. New York: Columbia University Press, 1999.

May, Roy, and Robin Cohen. "The Interaction between Race and Colonialism: A Case Study of the Liverpool Race Riots of 1919." *Race & Class* 16, no. 2 (1974): 111–26.

McAdam, Doug, John D. McCarthy, and Mayer N. Zald, eds. *Comparative Perspectives on Social Movements: Political Opportunities, Mobilizing Structures, and Cultural Framings*. New York: Cambridge University Press, 1996.

McClellan, Woodford. "Africans and Black Americans in the Comintern Schools, 1925–34." *International Journal of African Historical Studies* 36, no. 2 (May 1993): 371–90.

———. "George Padmore and the Hamburg Conference: Some Background." Paper presented at the international seminar "The Life and Times of George Padmore," University of the West Indies, Trinidad, October 2003.

McCracken, John. "African History in British Universities: Past, Present, and Future." *African Affairs* 92 (1993): 239–353.

McDaniels, Andrea. "Striking Cord with Youths, Brazil Rappers Nudge Reform." *Christian Science Monitor*, January 11, 1999, 7.

McDuffie, Erik S. "Black Women Radicals in the Garvey Movement and in the Left during the 1920s." In *Diasporic Africa: A Reader*, edited by Michael A. Gomez, 219–50. New York: New York University Press, 2006.

———. "Long Journeys: Four Black Women and the Communist Party, USA, 1930–1956." Ph.D. diss., New York University, 2003.

McKay, Claude. *A Long Way from Home*. London: Pluto, 1985.

McLeod, Marc. "Undesirable Aliens: Haitian and British West Indian Immigrant Workers in Cuba, 1898–1940." Ph.D. diss., University of Texas at Austin, 2000.

———. "Undesirable Aliens: Race, Ethnicity, and Nationalism in the Comparison of Haitian and British West Indian Immigrant Workers in Cuba, 1912–1939." *Journal of Social History* 31, no. 3 (1998): 599–623.

McMichael, Philip. *Development and Social Change: A Global Perspective*. Thousand Oaks, Calif.: Pine Forge Press, 2004.

Meeks, Brian. "The 1970 Revolution: Chronology and Documentation." In *The Black Power Revolution of 1970: A Retrospective*, edited by Selwyn Ryan and Taimoon Stewart, 135–77. St. Augustine, Trinidad: I.S.E.R., University of the West Indies, 1995.

———. *Caribbean Revolutions and Revolutionary Theory: An Assessment of Cuba, Nicaragua, and Grenada*. London: Macmillan Caribbean, 1993.

———. "The Development of the 1970 Revolution in Trinidad and Tobago." M.S. thesis, Mona, Jamaica, University of the West Indies, 1976.

———. "Lloyd Best, the People and the Road Not Taken in 1970." In *Independent*

Thought and Caribbean Freedom: Essays in Honour of Lloyd Best, edited by Selwyn Ryan, 71–88. St. Augustine, Trinidad and Tobago: Sir Arthur Lewis Institute of Social and Economic Studies, Trinidad, 2003.

———. *Narratives of Resistance: Jamaica, Trinidad, the Caribbean*. Mona: University of the West Indies Press, 2000.

———. "Obscure Revolt, Profound Effects: The Henry Rebellion, Counter-Hegemony, and Jamaican Society." *Small Axe* 2 (September 1977): 39–62.

———. *Radical Caribbean: From Black Power to Abu Bakr*. Kingston: The Press, University of the West Indies, 1996.

———. "Social Formation and People's Revolution: A Grenadian Study." Ph.D. diss., University of the West Indies, 1988.

Melish, Joanne Pope. *Disowning Slavery: Gradual Emancipation and "Race" in New England, 1780–1860*. Ithaca: Cornell University Press, 1998.

Meriwether, James H. *Proudly We Can Be Africans: Black Americans and Africa, 1935–1961*. Chapel Hill: University of North Carolina Press, 2002.

Miller, Floyd J. *The Search for a Black Nationality: Black Emigration and Colonization*. Urbana: University of Illinois Press, 1975.

Miller, James A., Susan D. Pennybacker, and Eve Rosenhaft. "Mother Ada Wright and the International Campaign to Free the Scottsboro Boys, 1931–34." *American Historical Review* 106, no. 2 (April 2001): 387–430.

Millette, David. "Guerrilla War in Trinidad: 1970–1974." In *The Black Power Revolution of 1970: A Retrospective*, edited by Selwyn Ryan and Taimoon Stewart, 625–54. St. Augustine, Trinidad: I.S.E.R., University of the West Indies, 1995.

Mitchell, Henry H. *Black Church Beginnings: The Long-Hidden Realities of the First Years*. Grand Rapids, Mich.: Eerdmans, 2004.

Mitchell, Michael. "Blacks and the Abertura Democrática." In *Race, Class, and Power in Brazil*, edited by Pierre-Michel Fontaine, 95–119. Los Angeles: Center for Afro-American Studies, University of California, 1985.

Mitchell, Tony, ed. *Global Noise: Rap and Hip Hop outside the USA*. Middletown: Wesleyan University Press, 2001.

Moeti, Moitsadi Thoane. "Ethiopianism: Separatist Roots of African Nationalism in South Africa." Ph.D. diss., Syracuse University, 1981.

Monestel, Manuel. "El calypso en Costa Rica." M.A. thesis, Universidad de Costa Rica, Maestría en Artes, 2003.

Moore, Barrington, Jr. *Social Origins of Dictatorship and Democracy: Lord and Peasant in the Making of the Modern World*. Boston: Beacon Press, 1966.

Moore, David Chioni, ed. *Black Athena Writes Back: Martin Bernal Responds to His Critics*. Durham, N.C.: Duke University Press, 2001.

Morgenthau, Ruth Schachter. *Political Parties in French-Speaking West Africa*. Oxford: Clarendon Press, 1964.

Moses, Wilson Jeremiah. *Alexander Crummell: A Study of Civilization and Discontent*. New York: Oxford University Press, 1989.

———, ed. *Classical Black Nationalism: From the American Revolution to Marcus Garvey*. New York: New York University Press, 1996.

Mullen, Bill V., and James Smethurst, eds. *Left of the Color Line: Race, Radicalism, and*

Twentieth-Century Literature of the United States. Chapel Hill: University of North Carolina Press, 2003.

Mullings, Leith. "Race and Globalization: Racialization from Below." *Souls* 6, no. 5 (2004): 1–9.

Munroe, Trevor. *The Workers Party: What It Is. Why It Is Necessary*. Kingston: Workers Liberation League, 1978.

Murphy, Martin F. *Dominican Sugar Plantations: Production and Foreign Labor Integration*. New York: Praeger, 1991.

Murrell, Nathaniel Samuel, William David Spencer, and Adrian Anthony McFarlane, eds. *Chanting Down Babylon: The Rastafari Reader*. Philadelphia: Temple University Press, 1998.

Musson, Doreen. *Johnny Gomas, Voice of the Working Class: A Political Biography*. Cape Town: Buchu Books, 1989.

NAACP. *Thirty Years of Lynching in the United States, 1889–1918*. 1919. New York: Arno Press, 1969.

Naison, Mark. *Communists in Harlem during the Depression*. New York: Grove, 1984.

Nascimento, Elisa Larkin. *Pan-Africanism and South America: Emergence of a Black Rebellion*. Buffalo: Afrodiaspora, 1980.

Nash, Gary B. *The Forgotten Fifth: African Americans in the Age of Revolution*. Cambridge, Mass.: Harvard University Press, 2006.

———. "Thomas Peters: Millwright and Deliverer." In *Struggle and Survival in Colonial America*, edited by Gary B. Nash and David G. Sweet, 69–85. Berkeley: University of California Press, 1981.

National Joint Action Committee. *Conventional Politics or Revolution?* Belmont, Trinidad and Tobago: The Vanguard, 1971.

Natsoulas, Theodore. "Patriarch McGuire and the Spread of the African Orthodox Church to Africa." *Journal of Religion in Africa* 12, no. 2 (1981): 81–104.

Neal, Mark Anthony. *What the Music Said: Black Popular Music and Black Public Culture*. New York: Routledge, 1999.

Nelson, William E., Jr. *Black Atlantic Politics: Dilemmas of Political Empowerment in Boston and Liverpool*. Albany: State University Press, 2000.

Nettleford, Rex M. *Identity, Race, and Protest in Jamaica*. New York: William Morrow, 1972.

Newman, Richard. "Archbishop Daniel William Alexander and the African Orthodox Church." *International Journal of African Historical Studies* 16, no. 4 (1983): 615–30.

———. "The Origins of the African Orthodox Church." In *The Negro Churchman: The Official Organ of the African Orthodox Church, 1921–1931*, 2 vols., edited by Richard Newman, iii–xxii. Millwood, N.Y.: Kraus Reprint Co., 1977.

Newman, Simon P. "American Political Culture and the French and Haitian Revolutions: Nathaniel Cutting and the Jeffersonian Republicans." In *The Impact of the Haitian Revolution in the Atlantic World*, edited by David P. Geggus, 72–89. Columbia: University of South Carolina Press, 2001.

Newton, Huey P. "Message to the Vietnamese." In *The Coming of the New International*, edited by John Gerassi, 539–95. New York: World Publishing Group, 1971.

————. *To Die for the People: The Writings of Huey P. Newton.* New York: Random House, 1972.

————. "The Women's Liberation and Gay Liberation Movements: August 15, 1970." In *To Die for the People: The Writings of Huey P. Newton,* 152–55. New York: Random House, 1972.

Newton, Velma. *The Silver Men: West Indian Labour Migration to Panama, 1850–1914.* Kingston: Ian Randle, 2004.

Nkrumah, Kwame. *Ghana: The Autobiography of Kwame Nkrumah.* New York: Nelson, 1957.

Northrup, David. *Indentured Labor in the Age of Imperialism, 1834–1922.* New York: Cambridge University Press, 1995.

Nzula, A. T., I. Potekhin, and A. Zusmanovich. *Forced Labour in Colonial Africa.* London: Zed Press, 1979.

Odendaal, Andre. *Black Protest Politics in South Africa to 1912.* Totowa, N.J.: Barnes and Noble, 1984.

Okonkwo, R. L. "The Garvey Movement in British West Africa." *Journal of African History* 21, no. 1 (1980): 105–17.

Okpewho, Isidore, Carole Boyce Davies, and Ali A. Mazrui, eds. *The African Diaspora: African Origins and New World Identities.* Bloomington: Indiana University Press, 1999.

O'Neale, Sondra A. *Jupiter Hammon and the Biblical Beginnings of African-American Literature.* Metuchen, N.J.: American Theological Library Association and the Scarecrow Press, 1993.

O'Reilly, Kenneth. *Racial Matters: The FBI's Secret File on Black America, 1960–1972.* New York: Free Press. 1991.

Osumare, Halifu. *The Africanist Aesthetic in Global Hip-Hop: Power Moves.* New York: Palgrave Macmillan, 2007.

Oxaal, Ivar. *Black Intellectuals and the Dilemmas of Race and Class in Trinidad.* Cambridge, Mass.: Schenkman, 1982.

Ozouf, Mona. *Festivals and the French Revolution.* Cambridge, Mass.: Harvard University Press, 1988.

Pacini Hernández, Deborah, and Reebee Garofalo. "Hip Hop in Havana: Rap, Race, and National Identity in Contemporary Cuba." *Journal of Popular Music Studies* 11/12 (2000): 18–47.

Padmore, George. *How Russia Transformed Her Colonial Empire.* London: Dennis Dobson, 1946.

————. *The Life and Struggles of Negro Toilers.* London: R. I. L. U. Magazine for the International Trade Union Committee of Negro Workers, 1931; reprint, Hollywood, Calif.: Sun Dance Press, 1971.

————. *Pan-Africanism or Communism? The Coming Struggle for Africa.* London: Dennis Dobson, 1956.

Page, Carol. "Black America in White South Africa: Church and State Reaction to the A.M.E. Church in Cape Colony and Transvaal, 1896–1910." Ph.D. diss., University of Edinburgh, 1978.

Page, Melvin E. *The Chiwaya War: Malawians and the First World War*. Boulder: Westview Press, 2000.

Painter, Nell Irvin. *The Narrative of Hosea Hudson: The Life and Times of a Black Radical*. New York: Norton, 1994.

Palmer, Colin. "Defining and Studying the Modern African Diaspora." *Perspectives: American Historical Association Newsletter* 36, no. 6 (1998): 22–25.

———. *Slaves of the White God: Blacks in Mexico, 1570–1650*. Cambridge, Mass.: Harvard University Press, 1976.

Palmié, Stephan. *Wizards and Scientists: Explorations in Afro-Cuban Modernity and Tradition*. Durham, N.C.: Duke University Press, 2002.

Pamphile, Leon D. "The NAACP and the American Occupation of Haiti." *Phylon* 67, no. 1 (1986): 91–100.

Paquette, Robert L. "Revolutionary Saint Domingue in the Making of Territorial Louisiana." In *A Turbulent Time: The French Revolution and the Greater Caribbean*, edited by David Barry Gaspar and David Patrick Geggus, 204–25. Bloomington: Indiana University Press, 1997.

Pardue, Derek. "Putting Mano to Music: The Mediation of Race in Brazilian Rap." *Ethnomusicology Forum* 13, no. 2 (2004): 253–86.

Patterson, Tiffany Ruby, and Robin D. G. Kelley. "Unfinished Migrations: Reflections on the African Diaspora and the Making of the Modern World." *African Studies Review* 43, no. 1 (2000): 11–45.

Payne, Charles M. *I've Got the Light of Freedom: The Organizing Tradition and the Mississippi Freedom Struggle*. Berkeley: University of California Press, 1995.

Peabody, Sue. *"There Are No Slaves in France": The Political Culture of Race and Slavery in the Ancien Regime*. New York: Oxford University Press, 1996.

Perotin-Dumon, Anne. "The Emergence of Politics among Free-Coloureds and Slaves in Revolutionary Guadaloupe." *Journal of Caribbean History* 25, no. 1–2 (1991): 100–135.

———. *Etre patriote sous les tropiques la Guadaloupe, la colonisation et la revolution 1789–1794*. Basse-Terre: Societe d'Histoire de la Gaudaloupe, 1985.

Perry, Jeffrey B. *Hubert Harrison: The Voice of Harlem Radicalism, 1883–1918*. New York: Columbia University Press, 2009.

———, ed. *A Hubert Harrison Reader*. Middletown, Conn.: Wesleyan University Press, 2001.

Perullo, Alex. "Hooligans and Heroes: Youth Identity and Hip-Hop in Dar es Salaam, Tanzania." *Africa Today* 51, no. 4 (2005): 75–101.

Pfeffer, Paula F. *A. Philip Randolph: Pioneer of the Civil Rights Movement*. Baton Rouge: Louisiana State University Press, 1990.

Phillips, Anthony De V. "'Go Ahead, England; Barbados Is Behind You': Barbadian Responses to the Outbreak of the Great War in 1914." In *Before and After 1865: Education, Politics, and Regionalism in the Caribbean*, edited by Brian Moore and Swithin Wilmot, 343–50. Kingston: Ian Randle, 1998.

Plummer, Brenda Gayle. "The Afro-American Response to the Occupation of Haiti, 1915–1934." *Phylon* 43, no. 2 (1982): 125–43.

———. *Haiti and the Great Powers, 1902–1915*. Baton Rouge: Louisiana State University Press, 1988.

———. *Rising Wind: Black Americans and U.S. Foreign Affairs, 1935–1960*. Chapel Hill: University of North Carolina Press, 1996.

Popkin, Jeremy D. *Facing Racial Revolution: Eyewitness Accounts of the Haitian Insurrection*. Chicago: University of Chicago Press, 2007.

Post, K. W. J. *Arise Ye Starvelings: The Jamaican Labour Rebellion of 1938 and Its Aftermath*. The Hague: Martinus Nijhoff, 1978.

Post, Ken. "The Bible as Ideology: Ethiopianism in Jamaica, 1930–1938." In *African Perspectives: Papers in the History, Politics, and Economics of Africa Presented to Thomas Hodgkin*, edited by Christopher Allen and R. W. Johnson, 185–207. Cambridge: Cambridge University Press, 1970.

Potkay, Adam, and Sandra Burr, eds. *Black Atlantic Writers of the Eighteenth Century: Living the New Exodus in England and the Americas*. New York: St. Martin's Press, 1995.

Pouchepadass, Jacques. *Champaran and Gandhi: Planters, Peasants, and Gandhian Politics*. New York: Oxford University Press, 2000.

Prashad, Vijay. *Everybody Was Kung Fu Fighting: Afro-Asian Connections and the Myth of Cultural Purity*. Boston: Beacon Press, 2001.

Presley, Cora Ann. *Kikuyu Women, the Mau Mau Rebellion, and Social Change in Kenya*. Boulder: Westview Press, 1992.

Price, Richard. *Maroon Societies: Rebel Slave Communities in the Americas*. Garden City, N.Y.: Anchor Press, 1973.

Proudfoot, Malcolm Jarvis. *Population Movements in the Caribbean*. New York: Negro Universities Press, 1970.

Pryke, Sam. "The Popularity of Nationalism in the Early British Boy Scout Movement." *Social History* (Great Britain) 23, no. 3 (1998): 309–24.

Pulis, John W. "Bridging Troubled Waters: Moses Baker, George Liele, and the African American Diaspora in Jamaica." In *Moving On: Black Loyalists in the Afro-Atlantic World*, edited by John W. Pulis, 183–221. New York: Garland, 1999.

———, ed. *Moving On: Black Loyalists in the Afro-Atlantic World*. New York: Garland, 1999.

Putnam, Lara. *The Company They Kept: Migrants and the Politics of Gender in Caribbean Costa Rica, 1870–1960*. Chapel Hill: University of North Carolina Press, 2002.

Pybus, Cassandra. *Epic Journeys of Freedom: Runaway Slaves of the American Revolution and their Global Quest for Liberty*. Boston: Beacon Press, 2006.

Quandt, William B. *Revolution and Political Leadership: Algeria, 1954–1968*. Cambridge, Mass.: MIT Press, 1969.

Quarles, Benjamin. *The Negro in the American Revolution*. Chapel Hill: University of North Carolina Press, 1961.

Queely, Andrea. "Hip Hop and the Aesthetics of Criminalization." *Souls* 5, no. 1 (2003): 1–15.

Quirós, Ronald Soto. "Inmigración e identidad nacional: Los 'otros' reafirman el 'nosotros.'" *Licenciatura* thesis, Escuela de Historia, Universidad de Costa Rica, 1998.

Rabe, Stephen G. *U.S. Intervention in British Guiana: A Cold War Story.* Chapel Hill: University of North Carolina, 2005.

Raboteau, Albert J. *Slave Religion: The "Invisible Institution" in the Antebellum South.* New York: Oxford University Press, 1978.

Radical History Review 87 (2003). Special issue on Transnational Black Studies.

Radical History Review 92 (2005). Special issue on the First Universal Races Congress of 1911.

Rael, Patrick. *Black Identity and Black Protest in the Antebellum North.* Chapel Hill: University of North Carolina Press, 2002.

Ranger, Terence. "The Myth of the Afro-American Liberator." Seminar Paper, UCLA, 1971.

Redding, Sean. "Government Witchcraft: Taxation, the Supernatural, and the Mpondo Revolt in the Transkei, South Africa, 1955–1963." *African Affairs* 95 (1996): 555–79.

Reddock, Rhoda. *Women, Labour, and Politics in Trinidad and Tobago—A History.* London: Zed Books, 1994.

Rediker, Marcus. *The Slave Ship: A Human History.* New York: Viking, 2007.

Redkey, Edwin. *Respect Black: The Writings and Speeches of Henry McNeal Turner.* New York: Arno Press, 1971.

Reinhardt, Catherine. "French Caribbean Slaves Forge Their Own Ideal of Liberty in 1789." In *Slavery in the Caribbean: Francophone World: Distant Voices, Forgotten Acts, Forged Identities,* edited by Doris Y. Kadish, 19–38. Athens: University of Georgia Press, 2000.

Rhodes, Leara. "Haitian Contributions to American History: A Journalistic Record." In *Slavery in the Caribbean Francophone World: Distant Voices, Forgotten Acts, Forged Identities,* edited by Doris Y. Kadish, 75–90. Athens: University of Georgia Press, 2000.

Rich, Paul. *State Power and Black Politics in South Africa, 1912–1951.* New York: St. Martin's Press, 1996.

Richards, Glen. "Friendly Societies and Labour Organisation in the Leeward Islands, 1912–19." In *Before and After 1865: Education, Politics, and Regionalism in the Caribbean,* edited by Brian Moore and Swithin Wilmot, 136–49. Kingston: Ian Randle, 1998.

———. "Race, Class, and Labour Politics in Colonial Jamaica, 1900–1934." In *Jamaica in Slavery and Freedom: History, Heritage, and Culture,* edited by Kathleen E. A. Monteith and Glen Richards, 340–62. Mona: University of the West Indies Press, 2002.

Richardson, Bonham C. "Caribbean Migrations, 1838–1985." In *The Modern Caribbean,* edited by Franklin W. Knight and Colin A. Palmer, 203–28. Chapel Hill: University of North Carolina Press, 1989.

———. *Panama Money in Barbados, 1900–1920.* Knoxville: University of Tennessee Press, 1985.

Rivera, Raquel. *New York Ricans from the Hip Hop Zone.* New York: Palgrave Macmillan, 2003.

Robaina, Tomas Fernandez. "Marcus Garvey in Cuba: Urrutia, Cubans, and Black Nationalism." In *Between Race and Empire: African-Americans and Cubans before* the *Cuban Revolution*, edited by Lisa Brock and Digna Castaneda Fuertes, 12–128. Philadelphia: Temple University Press, 1998.

Roberts, Rita. "Patriotism and Political Criticism: The Evolution of Political Consciousness in the Mind of a Black Revolutionary Soldier." *Eighteenth-Century Studies* 27 (1994): 569–88.

Robertson, David. *Denmark Vesey*. New York: Knopf, 1999.

Robinson, Cedric J. *Black Marxism: The Making of the Black Radical Tradition*. London: Zed Books, 1983.

Rock, Pete, with Black Ice. "Truth Is." *Soul Survivor II* CD. BBE Records/Rapster. May 11, 2004.

Rodney, Walter. *The Groundings with My Brothers*. London: Bogle L'Ouverture Publications, 1969.

———. *A History of the Guyanese Working People: 1881–1905*. Kingston: Heinemann Educational Books, 1981.

———. *How Europe Underdeveloped Africa*. London: Bogle-L'Ouverture Publications, 1969, 1973.

———. "Towards the Sixth Pan-African Congress: Aspects of the International Class Struggle in Africa, the Caribbean, and America." In *Pan-Africanism: The Struggle against Neo-Colonialism and Imperialism*, edited by Horace Campbell, 18–41. Toronto: Afro-Carib Publications, 1975.

Rogers, Shepherd Richard Athlyi. *Holy Piby: The Black Man's Bible*. Kingston: Research Associates School Times Publications, 2000.

Rohlehr, Gordon. *Transgression, Transition, Transformation: Essays in Caribbean Culture*. San Juan, Trinidad: Lexicon Trinidad Ltd., 2007.

Rojas, Fabio. *From Black Power to Black Studies: How a Radical Social Movement Became an Academic Discipline*. Baltimore: Johns Hopkins University Press, 2007.

Rolinson, Mary G. *Grassroots Garveyism: The Universal Negro Improvement Association in the Rural South, 1920–1927*. Chapel Hill: University of North Carolina Press, 2007.

Rose, Tricia. *Black Noise: Rap Music and Black Culture in Contemporary America*. Hanover: Wesleyan University Press, 1994.

Rosenthal, Michael. *The Character Factory: Baden-Powell and the Origins of the Boy Scout Movement*. New York: Pantheon, 1986.

Roth, Benita. *Separate Roads to Feminism: Black, Chicana, and White Feminist Movements in America's Second Wave*. Cambridge: Cambridge University Press, 2004.

Roth Gordon, Jennifer. "Hip Hop Brasileiro: Brazilian Youth and Alternative Black Consciousness Movements." *Black Arts Quarterly* 7, no. 1 (2002): 9–10.

Rothman, Adam. *Slave Country: American Expansion and the Origins of the Deep South*. Cambridge, Mass.: Harvard University Press, 2005.

Rout, Leslie B., Jr. *The African Experience in Spanish America, 1502 to the Present Day*. New York: Cambridge University Press, 1976.

Roux, Edward. *S. P. Bunting: A Political Biography*. Edited by Brian Bunting. Bellville, South Africa: Mayibuye Books, 1993.

Rugemer, Edward Bartlett. *The Problem of Emancipation: The Caribbean Roots of the American Civil War*. Baton Rouge: Louisiana State University Press, 2008.

Rustin, Bayard. "The Negro and Nonviolence." In *Time on Two Crosses: The Collected Writings of Bayard Rustin*, edited by Devon Carbado and Donald Weise, 6–10. San Francisco: Cleis, 2003.

Ryan, Selwyn, and Taimoon Stewart, eds. *The Black Power Revolution 1970: A Retrospective*. St. Augustine, Trinidad: I.S.E.R., University of the West Indies, 1995.

Saillant, John. "Origins of African American Biblical Hermeneutics in Eighteenth-Century Black Opposition to the Slave Trade and Slavery." In *African Americans and the Bible: Sacred Texts and Social Textures*, edited by Vincent L. Wimbush, 245–48. New York: Continuum, 2000.

Sanderson, Stephen K. *Revolutions: A Worldwide Introduction to Political and Social Change*. Boulder: Paradigm, 2005.

Sanneh, Lamin. *Abolitionists Abroad: American Blacks and the Making of Modern West Africa*. Cambridge, Mass.: Harvard University Press, 1999.

Sansone, Livio. "New Blacks from Bahia: Local and Global Afro-Bahia." *Identities* 3, no. 4 (1997): 457–94.

Santiago-Valles, Kelvin. "World-Historical Ties among 'Spontaneous' Slave Rebellions in the Atlantic." *Review* 28, no. 1 (2005): 51–83.

Satter, Beryl. "Marcus Garvey, Father Divine, and the Gender Politics of Race Difference and Race Neutrality." *American Quarterly* 48, no. 1 (1996): 43–76.

Schama, Simon. *Rough Crossings: Britain, the Slaves, and the American Revolution*. New York: Ecco, 2006.

Schmeisser, Iris. "'Ethiopia Shall Soon Stretch Forth Her Hands': Ethiopianism, Egyptomania, and the Arts of the Harlem Renaissance." In *African Diasporas in the New and Old Worlds: Consciousness and Imagination*, edited by Geneviève Fabre and Klaus Benesch, 263–86. Amsterdam: Rodopi, 2004.

Schmidt, Hans. *The United States Occupation of Haiti, 1915–1934*. New Brunswick: Rutgers University Press, 1971.

Schneider, Mark Robert. *We Return Fighting: The Civil Rights Movement in the Jazz Age*. Boston: Northeastern University Press, 2002.

Schultz, Bud, and Ruth Schultz, eds. *It Did Happen Here: Recollections of Political Repression in America*. Berkeley: University of California Press, 1990.

Scott, David. *Conscripts of Modernity: The Tragedy of Colonial Enlightenment*. Durham, N.C.: Duke University Press, 2004.

———. "The Dialectic of Defeat: An Interview with Rupert Lewis." *Small Axe* 10 (September 2001): 85–117.

Scott, Julius S. "The Common Wind: Currents of Afro-American Communication in the Era of the Haitian Revolution." Ph.D. diss., Duke University, 1986.

Scott, William R. *The Sons of Sheba's Race: African-Americans and the Italo-Ethiopian War, 1935–1941*. Bloomington: Indiana University Press, 1993.

Seale, Bobby. *A Lonely Rage: The Autobiography of Bobby Seale*. New York: Times Book, 1978.

———. *Seize the Time: The Story of the Black Panther Party and Huey P. Newton*. Baltimore: Black Classic Press, 1991.

Self, Robert O. "The Black Panther Party and the Long Civil Rights Era." In *In Search of the Black Panther Party: New Perspectives on a Revolutionary Movement*, edited by

Jama Lazerow and Yohuru Williams, 16–55. Durham, N.C.: Duke University Press, 2006.

Senior, Olive. "The Colón People." *Jamaica Journal* 11, no. 3 (1978): 62–71.

Sensbach, Jon F. *Rebecca's Revival: Creating Black Christianity in the Atlantic World.* Cambridge, Mass.: Harvard University Press, 2005.

Shannon, Magdaline W. *Jean Price-Mars, the Haitian Elite, and the American Occupation, 1915–1935.* New York: St. Martin's Press, 1996.

Shepperson, George. "Pan-Africanism and 'Pan-Africanism': Some Historical Notes." *Phylon* 23, no. 4 (1962): 326–58.

Shepperson, George, and Thomas Price. *Independent African: John Chilembwe and the Origins, Setting, and Significance of the Nyasaland Native Rising of 1915.* Edinburgh: University Press, 1958.

Sherwood, Marika. *Claudia Jones: A Life in Exile.* London: Lawrence & Wishart, 1999.

———. "The Comintern and the Colonies till c.1934." Paper presented to the African-History Seminar, School of African Studies, London University, December 1993.

———. "The Comintern, the CPGB, Colonies and Black Britons, 1920–1938." *Science & Society* 60, no. 2 (1996): 137–63.

———. "Racism and Resistance: Cardiff in the 1930s and 1940s." *Llafur* 4/5 (1991): 51–70.

Shick, Tom W. *Behold the Promised Land: A History of Afro-American Settler Society in Nineteenth-Century Liberia.* Baltimore: Johns Hopkins University Press, 1980.

Shridharani, Krishnalal. *My India, My America.* Garden City, N.Y.: Halcyon House, 1941.

———. *War without Violence: A Study of Gandhi's Method and Its Accomplishments.* New York: Harcourt, Brace, 1939.

Shukra, Kalbir. *The Changing Pattern of Black Politics in Britain.* London: Pluto, 1998.

Sidbury, James. *Ploughshares into Swords: Race, Rebellion, and Identity in Gabriel's Virginia, 1730–1810.* New York: Cambridge University Press, 1997.

Simons, Jack, and Ray Simons. *Class and Colour in South Africa, 1850–1950.* London: International Defence and Aid Fund for Southern Africa, 1983.

Singh, Nikhil. *Black Is a Country: Race and the Unfinished Struggle for Democracy.* Cambridge, Mass.: Harvard University Press, 2004.

———. "The Black Panthers and the 'Undeveloped Country' of the Left." In *The Black Panther Party [Reconsidered],* edited by Charles E. Jones, 57–105. Baltimore: Black Classic Press, 1998.

Sivanandan, Ambalaver. *Communities of Resistance: Writings on Black Struggles for Socialism.* London: Verso, 1990.

Sklar, Holly. *Washington's War on Nicaragua.* Boston: South End Press, 1988.

Skocpol, Theda. *States and Social Revolutions: A Comparative Analysis of France, Russia, and China.* New York: Cambridge University Press, 1979.

Smith, C. Calvin. "John E. Bush: The Politician and the Man, 1880–1916." *Arkansas Historical Quarterly* 54, no. 2 (1995): 115–33.

Smith, Mona Z. *Becoming Something: The Story of Canada Lee.* New York: Faber and Faber, 2004.

Sobel, Mechal. *Trabelin' On: The Slave Journey to an Afro-Baptist Faith*. Westport, Conn.: Greenwood Press, 1979.

Social Research 56, no. 1 (1989). Special issue on bicentennial of the French Revolution.

Solomon, Mark. *The Cry Was Unity: Communists and African Americans, 1917–1936*. Jackson: University Press of Mississippi, 1998.

South African Communist Party. *South African Communists Speak: Documents from the History of the South African Communist Party, 1915–1980*. London: Inkululeko Publications, 1981.

South African Students' Organization. "South African Students' Organization Amended Constitution, Adopted by General Students' Council, 4–10 July 1971." In *Africa Contemporary Record*, edited by Colin Legum, C210–C212. London: Rex Collings, 1972.

Spitzer, Leo, and LaRay Denzer. "I. T. A. Wallace-Johnson and the West African Youth League." *International Journal of African Historical Studies* 6, no. 3 (1973): 413–52.

———. "I. T. A. Wallace-Johnson and the West African Youth League." Pt. 2, "The Sierra Leone Period, 1938–1945." *International Journal of African Historical Studies* 6, no. 4 (1973): 565–601.

Springer, Kimberly. *Living for the Revolution: Black Feminist Organizations, 1968–1980*. Durham, N.C.: Duke University Press, 2005.

Squires, Mike. "Communists and the Fight against Racism during the Class against Class Period, 1928–33." *Communist Review*, Summer 2000, 12–19.

Starobin, Robert S., ed. *Denmark Vesey: The Slave Conspiracy of 1822*. Englewood Cliffs, N.J.: Prentice-Hall, 1970.

Stein, Judith. *The World of Marcus Garvey: Race and Class in Modern Society*. Baton Rouge: Louisiana State University Press, 1986.

Stein, Stanley J. *Vassouras: A Brazilian Coffee County, 1850–1900*. Cambridge, Mass.: Harvard University Press, 1957.

Stepan, Nancy Leys. *The Hour of Eugenics: Race, Gender, and Nation in Latin America*. Ithaca, N.Y.: Cornell University Press, 1991.

Stephens, Simon. "Kwaito." In *Senses of Culture*, edited by Sarah Nuttall and Cheryl-Ann Michael, 256–77. Cape Town: Oxford University Press, 2000.

Steward, T. G. "How the Black St. Domingue Legion Saved the Patriot Army in the Siege of Savannah, 1779." Occasional Paper No. 5. Washington, D.C.: American Negro Academy, 1899.

Stoddard, T. Lothrop. *The French Revolution in San Domingo*. Boston: Houghton Mifflin, 1914.

Stone, Carl. *The Political Opinions of the Jamaican People, 1976–1981*. Kingston: Blackett Publishers, 1982.

Stovall, Tyler. "Colour Blind France? Colonial Workers during the First World War." *Race & Class* 35 (1993): 35–55.

Strachan, Hew. *The First World War in Africa*. New York: Oxford University Press, 2004.

Stuckey, Sterling. *The Ideological Origins of Black Nationalism*. Boston: Beacon Press, 1972.

———. *Slave Culture: Nationalist Theory and the Foundations of Black America*. New York: Oxford University Press, 1987.

Sudbury, Julia. *Global Lockdown: Race, Gender, and the Prison-Industrial Complex*. New York: Routledge, 2005.

Suggs, Henry Lewis. "The Response of the African American Press to the United States Occupation of Haiti, 1915–1934." *Journal of Negro History* 73, no. 1–4 (1988): 33–45.

Suite, Winston. "The Arrogance of NJAC." In *The Black Power Revolution 1970: A Retrospective*, edited by Selwyn Ryan and Taimoon Stewart, 355–62. St. Augustine, Trinidad: I.S.E.R., University of the West Indies, 1995.

Summary of the Program and Aims of the African Blood Brotherhood. New York, 1920. Records of the CPUSA, Library of Congress, fond 515, reel 2, delo 37.

Sutherland, Bill. "Bill Sutherland: Tanzania." In *The Black Expatriates: A Study of American Negroes in Exile*, edited by Ernest Dunbar, 88–109. New York: Dutton, 1968.

Sutherland, Bill, and Matt Meyer. *Guns and Gandhi in Africa: Pan-African Insights on Nonviolence, Armed Struggle, and Liberation in Africa*. Trenton, N.J.: Africa World Press, 2000.

Swan, Maureen. *Gandhi: The South African Experience*. Johannesburg: Ravan Press, 1985.

Sweeney, Allison W. *History of the American Negro in the Great World War*. 1919. New York: Negro Universities Press, 1969.

Sweet, James H. *Recreating Africa: Culture, Kinship, and Religion in the African-Portuguese World, 1441–1770*. Chapel Hill: University of North Carolina Press, 2003.

Sweet, James I. "The Fourth of July and Black Americans in the Nineteenth Century: Northern Leadership Opinion within the Context of the Black Experience." *Journal of Negro History* 61, no. 3 (1976): 256–75.

Sykes, Bobbi. "Opening Statement." In *On Trial: Black Power in Australia*, edited by Ann Turner, 7–30. South Yarra: Heinemann Educational Australia, 1975.

Szok, Peter. *La última gaviota: Liberalism and Nostalgia in Early Twentieth-Century Panamá*. Westport, Conn.: Greenwood Press, 2001.

Taylor, Ula Yvette. *The Veiled Garvey: The Life and Times of Amy Jacques Garvey*. Chapel Hill: University of North Carolina Press, 2002.

Terry-Thompson, A. C. *The History of the African Orthodox Church*. New York: Self-published, 1956.

Thomas, Deborah A. *Modern Blackness: Nationalism, Globalization, and the Politics of Culture in Jamaica*. Durham, N.C.: Duke University Press, 2004.

Thomas-Hope, Elizabeth M. "The Establishment of a Migration Tradition: British West Indian Movements to the Hispanic Caribbean in the Century after Emancipation." *International Migration* 24 (1986): 66–81.

Thornton, John. *Africa and Africans in the Making of the Atlantic World, 1400–1680*. Cambridge: Cambridge University Press, 1992.

———. "African Soldiers in the Haitian Revolution." *Journal of Caribbean History* 25, no. 1–2 (1991): 58–80.

Tilly, Charles. *Social Movements, 1768–2004*. Boulder: Paradigm, 2004.

Tinker Salas, Miguel. "Relaciones de poder y raza en los campos petroleros venezolanos, 1920–1940." *Asuntos* (Caracas, CIED) 5, no. 10 (2001): 94–95.

Tolbert, Emory. *The UNIA and Black Los Angeles: Ideology and Community in the American Garvey Movement*. Los Angeles: Sage, 1980.

Trotter, Joe William, Jr., ed. *The Great Migration in Historical Perspective: New Dimensions of Race, Class, and Gender*. Bloomington: Indiana University Press, 1991.

Trouillot, Michel-Rolph. "From Planters' Journals to Academia: The Haitian Revolution as Unthinkable History." *Journal of Caribbean History* 25, no. 1–2 (1991): 81–99.

———. *Silencing the Past: Power and the Production of History*. Boston: Beacon Press, 1999.

Turits, Richard Lee. "A World Destroyed, a Nation Imposed: The 1937 Haitian Massacre in the Dominican Republic." *Hispanic American Historical Review* 82, no. 3 (2002): 589–635.

Turner, Joyce Moore. *Caribbean Crusaders and the Harlem Renaissance*. Urbana: University of Illinois Press, 2005.

Turner, Mary. *Slaves and Missionaries: The Disintegration of Jamaican Slave Society, 1787–1834*. Urbana: University of Illinois Press, 1982.

Turner, Richard Brent. *Islam in the African American Experience*. Bloomington: Indiana University Press, 1997.

Turner, Richard B., W. Burghardt Turner, and Joyce M. Turner, eds. *Richard B. Moore, Caribbean Militant in Harlem: Collected Writings, 1920–1972*. Bloomington: Indiana University Press, 1992.

Tyson, Timothy B. *Radio Free Dixie: Robert F. Williams and the Roots of Black Power*. Chapel Hill: University of North Carolina Press, 1999, 2001.

Ullman, Victor. *Martin L. Delany: The Beginnings of Black Nationalism*. Boston: Beacon Press, 1971.

Ulyanovsky, Rostislav. *Socialism and the Newly Independent Nations*. Moscow: Progress Publishers, 1974.

Urla, Jaqueline. "'We Are All Malcolm X!' Negu Gorriak, Hip-Hop, and the Basque Political Imaginary." In *Global Noise: Rap and Hip Hop outside the USA*, edited by Tony Mitchell, 171–93. Middletown: Wesleyan University Press, 2001.

Valentine, C. "Two Religions in Practice." *Crusader*, August 1921, 5–6.

Van Deburg, William L. *New Day in Babylon: The Black Power Movement and American Culture, 1965–1975*. Chicago: University of Chicago Press, 1992.

Van Tyne, Claude. *India in Ferment*. New York: Appleton, 1923.

Vincent, Theodore. *Black Power and the Garvey Movement*. Berkeley: University of California Press, 1972.

Vinson, Robert Trent. "'The Americans Are Coming': African Americans, Black West Indians, and Transnational Politics in Early 20th Century South Africa." Book manuscript, forthcoming.

———. "Citizenship over Race? African Americans in American–South African Diplomacy, 1890–1925," *World History Connected*, November 2004, <http://worldhistoryconnected.press.uiuc.edu/2.1/vinson.html>. Accessed February 1, 2008.

———. "In the Time of the Americans: Garveyism in Segregationist South Africa, 1920–1940." Ph.D. diss., Howard University, 2001.

Von Eschen, Penny M. *Race against Empire: Black Americans and Anticolonialism, 1937–1957*. Ithaca: Cornell University Press, 1997.

Wacquant, Loïc. *Deadly Symbiosis: Race and the Rise of Neoliberal Penality*. Cambridge: Polity Press, 2005.

Walker, David. *David Walker's Appeal to the Coloured Citizens of the World.* 1829. University Park: Pennsylvania State University Press, 2000.

Walker, James W. St. G. *The Black Loyalists: The Search for a Promised Land in Nova Scotia and Sierra Leone, 1783–1870.* New York: Africana Publishing, 1976.

Wallace, Michelle. *Black Macho and the Myth of the Superwoman.* New York: Dial Press, 1978.

Wallerstein, Immanuel. *The Modern World-System III: The Second Era of Great Expansion of the Capitalist World-Economy, 1730–1840s.* New York: Academic, 1988.

Walshe, Peter. *The Rise of African Nationalism in South Africa: The African National Congress, 1912–1952.* Berkeley: University of California Press, 1971.

Walters, Ronald W. *Pan Africanism and the African Diaspora: An Analysis of Modern Afrocentric Political Movements.* Detroit: Wayne State University Press, 1993.

Ward, Stephen. "The Third World Women's Alliance: Black Feminist Radicalism and Black Power Politics." In *The Black Power Movement: Rethinking the Civil Rights–Black Power Era,* edited by Peniel E. Joseph, 119–44. New York: Routledge, 2006.

Watkins, Lee. "'Simunye, We Are Not One': Ethnicity, Difference, and the Hip-Hoppers of Cape Town." *Race & Class* 43, no. 1 (2001): 29–44.

Watkins-Owens, Irma. *Blood Relations: Caribbean Immigrants and the Harlem Community, 1900–1930.* Bloomington: Indiana University Press, 1996.

Weinberg, Arthur, ed. *Attorney for the Damned.* Chicago: University of Chicago Press, 1989.

Wells-Barnett, Ida B. *On Lynching.* Amherst: Humanity Books, 2002.

Wendt, Simon. "Protection or Path toward Revolution?" *Souls* 9, no. 4 (2007): 320–32.

Wentink, D. E. "The Orthodox Church in East Africa." *Ecumenical Review* 20, no. 1 (1968): 33–43.

West, Michael O. "Ethiopianism and Colonialism: The African Orthodox Church in Zimbabwe, 1928–1934." In *Christian Missionaries and the State in the Third World,* edited by Holger Bernt Hansen and Michael Twaddle, 237–54. Athens: Ohio University Press, 2002.

———. "Like a River: The Million Man March and the Black Nationalist Tradition in the United States." *Journal of Historical Sociology* 12, no. 1 (1999): 81–100.

———. "Seeds Are Sown: The Garvey Movement in Zimbabwe in the Interwar Years." *International Journal of African Historical Studies* 35, no. 2–3 (2003): 335–62.

———. "Walter Rodney and Black Power: Jamaican Intelligence and US Diplomacy." *African Journal of Criminology and Justice Studies* 1, no. 2 (2006): 1–50. Online journal.

West, Michael O., and William G. Martin. "Introduction: The Rival Africas and Paradigms of Africanists and Africans at Home and Abroad." In *Out of One, Many Africas: Reconstructing the Study and Meaning of Africa,* edited by William G. Martin and Michael O. West, 1–36. Champaign: University of Illinois Press, 1999.

West-Durán, Alan. "Rap's Diasporic Dialogues: Cuba's Redefinition of Blackness." *Journal of Popular Music Studies* 16, no. 1 (April 2004): 4–39.

Westerman, George W. *Los inmigrantes antillanos en Panamá.* Panama: n.p., 1980.

Westmaas, Nigel. "Resisting Orthodoxy: Notes on the Origins and Ideology of the Working People's Alliance." *Small Axe* 14 (2004): 63–81.

White, Garth. "New World: Two Views." *New World Quarterly* 3, no. 4 (1967): 57–60.

White, Shane. "'It Was a Proud Day': African Americans, Festivals, and Parades in the North, 1741–1834.'" *Journal of American History* 81, no. 1 (1994): 13–50.

Whitfield, Harvey Amani. *Blacks on the Border: The Black Refugees in British North America, 1815–1860*. Burlington: University of Vermont Press, 2006.

Wickins, P. L. *The Industrial and Commercial Workers' Union of Africa*. Cape Town: Oxford University Press, 1978.

Wilder, Craig Steven. *In the Company of Black Men: The African Influence on African American Culture in New York City*. New York: New York University Press, 2001.

Wilkins, Fanon Che. "'In the Belly of the Beast': Black Power, Anti-Imperialism, and the African Liberation Solidarity Movement, 1968–74." Ph.D. diss., New York University, 2001.

———. "The Making of Black Internationalists: SNCC and Africa before the Launching of Black Power, 1960–65." *Journal of African American History* 92, no. 4 (2007): 468–90.

Willan, Brian. *Sol Plaatje: South African Nationalist, 1876–1932*. Berkeley: University of California Press, 1984.

Williams, Eric. *Capitalism and Slavery*. Chapel Hill: University of North Carolina Press, 1944.

Williams, Gavin. "Garveyism, Akinpelu Obisesan, and His Contemporaries: Ibadan, 1920–22." In *Legitimacy and the State in Twentieth-Century Africa: Essays in Honour of A. H. M. Kirk-Greene*, edited by Terence Ranger and Olufemi Vaughn, 112–32. London: Macmillan, 1993.

Williams, Robert. *Negroes with Guns*. Detroit: Wayne State University Press, 1998.

Wilson, Carlton. "Britain's Red Summer: The 1919 Race Riots in Liverpool." *South Asia Bulletin: Comparative Studies of South Asia, Africa and the Middle East* 15, no. 2 (1995): 25–35.

Wilson, Edward Thomas. *Russia and Black Africa before World War II*. New York: Holmes and Meier, 1974.

Wilson, Monica. *Reaction to Conquest: Effects of Contact with Europeans on the Pondo of South Africa*. London: Oxford University Press, 1961.

Wimbush, Vincent L., ed. *African Americans and the Bible: Sacred Texts and Social Textures*. New York: Continuum, 2000.

Winant, Howard. *Racial Conditions*. Minneapolis: University of Minnesota Press, 1994.

Wolf, Eric. *Europe and the People without History*. Berkeley: University of California Press, 1982.

Woodard, Komozi. "Amiri Baraka, the Congress of African People, and Black Power Politics from the 1961 United Nations Protest to the Gary Convention." In *The Black Power Movement: Rethinking the Civil Rights–Black Power Era*, edited by Peniel E. Joseph, 55–77. New York: Routledge, 2006.

———. *A Nation within a Nation: Amiri Baraka (LeRoi Jones) and Black Power Politics*. Chapel Hill: University of North Carolina Press, 1999.

Wright, Richard. "I Tried to Be a Communist." *Atlantic Monthly* 174 (August 1944): 61–70; 175 (September 1944): 48–56.

Wynter, Sylvia. "The Politics of Black Culture: From Myal to Marley." Mimeo, 1977.

Yelvington, Kevin. "The War in Ethiopia and Trinidad, 1935–1936." In *The Colonial Caribbean in Transition: Essays on Postemancipation Social and Cultural History*, edited by Bridget Brereton and Kevin A. Yelvington, 189–225. Mona: The Press, University of the West Indies, 1999.

Yun, Lisa. *The Coolie Speaks: Chinese Indentured Laborers and African Slaves in Cuba.* Philadelphia: Temple University Press, 2008.

Zachernuk, Philip S. *Colonial Subjects: An African Intelligentsia and Atlantic Ideas.* Charlottesville: University Press of Virginia, 2000.

Zangrando, Robert. *The NAACP Crusade against Lynching, 1909–1950.* Philadelphia: Temple University Press, 1980.

Zeleza, Paul Tiyambe. *Manufacturing African Studies and Crises.* Dakar: CODESRIA, 1997.

———. "Rewriting the African Diaspora: Beyond the Black Atlantic." *African Affairs* 104, no. 414 (2005): 35–68.

Zerai, Assata, and Horace Campbell. "The Black Radical Congress and Black Feminist Organizing." *Socialism and Democracy* 19, no. 2 (2005): 147–56.

Zips, Werner, ed. *Rastafari: A Universal Philosophy in the Third Millennium.* Kingston: Ian Randle, 2006.

HAKIM ADI is Reader in the History of Africa and the African Diaspora at Middlesex University, London. He is a founding member and chair of the Black and Asian Studies Association and a member of the Mayor of London's Commission on African and Asian Heritage. He is the author of *West Africans in Britain, 1900–1960: Nationalism, Pan-Africanism, and Communism* and coauthor of *The 1945 Manchester Pan-African Congress Revisited* and *Pan-African History: Political Figures from Africa and the Diaspora since 1787*. He has also written three history books for children.

SYLVIA FREY is Emeritus Professor of History at Tulane University, New Orleans. She is the author of *Water from the Rock: Black Resistance in a Revolutionary Age* and *The British Soldier in America: A Social History of Military Life in the Revolutionary Period* and coauthor of *Come Shouting to Zion: African American Protestantism in the American South and British Caribbean to 1830.*

WILLIAM G. MARTIN is Professor of Sociology at Binghamton University in Binghamton, New York. He is coauthor of *Making Waves: Worldwide Social Movements, 1750–2005* and *How Fast the Wind: Southern Africa and the World-Economy, 1975–2000*, editor of *Semiperipheral States and the World-Economy*, and coeditor of *Out of One, Many Africas: Reconstructing the Study and Meaning of Africa.*

BRIAN MEEKS is Professor of Social and Political Change in the Department of Government at the University of the West Indies, Mona, in Jamaica. He is chairman of the Michael Manley Foundation and director of the Centre for Caribbean Thought at the University of the West Indies, Mona. He is the author of *Caribbean Revolutions and Revolutionary Theory: An Assessment of Cuba, Nicaragua, and Grenada* and *Radical Caribbean: From Black Power to Abu Bakr*, coeditor of *New Caribbean Thought: A Reader*, and author of the novel *Paint the Town Red.*

MARC D. PERRY is Assistant Professor in the Afro-American Studies and Research Program and the Department of Anthropology at the University of

Illinois, Urbana-Champaign. His current book project explores Cuba's emergent hip hop movement as it expresses the global dynamics of race and social transformation in the post-Soviet era.

LARA PUTNAM is Associate Professor of History at the University of Pittsburgh in Pittsburgh, Pennsylvania. She is the author of *The Company They Kept: Migrants and the Politics of Gender in Caribbean Costa Rica, 1870–1960* and co-editor of *Honor, Status, and Law in Modern Latin America.* Her current research focuses on state racism, civil society, and policies toward British Caribbean youth at home and abroad from 1900 to 1970.

VIJAY PRASHAD is Professor and Director of International Studies at Trinity College, Hartford, Connecticut. His books include *The Darker Nations: A People's History of the Third World, Karma of Brown Folk,* and *Everybody Was Kung Fu Fighting: Afro-Asian Connections and the Myth of Cultural Purity;* he is coauthor of *Dispatches from Latin America: Experiments against Neoliberalism.* He is on the board of the Center for Third World Organizing (<www.ctwo.org>), United For a Fair Economy (<www.faireconomy.org>), and the National Priorities Project (<www.nationalpriorities.org>).

ROBYN SPENCER is Assistant Professor of History at Lehman College, City University of New York, in New York City. Her current book project is titled "Repression Breeds Resistance: The Rise and Fall of the Black Panther Party in Oakland, California."

ROBERT VINSON is Assistant Professor of History at the College of William and Mary in Williamsburg, Virginia, where his teaching and research are focused on the African Diaspora, South African history, and African American history. He is currently working on two monographs: *The Americans Are Coming! The Dream of "American Negro" Liberation in Segregationist South Africa* and the coauthored *Crossing the Water: African Americans and South Africa, 1890–1965. A Documentary History.*

MICHAEL O. WEST is Professor of Sociology and Africana Studies at Binghamton University in Binghamton, New York. His publications include *The Rise of an African Middle Class: Colonial Zimbabwe, 1898–1965* and the coedited *Out of One, Many Africas: Reconstructing the Study and Meaning of Africa.* His current research centers on the interconnections between black struggles in various parts of the world.

FANON CHE WILKINS is Associate Professor in the Graduate School of American Studies, Doshisha University, Kyoto, Japan, and was an active organizer of the Seventh Pan-African Congress in Kampala, Uganda, in 1994. His research is concerned with the transnational and transcontinental dimensions of black radicalism during the long 1960s. He is currently preparing for publication a manuscript titled "Freedom Was in the Air: Black Radicalism, Africa, and the Global Search for Black Power, 1957–1976."

National Front for the Liberation of Angola, 203

National Joint Action Committee (NJAC), 199–201, 212 (n. 10)

National Negro Congress (1930), 170

National Union for the Total Independence of Angola, 203

National Urban League, 170, 191

Nation of Islam, 13, 14, 25

Native Americans, 6, 37 (n. 26), 81

Native Baptist movement, 58

Natives Land Act (South Africa, 1913), 131

Natives (Urban Areas) Act (South Africa, 1923), 131–32

Ncwana, Samuel Bennett, 136, 146

Negritude, 99

Negro Factories Corporation, 140

Negro Welfare Association, 167–68, 171, 172

Negro Welfare Cultural and Social Association, 170, 172

Negro Worker (periodical): black liberation focus in, 166, 171; Caribbean articles in, 166–67, 172; editorship of, 19, 165–66; rise of fascism and, 20

Negro World (periodical): antiracism and anti-imperialism of, 122; British West Indian connections of, 107–8; circulation of, 10, 109, 139; contributors to, 39 (n. 48); demise of, 19; perspectives in, 12; promotion of, 137, 139; translations of, 138; on Wellington, 146

Negu Gorriak (rock group), 234

New Jewel Movement (NJM): failures of, 202, 203, 205–6, 211; Leninist tactics of, 204–5, 207; rise of, 200–201

Newton, Huey P.: arrest, trial, and imprisonment of, 29, 218, 220, 222; China visit of, 227–28; Cleaver's differences with, 226–27; intercommunalism theory of, 26, 222–24, 229; on nationalism, 25–26

New World movement, 198–99, 212 (n. 15)

New World Quarterly (journal), 212 (n. 7)

New York: Caribbean organizations in, 112; hip hop in, 232, 253, 258 (n. 56). *See also* Harlem

Nguyen Thi Dinh, 223

Nicaragua: British West Indian immigrants in, 108; liberation movement in, 211

Nixon, Richard, 228

NJAC. *See* National Joint Action Committee

NJM. *See* New Jewel Movement

"Nkosi' Sikeleli Afrika" (song), 144

Nkrumah, Kwame, 22, 23, 89

North Korea: Black Panther delegation to, 228; Black Panther support from, 221, 222, 226; as model, 224

NUFF (guerrilla group), 201

NWA (group), 33

Odd Fellows, 109, 111, 112

Odum, Howard, 189

Oilfield Workers Trade Union, 199

Organization of African Unity, 31

Organization of Afro-American Unity, 24

Outlet (newspaper), 200

Padmore, George: background of, 108; break with Comintern, 20, 175 (n. 77), 213 (n. 22); Comintern connections of, 172; declining influence of, 204; on Garveyism, 19; on Haitian Revolution, 87–90; at International Conference of Negro Workers, 165–66

Paisanos, Los (rap duo), 243–44, 255

Palestine: hip hop in, 234

Palmares, Republic of: creation of, 28

Pan-African Conference (1900), 37 (n. 13)

Pan-African Congresses (1919–45): Comintern compared with, 159, 165; communist attendees of, 15–16; ideals of, 47–48; new international order evidenced in, 22; organizers of, 89; UNIA opposed by, 14–15

Pan-African Congress (1974), 31

Pan-African Congress (1994), 34

Pan African Cultural Festival, 220–21

Pan-Africanism: black literary tradition as source of, 48, 55–60; Cold War–narrative on, 88–89; Comintern's engagement with, 155, 158–61, 164–65, 172; as communal defense, 120–21; definitions of, 47–48; evangelical Protestantism as source of, 48–52, 93; Haitian Revolution ignored in, 89–90; ideological foundations of, 48, 67–68; internationalization of, 16–17, 26–28; Italian invasion of Ethiopia and,

Manual of Hemostasis and Thrombosis

edition 3

ARTHUR R. THOMPSON, M.D., Ph.D.

Associate Professor of Medicine
University of Washington
Chief of Hematology
Seattle Public Health Hospital
Seattle, Washington

LAURENCE A. HARKER, M.D.

Director, Roon Research Center
 for Arteriosclerosis
Department of Clinical and Basic Research
Scripps Clinic and Research Foundation
La Jolla, California

F. A. DAVIS COMPANY • Philadelphia

Library of Congress Cataloging in Publication Data

Thompson, Arthur R.
  Manual of hemostasis and thrombosis.

  Rev. ed. of: Hemostasis manual / Laurence A. Harker, Ed. 2. 1974.
  Includes bibliographical references and index.
    1. Hemostasis—Handbooks, manuals, etc.
  2. Thrombosis—Handbooks, manuals, etc.   I. Harker, Laurence A. Hemostasis manual.   II. Title.
  [DNLM: 1. Hemostasis.   2. Thrombosis.   3. Blood coagulation disorders.   WH 310 T468m]
  RB144.T45   1982   616.1'3   82-14871
  ISBN 0-8036-8481-9

PREFACE

The purpose of this manual is to describe a pathophysiologic approach to the diagnosis and management of patients with hemostatic and thrombotic disorders. Since the approach is designed for students, house officers, physicians and other health professionals seeking an updated, concise review of this subject, the book is divided into sections. Fundamental concepts of hemostasis and thrombosis are presented in Section I. The clinical application of these fundamentals with regard to hemostatic disorders is presented in Section II, and, to thrombotic disorders, in Section III. Our intent is to provide in a single volume the source material needed throughout training and as a review. We have chosen to document the book with recent selected citations from the literature for two reasons. First, it is important to establish the scientific basis for the approach, and second, we feel that it is appropriate to date the current formulation, and thereby emphasize the inevitable evolution that must occur as the field develops in the years to come.

We are indebted to our associates who have contributed much to this work. In particular, we would like to acknowledge the intellectual input from Drs. Samuel A. Burstein, Richard B. Counts, John M. Harlan, and Thomas W. Malpass. We also express special appreciation to Paul Su for his art work, Lisa Jones for her editorial and secretarial help, Ruth Henderson for her technical assistance, together with Daphne Matlick and Lou Limtiaco for invaluable secretarial assistance.

Arthur R. Thompson
Laurence A. Harker

CONTENTS

PART 1
CONCEPTS OF HEMOSTASIS AND THROMBOSIS

The hemostatic mechanism is designed to arrest bleeding from vessels that have undergone a break in their integrity. The process is rapid and localized without compromising fluidity of the blood in circulation. Hemostasis involves a complex integrated interaction of (1) blood vessel, (2) platelets, and (3) coagulation cascade to form a localized stable mechanical seal that subsequently undergoes slow removal by (4) fibrinolysis. Rapid, localized hemostasis within a fluid medium is achieved by complicated systems of activation and inhibition whereby excessive bleeding and unwanted thrombosis are minimized. In this section, the components of the hemostatic mechanism will be considered with regard to their normal structure, function, interrelationships, and the mechanisms of their activation and inhibition.

1

BLOOD VESSELS
AND ENDOTHELIUM

STRUCTURE

Metabolic exchange depends upon the flow of blood through thin-walled capillaries. Their structure consists of a supportive basement membrane to which endothelial cells are tightly anchored (Fig. 1). Endothelial cells form a continuous monolayer that lines all blood vessels. However, endothelia differ in structure, function, and metabolic behavior in different organs, different parts of the same organ, and different segments of a single microcirculatory loop.[1] In general, the morphology predicts barrier function, and accordingly endothelium is classified as being (1) continuous, showing gap or tight intercellular junctions; (2) fenestrated; or (3) discontinuous. Continuous tight junctional endothelium is typical of the cerebral circulation, whereas fenestrated endothelium is illustrated by hepatic sinusoids.[2]

The larger vessels of the microcirculation (arterioles and venules) have a more complete structure consisting of: (1) the inner intima, including endothelium and subendothelium (basement membrane, elastic tissue, collagen fibers); (2) media composed of smooth muscle cells, collagen fibers, and occasional fibroblasts; and (3) the outer adventitia, consisting of fibroblasts and collagen fibers. As vascular size increases, noncollagenous microfibrils appear in the subendothelium and the elastic components condense into the well-defined internal elastic lamina, which separates the media from the intima.

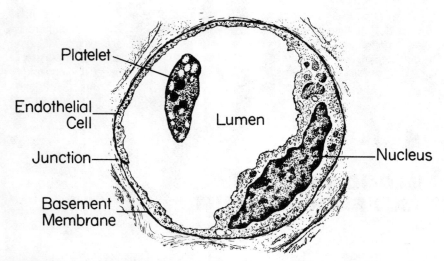

FIGURE 1. Structure of blood vessels. Vascular endothelium forms a cellular mono-layer that interfaces between blood and the underlying tissues. Endothelial cells function in the (a) transfer of metabolic substances, (b) formation of a barrier between the subendothelium and blood cells and macromolecules, (c) synthesis or metabolism of blood and subendothelial mediators, (d) thromboresistance of the vessel toward flowing blood, (e) repair processes, and (f) cellular immunity.

FUNCTION

Endothelial cells perform a number of critical functions including: (1) the material transfer of metabolic substances of varied molecular size between the circulating blood and the surrounding tissues; (2) the formation of a relative barrier to blood cells, plasma macromolecules, and particulate material; (3) the synthesis or metabolism of mediators that regulate the interaction between the vessel wall and blood components, for example, factor VIII/vWF, fibronectin, collagen, proteoglycans, and labile mediators of vascular tone; (4) the maintenance of thromboresistance; (5) mediation of vascular repair processes, such as cell migration, proliferation and thrombolysis; and (6) the processing of antigen in cellular immunity.[1-4]

The exchange of materials across the endothelium involves movement by active vesicles, transendothelial channels, or intercellular clefts. Maintaining the integrity of the vessel wall to the egress of blood cells depends upon the barrier function of the endothelium and the underlying vascular connective tissue, together with platelets that seal over gaps in the endothelial lining.[1]

One of the basic functional characteristics of intact, normal endothelium is its nonreactivity to platelets, leukocytes, and the coagulation factors. The thromboresistant character of the endothelium involves both passive and active mechanisms. The endothelial proteoglycans, primarily heparan sulfate, provide a surface that is passively nonthrombogenic.[5] Active thromboresistance of the endothelium is achieved through several mechanisms, including (1) the synthesis and release of prostacyclin (PGI_2); (2) secretion of plasminogen activators; (3) degradation of proaggregatory adenosine 5'-diphosphate (ADP) by membrane-associated apyrase (ADPase); (4) uptake and degradation of proaggregatory vasoactive amines; (5) uptake, inactivation, and clearance of thrombin; and (6) contribution of a cofactor (thrombomodulin) in the thrombin-dependent activation of protein C. The latter results in destruction of coagulation factors V and VIII and the release of plasminongen activators.[6-12]

PGI$_2$ is a labile prostaglandin that potently inhibits platelet adhesion and aggregation (Fig. 2). Modulation of PGI_2 production by injury factors, including activated clotting enzymes, serves to limit locally any hemostatic response.[13] The capacity of the endothelial lining to regulate PGI_2 production contributes to the nonthrombogenic properties of intact vascular endothelium. Endothelial denudation results in a loss of the nonthrombogenic surface as well as exposure of subendothelial connective structures to circulating blood.

The endothelium produces its own underlying connective tissue composed of several classes of collagen, proteoglycans, elastin, and microfibrils.[1,2] This connective tissue matrix modulates the permeability of the inner vessel wall and provides the principal stimulus to thrombosis following vessel injury.

Endothelial disruption activates directly all four components of the hemostatic apparatus: (1) Rapid vasoconstriction involves a direct vasoconstrictive response of the injured vessel and reflex stimulation of adjacent vessels. Reduced blood loss promotes more effective contact-activation of platelets and coagulation. Although vasoconstriction is not required for hemostasis to occur, it is critical in preventing exsanguination following severance of large vessels, especially arteries. (2) Platelets adhere immediately to exposed subendothelial connective tissue structures, particularly collagen fibers. Adherent and aggregated platelets enhance vasoconstriction by releasing thromboxane A$_2$ and vasoactive amines, including serotonin and epinepherine. (3) Coagulation is initiated both through the intrinsic system and the extrinsic system. (4) Fibrinolysis follows the release of tissue plasminogen activators from the vascular wall. Fibrinolytic removal of excess hemostatic material is necessary to reestablish vascular patency.

The relative importance of these reactions varies with vessel size. Capillaries, once ruptured, seal directly and immediately with little dependence on hemostasis. Breaks in arterioles and venules, on the other hand, become quickly occluded with a mass of fused platelets. Veins, which contain about 70 percent of the blood volume, may rupture with only modest trauma when subjected to increased hydrostatic pressure; hemostasis depends upon vascular contraction as well as perivascular and intravascular activation of hemostatic factors. Although arteries are the most resistant of all vessels to bleeding because of their thick, muscular walls, major trauma or erosive disease may precipitate arterial hemorrhage—the most severe test of hemostasis. Vasocon-

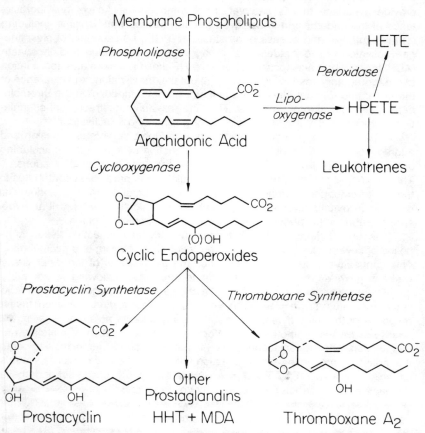

FIGURE 2. Prostaglandin metabolism. Phospholipase cleaves arachidonic acid-esters.[13] In the platelet, this enzyme is stimulated by low concentrations of ionized (non-bound) calcium, being further regulated by intracellular magnesium ion and cyclic AMP levels. Arachidonic acid is converted by an aspirin-sensitive cyclooxygenase to cyclic endoperoxides PGG_2 and PGH_2, or by a lipoxygenase to 12L-hydroxy-eicosatetraenoic acid (HETE) from its hydroperoxy intermediate (HPETE); the latter is also converted to leukotrienes. In the endothelial cell, these highly unstable cyclic endoperoxides are converted to PGI_2 (prostacyclin), a potent inhibitor of platelet aggregation and a vasodilator that is rapidly degraded to 6-keto-$PGF_{1\alpha}$ in vitro and multiple other metabolites in vivo. Within the platelet, thromboxane A_2 (TxA_2) is formed but spontaneously hydrolyzes to the stable, inactive, TxB_2. Thromboxane A_2 mediates vasoconstriction as well as platelet aggregation and release. PGG_2/PGH_2 are nonenzymatically transformed to 12L-hydroxy-5,8,10-heptadecatrienoic acid (HHT) and malondialdehyde (MDA) or the stable prostaglandins PGD_2, PHE_2, and PGF_2.

striction is of vital importance in establishing successful thrombus formation in arteries. In general, the larger the area of bleeding, the larger the vessel involved. For example, pinpoint petechial hemorrhage develops from arterioles and venules, whereas large, ill-defined soft tissue bleeding (ecchymoses) occurs from veins, and rapidly expanding "blowout" hemorrhage results from arteries.

2
PLATELETS

STRUCTURE

Platelets circulate as anuclear, cytoplasmic disks with an average diameter of 3 to 4 μm and volume of 10 fl. Platelet size distribution is very broad compared with other blood cells. In the nonstimulated state the discoid shape is maintained by a circumferential cytoskeleton of microtubules (Fig. 3).

Membrane glycoprotein receptors mediate the surface contact reactions of stickiness, shape change, adhesion, internal contraction, and aggregation. Contact activation of the membrane phospholipids also generates procoagulant activity and arachidonic acid (see Fig. 2, Chapter 1). The surface membrane is continuous with a sponge-like, open canalicular membrane system, and interdigitates with the dense tubular system that is not surface-connected. Channels of the open canalicular system and dense tubular system in platelets form interwoven membrane complexes morphologically identical to the association of transverse tubules and sarcotubules in embryonic muscle cells. This dual membrane system appears to constitute the calcium-regulating mechanism. Submembranous filaments and cytoplasmic filaments of the sol-gel zone constitute the contractile system of the platelet. Platelets contain substantial quantities of muscle proteins, including actin, myosin, tropomyosin, α-actinin, actin-binding protein, filamin, and troponin.[14]

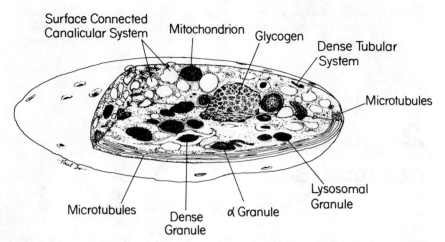

Surface Connected Canalicular System — Mitochondrion — Glycogen — Dense Tubular System — Microtubules — Lysosomal Granule — α Granule — Dense Granule — Microtubules

FIGURE 3. Platelet structure. Understanding platelet fine structure provides a morphologic basis for platelet function.[14] The peripheral surface coat mediates the membrane contact reactions of adhesion and aggregation. Plasma membrane, which also contributes the phospholipid procoagulant activity, forms an invaginated, sponge-like open canalicular membrane system that represents an expanded reactive surface to which plasma hemostatic factors are selectively adsorbed. Submembranous filaments and other cytoplasmic microfilaments of the sol-gel zone appear to constitute the platelet's contractile actomyosin system. Residual endoplasmic reticulum, free of ribosomes, forms a calcium binding dense tubular membrane system. Microtubules form a circumferential cytoskeleton that maintains the discoid shape. Following stimulation, the microtubules undergo a concentric central shift with an inner clustering of organelles; concurrently, cytoplasmic pseudopods form on the periphery. Constituents from the α-granules, dense granules, and lysosomal granules are then released into the open canalicular system in association with contraction of the actomyosin filaments, which results in a fused impermeable platelet mass. Energy for these events is derived by aerobic metabolism in the mitochondria and anaerobic glycolysis utilizing glycogen granule stores.

Energy for contraction is derived from aerobic metabolism in the mitochondria and anaerobic glycolysis utilizing glycogen granule stores. Three types of storage granules are present in platelets: (1) α-granules, the most numerous, containing platelet-specific proteins (platelet factor 4, β-thromboglobulin, platelet-derived growth factor) and proteins also found in plasma (fibronectin, albumin, fibrinogen, and coagulation factors V and VIII); (2) dense granules or bodies, containing storage ADP, serotonin, Ca^{2+}, and phosphates; and (3) lysosomal vesicles. Secretion involves the release of constituents from the storage granules into the open canalicular system.

Platelets are extremely sensitive cells and may respond to minimal stimulation by forming pseudopods that spontaneously retract. A somewhat stronger stimulus causes platelets to become reversibly sticky without loss of discoid shape. A change in shape to irregular spheres with spiny pseudopods occurs with an additional stimulus and may be accompanied by internal contraction (central clustering of organelles), that is triggered by an increase in the level of cytoplasmic calcium; it is also reversible. Extrusion of storage granule contents requires internal contraction. Secretory products facilitate platelet recruitment and lead to irreversible aggregation to form a fused, impermeable platelet mass.

FUNCTION

Platelets are essential for normal hemostasis and perform four distinct functions in response to vascular damage [13-16] (Fig. 4): (1) continual maintenance of vascular integrity by sealing over minor deficiencies of the endothelium; (2) initial arrest of bleeding through the formation of platelet plugs; (3) stabilization of the hemostatic plug by contributing procoagulant activity (platelet factor 3) to the coagulation cascade to form fibrin; and (4) promotion of vascular healing by stimulating endothelial cell migration, and medial smooth muscle cell migration and proliferation (through the release of the mitogen, platelet-derived growth factor, PDGF).

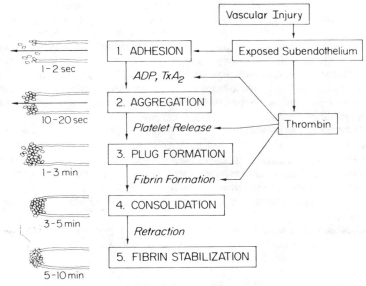

FIGURE 4. Hemostatic plug formation. The formation of a platelet plug proceeds through the sequence of: (1) platelet adhesion to exposed subendothelial connective tissue structures; (2) platelet aggregation by ADP, thromboxane A_2 and thrombin recruitment through transformation of discoid platelets into reactive spiny spheres that interact with one another through calcium-dependent fibrinogen bridges; (3) contribution of platelet coagulant activity to the coagulation process which stabilizes the plug with a fibrin mesh; and (4) retraction of the platelet mass to provide a dense thrombus.[15]

Platelet Adhesion. Vascular injury and endothelial denudation exposes subendothelial structures to circulating blood (Fig. 5). The process of platelet adhesion involves the interaction of platelet surface glycoproteins (GPI$_b$) with connective tissue elements of the subendothelium and requires factor VIII/von Willebrand factor (vWF) as a plasma cofactor.[17,18] Von Willebrand factor appears to be synthesized by endothelial cells and megakaryocytes, and is adsorbed to both circulating platelets and exposed subendothelial collagen. The platelet membrane GPI$_b$ acts as the surface receptor for vWF. Hereditary absence of GPI$_b$ (Bernard-Soulier syndrome) or absence of vWF results in defective platelet adhesion and serious abnormal bleeding.[17,18] Arachidonic acid metabolites do not appear to be involved in initial adhesion, spreading, or granule release of adherent platelets, although high concentrations of PGI$_2$ inhibit platelet adhesion to exposed subendothelium in vitro.

Platelet Aggregation. Vessel disruption not only induces platelet adhesion, but also initiates a series of complex and interdependent reactions including: (1) the release of dense granule ADP from adherent platelets; (2) the formation of small amounts of thrombin; and (3) the activation of platelet membrane phospholipase activity to generate thromboxane A$_2$. Release of ADP, thrombin formation, and thromboxane A$_2$ generation act in concert to recruit platelets from the circulation to produce the initial hemostatic plug (see Fig. 5).

Platelet aggregometry has been extensively used to examine this process in vitro. The addition of a platelet agonist to a stirred suspension of platelets results in the formation of platelet aggregates and an increase in light transmission through the opalescent platelet suspension (Fig. 6). Small concentrations of an agonist such as thrombin may induce only shape change manifested by a sudden narrowing and small deflection in the baseline aggregometry tracing. Such alterations reflect platelet shape change.

The primary wave of aggregation reflects a loose platelet-platelet attachment. Platelet shape change and early or primary aggregation are reversible. The secondary or recruitment wave of aggregation occurs with higher concentrations of agonist and represents largely irreversible aggregation mediated by released ADP and thromboxane A$_2$. ADP, epinephrine collagen, and thrombin are four well characterized aggregating agents or agonists and their specific effects follow.

ADP promotes platelet aggregation by binding to specific platelet receptors, inducing platelet shape change, and decreasing in adenosine 3':5' cyclic phosphate (cAMP) activity. The interaction of ADP with its membrane receptor mobilizes fibrinogen binding sites consisting of membrane glycoproteins GPII$_b$ and GPIII$_a$.[17-20] The platelet-platelet interaction is a process of Ca^{2+}-dependent ligand formation between bound fibrinogen molecules.[19,20] Platelets will not aggregate in the absence of platelet membrane GPII$_b$ and GPIII$_a$ (thrombasthenia), fibrinogen, or Ca^{2+}.[17-20] Binding of ADP also initiates phospholipase activity leading to the formation of thromboxane A$_2$.[21] Inhibition of thromboxane A$_2$ synthesis or deficiency of dense granule ADP will prevent the

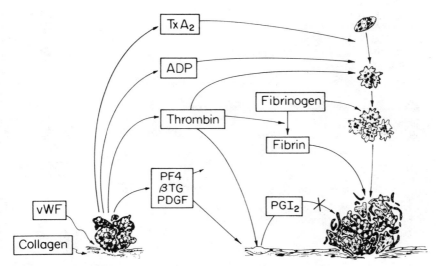

FIGURE 5. Hemostatic platelet functions. Platelets are normally nonreactive to intact vascular endothelium.[13] Vessel injury initiates platelet adherence with von Willebrand factor (vWF) as an important plasma cofactor.[16] Adherent platelets release dense granule contents, including ADP and α-granule constituents, including platelet factor 4 (PF4), β thromboglobulin (βTG), and platelet-derived growth factor (PDGF). Thrombin is generated locally through tissue factor, factor XII$_a$ and platelet procoagulant activity. Thromboxane A$_2$ (TxA$_2$) is synthesized from arachidonic acid liberated by membrane phospholipases. Released ADP, TxA$_2$ and thrombin recruit additional circulating platelets to the enlarging platelet mass. Thrombin-generated fibrin stabilizes the platelet mass. PGI$_2$ released by the vessel wall in response to thrombin limits thrombus formation by inhibiting further platelet deposition.

recruitment wave of aggregation induced by ADP, but not the initial internal transformation of organelles.

Epinephrine reacts with the platelet membrane α-receptor.[17,22] Agonist binding induces reversible aggregate formation by ADP-mediated mobilization of fibrinogren receptor sites and consequent platelet aggregation. It also produces inhibition of platelet cAMP activity. Irreversible platelet recruitment is mediated through and dependent on the release of endogenous ADP from dense granules and the synthesis of thromboxane A$_2$. Aspirin will inhibit the platelet contractile wave and secondary aggregation to epinephrine. The concentration of epinephrine required to induce platelet aggregation by itself is greater than that normally found in the circulation. It may, however, act synergistically at physiologic levels when combined with other aggregating agents.

In vitro, collagen induces a single wave of aggregation. Collagen causes a few platelets to adhere, releases ADP, and produces recruitment through fibrinogen binding. Dilute concentrations of collagen in vitro probably also initiate

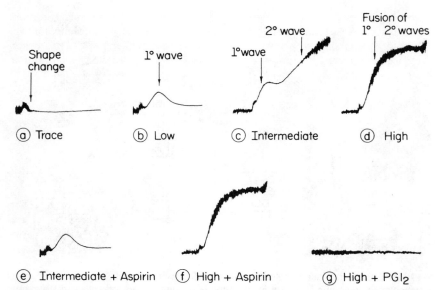

FIGURE 6. Platelet aggregation to thrombin. In vitro platelet aggregation is assessed by measuring light transmission through stirred, opalescent, platelet-rich plasma at 37°C. As aggregates form in response to the addition of an agonist, light transmission is increased, which is shown as an upward deflection. (*a*) Trace thrombin initiates only platelet shape change measuring by narrowing of baseline. (*b*) Low-dose thrombin produces shape change and primary wave reflecting a platelet contractile wave and loose platelet aggregates. (*c*) Intermediate-dose thrombin initiates shape change, primary wave, and the irreversible secondary wave. (*d*) High-dose thrombin produces irreversible aggregation. (*e*) Aspirin will prevent the secondary wave to intermediate-dose thrombin, but not shape change or the primary wave. (*f*) Aggregation to high-dose thrombin is not prevented by aspirin. (*g*) PGI$_2$, however, will prevent aggregation in response to high-dose thrombin (from Harlan and Harker,[13] with permission).

platelet phospholipase activity and the generation of thromboxane A$_2$.[21] Aspirin will block the initial internal transformation and aggregation induced by dilute collagen. Thromboxane synthesis inhibitors, however, will not inhibit platelet reaction to concentrated collagen, and platelets adherent to subendothelial collagen will release granule contents even in the presence of prostaglandin synthesis inhibitors.[23]

Thrombin plays an important pathophysiologic role in platelet aggregate formation.[15,16] At the site of vessel injury thrombin may be generated through activation of the intrinsic pathway by exposed collagen and damaged endothelium or the extrinsic pathway by tissue factor. Thrombin causes the appearance of platelet receptors for modified coagulation factor V, to which factor X$_a$ binds, thereby enhancing the conversion of prothrombin to thrombin on the platelet surface. The locally forming fibrin adheres to the surface of platelets and imparts stability to the platelet thrombus. Thrombin binding to the membrane surface receptor also induces ADP release from platelet dense granules, initiates phospholipase activity, and generates thromboxane A_2.[24,25] In low concentrations, thrombin-induced secondary platelet aggregation is blocked by cyclooxygenase inhibitors, although the primary wave is not. However, high-dose thrombin initiates platelet aggregation, including the secondary phase, which is not blocked by cyclooxygenase or thromboxane synthetase inhibitors.[23]

Platelet Release Reaction. The release reaction is a secretory process whereby substances stored in platelet granules are extruded from the platelet (see Figs. 5 and 6). ADP, epinephrine, subendothelial connective tissue, and thrombin are the physiologically important release-inducing agents. Alpha-granule contents (platelet factor 4, β-thromboglobulin, platelet-derived growth factor, factor VIII/vWF, factor V, thrombospondin, fibrinogen, albumin, and fibronectin) are readily released.[26,27] The dense granule contents (ADP, serotonin, and calcium) require greater platelet stimulation.[28] In vitro, lysosomal granules containing acid hydrolase are released only with concentrated collagen or thrombin. The exact mechanisms by which ADP, collagen, or thrombin initiate granule reaction is a membrane-mediated process involving specific glycoproteins located on the platelet surface. Receptors have been identified for the physiologically important agonists—ADP, epinephrine, collagen, and thrombin. The binding of these agonists initiates the formation of intermediates that activate the contractile-secretory apparatus.[14,21,29] Although thrombin and collagen can induce platelet aggregation and release directly, these agents also stimulate the platelet arachidonic acid pathway through activation of membrane phospholipase complex.[30] Generated arachidonic acid is rapidly converted to thromboxane A_2 which then mobilizes calcium from various intracellular storage sites.[14,21,29] Mobilized calcium is probably the final mediator of platelet aggregation and release. Elevated cytoplasmic calcium complexed with the calcium-binding protein, calmodulin, activates kinases producing phosphorylation of platelet myosin, triggering contraction, and initiating secretion.[29] Elevation of free ionized intracellular calcium activates the calcium-sensitive phospholipases, further amplifying the process. Thromboxane A_2 also lowers platelet cAMP probably through inhibition of membrane adenylate cyclase by mobilized calcium.[31]

Platelet Coagulant Activity. When platelets aggregate, platelet coagulant activity is produced, including a membrane phospholipoprotein (platelet factor 3) on the surface of the aggregated platelets. This phospholipoprotein accelerates two critical steps of the blood coagulation sequence (factor X activation and the conversion of prothrombin to thrombin).[32] Platelets also promote the proteolytic activation of factor XII by kallikrein and factor XI by both factor XII-dependent and factor XII-independent mechanisms.[33] The surface of the aggregated platelets serves as a site where thrombin can form rapidly in excess

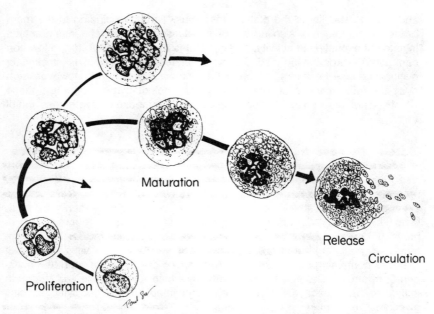

Maturation

Release

Circulation

Proliferation

FIGURE 7. Megakaryocyte formation and maturation. Megakaryocytes arise from self-renewing pluripotent diploid stem cells, and proceed through the stage of committed diploid precursors to become polyploid megakaryoblasts that exhibit some membrane and cytoplasmic features of the megakaryocyte-platelet series.[34] The degree of endoreduplication (upper and lower pathway arrows) is regulated by the platelet requirements in the peripheral blood. Cytoplasmic maturation involves the development of demarcation membranes, endoplasmic reticulum, storage granules, filaments, microtubules, and energy-generating structures. The preformed platelet subunits are released through marrow sinusoids to the peripheral circulation.

of the inhibiting capacity of anticoagulant mechanisms of blood. The thrombin has additional effects on the platelets and also generates polymerizing fibrin which adheres to the surface of the platelet mass.

PLATELET KINETICS

Platelet Production. In the process of producing platelets, marrow megakaryocytes proceed through five overlapping developmental phases (Fig. 7): (1) formation of identifiable polyploid cells from morphologically unrecognizable diploid precursors; (2) nuclear replication within each cell (endoreduplication); (3) cytoplasmic maturation and demarcation into platelet subunits; (4) release of preformed platelets into the circulation; and (5) final processing of the residual nuclear material by tissue mononuclear phagocytic cells.

Megakaryocytes arise from pluripotent hematopoietic stem cells that proceed through an intermediate phase of committed diploid precursors, and are

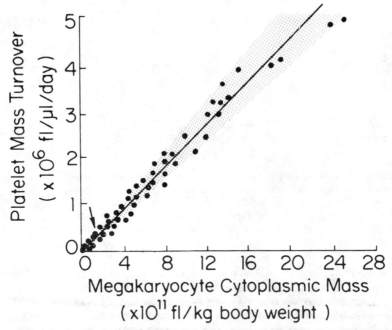

FIGURE 8. Megakaryocyte mass and platelet turnover. Two measures of platelet production are compared: platelet turnover in the blood and the generating megakaryocyte mass in the bone marrow.[35] The direct correlation indicates that these are equivalent determinations in steady state patients manifesting effective production with widely different rates of production. Platelet mass turnover represents the product of platelet turnover and mean platelet volume. Megakaryocyte cytoplasmic mass equals the mean megakaryocyte cytoplasmic volume multiplied by the total number of marrow megakaryocytes. The results in normal subjects are indicated by the arrow. The stippled area represents 95 percent confidence limits.

morphologically recognizable only after achieving polyploidy.[34] Endoproliferation occurs synchronously and early in development; the nucleus has a lobular configuration. Each megakaryocyte is analogous to a clone of cells undergoing common proliferation and maturation.

The amount of cytoplasm accumulated by each megakaryocyte is determined by the ploidy of that cell.[35] Since in general the mean platelet volume remains relatively constant over a wide range of perturbed rates of production, it follows that the number of platelets produced from a given mass of megakaryocytic cytoplasm remains about constant. An average-sized megakaryocyte in normal man produces about 1000 to 1500 platelets each. The marrow substrate available for platelet production (total thrombocytopoiesis) is therefore represented by the mass of megakaryocyte cytoplasm, which equals the product of the average megakaryocyte cytoplasmic volume and the total number of

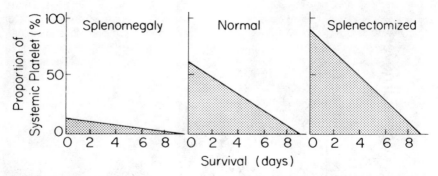

FIGURE 9. Normal platelet survival. Steady state, platelet population labeling with ⁵¹Cr results in a linear disappearance pattern of about 10 days in normal subjects[37] and reflects a 10-day finite platelet life span *(center panel)*. The proportion of injected ⁵¹Cr platelets not found in the circulation is a measure of the splenic platelet pool. Splenic pooling is increased with congestive splenomegaly *(left panel)* and absent following splenectomy *(right panel)*.

marrow megakaryocytes. There is a direct relationship between the generating mass of megakaryocytic cytoplasm and the circulating product (Fig. 8).

Platelet production in the marrow is regulated to meet the requirements for circulating platelets, presumably by a humoral stimulator ("thrombopoietin"), much as erythropoiesis is regulated by erythropoietin. This humoral stimulator acts to increase: (1) the rate of megakaryocyte formation from precursor cells; (2) endoreduplication and thus the amount of platelet-producing cytoplasm per megakaryocyte; and (3) the rate of cytoplasmic maturation and release.[34,35] It appears that cell numbers and cell size (ploidy) are independently regulated.[36] The changes observed in inflammation illustrate independent regulation, that is, a decrease in megakaryocyte size associated with a marked increase in megakaryocyte number.

Recently, in vitro clonal assays have been developed for a progenitor cell (CFU-M) which gives rise to colonies of identifiable megakaryocytes. The primary target cell for day-to-day regulation of the platelet count is the megakaryocyte or a cell immediately preceding the megakaryocyte, but not the CFU-M. This earlier progenitor is under the regulaton of some "second level" process.[36]

Platelet Survival and Turnover. Platelets circulate at a concentration of 250,000 ± 40,000 platelets per μl in normal subjects. Two thirds of the total platelets are in the systemic circulation, while the remaining third exists as a pool of platelets in the spleen.[37] That pool exchanges freely with the general circulation. The distribution between the systemic and the splenic compartments can be estimated by determining recovery, that is, the proportion of ⁵¹Cr-labeled platelets remaining in the circulation immediately after infusion (Fig. 9).

In normal individuals, isotopically labeled autologous platelets have a finite life span of about 9 to 10 days.[37] Platelet turnover, calculated from the platelet count divided by platelet survival time and corrected for splenic pooling, directly indicates the rate of removal from circulation (see Fig. 8). Moreover, in the steady state platelet turnover also measures the delivery of viable platelets from the marrow to the circulation and is thus used as a measure of effective thrombocytopoiesis (see Fig. 8). In normal subjects there is a turnover of 35,000 platelets per μl per day.

Platelet labeling is currently carried out with ^{51}Cr or ^{111}In. Labeling with ^{111}In also allows for the objective estimation of platelet distribution and localization of abnormal platelet deposition using standard gamma scintillation cameras for external imaging.[38]

3

COAGULATION

In the test tube at least 12 distinct plasma glycoproteins interact in a series of reactions leading to blood clotting. Their designation as Roman numerals was made before their role in the clotting scheme was appreciated. Their biochemical properties are summarized in Table 1. Initiation of clotting occurs either *intrinsically* by surface-mediated reactions or *extrinsically* through a tissue-derived factor pathway. The two systems converge upon a final common path which leads to the insoluble fibrin gel when thrombin acts on fibrinogen.[39] Distinction of these pathways is necessary in interpreting the clotting factor screening tests and for choosing appropriate blood components for therapy.

Except for the contact phase, *calcium* is required for most of the reactions and is the reason why chelators (e.g., citrate, EDTA) are used for blood collection and processing where *plasma* or cells are analyzed. It will be seen that for four of the clotting factors, the important calcium-binding properties are imparted through a vitamin K-dependent reaction. *Serum* is derived from clotted blood from which the fibrinogen has been converted to insoluble fibrin; the other clotting factors are at least partially activated or consumed during this process.

Two additional general principles apply to the variety of enzymatic reactions. First, in order to achieve a local concentration of these trace plasma proteins (i.e., of enzyme and substrate), various surface-mediated interactions with cofactors take place. The surfaces are either negatively charged (e.g.,

TABLE 1. Properties of human clotting factors

CLOTTING FACTOR (SYNONYM)	MOLECULAR WEIGHT (NUMBER OF CHAINS)	NORMAL PLASMA CONCENTRATION (µg/ml)	T₁/₂ ELIMINATION (HOURS)	ACTIVE FORM
INTRINSIC SYSTEM				
Factor XII (Hageman factor)	80,000 (1)	29	60	Serine protease
Prekallikrein (Fletcher factor)	80,000 (1)	50	?	Serine protease
High molecular weight kininogen (Fitzgerald factor)	120,000 (1)	70	?	Cofactor
Factor XI (Plasma thromboplastin antecedent)	160,000 (2, dimer)	4	65	Serine protease
Factor IX (Christmas Factor)	57,000 (1)	4	20	Serine protease
Factor VIII/VWF (Antihemophilic factor/ von Willebrand factor)	1–2,000,000* (series of 6–10 subunits)	7 (vWF)	10 (VIII:C)	Cofactor
EXTRINSIC SYSTEM				
Factor VII (Proconvertin)	55,000 (1)	1	5	Serine protease
Tissue factor (Tissue thromboplastin)	45,000 (1)	0		Cofactor

COMMON PATHWAY

Factor X (Stuart-Prower factor)	59,000 (2)	5	65	Serine protease
Factor V (Proaccelerin)	330,000 (1)	5–12	25	Cofactor
Prothrombin (Factor II)	70,000 (1)	100	100	Serine protease
Fibrinogen (Factor I)	340,000 (6: $A\alpha_2$, $B\beta_2$, γ_2)	2500 (250 mg/dl)	120	Clot structure
Factor XIII (Fibrin stabilizing factor)	300,000 (4: a_2, b_2)	10	150	Transglutaminase

*Subunit molecular weight of factor VIII/vWF is around 200,000 with a series of multimers found in circulation.

glass, kaolin or, in vivo, collagen) or phospholipid vesicles (provided in vivo as platelet factor 3), or part of the tissue factor complex.

Second, the clotting factors themselves can be divided into either cofactors or precursors of serine proteases. The latter are activated in turn by highly specific, limited proteolytic cleavages of a trypsin-like nature, that is, Arg-X peptide bonds.[40] Despite sequence identity in the catalytic regions of all of these proteases, they have developed distinct, highly specific selectivity which is presumably imparted by subtle differences in other portions of the enzyme such as substrate binding sites.

Fibrinogen is an exception to the second principle, as it is the precursor of the structural protein of the clot. The final step, which also differs from the above activation reactions, is the covalent stabilization of the fibrin matrix itself. Figure 10 presents a scheme of the clotting factor interactions involved in both intrinsic and extrinsic systems and their common path. It is becoming increasingly apparent that the in vitro factor interaction, *clotting*, is not identical with *coagulation* in vivo. Although it appears that platelets provide phospholipid in the latter, one of the most potent platelet aggregating agents is thrombin, a late stage clotting product, which is also effective in modifying and enhancing cofactors that lead to its formation. There are interrelationships between the intrinsic and extrinsic systems and, under some conditions, "crossover" activation reactions have been observed. The whole issue of what initiates coagulation in vivo in either system remains open, and some understanding of the mechanisms of pathologic alterations is just beginning to be appreciated. Although a great deal of information has been gleaned from studies of bovine clotting factors, this chapter emphasizes knowledge of the human system.

MECHANISMS OF COAGULATION

In the *intrinsic system,* contact activation refers to reactions following adsorption of contact factors to a highly negatively charged surface.[41,42] It should be stressed, however, that although the reactions are well understood in vitro, the physiologic or pathologic significance remains to be clarified. Involved are factors XII and XI, and the more recently described prekallikrein and high molecular weight kininogen (Fig. 11). All of the contact activations take place in the absence of calcium and, in vitro, represent the preincubation or surface interaction phase of intrinsic screening or specific clotting factor assays.

While procoagulant activities of each of these contact factors may be reduced by acquired or hereditary disorders, only low levels of factor XI are associated with abnormal bleeding. Kallikrein, it should also be noted, is also involved in the fibrinolytic system, inflammation, and has additional physiologic roles.[43]

A middle phase of intrinsic clotting begins with the first calcium-dependent step, activation of factor IX by factor XI_a. Factor IX is specifically cleaved by factor XI_a at two sites to produce factor IX_a (Fig. 12). Factor IX, with factors X, VII, and prothrombin, are the vitamin K-dependent clotting factors which have strikingly homologous sequences.[40] These four, after polypeptide chain synthe-

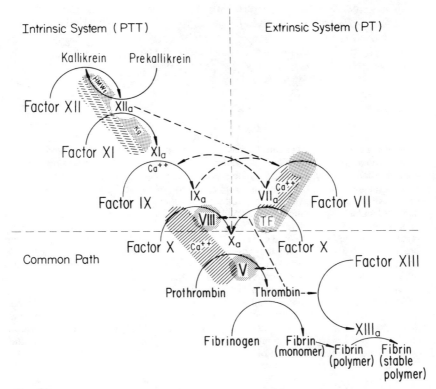

FIGURE 10. Mechanisms of clotting factor interactions. Clotting is initiated by either an *intrinsic* or *extrinsic* pathway with subsequent factor interactions which converge upon a final, *common path*.[39,40] The clinical screening tests are indicated as PTT for partial thromboplastin time and PT for prothrombin time. The factors circulate as (1) zymogens which are activated by specific cleavages to highly specific serine proteases, (2) cofactors (stippled for protein and hatched for phospholipid), or (3) the precursor of the structural protein of the clot (fibrinogen). A separate enzymatic system, generation of factor XIII$_a$, follows for clot stabilization. Protein cofactors include high molecular weight kininogen (HMWt Kg), tissue factor (TF), and factors VIII and V; each of the latter two require modification by thrombin. Other interactions between the intrinsic and extrinsic systems (arrows and dashed lines) can be demonstrated under some conditions.

sis but prior to secretion from the hepatocyte, are carboxylated at 10 to 12 specific glutamyl residues. The residues occur near the amino-terminal portion of the molecules. The new residue, a gamma-carboxy-glutamic acid is referred to as Gla. Due to the tertiary conformation, pairs of Glas form a charge density that tightly chelates calcium ions.[44]

Factor VIII is an essential cofactor in intrinsic factor X activation and is the largest protein involved in clotting.[45-47] It circulates as a series of multimers of at

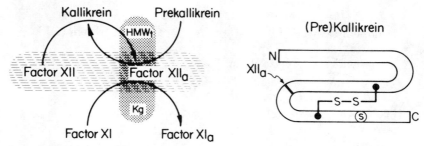

FIGURE 11. Contact activation. *Left:* The initial event in vitro is the adsorption of factor XII to a negatively charged surface (hatched, horizontal ovoid) where it undergoes a conformational change to expose its active site. Factor XII converts prekallikrein to kallikrein. Additional factor XII$_a$ and kallikrein are then generated by reciprocal activation. Factor XII$_a$ also activates Factor XI. Both prekallikrein and factor XI bind to a cofactor, high molecular weight kininogen (HMWt Kg; dotted, vertical ovoid), which serves to anchor them to the charged surface.[41,42] *Right:* Prekallikrein, as a typical contact activation factor, is activated by cleavage of an Arg-Ile bond by factor XII$_a$ to form an active serine protease of two chains with the amino-terminal (N) larger fragment being disulfide bonded (S—S) to the carboxy-terminal (C) smaller fragment. The latter contains the active center Ser (S). The structures of other contact factors (not shown) include factor XI, which is highly homologous to prekallikrein, but circulates as a disulfide bonded dimer of twice the molecular weight. Factor XII is of similar size, but the active form can also degrade itself to a lower molecular weight species that no longer binds to the negatively charged surface. High molecular weight kininogen has a different structure, including a nine amino acid, vasoactive peptide, bradykinin, which can be released after specific cleavages at each end by kallikrein.[43]

least several disulfide-bonded subunit chains which are of the same basic size.[48] The major portion of this protein should actually be regarded as the "von Willebrand factor" or a carrier protein, whereas a smaller moiety (presumably a separate, tightly associated protein or subunit) constitutes the clotting activity. Interestingly enough, factor VIII (as with factor V) first requires modification (m) by a serine protease, such as thrombin, to exert its reactivity independently.[49] These two cofactors bind independently to phospholipid vesicles, without ionic bridges, to facilitate the reaction between enzyme and substrate (e.g., factors IX$_a$ and X, for factor VIII$_m$, see Fig. 12).

Other properties of factor VIII include its ability to be concentrated by cryoprecipitation. It also appears to have a "marginal" pool in vivo. Stress, as exhibited by epinephrine infusion or strenuous exercise, can easily double the level of factor VIII/vWF protein and procoagulant activity (VIII:C) in circulating blood; under some conditions the specific activity (clotting units/given amount of protein) can also be markedly increased as is seen in vitro when trace amounts of thrombin are added. Once thrombin-modified, however, factor VIII$_m$ becomes less stable and its activity is easily destroyed. Factor VIII is sensitive to degradation by plasmin and activated protein C; its activity decreases pro-

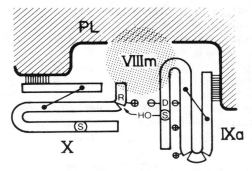

FIGURE 12. Intrinsic factor X activation. Factors IX_a and X are bound to the phospholipid surface (PL; cross hatched area) by calcium bridges through their γ-carboxyglutamic acid residues (Gla). Factor VIII, having been modified by thrombin (VIIIm; stippled circle) binds nonionically to the phospholipid surface and serves as the cofactor in the activation by an as yet undefined mechanism. The steps of catalysis established for tryptic-like cleavage involves binding of substrate (factor X) with an Arg (R) group ionically attaching to an Asp (D) residue in the bottom of the binding pocket near the active center Ser (S) of the enzyme (factor IX_a). The active center Ser forms an unstable acyl intermediate which is hydrolized, cleaving the Arg—Ile peptide bond to generate factor X_a. In the conversion of prothrombin to thrombin (not shown), factor X_a is the enzyme and factor V_m the modified cofactor.

gressively to around 20 percent over the first two days when whole blood or plasma is stored for transfusion at 4°C.

The *extrinsic system* is initiated by activation of factor VII, another vitamin K-dependent protein, which primarily differs from the others by its extremely low plasma concentration.[50] When factor VII interacts with tissue factor, an intracellular (hence extrinsic to plasma) microsomal lipoprotein, factor VII_a becomes a serine protease which is the extrinsic factor X activator.[39] Tissue factor is present in large amounts in the brain, lung, and placenta; it is also secreted by stimulated leukocytes,[51] and has been found in the intima of large blood vessels. Lipid comprises one third of the molecular weight of this factor and is essential for activity, providing the surface for calcium-vitamin K-dependent factor binding. Plasma samples from some individuals show factor VII_a generation at 4°C storage. This "cold-promoted" effect may involve factor XII_a or IX_a, or both.

The *common path* begins as factor X is activated by either factor VII_a-tissue factor or factors IX_a-VIII_m. Factor X is also vitamin K-dependent, but circulates as a disulfide-bonded two-chained zymogen.[40] Activation by either pathway generates factor X_a; intrinsic activation is depicted in Figure 12. Experimentally, an enzyme from the Russell's viper venom, as well as exposure to dilute trypsin, can also generate factor X_a.

After formation of factor X_a, the next step involves factor V, a cofactor, which (like factor VIII) has its activity manifest after modification by a proteolytic enzyme such as thrombin.[52,53] Factor V is a large protein, but its lability in the human system has made its isolation and subsequent characterization difficult. It markedly facilitates the activation of prothrombin, the final vitamin K-dependent factor in this cascade. The primary structure of prothrombin[39,40] is presented schematically in Figure 13.

The higher plasma concentration of prothrombin (see Table 1), as well as a biologic amplification of the clotting system, allows a few molecules of activated initiator or intermediate factors to generate a large burst of thrombin activity. Thrombin, in addition to its ability to modify factors V and VIII, is able to induce platelet aggregation. Its best charactererized interactions, however, are with two substrates, fibrinogen and factor XIII.[54]

Fibrinogen is a large, six-chained molecule whose primary sequence is depicted in Figure 14.[55] It is relatively cryo-insoluble (like factor VIII). Thrombin only removes about 3 percent of its molecular mass by releasing first the two A and then the two B peptides. The fibrin monomers so formed are able to polymerize nonenzymatically, leaving the fluid phase to become a gel (Fig. 14, lower portion). Denaturing agents such as urea, however, can still make the clot soluble at this point. A tough, insoluble fibrin polymer is formed by interaction of the fibrin polymer with factor XIII$_a$.

Factor XIII is either trapped within the clot or, alternatively, provided by platelets, and it is activated by thrombin cleavage of a single bond near the amino-terminal portion of its heavier (a) chain. This converts it to an active transamidase. In the presence of calcium, factor XIII$_a$ catalyzes peptide-like bond formation between E-amino groups of lysine from one fibrin monomer and the γ-amide groups of glutamine from adjacent molecules, splitting out NH$_3$.[56] These residues are located at the C-terminal portions of the α and γ chains of fibrinogen (see Fig. 14). Degradation of fibrinogen will be discussed in Chapter 4, under fibrinolysis.

PRODUCTION AND SURVIVAL

The liver cells synthesize all the plasma clotting factors with the probable exception of factor VIII (at least its von Willebrand portion), which is produced in multiple organs, possibly in endothelial cells.[45,46] Factor XIII appears in a smaller form, without the carboydrate-rich b chain, in platelets; the association of plasma factors V, VIII, X$_a$, thrombin, and fibrinogen with these cells relates either to the remarkable adsorptive properties of the platelet membrane, to specific binding sites for clotting factors, or to synthesis. As discussed under factor IX, the vitamin K-dependent factors are of special interest in terms of their generation of unique calcium-binding sites prior to secretion into the plasma. Furthermore, the carboxylase system involved is one of the more labile synthetic functions of the hepatocyte, such that the prothrombin time screening test, together with the serum albumin, are essentially the only clinical tests of liver function that correlate with more severe damage related to the synthetic capabilities of liver. Consistent with synthesis of other proteins, experiments with animal polysomes indicate that fibrinogen chains are first syn-

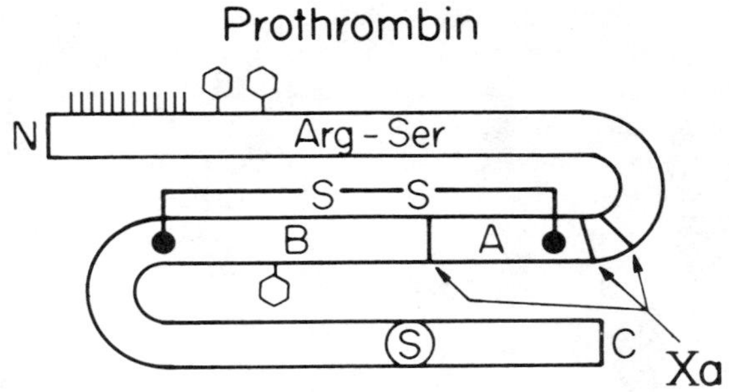

Prothrombin

FIGURE 13. Structure of prothrombin. Prothrombin is the largest of the vitamin K-dependent proteins and is depicted from its amino terminus (N) to its carboxy terminus (C). The aminoterminal region contains 10 Gla (vertical bars). In its conversion to thrombin, factor X_a cleaves two bonds (Arg—Thr and Arg—Ile) to form disulfide bonded A and B chains, respectively, that represent the carboxy-terminal half of the precursor. In the human enzyme, a second Arg—Thr cleavage near the amino-terminal portion of the A chain occurs which does not alter its activity. Once it is generated, thrombin is no longer covalently linked to the Gla region so that it enters the soluble phase to interact with fibrinogen. The amino-terminal "pro-piece" (fragment 1 • 2) remains bound to phospholipid, where thrombin cleaves an Arg—Ser bond in this half of the molecule, generating two separate fragments; a physiologic role for these peptides remains to be identified. The hexagonal structures represent Asn-linked carbohydrate chains.

thesized with amino-terminal, "signal" peptides; noncoding regions in genes for fibrinogen and prothrombin have also been observed.

The turnover of clotting factors has been evaluated either by following survivals of isotope-labeled purified protein (e.g., radioiodinated fibrinogen), or by transfusing normal plasma or concentrates of partially purified factors into patients with isolated deficiencies. The disappearance rates of the members of the vitamin K-dependent group have also been measured after this reaction has been blocked with antagonists or re-established by subsequent administration of vitamin K itself. The results of these various techniques are in reasonably good agreement. With the exception of the higher molecular weight factors such as factor VIII, which follow more simple kinetics,[45] disappearance curves are double exponential functions, representing equilibration with an extravascular pool and metabolic turnover from the central volume. The late phase is prolonged by reentry from the larger volume of distribution.[57] Concentration and survival data of the coagulation factors are summarized in Table 1.

Consideration of these characteristics is particularly relevant to blood component replacement therapy, as will be discussed in Chapter 10. It should be emphasized that even sensitive kinetic studies in experimental animals have been unable to demonstrate consumption of the clotting factors as a significant mechanism for their normal disappearance; for several of them (especially factors VII, VIII and IX) this disappearance is unusually rapid when compared with other plasma proteins.

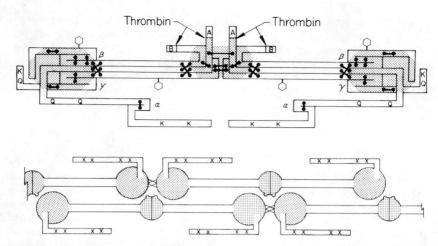

FIGURE 14. Fibrin(ogen) structure and polymerization. *Upper:* Depicts the primary structure of fibrinogen[55] arranged to correspond to its image on electron microscopy, which includes a central and two terminal domains (stippled) with rod-like connections. This 340,000 mol wt glycoprotein is a paired structure of three highly homologous chains, Aα, Bβ and γ, respectively. Complete amino acid sequence has been solved and arrangement of the disulfide bonds (lines connecting dots) proposed. The central or "E" region contains the amino-terminal portions of each set of three chains, including three disulfide bridges between the sets. The A and B fibrinopeptide portions (16 and 14 amino acids, respectively) are also found protruding from this region. Each set of three chains then forms a rope-like rod, lashed at each end by a disulfide ring. The carboxy-terminal domains ("D" regions) are formed by the β and γ chains; the carboxy-terminal ends of the longer α chains extend out from these regions. Crosslinking sites include donor Gln (Q) and acceptor Lys (K) residues. Thrombin cleaves the A (and then the B) peptides, as indicated by arrows. *Lower:* Newly formed amino terminal "knobs" of the α chains interact with and orient two D regions of different monomers to form alternate rows of a fibrin strand. Factor XIIIₐ covalently crosslinks two γ-chain ends from adjacent D regions by reciprocal transamidation of Gln and Lys residues. Subsequent interactions and crosslinkings (x) occur between the extended ends of the α-chains to other fibrin strands to form a three-dimensional fibrin mesh.

CONTROL MECHANISMS

Obviously, the body has mechanisms of avoiding massive thrombus formation once coagulation is initiated. Although fibrinogen, prothrombin, and factors V and VIII are largely consumed (for the latter two this may also reflect destruction) when blood or plasma is clotted in a test tube, cleavage of other intermediate enzymes is somehow blocked after 5 to 20 percent activation has occurred. At least three types of mechanisms which affect rates of coagulation can be considered.

First, increased blood flow reduces the chance of localized concentration of precursors and removes activated materials by dilution into a larger volume. This is demonstrated by the absence of fibrin thrombi in damaged, but patent, arteries and arterioles, as opposed to their presence in the venous system. Related to the blood flow consideration is the rapid disappearance of inactivated clotting factors by passage through the liver. Here they are presumably taken up by mononuclear phagocytic cells, perhaps while adsorbed to surfaces or vesicles as particle-like materials, or to inhibitors.

Second, during the process of activation, proteolytic enzymes are generated which not only activate clotting factors, but also degrade cofactors. Plasmin, for example, degrades fibrinogen and fibrin monomers, and can rapidly inactivate cofactors V and VIII by relatively specific cleavages. Of interest is the recently discovered protein C. This is a vitamin K-dependent precursor of a serine protease,[58] which is another substrate for thrombin activation in the presence of an endothelial cofactor.[11] The active form, not a procoagulant, rapidly destroys factor V and probably factor VIII. Further physiologic studies are necessary to determine the relative importance of these and other neutral proteases (such as from granulocytes) in limiting coagulation.

The third category of regulation involves naturally occurring circulating protease inhibitors. These plasma proteins have been compared to families of naturally occurring tissue and plant protease inhibitors. The major ones which inactivate the proteases involved in hemostasis are summarized in Table 2.

Alpha$_2$-macroglobulin, which contains two sets of disulfide-bonded dimers, competes with macromolecular substrates and envelops a broad spectrum of serine, thiol, carboxy, or metallo-proteases in a "trap" that is rapidly cleared from plasma.[59] Alpha$_1$-antitrypsin is best known for its deficient (more active) form which leads to lung or liver diseases; its major action appears to be the inhibition of neutral proteases from inflammatory reactions, including neutrophil elastase or tissue enzymes. Because of its broad specificity, it is often referred to as the α_1-proteinase inhibitor. Like the next three inhibitors, it inhibits serine proteases by forming 1:1 stoichiometric complexes that inactivate the inhibitor upon association; affinity of α_1-antitrypsin for active coagulation factors is relatively weak. Antithrombin III shares sequence homology with α_1-antitrypsin and, by itself, antithrombin can progressively inactivate all serine proteases of hemostasis by forming high-molecular-weight, stable complexes.[60] As will be discussed in Chapter 13, heparin and contact with damaged endothelium markedly accelerate this reaction, accounting for an immediate, potent, anticoagulant effect. Congenital deficiency of antithrombin III predisposes individuals to venous thromboembolism. C$_1$ esterase inhibitor is primarily known for its congenital deficiency which causes hereditary angioedema. This complement-system protease inhibitor is a potent inhibitor of plasma kallikrein, particularly when it is not bound to high-molecular-weight kininogen.[59] Although the recently described α_2-antiplasmin circulates in the lowest concentration of these inhibitors, its inactivation of plasmin is the most avid and immediate inhibition known.[61] In purified systems, α_2-antiplasmin will

TABLE 2. Plasma protease inhibitors

PROTEIN	MOLECULAR WEIGHT (NO. OF CHAINS)	PLASMA CONCENTRATION (mg/dl)	MECHANISM OF INHIBITION
α_2-macroglobulin	725,000 (4)	210*	Non-active site binding of virtually any proteolytic enzyme
α_1-antitrypsin	54,000 (1)	200*	
antithrombin III	62,000 (1)	29	More specific active site, stiochiometric complex with serine protease(s)
C_1 esterase inhibitor	105,000 (1)	18	
α_2-antiplasmin	63,000 (1)	6	

*Because of its size, relative μ molar concentration of α_2-macroglobulin is one-twelfth that of α_1-antitrypsin despite the same mg/dl.

inactivate most of the contact proteases when they are no longer surface bound.

In comparing the different inhibitors with thrombin, for example, relative kinetics of inhibition show that antithrombin III is more potent than α_1-antitrypsin or α_2-macroglobulin when small synthetic substrates are used for the assay. In comparing the effect of thrombin on fibrinogen, however, α_2-macroglobulin becomes the most potent of these inhibitors.[59] The relative physiologic effects of the different inhibitors as they circulate in blood are only beginning to be sorted out, but are clearly relevant to disorders of thrombosis.

4

FIBRINOLYSIS

The fibrinolytic system removes unwanted fibrin deposits to re-establish flow in vessels occluded by a thrombus and to facilitate the healing process following inflammation and injury. It is a multicomponent enzymic system composed of a circulating zymogen, activators, cofactors, and inhibitors.[62] Although a variety of proteases are associated with inflammatory reactions, the best characterized is plasmin. This enzyme circulates as the proenzyme plasminogen, and is then converted to an active serine protease by limited proteolysis. The fibrinolytic system interacts with the coagulation system at the level of contact activation. After modification, plasminogen adheres to a fibrin clot, being incorporated within the mesh during polymerization. Plasminogen activation may occur by three different pathways: an intrinsic pathway in which all components involved are present in precursor form in the blood; an extrinsic pathway in which the activator originates from tissues or from the vessel wall and is released into the blood by certain stimuli or trauma; and an exogenous pathway in which the activating substances streptokinase or urokinase may be infused for therapeutic purposes.

PROPERTIES AND ACTIVATION
OF PLASMINOGEN

Plasminogen is a single-chain plasma glycoprotein which is similar in size to the contact activation factors. Its molecular weight is 90,000 and its primary

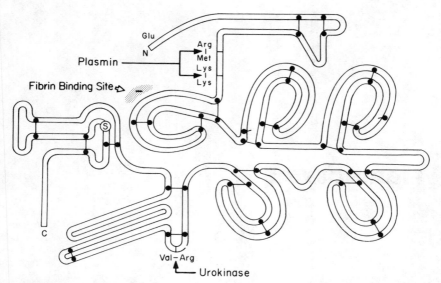

FIGURE 15. Plasmin(ogen) structure. The primary structure of plasminogen is represented diagrammatically. Near the amino terminus (N), and amino-terminal residue Glu, two bonds, Arg—Met and Lys—Lys, are quite susceptible to cleavage by plasmin. The next domain contains five loop-like regions ("kringles," from their similarity to a Scandinavian pastry), which are homologous with each other and similar to two looped regions in a similar part of prothrombin. In plasminogen, these loops contain at least two negatively charged fibrin (lysyl-) binding sites (stippled area) which are exposed by cleavage of the amino-terminal peptide. Beyond the kringles, the next region begins with the Arg—Val peptide bond which is cleaved by activators such as urokinase to convert plasminogen to its active form, plasmin. The active center Ser (S) is then able to exert its proteolytic function. Disulfide bonds are indicated by the connected dots; the carboxy terminus, by C.

structure[62] is depicted in Figure 15. It is produced by the liver and has a biologic half-life of about two days. Its plasma level (120 μg per ml, or comparable to that of prothrombin) increases with chronic inflammation and falls with either consumption or decreased liver production, paralleling changes in fibrinogen concentration.

Intrinsic activation of plasminogen may occur by one or more pathways involving factor XII, prekallikrein, high-molecular-weight kininogen, and a distinct plasma protein (proactivator). The plasma proactivator is converted to an active form by kallikrein, derived from contact activation. An endothelial cell protease which has recently been described, can generate kallikrein through factor XII-activation.[63] An intrinsic mechanism presumably accounts for circulating degradation products and fibrin monomers found during disseminated intravascular coagulation.

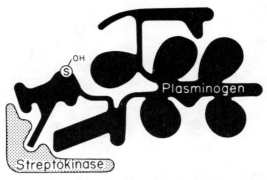

FIGURE 16. Activation of plasminogen by streptokinase. Streptokinase binds to the carboxy-terminal portion of plasmin(ogen), making the active center serine (S—OH) more reactive. This occurs without the specific Arg—Val activation cleavage. The complex is thus capable of converting other molecules of plasminogen to plasmin (not shown). Free plasmin enhances fibrinolysis by its secondary cleavage of peptide bond(s) releasing the amino-terminal fragment of Glu-plasmin(ogen) and exposing the fibrin binding site(s); when Lys-plasminogen is bound to fibrin, tissue activator is also able to form the active, degradative enzyme, which is protected from α_2-antiplasmin through prior binding to fibrin (not shown).

Extrinsic plasminogen activator found in blood probably represents released vascular plasminogen activators. These activators are similar or identical to the activator isolated from other tissues. Extrinsic (tissue) plasminogen activator has a high affinity for fibrin.

The activation mechanism is best established for the protease found in minute concentration in normal urine, urokinase. Urokinase is a trypsin-like protease that activates plasminogen by cleaving a specific Arg-Val bond (Fig. 15), and differs from the tissue plasminogen activators in that the tissue activator must bind with fibrin before the activation can occur. Urokinase reacts with plasminogen in the fluid phase of blood.[62]

Streptokinase is a nonenzymatic protein that activates the fibrinolytic system indirectly by forming a 1:1 stoichiometric complex with plasminogen or plasmin and thereby converts the inactive proenzyme into an efficient plasminogen activator (Fig. 16).

The physiologic activator of plasminogen appears to be the tissue-derived protease present in endothelial cells and other tissues.[63] By activating the plasminogen within a thrombus, it allows for gradual dissolution during the time in which tissue repair processes occur. Fibrinolytic activity can also be generated experimentally by infusion of activated protein C.[12]

ROLE AND FATE OF PLASMIN

Once plasmin is formed, it becomes an active serine protease with relatively broader specificity than thrombin. It hydrolyzes not only Arg-X but Lys-X bonds,

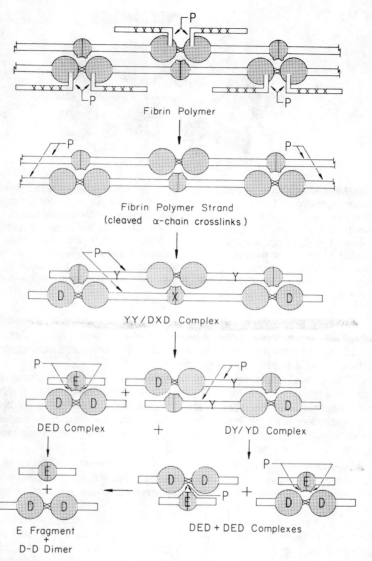

FIGURE 17. Degradation of fibrin by plasmin. Plasmin digestion of a fibrin polymer proceeds by cleavage of the extended carboxy-terminal portions of the α-chains to produce isolated fibrin stands. Early in the digestion of the strands, complexes which correspond to YY/DXD and DY/YD are formed, followed by smaller DED complexes, DD dimers, and E fragments.[64] On electron microscopy, images of X, Y and D fragments, DD dimers, and DED complexes have been visualized.[65] When fibrinogen is degraded by free plasmin, the same fragments appear although the Aα and Bβ chains may remain intact.

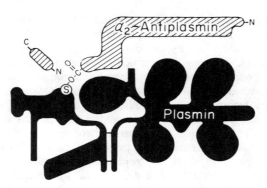

FIGURE 18. Inhibition of plasmin. Interaction of α_2-antiplasmin with plasmin[61,62] is a rapid reaction that involves binding of the amino-terminal portion of the inhibitor to the fibrin binding site on the heavy (H) chain of plasmin as illustrated (first loop-like structure) and the formation of an acyl intermediate between a specific Met—Val peptide bond of the inhibitor and the active center Ser (S) on the light chain of plasmin. The fibrin binding site needs to be exposed by the removal of the amino-terminal portion of Glu-plasmin(ogen). Upon inhibition, a carboxy-terminal peptide is cleaved from the inhibitor and a shift of its antigenic determinants is observed.

and can dissolve insoluble fibrin polymers[64] as shown in Figure 17. Cleavages of fibrin monomers occur in restricted regions and produce first the larger X and Y fragments and then smaller D and E fragments. Anticoagulant effects, particularly as seen in screening tests such as the thrombin and bleeding times, reside predominately in the soluble X and Y fragments and intermediate complexes thereof. Once the lower molecular weight fragments are formed, they are rapidly cleared from plasma. In vivo, it appears that a fibrin mesh can be solubilized with incomplete digestion, since cleavage of only some of the rods within a given strand is needed, producing a variety of crosslinked complexes.[64] On electron microscopy, images of X, Y, and D fragments, DD dimers and DED complexes have been visualized.[65]

Factors V and VIII also serve as substrates for plasmin degradation in the circulation. Indeed, in secondary fibrinolysis associated with severe disseminated intravascular coagulation, circulating levels of these factors may become sufficiently low to compromise hemostasis. In such situations, the fibrinogen levels are also severely depressed due to simultaneous consumption.

INACTIVATION OF PLASMIN

In plasma, plasmin is immediately inactivated by the very potent α_2-antiplasmin (Fig. 18); inhibition can also be demonstrated with α_2-macroglobulin. The potency and concentration of the more specific antiplasmin inhibitor, however, is such that it would rapidly neutralize half of the total amount of plasminogen if it were all suddenly converted to plasmin.[61,62] This undoubtedly represents the major control mechanism preventing generalized, systematic, degradative effects of plasmin. Pharmacologically, plasmin is inhibited by agents such as epsilon-aminocaproic and tranexamic acids, which compete with fibrin for the lysyl-binding sites. Clinically, such drugs have been tried in acute subarachnoid hemorrhages. They decrease the transfusion requirements following dental extraction in patients with hemophilia, but do not appear to help in the management of bleeding from other sites. They also inhibit C_1 esterase, in the complement pathway, and have been used to control episodes in some patients with deficiency of the C_1 esterase inhibitor (hereditary angioedema).

Within the microenvironment of a thrombus, the plasmin formed is capable of digesting the fibrin mesh. The tremendous potential for fibrinolysis in the microcirculation probably relates to the high ratio of endothelial cells to the surface of the fibrin thrombus so that tissue activators can enter the thrombus in high concentrations. Excess plasmin released to the circulation, moreover, is rapidly inactivated.

5

INTEGRATED REACTIONS AMONG HEMOSTATIC COMPONENTS

The endothelial, platelet, coagulation, and fibrinolytic systems interrelate in a number of ways, many of which serve to promote localized hemostasis while preventing generalized thrombosis. Figure 19 depicts many of these reactions and serves as the basis for the discussion in this chapter.

The luminal surface of normal *endothelium* is an inert barrier preventing constituents of the blood from interacting with subendothelial structures and forming thrombus on the vessel wall.[5] Moreover, intact endothelium actively resists thrombus formation locally whenever activated species of the platelet or coagulation systems circulate. For example, platelet aggregate formation is prevented by the endothelium despite the presence of ADP, epinephrine, or thrombin, through the inactivation of ADP,[8] active clearance of vasoactive amines,[9] facilitated complexing of thrombin with antithrombin III,[10] and the explosive thrombin-mediated synthesis and release of inhibitory PGI_2.[66] These mechanisms markedly decrease the possibility of thrombus forming at distal sites and limit the local extension of thrombus.

Endothelial disruption initiates thrombus formation (see Fig. 19). This process initially involves the attachment of *platelets* to the subendothelium through the interaction of a platelet receptor (GPI_b), subendothelial collagen, and a plasma cofactor, factor VIII/vWF.[15-18] Fibronectin and thrombospondin derived from plasma, platelets, and endothelium may also play roles in this process.[67] An unstable platelet mass forms through several interactive but independent recruitment mechanisms, including the generation of thromboxane

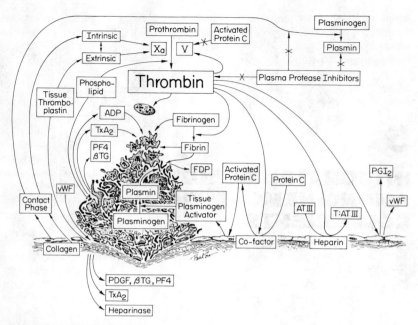

FIGURE 19. Interactions among hemostatic components.

A$_2$, release of dense granule ADP, and thrombin-mediated platelet activation.[19-25] Aggregation requires the rapid generation of platelet membrane fibrinogen receptor complex (GPII$_b$ and GPIII$_a$) and calcium-dependent interplatelet bridging by fibrinogen.[17,19,20,68,69] This binding reaction may also involve the α-granule proteins thrombospondin and fibronectin.[70,71] Regulation of fibrinogen receptors appears to play an important role in modulating platelet function. The appearance of platelet specific α-granule proteins in plasma and urine serves as an indicator of platelet activation in vivo.[27] The deposition of platelet factor 4 in the subendothelium may play a role in neutrophil and macrophage chemotaxis[72] and platelet-derived growth factor appears to be important in the intimal migration and proliferation of smooth muscle cells.[3,73]

Thrombin plays a pivotal role in the formation of hemostatic plugs (see Fig. 19). Thrombin is generated locally on the platelet surface through both extrinsic and intrinsic pathways.[39,40] All injured cells release tissue thromboplastin to activate extrinsic coagulation. Hageman factor is activated both by disrupted endothelial cells[63] and by subendothelial connective tissue.[41] Platelets promote subsequent activation of the early stages of intrinsic coagulation[33] by a process that may involve a factor XI receptor and high-molecular-weight kininogen. Factors V and VIII also specifically bind to platelets; they act with membrane phospholipid to facilitate the activation of factor X to X$_a$ and in the final conversion of prothrombin to thrombin.[32,74] Low concentrations of thrombin are formed within seconds of exposing blood to nonendothelialized surfaces, long before fibrin is formed. These concentrations are sufficient to stimulate platelet release of α-granules at levels below which fibrinogen is cleaved.[75-77] Thrombin-modified factor V (factor V_m) binds to platelets with much higher affinity than the unmodified form. Platelet-bound factor V_m serves as a high affinity platelet receptor for factor X_a. Indeed, the rate at which thrombin is generated is increased more than 300,000-fold in the presence of factor V_m bound to platelets.[32,74] Thus, the generation of thrombin initiates potent positive feedback mechanisms on the platelet surface for explosive activation of the coagulation cascade and fibrin formation.

The potent effects of thrombin are actively limited to the site of vascular injury by three important protective mechanisms. The first involves direct inactivation of circulating thrombin by the plasma protease inhibitors (see Chapter 3). The second reaction preventing the escape of thrombin into the circulation involves the enhancement by the endothelial surface of thrombin-antithrombin III complex formation.[10] Third, thrombin released into the circulation binds to thrombomodulin, a receptor on the luminal surface of the endothelial cells. The resultant complex activates protein C[11] which destroys factors V and VIII. Thus, thrombin initiates negative feedback mechanisms controlling its own generation.

Fibrinolysis is localized within the thrombus. Plasminogen binds to fibrin in the consolidating thrombus, and tissue plasminogen activator, derived from the endothelium adjacent to the forming thrombus, is specifically coupled to fibrin. Direct activation of associated plasminogen proceeds with the local release of plasmin within the thrombus (see Figure 19), where inactivation by α_2-antiplasmin is delayed. Moreover, thrombin-dependent activation of protein C markedly increases the release of tissue plasminogen activator[12] and platelet-dependent retraction enhances thrombolysis.[78]

Within the *coagulation* system there are several lines of evidence which indicate that coagulation in the body does not proceed entirely as clotting does in the test tube, despite the clinical utility of in vitro factor tests. The initiation reactions are obvious cases in point; however, the modification of cofactors and the mechanisms limiting complete consumption of clotting factors also need to be considered.

The activation of factor VII to initiate extrinsic clotting is poorly understood, even in vitro. Under certain conditions, factors XII_a and IX_a can generate factor VII_a activity and factor VII_a itself may influence intrinsic clotting by activating factor IX.[39] Although such interactions can be demonstrated in highly purified, in vitro systems, their relevance to complex conditions remains to be assessed. They do suggest that the simple, intrinsic-extrinsic system model of clotting is an oversimplification of an even more complex physiologic process.

Just as one may wonder how thrombin can be initially generated to induce platelet aggregation, which then releases platelet factor 3 to allow coagulation to occur, the same question can be raised as to what enzyme in vivo is able to modify the cofactors V and VIII, allowing them to assume their active forms. These reactions are even more difficult to study in the test tube because of susceptibility of these molecules to inactivation by further proteolytic cleavage by various plasma and cellular proteases.

Surface-mediated reactions also deserve consideration in the binding of active enzymes. For example, once factor XII is cleaved to a low-molecular-weight enzyme, it is released from the portion of the molecule that binds to the negatively charged surfaces. Although it retains activity in other systems, it is no longer able to activate factor XI.[43] Another question is how does factor XI$_a$ interact with factor IX in vivo since in vitro this is lipid-independent and cofactor-independent. Whereas vitamin K-dependent factors require calcium to bind to lipid, factors V and VIII do not, leading to questions of specificity and the nature of binding to phospholipids. Interactions of coagulation and other components, especially the platelet, also need to be considered. More recently, it has been appreciated that other enzymes derived from cellular elements of the blood or tissues, for example, can activate certain coagulation factors, with potential pathologic implications.[79] For the time being, at least, one must assume that the in vivo correlate(s) to contact activation in a test tube remains to be identified.

Factor XIII$_a$ crosslinks other factors and inhibitors within the region of the thrombus. One such reaction is the binding of fibronectin to collagen.[68]

Through its activation of prekallikrein and reciprocal activation leading to a final, soluble (non-surface bound) factor XII$_a$, there are additional pathways involved. The first relates to the effect of kallikrein on kininogens to release kinins that mediate inflammatory responses. In this regard, the C'-1 esterase inhibitor functions to inhibit kallikrein, linking clotting to the complement system. One of the smaller factor XII fragments itself may enhance vascular permeability as well.[42] Other established pathways involve the formation of a plasminogen activator from a proactivator; again this activation is kallirein-dependent. The significance of this plasma reaction (or its relationship to tissue-derived activator substances) to in vivo clot dissolution is unclear, yet it may well explain the generation of plasmin which leads to the soluble fibrin degradation products seen in disseminated intravascular coagulation. It has been postulated (but not yet conclusively shown) that the prorennin-rennin (angiotensin) and even proinsulin systems may depend upon kallikrein for activation.

There are also several well established interactions between inflammation and hemostasis. Activated mononuclear leukocytes release tissue factor and thus activate extrinsic coagulation,[51] and generate thrombin locally by secreting a direct prothrombin activator.[80] The generation of thromboxane A$_2$ and PGI$_2$ by activated leukocytes (or the effects of activated neutrophils on vascular tissues) affect platelet-endothelial interactions.[13] The production of acetyl glyceryl ether phosphorycholine (AGEPC) activates platelets.[81] The mononuclear phagocytic system also functions in pathologic processes as an avid scavenger of α_2-macroglobulin-active protease complexes,[59] whereas granulocyte peroxides can inactivate α_1-antitrypsin.[82] Conversely, the hemostatic mechanism affects inflammation. Chemotaxis of leukocytes is induced by fibrinopeptide B[51] and platelet factor 4.[72] Platelet factor 4 also stimulates elastase from leukocytes.[83] Permeability is increased by platelet cationic protein.[84] Platelets also possess F_c receptors and initiate complement complex formation, a process that may enhance platelet coagulant activity.[85] One complement component complexes with vitamin yet another K-dependent protein S.[86]

Thus, the blood vessels, platelets, clotting factors, and fibrinolytic components and inhibitors interact physiologically and pathologically in a variety of ways in order to promote and limit normal hemostasis. Alterations of any of the various components lead to bleeding disorders or thrombotic diseases.

6

THROMBUS FORMATION, DETECTION, AND RESOLUTION

A thrombus is a blood-derived mass formed on endovascular or endocardial surfaces. It probably represents an excessive response of the hemostatic mechanism to altered vascular surfaces under variable flow conditions. Thrombi may occur anywhere in the circulation, in arteries, veins, capillaries, or chambers of the heart. The thrombus may occlude a blood vessel, causing ischemia or infarction, or a thrombus may be adherent to one side of the vessel or heart chamber, allowing blood to flow past its free borders (mural thrombus). Thrombi may embolize downstream, to occlude vessels distally. It is unusual for an occlusive thrombus to form in a larger artery; occlusive thrombi tend to form in medium-sized, stenosed arteries or smaller vessels in the microcirculation. Occlusive thrombi form more readily in veins. Thrombotic and thromboembolic vascular occlusion play important roles in the pathogenesis of heart attacks and strokes, and are, therefore, important causes of morbidity and mortality in Western man.[87,88]

THROMBOGENESIS

Whereas normal endothelium is nonreactive with circulating blood, vascular damage initiates activation of platelets and the coagulation cascade that is fundamental to thrombus formation. Three major factors determine the site and extent of a thrombus: (1) mechanical effects in which blood flow is predominant; (2) alterations in the constituents of the blood; and (3) changes in the vessel wall (Virchow's triad). It is the interaction among these three factors that determines the kind of thrombus that forms within the vascular compartment. For example, vessel injury in a vein with slowed or arrested blood flow will usually lead to a thrombus that is rich in fibrin and red blood cells ("red thrombus"). Conversely, a thrombus that forms in the arterial circulation where flow is relatively undisturbed will consist primarily of platelets and some fibrin ("white thrombus").

Blood Flow. The structure and localization of thrombi are profoundly influenced by blood flow. In normal vessels, blood flows with a characteristic streaming pattern (so-called "laminar flow"). This pattern reflects the tendency of the blood to flow in concentric cylindrical layers with the innermost stream moving most rapidly and each successive layer moving more slowly, out to the vessel wall where flow is minimal. The cellular components of the circulating blood are mutually repelled by their electric charges, remaining separate from one another and from the endothelial lining. Of particular importance in laminar flow is the effect of red cells that tend to occupy the central portion of the lumen and selectively displace platelets towards the vascular surface.[89] Because velocity in the vortex is minimal close to the vessel wall, formed elements have little tendency for inward radial migration, thus increasing the likelihood that a platelet mass once formed will adhere to the wall. Irregularities in arterial walls produce a turbulent flow pattern that promotes thrombus formation.[90] Platelets collide in such areas of disturbed flow, especially with vortex flow patterns. When flow is arrested by an occlusive thrombus in an artery, clotting of blood distal and proximal to the occlusion in stagnant, interrupted flow areas gives rise to an extension of "red" thrombus from the initial occluding "white" thrombus.

Another important effect of flow in relation to the vessel wall is that areas of altered flow may concentrate agents that damage endothelium.[91]

In arteries, another effect of blood flow is to limit size of thrombi. When a thrombus grows and interacts with flowing blood, platelets on the surface will tend to be dislodged because of the shear effects of flow. In situations in which flow is not slowed or arrested, the stimuli that cause platelet aggregate formation and activation of coagulation will be rapidly diluted by the flowing blood. Thus, it is difficult for an occlusive thrombus to form except at sites where blood flow is disturbed or arrested.

In veins, thrombi tend to be initiated in valve pockets and at points of maximum stasis in relatively stagnant channels. Some venous thrombi may begin as platelet aggregates in the pockets of vein valves or in the intramuscular venous sinuses of the leg veins.[92] Stasis coupled with vascular injury is known to be an important factor in causing the formation of venous thrombi. Because of the sluggish blood flow in veins, the activation of coagulation can lead to extensive fibrin formation, with trapped red cells producing characteristic red thrombi.

Alterations in the Blood. Platelets and coagulation factors become activated by thrombogenic endovascular surfaces or by the massive entry of activators into the blood stream. These activated species may circulate temporarily in a partially or fully activated state, and the activated constituents may contribute directly to the development of thrombosis, especially in association with stasis.[91] Under some conditions, the clinical presentation is that of intravascular coagulation (DIC), rather than thrombosis.

Clinical thrombosis or DIC may follow the entry of some activators of coagulation into the blood stream. Examples of such associations include acute severe brain trauma (brain thromboplastin), infusion of concentrates of vitamin K-dependent factors (activated serine proteases), neoplasms (release of breakdown or secretory products), bacteremia (monocyte and neutrophil-derived tissue thromboplastin), and some snake venoms.

Defects in the mechanisms that inhibit or remove activated factors from blood may also contribute to the risk and extent of thrombosis. To illustrate, familial partial deficiency of the serine protease inhibitor, antithrombin III, carries a high risk of recurrent venous thrombosis. Likewise, recurrent thrombophlebitis and pulmonary embolism are associated with hereditary deficiency of protein C (which in its activated form limits activation of the coagulation process by destroying factors V and VIII).

Increased clinical thrombosis is also associated with a decrease in plasma fibrinolytic activity because of impaired generation of activators of plasminogen, deficiency of or defective plasminogen, or increased levels of inhibitors to plasmin or its formation. For example, a hereditary excess of antiplasmin or presence of dysfunctional plasminogen are associated with increased frequency of thrombosis. These conditions are discussed in Chapter 12.

Vascular Injury. When the subendothelium of a vessel is exposed, platelets adhere to the microfibrils, basement membrane, and collagen.[3,15] Collagen is capable of inducing the synthesis of platelet thromboxane A_2 and the release of dense granule contents (ADP), together with activation of the coagulation cascade, through both the intrinsic system (by collagen and endothelial-derived enzymic activation of the contact phase), to produce thrombin. Thrombin converts fibrinogen to fibrin and induces fibrin and thrombus stabilization by activation of factor XIII. Phospholipid on the surface of platelets profoundly accelerates the reactions leading to the formation of thrombin, so that thrombin can be generated at a rate faster than its neutralization by antithrombin III. Moreover, the reactions that occur on the surface of the platelets are not easily inhibited by the natural anticoagulants in blood. Within hours the denuded vascular surface loses much of its capacity to activate platelets and coagulation owing to changes in the properties of the denuded vascular surface, perhaps by the action of plasma or blood cell-derived enzymes.[15]

Vascular injury is fundamental in determining location and extent of thrombus formation. Some of the mechanisms underlying endothelial denudation have been identified and include: (1) mechanical, (2) immunologic, (3) chemical, and (4) infectious processes.[3]

Mechanical injury that results in thrombosis is illustrated by the direct vascular injury associated with trauma or surgery, thermal injury, vascular instrumentation by needles or catheters, and possibly acute hypertension. Very high shear can also cause endothelial injury. It is possible that in larger arteries with marked stenosis, the shear at the stenosis might be sufficiently high to dislodge the endothelium, particularly in a diseased vessel in which the adherence of the endothelium to the wall may be compromised.[87,89]

Endothelial cells may be injured by specific antibodies against them, or by sensitized lymphocytes. Circulating immune complexes also cause injury, which tends to be localized to regions of disturbed blood flow. Products of tobacco smoking have been postulated to injure endothelial cells through immune mechanisms. It has been proposed that IgE-mediated response to an antigen in cigarette smoke may be causally related to the development of vascular injury in hypersensitive smokers.[93]

Chemical endothelial injury has been described for hyperlipidemia, homocystinemia, bile salts, radiologic contrast dyes, and some chemotherapeutic agents.[3] In addition, under anoxic conditions, gaps form between endothelial cells, the cells swell, and platelets are deposited.[94]

Thrombi form in the microcirculation with some bacterial infections, particularly with Gram-negative bacteria. Intravascular platelet aggregates can also be produced directly by bacteria. Endotoxin can interact with the leukocytes and platelets, damage the endothelium, and activate the coagulation pathway. The lipid A-rich bacterial polysaccharide from Gram-negative bacteria causes platelet aggregation in the presence of immune complexes or aggregated IgG.[95] With human platelets, the lipopolysaccharide interaction with platelets is believed to be independent of the complement pathway. Endotoxin may also activate the coagulation system, either through activation of factor XII, or through leukocytes.[96] Although the relative importance of the contributions of leukocytes and platelets to endothelial injury has not been fully established, activation of the complement pathway causes the formation of $C5_a$, which promotes leukocyte adherence to the endothelium and detachment of endothelium through the granular release of neutral proteases and oxygen radicals at the injured sites. Viruses and microtatabiotes have also been proposed to injure endothelial cells directly.[87]

TURNOVER OF A THROMBUS

Studies of thrombus formation have shown that when the vessel wall is injured, a platelet-rich thrombus forms rapidly and undergoes episodes of dissolution and reformation. The constituents comprising permanent thrombi turn over. For example, as fibrin and platelets are lost from experimental pulmonary emboli through fibrinolysis, new fibrin and platelets are laid down through activation adjacent to the embolus. Fibrin continues to be laid down in coronary artery thrombi in man several hours after initiation of the thrombus. Experimentally, the most rapid removal of such an embolus can be achieved with a combination of heparin and activators of the fibrinolytic mechanism.[87,88]

The distinctions between arterial and venous thrombogenesis are illustrated by kinetic studies using labeled platelets and fibrinogen (Fig. 20). In patients with ongoing arterial thromboembolism, the principal role of platelets in the thrombotic process is reflected as isolated platelet consumption, that is, shortened platelet survival and increased platelet turnover. Circulating fibrinogen is not detectably consumed in this setting, presumably because procoagulant material is swept away from the thrombogenic focus by the rapid arterial flow before coagulation becomes fully activated. Ongoing venous thrombosis is manifest kinetically as consumption of both platelets and fibrinogen at equivalent rates, since it reflects fibrin extension under static or low shear flow conditions.[37,97]

The composition of the thrombus has important therapeutic implications, that is, fibrin formation in venous thrombosis is most effectively inhibited by anticoagulants such as heparin or warfarin, whereas some arterial thrombi may be prevented by agents that modify platelet behavior. Antithrombotic agents will be discussed in Chapter 13.

The fate of a thrombus also depends on its nature and site. In an arterial thrombus, platelet deposits undergo changes of cell disruption and lysis such that the platelet mass becomes changed morphologically to a "fibrin" thrombus within 12 to 24 hours. The thrombus is also invaded by polymorphonuclear leukocytes and mononuclear cells, perhaps through the chemotactic effects of fibrinopeptide B and platelet factor 4.[51,72] These cells phagocytize cellular debris. Thus after two to three days, the amount of fibrin is markedly reduced and phagocytic cells are present in increasing numbers. By four to seven days the margins of the thrombus are covered with endothelium, and may show the appearance of elongated smooth muscle cells. Thereafter, the amount of fibrin is further reduced and there is evidence of collagen and elastin formation. A week or so later, the initial platelet mass has organized into a thickening of the arterial intima, rich in collagen, smooth muscle cells, and elastic fibers, that is, a nonspecific intimal lesion. The intimal migration and proliferation of smooth muscle cells may be mediated by the platelet-derived growth factor released from platelet α-granules.[98]

When smaller vessels are injured, the platelet mass formed at the site of damage readily builds up and breaks down. The mass may be so unstable that it fragments before sufficient fibrin accumulates to stabilize it, or alternatively, fibrin may be digested through fibrinolytic activity, leading to fragmentation of the thrombus. These processes may proceed simultaneously; the sequence in any given instance depends on whether factors leading to the growth and persistence of the thrombus overcome those causing its disruption. The microcirculation could be obstructed by thrombosis or thromboembolic processes involving at least three mechanisms: (1) embolic material derived from mural thrombi in larger proximal arteries; (2) intravascular stimuli that cause platelet aggregation; and (3) direct injury to the endothelium in the microcirculation.

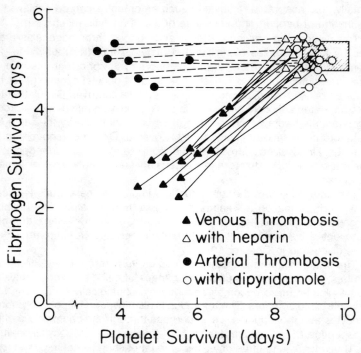

FIGURE 20. Platelet and fibrinogen kinetics. Patients with venous and arterial thrombosis had their ^{51}Cr-platelet and ^{125}I-fibrinogen survivals simultaneously measured. Arterial thrombosis is characterized by selective platelet utilization that is interrupted by dipyridamole, but not heparin, whereas venous thrombosis involves combined and equivalent platelet and fibrinogen consumption that is blocked by heparin, but not by dipyridamole. The results in normal subjects are shown by the hatched area (mean $\pm$ 2 SD).

An example of embolic phenomena affecting the microcirculation involves mural thrombi in diseased carotid arteries which release embolic fragments of platelet aggregates or platelet-fibrin emboli into the microcirculation of the eye and the brain. These can be seen passing through the microcirculation of the retina, associated with transient disturbances in vision. It is believed that such aggregates in the microcirculation of the brain can cause transient attacks of cerebral ischemia. Such aggregates might release thromboxane A_2, which could cause vasoconstriction of the microcirculation and impair the passage of the emboli through it. Evidence in man about this process causing obstruction of the microcirculation in other organs comes from postmortem studies indicating that some chronic nephrosclerosis in older humans is caused by embolic material passing into the renal circulation from mural thrombi in the aorta proximal to the renal arteries. In addition, platelet emboli in the microcirculation may be a cause of some instances of the sudden death seen in humans with advanced coronary artery atherosclerosis.

DETECTION OF ONGOING THROMBOSIS AND THROMBOEMBOLISM

Since activation of the coagulation mechanism and the fibrinolytic pathway leads to changes in plasma proteins, numerous approaches have been developed to detect activated clotting factors and fragments of fibrinogen or fibrin in blood as an indication that thromboembolic processes are occurring.[87,99] In venous thrombosis it is possible to detect increased activity of clotting factors in the plasma and fibrinopeptides which are cleavage products of the action of thrombin on fibrinogen.[100] Degradation products of fibrinogen and fibrin formed by activation of plasminogen have been found in the plasma of patients with clinical evidence of thromboembolic processes.[62]

Attempts to detect altered platelets during thromboembolism have followed three main lines of study. These approaches include detection of hypersensitive platelets in terms of platelet aggregation and the release reaction,[87] changes in platelet survival,[37] and the detection of products released from platelets such as β-thromboglobulin and platelet factor 4.[27] The involvement of the platelet release reaction in thromboembolic processes has been shown by the increased levels of platelet factor 4 and β-thromboglobulin in the plasma of some individuals during what appear to be thromboembolic episodes.

Decreased platelet survival has been shown to correlate with clinical manifestations of arterial disease.[37] The mechanisms responsible for shortened platelet survival appear to be related to the factors involved in thrombosis and loss of the endothelium.

However, our ability to detect individuals predisposed to clinical thrombosis is limited at present. Despite the large number of blood tests that have been proposed, few of these are predictive or practical. Moreover, those tests that may be useful for identifying risk of venous thrombosis have little or no predictive value in individual patients with arterial thrombosis and vice versa.

Certain clinical and pathophysiologic states have been associated with an increased frequency of arterial or venous thrombosis (see Chapter 12). Unfortunately, the relative importance of these various risk factors and their interactions remains unclear.

RELATIONSHIP OF THROMBOGENESIS TO ATHEROSCLEROSIS

Injury to the endothelium is postulated to play an important part in atherogenesis.[3,98] Platelet adhesion and release of a platelet-derived growth factor at sites of endothelial denudation may mediate in part the migration of smooth muscle cells from media to the intima, stimulating the proliferation of intimal smooth muscle cells to form new connective tissue by these cells. In injury resulting from chronic hyperlipoproteinemia, lipids deposit within the cells and in the extracellular material. If the injury is a single event, the lesions may be reversible, whereas chronic or repeated injury over an extended period may result in progressive lesion formation and, ultimately, mature atherosclerotic disease. The platelet-derived growth factor is mitogenic for smooth muscle cells and fibroblasts, but not endothelial cells. The growth factor does not appear to be present in plasma in significant amounts unless the platelets have undergone the release reaction. Thus, the localized release of this material when platelets adhere to subendothelial connective tissue may be an important factor in smooth muscle cell migration into the intima and proliferation in response to endothelial injury.

The macrophage and the endothelial cell itself may represent alternative or additional sources of mitogens that also stimulate smooth muscle cell proliferation.[98] Hence, the endothelium might stimulate the underlying smooth muscle cells directly to proliferate in the absence of endothelial denudation. Experimentally, endothelial desquamation and intimal lesion formation have been induced mechanically by surgical procedures, chronic indwelling cannulae, or intra-arterial balloon catheters; chemically by chronic homocysteinemia; immunologically by humoral or cell-mediated mechanisms; or by diet-induced chronic hyperlipidemia.

PART 2
CLINICAL BLEEDING DISORDERS

Excessive bleeding caused by alterations of any of the hemostatic components can be massive following vessel disruption by trauma, surgery, penetrating ulcers, or spontaneous hemorrhages in the presence of severe thrombocytopenia or factor deficiency. Problems of recognition occur when bleeding from surgery, trauma, or other lesions is aggravated by a mild hemostatic defect. In the latter, more subtle situations, proper diagnosis and use of blood component therapy are also important to achieve hemostasis. Milder defects occur much more commonly than is usually appreciated. Whereas mild, inherited disorders are infrequently encountered, when they do occur a high index of suspicion and accurate diagnostic evaluation are needed. In patients who are being massively transfused, whether for bleeding associated with cardiovascular surgery or severe trauma, it is important to screen whenever possible for pre-existing or developing defects.

This section deals with the practical approach to bleeding disorders and the appropriate use of screening tests, followed by specific disorders of platelets and coagulation factors. Emphasis is placed upon recognition, specific diagnosis, and treatment.

7

APPROACH TO BLEEDING DISORDERS

Since hemostatic competence is frequently questioned in clinical medicine, the initial evaluation is designed to establish the presence or absence of any measurable inadequacy of the hemostatic components. The history and physical examination often suggest the presence of a bleeding disorder, but laboratory testing is essential to establish the nature of the defect.

CLINICAL ASSESSMENT

A thoughtful, careful history provides critical information in focusing subsequent investigation.[101,102] The historical evaluation should establish: (1) the type of bleeding present (petechiae, purpura, ecchymosis, single or generalized bleeding sites); (2) the course or pattern of bleeding (spontaneous or post-injury onset, frequency, short-term or life-long duration, severity); (3) family history of bleeding, and if positive, whether X-linked, autosomal dominant, or recessive inheritance pattern; (4) previous or current therapy (drugs, e.g., aspirin, coumarins, cancer chemotherapy, immunizations, transfusions); and (5) local or systemic associated diseases (such as leukemia, uremia, liver disease, infections, malignancy). When obtaining the patient's history one should take into consideration the many challenges to the hemostatic mechanism that occur, since such episodes may be a more significant test of hemostasis than any laboratory determination. Because some bleeding always accompanies tissue

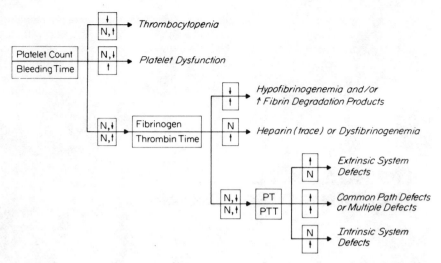

FIGURE 21. Strategy for use of hemostatic screening test. Hemostatic defects reflect platelet, or late or early stage factor disorders. Quantitative and functional abnormalities of platelets are the first consideration owing to the importance of plug formation in initial hemostasis. For factor defects, the late stage is considered first, since a low fibrinogen can prolong all other kinetic tests. Combined defects include thrombocytopenia with hypofibrinogenemia (disseminated intravascular coagulation), platelet dysfunction with an intrinsic factor defect (von Willebrand disease) and a prolonged thrombin time with either multiple other defects (liver disease), or delayed intrinsic clotting (therapeutic heparinization). It should also be noted that clot stabilization is not assessed in this scheme, and that inhibition, particularly of the intrinsic system, needs to be considered by repeating the PTT with a 1:1 mix of patient and normal plasmas (from Thompson,[102] with permission).

disruption, the important question to be answered is whether the bleeding has been out of proportion to the injury. Specific inquiry should be made about circumcision, tooth extraction, menstruation, severe trauma, operative procedures, blood transfusions, and iron deficiency anemia. For example, prolonged or delayed bleeding is characteristic of many coagulation defects. This feature may cause both patient and physician to underestimate initially the severity of the bleeding episode.

On *physical examination,* the type of bleeding may suggest its cause. Petechial or purpuric bleeding occurs with platelet and vascular abnormalities. Petechiae due to vasculitis are often palpably elevated as a result of an associated increase in capillary permeability. Petechial lesions of severe thrombocytopenia are not elevated and, while often widespread, they may first appear over the ankles or submucosally. Minor cuts bleed for a long time in patients with platelet disorders because platelet plugs do not form. Mucosal, renal, and gastrointestinal bleeding are common in thrombocytopenia and are also seen in the more generalized vascular purpuras.[103]

Widespread ecchymotic bleeding (from veins), with or without bleeding from the gastrointestinal and urinary tracts, is most often associated with acquired coagulation defects. Single large bleeding episodes (arteriolar) into the joints are characteristic of congenital coagulation defects, especially deficiencies of factors VIII and IX. Residual joint deformities from old hemarthroses may also be present. Other physical findings with possible hemostatic relevance include splenomegaly, lymphodenopathy, and signs of hepatic failure.

LABORATORY SCREENING TESTS

Despite the leads derived from the clinical examination, diagnosing the type of hemostatic incompetence ultimately depends on laboratory testing (Fig. 21). A battery of tests is used as a screen for hemostatic defects.[102,104] Platelet plug formation reflects the primary hemostatic event and is evaluated by the bleeding time and the platelet count. Abnormalities of coagulation are then screened for by measuring the fibrinogen concentration, thrombin time, prothrombin time, and partial thromboplastin time. The presence of factor XIII is screened for by a separate procedure. One must be suspicious of sample or laboratory errors if the results are inconsistent within themselves or with the clinical situation. In addition, if the history is particularly striking, and screening tests are normal, consultation and further studies may well demonstrate a mild defect. Details of the screening tests and their limitations are presented in Appendix A. Once screening tests have indicated the type of disorder, additional studies and factor assays are used to establish a specific diagnosis. Uncommonly, vascular disorders[103,105] or emotional factors[106] may contribute to abnormal bleeding or purpura.

SCREENING FOR PLATELET ABNORMALITIES

Incompetence of platelet plug formation is detected by prolongation of the template bleeding time. Since the defect may be qualitative or quantitative, an assessment of platelet number is also included in the preliminary evaluation.

The standard template bleeding time assesses the overall hemostatic role of platelets in vivo (Fig. 22). The bleeding time in normal subjects is 5.0 ± 1.5 min. Platelet plug formation appears to be unimpaired when there are normal platelets with a concentration of 100,000 per μl or more of blood. Below this level, bleeding increases linearly with decreases in platelet count according to the formula:

$$\text{bleeding time (min)} = 30 - \frac{\text{platelet count per } \mu l}{4000}$$

The relationship does not apply below a level of 10,000 platelet per μl. Disproportionate prolongation reflects platelet dysfunction, while bleeding times

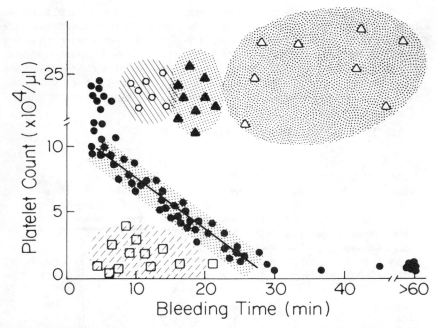

FIGURE 22. Relationship of bleeding time to platelet count. The bleeding time is inversely related to circulating platelet count in patients with thrombocytopenia owing to decreased production *(closed circles,* which also include 8 normal subjects) when the count is between 100,000 per μl and 10,000 per μl. Platelet function defects are represented by subjects taking aspirin *(open circles)* and patients with uremia *(closed triangles)* and inherited severe von Willebrand disease *(open triangles).* Many patients with idiopathic thrombocytopenic purpura have platelets with increased hemostatic competence *(open squares).*

shorter than predicted indicate platelets with increased hemostatic competence (see Fig. 22).

Thrombocytopenia (fewer than 100,000 platelets per μl) is the most common cause of ~~serious bleeding~~. The resultant impairment in primary hemostatic plug formation is evident from the inverse relationship of the count to the bleeding time; correlation with the platelet concentration is important to determine specific platelet functional activity. A preliminary estimate of the platelet count can be determined from the blood film, but more precise measurements are needed. These include particle enumeration, and, for counts below 50,000 μl, phase microscopy.

The blood film may show abnormalities of other blood cells reflecting a common underlying etiology. For example, widespread vasculitis may cause consumptive platelet destruction and fragmented red cells, while vitamin B_{12} or folate deficiency is associated with red cell macro-ovalocytes and poikilocytes.

Concomitant granulocytopenia and thrombocytopenia can occur in lupus erythematosus, or as part of a pancytopenic marrow depression from drugs or neoplastic infiltration. Marrow disruption by invading tumor may be manifest by the appearance of nucleated red cells in peripheral blood. Lymphoproliferative disorders with increased circulating lymphocytes or lymphadenopathy may be accompanied by immune thrombocytopenia or marrow replacement. Replacement of marrow by myeloid leukemic cells causes thrombocytopenia in association with immature myeloid forms on blood film.

Bone marrow examination provides additional insight into the thrombocytopenic process. A normally functioning marrow responds to thrombocytopenia by compensatory increases in megakaryocyte number, size, cytoplasmic maturation, and release, with a shift to cytologically immature megakaryocytes. Ineffective thrombocytopoiesis represents an exception, showing increased megakaryocytopoiesis without delivery of viable platelets to the blood. Reduced thrombocytopiesis is verified by finding decreased numbers of megakaryocytes, which is most often associated with intrinsic marrow disease. Increased numbers are seen with ineffective production or increased destruction.

Antibody tests may be helpful to establish an immune mechanism in the remaining patients with increased destruction. Besides the established tests to confirm the presence of drug-related antibodies and alloantibodies, more sensitive tests of autoantibodies have been developed.

Platelet dysfunction is defined as a long bleeding time with platelet count greater than 100,000 per μl. It is usually acquired and reversible as part of an associated disease or drug therapy. A functional abnormality superimposed on thrombocytopenia manifests as an inappropriately prolonged bleeding time for the degree of thrombocytopenia. Further characterization of acute acquired dysfunction may be difficult; the nature of the defect is usually evident from the associated clinical setting. Serial monitoring of the bleeding time may be helpful to indicate when platelet transfusion therapy is required or successful. Hereditary functional defects need additional testing of platelet function in order to establish a specific diagnosis. These tests include: (1) in vitro platelet aggregation induced by ADP, collagen, epinephrine, thrombin, and ristocetin; (2) factor VIII/coagulant and factor VIII/vWF antigen activity; (3) platelet coagulant activity; (4) dense-granule content of ADP and ATP and the capacity for release; (5) α-granule contents of platelet factor 4 and β-thromboglobulin; and (6) electron microscopy.

SCREENING FOR COAGULATION ABNORMALITIES

Three overlapping test systems are selected to assess the overall competence of the coagulation process. These include the conversion of fibrinogen to fibrin and tests of extrinsic and intrinsic coagulation. Abnormalities are determined as prolongations of the clotting times beyond normal when compared with a pool of plasma from normal donors. Abnormal tests are repeated with an equal mixture of patient and normal plasma (1:1 mix) to differentiate clotting factor deficiency from inhibition. Prolonged clotting times owing to factor deficiency are completely corrected to the normal range by the addition of an equal volume of normal plasma. In contrast, abnormal clotting times owing to factor inhibition show little if any correction by normal plasma. In addition to tests in Figure 21, two other screening tests and factor assays are discussed below.

Fibrinogen. For routine screening, the functional level of fibrinogen is measured kinetically. Normal values are 250 $\pm$ 50 mg per dl. Concentrations below 100 mg per dl may significantly limit fibrin formation. Partially clotted samples give low values. Since all clotting screening tests depend upon this reaction to provide an end point (whether visible or physical-chemical), fibrinogen levels below 80 mg per dl prolong the clotting time of the other clotting tests, making their results uninterpretable. In the presence of large amounts of fibrin(ogen) degradation products, a falsely low level of fibrinogen will be observed. The absolute level of fibrinogen can be determined by nonkinetic, total clottable protein tests (see Appendix A). The protein tests are also helpful in that they give normal values in dysfibrinogenemia.

Thrombin time. This test is performed like the functional (kinetic) fibrinogen test by adding exogenous thrombin to the patient's plasma. The thrombin time differs from the fibrinogen screen in that the limiting factor is enzyme, rather than substrate. Normal plasma should have a thrombin time of 18 to 25 seconds. The thrombin time is most useful to screen for heparin contamination, which can occur when a sample is drawn from cannulae (such as arterial lines) that has been previously flushed with a dilute heparin solution. The thrombin time will also be prolonged by fibrin(ogen) degradation products, congenital or acquired dysfibrinogenemia, or severe hypofibrinogenemia, and is used to monitor thrombolytic therapy.

Prothrombin Time (PT). This test screens the extrinsic system, as it involves a tissue activator that is normally "extrinsic" to the circulation. It will be prolonged by decreased levels of factor VII as well as those in the common path (factors X, V, prothrombin, and fibrinogen). Values in normal plasma usually average 12 to 14 seconds. Isolated prolongation of this screening test reflects factor VII deficiency as a rare congenital state or an early acquired production defect in which related factors are not yet significantly depressed. Extrinsic system tests are used to monitor oral anticoagulant dosage and are the most sensitive measurement of decreased synthesis in severe liver disease.

Partial Thromboplastin Time (PTT). The PTT measures intrinsic coagulation factors (XII, XI, IX, and VIII) and factors of the common path. The term "partial thromboplastin" refers to the addition of phospholipid without tissue factor. It is also referred to as an "activated" PTT to indicate addition of a

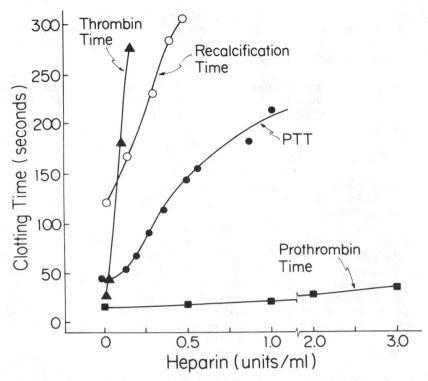

FIGURE 23. Effect of heparin on coagulation screening tests. Dilutions of heparin were added to normal plasma and the screening tests performed (see Appendix A). Note the extreme sensitivity of the thrombin time compared with the relative insensitivity of the prothrombin time. Intrinsic system tests average around twice prolonged at therapeutic levels (0.2 to 0.5 U per ml) of the anticoagulant when performed as indicated in Appendix A. (Henderson, RA, Counts, RB, with permission.)

contact-active, negatively charged surface such as kaolin or ellagic acid. Normal values average 35 to 42 seconds. Greater than 10 seconds of prolongation is abnormal for most of the PTT reagents and should represent the point at which a 30 percent level or less of a given factor is present. Sensitivity of this test is highly variable from laboratory to laboratory and among different reagents. A simplification of this test is the whole blood recalcification time. Intrinsic system tests are most commonly affected when a circulating anticoagulant (inhibitor) or congenital factor deficiency is present. After a 1:1 mix of patient and normal plasma, the PTT usually remains prolonged when inhibitors are present and corrects for simple deficiency. By virtue of their intermediate sensitivity to heparin (Fig. 23), the intrinsic system tests are commonly used to monitor the therapeutic effect of this anticoagulant.

Factor XIII. A separate screening test for the fibrin-stabilizing factor is required since this enzyme acts at a step after fibrin polymerization. Despite its rarity, deficiency can easily be checked by determining if a clot is soluble in urea on overnight incubation.

Fibrin(ogen) Degradation Products (FDP). Routine tests are semiquantitative and are performed by slide agglutination. All normal individuals manifest weakly positive results, and stronger reactions are seen in many patients with liver disease or disseminated intravascular coagulation, or both. The limited clinical utility of these tests will be discussed under disseminated intravascular coagulation in Chapter 11.

Specific Assays. If definite abnormalities are present in the screening tests, or if clinical suspicion is high, specific factor assays are usually required. Factor and inhibitor assays are difficult to perform because of the care required in preparation of reagents and execution of the procedures. Reliable results are obtainable only from laboratories that perform these tests regularly. Factor assays are based upon either the extrinsic (prothrombin time) or intrinsic (partial thromboplastin time) activation conditions in which dilutions of the patient plasma are added to a known deficient substrate plasma. Such substrates are usually obtained from patients with severe congenital deficiency. The capacity of the test plasma to correct the prolonged clotting time of the known deficient plasma is compared with the effect of dilutions of normal plasma on the same deficient substrate plasma. Results are expressed as a percentage of the normal result or the equivalent number as units per deciliter.

8
QUANTITATIVE PLATELET DISORDERS

Alterations in the platelet concentration of circulating blood affect the hemostatic, thrombotic, and repair functions of the platelet. Mechanisms underlying thrombocytopenia include disturbances of platelet production, distribution and dilution, or destruction (Table 3). Thrombocytosis is either reactive or autonomous. This chapter outlines the general approach to quantitative platelet defects. Recognition of thrombocytopenia is followed by a discussion of the thrombocytopenic disorders[35] and platelet transfusion therapy. The chapter concludes with a consideration of thrombocytosis.

THROMBOCYTOPENIA

Clinical Approach To Thrombocytopenia

The sequence for evaluating the patient with severe thrombocytopenia includes: (1) history and physical examination; (2) platelet count and blood film evaluation; (3) bleeding time; (4) coagulation tests; (5) bone marrow examination; and (6) trial transfusion of platelets with follow-up serial platelet counts. The hallmark of thrombocytopenic bleeding is the appearance of petechiae, and a search should be made for these lesions on exposed and easily traumatized areas. On physical examination special attention to the oral mucosal and ankles for petechiae, a search for adenopathy and organomegaly, and a rectal examination with stool guaiac test should be included. A complete blood

TABLE 3. Thrombocytopenia

MECHANISM	SPECIFIC DISORDERS
Disorders of production Megaryocytic hypoplasia	Congenital (Fanconi's anemia, TAR syndrome, intrauterine drugs or infection) Acquired (radiation, chemicals and drugs, alcohol, insecticides, infections, lupus erythematosus, heroin, idiopathic aplasia, neoplastic or fibrotic marrow replacement)
Ineffective production	Hereditary (autosomal or sex-linked types, May-Hegglin anomaly, Wiscott-Aldrich syndrome) Acquired (vitamin B_{12} or folate deficiency, Di Guglielmo's syndrome paraxysmal nocturnal hemoglobinuria, preleukemia)
Disorders of distribution or dilution	Splenic pooling (congestive, infiltrative, or imflammatory splenomegaly) Vascular pooling (hypothermia) Dilution (massive transfusion)
Disorders of destruction	Combined consumption of DIC (snake venoms, tissue injury, obstetrical complications, neoplasms, infections, intravascular hemolysis) Isolated platelet consumption (thrombotic thrombocytopenic purpura, hemolytic-uremic syndrome, purpura fulminans, vasculitis, prosthetic valvular or vascular devices) Immune platelet destruction (autoimmune disorders, post-transfusion and isoimmune neonatal purpuras, drugs, infection and solid tumor induced antibodies)
Multiple disorders	Decreased production and increased destruction (lymphoproliferative and other malignancies, infections) Increased pooling and destruction (lupus erythematosus, cardiopulmonary bypass surgery) Decreased and ineffective production with increased splenic pooling and destruction (alcoholic liver disease)

count, including a platelet count and blood film examination comprise the initial screening evaluation. It is important to confirm low platelet counts by examining a well-prepared blood film. In addition, platelet size and shape should be noted.

The template bleeding time is an important bedside test in the initial assessment of thrombocytopenia, since bleeding times may be longer or shorter than predicted, indicating platelet disfunction or increased hemostatic competence respectively. A bone marrow examination is usually required to assess production. Marrow biopsy is needed to accurately determine megakaryocyte number and size. Abundant megakaryocytes in the presence of thrombocytopenia implicates either platelet destruction or ineffective production as the underlying pathophysiologic mechanism. Coagulation screening tests may be necessary to distinguish combined platelet and fibrinogen consumption from isolated platelet consumption. Platelet survival studies may be needed to establish the presence of ineffective production. Useful information regarding platelet viability may be obtained in patients without platelet alloantibodies by transfusing a pool of platelet concentrates and following their disappearance using serial platelet counts. However, this approach exposes the patient to platelet antigens and occasionally to hepatitis viruses.

The clinical approach described will usually suffice to categorize provisionally the thrombocytopenia into at least one of the three major pathophysiologic categories—disorders of production, distribution, or destruction—and may specifically establish the diagnosis (see Table 3). In many centers, specific platelet antibody studies are now available to confirm the diagnosis of immune-mediated thrombocytopenia, although their sensitivites and specificities vary. Blood or marrow cultures, folate or vitamin B_{12} levels, cytogenetics, ultrastructural examination, and other tests may be necessary to clarify the specific disorder.

Disorders Of Production

Defective platelet production occurs when the number of viable platelets entering the circulation is less than expected from a normally functioning marrow. In this category platelet survival in the peripheral blood is relatively normal but platelet turnover is decreased.[37,107] Production, distribution, and survival parameters for quantitative disorders are represented schematically in Figure 24. Typical kinetic profiles appear in Table 4.

Decreased Megakaryocytopoiesis. Marrow hypoproliferation occurs secondary to marrow damage, marrow replacement, or intrinsic marrow abnormalities (see Table 3). Megakaryocyte size and ploidy are characteristically increased because of the thrombocytopenic stimulus, although the overall cytoplasmic mass is decreased (see Fig. 24). In addition to megakaryocytic hypoplasia, however, platelet survival may be somewhat shortened when thrombocytopenia is severe, perhaps through associated consumption.[108]

Congenital megakaryocytic hypoplasia is associated with the Fanconi's syndrome and its variants, congenital hypoplastic thrombocytopenia with absent radii (TAR syndrome), macrothrombocytopenia, congenital intrauterine rubella or other infections, and maternal administration of drugs such as the thiazides.

Marrow damage resulting in decreased marrow hematopoiesis, including reduced megakaryocytopoiesis as part of an overall marrow aplasia, is seen in relationship to drugs (cancer chemotherapy,[296] benzene, chloramphenicol), toxins, radiation, infections including hepatitis, thymoma, and unknown causes, that is, idiopathic aplastic anemia. In these settings, thrombocytopenia is seen

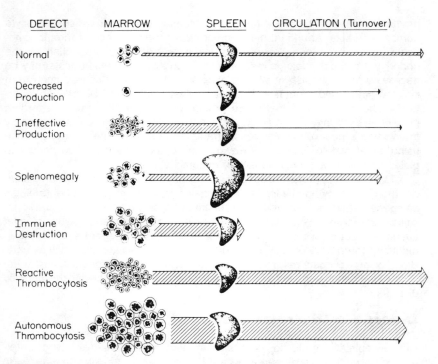

DEFECT	MARROW	SPLEEN	CIRCULATION (Turnover)

Normal

Decreased
Production

Ineffective
Production

Splenomegaly

Immune
Destruction

Reactive
Thrombocytosis

Autonomous
Thrombocytosis

FIGURE 24. Kinetic mechanisms underlying quantitative disorders of platelets. The relative number and volume of marrow megakaryocytes is depicted in the marrow column. The area of the hatched bar that follows represents the megakaryocytic substrate cytoplasm available for platelet formation. The size of the splenic pool is depicted by the size of the spleen. Platelet survival in the peripheral blood is shown by the length of the arrow in the circulation column. Platelet turnover is graphically displayed as the width of that arrow. These typical examples are profiled numerically in Table 4.

in association with cytopenias of other marrow-derived blood cells, although isolated thrombocytopenia may appear first. The mechanisms underlying marrow aplasia are not known.

Acquired *isolated megakaryocytic hypoplasia* has been reported following exposure to drugs, chemicals, insecticides, in association with systemic lupus erythematosus, or without a recognized cause. Recovery of such patients has been observed following long-term support with platelet transfusions. Selective megakaryocytic suppression may follow melphalan, thiazide diuretics, alcohol, or possibly estrogens.

Idiopathic aplastic anemia is a diagnosis of exclusion after the aforementioned associations are excluded. Nearly one half of the patients with aplastic anemia are classified as idiopathic.[109] One third of these patients are over age 60 and one quarter are under age 20. A bleeding diathesis is the most com-

TABLE 4. Typical kinetic profiles of patients with quantitative platelet disorders

CATEGORY	MEGAKARYOCYTES			PLATELETS			
	CELL NUMBER ($\times 10^6$/kg)	CYTOPLASMIC VOLUME (fl)	CYTOPLASMIC MASS ($\times 10^{11}$ fl/kg)	CONCENTRATION (plat/μl)	VOLUME (fl)	SURVIVAL (days)	MASS TURNOVER ($\times 10^5$ fl/μl/day)
Normal	15 ± 4	12,000 ± 1700	1.8 ± 0.4	250,000 ± 40,000	8.7 ± 0.8	9.6 ± 0.6	3.2 ± 0.5
Decreased megakaryocytopoiesis — damaged marrow	2	14,000	0.3	22,000	9.1	5.2	0.7
Ineffective production Autosomal dominant	49	9,400	4.6	64,000	8.9	8.4	1.1
Wiscott-Aldrich syndrome	20	9,000	1.8	40,000	4.0	5.0	0.4
Vitamin B$_{12}$ deficiency	51	8,900	4.5	62,000	8.5	8.4	0.8
Preleukemia	18	13,300	2.4	16,000	9.0	6.7	0.4
Splenic pooling	29	15,100	4.4	75,000	8.6	7.0	6.2
Immune destruction	41	19,000	7.8	15,000	9.9	0.1	14.0
Reactive thrombocytosis	90	8,900	8.1	1.2×10^6	8.0	9.0	15.1
Autonomous thrombocytosis	84	20,000	16.4	1.5×10^6	9.0	8.2	29.6

mon presenting symptom in aplastic anemia, with the platelet count usually less than 30,000. Both anemia and leukopenia are usually associated. One quarter of the patients die within four months of symptoms and only one third of the patients survive for five years. About 10 percent achieve complete remission with good supportive therapy.

Bone marrow transplantation is the treatment of choice for young patients with severe aplastic anemia who have a histocompatible sibling donor. Long-term survival can be expected in about 45 percent of patients who have received prior blood transfusions and up to 75 percent of those who have not.[109] Patients who are diagnosed as having aplastic anemia should have histocompatibility testing performed on their siblings and blood transfusions should be avoided if at all possible to prevent sensitization. Corticosteroids have no influence on the course of the aplastic anemia, and therefore should not be given. A randomized, prospective study showed that oral or intramuscular androgens have no benefit with respect to the time or rate of response, percentage of patients responding, median, or long-term survivor period in severe aplasia.[109]

Platelet transfusions are often required for severely thrombocytopenic patients who do not have a suitable marrow donor. Measurements of fecal blood loss in such patients suggest that prophylactic platelet transfusions should not be given when the platelet count remains above 5000 per μl, and that all nonessential medications should be avoided. When the platelet count falls below 5000 per μl, however, prophylactic platelet transfusions are usually required.[108]

Disorders associated with *marrow displacement* include: (1) metastatic carcinoma, (2) multiple myeloma, (3) leukemia or lymphoma, (4) myelofibrosis, and (5) less common disorders such as systemic histiocytosis, Gaucher disease, or osteopetrosis. Marrow replacement by abnormal cells or fibrosis may be only one of several processes involved in such a production abnormality. Other possibilities include the local formation of toxic substances that inhibit megakaryocytopoiesis, or interference with normal regulatory mechanisms of production. Diagnosis of these disorders is often suspected on the basis of a leukoerythroblastic blood film. Treatment of the underlying disorder may allow the megakaryocytes to repopulate.

Ineffective Platelet Production. Ineffective thrombocytopoiesis is characterized by increased marrow megakaryocytic substrate cytoplasm in association with decreased delivery of viable platelets to the circulation (Figs. 24 and 25). The defect may involve disordered platelet formation, abnormal marrow release of platelets, or intramedullary destruction of platelets. Ineffective platelet production is found in vitamin B_{12} and folate deficiencies, di Guglielmo syndrome, and most of the hereditary thrombocytopenias, and may herald impending leukemia.[37,108]

The *hereditary thrombocytopenia syndromes* characterized by ineffective platelet production include autosomal dominant thrombocytopenia, May-Hegglin anomaly, and Wiscott-Aldrich syndrome. There is an associated defect in endoreduplication of the megakaryocytes that is manifested as decreased

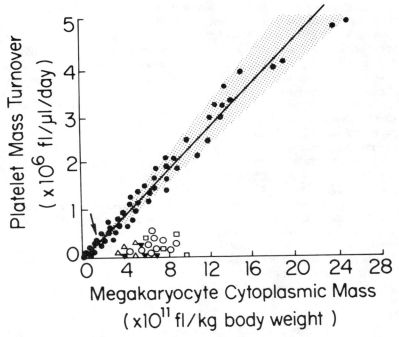

FIGURE 25. Ineffective platelet production. In thrombocytopenia, there is usually a direct relationship between marrow megakaryocyte cytoplasmic mass and the turnover of platelet mass in the peripheral blood. Platelet mass turnover represents the product of platelet turnover and mean platelet volume. Megakaryocyte cytoplasmic mass equals the mean megakaryocyte cytoplasmic volume multiplied by the total number of marrow megakaryocytes. The results in normal subjects are indicated by the *arrow*, and the *stippled area* represents 95 percent confidence limits in thrombocytopenic patients with effective production. Ineffective thrombocytopoiesis is identified as disparity between available marrow substrate (megakaryocyte cytoplasmic mass) and delivery of platelet mass to the peripheral blood (platelet mass turnover). Results in patients with autosomal dominant thrombocytopenia *(open circles)*, Wiscott-Aldrich syndrome *(open triangles)*, megaloblastosis *(open squares)*, and preleukemia *(closed triangles)*, are characterized by ineffective platelet production.

megakaryocytic ploidy and size compared with what should be expected for the platelet count (see Fig. 24 and Table 4). Although morphologic dyspoiesis is usually present, patients with ineffective thrombocytopoiesis may be mistakenly thought to have a disorder of destruction because of the pronounced marrow megakaryocytosis. Determination of the platelet survival time may be required to distinguish between destructive thrombocytopenia and ineffective platelet production.

In patients with autosomal dominant thrombocytopenia, platelet survival is relatively normal and there are abundant immature marrow megakaryocytes. Kindred with this disorder reveal about threefold increase in megakaryocyte cytoplasmic mass with a platelet turnover of one-third normal.[108] Other examples of hereditary thrombocytopenia with autosomal dominant transmission have been reported in association with nephritis, deafness, large platelets, and abnormal platelet function.[37]

The May-Hegglin anomaly is an autosomal dominant disorder in which all affected patients have Döhle bodies in their neutrophils and large platelets on peripheral blood film. Thrombocytopenia is present in about one third of these patients. In some patients megakaryocytes are increased in numbers and have abnormal ultrastructure. Most patients are asymptomatic, but bleeding times may be discordantly prolonged in some patients and associated with clinically significant bleeding.

The Wiscott-Aldrich syndrome is an X-linked hereditary disorder characterized by thrombocytopenia, eczema, and increased susceptibility to infection due to an immunologic deficiency. Platelet volumes and platelet survival are reduced to about half of normal.[110] The resultant platelet mass turnover is one quarter of normal, but is associated with normal marrow megakaryocytic cytoplasmic mass. The modestly reduced platelet survival does not explain the degree of thrombocytopenia. Thus, ineffective production is the major pathophysiologic defect. Variants of the syndrome consisting of sex-linked thrombocytopenia with failure to respond to microbial antigens and sex-linked thrombocytopenia have been reported. Other X-linked thrombocytopenias occur such as that associated with platelet dysfunction and a thalassemia-like picture, but it is not known to what extent production may be ineffective.

Ineffective thrombocytopoiesis is characteristic of *vitamin B₁₂ or folate deficiency*.[37,108] Marrow megakaryocyte mass is increased several fold and platelet turnover is greatly reduced, indicating that only about 10 percent of the platelet production expected from the available megakaryocytic cytoplasm actually occurs. Platelet survival is generally normal, although modestly decreased survival times have been reported in some patients, possibly related to alcohol ingestion. Different hematopoietic cell lines may be affected variably. Predominant impairment in megakaryocytes may occur with little identifiable alteration in megakaryocyte morphology. Patients respond to vitamin replacement within one to two weeks. In the bleeding alcoholic patient with thrombocytopenia, immediate parenteral administration of folate is indicated to optimize platelet production.

Disorders Of Distribution Or Dilution

Normally, the spleen sequesters one third of the circulating platelet mass in dynamic equilibrium with the circulation (see Fig. 9). With *splenomegaly*, pooling is proportionately increased. It is unusual, however, for the platelet count to fall below 50,000 per μl with splenomegaly alone, because platelet production usually increases in hypersplenic states (see Fig. 24 and Table 4). However, it rarely increases to more than two to three times basal production rates. Platelet survival is relatively normal.[37,108] Although there is no absolute correlation between spleen size and degree of thrombocytopenia, the absence of palpable splenomegaly rules out increased splenic pooling as a principal cause of thrombocytopenia. The significance of abnormal splenic pooling in a setting of complex thrombocytopenia can best be evaluated by platelet kinetic studies (see Table 4). Normally, about 65 percent of radiolabeled platelets can be recovered immediately after injection into the circulation, but in patients with splenomegaly, less than 30 percent recovery is usually observed. Treatment of thrombocytopenia secondary to splenic pooling is directed to the underlying disease. Since pooling alone does not usually lead to severe degrees of thrombocytopenia, splenectomy is rarely required.

Lowering of the body temperature to less than 25°C, as with *hypothermia* for cardiovascular surgery, results in a transient, modest thrombocytopenia in man secondary to platelet sequestration in the liver. There is also an associated transient defect in function that occurs with hypothermia.[112] Platelet count and function return to baseline values upon rewarming.

Treatment of massive blood loss by *transfusion* of large volumes of stored blood *dilutes* the platelet count progressively in proportion to the amount of blood given. This phenomenon is explained by the fact that stored blood contains platelets with severely impaired viability owing to the effects of the requirements for processing and storage temperature,[113] and by the fact that compensatory increases in endogenous platelet production do not occur acutely. Thrombocytopenia is not produced by blood loss per se in the absence of transfusions. Excessive bleeding due to dilutional thrombocytopenia can be prevented in most patients receiving large amounts of blood by assessing platelet counts after 8 to 10 units of blood, and transfusing platelet concentrates when the platelet count becomes marginal for hemostasis, that is, less than 100,000 per μl.

Increased Platelet Destruction

An acute shortening of platelet survival time produces a proportional decrease in the circulating platelet count. Within a few days of continuing platelet destruction, increases of two to eight times normal platelet production may occur, but thrombocytopenia persists if the production rate does not compensate for the increased rate of destruction. Platelet destruction may be selective as an isolated consumptive or immune-mediated process, or may occur in concert with localized or systemic activation of the coagulation cascade (see Fig. 24 and Table 3).

Combined Consumption. Platelet consumption secondary to the activation and consumption of coagulation factors is the most common cause of destructive thrombocytopenia. These disorders have been referred to as *disseminated intravascular coagulation* (DIC), or consumptive coagulopathies.[114] These terms should not be applied to clinical entities involving isolated platelet consumption, such as hemolytic uremic syndrome or thrombotic thrombocytopenic purpura. The term "disseminated" intravascular coagulation may be misleading because the consumptive process frequently occurs locally, as within a diseased organ.

Activation of the coagulation cascade and the destruction of at least some of the consumable coagulation factors (fibrinogen, prothrombin, and factors V, VIII, and XIII) are considered characteristic of combined consumption. In general, platelets are secondarily involved in this type of consumptive process through platelet trapping in the fibrin mesh, and in vivo activation of platelets by factor X_a and thrombin.

These disorders are kinetically characterized by an equivalent reduction in both platelet and fibrinogen survivals (Fig. 26). Initially, the degree of thrombocytopenia is determined by the rate of consumption and changes in distribution. After several days the platelet count also reflects increases in platelet production, unless there is associated marrow suppression, as with cancer chemotherapy.

Combined consumption follows activation of coagulation, initiated either locally or by direct activation of the intrinsic system or the extrinsic system, (e.g., release of thromboplastin or cellular procoagulants). Commonly associated conditions are shock and stasis, crush injury, surgical trauma, anoxic necrosis, brain injury, or other causes of tissue infarction. Examples of obstetric disorders include abruptio placentae, amniotic fluid embolism, retained dead fetus, or toxemia of pregnancy. Malignant diseases may be associated with activation of factor X, release of thromboplastin from granules in leukemic cells, or discharge of necrotic tumor debris. Bacterial, viral, rickettsial, and protozoal infections can also result in combined consumption. The mechanism of consumption in the various infectious disorders, however, is complex. Endotoxin from bacterial organisms has been shown to affect the vessel wall, platelets, granulocytes, coagulation cascade, and other systems thought to participate in the pathogenesis of consumption.

Pathogenetic, diagnostic, and management aspects of combined consumption will be described in Chapter 11. It should be emphasized that bleeding is the major clinical complication of severe intravascular coagulation, and that treatment is first directed at the underlying cause. Blood components, especially platelet concentrates, are most useful in managing blood loss or life-threatening hemorrhage.

Isolated Platelet Consumption. In disorders associated with vascular injury in areas of high shear flow, thrombocytopenia occurs as a result of platelet consumption at sites of endothelial disruption.[35,37] Circulating fibrinogen is usually not measurably destroyed, presumably because there is insufficient time for activation to be completed during rapid blood transit. Isolated platelet consumption is seen with thrombotic thrombocytopenic purpura, hemolytic-uremic syndrome, other vasculitis syndromes, and occasionally with intravascular prosthetic devices. The relationship between fibrinogen and platelet destruction in these disorders is shown in Figure 26.

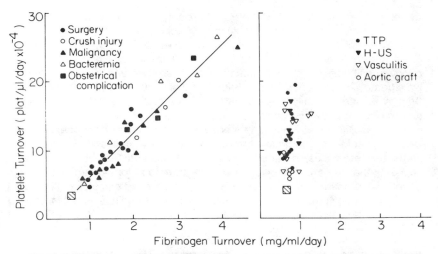

FIGURE 26. Combined platelet and fibrinogen versus isolated platelet consumption. There is a direct relationship between platelet and fibrinogen turnover calculations in patients with surgical or traumatic injury, metastatic malignancy, bacteremia, and obstetric-related activation of the coagulation cascade *(left panel)*. Turnover is calculated by dividing the concentration in blood by the mean time in circulation (survival time). Platelet destruction (turnover) is selectively increased over fibrinogen destruction (turnover) in patients with abnormal endovascular surfaces exposed to high shear (arterial) blood flow *(right panel)*. Marked isolated platelet destruction is characteristic of thrombotic thrombocytopenic purpura (TTP) and hemolytic uremic syndrome (H-US). Results in normal subjects are shown in the hatched *squares*.

Thrombocytopenia, neurologic abnormalities, microangiopathic hemolytic anemia, renal abnormalities, and fever comprise the classical pentad of *thrombotic thrombocytopenic purpura* (TTP). The major pathologic finding of TTP is thrombi in the microcirculation. There is extensive organ involvement, so that microthrombi are easily found on postmortem examination. While primary endothelial cell damage with subsequent platelet thrombus formation may account for all of the clinical features of the syndrome, the nature of the mechanism of endothelial injury is not clear. Immune platelet destruction has also been proposed. The syndrome tends to occur in young adults, but is seen at all ages, with a slight female predominance. Many patients have a viral-like prodrome. Coagulation studies are normal. Therapy consists of plasma exchange (plasmapheresis), plasma infusion, and high-dose corticosteroids in combination with pharmacologic inhibitors of platelet function.[115]

Hemolytic-uremic syndrome is clinically and pathologically similar to TTP. This syndrome occurs primarily in children, but has also been described in adults. Although the pathogenesis is also proposed to be immunologic or infectious, direct evidence is lacking. Pathologic examination reveals vascular endothelial damage in glomerular capillaries and renal arterioles, with local deposition of platelets and fibrin. Microangiopathic hemolytic anemia, thrombocytopenia, fever, and occasionally a prodromal viral illness, are often seen in hemolytic-uremic syndrome. As opposed to TTP, hypertension is frequent and renal failure is more common than hepatic involvement, while neurologic manifestations are less common and less severe. In children, supportive therapy with hemodialysis, blood transfusions, and antihypertensive therapy is most effective; heparin should not be given. Platelet function inhibitors may be effective in adults.[116]

In *vasculitis,* selective mild to moderately severe thrombocytopenia due to isolated platelet consumption has been noted in some patients with systemic lupus erythematosus, rheumatoid arthritis, or polyarthritis. This association suggests that the process involves platelet thrombus formation secondary to endothelial damage that is perhaps induced by immune complexes. Vasculitis is differentiated from TTP on the basis of clinical findings and biopsy that reveals fibrinoid necrosis and inflammation, findings not associated with typical TTP.

Immune Platelet Destruction. Immune-mediated platelet destruction[117,118] is characterized by shortened platelet survival, an increased megakaryocytic mass due to both an increased number and volume of megakaryocytes, together with at least some objective evidence of an immune process underlying platelet destruction.[35] While in the past a therapeutic response to high dose steroids has usually provided the evidence for an immune mechanism, establishment of an immune etiology by in vitro testing is becoming increasingly useful as newer techniques for detection of platelet antibodies are made available.[117-119]

Autoimmune (idiopathic) thrombocytopenic purpura (ITP) manifests itself either as an acute self-limited or chronic disorder. The acute illness most often occurs in children, whereas the chronic syndrome presents in adults. In ITP platelet survival is extremely short and is usually measured in minutes to hours.[37]

Acute ITP may present at all ages, but most frequently is seen in children between two and six years of age. The disease is preceded by viral infection in over 80 percent of the cases. When symptomatic, patients most frequently present with a sudden onset of petechiae, purpura, epistaxis, gastrointestinal, or genitourinary bleeding, most often one to six weeks after the symptoms of the viral illness itself. Intracranial hemorrhage occurs only rarely. A palpable spleen may be present as a separate manifestation of the antecedent viral illness. The prognosis of acute ITP is excellent; over 80 percent of the patients will recover within six months without treatment. The usual period of thrombocytopenia is four to six weeks. Recurrence after recovery is rare. Mortality is considered to be approximately 1 percent.

Over 90 percent of adults with ITP fail to undergo spontaneous remission, whereas fewer than 10 percent of affected children develop chronic or recurrent disease. The clinical and pathologic manifestations of *chronic ITP* appear to be due to continued formation of antiplatelet IgG antibody and subsequent clearing of the antibody-damaged platelets by the mononuclear-phagocytic system. Platelet destruction occurs mainly in the spleen, probably because the spleen is both a major site of antiplatelet antibody synthesis and a major phagocytic organ; however, palpable splenomegaly is essentially never found. Hepatic removal of antibody-coated platelets occurs when the antibody level is very high, and is the presumed explanation for continued disease in patients who fail splenectomy and a hypertrophied accessory spleen is not present. There may be a role for cell-mediated immunity or immune complexes in the pathogenesis of chronic ITP in some patients. Chronic ITP has a female to male predilection of three to one, and occurs most frequently in young and middle-aged adults.

In the *differential diagnosis,* immunologic thrombocytopenia secondary to drugs, transfusion, lymphoma, or systemic lupus erythematosus can often be established by careful history, marrow biopsy, and antinuclear antibody tests. Chronic combined consumption can occasionally be confused with ITP, but appropriate coagulation studies will rule out this entity. Thrombotic thrombocytopenic purpura and hemolytic-uremic syndrome can be differentiated on the basis of clinical findings and the peripheral blood film showing the absence of characteristic microangiopathic changes (red cell fragmentation).

Regarding *therapy* for ITP, the response to corticosteroids in doses of 1 to 2 mg per kg per day of prednisone provides useful initial confirmation of the immune nature of this disorder. The platelet count increases convincingly in over 80 percent of patients within one to two weeks. However, only 10 to 15 percent achieve a permanent remission. After a few months patients who fail steroid therapy or who require toxic doses to maintain a reasonable platelet count should undergo splenectomy. About 80 percent of patients respond to splenectomy within a week and two thirds enter permanent remission. Of the one third of the patients who do not undergo complete permanent remission, many are relieved of bleeding symptoms despite mild to moderate thrombocytopenia and require either no therapy or well-tolerated doses of corticosteroids (less than 10 mg of prednisone per day). During splenectomy, bleeding in these thrombocytopenic patients is predictably less than might be expected from the degree of thrombocytopenia because of the hemostatically more competent platelets in circulation. Nevertheless, a platelet count above 100,000 per μl is desirable for surgery, even if high-dose steroids are needed transiently before surgery to achieve that level.

Immunosuppressive therapy with cyclophosphamide, azathioprine, or other agents has occasionally been reported to be useful in refractory cases, although there are no controlled studies. Three to six weeks may be required before response is noted. Vincristine has been reported to be effective within one to two weeks in some patients with refractory ITP, although the remissions are generally not maintained. Cyclophosphamide has been used with some success for maintenance of remissions initially induced by vincristine. Recent attempts to treat refractory ITP by transfusing platelets loaded with vinblastine have been reported with high response rates. Unfortunately, subsequent experience has indicated that only a few patients respond to this mode of therapy.

Although plasmapheresis and plasma exchange have been reported to induce remission in several refractory patients,[120] this has not been the usual experience. Platelet transfusions are of little use in ITP, as transfused platelets are rapidly destroyed and impose the risk of alloimmunization. However, in situations of life-threatening hemorrhage, such as intracranial bleeding, platelet concentrates may occasionally promote hemostasis despite the absence of a measurable increment in the platelet count.

In *transplacental ITP*, thrombocytopenic purpura occurs at birth in as many as 50 percent of the offspring of mothers with ITP. The chance of the neonate being affected is higher if the mother is thrombocytopenic at delivery. However, about 20 percent of infants will be thrombocytopenic despite a normal platelet count in the mother. The etiology appears to be transplacental transfer of maternal autoantibody.[121] Usually treatment is unnecessary because the disorder is of short duration.

A separate clinical entity is *isoimmune neonatal thrombocytopenia*. The pathogenesis of this disorder is analogous to that of erythroblastosis fetalis. In this uncommon condition, platelet antigens inherited from the father (usually PI^{A1}) evoke a maternal antibody response and transplacental transfer of maternal antibody that results in transient thrombocytopenia.[122]

Secondary *autoimmune thrombocytopenia* occurs in chronic lymphocytic leukemia, lymphomas, and systemic lupus erythematosus often enough to warrant careful examination to rule out lymphoproliferative disorders, and serologic tests to rule out lupus erythematosus.[117-119] Occasionally, patients with solid tumors may also develop immune-mediated thrombocytopenia. An immunologic etiology of the thrombocytopenia in these disorders has been suggested by the presence of platelet-associated immunoglobulin in some of these patients. The clinical picture is indistinguishable from chronic ITP.[123]

Numerous *drugs* have been associated with thrombocytopenia.[124] Gold salts, quinine, quinidine, sulfonamide derivatives, and possibly heparin are the most frequently associated medications thought to produce thrombocytopenia by immune mechanisms. The most likely pathogenetic mechanism of thrombocytopenia appears to be the formation of immune complexes composed of drug and antidrug antibody which stimulate lymphocyte proliferation. The platelets bearing immune complexes are subsequently recognized and cleared by the mononuclear-phagocytic system in a reaction dependent upon factor VIII/vWF.[125] Once sensitized, the onset of thrombocytopenia in most cases is within 24 hours after use of the offending drug. Gold salts represent an exception, and thrombocytopenia may occur several months after the drug is administered.

Diagnosis is often suspected on the basis of the clinical history. Frequently it is difficult to ascertain which of a number of drugs is responsible for the thrombocytopenia. Unfortunately, in vitro tests are frequently negative when drugs other than quinine or quinidine are involved. Challenge of patients with a suspected offending agent should not be undertaken in most instances. All nonessential medications should be discontinued in patients suspected of having drug-induced thrombocytopenia. Corticosteroids do not shorten the duration of the thrombocytopenia. Platelet transfusions may be helpful for life-threatening hemorrhage.

An interesting disorder of uncertain pathogenesis is *post-transfusion purpura*.[126] The vast majority of patients are lacking a platelet antigen (PI^{A1}) which is present in 98 percent of normal donors. It is generally thought that the patient produces an antibody to PI^{A1} in response to a preceding transfusion. Most cases reported are women who have had previous pregnancies. Approximately one to two weeks after transfusion, thrombocytopenic bleeding occurs which may be life-threatening and can last for several months. Exchange transfusion and plasmapheresis have been of benefit.

Thrombocytopenia Due To Multiple Causes

Alcoholic liver disease is a common problem in which the patient may exhibit thrombocytopenia due to concurrent abnormalities in two or more pathophysiologic categories. Decreased production may occur by the direct toxic effect of alcohol, as well as through ineffective production secondary to folate deficiency. Congestive splenomegaly secondary to cirrhosis with portal hypertension increases splenic platelet pooling and contributes further to the thrombocytopenia. Decreased platelet survival due to the direct effect of alcohol, and consumption related to hepatocellular disease cause additional platelet destruction and contribute to the development of thrombocytopenia. The relative contribution of each of these mechanisms may be clarified using ^{51}Cr-platelet kinetic studies (see Fig. 24 and Table 4). Withdrawal of alcohol and administration of folate will generally allow the platelet count to normalize within one to two weeks. A transient "overshoot" thrombocytosis may follow.

Lymphoproliferative disorders, lymphomas, and chronic lymphocytic leukemia are frequently associated with thrombocytopenia resulting from defective production, destruction, and pooling. Production abnormalities are due to marrow infiltration with leukemic cells or chemotherapy. Increased splenic pooling from infiltrative splenomegaly is less frequent than with congestive splenomegaly. Destruction of platelets by antiplatelet antibodies synthesized by the malignant cells is also seen in some of these patients.[117-119]

The use of *extracorporeal bypass* oxygenator apparatus produces thrombocytopenia by dilution, platelet sequestration, and consumption.[112] Dilution of blood platelets by large volumes of priming solutions usually results in an immediate lowering of the platelet count at the onset of bypass. Platelet activation during passage through the extracorporeal apparatus produces transient dysfunction, selective release and depletion of α-granule contents, and sequestration of platelets, probably in the liver and spleen. In addition, platelets are destroyed in the oxygenator and surgically traumatized tissue. Platelet counts remain reduced for several days after bypass because of the continued platelet utilization in the injured tissues.

Metastatic tumor is commonly associated with thrombocytopenia consequent to several mechanisms. Production defects may occur owing to bone marrow infiltration or chemotherapy. Platelet destruction may be due to autoantibody, isolated platelet consumption, or combined platelet and fibrinogen consumption; the latter may remain subclinical.

Serious *infections* are often associated with isolated or combined consumption.[127] Splenomegaly of infectious etiology in some parts of the world is commonly associated with mild thrombocytopenia. A production abnormality may possibly result from marrow infiltration with granulomas, or from bone marrow necrosis, as an unusual consequence of some infections.

Platelet Transfusions

Thrombocytopenic bleeding is readily controlled by transfusing adequate numbers of viable, functional platelets. The minimal platelet concentration needed to maintain hemostasis depends on the functional capacity of the platelets and the hemostatic challenge.[108] In patients with marrow aplasia, for example, a platelet count of 5000 per μl or greater is usually sufficient to prevent serious bleeding in the absence of complicating factors, while some patients with immune thrombocytopenia may need no more than 1000 per μl to prevent spontaneous bleeding. In contrast, patients with thrombocytopenia and associated platelet dysfunction (e.g., leukemia, uremia, drug ingestion), may require a platelet count of 20,000 per μl or higher to prevent fatal spontaneous hemorrhage. Determination of the bleeding time may be helpful in establishing the minimal essential platelet concentration required in an individual patient. When additional hemostatic burdens are superimposed, such as trauma, infection, ulcerative local lesions, and so on, the platelet count required to prevent bleeding increases.

Although fresh whole blood transfusions have been successfully used to treat thrombocytopenic bleeding, platelet concentrates are now preferred because they are not only more efficient, but they also allow optimal platelet storage and proper use of other blood components. Eighty-five percent of the platelets from an individual 500-ml blood donation may be concentrated and stored at room temperature for up to 72 hours without loss of viability or function.[128] These platelets must be prepared in special plastic bags, suspended in 70 ml of plasma, and maintained with gentle, continuous mixing throughout the storage period. The risk of bacterial growth during the storage period is avoided by processing the platelets in a closed-bag system. Infusion of one such platelet concentrate into an adult without splenomegaly increases the peripheral platelet count by about 10,000 per μl. Since platelets lose both viability and function when exposed to 4°C, whole blood processed or stored at refrigerated temperatures provides effectively no platelets on transfusion. After massive transfusions with such blood, the platelet count falls, owing to dilution. The number of transfused platelets needed to maintain an appropriate circulating level varies with (1) the increase required in the peripheral count, (2) blood volume, (3) the survival time in vivo, and (4) the proportion of transfused platelets destined for pooling in the spleen.

Since currently unresolved technical and biologic complexities of platelet typing do not permit easy selection of compatible platelet donors, random donor platelets are usually given initially. Consequently, the recipients may become refractory to platelet transfusions owing to alloantibody formation. This generally occurs after exposure to about 20 separate donors. Because alloimmunization is the principal problem currently limiting long-term platelet support, platelet transfusion is most successful in patients with transient hypoproliferative thrombocytopenia, such as acute reversible marrow injury due to drugs or chemicals. Platelet transfusions are particularly useful in patients receiving chemotherapy for malignant disease because they allow the patients to be carried through more aggressive intermittent antitumor regimens. There has been some success in selecting platelet donors for long-term support of aplastic patients. HL-A typing identifies potential compatible donors from family members or the community at large when the recipients are unsuitable for marrow transplantation. Subsequent specific typing to select appropriate compatible donors may provide indefinite platelet support, although it is impossible to predict which patients will rapidly develop alloantibodies to all potential donors.

Once the decision has been made to begin platelet transfusions in a patient who may require long-term platelet transfusions, it is important to develop a strategy for support. In theory, it might be expected that limiting platelet antigen exposure through sequential single donor platelet support would delay platelet alloimmunization. However, there are no reported data to prove the effectiveness of this approach, and since red cell transfusions (which contain platelet membrane) are often required for these patients, it would be difficult to limit antigen exposure effectively. Moreover, it has been shown that: (1) the time for sensitization to random donors is variable but may require months to years; and (2) the use of random donors does not impair the subsequent identification of compatible donors.[108] Therefore, random donor platelets are used until sensitization is demonstrated, that is, there is no platelet increment at one hour after the transfusion of a platelet concentrate derived from six donors on two separate occasions. Thereafter, compatible donors are selected.

On the basis of in vitro testing with patient transfusion studies in the support of alloimmunized thrombocytopenic patients it has been found that: (1) family members provide compatible platelet transfusions for about half of the patients, but HL-A matching is not always sufficient to predict compatibility; and (2) compatible unrelated random donors are often identified by platelet crossmatching procedures from individuals who share at least two HL-A antigens with the thrombocytopenic patient.

THROMBOCYTOSIS

Platelet counts greater than normal can only result from increased production, since platelet survival does not become prolonged beyond normal values. In the majority of cases, production is effective, although about one fourth of the patients with thrombocytosis occurring in the myeloproliferative diseases may have a component of ineffective production. The increased production of platelets is either autonomous or reactive (Table 5). There is no evidence at

TABLE 5. Thrombocytosis

Reactive thrombocytosis
   Iron deficiency
   Inflammatory disease
   Malignancy
   Splenectomy
   Drugs
   Redistribution
   Rebound thrombocytosis
   Others
Autonomous thrombocytosis
   Essential thrombocytosis (thrombocythemia)
   Myeloproliferative disorders (polycythemia vera, myelofibrosis, chronic
      myelogenous leukemia, myelodysplasias)

present that thrombocytosis occurs as a compensatory response to hereditary disorders of defective platelet function. This suggests that the normal regulatory processes of platelet production are keyed to circulating concentration or mass, rather than some aspect of hemostatic function.

Reactive Thrombocytosis

Thrombocytosis has been reported in association with many pathologic conditions, some of which are listed in Table 5. In these reactive or secondary thrombocytotic states, megakaryocyte number is increased, but volume is decreased (see Fig. 24). Production is effective and platelet survival is normal.[35] The biologic significance of reactive thrombocytosis is not understood.

Iron Deficiency. Thrombocytosis may be seen in association with iron deficiency, usually secondary to blood loss, but occasionally with nutritional deficiency. Since severe iron deficiency has also been associated with thrombocytopenia in some instances, especially in children, it is possible that iron may have some regulatory role in thrombocytopoiesis.

Inflammatory Disease and Malignancy. Acute, and especially chronic inflammatory diseases, have been associated with elevated platelet counts. Occasionally, the platelet count will vary according to the activity of the underlying disease. The injection of foreign substances which produce inflammation in experimental animals has resulted in thrombocytosis that is associated with an increase in megakaryocytic colony-forming units in vitro. The process is blocked by cyclosporin A (inhibitor of T lymphocytes) in vivo and in vitro.[129] These results suggest that a nonspecific release of a mitogen from T lymphocytes in the marrow mediates the megakaryocytic hyperplasia. The possible role of inflammatory iron block in the pathogenesis of this disorder has not been explored. Chronic inflammation may also be related to the thrombocytosis seen with malignancies. Extremely elevated counts have been reported without symptoms referable to the platelet count per se. Tumors of the lung, ovary, breast, stomach, and Hodgkin disease are the more frequently associated malignancies.

Splenectomy and Redistribution. Thrombocytosis following splenectomy is of interest in that the degree of elevation of the platelet count may be greater than can be accounted for by the absence of the splenic platelet pool, the surgical procedure, or interval since splenectomy. The platelet count is frequently one million per μl or greater and thrombocytosis may last for a period of months. Splenectomy for hemolytic anemia may result in persistent thrombocytosis if the hemolytic process is not corrected by the procedure. Occasionally, splenectomy unmasks essential thrombocytosis. Thrombocytosis is seen following exercise and after epinephrine. The platelet count may rise to levels 50 percent greater than basal and rapidly returns to normal. Splenectomy abolishes the thrombocytotic response to epinephrine, but not to exercise.

Drugs. The administration of vinca alkaloids, through unclear mechanisms, occasionally results in an elevated platelet count in man and experimental animals. Miconazole, an antifungal agent, has been associated with reversible anemia and thrombocytosis.

Rebound Thrombocytosis. Thrombocytosis may follow a period of thrombocytopenia, for example, cytotoxic drugs, treatment of folate or vitamin B_{12} deficiency, recovery from thrombocytopenia occurring during surgery, or withdrawal from alcohol. Since platelet production appears to be regulated by a feedback mechanism, it is likely that rebound thrombocytosis is due to the poor damping characteristics of megakaryocytopoietic regulation. In addition, a chronic thrombocytopenic stress may result in the synchronization of megakaryocytes, which may continue to mature until platelet production occurs, despite cessation of the thrombocytopenic stimulus.

Other Disorders. Hemorrhage and hemolytic anemia have been associated with mild thrombocytosis; however, the pathogenesis of the increased platelet count is obscure. There has been speculation concerning the possible relationship between erythropoiesis and thrombocytopoiesis. Clarification of this issue will require the isolation and purification of the putative thrombocytopoietic regulatory substance(s).

Thrombocytosis is occasionally found in the various preleukemic and refractory marrow states, and is seen in up to one third of patients with idiopathic refractory sideroblastic anemia. It is possible that patients with this latter disorder and thrombocytosis are less likely to develop leukemia. It is not known whether the thrombocytosis is autonomous or reactive in these conditions.

Management. Since there is little documented evidence to suggest that reactive thrombocytosis results in any clinical sequelae, therapy should be directed towards the underlying illness, rather than the elevated platelet count. There is no evidence that a reactive elevation in platelets per se predisposes to thrombosis.

Autonomous Thrombocytosis

Essential Thrombocytosis (Thrombocythemia). In this disorder, platelet production appears to be autonomous. Megakaryocyte numbers and volume are both increased, contributing to the marked increase in megakaryocyte mass.[25] Platelet survival is relatively normal (see Fig. 24). As in other myeloproliferative syndromes, the disorder will probably prove to be of clonal origin.[130]

This disease predominantly affects middle-aged patients with an equal sex predilection. Young patients with the disorder may have a long period of survival. There does not appear to be any correlation between bleeding or thromboembolic events and the level of the platelet count, the bleeding time, or platelet aggregation studies in either autonomous thrombocytosis or thrombocytosis secondary to other myeloproliferative disorders.

In essential thrombocytosis, platelet counts are frequently over one million and the platelets are often found in clumps on blood films. They may exhibit marked anisocytosis and poikilocytosis. In 90 percent of the cases, there is an associated neutrophilia. The hematocrit is occasionally slightly increased. Basophilia and eosinophilia may be seen. Iron deficiency anemia secondary to bleeding occurs. The bone marrow frequently reveals panmyelosis. Megakaryocytes are numerous and may exhibit bizarre morphology. Fibrosis is infrequently observed. Cytogenetic analysis may reveal an abnormality of G group chromosomes. Serum acid phosphatase and uric acid are occasionally elevated. Pseudohyperkalemia, owing to in vitro potassium release from platelets, may occur. The bleeding time may be prolonged but is seldom over 15 minutes. Platelet function tests in essential thrombocytosis are usually abnormal. A lack of responsiveness to epinephrine is most characteristic and may be related to a deficiency of α-adrenergic receptors on the platelet.[22] Abnormalities in ADP-induced aggregation are less common, whereas collagen-induced aggregation is often normal. In patients with thromboembolic phenomena, in vivo platelet aggregate formation and spontaneous in vitro aggregation has been demonstrated, although difficulties in sample collection and preparation make these tests difficult to evaluate. Ultrastructural studies have demonstrated profound abnormalities of granules, mitochondria, and microfilament arrangement.

Treatment directed at lowering the platelet count is usually justified when symptoms of bleeding or thromboembolism are associated with a count of one million or greater. Alkylating agents or ^{32}P are usually employed for this purpose. Chronic alkylator therapy, especially in younger patients, should be used judiciously in view of the increased risk of malignancy with this mode of treatment in polycythemia vera.[131] More recently, hydroxyurea has been recommended, although control may be transient and the long-term effects are unknown. Thrombocytopheresis has been used in essential thrombocytosis with variable success, but may occasionally be useful to lower acutely the platelet count. Platelet function inhibitors may decrease symptoms in patients with digital pain, but have been found not to reduce the thromboembolic complications.[132]

Thrombocytosis Associated with Other Myeloproliferative Disorders. High platelet counts have been associated with polycythemia vera, chronic myelogenous leukemia, and myeloid metaplasia. Megakaryocyte mass is increased in polycythemia vera and myeloid metaplasia; this is due to an increase in both megakaryocyte number and volume. Chronic myelogenous leukemia is an interesting exception, since the increase in megakaryocyte mass is totally accounted for by an increase in megakaryocyte number with an actual reduction found in average megakaryocyte volume. The clinical manifestations of thrombocytosis in patients with polycythemia vera are similar to those with essential thrombocytosis, except that the bleeding time is more frequently prolonged, usually because of a reduction in dense-granule ADP content. In myeloproliferative disorders, platelet function may not be adequately reflected by the bleeding time.

9

QUALITATIVE PLATELET DEFECTS

Qualitative platelet disorders are identified clinically by measuring a disproportionately prolonged template bleeding time with respect to the platelet count. These abnormalities may be inherited or acquired, and may be intrinsic or extrinsic to the platelet.[13,18,28,133,134] A wide spectrum of acquired and congenital abnormalities of platelet function have been identified, most of which result in mild bleeding disorders (Table 6). This chapter presents the clinical approach to platelet dysfunction and considers hereditary and acquired disorders, with some comments about management.

CLINICAL APPROACH TO PLATELET DYSFUNCTION

The congenital disorders of platelet function have been extensively studied and have provided important insights into platelet physiology and pathophysiology, but these defects are uncommon in clinical medicine. On the other hand, acquired syndromes of platelet dysfunction are more complex, inadequately studied, more difficult to classify, but occur frequently in a wide variety of clinical settings.

The severity of bleeding disorders caused by platelet dysfunction depends not only on the nature of the platelet defect itself, but also upon the severity of the hemostatic challenge. Disorders of platelet function vary in severity from the mild syndromes of easy bruisability seen, for example, in the storage pool

TABLE 6. Disorders of platelet function

MECHANISM	HEREDITARY DEFECTS	ACQUIRED DEFECTS
Substrate vascular connective tissue	Ehlers-Danlos syndrome Hereditary hemorrhagic telangiectasia	Scurvy Amyloidosis
Adhesion	Bernard-Soulier syndrome von Willebrand Disease	Acquired von Willebrand disease Uremia Drugs, (PGI_2dipyridamole)
Platelet aggregation	Thrombasthenia Afibrinogenemia	Fibrin(ogen) degradation products, (DIC, liver disease, fibrinolytic liver disease, fibrinolytic therapy) Macromolecules (paraproteins, dextran) Drugs (semisynthetic penicillins)
Release of granular constituents Storage pool deficiency α-granule	Gray platelet syndrome Autosomal recessive disorders	Cardiopulmonary bypass
dense granule	Albinism Familial disorders	Immune mediated release, (ITP, collagen vascular disease) Drugs, (reserpine, methysergide, tricyclic antidepressants, phenothiazines)

Defective release	Cyclooxygenase deficiency	Platelet dyspoiesis, e.g., leukemia, myeloproliferative syndrome
	Thromboxane synthetase deficiency	Drugs (aspirin, other nonsteroidal anti-inflammatory agents, furosemide, nitrofurantoin)
		Ethanol
		Diet
Altered nucleotide metabolism	Glycogen storage disease	Drugs (phosphodiesterase inhibitors), stimulators of adenylcyclase, (PGI_2, PGE_1)
	Fructose-1,6-diphosphate deficiency	
Other mechanisms	Platelet factor 3 deficiency	Drugs (heparin, sympathetic blockers, clofibrate, hydroxychloroquine)
	Deficiency of factor V receptors	Diet
		Viral infections
		Hypothyroidism

deficiencies, to the severe and sometimes fatal hemorrhages seen in conditions such as autosomal recessive von Willebrand disease. The bleeding tendency in any of the platelet function disorders may be aggravated by the introduction of additional hemostatic defects, for example, chemotherapy-induced thrombocytopenia, the administration of aspirin, or anticoagulants. Gastrointestinal or genitourinary bleeding may be a manifestation of defective platelet function; such bleeding may be precipitated by an underlying structural abnormality such as an ulceration, or colonic bladder polyps.

The diagnostic approach to patients with platelet dysfunction will depend somewhat on the urgency with which the provisional diagnosis must be made in order to manage the bleeding diathesis. For example, the diagnostic workup of a patient with an acute bleeding episode may be limited to screening test evaluation of hemostasis, followed by a decision as to the possible role that a platelet defect may play in causing the bleeding. Since acute disorders are usually transient, comprehensive evaluation may not be possible. In contrast, the diagnostic workup in a patient with chronic or recurrent bleeding should be definitive. Most often the diagnosis can be suggested on the basis of information obtained in the history, physical examination, and simple laboratory assessment, but confirmation frequently requires diagnostic tests that are available only in specialized laboratories. However, patients in whom von Willebrand disease has been excluded and who have a mild congenital bleeding disorder for which there is no specific therapy, may receive laboratory characterization at some convenient time.

The *diagnosis* of platelet dysfunction in most instances is made by the systematic analysis of information obtained in the history, physical examination, and laboratory evaluation of hemostatic function. The bleeding time is the appropriate screening test. It is prolonged in patients with significant platelet function defects and adequate platelet counts, and is disproportionately prolonged with thrombocytopenia.

Light microscopic examination of a stained blood film may be useful. Large-appearing platelets may suggest the Bernard-Soulier syndrome, gray platelets implicate α-granule deficiency, and marked platelet anisocytosis may be seen in the myeloproliferative syndromes. In most situations of suspected platelet dysfunction a screening evaluation of the coagulation cascade is required, consisting of thrombin, fibrinogen determination, and prothrombin partial thromboplastin times. Any patient with a history of abnormal bleeding and a prolonged bleeding time should also be evaluated for the presence of von Willebrand disease. The diagnosis is best established by the simultaneous measurements of factors VIII:C and VIII/vWF:Ag. These measurements, combined with decreased platelet aggregation to ristocetin, allow a diagnosis to be made in the majority of patients with von Willebrand disease.

Platelet aggregation is widely available for the evaluation of platelet function and may provide useful diagnostic information, especially in the congenital disorders of platelet function. For example, in vitro aggregation to ADP, epinephrine, and collagen is absent with thrombasthenia and may be decreased in aspirin-like defects and storage pool deficiencies. Ristocetin-induced aggregation is decreased to absent in most patients with von Willebrand disease and in the Bernard-Soulier syndrome. Epinephrine fails to aggregate platelets in most patients with essential thrombocytosis, a fact of some diagnostic utility. Although in vitro platelet aggregation testing may provide important diagnostic clues, the technique is difficult to reproduce and to standardize, and the abnormalities seen with such tests may have little or no relationship to the actual mechanism of the hemostatic defect in vivo. Abnormalities of platelet aggregation need to be interpreted in light of the observed bleeding time.

Electron microscopy has been used in the enumeration of platelet α-granules and dense granules to confirm storage pool deficiencies. Direct measurements of dense-granule ADP and ATP are required to differentiate storage pool deficiency from aspirin-like defects. Platelet α-granule contents may be evaluated by measuring releasable pools of platelet factor 4 and β-thromboglobulin by radioimmunoassays; tests that are now available commercially. Platelet arachidonate metabolism may be evaluated by measuring its stable end-product thromboxane B_2 by radioimmunoassay or by the finding of absent in vitro platelet aggregation to added arachidonic acid or endoperoxides.

HEREDITARY DISORDERS OF PLATELET FUNCTION

Disorders of Connective Tissue Substrate. *Defective connective tissue* support leads to a propensity for vessel wall disruption, impaired vessel wall retraction after vascular breakage, and dissection of hematomata along tissue planes. Whereas in vitro platelet function is usually normal in this syndrome, platelets do not adhere properly to the defective collagen, leading to a bleeding diathesis that resembles qualitative platelet defects. The mild bleeding tendency that often occurs in the Ehlers-Danlos syndromes appears to be due to abnormalities of collagen.[103,134]

Disorders of Adhesion. The *Bernard-Soulier syndrome* is an autosomal recessive trait characterized by a long bleeding time, a normal or variably reduced platelet count, failure of platelets to adhere to subendothelium, and impaired platelet aggregation to ristocetin. In contrast to von Willebrand syndrome, however, these patients have normal levels of factor VIII/von Willebrand factor, and the abnormal ristocetin aggregation is not corrected by addition of this protein. The Bernard-Soulier syndrome is due to a deficiency of platelet surface receptors for the von Willebrand factor. A reduction in GPI complex in platelet membrane fractions isolated from patients with the Bernard-Soulier syndrome has been demonstrated. The GPI complex appears to include the receptor for factor VIII/vWF factor.[17,18,135]

The *von Willebrand syndrome* is a disorder classically characterized by a decrease in factor VIII coagulant activity (VIII:C) and parallel decreases in the factor VIII-related antigen, or von Willebrand factor (VIII/vWF:Ag). The defect in platelet-plug formation is due to decreased platelet adherence to subendothelial surfaces.[17,18,45-48] A characteristic feature of the disease is its variable nature in both clinical presentation and laboratory manifestations. This variability is seen among affected individuals within the same family (unlike hemophilia A), as well as from family to family. The classical form of von Willebrand disease is inherited as an autosomal dominant trait, and is characterized by a mild to moderate bleeding tendency. Two main variants can be defined on the basis of laboratory findings. In type 1 there are concordant decreases in VIII:C and VIII/vWF:Ag. In type 2 there is a qualitative abnormality of the factor VIII/vWF complex which can be demonstrated on crossed immunoelectropheresis.

A more severe but less common form of von Willebrand disease is transmitted as an autosomal recessive trait and is clinically similar to hemophilia. Both quantitative and qualitative abnormalities of factor VIII/vWF complex can be demonstrated. Unlike Bernard-Soulier syndrome, the decreased adherence in von Willebrand disease is due to the decreased plasma von Willebrand factor, which mediates the platelet interaction with subendothelium. This defect is particularly apparent under high shear conditions characteristic of the microcirculation. Infusion of normal plasma or cryoprecipitate containing factor VIII/vWF complex temporarily corrects the defect in platelet function. Bleeding in von Willebrand disease, however, is due to both the decrease in factor VIII coagulant activity and the defect in platelet plug formation (see Chapter 11).

Disorders of Platelet-Platelet Interaction. *Thrombasthenia* (Glanzmann disease) is an autosomal recessive disorder resulting in a moderately severe lifelong hemorrhagic tendency and is one of the most rare congenital bleeding disorders. The platelet count is normal but the bleeding time is greatly prolonged and clot retraction is defective. The platelets fail to aggregate in response to ADP, epinephrine, collagen, or thrombin. In direct contrast to the Bernard-Soulier syndrome, thrombasthenic platelets adhere normally to subendothelium, but fail to show recruitment into hemostatic plug formation.[15-20] The reason that thrombasthenic platelets do not aggregate is related to an impairment in the binding of fibrinogen to the platelet membrane, owing to a specific membrane receptor defect manifested as a decrease in platelet membrane glycoproteins II_b and III_a.[17,18] Impaired binding of fibrinogen prevents bridging between platelets during aggregation.

The hereditary absence of circulating fibrinogen *(afibrinogenemia)* blocks the capacity of platelets to aggregate, evidencing the critical role of fibrinogen in the formation of interplatelet binding necessary for aggregation.[18-20]

Disorders of Release. The hereditary disorders of the *release reaction* are subdivided on pathogenetic grounds into three categories: those due to granule "storage pool" deficiency in which the failure of release is due to a lack of α-granules or dense granules within the platelet, those due to an abnormality of the release mechanism in the presence of a normal storage pool (the aspirin-like syndrome), and those disorders of nucleotide metabolism.[28,133,134]

Storage pool deficiencies of both α-granules or dense granules are well known.[28,136] The so-called gray platelet syndrome is characterized by a nearly total congenital absence of α-granules.[137] Platelet aggregation is only modestly impaired and bleeding times are nearly normal. Hereditary deficiency of dense granules, on the other hand, imposes a major defect in platelet hemostatic function as manifested by long bleeding times and a defect in aggregation that is proportionate to the reduction in dense granules.[28] The most severe form is associated with albinism and an accumulation of ceroid-like pigment in macrophages (Hermansky-Pudlak syndrome). The characteristic pattern of aggregation demonstrates the failure of platelets to aggregate in response to usual concentrations of collagen, or to produce a second phase of aggregation with ADP, epinephrine, or dilute thrombin. The chief diagnostic feature of this type of storage pool disease is the greatly reduced platelet dense-granule content of ADP. Other dense-granule substances such as serotonin, calcium, and pyrophosphate are also decreased. The congenital platelet storage pool deficiencies are not a homogenous group of disorders, and have recently been separated into a number of subgroups on the basis of associated biochemical abnormalities and abnormalities in other types of granules.[136] Bleeding times are prolonged proportionate to the decrease in dense-granule ADP.

The release reaction triggered by collagen or thrombin depends on the synthesis within the platelets of the cyclic endoperoxides prostaglandin G_2 and prostaglandin H_2 by the enzyme cyclooxygenase. These unstable endoperoxides are converted by thromboxane synthetase to thromboxane A_2. Several patients have been described with a *deficiency of cyclooxygenase*[138] or *thromboxane synthetase,*[139] characterized by the inability to form thromboxane A_2 while retaining the ability to form the less potent cyclic endoperoxides. The fact that the absence or blockade of these enzymatic pathways induces only a mild to moderate defect in hemostasis suggests that activation of platelet release and aggregation also occurs physiologically by mechanisms independent of the arachidonate pathway.

Defects in *platelet procoagulant activity* may also be hereditary. Platelets contribute significantly to the rapid generation of fibrin by providing platelet surface phospholipid receptor sites for activated clotting factors V_m and X_a, which bind to the platelet surface and rapidly catalyse the conversion of prothrombin to thrombin. Fibrin formed by thrombin stabilizes the platelet aggregate and allows for the formation of a stable hemostatic plug. The complex interaction of platelet surface receptors and activated clotting factors has in the past been called platelet factor 3 activity and a kindred deficient in this activity has been reported.[140] This disorder represents a congenital deficiency of receptors for factor V_m.[141] The patient had a normal bleeding time, but had a significant history of menorrhagia and postoperative bleeding as well as easy bruising.

ACQUIRED DISORDERS OF PLATELET FUNCTION

Acquired disorders of platelet function probably occur much more commonly than is recognized clinically, and are associated with a wide range of clinical settings, diseases, and drugs.[134] The defective mechanism is less clearly identified in many of these circumstances than in the hereditary platelet disorders, and several of the conditions affect more than one aspect of hemostasis. Nevertheless, the pathophysiologic scheme that has been used to classify the hereditary disorders will be applied as the framework for the classification of acquired platelet dysfunction (see Table 6).

Disorders of Connective Tissue Substrate. Although now rarely seen in western nations, *scurvy* may be associated with severe gingival bleeding and hemorrhage into subcutaneous tissues and muscles. In children, subperiosteal hemorrhages are the characteristic manifestation of the disease. Involvement of the skin is characteristic of primary *amyloidosis,* and may give rise to purpura and ecchymoses without apparent traumatic provocation. Amyloid infiltration of the liver may make liver biopsy an especially hazardous diagnostic maneuver because of the risk of hemorrhage. Some patients with amyloidosis develop an associated acquired factor X-deficiency. Painful purpuric lesions are characteristic of the rare autoerythrocyte sensitization syndrome.[106]

Disorders of Adhesion. Several patients have been described with *acquired von Willebrand disease,* usually associated with autoimmune or lymphoproliferative diseases. The pathogenesis may involve antibodies against a portion of the factor VIII/vWF complex, or accelerated clearance of the larger, more physiologically active factor VIII/vWF.[142] These patients differ from the inherited disorder in that they fail to have a sustained rise in factor VIII clotting activity after plasma infusion.

Uremia produces an extrinsic platelet defect that parallels the progressive accumulation of metabolic products in the blood. In untreated uremic patients the template bleeding time is usually longer than 30 minutes, and predictably shortens to normal in patients treated with peritoneal dialysis. The bleeding normalizes incompletely with hemodialysis. The mechanism of the platelet defect in uremia appears to be due at least in part to the accumulation of uncleared metabolites. Guanidinosuccinic acid in concentrations similar to those found in uremic plasma can inhibit platelet factor 3 availability, and in vitro aggregation to ADP, collagen and epinephrine. Similar abnormalities have been demonstrated with phenol and phenolic acids.

Drug effects constitute the largest category of acquired platelet disorders encompassing a wide variety of mechanisms. The best characterized of these drugs are those which have been used therapeutically as antithrombotic agents (see Chapter 13). Even though the biochemical mechanisms of some of these platelet-affecting drugs are relatively well understood, the clinical effect on hemostasis has not been well characterized.

Disorders of Platelet Interaction. Proteolytic *degradation products of fibrin(ogen)* inhibit platelet plug formation. These complexes may be increased in a variety of clinical situations such as intravascular coagulation, fibrinolytic therapy, and liver disease. The relative importance of platelet dysfunction in the pathogenesis of bleeding in these patients is difficult to determine, since the defect is usually mild and other associated hemostatic defects are present. Plasmin digestion of fibrin in vitro transiently produces a number of intermediate products, fragments X and Y, which are digested further to lower-molecular-weight products, DD dimers and E fragments (see Fig. 17, Chapter 4). Fragments X, Y, and to a lesser extent D, manifest anticoagulant properties by binding to fibrin monomers and interfering with their subsequent polymerization to fibrin. Patients suffering from hepatic cirrhosis frequently have enhanced plasminogen-plasmin system activity as evidenced by rapid lysis of clotted blood and elevated fibrin-fibrinogen degradation products. The mechanism of this fibrinolytic state is not clear, but may be related to poor clearance of plasminogen activators by the liver. Patients with severe liver disease have a complex hemostatic defect which may consist of thrombocytopenia, decreased vitamin K-dependent clotting factors, increased fibrinolytic activity, and defective fibrinogen polymerization, as well as qualitative platelet defects, as discussed in Chapter 11.

Abnormal bleeding occurs commonly in *dysproteinemias*. Platelet dysfunction, as demonstrated by a prolonged bleeding time, abnormal ex vivo adhesion and aggregation, and reduced platelet membrane phospholipid availability, is usually responsible. Although abnormalities in fibrin formation are more frequently demonstrated, these findings correlate poorly with clinical bleeding syndromes. The mechanism of platelet dysfunction has not been well characterized, but has been assumed to be secondary to the interference of the paraprotein with the reactions occurring at the platelet membrane surface. In addition to platelet dysfunction, hyperviscosity and thrombocytopenia may contribute to the hemorrhagic diathesis.

Dextran, a polysaccharide of varying molecular weight used as a plasma expander, increases the bleeding time and decreases platelet retention in glass bead columns. It also decreases the availability of platelet procoagulant activity. Bleeding complications of dextran therapy are approximately equal to those of oral anticoagulants. The mechanism of platelet inhibition is not specifically known, but may be related to platelet membrane changes or alterations in plasma constituents necessary for normal platelet aggregation.

Of particular importance to patients undergoing intensive cancer chemotherapy is the effect of *antibodies* on platelet function. Carbenicillin, a drug frequently used in patients with suspected sepsis and limited marrow reserves, is the most extensively studied of the antibiotics reported to cause platelet dysfunction.[143] The majority of hemostatically normal subjects exposed to concentrations of carbenicillin commonly used to treat Gram-negative sepsis will have a prolonged bleeding time. The defect appears within 24 hours after the start of therapy and persists for days. Penicillin G has also been implicated as a platelet inhibitor, but to a lesser degree than carbenicillin, possibly because the dosage is much less than that typically employed with carbenicillin. Ampicillin and cephalothin have also been demonstrated to produce a significant increase in spontaneous stool blood loss when administered to profoundly thrombocytopenic patients, presumably through similar mechanisms.[108]

Disorders of Platelet Release. *Defective α-granule storage* develops in patients undergoing open heart surgery and pump oxygenator bypass, placing them at risk of serious bleeding because of surgical damage to blood vessels and acquired defects in hemostasis.[112] A number of hemostatic defects may promote nonsurgical bleeding during the perioperative period including: (1) reduction in the levels of coagulation factors; (2) heparinization and the potential for subsequent inadequate neutralization or protamine excess; (3) increased fibrinolytic activity; (4) thrombocytopenia; and (5) acquired platelet defects. With the onset of cardiopulmonary bypass a marked prolongation in bleeding time predictably occurs in all patients that parallels platelet α-granule release. At the end of bypass, circulating platelets are partially depleted of α-granules without release of dense granule constituents. Interestingly, the bleeding time rapidly normalizes without reaccumulation of α-granules or their contents, suggesting that this acquired α-granule storage pool deficiency and the transient functional defect are independent consequences of platelet activation. Both the prolonged bleeding time and the bleeding diathesis responded quickly to transfused platelets.

Dense-granule storage pool defects are occasionally seen in association with autoimmune diseases, including autoimmune hemolytic anemia and systemic lupus erythematosus. These defects are characterized by a prolonged bleeding time and decreased aggregation to collagen, thrombin, and ADP.[144] It has been suggested that antiplatelet antibodies or antigen-antibody complexes may act on circulating platelets, inducing dense granule release. It is evident that different disease processes may induce a spectrum of storage pool defects, characterized by diminution of secretable substances that are stored in platelet granules. The specific substances that are depleted appear to explain the functional changes.

Primary disease of the bone marrow *(dyspoiesis)* has been shown to produce functional defects in all three cell lines, and is frequently associated with a bleeding tendency, owing to dense granule depletion, defective arachidonate pathway, deficiency of α-adrenergic or F_c receptors.[22,145] There have been several reports of morphologic and functional platelet abnormalities in acute leukemia and preleukemia. Although most often described in granulocytic leukemia, platelet abnormalities also appear in lymphocytic leukemias, and even leukemic reticuloendotheliosis.[146]

Bleeding due to defective dense granule release mechanisms has long been recognized as a complication of the *myeloproliferative disorders* (polycythemia vera, chronic myelogenous leukemia, agnogenic myeloid metaplasia, and essential thrombocytosis). The latter is associated with a marked elevation in platelet count (often greater than 1,000,000 per μl) and prolongation in the bleeding time that may sometimes parallel the elevation of the platelet count. Platelet survival is relatively normal and megakaryocytic volume is abnormally large relative to the platelet count. In vitro studies have shown that defective epinephrine-induced aggregation is the most consistent functional abnormality.[22] Polycythemia vera and myeloid metaplasia may show some of these same abnormalities in platelet function, whereas chronic myelogenous leukemia patients are more likely to have normal platelet aggregation.

Individuals who drink large quantities of *alcohol* over substantial periods may develop platelet dysfunction demonstrated by prolongation of the bleeding time, impaired secondary aggregation, reduced platelet procoagulant availability, and decreased platelet survival.[147] These effects occur in the absence of thrombocytopenia, but become more profound when thrombocytopenia is present. The mechanism of this action is unknown but may be through inhibition of platelet prostaglandin endoperoxide synthesis.

Aspirin produces a platelet abnormality characterized by defective second wave aggregation and mild prolongation in the bleeding time.[23] A single 200-mg dose of aspirin irreversibly acetylates approximately 90 percent of platelet cycoloxygenase, resulting in failure of platelets to synthesize cyclic endoperoxides and thromboxane A_2. The fact that the ingestion of aspirin by normal individuals results in only a mild prolongation in bleeding time suggests that prostaglandins and thromboxanes do not constitute a critical single pathway for aggregation and release. Therefore, the platelet arachidonic acid pathway appears to act as a mechanism of potentiation or amplification of physiologic stimuli leading to aggregation and release.

Sulfinpyrazone is another drug in the class of nonsteroidal anti-inflammatory agents. Like aspirin, sulfinpyrazone inhibits the platelet release reaction in vitro, although in contrast to aspirin it is a competitive inhibitor or cycoloxygenase and does not prolong the bleeding time.[23] Indomethacin, phenylbutazone, and many of the newer nonsteroidal anti-inflammatory agents inhibit platelet aggregation induced by collagen and arachidonic acid, as well as the second wave of aggregation induced by ADP and epinephrine. Furosemide and nitrofurantoin inhibit platelet aggregation by competitive inhibition of the interaction of ADP with platelets.

The effect of *diet* on platelet function has been largely speculative and has centered around thrombosis and atherogenesis rather than hemostasis; however, in rare instances diet may be associated with platelet dysfunction. Thromboxane A_2 is generated from membrane arachidonic acid. Dietary eicosapentaenoic acid (found primarily in some seafoods) incorporates into membrane phospholipids and results in the synthesis of thromboxane A_3, which is inactive towards platelets, and PGI_3, an inhibitor of platelet function.

Other causes of platelet dysfunction. A number of drugs and conditions do not fit well into the above categories because little is known regarding their mechanism of action. Heparin is used therapeutically for its inhibitory effect on coagulation. However, some fractions of the commercial preparations also appear to inhibit platelet function.[148] Some patients develop thrombocytopenia when treated with heparin through mechanisms that may be immunologic, or due to activation by a polysaccharide fraction that is less active as an anticoagulant. The bleeding time may be prolonged with high doses of heparin. Hydroxychloroquine, an antimalarial agent, inhibits in vitro aggregation to ADP and collagen, but does not prolong bleeding time.

Sympathetic blocking agents, such as phentolamine and dihydroergotamine, that inhibit primarily α-adrenergic receptors, have been shown to inhibit in vitro and ex vivo platelet aggregation. The effect of beta blocking agents such as propranolol on platelet function remains controversial, as some workers have shown that this drug does not inhibit aggregation except at concentrations that exceed usual blood levels of the drug; however, propanolol has been found to inhibit aggregation in patients showing enhanced platelet aggregations by mechanisms other than its beta blocking properties.

MANAGEMENT

Proper treatment of the disorders of platelet function depends on an accurate diagnosis and varies from patient to patient and from disease to disease. Generally, treatment is directed at removing the cause of the platelet dysfunction where possible. For example, this would include treating such systemic diseases as uremia or multiple myeloma, and removing drugs that may be causally implicated. Steroids or immunosuppressive therapy may be indicated in immune-mediated dysfunction. In patients with platelet dysfunction owing to a deficiency of a required plasma cofactor such as von Willebrand disease, therapy consists of replacement with cryoprecipitate. If, on the other hand, an extrinsic factor acts as an inhibitor, as with plasma dysproteinemia, replacement using platelet concentrates may be ineffective and removal of the inhibitor by plasmapheresis is necessary. If the hemostatic disorder is due to an intrinsic platelet defect and the patient is bleeding, platelet concentrates are indicated.

If both qualitative and quantitative platelet defects are present, the guidelines for use of platelet concentrates remain unclear. If even a mild qualitative defect is superimposed on thrombocytopenia, as with carbenicillin therapy in the pancytopenic chemotherapy patient, the risk of bleeding increases considerably, and platelet transfusions may be needed at a platelet count of 20,000 per μl or more. If the patient is bleeding, and this is due in whole or in part to a functional platelet defect, platelet concentrates are indicated irrespective of the platelet count. In general, platelet concentrates should be used judiciously, since alloimmunization to platelets (see Chapter 8) is to be expected, and will result in refractoriness to subsequently transfused platelet concentrates.

10

HEREDITARY COAGULATION DISORDERS

The congenital coagulation factor deficiencies occur in about 1 per 10,000 population. Their clinical manifestations are highly variable, ranging from frequent, spontaneous bleeding in the severe forms of hemophilia, to totally normal hemostasis in certain defects of contact activation factors. The more severe disorders are easily recognized clinically and readily identified by clotting assays. Moderately severe or milder forms are twice as prevalent as are severe deficiencies; true prevalence of mild hemophilia and von Willebrand disease is probably underestimated, as many patients go unrecognized. In contrast to the pain, morbidity, and frequent chronic complications found in patients with severe hemostatic defects, the major risk to most patients with milder forms (particularly when their presence is not suspected) is unanticipated bleeding following trauma, surgery, or dental extractions.

This chapter reviews the approach to recognizing a bleeding disorder and confirming this suspicion, followed by specific discussions of clinical aspects of hemophilia A and B and von Willebrand disease. Types of bleeding episodes in these congenital defects can be generalized to certain acquired coagulation defects (see Chapter 11) and complications of anticoagulant therapy (see Chapter 13). The management of the hereditary disorders is then outlined. The final section summarizes the rare congenital defects of hemostatic proteins, other than factors VIII and IX, which may be associated with a hemorrhagic tendency.

CLINICAL APPROACH TO COAGULATION DISORDERS

History. Inherited coagulation deficiencies are uncommon or rare, and may be difficult to recognize, even with laboratory screening. As discussed in Chapter 7, the most sensitive screen is a careful history.[101] In particular, evidence of delayed, intermittent, or prolonged microvascular oozing should be sought. Because platelet plug formation is intact, initial hemostasis is often achieved with subsequent oozing several hours to days later.

Spontaneous bleeding, major muscle hematomas, or hemarthroses in the absence of severe joint trauma are strongly suggestive of the moderate or severe hemophilias, being rarely seen in other disorders. Patients with milder disorders may give a negative history in the absence of previous surgery, or may not have bled abnormally despite some trauma. A history of prolonged hospitalizations and of blood transfusions needed for minor operations or dental extractions should always make one suspicious of an abnormality of hemostasis. In addition to the patient's own history, an extensive family pedigree should be recorded for each patient in which a hereditary bleeding problem is suspected.

Laboratory Diagnosis. In screening for congenital factor defects, the prothrombin time and partial thromboplastin time may be used together to place a suspected deficiency in either the extrinsic or intrinsic activation pathways, or in the common pathway that includes factors X, V, and prothrombin. As discussed in Chapter 7 and in Appendix A, an appreciation of the limitations and sensitivities of the particular kinetic assays run by a given laboratory is essential.

Hereditary abnormalities of fibrinogen that affect late-stage clotting screening tests are less frequently encountered. These disorders usually show a prolonged thrombin time, and can be identified by discrepancies between kinetic (Clauss) and total clottable fibrinogen determinations. A separate screening test, which also suffices for definitive diagnosis, is necessary to detect factor XIII (fibrin stabilizing factor) deficiency. Screening for congenital platelet dysfunction is also necessary as, for example, a mild factor deficiency does not differ clinically from a platelet functional defect.

If the screening tests are equivocal, or if they are normal and the clinical suspicion is sufficiently strong, specific assays are indicated to establish: (1) the precise factor which is deficient and (2) the level of that factor in the patient's plasma (usually expressed as a percentage of the normal clotting activity). Whereas the former is essential to define specific therapy, the latter is important in prognosis and in planning the amount and type of treatment necessary.

HEMOPHILIA A AND B AND VON WILLEBRAND DISEASE

The term hemophilia was originally applied to any lifelong hemorrhagic disorder. In the early 1950's, it was demonstrated in clinical laboratories in Oxford, San Francisco, and Philadelphia that there were two types of hemophilia. The initial observation was that in mixing plasmas from different patients, correction of clotting would occasionally be observed. It was possible to demonstrate that these different types of hemophilias were due to deficiencies of plasma proteins with different properties. Type A was deficient in the protein which lost activity when plasma was clotted to serum and was later identified as factor VIII, whereas the less common one (type B, initially described in an individual with the surname of "Christmas"), retained this activity in normal serum, but lost it when the serum or plasma was adsorbed with insoluble barium or aluminum salts. Prior to the availability of specific assays, mixing of various patient versus normal fractions formed the basis of a thromboplastin generation test to distinguish the types.

Prevalence. By far the most common congenital bleeding disorder is factor VIII deficiency, or hemophilia A, which accounts for three fourths of all congenital defects. Factor IX deficiency (hemophilia B) is about one fourth as frequent. The prevalence of hemophilia appears to be the same in all populations, races, and countries, around 1 in 10,000 persons. In contrast, prevalence of von Willebrand disease varies. Severe deficiencies of factor VIII and IX probably account for only one third or less of all patients with hemophilia, but such individuals are more likely to have been identified and receiving blood products than patients with milder forms.

Inheritance of Hemophilia. Both hemophilia A and B are sex-linked recessive disorders (Fig. 27), although 20 percent of affected individuals have a negative family history. The degree of severity, once the gene is established in a pedigree, is the same in all affected males. However, carriers may be symptomatic if their normal X chromosome is inactivated to a much greater extent than the one containing the gene for hemophilia. As this is a random event, it is not predictable what a carrier's factor VIII or IX level will be, but it can be in the range of mild hemophilia; levels as low as 2 to 5 percent have been reported. Clinically, symptomatic carriers should be treated like affected males. Carriers of hemophilia B are more likely to have significantly lower levels than normal compared with women heterozygous for hemophilia A; this may be caused by the more pronounced hormonal effects on factor VIII:C levels.

Clinical Manifestations. Hemophilia A and B are clinically indistinguishable.[149] The manifestations of the disorder depend on the severity of the deficiency. Patients having less than 1 percent of the normal mean level are subject to spontaneous bleeding episodes; their clinical picture tends to be

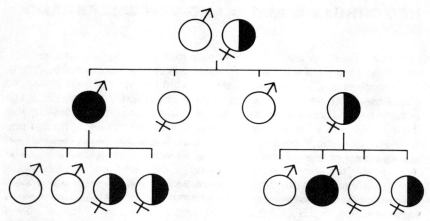

FIGURE 27. Inheritance of hemophilia. X-linked inheritance is shown where carrier (heterozygous) females have an average of half their sons affected *(solid symbols)* and half their daughters as carriers *(half-shaded symbols)*. Daughters of an affected male are obligate carriers. For 20 to 25 percent of patients with hemophilia A or B, however, family history will be negative, reflecting a high spontaneous mutation rate.

dominated by the problems and complications of repeated acute bleeding. Individuals with factor levels in the 1 to 4 percent range seldom have spontaneous bleeding, but may develop some of the chronic complications of bleeding, such as arthritis. Hemophiliacs having factor levels between 5 and 30 percent do not have spontaneous bleeding and may go for years without bleeding, or may not recognize that they have a bleeding problem.

Severe hemophilia ordinarily becomes obvious in infancy or early childhood. Prolonged bleeding from circumcision is the rule, but does not invariably occur. During the first year of life, there are usually few, if any, problems of spontaneous bleeding and, indeed, the presence of this defect may not be suspected until the child becomes an active toddler. At this point frequent, large ecchymoses are noted, and oral lacerations, including tearing of the frenulum, can be particularly troublesome. Hemarthroses and muscle hematomas also occur, but may only be suspected when a child is limping or showing signs of pain.

In older children and adults, the knees, elbows, and ankles are more prone than other joints to develop hemarthroses, and if repeated bleeding episodes are not treated promptly, they may develop chronic synovitis and even arthritis (Fig. 28). Such joint disease is the most common cause of physical disability in patients with hemophilia. Muscle hematomas may occur spontaneously, or follow trauma. Early detection may be difficult, since patients present with pain within the muscle unaccompanied by swelling or ecchymoses. Deep muscle hematomas can be quite serious, particularly when involving the iliopsoas and quadriceps groups. These may lead to contractures,

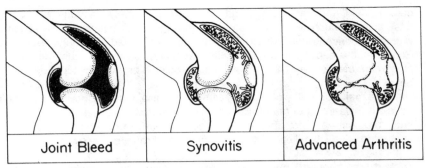

| Joint Bleed | Synovitis | Advanced Arthritis |

FIGURE 28. Progression of hemophilia arthropathy. A side section of a knee is shown. *Left: Hemarthrosis* involves the accumulation of blood *(black)* in the synovial space of a normal joint. *Center:* After recurrent episodes, a stage of *synovial thickening* occurs. The lining is more friable and prone to bleeding. This pathologic change presents clinically as a chronically swollen joint. *Right:* Once cartilage and bone are eroded, a roughened and cystic articulation occurs leading to chronic *arthritis.* (Clements, MJ, Counts, RB, with permission).

muscle atrophy, peripheral nerve entrapment, or even chronic hematomas ("pseudotumors"). Femoral nerve palsy from an iliopsoas hematoma is an especially serious problem. This may cause permanent weakness and atrophy of the quadriceps muscles, thus predisposing the individual to further bleeding and damage in the knees, and limiting other activities such as climbing and running. Without prompt and adequate treatment, muscle hematomas become chronic and sometimes encapsulated, which can cause severe disability, requiring surgical resection. Prior to adequate replacement therapy and surgical techniques, chronic hematomas frequently ruptured externally and became infected, usually with a fatal outcome. Large bony erosions also occurred. Early, aggressive replacement therapy in children will prevent chronic hematomas and, when begun in childhood, will dramatically decrease arthropathy,[150] at least through adolescence.

Injuries of the mouth and pharynx, including local injections for dental anesthesia, can lead to soft-tissue hematomas; in the posterior mandibular region, these hematomas have the potential for causing airway obstruction in the neck. Intracranial bleeding, usually following trauma, is not common, but has high mortality and is one of the major causes of death in patients with hemophilia. An increased incidence of seizure disorders has not been documented in these patients, but when encountered, it is attractive to assume that an epileptic focus might have occurred from a minor bleed that arrested and healed spontaneously. Thus, in a variety of ways, acute bleeding episodes can lead to chronic physical problems.

Additional complications of hemophilia include poor dental care, which in the past has commonly led to severe dental and periodontal disease, necessitating extensive extractions at a young age. Although severe problems with chronic pain and narcotic dependence were frequently encountered in the past, this is much less common today owing to the availability of specific treatment concentrates and preventive measures aimed at younger patients. Some adults, especially patients with inhibitors, which preclude routine replacement therapy, still have chronic pain problems or narcotic dependency, or both.

The major disability of patients with hemophilia is not associated with their physical limitations but rather with chronic social and behavioral problems. The latter problems are not unique to hemophilia, but are common problems accentuated within families having children with chronic diseases.

Inhibitors. About 10 percent of patients with severe hemophilia A develop alloantibodies, usually within the first few years after initial treatment.[151] The first clue may be lack of response to routine bleeding episodes following an ordinary treatment dose. If a patient begins to respond less well than expected to therapy, an inhibitor assay should be obtained. Some inhibitors show in vitro neutralization effects at low titers, no boost response, and are either not clinically significant or may be overcome with larger doses of factor VIII. Severe inhibitors, however, rise to high titers (e.g., 50 Bethesda U per ml or more) within five to seven days of re-exposure to concentrated factor VIII:Ag and the titer can remain high for several months. Such levels preclude effective treatment, as even massive doses of factor VIII are rapidly inactivated. Treatment should therefore be reserved for life-threatening situations.

Since hemophilic factor VIII inhibitors are alloantibodies, immunosuppression has not been as useful as in treating the acquired autoantibodies to factor VIII. It is difficult to lower significantly the antibody titer by plasmapheresis because of the large volume of distribution of IgG (and other problems in a life-threatening bleeding episode), but this approach may be helpful. Large doses of concentrates of the vitamin K-dependent factors have been used to "bypass" the inhibitor; the current products are not uniformly effective[152] and one runs the risk of inducing thrombosis, disseminated intravascular coagulation, or boosting the antibody titer. Experimentally, "activated" concentrates offer some promise, but the same limitations apply.

Thus, routine bleeding episodes in patients with such inhibitors should be managed as far as possible by immobilization and analgesia. Although bleeding frequently abates in time, this approach causes further muscle weakness and the need for rehabilitation. Preventive measures such as exercise programs and dental prophylaxis are thus even more important for individuals with factor VIII inhibitors than for other patients with hemophilia.

Carrier Detection. Testing of plasma samples is recommended for women in pedigrees with hemophilia. This holds for the "spontaneous" forms as well since the mutation may have occurred in a previous generation, being passed "silently" among women, or it may have occurred in the patient or his mother. Antigen level testing can assist in the diagnosis, but some carriers will still test as completely normal (Fig. 29).

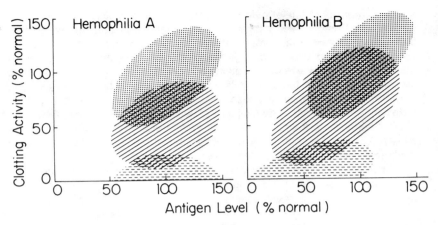

FIGURE 29. Clotting activities versus antigen levels for factors VIII and IX. Because of variability in either factor VIII or IX clotting assays, it is helpful to have independent antigen test confirmation, and for carrier detection, to repeat testing on at least three separate samples. Note that ellipses represent ranges of values encountered, not frequencies of abnormal values. Testing factor VIII/vWF:Ag in addition to factor VIII:C in families with hemophilia A improves the ability to diagnose a carrier to around 75 percent; VIII/vWF:Ag to VIII:C ratios are as high as 2:1 in many carriers. The newer factor VIIIC:Ag test remains to be evaluated in this regard. For potential carriers of hemophilia B, a low factor IX:C activity can often establish the diagnosis; factor IX:Ag testing is particularly helpful in pedigrees in which the abnormal gene produces crossreacting material which circulates in excess of clotting activity.

In genetic counseling it is advisable to spend several sessions with the patient and family members in order to cover thoroughly current clinical aspects of the disease, its inheritance, and the concepts of relative risk and probability. It needs to be re-emphasized that negative tests do not exclude the carrier state, but only decrease the probability of a woman being a carrier. It is important to assess the level of understanding and emotional factors in helping such individuals reach decisions. Some women may elect to become pregnant and undergo amniocentesis. Should the fetus be a male, elective abortion may be offered. Experimentally, fetoscopy has recently been used to obtain fetal blood samples at around 20 weeks and the factor VIIIC:Ag test used to identify affected males.[45,153] Abortion can then be offered when the test is positive and it is known that affected members of that pedigree do indeed have low factor VIII coagulant antigen (VIIIC:Ag) levels. The risk of this testing and its accuracy remain to be determined on a larger scale, however. For hemophilia B, factor IX is relatively less developed at this stage of fetal life, which makes such an approach less helpful.

von Willebrand Disease. In 1926, von Willebrand noted an autosomally inherited tendency in families from the Aland Island near Finland. Bleeding suggestive of poor platelet plug formation was noted clinically, leading to the designation "vascular hemophilia." It was later found that the factor VIII:C levels were low which, together with a long bleeding time and prolonged response to infused plasma or cryoprecipitate, became the hallmarks of the diagnosis. The von Willebrand protein can now be measured directly, either by immunoassay (as the factor VIII-related/vWF antigen), or by an assay in which normal, fixed platelets aggregate in response to the antibiotic ristocetin, reflecting vWF concentration in the subject's plasma. These newer tests, included in Table 7, have led to the recognition that there are several different types of the disease,[46,154] and offer a ready distinction from hemophilia A. Being autosomally transmitted, von Willebrand disease occurs in both sexes.

In the most common form, a mild bleeding disorder is present with a bleeding time usually in the range of 12 to 24 minutes and a factor VIII:C between 10 and 40 percent. Factor VIII/vWF:Ag is likewise decreased, as is ristocetin cofactor activity. After cryoprecipitate infusion, factor VIII:C levels rise appropriately for the amount transfused and remain elevated, usually for a few days. Bleeding times are transiently corrected (for four to six hours), but the response to clinical bleeding, as in elective surgery, relates more to the correction of the factor VIII:C level. This form of von Willebrand disease is inherited in an autosomal dominant pattern and clinically behaves like the mild forms of hemophilia.

A more severe, autosomal recessive type of von Willebrand disease also occurs. Here the factor VIII:C levels are 2 to 5 percent, bleeding times are greater than 30 minutes, factor VIII/vWF:Ag levels are barely detectable by the most sensitive radioimmunoassays, and the plasma shows no ability to promote ristocetin-induced platelet aggregation whatsoever. As in the mild form, a prolonged rise of factor VIII:C activity is observed after cryoprecipitate infusion, but clinically such individuals behave as if they have moderately severe hemophilia. Even chronic joint disease can occur. The parents of severely affected patients occasionally have some mild abnormalities in the above-mentioned tests, but are usually without any bleeding disorders themselves. This group is heterogenous and may result from inheritance of a double dose of one of the variant types (discussed below), or from "compound heterozygosity" of two distinct variant types.

Several variants of von Willebrand disease have been noted that may produce mild bleeding disorders and do not follow the characteristic patterns described above. In such disorders, it is even possible to see affected members within the same pedigree with differing degrees of severity. More often, the pattern is to have factor VIII:C activity levels in the 40 to 60 percent range with factor VIII/vWF:Ag levels about half the concentration. The von Willebrand protein in some pedigrees shows more rapid migration on crossed immunoelectrophoresis, and probably circulates in these patients as lower molecular weight multimers.[154] Variants in which normal ristocetin-induced platelet aggregation occurs with abnormal subendothelial platelet adhesion have recently been described.

TABLE 7. Comparison of hemophilia and von Willebrand disease

	HEMOPHILIA A	VON WILLEBRAND DISEASE
Procoagulant defect		
Partial thromboplastin time	Prolonged	Prolonged
VIII:C, Clotting activity	1 to 30%	2 to 50%
VIIIC:Ag, Coagulant antigen (human alloantibody or monoclonal antibody)	Reduced	Reduced
Platelet defect		
Bleeding time, Ivy template	Normal	10 to 30 minutes
VIII:R(vWF), ristocetin aggregation	Normal	Decreased
VIII/vWF:Ag, VIII-related antigen (rabbit or heteroantibody)	50 to 150%	1 to 40%
Mode of inheritance	X-Linked recessive (25% spontaneous)	Autosomal dominant, mild (more common, several "variants") Autosomal recessive, severe (rare)
Response to cryoprecipitate Infusion	8 to 12 hour T$\frac{1}{2}$	Prolonged correction of VIII:C (2 to 4 days) Transient correction of platelet defect (4 to 6 hours)

MEDICAL MANAGEMENT OF BLEEDING EPISODES

An accurate laboratory diagnosis is necessary before proper treatment can be selected because deficiencies of factor VIII and IX are clinically indistinguishable, but concentrates of factor VIII contain essentially no factor IX, and vice versa.[155] In addition, patients with von Willebrand disease will require less frequent transfusions. Additional considerations in determining a treatment plan involve the patient's baseline level, knowledge of the recovery and half-life of the given factor, and a somewhat empiric schedule that has proven successful in the particular patient and others like him.[156] Not only should the site of a bleed be considered, but also the duration of symptoms and nature of any antecedent trauma. Established bleeds in chronically damaged joints or those in the deep muscle groups seldom respond to a single dose. The number and frequency of infusions is also influenced by the indication, whether prophylaxis, maintenance, a bleed, or surgery.

For isolated, routine bleeding episodes at various sites, the usual dosage and schedule are summarized in Table 8. A rule of thumb is that if pain has not

TABLE 8. Recommended therapy for hemophilia

TYPE OF BLEEDING	INITIAL FACTOR VIII OR IX LEVEL NEEDED (% OF NORMAL)	MAINTENANCE SCHEDULE*
Uncomplicated hemarthroses	30 to 40	Repeat dose in 24 hours if not improved
Hemarthroses with synovitis	30 to 40	Repeat dose every other day for 1 to 3 months until chronic effusion resolves
Hematuria	30 to 50	Repeat daily until bleeding stops
Muscle hematoma	50 to 70	Treat every 12 hours to keep level >30% until hematoma resolves
Head trauma	40 to 50	Depends on clinical situation
Surgery	80 to 100	One half of initial dose every 12 hours for 10 to 14 days (until scar tissue is formed) and additional doses for postoperative rehabilitation
Dental extraction	30 to 40	Epsilon-aminocaproic acid 3 to 6 gm by mouth every 6 hours P.O. reduces need for additional transfusions although oozing may still occur requiring repeat dosage of blood components

*A bag (or "unit") of plasma contains about 250 ml (200 ml if from platelet-poor plasma) at an average of 1 clotting Unit per ml. Thus, cryoprecipitate averages 100 to 125 factor VIII clotting Units per bag (50 to 60% yield). Commercial concentrates have the number of clotting Units stamped on their labels.

been relieved in a few hours, additional therapy is usually needed. An exception would be pains due to arthritis, which can be difficult for patients to distinguish from hemarthroses. For dental extractions, a 10-day course of epsilon aminocaproic acid following a preoperative dose of the clotting factor decreases the need for blood products.[157]

To calculate the blood component dose, one simply multiplies the estimated plasma volume times the desired increment times the unit of clotting activity, defined as the amount of the factor in 1 ml of a normal plasma pool. For an adult, 40 ml per kg is the usual plasma volume, whereas this conversion factor is slightly larger for infants. The desired level minus the baseline level represents the increment. For factor VIII, complete recovery is assumed, whereas the larger volume of distribution of factor IX results in a 35 to 40 percent recovery[57] and the need for larger dosage. The frequency of transfusion depends upon the half-life (see Table 1) and length of time a minimum level needs to be exceeded.

An example would be a 70-kg adult with severe hemophilia A and acute knee pain over the past hour. The dose would be: 70 kg × 40 ml per kg × 0.35 unit per ml increment = 980 clotting units. For cryoprecipitate, this would mean 10 bags dissolved and pooled; two bottles of 500 units lyophilized factor VIII concentrate would also be sufficient. The same patient undergoing surgery would receive a larger dose immediately preceding surgery and repeated doses every 12 hours; therapy would then be maintained for 10 to 14 days.

Factor VIII Deficiency and von Willebrand Disease. Fresh frozen plasma contains normal amounts of factor VIII:C and von Willebrand factor. In order to raise the deficient level to the hemostatic minimum, however, concentrated factor VIII preparations can be used to avoid circulatory overload. The specific components (see Appendix B) prepared from plasma allow a more optimal, multiple use of blood as well. Cryoprecipitate has the advantage of being of higher yield and from a small donor pool, which minimizes exposure to hepatitis viruses. It appears to be more effective than other concentrates in patients with von Willebrand disease.[155] When care is taken in preparation, one bag contains an average of at least 100 units of factor VIII.

Factor IX Deficiency. Plasma should be considered for routine treatment of most patients with milder forms of hemophilia B because of the hazards associated with commercial concentrates. However, the volume required for plasma infusion is large, and volume overload may occur. In adults, uncomplicated joint bleeds and smaller muscle hematomas can usually be adequately treated with a single dose of three to four bags of plasma.

In the United States, lyophilized concentrates of the vitamin K-dependent factors are currently available only from the Red Cross or commercial sources. As they are derived from blood from a large pool of donors, they have an inherently high risk of hepatitis virus transmission. An additional risk of the concentrates containing factor IX is of thrombotic diseases (deep vein thrombophlebitis, pulmonary embolism, or disseminated intravascular coagulation). These complications appear to be greatest in patients with poor liver function, or those receiving large and repetitive doses such as for surgery. As with hemophilia A, minimal hemostatic levels postoperatively must be exceeded for 10 to 14 days to allow complete wound healing and to avoid delayed bleeding problems. Thus, the concentrated forms should be reserved for hemophilia B patients with demonstrated antibody to the hepatitis B surface antigen, with severe allergic reactions to plasma, or for major surgical procedures.

Complications of Therapy. Immediate complications of blood components include allergic and hemolytic reactions and, for vitamin K-dependent factor concentrates, a thrombotic tendency.[155] Urticaria is a commonly encountered allergic reaction with plasma, cryoprecipitate, and sometimes even lyophilized concentrate infusion. In susceptible individuals, its incidence is higher with more rapid infusion, but it is usually short-lived and responds readily to antihistamines. Individuals who develop hives frequently usually avoid them by taking an oral antihistamine one hour prior to the infusion. Other, fortunately uncommon, allergic manifestations are the anaphylactoid reactions. They are not related to the frequency of urticaria and may occur in its absence. When anaphylaxis occurs after multiple exposures to plasma, as in an individual with factor IX deficiency, this is an indication for concentrate therapy. To avoid hemolytic reactions, ABO group-specific plasma should be used whenever possible. Hemolysis following cryoprecipitate therapy has also been documented when this material is stored with plasma to serve as its diluent, as opposed to dissolving it in saline. Occasionally, acute febrile reactions with chills occur; these are presumably due to granulocyte antigens or products. They may last up to a few hours and are comparable to granulocyte reactions in patients who have had numerous red cell transfusions.

Chronic complications of treatment include inhibitors and liver disease. The occurrence of inhibitors has also been discussed above; it should be emphasized that any blood product or concentrate contains at least trace amounts of all plasma proteins, so that the potential for a boost response of an inhibitor or allergic reactions is always present. The problem of chronic liver disease deserves comment. It has been noted that most patients with hemophilia who have fairly frequent transfusions have a high incidence of mild to moderately elevated liver transaminase enzymes and serologic evidence of exposure to hepatitis B.[158] Where liver biopsies have been performed, these have shown the histiologic criteria of chronic persistent hepatitis, although in some individuals chronic active disease has been diagnosed. As clinically overt liver failure in patients with hemophilia is quite uncommon, it is not yet clear what these abnormal chemistries or histologies mean in a prognostic sense. They presumably relate to the transfusion of hepatitis viruses, as nearly all multiply-transfused patients will show antibody to the hepatitis B surface antigen; some show persistent antigenemia itself.

COMPREHENSIVE CARE

With any chronic disorder, the multiple facets and potential problems of patients with hereditary bleeding disorders are difficult to address in a coherent manner. As blood components have become readily available for the medical management of bleeding episodes, it has been possible to focus upon other chronic complications and, more recently, to place increasing emphasis on the preventive aspects of care. Comprehensive care centers for hemophilia have recently proliferated, and the current challenge for the centers is to provide expertise in diagnosis, treatment, home training, and monitoring of chronic problems, while also addressing the social and emotional complications for both patients and family members, and to deliver quality care without excessive cost.

While all health professionals need to be able to recognize congenital bleeding disorders and be aware of the limitations of screening tests, specific factor assays are best performed by reference laboratories. Within a given region, routine bleeding episodes can often be managed by the patient or family, or supervised by a community physician knowledgeable in the care of hemophilia. Routine dental care can likewise be provided at a local level, again if certain principles are applied and precautions taken. In these situations a center must provide expertise and also maintain continuity and focus upon the particular problems of each patient. A clearly defined treatment plan for each patient is therefore necessary, regardless of the degree of severity. A center staff appreciative of each of the many types of problems and available community resources is needed to optimize and coordinate care.[149,156]

BLEEDING DISORDERS FROM OTHER HEMOSTATIC PROTEIN DEFECTS

Contact Phase Proteins. As mentioned in Chapter 3, defects of factor XII, prekallikrein, or high-molecular-weight kininogen are autosomally inherited deficiency states which have no bleeding tendency whatsoever. They must be kept in mind, however, as causes of prolonged partial thromboplastin time. Deficiency of factor XI is usually associated with a mild bleeding tendency inherited in an autosomal recessive manner. Occasionally, a patient with in vitro assay levels, up to even 20 percent, will have a moderately severe disease. Heterozygotes are frequently detectable, but asymptomatic. The true prevalence of factor XI deficiency has not been determined, but a survey in Israel found a high frequency in Ashkenazi Jews.[159] The bleeding manifestations are usually not a problem except with surgery. There is little specific advice on treatment available in the literature, but plasma transfusion (15 to 20 ml per kg) usually is sufficient to control bleeding episodes; the half-life of factor XI is about 2.5 days.

A mild bleeding disorder with autosomal dominant inheritance was described by Hougie as Passovoy deficiency. The etiology remains unknown, and it is difficult to detect because the partial thromboplastin time is only slightly prolonged.[160] The duration of in vitro clot formation (or end point of the screening test) is visually longer than normal, but this observation also applies to patients with lupus inhibitors.

Other Vitamin K-dependent Factors. Deficiencies of factors VII and X are rare and are transmitted by autosomal recessive inheritance. Plasma transfusion is the preferred treatment, and as the minimum level required for surgery is somewhat lower than that needed for factors VIII and IX, a concentrate is less frequently necessary. Furthermore, the vitamin K-dependent factor concentrates used for factor IX contain approximately the same concentration of factor X, but are frequently low in factor VII.[155] Other distinctions are that factor VII defects are usually milder clinically than those of factor X, and factor VII has a much shorter half-life following infusion (see Table 1). Factor X defects are of further interest, as this protein represents the central enzymatic step at which intrinsic and extrinsic clotting systems enter a common pathway. When an abnormal protein circulates, it may participate more efficiently in one or the other system, or in its ability to be activated by an exogenous protease, such as the procoagulant from Russell's viper venom.[161]

Abnormalities of prothrombin[54] occur as low circulating levels of protein (hypoprothrombinemia), or as circulation of abnormal protein (dysprothrombinemia). These autosomal traits are not usually associated with a bleeding tendency. Compound heterozygosity has also been noted to account for at least three types of dysprothrombinemia that were also associated with a mild bleeding disorder. Of note, the one-stage prothrombin times may be relatively insensitive to either prothrombin defect, since levels around 10 percent are only associated with prolongations of a few seconds. Immunoassays are used to detect a population of circulating but dysfunctional protein; mechanisms of this abnormality can range from decreased activation or interaction with one portion of the activator complex, to decreased activity in the thrombin moiety once it is formed. As might be predicted, congenital defects of vitamin K-dependent carboxylation with low levels of all four of the vitamin K-dependent factors have been described; in one case, long-term treatment with high doses of oral vitamin K raised factor levels to the range of a mild deficiency.[162]

Factor V. This deficiency has in the past been referred to as "parahemophilia," and also represents a rare autosomal recessive disorder. Severity is usually moderate to mild as spontaneous bleeding is rare. The treatment is transfusion of fresh frozen plasma in doses of 15 to 20 U per kg, as no satisfactory concentrate is available. The minimum level needed for surgical hemostasis is in the 10 to 15 percent range, levels easily attained by plasma infusion of this relatively large molecule with a high intravascular recovery.

Even more rarely, individuals with a combined, usually mild deficiency of both factors V and VIII have been described. This curious double deficiency appears to be mainly of biochemical and genetic interest; a deficient inhibitor of activated protein C has been proposed.[162] Clinically, most of these individuals have responded well to treatment of the factor VIII deficiency alone; the factor V is seldom low enough to contribute to abnormal bleeding. Other reports of multiple deficiencies are usually due to chance inheritance of genetically distinct defects.[162] Likewise, discovery of hemophilia in women most often reflects a symptomatic carrier state, but chromosomal abnormalities and consanguinity have also been responsible.

Fibrinogen. A number of hereditary abnormalities of fibrinogen have been reported in the past 15 years.[163] Congenitally low levels of immunoreactive fibrinogen occur, are usually without any bleeding tendency whatsoever, and are referred to as *hypofibrinogenemia;* they may represent heterozygotes for *afibrinogenemia.* The latter is a rare but recognized autosomal recessive trait which is usually a severe disorder, with frequent bleeding episodes even in infancy (e.g., from the umbilical stump). Most patients with an abnormal protein, *dysfibrinogenemia,* are asymptomatic, but a mild bleeding problem or tendency to thrombosis is sometimes found. Most often, the abnormality presents as a prolongation of the thrombin time with or without a low fibrinogen level by the kinetic method. The total clottable fibrinogen is normal. When abnormal bleeding occurs, such patients can be treated with cryoprecipitate as a concentrated source of fibrinogen.

Delayed fibrin monomer polymerization as well as slow fibrinopeptide release have been identified. In a patient homozygous for fibrinogen "Detroit," in which an Arg to Ser substitution in the 19th position of the Aα-chain was found, this alteration of the α-knob structure prolonged polymerization (DD interaction), which also delayed the Bβ cleavage by thrombin. Aα cleavage was normal.[163]

Factor XIII. Deficiency of the fibrin stabilizing factor is a rare bleeding disorder that may be mild to moderately severe but is not detected by routine screening tests. Diagnosis is made by simply adding denaturing agents, such as 5M urea, to the fibrin clot. In normal plasma, fibrin is rapidly crosslinked such that the clot is insoluble in urea. In plasma from a patient deficient in factor XIII, where covalent crosslinking is impaired, urea dissolves the clot by breaking the noncovalent bonds of polymerized fibrin.

Clinical hallmarks of factor XIII deficiency include delayed bleeding and poor wound healing; cheloid scar formation frequently occurs. Inheritance of factor XIII deficiency appears to be autosomal recessive. Levels 5 to 10 percent of normal are sufficient to prevent or control bleeding. The long half-life further simplifies treatment such that a single transfusion, for example, two units of plasma, is sufficient to treat any bleeding episode in an adult.[164]

Other Hemostatic Proteins. Of nonprocoagulant proteins, one might suspect deficient inhibitors of fibrinolysis to cause a bleeding abnormality. Indeed, individuals with deficient α_2-antiplasmin have been reported. Consanguinity was present in one pedigree and, unlike the proband, none of several heterozygotes had clinically abnormal bleeding.[165]

11

ACQUIRED ABNORMALITIES OF COAGULATION

Acquired coagulation factor defects can occur throughout life, and are frequently associated with specific clinical settings. They may be mild and present simply as enhanced operative bleeding, and if the individual's hemostatic response has not been previously challenged, they must be distinguished from congenital disorders. They can also present as acute generalized bleeding, and are often associated with abnormalities of more than one screening test. Acquired disorders are summarized in Table 9, which categorizes congenital and acquired factor disorders. Deficiency states are listed according to stage of coagulation involved, that is, intrinsic or extrinsic system defects, both system or common path defects, and defects of the late-stage reactions. It should be noted that, as presented in Chapter 9, results of the late-stage screening tests should be evaluated first, as a low fibrinogen can prolong other kinetic screening tests.

This chapter discusses four general categories: (1) production defects of hepatic synthesis; (2) destructive or consumptive disorders, that is, disseminated intravascular coagulation; (3) inhibition by circulating anticoagulants; and (4) abnormalities in the massively transfused patient. Diagnostic, clinical, and management aspects are considered within each category.

DISORDERS OF PRODUCTION

Liver Disease. Abnormalities of hepatocellular protein synthesis are best correlated with the prothrombin time. In severe liver disease, the prothrombin

TABLE 9. Coagulation factor disorders*

MECHANISM AND EFFECTS ON SCREENING TEST RESULTS	ACQUIRED DEFECTS	CONGENITAL DEFECTS
Intrinsic system defect Prolonged PTT and normal prothrombin time	Autoantibodies (Nephrotic syndrome) (Contact phase factor defect)	Hemophilia A or B von Willebrand disease (Contact phase factor defects)
Extrinsic system defect Normal PTT and prolonged prothrombin time	Liver disease—mild Vitamin K defect—early	(Factor VII deficiency)
Common path or multiple defects Prolonged PTT and prolonged prothrombin time	Liver disease Vitamin K defect DIC—late (Amyloidosis) (Autoantibodies) lupus inhibitors	(Common path factor defect)
Late age defects Prolonged thrombin time and low fibrinogen level	Disseminated intravascular coagulation-DIC	Hypofibrinogenemia (afibrinogenemia)
Prolonged thrombin time and normal fibrinogen level	Dysfibrinogenemia-liver disease Heparin effect Fibrin(ogen) degradation products DIC—late (Autoantibody)	Dysfibrinogenemia
Decreased clot solubility in urea		(Factor XIII deficiency)

*Extremely uncommon conditions appear in parentheses.

time and the partial thromboplastin time remain prolonged despite parenteral therapy with water-soluble vitamin K. These screening tests largely reflect the depression of factors II, VII, IX, and X, and when levels of circulating protein are assessed antigenically, for example, they are usually low as well (i.e., an absolute production defect). Earlier in the course of liver disease, the screening tests may partially correct a few days following vitamin K therapy, suggesting that the carboxylase system (see vitamin K deficiency below) can be enhanced with excess cofactor. In early liver failure, it is possible to depress levels of factor VII out of proportion to other vitamin K-dependent factors. In this case, the prothrombin time is disproportionately prolonged. Probably the most sensitive early marker for hepatocyte disease is the demonstration traces of immunoreactive des-γ-carboxyprothrombin.[166]

Several hemostatic defects occur in liver disease (Table 10). These include the accumulation of higher than normal levels of fibrinogen-fibrin degradation products in the plasma, presumably related to decreased clearance. These or other catabolic products may lead to some platelet and fibrinogen dysfunction, prolonging bleeding time and thrombin time to up to twice normal. Another mechanism which produces fibrinogen dysfunction involves production of fibrinogen with increased levels of carbohydrate (sialic acid) content, which then behaves in vitro as a defective fibrinogen molecule. This type of dysfibrinogenemia is seen in patients with severe cirrhosis complicated by ascites or frequent variceal bleeding, or both, and has also been found in several patients with hepatoma.[167] It behaves kinetically like fetal fibrinogen, and is thus reminiscent of α-fetoprotein. Finally, decreased platelet production, ineffective folate-deficient production, increased splenic pooling, and a direct toxic effect of alcohol may all contribute to moderately severe thrombocytopenia in patients with alcoholic liver disease.[147]

Management of bleeding in patients with liver disease can be extremely difficult. For upper gastrointestinal hemorrhage, iced saline lavage, balloon compression, or local arterial infusions of angiotensin may be life-saving maneuvers. It is essential to consider in all such patients, however, that the amount of bleeding may be enhanced by one or more of the above hemostatic defects. In severe liver disease the defects are frequently multiple, and attempts to treat with concentrates of the vitamin K-dependent clotting factors, for example, have corrected the prolonged prothrombin and partial thromboplastin times, while failing to promote hemostasis. For thrombocytopenic patients, platelet concentrates are indicated, although the recovery in vivo may be decreased by splenomegaly or consumptive processes, or both. Clotting factors are best replaced by transfusion of whole blood (or packed cells with plasma), as these contain hemostatic levels of all the clotting factors lowered in this state. Levels of factor VIII, for example, are well maintained even in severe liver disease, so that deficiency is not encountered in the absence of its consumption. Factor V is labile to storage, but relatively low levels of this factor, compared with the others, are adequate for normal hemostasis, so that its role in replacement therapy is less critical.

TABLE 10. Hemostatic defects in liver disease

SCREENING TEST RESULTS	DEFECT(S)
Low platelet count	Folate deficiency Toxic ETOH effects Increased splenic pooling
Prolonged bleeding time	Increased fibrin(ogen) degraditon products and bilirubin; ethanol
Prolonged prothrombin time and PTT	Decreased vitamin K-dependent carboxylation and factor production
Prolonged thrombin time	Dysfibrinogenemia (increased sialic acid content) decreased clearance of fibrin(ogen) degradation products and plasminogen activators
Low fibrinogen	Exclude concomitant DIC (as due to necrosis, sepsis, or shock)

Vitamin K. Vitamin K is a fat-soluble vitamin. The mechanism of its action has been elucidated in studies of prothrombin (Fig. 30)[44] and factors VII, IX, and X following coumarin antagonists. It is of interest that two other Gla-containing plasma proteins have been identified: protein C and protein S, a proenzyme which when activated becomes an anticoagulant. These Gla have also been found in proteins in bone matrix,[168] the lens of the eye, and even atherosclerotic plaques. Interference with a bone matrix protein is presumably the mechanism of the abnormalities found in the specific embryopathy associated with coumarin ingestion during the first trimester of pregnancy.[169]

Deficiency may occur as an acquired defect in association with generalized fat malabsorption of the intestine in which vitamin D, A, and E are also poorly absorbed. Many plants provide dietary vitamin K. It is also synthesized by gastrointestinal flora and absorbed. Thus, in the absence of malabsorption, vitamin K deficiency only occurs with inadequate oral intake in the presence of broad spectrum antibiotics. This is most frequently encountered after these conditions are met for approximately two weeks, during which stores of the vitamin are depleted. When vitamin K has not been added to hyperalimentation fluids in acutely ill patients on antibiotics, they frequently present with oozing, or at least prolonged intrinsic and extrinsic screening tests, some 10 to 15 days into their course. A fibrinogen level should be checked to exclude prolongation due to hypofibrinogenemia, as seen in clinically significant disseminated intravascular coagulation. Slow intravenous administration of water-soluble vitamin K is the treatment of choice. Rare anaphylactoid reactions have occurred with parenteral water-soluble vitamin K administration; epinephrine treatment should be available.

Less commonly, an occasional patient on high doses of aspirin, usually 16 or more tablets per day (as in severe rheumatoid arthritis), will show a vitamin

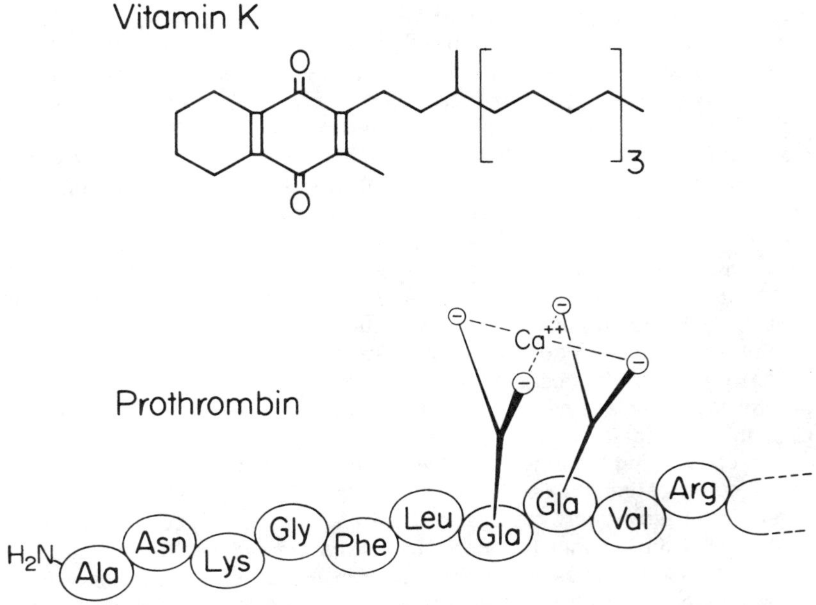

Vitamin K

Prothrombin

FIGURE 30. Structure and action of vitamin K. Vitamin K *(upper view)* is a naptho-quinone derivative with a hydrophobic side chain which differs in plant (K_1) and bacterial (K_2) forms; a synthetic water-soluble form is used therapeutically. Once a vitamin K-dependent protein is produced in the hepatocyte, specific glutamyl residues are carboxy-lated in a post-protein synthesis reaction. Sterically adjacent dicarboxylic residues (Gla) form a negative charge density which serves as a tight calcium-binding site as shown for prothrombin *(lower view)*. This allows these trace plasma proteins to form calcium bridges to phospholipid surfaces and thus achieve a sufficient local concentration to be activated and in turn interact with their cofactors and substrates. In vitamin K deficiency or antagonism, this extra carboxylation is incomplete, and abnormal proteins (e.g. des-γ-carboxy prothrombin), then circulate with markedly impaired clotting activity.

K synthesis defect. In this situation, and in some patients with mild or moder-ately severe malabsorption, oral administration of water-soluble vitamin K is sufficient to correct the acquired defect. Although hereditary resistance to war-farin therapy may occur in persons with markedly increased requirements for vitamin K, such individuals have normal levels of the vitamin K-dependent factors when not on an antagonist. Overdosage of coumarin anticoagulants, whether accidental in children, an error in therapeutic regulation, or even sur-reptitious ingestion,[106] can lead to bleeding within several hours (see Chap-ter 13).

Deficiency of vitamin K has also been implicated in hemorrhagic disease of the newborn. However, this situation is complicated by the immaturity of the liver at birth. In the normal fetus, increasing levels of vitamin K-dependent factors parallel increased hepatic protein synthetic function around the 25th week of life. By full-term birth, an average of only 30 to 40 percent of these factors is present, and levels rise gradually over the first year of life. Levels of other clotting factors, such as factor VIII, for example, average over twice as high. Thus, although vitamin K administration to all newborns is a legislated reality in most states, the actual incidence of deficiency or therapeutic benefit, particularly in relationship to liver immaturity, has not been established. Specific immunoassays of normal versus des-γ-carboxyprothrombin[166] should help clarify this issue.

Bleeding in premature infants is even more complicated.[170] Consumptive disorders are frequently encountered and volume considerations are extremely critical. Hypofibrinogenemia, with or without thrombocytopenia, may occur. It is helpful that platelet concentrates contain up to 50 ml of plasma which has essentially normal hemostatic levels of all factors; this volume provides a degree of factor replacement as well. Cryoprecipitate is occasionally needed to raise the fibrinogen.

In considering management of vitamin K deficiency, one must first assess for bleeding or immediate risk of bleeding (as with emergency surgery) to determine if more rapid reversal of the deficiency is indicated. The rates of synthesis of the vitamin K-dependent factors are indeed the inverse of the disappearance half-lives, determined after institution of antagonists or factors following infusion, so that in the massively bleeding or operative setting, more rapid correction of the defect with plasma or whole blood transfusion may be necessary. The volume load of replacement becomes critical, as sufficient factors must be infused to raise levels to the 30 to 50 percent range, and in an adult this usually means 4 to 6 units of plasma or whole blood. Parenteral vitamin K should, of course, also be administered immediately.

DISORDERS OF DESTRUCTION

Disseminated Intravascular Coagulation (DIC). DIC is a frequently encountered entity in which platelets and fibrinogen are consumed.[114] It is also referred to as "defibrination syndrome" or "consumption coagulopathy." It is important to consider this entity in terms of its severity, because in many clinical situations there is increased utilization of these hemostatic components that is subclinical. For severe defects, abnormal or generalized bleeding may occur.

The pathogenesis of DIC involves the activation of the coagulation system, thrombin generation, and platelet interaction with consumption of platelets and fibrinogen. As a secondary phenomenon, fibrin polymers, smaller fibrin strands, and even fibrinogen are degraded by the lytic mechanism. The stimulus or "trigger" of clotting can occur either by direct enzymatic activation of a clotting factor or by the release of an activator procoagulant such as tissue factor. The latter occurs in vitro with stimulated leukocytes.[51,80] Alternative mechanisms would involve initiation of the contact system through an endothelial cell protease that can activate factor XII,[63] or direct activation of intermediate clotting factors by neutral proteases from granulocytes. It may well be that under different circumstances the specific trigger reaction or reactions vary.

The sequence of events in DIC and its relationship to thrombosis are best illustrated by studies of women undergoing intrauterine infusion of hypertonic saline for abortion.[100] The placenta is rich in tissue thromboplastin, but it is not clear if extrinsic activation is the major mechanism for the limited DIC that occurs in this situation. Within minutes after infusion, free fibrinopeptide A can be detected, signaling that thrombin has been produced; about the same time levels of β-thromboglobulin and platelet factor 4 rise as thrombin stimulates platelets to undergo the release of their α-granules. Once fibrinogen has had its A peptides removed it is referred to as fibrin I, and can form small polymers and either be converted to normal fibrin with thrombin induced B peptide release, or, alternatively, form degradation product X by plasmin. A Bβ peptide, which contains three times as many amino acids as the B fibrinopeptide, is also released by plasmin action on fibrin I. The peak time of the thrombin-mediated reactions occurs one to two hours post-saline, whereas the Bβ peptide peaks at four hours, paralleling the formation of other fibrin degradation products, Y, D, and E. Plasmin action is thus secondary. The hypertonic saline infusion constitutes a situation in which thrombin generated within a damaged organ produces a systemic effect in which fibrinopeptides and platelet granule contents circulate. Fortunately, DIC in this situation is almost always subclinical.

Although bleeding is the major complication of consumptive states, it has been argued that fibrin deposition, particularly in the small vessels of the kidney, may lead to ischemic damage, analogous to the Schwartzman reaction in rabbits. Thrombotic complications in the microcirculation, however, are most frequently associated with disorders in which platelet consumption occurs predominantly, if not exclusively, independent of fibrinogen destruction (e.g., thrombotic thrombocytopenic purpura). A final complication that is rarely of clinical significance, but may serve as a diagnostic aid, is microangiopathic hemolytic anemia, that is, the appearance of red cell fragments on peripheral smear. As discussed below, this finding is frequently not present and should not be regarded as diagnostic. Consumptive coagulopathies will be discussed in terms of laboratory diagnostic tests and their limitations, underlying and associated disease states as related to various trigger mechanisms, and management.

The *laboratory diagnosis of DIC* requires demonstration of increased utilization of platelets and fibrinogen. This is reflected in the research setting by using ^{51}Cr-platelets and ^{125}I-fibrinogen with simultaneous survival studies over several days. With these techniques, it has been possible to demonstrate increased consumption in patients undergoing elective surgery, for example, where the degree of consumption is at least semiquantitatively related to the degree of surgical injury (see Fig. 26, Chapter 8). With normal liver and bone marrow function, however, increased production readily compensates for mildly increased destruction, so that levels of fibrinogen and platelet counts are not altered in these situations. When the synthetic capacities are exceeded, however, platelet count and fibrinogen levels fall; these tend to decrease in concert. In the acute, severe forms of this syndrome, thrombocytopenia to well below 100,000 platelets per μl and hypofibrinogenemia to below 100 mg per dl will occur. With the accumulation of fibrin-fibrinogen degradation products, as evidence of secondary fibrinolysis, inhibition of platelet function further limits hemostasis. At levels of fibrinogen below 80 to 100 mg per dl, these degradation products can also significantly interfere with the routine kinetic screening test for fibrinogen, so that a falsely low level is encountered when compared with the total clottable protein method for fibrinogen determination. The thrombin time is, of course, also prolonged by the antithrombin effect of X and Y fragments.

Routine tests for fibrin-fibrinogen degradation products are only semiquantitative and not necessarily specific. If one regards any normal individual as 1 +, most patients with liver disease have 2 + reactions, and in DIC 3 + reactions may be encountered in the commonly used agglutination assay. With further degradation of fibrin-fibrinogen molecules, however, smaller D and E fragments are produced that are rapidly cleared, and may not react in the commonly employed latex screening test; thus, DIC may exist in the absence of a positive test. On the other hand, certain individuals with elevated levels of gamma-globulins, as in chronic inflammatory conditions, may give false positive tests when the latex particles are used. The problems of specificity can be circumvented by more specific immunologic assays of fibrinogen, fibrin, or fibrinopeptides, but such tests are time consuming and not yet readily available to clinical laboratories. Tests of serum fibrin monomers by ethanol gelation or protamine precipitation (so-called paracoagulation tests) may also be used, but are even less direct. Experimentally, thrombin cleavage of factor XIII can also be followed as a marker of DIC or thrombosis that, along with immunologic assays for detection of inhibitor-enzyme complexes, will provide greater insight into the events occurring in vivo. Antibodies to pairs of degraded D regions (covalently crosslinked DD dimers) or D-E-D complexes,[64] as well as to the 42 amino acid Bβ peptide,[100] are clearly more specific for detection of cleavage products. Detection of plasmin-α_2-antiplasmin[171] or elastase-α_1-antitrypsin complexes constitutes an additional, sensitive means to characterize events associated with active DIC.

Further comment on the presence of fragmented red cells on smears is necessary. A microangiopathic smear may be seen in vasculitis or diseases of primary platelet consumption, as well as in individuals with hypertension. Their presence is thus not specific for DIC; conversely, they are frequently absent in patients with documented consumption. In summary, the best laboratory diagnostic indicators for clinically significant DIC are a decreased platelet count and decreased fibrinogen level. Provided that the synthetic capacities of the marrow and liver are not impaired, and recognizing that recovery of the fibrinogen level occurs more rapidly than the platelet count, the degree of depression is similar.

DIC can be found to complicate a vast array of underlying or *associated diseases*. The major implication of this is to avoid delays in recognition. Not infrequently, a fall in the platelet count and fibrinogen level may herald the onset of the condition itself, as is frequently seen in bacterial sepsis. The problem for the clinician, once DIC has been recognized, is to identify possible trigger mechanisms and, for those that are treatable, to correct the underlying condition rapidly while providing supportive measures as discussed below.

It is useful to consider conditions in terms of their possible mechanisms of triggering DIC, as shown in Table 11. Experimental infusion of activated clotting factors into animals produces the typical changes of DIC, once the levels exceed the normal defense mechanisms of inhibition. Although uncommon clinically, the direct procoagulant effect is best represented by the occasional occurrence in acute hemorrhagic pancreatitis, in which tryptic-like enzymes overwhelm the naturally occurring plasma inhibitors and activate the clotting cascade. Pancreatitis secondary to L-aspariginase therapy has also been associated with DIC. In certain snake bites, venom proteases activate factor X or prothrombin directly, even without a requirement of phospholipid. This mechanism may also account for the DIC occasionally seen after infusion of crude, commercial concentrates of vitamin K-dependent clotting factors that contain variable amounts of activated factors VII, IX, and X.

Disruption of cells with release of neutral proteases occurs in tissue injury or intravascular cell lysis, and may also lead to DIC. The former includes a variety of disorders, from simple surgical wounds to massive ischemic necrosis. In these conditions, the degree of tissue injury is directly related to the severity of the DIC. Tissue ischemia or necrosis is also associated with DIC in obstetrical complications, including retained dead fetus, abruptio placenta, and amniotic fluid embolism. To a large extent this may reflect the high levels of tissue thromboplastin found in the placenta; a tissue factor can also be implicated in consumption induced by massive injury to the brain or lungs. In peritineo-venous shunts, ascitic fluid contents can induce DIC. Occasionally, specific proteases[79] or necrosis from solid tumors may trigger DIC.

Although uncommon in occurrence, the malignancy most frequently complicated by severe DIC is acute promyelocytic leukemia. This appears to be related to intravascular release of a tissue factor or neutral proteases in the nonspecific granules and direct activation of coagulation and damage to endothelial cells. DIC may become overt during initial chemotherapy and rapid cell lysis. Other forms of acute leukemia generally have less marked DIC, although it is usually present; it is frequently clinically significant as an added hemostatic defect, in addition to the underlying compromise in platelet production. In acute intravascular hemolysis, cellular contents are again released into the circulation and clinically significant DIC can occur.

The vasculature is an especially important area for consideration, as shock, hypotension, and acidosis lead to increased venous stasis and thus promote coagulation. Endothelial cell injury occurs in patients with burns and is, at least theoretically, one mechanism by which endotoxin in Gram-negative sepsis can induce DIC. Once the collagen basement membrane is exposed,

TABLE 11. Trigger mechanisms in disseminated intravascular coagulation

---

Direct intravascular activation by specific proteases
  Snake venoms (e.g., Russell viper venom)
  Hemorrhagic pancreatitis (trypsin)
  Crude, commercial concentrates of vitamin K-dependent factors
    (factors IX_a, X_a, VII_a)

Release of cellular procoagulants (thromboplastins, neutral proteases)
  Extravascular tissue injury (surgery, trauma, tumor necrosis)
  Intravascular cell lysis (acute leukemias, hemolysis)
  Granulocyte lysis or monocyte stimulation (sepsis)
  Circulation of ascitic or amniotic fluid

Vascular factors
  Shock, hypotension, and stasis (volume depletion, sepsis)
  Endothelial cell damage (endotoxin)
  Other (cyanotic congenital heart disease, giant hemangioma)

---

contact activation as well as platelet consumption can occur. Among pediatric syndromes, cyanotic congenital heart disease and giant hemangiomas constitute additional diseases which could be added informally to this category.

The mechanisms of inducing DIC by different infectious agents are frequently complex and varied. In falciparum malaria, acute intravascular red cell hemolysis occurs. Endothelial cell damage is a striking feature of Rocky Mountain spotted fever. Endotoxin causes several effects which could account for DIC. Falling platelet counts and fibrinogen levels may be the early signs of the acute onset of sepsis, whether with an endotoxin-producing organism or other bacterial strains. This is encountered frequently in patients with bone marrow granulocyte suppression due to leukemia or cancer chemotherapy, or both. It should be emphasized, moreover, that the most common treatable conditions causing overt DIC are hypotension and sepsis, even in patients with malignancies.

In *managing patients with severe DIC,* attention to the underlying condition is essential as an immediate step. Blood volume may require expansion to elevate blood pressure. If sepsis is a strong possibility, antibacterial therapy should be initiated immediately, prior to confirmatory culture results. Beyond these and other immediate supportive measures, however, the clinical severity of DIC as related to the clinical condition of the patient must be assessed. If the patient is not bleeding actively, either in a generalized fashion or from a localized lesion, no further hemostatic therapy may be indicated. However, as the major complication of DIC is bleeding, blood component replacement becomes the next line of defense. Transfusion with whole blood (or red cells and plasma) for blood loss is generally sufficient to maintain hemostatic levels of clotting factors in moderately severe DIC. When the fibrinogen level is extremely low, additional hemostatic benefit can be achieved by a concentrated form of fibrinogen (cryoprecipitate). Platelet concentrates are frequently the major replaceable hemostatic component that controls bleeding. Although platelet dysfunction induced by fibrinogen-fibrin degradation products, for example, would also apply to transfused platelets, this should only lead to their use at somewhat higher counts than if an individual had normally functioning platelets. The concept that treating with blood components will only add "fuel to the fire" and enhance the process of microvascular damage, as occurs in the rabbit, has not proved to apply clinically as indicated in a recent series with careful observations at autopsy.[172] Indeed, in situations in which hemorrhagic shock may be triggering DIC, it is of the utmost importance to attempt to achieve a normal hemostatic mechanism as quickly as possible.

Attempts to inhibit clotting or fibrinolysis were formerly common approaches in DIC. Heparin therapy, especially by continuous intravenous infusion, has been used to disrupt the effect of an ongoing stimulus for consumption of coagulation factors. Levels of fibrinogen and factors V and VIII improve rapidly after institution of this anticoagulant, but its use in the management of DIC is hazardous. In effect, one substitutes one severe hemostatic defect, that of heparinization, for that accompanying DIC. When DIC is severe enough to produce bleeding, the results of the additional defect can be catastrophic. In patients in whom bleeding is not a prominent clinical feature, there is probably little need to intervene, except for measures directed at the underlying associated disease. Another former approach to DIC that was widely used in obstetrical complications was an attempt to inhibit fibrinolysis with epsilon-aminocaproic acid (EACA). This drug is a potent inhibitor of plasmin but, as mentioned above, fibrinolysis is a secondary phenomenon. In addition, acute severe DIC is frequently produced by a rather sudden event such as lysis of leukemic cells or by bacteremia. Thus, the underlying clinical stimulus may have diminished by the time the clinical syndrome is recognized, so that any intervention directed towards the clotting factor or fibrinolytic mechanisms may be too late. Clinically significant bleeding, as the major complication of DIC, is best managed by blood component replacement.

Other Degradative or Consumptive States. There is no evidence that normal catabolism of clotting factors occurs by in vivo clot formation, but in some clinical situations, rather specific factor consumption has been observed. Although fibrinolysis in DIC is a secondary event, on rare occasions fibrinogen can be degraded out of proportion to platelet consumption. This is seen after massive brain or tissue trauma where, in effect, a bolus of tissue factor is delivered to the circulation. It can also occur after envenomation with fibrinogen-cleaving enzymes, such as following crolatus (rattlesnake) bites. A second consumptive situation is the alteration of contact activation and factor XII seen in some patients with the nephrotic syndrome.[173] It is unclear if this represents a pathogenic effect or a secondary phenomenon. Increased turnover of contact factors also occurs in some patients with DIC. A final mechanism leading to deficiency has been reported in a few patients with amyloidosis and an acquired factor X deficiency.[174] Factor IX levels are sometimes depressed as well. This seems to reflect a tremendous capacity of the amyloid substances to bind these factors, possibly by calcium bridges or other interactions, to mucopolysaccharides such as heparan sulfate or amyloid fibrils.

CIRCULATING ANTICOAGULANTS

Inhibitors of clotting are found in normal plasma and include antithrombin III, α_1-antitrypsin, α_2-macroglobulin, C1 esterase inhibitor, and α_2-antiplasmin. Epidemiologic screening has demonstrated significant decrease of antithrombin III in patients taking birth control pills, for example, but the differences are not marked, and other inhibitor levels are increased. The mildly increased risk of thrombosis has not been directly related to these changes. Thus, these inhibitors primarily function to control hemostatic processes that result as localized phenomena (e.g., from increased concentrations of platelet phospholipid membrane vesicles at a site of injury) from spreading to thrombus formation in the general circulation.

Circulating anticoagulants can also be encountered pathologically and present as acquired hemostatic defects.[151] These are usually immunoglobulins, and can be recognized in screening tests such as the partial thromboplastin time, where prolongation is not corrected by a 1:1 mix of the patient's plasma with a normal plasma pool. The pathologic inhibitors can either be directed against a specific clotting factor, or have a less well-defined mechanism, as seen in lupus erythematosus. Therapeutic anticoagulants as additional forms of inhibition will be discussed in Chapter 13.

Specific factor inhibition most commonly involves antibodies against factor VIII. These may occur spontaneously, particularly in elderly individuals, as one of the postpartum autoimmune phenomena, or in association with chronic inflammatory conditions such as rheumatoid arthritis. They also occur in 10 percent of patients with severe hemophilia A as alloantibodies after exposure to transfused factor VIII. Antibodies against the von Willebrand portion of the factor VIII/vWF complex which may not inhibit the procoagulant activity have been described (leading to an acquired bleeding tendency). These mild defects are sometimes noted as they produce excessive bleeding from vascular lesions, such as angiodysplasia in the gastrointestinal tract. Less commonly, specific inhibitors of factors V, VII, IX, XI, or XIII are found as autoantibodies.

In *systemic lupus erythematosus,* patients with active disease frequently demonstrate prolongation of both prothrombin time and, to a greater extent, the partial thromboplastin time. Although not corrected by the 1:1 mixture, a specific site of interaction in the clotting mechanism has not been identified. In some patients, evidence for phospholipid specificity has been found.[175] An intermediate of prothrombin activation has also been implicated, and in other cases contact activation is primarily interfered with. Thus, there may be more than one antibody or site of action of these inhibitors. In clotting factor assays they clearly behave differently than specific factor VIII inhibitors, although the latter are occasionally found in patients with lupus. The classic lupus inhibitor has been seen as the presenting symptom of the disease and has also been found in the drug-related lupus syndromes. The severity of the hemostatic defect cannot be predicted by the degrees of screening test prolongation, as some patients have undergone surgery without abnormal bleeding. On the other hand, and particularly if discovered in the course of evaluation for elective surgery, the more conservative approach is to treat first, since a significant proportion of patients will have abnormal bleeding. More recently, an increased risk of thrombosis has also been noted.[176]

Treatment of patients with nonhemophilic acquired inhibitors using high-dose steroids is frequently successful in several days to a few weeks. For the lupus inhibitor, complete normalization of the partial thromboplastin time is usually observed, but mild prolongation of the prothrombin time may persist. Acutely, massive doses of factor VIII may achieve hemostasis in bleeding patients with specific inhibitors of relatively low anti-factor VIII titer. Plasmapheresis should be reserved for extenuating circumstances, but may be helpful for life-threatening, uncontrollable hemorrhages.

THE MASSIVELY TRANSFUSED PATIENT

Transfusion of large quantities of blood into an actively bleeding patient can lead to alterations of the clotting factor screening tests, despite the fact that hemostatic levels of the factors themselves are usually well preserved. Local lesions are often responsible for the blood loss, but after 10 to 20 units of whole blood or its equivalent have been transfused, most patients will become thrombocytopenic. Platelet dysfunction is a frequent concomitant disorder. Thus, the major hemostatic defect involves platelets such that initial therapy should be directed at monitoring and maintaining a count near 100,000 per μl.[177]

Low levels of clotting factors are uncommon without underlying defects, unless the predominant transfusion products are packed red cells and albumin. Whole blood stored at 4°C for 21 days, maintains normal levels of all factors except V and VIII. The former remains at levels above its minimum for hemostasis (around 15 percent), whereas factor VIII falls to around 20 percent in the first 48 hours. Without concomitant severe DIC, the recipient rarely has factor VIII levels below 50 percent. When levels fall below 25 to 30 percent, excessive bleeding may be controlled by cryoprecipitate. This is the safest blood product to transfuse, and also provides a concentrated form of fibrinogen, which is usually needed at this point.

The screening tests affected include the bleeding and thrombin times, reflecting some degree of DIC usually associated with hypotension; fibrinogen degradation products may also be elevated. In the emergent setting, it is not uncommon to have errors in sample collection or inadvertent heparin contamination, or both, so that results must always be compared to the clinical picture of bleeding. On the whole, however, fibrinogen levels, and certainly those of the vitamin K-dependent factors, are essentially normal in whole blood or plasma infused which tends to maintain them in the recipient.

Citrate toxicity is another consideration in the massively transfused patient. This rarely becomes a problem except in newborns or patients with liver disease, in whom toxic levels can occasionally be reached. For normal adults it has been calculated that this would occur if two units (1000 ml) were transfused in 10 minutes or less. Calcium can be given to avoid or reverse this toxicity, but is seldom needed clinically.

There are local, nonsurgical measures to produce hemostasis, as with upper gastrointestinal bleeding.[178] On the other hand, continued rapid blood loss only leads to hypotension, DIC, and massive transfusion requirements that might be minimized by an early operative procedure. In either event, screening for mild hemostatic defects is imperative, as specific blood components may be indicated.

PART 3
CLINICAL THROMBOTIC DISORDERS

Thromboses with or without embolism of either the venous or arterial systems are a major cause of morbidity and mortality in Western man. This section presents the clinical approach to venous and arterial thrombotic and thromboembolic disease, followed by a discussion of fibrinolytic agents, anticoagulants, and platelet function inhibitors used in antithrombotic therapy. A final chapter outlines the clinical management of specific disorders, including deep venous thrombosis and pulmonary embolism as well as arterial thrombosis and thromboembolism as they present in the coronary, cerebral, and peripheral circulatory systems.

12

CLINICAL APPROACH TO THROMBOSIS AND THROMBOEMBOLISM

VENOUS THROMBOSIS AND THROMBOEMBOLISM

Pulmonary embolism is responsible for 50,000 to 100,000 deaths per year in the United States. In one fourth to one half of these patients, the fatality is particularly tragic because it develops in the absence of any established, life-threatening condition. Fatal pulmonary embolism occurs as a complication of general surgery in 0.1 to 0.8 percent of patients, and in emergency hip surgery, the frequency in some series has been near 5 percent. Pulmonary embolism arises from thrombi in the deep venous system, usually of the lower extremities. Although risk of embolization is least from distal calf thrombi, this vascular bed shows fibrin deposition in 10 to 40 percent of all patients over 40 years of age undergoing routine surgical procedures. It is therefore important to identify factors that predict relative risk for clinically significant deep venous thrombosis and to design effective prophylactic regimens for venous thrombotic and thromboembolic disease.

Clinical Recognition of Deep Venous Thrombosis (DVT). The symptoms and signs of DVT are consequences of both venous obstruction and local inflammation. Venous obstruction causes swelling and venous distention; the reactive inflammatory response causes pain, tenderness, erythema, and warmth. With the physical signs of obstruction, the clinical diagnosis of DVT is much more likely to be accurate than when only the signs and symptoms of inflammation are present. The traditional physical findings of DVT such as the Homan sign are unreliable, being both nonspecific and insensitive. Indeed, up to one half of the patients with DVT postoperatively will have no signs whatsoever. Conversely, half of all patients with "typical" signs of calf pain and tenderness do not have DVT, but have instead cellulitis, a ruptured popliteal cyst, or inflammation involving muscle, tendon, joint, bone, or soft tissues. Laboratory procedures are thus necessary to establish the diagnosis of DVT.[179]

Laboratory Detection of DVT. Widely available methods for detecting DVT include contrast and isotopic venography, Doppler flow studies, and impedance plethysmography. Labeled fibrinogen uptake may also be useful in patients at known risk, but this latter test is reserved largely for experimental studies, since observations must be accumulated over several days to identify thrombus formation (see later section on experimental evidence of ongoing thrombotic states). Because thermography is positive with any local inflammatory process,[179] it lacks the necessary specificity to be used as a screening test. Experience with different detection procedures is surprisingly variable, even among large centers. Consequently, if equivocal results are obtained, or clinical suspicion is high, serial studies may be helpful in establishing the diagnosis.

The *contrast venogram* remains the reference standard for the detection of deep venous thrombosis and is the method against which all other techniques are compared. The test involves the injection of radiopaque contrast material into a superficial foot vein, thereby filling the deep veins with contrast media. Thrombosis is diagnosed by the presence of an intraluminal filling defect on more than one projection, or the presence of dye above and below a completely occluded venous segment. The presence of collateral flow suggests chronicity for a specific lesion, although pre-existing venous disease compromises that interpretation. Withholding anticoagulants in patients with negative venograms has been shown to be without significant risk of embolization.[180] The disadvantages of venography include the requirement for x-ray equipment and radiologist's time, the discomfort produced in the patient, the possible initiation of DVT itself, and the fact that some thrombi may be missed. Also, minor degrees of superficial phlebitis may follow at the site of injection, and rarely there may be superficial necrosis. Despite the accuracy and sensitivity of this examination, it is obvious that not all patients presenting with pain in the calf should be subjected to an expensive and invasive procedure. The sensitivity and complication rate will also depend upon the skill and experience of the radiologist.

Isotopic venography is performed as for a pulmonary lung scan by injecting technetium (^{99}Tc)-labeled macroaggregated albumin into a foot vein. If a major venous occlusion is present, the isotope fails to fill the occluded vein, but fills collateral veins, as shown by external scanning. In addition, the possible presence of pulmonary emboli is assessed because a lung scan is subsequently obtained. Studies comparing this technique with contrast venography indicate that the isotopic procedure detects major occlusive thrombi in the large veins of the pelvis or thigh with about 90 percent accuracy. False-negative results are common when mural thrombi fail to obstruct venous blood flow completely, and calf-vein thrombi are usually missed. False-positive results sometimes occur in areas of inflammation, hematoma, or edema.

The *Doppler ultrasound flow detector* measures changes in venous or arterial blood flow. Compression of a vein downstream will cause increased blood flow proximally that may be detected with the Doppler device. Obstruction prevents the compression-induced increase in flow. This technique is reasonably sensitive for the detection of major occlusion in veins above the knee in symptomatic patients.[181] However, it will not reliably detect thrombi in the calf or early nonadherent thrombi that do not substantially obstruct flow. Since the end point is subjective, the technique requires an experienced operator. The method may be useful in giving the clinician reasonable assurance that no major thrombus is present in the deep veins of the proximal thigh.

Impedance plethysmography compares proximal and distal electrical resistance in the calf that reflect reciprocal changes in calf volume produced by venous congestion induced by inflation and deflation of a thigh pressure cuff. It is reasonably accurate in detecting major thrombi in the proximal thigh of symptomatic patients but, like the ultrasound study, it is insensitive to distal thrombi in the calf. Although not as widely used as the Doppler flow detector, laboratories proficient in plethysmography have found this approach to be more objective, sensitive, and specific when compared with Doppler studies or isotope venography.[182] False-positive results are produced by any condition that compromises arterial flow to, or venous return from, the extremity. In addition, plethysmography is not useful in an extremity that bears a cast or cannot be relaxed because of pain or traction.

Strategy for Establishing Diagnosis of DVT. In view of the hemorrhagic risks associated with antithrombotic therapy, together with the diagnostic limitations of the clinical symptoms and signs, it is imperative to obtain objective evidence for the presence of DVT or PE prior to committing patients to a course of anticoagulants. The upper half of Figure 31 outlines a strategy to approach DVT. The diagnosis is considered to be established with positive tests in two of the three noninvasive laboratory examinations, or by direct contrast venography itself. Some centers with a special skill using a particular noninvasive technique may accept a single positive study. The contrast study is usually reserved for situations with high clinical likelihood but equivocal noninvasive test results. Since a diagnosis of either deep venous thrombosis or pulmonary emboli leads to anticoagulant therapy, a positive perfusion scan with equivocal findings for deep vein thrombosis establishes the diagnosis and renders a contrast venographic study unnecessary.

Clinical Recognition of Pulmonary Embolism (PE). The clinical presentation of pulmonary embolism may vary from the classical onset of pleuritic

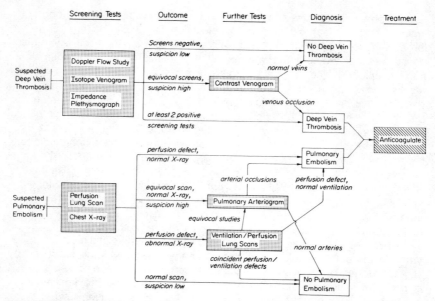

FIGURE 31. Strategy of approach to venous thrombosis and thromboembolism. The approach to patients with suspected deep venous thrombosis or pulmonary embolism involves the utilization of screening procedures. Depending upon the results of these tests, further testing with contrast studies or double isotope scanning may be indicated. Antithrombotic therapy needs to be instituted once the diagnosis is made; alternatively, if the suspicion is high and there are no major contraindications, heparinization can be started while confirmatory noninvasive screening procedures are being performed. The pulmonary angiogram is not necessary when deep venous thrombosis is documented, since anticoagulant therapy is indicated in both.

chest pain, cough, dyspnea, and hemoptysis in a patient with pre-existing deep vein thrombosis, to an asymptomatic pleural effusion or a low-grade fever and tachycardia in an otherwise typical postoperative patient. None of the presenting symptoms and signs are sufficiently specific or sensitive to make a definitive clinical diagnosis of pulmonary embolism. However, when clinical suspicion is high in an urgent setting, heparin therapy should be initiated before diagnostic confirmation has been completed. Emergent therapy is particularly relevant when PE is associated with cardiovascular collapse, since this setting usually reflects massive embolization occluding one half to two thirds of the pulmonary circulation.

Laboratory Detection of PE. Perfusion lung scans or pulmonary angiograms are required to establish the diagnosis of pulmonary embolism. Sometimes it is useful to demonstrate a low arterial oxygen level, although this in itself is nonspecific. When arterial partial pressures of oxygen are above 90 to

95 mm Hg, one can be relatively certain that major embolization to the lungs has not occurred. Although elevated bilirubin and lactic dehydrogenase levels and a right axis shift in the electrocardiogram can all be associated with PE, they are late findings and are not routinely found in PE patients. The chest roentgenogram is typically normal, since perfusion but not ventilation is impaired, but parenchymal infiltrates can be seen if the embolus is complicated by pulmonary congestion or infarction.

A normal *perfusion lung scan* is highly reliable in excluding significant pulmonary embolism. The major diagnostic problem associated with lung scans is false positive or equivocal scans. In one large series,[183] the majority of patients with questionably positive perfusion lung scans failed to show defects on pulmonary arteriograms. Any pre-existing lung disease may be associated with perfusion scan defects. The interpretation of abnormal findings in the lung perfusion scan can be facilitated by comparing them with the results of ventilation scans, particularly when infiltrates or other abnormalities are present on the chest roentgenogram. A classic pulmonary embolus produces a perfusion defect in an area of normal ventilation, that is, mismatched or discordant defects. When the lung scan shows segmental or lobular perfusion defects with a normal chest roentgenogram or without matching ventilation defects, there is a high probability of pulmonary embolism. Selective angiography in such situations confirms that up to 90 percent of such patients will indeed have pulmonary embolism.

The reference standard for the diagnosis of pulmonary embolism remains the *pulmonary angiogram*. As opposed to perfusion scans, interpretation of radiographs of the pulmonary arterial tree is remarkably uniform, even among radiologists at different institutions.[183] Pulmonary angiography is both sensitive and specific for pulmonary embolism, but is expensive, invasive, and carries some risk to the patient. It is therefore not indicated if the diagnosis can be either established or excluded by other techniques.

Strategy for Establishing the Diagnosis of PE. It is important that the diagnosis of PE be clearly established, since antithrombotic therapy is associated with some definite risk of serious or fatal bleeding. The branching approach to the diagnosis summarized in the lower portion of Figure 31 begins with the perfusion lung scan. A typical lobar perfusion defect or multiple segmental defects in an area that is clear on the chest roentgenogram, is sufficient to establish the diagnosis. When pre-existing lung disease is present, and the chest roentgenogram is abnormal, combined ventilation and perfusion lung scans may be useful. When the suspicion of PE is high and one is not able to establish conclusively a diagnosis by noninvasive approaches, pulmonary angiography is necessary. Indications for angiography include: (1) clinically convincing presentation with the absence of a defect on perfusion scan; (2) significant pulmonary parenchymal disease that precludes the definitive interpretation of the lung scan; (3) clinical presentation and perfusion scan that strongly suggest the diagnosis in a patient with no predisposing risk factors or evidence of deep venous thrombosis by venography; and (4) patients with positive noninvasive tests and a very high risk of bleeding if anticoagulant therapy were to be given. Since a positive venogram would allow one to decide to treat for venous thromboembolism in patients who may also have positive angiography, contrast venography, a lower risk procedure, may be preferred.

Other Types of Venous Thrombosis. DVT is uncommon in the *upper extremity,* but may follow trauma to axillary or subclavian veins. When it occurs spontaneously or in young individuals, an underlying thrombotic predisposition should be considered (see later section on experimental evidence of ongoing thrombotic states), such as an abnormality in vascular plasminogen activator.[184]

Renal vein thrombosis can lead to acute organ dysfunction and occur spontaneously or in "hypercoagulable" states, most notably in patients with nephrotic syndrome; nephrotic syndrome is less frequently caused by renal vein thrombosis.[185] Thrombosis of *portal or mesenteric veins* can complicate conditions with stasis (e.g., portal hypertension, cirrhosis) or be seen postoperatively, as after splenectomy. Only about 10 percent of intestinal ischemia, however, is due to mesenteric venous occlusions.[186]

Thrombosis of *superficial veins* in the absence of detectable extension to the deep venous system does not appear to be associated with a risk of embolization to the pulmonary circulation. It may follow trauma or intravenous injections, or may occur in varicose veins. Spontaneous, multiple, or recurrent superficial thrombophlebitis may be a manifestation of underlying malignancy.[187] Finally, *retinal vein thrombosis* can present as an emergent ophthalmologic problem and subsequent "neovascularization" can also lead to blindness.

ARTERIAL THROMBOSIS AND THROMBOEMBOLISM

The clinical presentation and recognition of arterial thrombotic or thromboembolic disease is usually more clear-cut than the presentation with venous thrombosis or thromboembolism. The process may involve mural thrombosis, such as thrombus covering an atherosclerotic plaque, or an area of previous transmural infarction of the heart secondary to myocardial infarction. Total occlusion may occur acutely, producing organ symptoms of ischemia. Embolization into the arterial system also occurs acutely, leading to sudden loss of organ function, as illustrated by some instances of transient ischemic attacks or stroke. When the coronary circulation is involved, the clinical presentation is that of typical evidence for angina versus infarction. Acute occlusion of other vessels, including arteries to a lower extremity, can occur from embolization of mural thrombi associated with abdominal aortic atherosclerotic plaques, or from prosthetic devices. Acutely, atherosclerosis and vasospasm cannot be distinguished from thrombotic disorders; both processes may coexist. Although Doppler flow studies may be helpful in documenting the occlusion,[188] the specific diagnosis is most readily provided by contrast angiography. Moreover, thromboemboli in larger vessels may be removed mechanically or by thrombolytic therapy immediately following the diagnostic procedure.

Coronary Artery Thrombosis or Thromboembolism. Coronary artery atherosclerotic disease (ischemic heart disease) is the leading cause of mortality in the United States, accounting for 700,000 deaths each year. More than half of such deaths occur suddenly, before the victim can reach the hospital, or within hours after the onset of acute myocardial infarction. Recent public health statistics indicate that the death rate from coronary artery disease, adjusted for age, reached a peak in 1963, and has declined since that time, presumably related to preventive and therapeutic measures. It is not clear what the relative importance of preventive factors might be in producing this decline in mortality, that is, less atherogenic diet, less cigarette smoking, more exercise, compared with treatment factors such as out-of-hospital cardiopulmonary resuscitation, improved management in emergency rooms and coronary care units, and cardiac surgery.

It is now clear that thrombosis is the most common immediate cause of acute myocardial infarction.[189] The thrombi essentially always occur in vessels with markedly stenotic lesions. Hemorrhage into an atheromatous plaque, rupture of an atheromatous plaque with distal embolism of atheromatous material, and thromboembolism from the heart are considered to be uncommon causes of coronary artery occlusion. It is of interest that a number of patients with coronary spasm early in myocardial infarction have been described. However, vasospasm is thought to be an infrequent cause of myocardial infarction, since infarction is rare in patients with variant (vasospastic) angina.

Although the factor or factors that immediately precipitate terminal dysrhythmias in victims of out-of-hospital ventricular fibrillation—"sudden death"—remain largely unidentified, coronary atherosclerosis is the dominant (or sole) cardiac pathologic condition. Postmortem studies of individuals who die suddenly from cardiac causes do not show gross thrombosis of the coronary arteries. With the advent of mobile coronary care systems and successful resuscitation of many patients experiencing out-of-hospital ventricular fibrillation, studies have shown that such episodes are usually not associated with acute myocardial infarction. In addition, the subgroup of survivors without associated acute infarction has had an extraordinarily high rate of recurrence of ventricular fibrillation in subsequent years. The traditional risk factors linked with coronary atherosclerosis per se (smoking, hypertension, and hyperlipidemia) are also associated with sudden death. Unfortunately, an analysis of these factors fails to distinguish between patients who are likely to die suddenly and those who will suffer other coronary events.

Platelets may contribute to the pathogenesis of myocardial infarction in several ways: (1) Platelets appear to be important in the thrombotic occlusion of diseased coronary arteries. (2) They may play a role in the development of the atherosclerotic plaque through the release of platelet-derived growth factor that stimulates the proliferation of intimal smooth muscle cells and consequent lesion formation. (3) Acute platelet deposition on a proximal plaque could produce platelet microemboli downstream, leading to ischemia, infarction, or transiently, arrhythmia. (4) Vasospasm may be produced by the potent vasoconstrictor, thromboxane A_2, released by activated platelets. These concepts have prompted a number of studies examining antiplatelet agents in the secondary prevention of myocardial infarction.

Patients who develop typical cardiac pain accompanied by Q waves with or without serial T and S-T segment changes in their electrocardiograms and by increased concentrations of cardiac enzymes, will be found to have transmural myocardial infarction with subtending thrombotic occlusion of a diseased artery. Such patients will also have extensive coronary atherosclerosis. Isotopic studies indicate that thrombus formation antedates the episode rather than being consequent to it. Moreover, recent studies using thrombolytic therapy in patients with acute myocardial infarction show that reperfusion of the occluded vessel is frequently associated with at least partial reversal of electrical changes and some improvement in myocardial function (see Chapters 13 and 14). Patients with transmural infarcts may die suddenly and may be confused with patients with unheralded "sudden death." In such patients the findings at necropsy will depend on the interval between infarction and death, because an occluding thrombus may be lysed within a few days. At present there is little evidence that angina pectoris or "sudden death" per se are caused by acute coronary artery thrombosis. A crescendo angina pattern may, however, precede infarction.

Cerebral Artery Thrombosis or Thromboembolism. Approximately 400,000 persons in the United States suffer a stroke (cerebral infarction) each year; 40 percent of these individuals will die within 30 days following the stroke. It has been estimated that about 80 percent of cerebral infarctive events are due to thrombotic processes (65 percent due to thrombosis in situ and 15 percent due to thromboemboli). About 15 percent of strokes are due to hemorrhagic infarction (intracranial hemorrhage).[190,191] The frequency with which hemorrhage complicates infarction is not known. The overall frequency of stroke has decreased by about one fourth over the past 25 years.[192] Although the decline has involved both sexes and all age groups, the most marked reduction has occurred in the incidence of hemorrhagic infarction. The decrease probably relates in part to wider recognition and control of hypertension.

Thrombus formation in cranial supply vessels typically occurs in association with severely diseased vessels, and the thrombi have the characteristic structure of arterial thrombi elsewhere. This process is thus the counterpart of transmural myocardial infarction with thrombotic occlusion of a diseased supply artery. Thrombosis is most likely to occur where atherosclerotic narrowing is greatest. The most common sites are the internal carotid artery at the carotid sinus, the junction of vertebral and basilar arteries, and the main bifurcation of the middle cerebral artery. The evolution of the clinical picture of cerebral thrombosis is much more variable than embolism or hemorrhage. Usually the stroke is preceded by some transient ischemic attacks that last from seconds to hours. The final stroke may become established as a single attack that develops over hours, or less commonly it may evolve in a stuttering, intermittent pattern over hours to days (stroke in evolution).

Cerebral artery thromboemboli may arise from several sites. Some may originate in the stagnant, slowly flowing blood in the atria of patients with mitral valvular disease and atrial fibrillation. These emboli are subject to modification by the administration of anticoagulants. Other thromboemboli may arise on the surface of transmural myocardial infarctions, while others form on damaged or prosthetic heart valves. Some may form in the carotid vessels themselves, especially the carotid sinus. It is important to note, however, that occasionally atheromatous material may embolize to the eye or brain, without any thrombotic process being involved. Thus, cerebral infarction does not constitute a single coherent condition, but is caused by thrombosis in situ and by a wide range of diseases where emboli of differing types come from different sources. Nevertheless, a sustained neurologic deficit, or completed stroke, is most commonly due to thrombosis in situ or embolization from the heart or neck vessels.

It is important to recognize that cerebral hemorrhage cannot be reliably distinguished from cerebral infarction on the basis of history and physical findings. The absence of neck stiffness and blood in the cerebrospinal fluid (CSF) does not exclude intracerebral bleeding, since these signs indicate only that the hemorrhage has been massive enough to break through into the ventricles. Until recently, carotid arteriography provided the most certain clinical differential between thrombotic stroke and hemorrhagic stroke. The advent of computerized axial tomography (CAT scanning) represents an important advance in this regard. It separates hemorrhagic from infarctive stroke without the need for time-consuming or invasive procedures, with greater confidence than with any other technique, and can discriminate soon after the onset of the neurologic deficit.[297]

Transient Ischemic Attacks (TIA). Episodes of neurologic dysfunction that develop suddenly, last five minutes to many hours, and clear completely, are designated as transient ischemic attacks. Symptoms during an attack generally point to disturbances of circulation in either the carotid or vertebrobasilar arterial systems. The characteristic presence of disease in the subtending neck vessels contrasts with its frequent absence in completed strokes; thus the nature of the embolic masses may well differ. The incidence of stroke in patients with TIA has been reported to vary from 10 to 70 percent. In general, if untreated, about one third of patients will suffer a completed stroke, one third will continue to have TIA without infarction, and one third will have a spontaneous remission. It is believed that TIA results largely from thromboembolism. The transient nature of the attack is explained by the rapid fragmentation and dissolution of microemboli. Finally, it is not always easy to separate transient episodes that have an embolic or occlusive origin from other short-lived neurologic problems, such as epilepsy, migraine, hypoglycemia, or hypotension.[193]

Peripheral Arterial Disease. Acute occlusion of peripheral arteries may threaten limb viability if the collateral arterial circulation around the obstruction is inadequate. Arterial occlusion may be due to thrombosis at the site of underlying atherosclerotic vascular disease, or may be the result of thromboembolism arising from a more proximal site in the arterial circulation, usually the heart. Local thrombotic occlusion may be precipitated by transient statis associated with atherosclerotic plaque ulceration, hemorrhage, dissection or aneurysm formation. Rarely, occlusion may follow direct arterial trauma. As with cerebral emboli, acute peripheral arterial embolism is most commonly related to atrial fibrillation, (secondary to atherosclerotic heart disease, mitral valvular disease, or cardiomyopathy). Transmural anterior or anteriolateral myocardial infarction is frequently associated with mural thrombus, and the frequency of embolization is directly related to infarct size.[194] Embolization may continue if a left ventricular aneurysm develops subsequently. Less common causes of embolization include left atrial myxoma, bacterial endocarditis, prosthetic heart valves, or vascular grafts.[195]

Clinically, acute peripheral arterial occlusion is manifest by pain, cold, pallor, paresthesias, paralysis, and pulselessness. Often the clinical history of the sudden onset of pain in a previously asymptomatic limb characterizes embolization. The patient may also have a history of atherosclerotic or valvular heart disease, or manifest atrial fibrillation. Mural thrombi or atherothrombotic fragments from the aorta can also serve as an embolic source.[196] Intact pulses in the affected limb are more frequently seen in acute embolic occlusion. Tibial artery occlusion may be silent until irreversible ischemia has occurred. Thrombosis, on the other hand, typically presents more gradually, in association with previous symptoms of claudication, absent peripheral pulses, and ischemic skin changes.

The Doppler ultrasonic velocity detector provides rapid bedside evaluation in patients with suspected vascular occlusion.[188] In acute occlusion with adequate collateral circulation, the distal arterial velocity may be detectable, but without discrete diastolic sounds. In the absence of adequate collateral flow, arterial velocity signals may not be heard. Definitive confirmation of acute occlusion requires contrast arteriography, and is indicated in most instances, inasmuch as management generally involves vascular surgery.

CLINICAL RISK FACTORS FOR THROMBOSIS

In either venous or arterial thromboembolic disease, a major problem for the clinician and clinical investigator is to identify and provide relative significance to specific predisposing risk factors. In addition, the specificity of diagnostic laboratory tests manifesting ongoing thrombosis requires elucidation. Those clinical states associated with established risk of thrombotic disease are listed in Table 12.

In *venous thrombosis,* increased stasis is produced by immobilization, obesity, congestive heart failure, or pregnancy. Other important risk factors include recent surgery, neoplastic disease, myeloproliferative disorders, or the

TABLE 12. Conditions associated with increased risk of thrombosis

VENOUS THROMBOSIS AND THROMBOEMBOLISM	ARTERIAL THROMBOSIS AND THROMBOEMBOLISM
Increased venous stasis	Abnormal vascular surface
Immobilization	Atherosclerotic cardiovascular disease
Trauma	Hypertension
Surgery	Cigarette smoking
Pregnancy	Hyperlipidemia
Congestive heart failure	Diabetes
Varicosities obesity	Lack of physical exercise
	Lack of physical exercise
Coagulation activation	Homocystinemia
Malignancies	Type A personality
Concentrates containing factor IX	?Male sex
?Myeloproliferative disorders	?Family history
?Homocystinemia	
	Vascular occlusive and hyperviscosity disease
Decreased control of coagulation	Sickle cell disease
Antithrombin III deficiency	Polycythemia
Protein C deficiency	Plasma cell dyscrasias (esp.
?Nephrotic syndrome	macroglobulinemia)
?Oral contraceptives	
	Increased platelet reactivity
Delayed clot lysis	?Essential thrombocytosis
Defective plasminogen	?Nephrotic syndrome
Deficient tissue plasminogen proactivator(s) some dysfibrinogenemias	

nephrotic syndrome. Occasionally congenital abnormalities are seen, such as dysfibrinogenemia or homocystinuria. More recently recognized are patients with inherited low levels of antithrombin III or protein C. These patients have impaired control mechanisms that normally limit the growth of thrombus formation. Consequently, thrombi extend beyond that required to achieve hemostasis. One additional group of patients at risk for recurrent thrombophlebitis, particularly in early life, is a subpopulation with impaired fibrinolysis.

Risk factors for *arterial disease* include hypertension, cigarette smoking, hyperlipidemia, diabetes, and occasionally, essential thrombocytosis. Of these, high blood pressure causes a greater risk for cerebral arteries, smoking and diabetes for peripheral arteries. Lack of physical exercise has been implicated in the increased risk of coronary artery disease. The frequency of arterial thrombosis in nephrotic syndrome is also increased, and this has been attributed to hyperresponsive platelets.[197] The rare genetic recessive disorder of homocystinemia leads to a vascular defect involving both the arterial and venous endothelial surfaces such that thrombotic events in either or both systems may be observed. Patients with sickle cell disease may undergo microvascular occlusion owing to direct sludging and stasis of small vessels by the abnormal red cells. Since platelets represent the primary response within the arterial system, congenital disorders of platelet metabolism are at least a theoretic explanation for increased risk of accelerated arterial thromboembolic disease in some patients; none have been described to date.

A major controversial clinical problem relates to the question of the degree of risk imposed by the estrogens in *oral contraceptive agents* in predisposing women to arterial or venous thromboembolic disease.[198] For example, significantly lower levels of antithrombin III are found in women who are on oral contraceptives, but a convincing correlation between changes in antithrombin III and venous complications has not been established; indeed, levels of other inhibitors are usually elevated. Nonetheless, use of oral contraceptives is presently viewed as a definite risk factor contributing to thrombosis. It appears that decreasing the content of estrogens may decrease the risk of venous, but not arterial, complications.[199] In women, the risk of arterial thrombosis appears to be potentiated by cigarette smoking.

Laboratory Detection of Thrombotic Predisposition. With few exceptions, tests to identify patients with increased risk of thromboembolic disorders are not generally useful. Whole blood viscosity may represent an increased risk when caused by a high hematocrit (e.g., >60 percent), or rouleaux from dysproteinemia. Patients with essential thrombocytosis also have an increased tendency to thrombosis, in association with atherosclerotic vessels. It has been proposed that "hypercoagulable states" are associated with high (two- to threefold elevated) levels of fibrinogen, factors V or VIII, or by reactive thrombocytosis. However, a large body of evidence indicates that these changes simply reflect nonspecific host inflammatory responses, and do not in themselves correlate with thrombotic risk.

Currently, only a few specific tests are indicated in the workup of young patients with recurrent thromboembolism, or patients with a positive family history of recurrent disease. These tests are identified in Figure 32 in the context of possible underlying mechanisms. Measurements of homocystine in urine and plasma are required to identify this rare recessive disorder, typically found in patients with physical features of bilateral dislocated lenses, frontal baldness, and impaired mental capability. Decreased control of normal hemostasis could explain the high frequency of DVT and PE associated with familial low levels of antithrombin III (40 to 60 percent of normal),[200] or in the recent report of partial protein C deficiency.[201] Replacement of antithrombin III by transfusion is currently under study; the results should help to clarify the role of antithrombin III deficiency in thrombotic predisposition. Acquired antithrombin III deficiency appears to explain the risk of venous thrombosis in patients with nephrotic syndrome.[201] Low levels in liver disease are not associated with increased thrombotic risk; a modest reduction is seen with heparin therapy alone such that levels should not be determined acutely. Partial resistance to fibrinolysis may represent another thrombotic mechanism in some patients with certain dysfibrinogenemias[163] or low levels of tissue plasminogen activator.[202] One family with a genetically abnormal plasminogen has also been studied.[203] En-

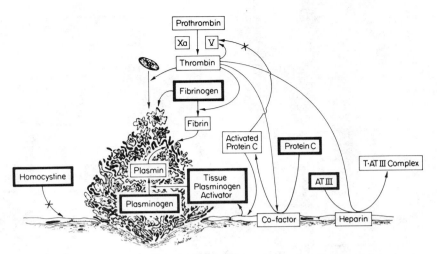

FIGURE 32. Congenital abnormalities associated with increased risks of thrombosis. Relatively few congenital defects have been identified which predispose individuals to thrombotic disorders. These are summarized according to the defects involved as related to the overall interactive scheme of hemostasis presented in Figure 19 (Chapter 5). The defects outlined in the *heavy boxes* include the effects of *homocystinemia* on endothelial cells, the reduced control of normal hemostasis in partial deficiencies of *antithrombin III* or *protein C,* and abnormal formation or lysis of fibrin clots, or both, in *dysfibrinogenemia* and abnormalities of *plasminogen or tissue plasminogen activator(s).*

hanced inhibition of plasmin has been proposed as an additional theoretic cause of a thrombotic predisposition. The net effect of modest changes in several modulating processes is not known. As expected, clinical manifestation of an inherited thrombotic tendency will frequently be associated with acquired risk factors (e.g., age, atherosclerosis, surgery).

EXPERIMENTAL EVIDENCE OF ONGOING THROMBOTIC STATES

Additional tests for thrombosis may be clinically useful in the future. These are summarized in Figure 33 with respect to the interactive scheme (see Fig. 19, Chapter 5).

Evidence for *coagulation factor activation* in vitro is largely based upon highly selective immunoassays. When prothrombin is activated, the aminoterminal portion (fragment 1 • 2, see Fig. 13) is formed and can be detected in native whole blood.[77] This, and the release of fibrinopeptide A,[100] however, are not specific, since they occur in disseminated intravascular coagulation as well as thrombosis. Specific fibrin degradation products are identified as DD-dimers and circulate when thrombi are lysed, but substantial elevations usually reflect

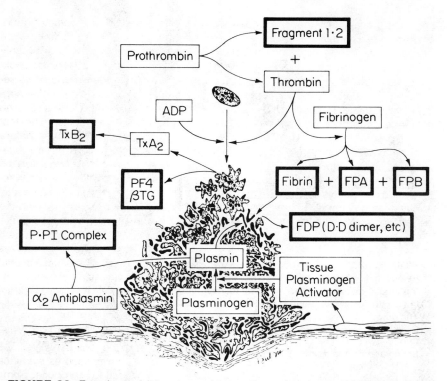

FIGURE 33. Experimental laboratory evidence of ongoing thrombotic disease. Evidence can arise from specific immunoassays of protein metabolites indicated in the *heavy boxes.* These include the amino-terminal half of prothrombin (fragment 1 • 2) from thrombin generation, or from the effects of thrombin to stimulate platelet release of *β-thromboglobulin* (βTG) or *platelet factor 4* (PF4). Platelet reactivity can be further documented by measuring plasma levels of the more stable metabolite, *thromboxane* B_2. Blood levels of *fibrinopeptides A and B* reflect the proteolysis of fibrinogen by thrombin, and soluble *fibrin monomers* can also be detected. As the result of fibrinolysis, circulating levels of *plasmin-$α_2$-antiplasmin* complex (P-PI) as well as specific *fibrin degradation products* (FDP) can be shown. With the exception of the Bβ form of fibrinopeptide B, which is found after plasmin degradation of the amino-terminal portion of the Bβ-chain of fibrinogen (following thrombin cleavage of the Aα-chain), other tests cannot distinguish between thrombin formation in disseminated intravascular coagulation and on-going thrombotic disorders.[100]

DIC. Although not yet exploited, specific assays for enzyme-inhibitor complexes, such as thrombin-antithrombin III[298] and plasmin-antiplasmin[171] complexes also serve to detect coagulation factor activation. Fibrinopeptide B, a regular thrombin cleavage product of fibrinogen (as opposed to the larger Bβ peptide from plasmin digestion), is a much more specific marker of ongoing venous thrombosis,[100] although its clearance from the circulation is rapid.

Uptake of ^{125}I-fibrinogen depends on the incorporation of labeled fibrinogen into a forming or recently formed thrombus in sufficient amounts to be detected by external scanning. Below the knee, this dynamic method is highly accurate when compared with contrast venography; above this level the background counts from soft tissues, blood vessels, and bladder interfere. False-positive results occur with inflammation, hematomas, or edema. False-negative results can occur if the thrombus is more than five days old, and is no longer incorporating sufficient labeled fibrinogen to be detectable. The test requires at least 24 hours following injection of the labeled fibrinogen before scanning can be performed; uptake on each limb is compared for three subsequent days with precordial (heart) measurements serving as control for the background blood pool. It also requires a continuous supply of labeled fibrinogen from donors who have been proven to be hepatitis-free. Because this technique is not sensitive to proximal thrombi, the thrombi associated with the greatest risks of pulmonary embolism, it is not suitable for routine use. Primarily, the technique has been helpful in screening patients at increased risk, and in defining the extent of deep venous thrombosis. If used clinically, it is always necessary to couple the test with a noninvasive technique sensitive to proximal lower extremity thrombi.[181,182]

Stimulation of platelets may be detected by immunoassays of platelet secretory products such as platelet factor 4 and β-thromboglobulin.[204] However, care must be taken to avoid in vitro or sample collection artifacts. Urinary levels of these products and for the more stable arachidonic acid metabolite thromboxane B_2 may be more specific, but appear to be less sensitive. The detection of "circulating platelet aggregates" has been proposed as evidence of platelet activation in vivo, but the test has been difficult to reproduce. Some of the best experimental evidence to date is derived from the tedious procedure of measuring ^{51}Cr-platelet survival (see Fig. 20, Chapter 6). In arterial disease, platelet survival may be shortened while simultaneous studies of ^{125}I-fibrinogen survival typically are normal.[37] More recently, ^{111}In-labeled platelets have led to in vivo localization of thrombi, for example, mural thrombi in the heart[38] and vascular grafts, providing dynamic evidence of arterial thrombus formation.

13

MECHANISMS OF ACTION OF ANTITHROMBOTIC AGENTS

There are three classes of antithrombotic agents, each directed at different aspects of the thrombotic process (Table 13). Moreover, a specific agent may affect only one of several activation pathways for a given component. This chapter deals with the mechanism of action for each class of agents used, changes occurring in hemostatic screening tests, tests to monitor the effects produced, and the risks and contraindications. Since thrombolytic therapy potentially represents the means for removing recently established thrombus, and therefore is the initial therapeutic consideration, it is discussed first, despite the present uncertainty regarding many of the proposed indications and risks. Anticoagulant therapy is much more clearly defined with respect to its indications and efficacy, especially in venous disease. Currently available drugs that affect platelet function have few well-established clinical indications at present. Specific clinical indications are covered in Chapter 14.

FIBRINOLYTIC THERAPY

Theoretically, thrombi and thromboemboli can be effectively removed by thrombolytic therapy, and two agents, streptokinase and urokinase, are available clinically. Urokinase is a trypsin-like enzyme found in trace amounts in human urine. Of experimental interest is the tissue culture-derived plasminogen activator preparation that differs from urokinase in its ability to localize in established thrombi by binding to fibrin; it is currently under study in animals.

TABLE 13. Antithrombotic agents

AGENT	ACTION	ADMINISTERED ROUTE	MAJOR INDICATIONS
Fibrinolytic			
Streptolinase Urokinase (Tissue activator)	Plasminogen activators	Intravenous, continuous infusion for 24-72 hours followed by heparin	*Acute, massive PE ?DVT (may decrease risk of postphlebitic symptoms)
		Intracoronary artery infusion at low doses	Acute myocardial infarction (under study)
Anticoagulant			
Heparin	Markedly enhances inhibition of proteases by antithrombin III	Intravenous, continuous infusion	*Deep venous thrombosis (DVT) *Pulmonary embolism (PE) (7-12 days)
		Subcutaneous Full doses	*DVT during pregnancy or long term prevention when oral agents are inadequate
		Low doses	Preventive use in high risk patients during surgery or bed rest
Warfarin	Vitamin K antagonist	Oral, daily	*Longer term prevention of recurrence (2-3 months with uncomplicated, distal DVT; 3-6 months with PE or proximal DVT)

Antiplatelet			
Aspirin	Decreases platelet aggregation and release	Oral	*Transient ischemic attacks
Sulfinpyrazone		Oral	?Prevention of recurrent myocardial infarction
Dipyridamole	Decreases platelet adhesion	Oral	*Systemic and cerebral emboli from old-style artificial heart valves (in addition to warfarin)
Ticlopidine	Blocks ADP induced platelet, interactions with fibrinogen and VWF	Oral	?Under investigation
PGI$_2$	Activates adenyl cyclase	Local intravenous infusion	Under study for hemodialysis, cardiopulmonary bypass, peripheral vascular disease

*Well established indication

Streptokinase is a nonenzymatic protein excreted by group C beta-hemolytic streptococci. Streptokinase acts by forming a complex with plasminogen allowing its active site to become exposed, generating plasmin from other plasminogen molecules (see Fig. 17, Chapter 4). In contrast, urokinase and tissue activator(s) directly activate plasminogen to plasmin by limited proteolysis (see Fig. 15). There is no demonstrated difference in efficacy between streptokinase and urokinase, except in patients with high antistreptococcal-antibody titers in whom only urokinase is effective. Both drugs are administered by an initial loading dose, followed by continuous intravenous infusion, required because of the rapid clearance from the circulation. Both agents are currently approved by the Food and Drug Administration for use in massive pulmonary emboli,[205] and streptokinase is approved for use in extensive deep venous thrombosis[206] and AV-cannula occlusion. The bacteria-derived product is about one tenth as expensive for a comparable dose, but patients may become transiently refractory to subsequent administration.

The amount of plasmin generated by streptokinase or urokinase must first exceed the ability of plasma α_2-antiplasmin to inactivate the enzyme. Free plasmin not only digests fibrin, but also destroys circulating fibrinogen, factor V, and factor VIII, producing a potentially serious hemostatic defect. Although several coagulation screening tests are altered by the proteolytic effects of plasmin,[206] it is sufficient to follow therapy with the thrombin time. This test becomes prolonged by the inhibitory effects of higher molecular weight fibrinogen degradative products and hypofibrinogenemia. Typically, the infusion of 250,000 units of streptokinase over 30 minutes followed by 100,000 units per hour, or 5000 units per kg of urokinase over 10 minutes, followed by 5000 units per kg per hour will prolong the thrombin time two- to six-fold over baseline. Continuous infusion is generally maintained for 24 to 72 hours.[207]

Patients receiving fibrinolytic therapy are at significant risk of bleeding if they are subjected to invasive procedures or trauma. Perhaps of greater importance is the risk of bleeding from sites of previous vascular injury, since fibrin-stabilized platelet thrombi may be readily lysed. The latter consideration applies to postoperative wounds less than two weeks old.

Patients considered for thrombolytic therapy must be carefully selected if serious hemorrhagic complications are to be avoided. Thrombolytic therapy should not be used in any patient following recent surgery, parturition, cardiopulmonary resuscitation, percutaneous biopsy, or central nervous system lesions, (including recent stroke). Relative contraindications include mitral valve disease with atrial fibrillation, subacute bacterial endocarditis, hypertension, cavitating lung disease, acute or chronic renal or hepatic insufficiency, ulcerative cutaneous or mucous membrane lesions, recent bleeding from any site, or a history of allergic reaction to the thrombolytic drug. These exclusions will eliminate many of the patients being considered for thrombolytic therapy, for example, postoperative patients with massive pulmonary emboli. At present, thrombolytic therapy should not be administered together with any other antithrombotic agent, and probably should be given in an intensive care facility.

The patient should have normal hemostatic screening tests prior to therapy, and invasive diagnostic procedures should be minimized.

Because of the many exclusions and potential dangers involved in fibrinolytic therapy, clinicians have been hesitant to use it for venous thrombosis and thromboembolism except in situations in which the benefit clearly outweighs the risk. As will be discussed in Chapter 14, this situation may only be met in an occasional patient with acute massive pulmonary embolism, or submassive embolism associated with shock. The risks of hemorrhage appear to be greatly reduced with tissue plasminogen activator therapy.

There is growing interest in the localized administration of thrombolytic agents directly into coronary vessels in patients with acute myocardial infarction. When 2000 to 8000 units per minute of streptokinase are infused by coronary catheter directly proximal to an occluding thrombus, reperfusion of the occluded vessel is achieved within 30 to 60 minutes in more than 80 percent of patients. If vascular patency is re-established within three to six hours of initial symptoms, there is increasing evidence that ischemic myocardium may be preserved.[208,209] At the end of the infusion there may be little detectable systemic fibrin(ogen)olytic effect at this low infusion rate, thus the risk of systemic hemorrhage may be reduced. Although 10 to 20 percent of patients will reocclude within subsequent weeks, the interval provides time to carry out a more definitive procedure, such as aortocoronary bypass grafting, or transluminal angioplasty.[210]

ANTICOAGULANTS

Heparin. This sulfonated mucopolysaccharide has repeating disaccharide units that are primarily iduronic acid and N-acetyl-glucosamine. Two to three sulfate groups are attached per disaccharide unit and, at the reducing end of the sugar, the molecules are bound in vivo to several seryl residues present throughout specific binding proteins. It should be noted that the molecules are "polydisperse" with a molecular weight range between 6000 and 14,000. A specific tetrasaccharide sequence with two nonsulfonated uronic acid residues is required for the anticoagulant activity that is mediated through its binding to antithrombin III (Fig. 34). The heparin-antithrombin complex is an immediate, potent inhibitor of activated coagulation proteases.[60]

Anticoagulant-active fractions of heparin represent a variable, relatively small portion of commercial preparations. Organ or species of origin, or the preparative process itself may produce heparins of different specific activity, although there is no clear therapeutic benefit from any of the preparations over the commonly available type from porcine intestine. Consequently, doses are standardized for anticoagulant effect, that is, units as opposed to weight, using clotting screening tests.

A *physiologic effect* of heparin is manifest by the immediate inhibition of screening clotting tests (see Fig. 23, Chapter 7). The thrombin time is the most sensitive, as it is markedly prolonged at even 0.01 unit per ml of heparin. The

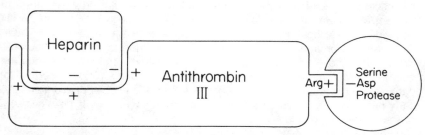

FIGURE 34. Structure and mechanisms of action of heparin. *Upper view:* Structure of heparin. A tetrasaccharide portion of the repeating uronic-glucosamine units is shown. One or two of these, or closely related sequences, occur in low or high molecular weight heparin fractions, respectively, and serve as the antithrombin III binding sites. A somewhat larger sequence may also be involved.[60] *Lower view:* Mechanism for the interaction of heparin with antithrombin III. The specific sites on heparin ionically bind to the amino groups of Lys residues in antithrombin III, enhancing the reactivity of a specific Arg (+) residue. This binds to the Asp (–) pocket of the serine proteases (e.g., thrombin, factors IX_a, X_a, VII_a, XI_a, and plasmin) forming a stable, covalent inhibitor-enzyme complex. In addition, heparin may interact independently with thrombin or factor IX_a to modulate the protease-inhibitor reactivity, but kinetically, these reactions may be of secondary importance in its anticoagulant effect.[60]

next most sensitive are tests of intrinsic clotting, such as the partial thromboplastin time (PTT) or recalcification time. These are usually doubled by about 0.2 unit per ml of heparin; therapeutic levels are 0.2 to 0.5 unit per ml of whole blood. The extrinsic screening test, the prothrombin time, is only slightly prolonged by even 0.5 unit per ml. Thus, the prothrombin time can be used to assess the status of oral anticoagulation without interrupting anticoagulation with continuous heparin infusion. In general, the more thrombin added or generated in these tests, the less sensitive that test will be to inhibition by heparin. Another important factor in screening test sensitivity to heparin may relate to the specific rates of inhibition of the various steps in each pathway; the amounts of factors X_a or IX_a generated are much smaller than thrombin, and the earlier enzymes may be more reactive to heparin inhibition, especially in intrinsic coagulation.

For *monitoring* heparin therapy, an intrinsic clotting screening test is performed prior to institution of treatment, four hours following any adjustment in dosage, and daily during maintenance therapy. The partial thromboplastin time (PTT) is the most precise screening test for monitoring heparin therapy, but it is rather expensive and time consuming. Therefore, recalcification times are substituted by some centers. Since contact activation is suboptimal in the recalcification test, the normal times are more than twice as long as the PTT. Recalcification times depend on platelet phospholipid, such that severe thrombocytopenia can falsely prolong the result. Nevertheless, this test is sufficiently sensitive to determine whether an adequate amount of heparin is being administered. The whole blood variation of this test can easily be run in five minutes; alternatively, platelet-rich plasma may be used. Whatever intrinsic clotting test is chosen, it should be emphasized that the sensitivity of the test varies considerably with different reagents (even among different lots), so that one needs to be familiar with the standardization data for a specific laboratory (see Appendix A).

There is considerable *variability of response* to heparin among different individuals, and even in the same individual at different times in the course of illness. Besides variability in heparin pharmacokinetics,[211] this reflects, at least in part, other basic proteins in plasma that bind heparin and thus compete with antithrombin III. Such proteins probably include "acute phase reactants," such as C-reactive protein, which is elevated several hundredfold during the first few days of an acute illness. These transiently high levels may explain the occasional phenomenon of a decreased heparin requirement to achieve the same prolongation of the intrinsic system screening test time a few days following the onset of therapy for thromboembolic disease. The larger average dose needed in the patients with pulmonary embolism, compared with deep venous thrombosis without emboli, is explained by an increased rate of heparin clearance in patients with pulmonary emboli.[221]

Heparin may be *administered* intravenously by continuous infusion, or by subcutaneous injection. The subcutaneous route is usually reserved for low-dose heparin except for the occasional patient who requires chronic, long-term administration of full doses as an outpatient. Continuous infusion is associated with fewer bleeding complications than intermittent bolus injection,[212] while providing equal protection against recurrent venous disease. The half-life of heparin following an intravenous administration is short, around 90 minutes, depending on the dose and the patient. If administered by intravenous bolus injection, the usual dose is 4000 to 8000 units every four hours. Initially, this dose prolongs the intrinsic clotting test to infinity. By one-half hour before the next dose, the intrinsic clotting test should be reduced to about twice normal. The bolus regimen requires an average of 50 percent more heparin daily, than continuous infusion. When given by continuous infusion, an initial loading dose of 75 units per kg body weight is given as an intravenous bolus, and then heparin is infused at a rate of 10 to 25 units per kg per hour, depending upon the clinical situation. When administered by continuous infusion, it is mandatory to prolong the PTT or recalcification time to therapeutic levels of about twice baseline. Infusions require an accurate infusion gauge or administration system and close observation of the patient; it should be given in an intravenous line separate from other drugs or fluids. To adjust the PTT or recalcification time, it is usually sufficient to change the infusion rate and not necessary to give a new bolus. After each adjustment, the recalcification time or PTT should be checked in another four hours to assess the effect of the change in administered dose. Usually the appropriate therapeutic recalcification time is in a range of 200 to 300 seconds, and the partial thromboplastin time is in the range of 80 to 100 seconds. Once this has been achieved, daily monitoring is sufficient.

Currently, heparin is *indicated* acutely (and in some instances, chronically) in patients with venous thromboembolism to prevent recurrence or extension while endogenous fibrinolysis occurs. It is also used during open heart surgery and renal dialysis. Low doses have been administered in attempts to prevent venous thromboembolism. These indications are discussed in Chapter 14.

Warfarin. The coumarin nucleus is similar chemically to the naphthoquinone derivative, vitamin K (see Fig. 30, Chapter 11), and indirect evidence strongly suggests that they interact at a common receptor site. The four vitamin K-dependent clotting factors, II (prothrombin), VII, IX, and X have specific glutamyl residues near their amino-terminal ends that are carboxylated in a postprotein synthesis reaction, forming tight calcium-binding sites. In the absence of vitamin K or in the presence of its antagonists such as coumarin derivatives, this final carboxylation is incomplete, and abnormal proteins then circulate with markedly impaired activity.

The *pharmacologic response* depends upon the net effect of factor levels achieved. Since the four factors have different half-lives, depletion of factor VII, which has the shortest half-life, can prolong the prothrombin time within 24 hours following large doses of warfarin prior to having a significant effect upon the other factors. It is therefore common practice to begin warfarin therapy with two daily doses of 10 mg each and re-evaluate the dose based upon the results of the daily prothrombin time until it equilibrates in the therapeutic range. Prothrombin times vary considerably in their dose-response curves, however, so that they need to be carefully standardized (see Appendix A). Approximately one to two weeks of coumarin administration are required for all four factors to reflect completely a given dosage. The range of response among different individuals is particularly wide; from 2 to 18 mg per day may be required to maintain a patient in therapeutic range once equilibration has been achieved. The monitoring prothrombin time reflects the dose given 36 to 48 hours previously. To prevent inordinant risks of bleeding, a partial hemostatic defect is produced, that is, approximately 10 percent levels of factors II, VII, IX, and X, which is clinically similar to mild hemophilia.

Screening tests for extrinsic system clotting are helpful in *monitoring* warfarin therapy, and these include the prothrombin time, and, particularly in Europe, the Thrombo-test. A properly standardized prothrombin time (see Appendix A) should be used in monitoring warfarin therapy. The therapeutic antithrombotic range for the prothrombin time is 15 to 20 percent of the normal calibration curve after in vivo equilibration has been achieved. The variability among commercial thromboplastins renders the prolongation in absolute times less satisfactory in following changes in the prothrombin time, especially if the test has not been standardized. Because of the relatively greater sensitivity to lower levels of factor VII, however, the prothrombin time does not always reflect a patient's overall degree of anticoagulation. Newer tests such as the use of chromogenic substrates or immunoassays for normal versus des-γ-carboxy prothrombin levels,[213] may prove more useful in predicting patients at risk for hemorrhage or recurrent thrombosis.

Drug interactions play an important role in coumarin therapy (Table 14). Since warfarin contains an asymmetric carbon atom, there are two optically active isomers. In the presence of some drugs the metabolic effects are different for the two isomers. Thus, the potentiating effect of phenylbutazone, for example, is due in part to the increase of enzymes that metabolize the less active form in preference to the more active form. This leads to no net change of plasma warfarin yet a potentiation of the anticoagulant effect.[214] Other drugs can compete with the hydroxylase that initiates breakdown of either isomer of the active anticoagulant (Fig. 35). Aspirin has a variable effect on synthesis, and occasionally some individuals on large daily doses of aspirin alone demonstrate vitamin K antagonism. Nearly any strongly acidic drug can displace albumin-bound warfarin in vitro, but interactions at other sites may predominate. Antagonism, leading to a shorter prothrombin time can also occur. Barbiturates induce microsomal enzymes in the hepatocytes, which increase the metabolism of both forms of warfarin and thus antagonize the anticoagulant effect of the drug.

Disease states, blood lipid levels, and dietary factors may also influence interactions, perhaps explaining effects observed occasionally in patients. It should be emphasized that patients on warfarin frequently have multiple medical problems, and in a six-month Medicaid survey, one third of nearly 500 patients were exposed to a potentially interacting drug.[215] Barbiturates and barbiturate-containing compounds accounted for three quarters of the interacting drugs, and there was a strong correlation between total number of drugs prescribed to a patient and the likelihood that an interacting drug would be taken.

It should be emphasized that any drug independently impairing hemostasis potentiates the risk of bleeding, usually without further prolonging the prothrombin time. This includes other antithrombotic agents and marrow suppressive drugs or drug-induced thrombocytopenias. Thus, additional hemostatic defects must be considered when bleeding occurs in patients who are taking warfarin.

TABLE 14. Drug-warfarin interactions

SITE OF INTERACTION	ANTAGONIZING WARFARIN EFFECT	MECHANISM OF EFFECT	POTENTIATING WARFARIN EFFECT
Absorption	*Cholestyramine	Binds W in gut	Antibiotics (broad spectrum)
		Reduces colonic vitamin K_2 (Specific metabolic effects)	
		Reduces dietary vitamin K_1 (unless replaced)	Hyperalimentation (NPO)
Transport		Displace albumin-bound W	*Thyroxine (D, L)
			Clofibrate
			Sulfunamides
Metabolism	*Barbiturates	Induces P-450 system, clears both enantiomers more rapidly	*Phenylbutazone
	EtOH (chronic)	Enhances metabolism of less active enantiomer (R) and/or clears more active one (S) less rapidly	*Trimethoprim-sulfamethoxazole
			Metronidazole
			*Sulfinpyrazone
		Competes with microsomal enzymes	Phenytoin
			Tolbutamide
			Cimetidine
			Disufiram
Factor synthesis	Vitamin K	Synthetic carboxylase cofactor	Salicylates (high doses)
		Suppress effective production	EtOH (acute)
Other or unclear	Glutethamide		Quinidine
	Rifampicin		Griseofulvin
			Ethylchlorvynol

*Predictable, well documented effect and mechanism.

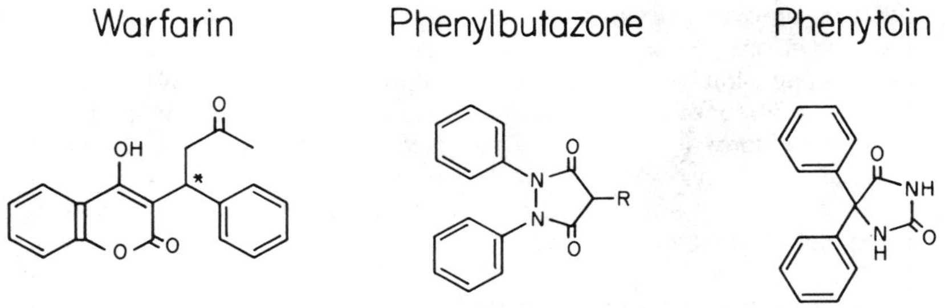

Warfarin   Phenylbutazone   Phenytoin

FIGURE 35. Structure of warfarin and interacting drugs. Warfarin has a coumarin nucleus which is similar to the naphthoquinone, vitamin K. Its side chain contains an asymmetric carbon (*) and stereoisomers of differing reactivity have been identified. S (the three- to fourfold more active enantiomer) normally has a longer half-life than R but a less steep dose-response curve. Other drugs, including phenylbutazone and diphenyl-hydantoin (phenytoin), undergo initial parahydroxylation by a liver enzyme which is also active on the coumarin nucleus, thereby potentiating the effect of the anticoagulant. A similar vitamin K antagonist, phenanedione (not shown) is structurally and metabolically different and has a different pattern of drug interactions.

Warfarin is *indicated* chronically for three to six months to prevent recurrence of venous thromboembolism and for longer periods in some high-risk patients. It also reduces arterial emboli from the heart (see Chapter 14).

Complications of Anticoagulant Therapy. The major risk of anticoagulant therapy is *bleeding*.[216] Large series of patients indicate a 2 to 4 percent per year frequency of major bleeding episodes (those requiring transfusion) in patients treated with standard doses of either heparin or warfarin; the risk of a fatal hemorrhage is about 0.2 percent per year for patients on oral anticoagulants.[217] The incidence of complications from warfarin is higher in patients monitored infrequently; frequency of bleeding episodes increases with prolongation of the prothrombin time beyond the therapeutic range. The frequency of bleeding with heparin therapy is reduced when administered by continuous infusion and adjusted by monitoring, as opposed to the intermittent bolus regimen.[212] Bleeding episodes in patients on warfarin occurring while the anticoagulant effect is within the therapeutic range are frequently due to focal pathologic lesions, such as an occult neoplasm being unmasked by the therapy, especially in the gastrointestinal or genitourinary tracts. The most common minor episodes involve urinary, gastrointestinal, and vaginal bleeding.

In general, any new or painful symptom in an anticoagulated patient should be considered a manifestation of a potential bleeding complication until proven otherwise. Uncommon presentations from bleeding parallel those in patients with milder congenital coagulation factor disorders (see Chapter 10) and include airway obstruction in the neck from a retropharyngeal hematoma, mediastinal masses on chest roentgenograms, alveolar infiltrates without hemoptysis, or pericardial effusions. An acute abdomen can follow rupture of liver or spleen, an ovarian cyst, or diverticuli, and intramural bleeding can lead to small bowel obstruction. Iliopsoas hematomas can present with right lower quadrant pain simulating appendicitis and produce femoral nerve entrapment, while other retroperitoneal hemorrhages cause back pain and blood loss anemias. Acute adrenal insufficiency has been observed, and partially clotted blood has formed pseudotumors of the renal pelvis seen on intravenous pyelography. Arthritis or arthralgias, with or without swelling, can occur. Finally, intracranial or epidural hematomas without specific trauma have been reported.

Additional complications of *heparin* include thrombocytopenia, alopecia, and osteoporosis. The frequency of heparin-associated thrombocytopenia is about 2 to 3 percent,[218] but it is prudent to check a platelet count prior to therapy, on the fifth day, or with any bleeding episode. Where recalcilfication times are used to monitor heparin effect, moderately severe thrombocytopenia will falsely prolong the test result, since it is dependent upon platelets to provide phospholipids. Alopecia or osteoporosis may occur after prolonged usage of full-dose heparin over several months. Rarely, "paradoxical" thrombosis occurs.

Warfarin therapy is associated with a fetal bony embryopathy when administered to women during their first trimester of pregnancy. Marginal hemostatic levels of the vitamin K-dependent clotting factors are not attained in the fetus until the last trimester of pregnancy, so that it is tempting to speculate that the developmental bony abnormalities are associated with dysfunction of bone matrix proteins known to contain Gla residues.[168] Women receiving warfarin should be advised against pregnancy because of this risk.[169] Poisoning with warfarin has occurred in children ingesting coumarin-type rat poisons and, occasionally, with factitious ingestion.[106] Rarely, areas of skin necrosis are seen, particularly after large loading doses of warfarin. These are associated with thrombi in vessels and extremely low factor VII levels.[219] A similar dermal necrosis has been seen less frequently in patients on heparin alone. Perhaps this represents a *forme fruste* of autoerythrocyte sensitization.

Reversal of heparin is achieved by *protamine* sulfate, a basic nuclear histone which contains one third of its residues as arginine. Protamine binds heparin more tightly than any plasma protein, including antithrombin III. It is routinely given after heparinization during cardiopulmonary bypass surgery in approximately equal weight amounts to administered heparin. The protamine may metabolize more rapidly than heparin, however, thereby accounting for the occasional open-heart surgical patient who exhibits "rebound" heparinization seen a few hours after surgery. Excess protamine sometimes prolongs coagulation screening tests, but rapid methods for removing heparin or protamine, or both, from plasma can be used to allow assessment of the underlying coagulation system which is otherwise masked by inhibition[220] (see Appendix A).

Management of bleeding in patients on *warfarin* depends on the seriousness of the bleeding episode. For immediate reversal, as for massive or life-threatening hemorrhage or emergent surgery, plasma (or whole blood) should be given. In adults, four to six bags of 250 ml plasma each are usually required to raise the vitamin K-dependent factors to hemostatic levels, that is, above 30 to 40 percent. Vitamin K administration should also be given in this situation. Treatment with vitamin K alone will correct factor VII levels in several hours, and within one to two days hemostasis will be sufficiently normalized to limit bleeding. If oral anticoagulants are truly indicated to prevent thrombosis, however, it becomes extremely difficult to re-equilibrate the patients on warfarin following injection of vitamin K. Thus, for relatively minor bleeding, or an abnormally prolonged prothrombin time alone, it is often more useful to reduce or withhold a warfarin dose, or that of a potentiating drug, and follow the prothrombin time until it returns to the therapeutic range.

AGENTS THAT MODIFY PLATELET BEHAVIOR

Inhibitors of Platelet Function. Antiplatelet agents may interfere with thrombus formation at several steps. They may prevent platelet adherence to exposed subendothelium, inhibit primary platelet aggregation or secondary platelet release, and perhaps disaggregate platelets already present in a thrombus. Currently, the three agents available for clinical use are aspirin, dipyridamole, or sulfinpyrazone. All of these agents are available for use orally, are relatively safe, and have shown therapeutic benefits in some clinical trials and laboratory models of thrombosis. A more potent agent, ticlopidine, is currently being studied to assess its clinical utility versus complication rate. Infusions of the short-lived PGI_2 have also been performed experimentally in selected patient groups. The mechanisms of actions of these agents are summarized in Table 15. Clinical trials of the more common agents in cardiac or cerebrovascular diseases will be discussed in Chapter 14.

Aspirin irreversibly acetylates cyclooxygenase in platelets and thus blocks synthesis of thromboxane A_2 (see Fig. 2, Chapter 1). Inhibition occurs at very low doses; 80 mg in an adult will produce an 86 percent inactivation of cyclooxygenase, and the standard 325-mg tablet administered once daily produces a greater than 95 percent inactivation. Since platelets are not capable of synthesizing new protein, the inhibition is irreversible and lasts for the lifetime of the platelet. Megakaryocytes in the marrow may also be affected. Following a single dose of aspirin in a normal individual the bleeding time may be prolonged to 8 or 10 minutes and remain detectably prolonged for two or more days until enough new, unaffected platelets are produced to normalize the bleeding time. Aspirin, however, will not correct shortened platelet survival times in patients with ongoing platelet consumption due to active thrombus formation.

Theoretically, single, small doses of aspirin could have a greater antithrombotic effect than larger, more frequent doses. At 80 to 325 mg daily, arachidonate metabolism is virtually blocked in all circulating platelets, but endothelial prostacyclin production is either less affected or recovers rapidly. Low-dose aspirin has been shown to be antithrombotic in patients with arteriovenous silastic cannulae.[221] Thus, it is postulated that large or frequent doses

TABLE 15. Mechanisms of action of antiplatelet agents

	ASPIRIN	DIPYRIDAMOLE	SULFINPYRAZONE	TICLOPIDINE	PGI$_2$
Mode of action	Irreversible acetylation of cyclooxygenase	Inhibitor of platelet phosphodiesterase	Competitive (reversible) inhibition of cyclooxygenase	?Alters platelet membrane binding sites	Stimulates adenyl cyclase
Platelet aggregation	Blocks except with thrombin	Weak effect	Inhibits dilute collagen	Blocks	Blocks
Platelet adhesion	No effect	Decreases	No effect	?	Blocks
Platelet survival	No effect	Improves	Improves	?	Improves
Bleeding time	Prolongs	No effect	No effect	Prolongs	Prolongs

of aspirin could be less antithrombotic by completely inhibiting prostacyclin production by endothelium. However, this has never been directly demonstrated in vivo, and studies of patients taking large doses of aspirin for rheumatoid arthritis do not show any increase in thrombotic events. Similarly, the two British trials of secondary prevention of myocardial infarction gave similar results despite a threefold difference in the aspirin dose (see Chapter 14). Indeed, aspirin in larger doses has been shown to have antithrombotic effects apart from inhibition of platelet thromboxane production in primate models of arterial thromboembolism. On the other hand, a once-daily, low-dose regimen may reduce the gastrointestinal side effects associated with larger, more frequent doses in clinical trials. None of the controlled clinical studies available have yet resolved the question of high-dose versus low-dose aspirin.

Sulfinpyrazone, a uricosuric agent, was first used in the management of gout. Structurally, it is similar to anti-inflammatory agents such as phenylbutazone. Like other nonsteroidal anti-inflammatory agents, sulfinpyrazone acts as a competitive inhibitor of cyclooxygenase. This means that the effect on platelets is reversible; sulfinpyrazone is effective only when drug levels are adequate. Patients taking therapeutic doses of sulfinpyrazone do not show prolonged bleeding times, but, like dipyridamole, shortened platelet survival times are prolonged by sulfinpyrazone in patients with ongoing thrombus formation.[222] The usual dose of sulfinpyrazone in antithrombotic therapy is 200 mg four times daily. Sulfinpyrazone appears to have fewer gastrointestinal side effects than aspirin, perhaps because it is a less potent inhibitor of gastric prostaglandin synthesis.

Dipyridamole is officially classified as a coronary vasodilator. In vivo it inhibits platelet adhesion, and in high concentrations in vitro it inhibits platelet aggregation and release. It can also normalize shortened platelet survival times in patients with ongoing clinical arterial thromboembolism (see Fig. 20, Chapter 6). Interestingly, in patients taking dipyridamole, the bleeding times are generally normal. Dipyridamole inhibits platelet phosphodiesterase, the enzyme which degrades cAMP to AMP. It has been proposed that dipyridamole may act in vivo by potentiating the effect of endogenous prostacyclin, since prostacyclin elevates platelet cAMP and dipyridamole prevents its breakdown.[6,223] Dipyridamole, with warfarin, reduced the thromboembolic complications of old-style artificial heart valves,[224] but other clinical studies using dipyridamole as a single platelet function inhibitor have generally been disappointing. It is currently used only in combination with other antiplatelet agents. There is platelet survival evidence in patients and in animal models of thrombogenesis that dipyridamole and aspirin are synergistic. Normalization of platelet survival in patients with ongoing platelet consumption is optimally produced by the regimen aspirin (325 mg) and dipyridamole (75 mg) given together three times daily.[225]

Ticlopidine, a new, potent platelet function inhibitor, has recently been introduced for clinical trials. It prolongs the bleeding time and abolishes in vitro primary aggregation of platelets to nearly all agonists. The mechanism of action appears to relate to the blocking of fibrinogen and von Willebrand factor interactions with membrane glycoproteins.[226] It is anticipated that the risk of hemorrhagic complications of this more potent agent may be increased, although relative risks and potential benefits remain to be clarified.

Prostacyclin (PGI₂), a biologic substance, has been chemically synthesized and is available for experimental studies.[6] Its half-life in vivo is probably 30 seconds to 2 minutes. Unlike prostaglandins of the E series it is not metabolized by the lung, but approximately 50 percent is lost during a single transit through the circulation, probably being metabolized in the liver and the vasculature. In vitro, it is nonenzymatically oxidized to 6-keto $PGF_{1\alpha}$, a stable, inactive metabolite unique to PGI_2. In vivo, numerous other metabolites are also produced. PGI_2 is produced by a number of cells in the body, including endothelial cells, smooth muscle cells, fibroblasts, and macrophages. It is the most potent antiaggregating agent yet described in nature, and is also a potent vasodilator in all vascular beds. Whether PGI_2 is present as a circulating hormone in vivo is yet uncertain, but it is clear that infusions of PGI_2 have potent hemodynamic and antithrombotic effects.

PGI_2 may be stabilized for experimental use by maintaining the compound at high pH and low temperature before infusion. It has been studied experimentally as an antithrombotic agent[13] in charcoal hemoperfusion,[227] cardiopulmonary bypass,[228] renal hemodialysis,[229] and peripheral vascular disease.[230] Whether PGI_2 has any real advantage over the more stable antiaggregating and vasodilating prostaglandin PGE_1 is not yet clear. PGI_2 is currently available only as an investigational drug.

Perspective. Combination chemotherapy with multiple antiplatelet agents in experimental animals produces enhanced effects by interfering with platelet thrombus formation at multiple steps. However, controlled clinical studies to date have not demonstrated an effect in human arterial thrombotic disorders (see Chapter 14).

It is apparent that the ideal antiplatelet agent has not yet been found. Although aspirin completely blocks platelet thromboxane A_2 production, it does not block collagen or thrombin-dependent pathways of activation, and thrombin plays a critical role in thrombus production in vivo. Aspirin also does not affect platelet adherence to exposed subendothelium or release of ADP from adherent platelets. Current research is directed at drugs which: (1) produce selective inhibition of thromboxane synthetase without affecting prostacyclin synthetase; (2) affect platelet adherence as well as aggregation and release; (3) enhance vascular PGI_2 production; and (4) inhibit both thrombin and thromboxane-mediated platelet aggregation. There are few such candidates presently available for clinical trials.

14

MANAGEMENT OF PATIENTS WITH THROMBOTIC DISORDERS

Once the diagnosis of thrombosis is established, the appropriate antithrombotic strategy must be formulated. Treatment will vary depending upon whether the venous or arterial circulatory system is involved, the size and location of the involved vessel(s), and the risks of extension, embolization, or recurrence. The complication rate of antithrombotic therapy will also need to be carefully weighed and balanced against these risks.

Initially, a decision should be made regarding the possible indications for rapid thrombus dissolution using fibrinolytic agents. An assessment of potential indications and benefit should be considered with respect to the alternative of conventional anticoagulants only. For example, direct perfusion of recently occluded coronary arteries with streptokinase has shown dramatic lysis of thrombi,[208,209] although its overall role in the management of acute myocardial infarction remains to be established through controlled trials and longer term follow-up with respect to mortality, myocardial salvage, and reocclusion.

For established DVT and PE, heparin remains the mainstay of acute treatment, followed by warfarin therapy to reduce the risk of recurrence.[231] Oral anticoagulants are also effective in reducing arterial thromboemboli from artificial surfaces, including heart valves, or from mural thrombi. A major controversial area of management involves the question of prophylaxis of venous thrombosis by low-dose heparin or physical measures. Whether the fatality rate from pulmonary embolism can be reduced remains unclear, despite a number of clinical trials.

Although platelet function inhibition is theoretically an attractive means of reducing the formation and embolization of arterial thrombi, the drugs available for clinical use are limited with respect to potency and mechanism of action. Results from large-scale, controlled clinical trials of secondary prevention of myocardial infarction have been inconclusive. More potent and specific platelet function inhibitors are becoming available and their potential role is under study. This chapter discusses therapeutic issues according to specific venous or arterial thrombotic diseases.

VENOUS THROMBOSIS
AND THROMBOEMBOLISM

Indications for Fibrinolytic Therapy. Systemic use of streptokinase or urokinase in patients with massive pulmonary embolism was studied in a large, randomized, cooperative trial in the early 1970s. The results of this trial[183] provided considerable information about the clinical nature of PE and the accuracy of various diagnostic procedures. For patients with recent, large emboli, infusion with either 12 or 24 hours of urokinase or streptokinase showed accelerated reperfusion by both lung scans and pulmonary angiograms in the first 24 hours, compared with patients treated with heparin alone. Reperfusion became identical in the thrombolytic and heparin-only treatment groups after a few days, and there was no difference in mortality. It should also be emphasized that patients given systemic fibrinolytic therapy were also given conventional treatment consisting of full-dose heparin and warfarin subsequent to thrombolytic therapy. In addition, it was also found to be important to monitor lytic therapy with thrombin times to document that a fibrinolytic effect had been achieved.[207]

In the large-scale pulmonary embolism trials, a greater incidence of hemorrhagic complications was noted in patients receiving fibrinolytic agents, although to some extent, this was related to the use of invasive procedures such as follow-up pulmonary angiograms.[183] For either fibrinolytic therapy followed by heparin, or heparin alone, the risk of recurrence or extension was equally low. Suggestive evidence of long-term beneficial effects on pulmonary function in a small series of patients initially treated with fibrinolytic therapy (as opposed to those receiving anticoagulants alone) are intriguing[232] but it remains to be demonstrated that the increased risk of severe hemorrhage is offset by the measured increments in pulmonary capillary perfusion, and whether or not the observed differences are of long-term clinical significance. At present, it is therefore recommended that systemic fibrinolytic therapy be reserved for patients with massive, life-threatening pulmonary emboli and circulatory collapse, provided there are no major contraindications to its use. Treatment details are specified in Chapter 13.

In deep venous thrombosis, it has been argued that early thrombolytic therapy will restore flow more rapidly, and thus decrease the frequency of damage to venous valve cusps, and consequently decrease the incidence of the postphlebitic syndrome.[206] The prevalence of this serious complication, however, is not known, and it has been observed in the absence of clinically apparent deep venous disease.[233] Furthermore, attempts to characterize venous function in patients who have received streptokinase suggest that venous insufficiency cannot be prevented by this mode of therapy.[234] Thus, judgment should be reserved until more is known about the natural history of postphlebitic syndrome and whether or not early fibrinolytic therapy, with its attendant greater risks, should be used routinely. Alternatively, if risk factors for this syndrome could be delineated and stratified, trials on patients at high risk would provide extremely useful clinical data.

Anticoagulant Therapy for Venous Thrombotic Disorders. For the past two decades, immediate heparinization has been used as the initial therapy of pulmonary emboli, with a striking reduction of mortality from recurrence.[235] Likewise, heparinization is used in deep vein thrombosis to prevent extension or embolization of thrombi while endogenous fibrinolysis gradually removes thrombotic material. Treatment is associated with normalization of tests of ongoing thrombosis (see Chapter 12), including circulating levels of fibrinopeptide A.[236] Incomplete normalization of this determination by therapy appears to predict a high risk of recurrence.

The standard approach to heparinization initially involves immediate anticoagulation with an intravenous bolus of heparin. This is followed by a continuous intravenous infusion with doses as specified in Chapter 13, recalling that the average requirement in PE is increased about 50 percent over that in DVT.[211] Individual variability in response to the standard dosage is great, but can be monitored by the recalcification time or PTT four hours after initiating or adjusting the dosage, and then daily to maintain the intrinsic clotting test close to twice baseline values. Platelet counts should be obtained prior to therapy, on day five, or with any bleeding complication. The infusion is maintained 7 to 10 days. Figure 36 presents a typical example of heparinization that includes the switching to oral anticoagulation using warfarin. The latter drug is begun at least three to four days before heparin is discontinued, and doses are adjusted according to the response of the prothrombin time which, in itself, is relatively insensitive to heparin (see Fig. 23, Chapter 7).

Recommendations for the length of time to maintain patients on oral anticoagulants are not precisely known. The risk of recurrence even in uncomplicated cases remains high for several weeks.[237] For straightforward, distal DVT, six weeks will usually suffice, whereas three to six months of treatment are generally recommended for proximal DVT or PE. In patients with greater risk of recurrence, longer periods may be necessary.

In the patient who continues to show new emboli despite adequate heparinization, or in whom there is an absolute contraindication to antithrombotic therapy, an inferior vena caval umbrella or plication may protect the patient transiently from pulmonary emboli. Recurrences of venous thrombosis or thromboemboli in patients on warfarin (in anticoagulant range) usually reflect a thrombotic tendency that exceeds the limited antithrombotic capacity of this drug. Monitored, full-dose heparinization may be continued as subcutaneous

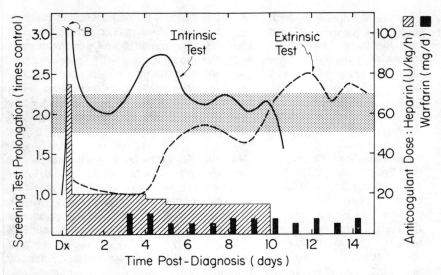

FIGURE 36. Typical use of anticoagulant therapy in venous thrombotic disorders. After diagnosis (Dx) a bolus (B) of heparin (75 units per kg) is given to patients with extensive proximal DVT. The intrinsic system test (recalcification or partial thromboplastin times) is then monitored each day to maintain the patient in the therapeutic range (stippled) using 20 decreasing to 15 units per kg per hour by continuous intravenous infusion. After checking the extrinsic system test (prothrombin time) on the third day, warfarin is begun with two initial daily doses of 10 mg followed by amounts predicted to maintain the prothrombin time in range some 48 hours after each dose. It should be emphasized that these represent typical dosage maneuvers; owing to wide individual variation in sensitivity to both anticoagulant agents, the doses themselves will vary considerably among different patients. Also note that clotting tests lower than the therapeutic range are associated with increased risk of thromboembolic recurrence, whereas levels above this range represent increased risk of bleeding secondary to the anticoagulant therapy itself. Finally, as pointed out in Chapter 13 and Appendix A, reagent variability necessitates that each hospital laboratory carefully standardize its particular monitoring tests and that the clinician be aware of their therapeutic ranges.

heparin in the outpatient management of such patients, and this treatment may even have a lower incidence of hemorrhagic complications than warfarin.[237] Low-dose heparin should never be substituted for warfarin, as it does not prevent recurrence following 10 days of full-dose, intravenous heparinization.[238]

Prevention. A great deal of attention has been focused upon prophylactic measures for DVT. Using ^{125}I-fibrinogen calf scanning results, dramatic reductions in fibrin accumulation in the calf have been achieved using both physical and pharmacologic measures. It is not yet clear, however, to what degree calf-vein thrombi reflect the risk of pulmonary embolism.

For the operative and immediate postoperative periods, mechanical devices are being developed which intermittently compress the calves.[239,240] When radioiodinated fibrinogen accumulation in the calves was taken as an index of a tendency towards venous thromboembolism, the frequency of positive scans was markedly reduced.

Low-dose subcutaneous heparin (5000 units every 8 to 12 hours), beginning before surgery and continuing until a patient is fully ambulatory, has been advocated to reduce the incidence of venous thrombosis and pulmonary embolism in patients undergoing major abdominal and thoracic surgery. The incidence of labeled fibrinogen scanning defects routinely decreases from 20 to 30 percent to 5 to 10 percent with low doses, and in a large European cooperative study[241] the occurence of fatal pulmonary emboli was 2 per 2000 treated versus 16 per 2000 control surgical patients (over age 40 and based on 72 versus 53 autopsies, respectively). These observations may apply to medical patients at prolonged bed rest as well. Abnormal calf scanning results have been unaffected in patients undergoing hip surgery, however. Because fatal PE occurs in about 1 per 1000 surgical patients in the United States and Canada, the European results may not strictly apply. It would be more helpful to stratify patients by risk factors in future studies. Another consideration relates to the individual variation in heparin levels during administration of the low-dose regimen. Some persons will have no detectable heparin, while others occasionally have significantly prolonged PTTs from low-dose administration[242], and a small increased risk of bleeding is encountered in them. A final concern regarding the large-scale trial relates to the fact that the frequency of nonfatal PE at autopsy (including those that may have contributed to but not caused death) was equal in control and treated groups.

In patients with low risk of bleeding but high risk for venous thromboembolism, low-dose heparin is generally safe, but should not be given without attention to exercising the lower extremities as well. Even then, occasionally a "hypercoagulable" patient will develop venous thromboembolism. It may be that such patients are among the 5 percent with unaffected calf scans found in all low dose heparin treated series. It should be re-emphasized that low-dose heparin is totally inadequate anticoagulation for established DVT or PE. Furthermore, it is clearly less effective than warfarin in preventing recurrence.[238] Considerations of cost-effectiveness for large-scale prophylaxis need to be tempered by risk factors,[243] but in general, one should strive for early mobility or leg exercises, or both, in any hospitalized patient, even if it is elected to use low-dose heparin. Earlier ambulation may be credited with the impressive reduction in PE post-myocardial infarction.

ACUTE MYOCARDIAL INFARCTION

Thrombosis has been implicated frequently in the pathogenesis of acute transmural myocardial infarction. Both autopsy studies in patients dying of transmural infarction and coronary angiography in the first hours postonset have shown acute occluding thrombosis in 85 to 90 percent of these patients.[189] However, acute thrombosis is not as often noted in patients with subendocardial infarction, and in patients with sudden death, acute thrombosis is seldom seen. Sudden death victims frequently have no evidence of acute infarction, although they usually have severe atherosclerotic coronary artery disease. The role of thrombosis in patients with sudden death is unclear; there is some evidence suggesting that diffuse platelet microembolization may be involved in at least some patients, although other mechanisms of arrhythmias and vasospasm appear to be more important.

Because of the enormous morbidity and mortality associated with myocardial infarction, there has been great interest in antithrombotic therapy in the secondary prevention of recurrent myocardial infarction. At present there is no clear evidence to support the routine use of anticoagulant, antiplatelet, or systemic thrombolytic therapy in acute myocardial infarction.[244,245] Anticoagulant therapy has been claimed to reduce the mortality in patients with myocardial infarction primarily by reducing thromboembolic events. However, since such events occur in only 5 to 10 percent of patients, the benefit is quite small; most physicians do not feel that long-term therapy justifies the 2 to 4 percent risk per year of serious bleeding complications. However, there are subgroups of patients at high risk of mural thrombus formation and systemic emboli, that is, those with large transmural anterior or anteriolateral infarcts[194] with or without a ventricular aneurysm. Patients at risk of venous thrombosis and pulmonary embolism, for example, those with congestive heart failure or prolonged bed rest, probably benefit from anticoagulation during the acute phase. For example, in men over 60 years of age, despite the increased incidence of hemorrhagic complications in orally anticoagulated patients, total morbidity due to intracranial events was greater in the placebo group.[246] This Dutch series, which had a remarkably low incidence of hemorrhage, attributed their success to very careful monitoring with Thrombo-tests. Nevertheless, small differences between treated and untreated in a relatively uncommon complication[245] and the lack of an effect on postmenopausal women make it difficult to generalize from these results.

Thrombolytic therapy has been used in an attempt to reduce infarct size and thus decrease mortality. Large-scale, controlled trials of systemic thrombolytic agents in acute infarction have failed to show benefit, and such therapy is not recommended.[244,247] However, the potential for tissue plasminogen activator has not been assessed. Recent trials of direct intra-coronary artery infusions of thrombolytic agents within a few hours of onset of the occlusion have demonstrated dramatic results with thrombus dissolution and some myocardial "salvage."[208,209,299] Whether such aggressive therapy will have long-term benefits in preserving myocardium and reducing mortality needs to be determined in future controlled trials with longer term follow-up.

Several anecdotal reports in the past have suggested that aspirin may reduce the frequency or severity of infarction or death in these patients. However, the recent large, randomized, cooperative trial of the Aspirin Myocardial

Infarction Study (AMIS) group,[248] failed to demonstrate any reduction in death or reinfarction in patients randomized to receive aspirin following myocardial infarction. In this study aspirin was not begun until at least two months and generally after six months postinfarction. In contrast to the AMIS study, the Anturane Re-infarction Study[249] noted a significant reduction in sudden death in patients who began sulfinpyrazone 200 mg four times daily within the first six weeks of myocardial infarction. The benefit was noted only in the first six months of therapy, and the effect was found only in sudden death patients and not on reinfarction. The results of this study have been seriously challenged, however, because of irregularities in the assignment of patients to the sudden death category. Consequently, this drug is not approved by the Food and Drug Administration for this indication. The recently concluded Persantin-Aspirin Re-infarction Study (PARIS)[250] and British Medical Research Council Study[251] suggested a modest trend for benefit with aspirin or aspirin-dipyridamole begun early postinfarction. Of the 10 percent of patients who die in the first year post-myocardial infarction, most die in the first six months. It is possible that treatment in the first weeks following infarction is critical for any antithrombotic regimen. Currently, however, the data do not establish benefit from the routine use of antiplatelet agents in the secondary prevention of myocardial infarction.[244,245]

For acute myocardial infarction, one is left with the possibility that acute thrombolytic therapy within the first few hours of occlusion may have a role in limiting ischemic necrosis. In addition, patients with large transmural anterior myocardial infarctions have sufficient risk of cerebral embolization from mural thrombus to justify a course of full-dose anticoagulation. Although it appears that many of these thrombi may not embolize, the repercussions of a cerebral or major peripheral embolus may be disastrous. Anticoagulant therapy should also be considered in patients with marked increased risk factors for development of deep venous thrombosis (e.g., congestive heart failure, anticipated prolonged bed rest, and perhaps age) and low-dose heparin may be used as a more general prophylactic measure in this setting. Despite low-dose heparin treatment, however, physical measures, including regular exercise of the lower extremities, should be stressed. Finally, current therapeutic attempts with available platelet function inhibitors have been inconclusive, but results with more potent agents will be forthcoming.

OTHER HEART DISEASES

As with anticoagulant therapy for ventricular mural thrombi following a transmural infarct, anticoagulant therapy for thromboemboli arising from the left atrium is often indicated. *Atrial fibrillation* secondary to ischemic heart disease is now more prevalent than mitral valvular disease as an etiology, although the former also carries a risk of up to 35 percent of patients having clinically significant systemic embolization.[252] It has been appreciated that the incidence of atrial fibrillation is rare when the left atrium measures less than 40 mm in diameter by echocardiography, but the arrhythmia was found in over half of the patients in one series with chamber enlargement beyond this measurement.[253] Thus, left atrial size is an important determinant in the development of atrial fibrillation or mural atrial thrombus formation, or both. Embolic strokes have been noted in some patients with the onset of fibrillation, or with the change back to normal sinus rhythm. Left atrial enlargement alone constitutes a rationale for long-term anticoagulant therapy. The bradycardia-tachycardia syndrome is also associated with systemic arterial emboli, particularly in older patients.[254] In the latter settings, however, relative contraindications to long-term anticoagulant therapy should be weighed more heavily than in the venous thrombotic disorders.

Heart valve replacement with prosthetic devices[255,256] and tissue heterografts[257,258] has evolved considerably over the past 20 years. Advances in design such as the cloth covering of Starr-Edward valves[255] and convexed-concaved modification of the Bjork-Shiley prostheses,[256] as well as the materials within the prosthetic surfaces themselves, have decreased the overall risk of arterial thromboembolism following replacement, and of thrombosis of the prosthetic device itself. Thus, patients can be expected to survive several years with artificial valve replacement but must be maintained on oral anticoagulants for life. Unfortunately, clinically significant embolic events usually involve the cerebral circulation such that the morbidity of this complication is particularly high. Significant bleeding is often encountered during the years of therapy with long-term oral anticoagulant.[217]

Heterograft-tissue valve replacement further reduces the risk of late arterial embolic complications. In the absence of a large left atrium or persistent atrial fibrillation long term anticoagulants are often unnecessary. As shown in one large series, a third of all patients with mitral valve replacement required long-term therapy with oral anticoagulants, whereas only one tenth of those with isolated aortic valve replacement required this therapy.[258]

The possibility of augmenting the antithrombotic effect of warfarin with platelet function inhibitors was considered in old style valves a decade ago, and, in a small series, the addition of dipyridamole to warfarin reduced arterial embolization from 14 to 1 percent in a follow-up period of one year.[224] It is clear that this and other early experience with platelet function inhibitors is irrelevant to the current generation of prostheses, although aspirin was a helpful adjunct in a more recent series.[259] Additional studies of combinations of agents to reduce further the current risk of thromboembolism-related fatality are clearly needed. It will be important to consider other cardiac variables such as rhythm, atrial chamber size, and ventricular disease, and to weigh the relative risks of hemorrhage against the potential benefit of reducing the incidence of a rather infrequent complication.

STROKE AND TRANSIENT ISCHEMIC ATTACKS (TIA)

The most characteristic feature of stroke is its speed of evolution, in that the deficit appears in seconds or minutes, rarely hours, or at most a few days.

Embolic and hemorrhagic stroke characteristically begin suddenly, with the deficit reaching its maximum almost immediately, whereas thrombotic strokes most often are preceded by some transient ischemic herald and may develop in a stepwise fashion over hours to days. In hemorrhage related to hypertension, the deficit evolves smoothly over minutes to hours. The neurologic deficit reflects the location and size of the infarct or hemorrhage.

Computerized axial tomography (CAT) is the diagnostic tool to identify acute hematomas or acute hemorrhagic infarcts. It also is useful to localize ischemic infarcts once swelling of the necrotic tissue appears in a few days. Arteriography demonstrates stenoses and occlusion of larger vessels, and occasionally shows embolic occlusion. The risks associated with arteriography are increased in patients with stroke in evolution. Visualization of the carotid arteries near the bifurcation in the neck has a high yield potential for surgical correction. In this regard, noninvasive ultrasonic duplex scanning has been shown to have some usefulness to detect and categorize the severity of carotid artery atherosclerosis[260] as related to sources of stenosis or emboli.

Thromboembolism has been implicated in the pathogenesis of stroke most prominently in the production of platelet-fibrin emboli from extracranial vascular lesions, and in the development of thrombus in a stenotic or ulcerated intracranial vessel. Antithrombotic therapy is designed to prevent propagation of the pre-existing thrombus or formation of new thrombus, and to decrease the formation of platelet-fibrin emboli.

The rationale for antithrombotic therapy in transient ischemic attacks (TIA) is based on the observation that TIA may herald thrombotic strokes. In a large proportion of patients, TIA appear to be caused by platelet-fibrin emboli from extracranial vessels that are amenable to antithrombotic therapy. In patients with TIA, approximately 10 percent a year will have a nonfatal stroke and 5 to 10 percent a year will die of stroke or myocardial infarction.[261,262]

A number of uncontrolled, nonrandomized, or retrospective trials have reported benefit from anticoagulant therapy with heparin or warfarin in patients with TIA.[263,264] When the randomized trials are considered, there appears to be no clear-cut effect on survival, no clear reduction in stroke, but a possible decrease in the frequency of TIA. Since these conclusions are not universally accepted, a number of centers continue to anticoagulate patients with TIA for three to six months unless there are specific contraindications. However, the uncertain benefit, the risk of hemorrhage, and the need for diligent patient cooperation and laboratory monitoring have dissuaded most physicians from this form of prophylaxis in deference to antiplatelet therapy.

Recently, there have been two large-scale, double-blind, randomized studies on the use of antiplatelet agents in the prevention of TIA, stroke, and death in patients presenting with a TIA.[265,266] The earlier study suggested some benefit from aspirin in reducing death or stroke in patients with TIA.[265] In the other study,[266] significant reduction in the risk of stroke, death, or TIA with aspirin therapy was clearly demonstrated. Aspirin reduced the risk of stroke or death by 31 percent. These effects were largely restricted to men in whom there was a 48 percent reduction of stroke or death. In women there was no statistical proof of benefit from aspirin. Sulfinpyrazone alone in this study was ineffective. Moreover, there was no significant benefit from the combination of sulfinpyrazone and aspirin compared with aspirin alone. These studies have led to the recommendation that aspirin in doses of 325 mg q.i.d. or 650 mg b.i.d. be used in men with TIA. Whether aspirin would have a similar protective effect on patients with completed strokes who are at similar risk of a recurrent stroke is yet uncertain, but some clinicians recommend such therapy in this situation. The dramatic sex difference noted in that study is difficult to explain. Most clinicians at this point, however, continue to prescribe aspirin or an aspirin-containing regimen to women who have had TIA. This approach is supported by the AMIS trial, which noted a reduction in stroke and TIA in both men and women taking 1 gram of aspirin daily.[248] Some centers recommend a combination of aspirin and dipyridamole on the basis of the aspirin trial, together with the theoretical benefit of using a regimen that normalizes shortened platelet survival (see Chapter 13). Clinical trials with combinations of agents are in progress to resolve these issues.

PERIPHERAL VASCULAR DISEASES AND VASCULAR GRAFTS

The treatment of acute arterial occlusion usually involves prompt surgical intervention to restore arterial circulation, and such therapeutic intervention is mandatory if ischemic threatens limb viability.[267,268] Since stasis is a consequence of occlusion, heparin is usually given to prevent extension of the thrombotic process and as possible treatment of an underlying source of emboli such as cardiac disease. The development of the balloon catheter has simplified the treatment of acute arterial embolization. The procedure usually involves common femoral arteriotomy performed under local anesthesia. The catheter is passed proximally and distally in the arterial system, and embolic material is retrived by withdrawing the inflated balloon, using care to avoid overinflation and consequent arterial injury. Arteriographic visualization is important to document complete retrieval of emboli. Follow-up antithrombotic therapy is important to avoid recurrence. In the past, heparin has been used for this purpose, but the role of newer antiplatelet drugs in the prevention of recurrences is being tested in controlled clinical trials.

In acute arterial thrombosis, arteriography is necessary to define the location and extent of the arterial occlusion, and status of the inflow and runoff vessels. Although reperfusion using fibrinolytic therapy is an attractive course and has been reported, surgery provides the most rapid treatment for large artery occlusion and a viable ischemic limb, while thrombolytic therapy may be indicated for small artery occlusion.[269] Based upon limited experience, it is concluded that thrombolytic therapy is more likely to be successful when the occlusion is embolic rather than thrombotic. In addition, the likelihood of lysis is influenced by the duration of arterial occlusion, that is, greatest success occurs when the occlusion is less than 12 hours in duration. If reperfusion is delayed and the degree of ischemia threatening, irreversible damage may supervene before lysis is completed. There is recent renewed interest in the acute, local infusion of lytic agents intra-arterially proximal to the occlusion, but controlled data are not yet available.

The underlying arterial disease often requires major arterial reconstruction including bypass procedures to correct the arterial insufficiency.[267] Subsequent postoperative antithrombotic therapy with antiplatelet drugs has been proposed but there are no controlled clinical trials available to date. While arterial revascularization should ideally be carried out within the first few hours following acute arterial occlusion, reconstruction may be possible after several days if collateral circulation has maintained limb viability.

Thrombotic occlusion seldom occurs in high-flow, aortofemoral prostheses, but is common in smaller caliber grafts such as femoropopliteal bypass vascular grafts.[195,267] In man, these vascular graft surfaces remain thrombogenic for at least several years, as evidenced by ongoing platelet consumption and ^{111}In-platelet deposition. Although antiplatelet drugs can reduce platelet deposition on the vascular grafts, the low frequency of clinical embolic events has limited data from controlled clinical trials with respect to the capacity of platelet active drugs to increase the patency rate of grafts.[270] Thrombi remain a common, early complication of hemodialysis grafts, prompting research to develop less thrombogenic biomaterials.

Prevention of acute arterial occlusion depends upon successfully modifying atherosclerotic peripheral arterial diseases that lead to arterial occlusion. In this regard, prostacyclin infusions have been proposed in the management of chronic peripheral vascular disease.[230] To demonstrate that such therapy or that involving other drugs that modify platelet function will indeed alter the course of arterial vascular disease remains to be tested with long term treatment by more potent agents.

APPENDIX A

TESTS FOR HEMOSTASIS

While the presence of a bleeding disorder may be suspected from the history and clinical observation, accurate diagnosis depends upon specific laboratory tests. Since most of the tests are complex assays, the physician needs an appreciation and understanding of the sensitivity and variabilities of the tests to evaluate accurately the laboratory results. This appendix describes representative screening test procedures. Discussion on clinical relevance appears in Chapter 7 and is reviewed elsewhere.[102,104] General methodologic issues have also been published.[271] The strategy for consideration of test results in Chapter 7 (see Fig. 21) serves as an organizational framework for this appendix.

PLATELET SCREENING TESTS

Platelet Count

Since defective plug formation is usually caused by thrombocytopenia, it is important to assess platelet concentration as part of the hemostatic screening profile. Blood for platelet counting should be collected in EDTA (lavender top tube). Platelet enumeration remains reliable for up to 18 hours if kept unagitated at room temperature. The concentration of platelets can be estimated at three levels of precision depending upon available time, equipment, and needs.

Blood Film Estimation. When bleeding necessitates urgent evaluation, platelet number can be estimated from the Wright-stained peripheral smear. A ratio of 1 platelet to 20 red cells corresponds to a normal platelet count. Smears are read as showing absent, reduced, adequate, or increased platelets. With experience, the platelet count may be approximated within 25 to 50 percent.

Chamber (Hand) Counts by Phase Contrast Microscopy. *Principle:* Platelets are counted in a special counting chamber using phase microscopy after lysing the red blood cells with 1 percent ammonium oxalate. The error in the method is approximately 10 to 15 percent. It remains the most precise method to assess severe or moderately severe thrombocytopenia.

Material: Red cell pipette; 1 percent ammonium oxalate; special hemocytometer; phase contrast microscope; hand tally.

Procedure: Draw blood up to the 1 mark in a red blood cell pipette and dilute with 1 percent ammonium oxalate to the 101 mark. Shake pipette for three minutes. Charge counting chambers and allow to stand 15 minutes in moist chamber. Count platelets in the four corners and center squares of the hemocytometer.

$$\text{Calculation: platelets}/\mu\text{l} = \frac{\text{cells counted} \times \text{dilution}}{0.004 \times \text{squares counted}}$$

Particle Counting. Electronic particle enumeration increases precision owing to increased number of particles detected in a short counting period. Because of the equipment required, electronic enumeration[272] is most practical in laboratories where a large number of platelet counts are performed daily. For separate platelet counters, platelet-rich plasma (from blood settled by gravity for 30 minutes) is diluted and added. Some hospital laboratories are now obtaining routine platelet counts on whole blood, using newer counting devices which measure a size distribution range by electronic impedance or laser light scattering,[273] which are simple, rapid techniques with some compromise of accuracy and a resultant broader normal range.

Interpretation. The normal platelet count (by any method) is 250,000 per μl $\pm$ 60,000. For automatic procedures, results of individual determinations have a variance of ± 2 to 3 percent. Reliable platelet counts will not be obtained below 50,000 per μl without special care in handling particle-free material and using larger volumes of plasma, that is, 25 to 100 μl, to reduce dilution error. Platelet counts are unreliable when white cell counts are greatly elevated (>100,000 per μl). Severe red cell fragmentation may produce an artificially increased count. Results from particle counting devices need to be consistent with a smear estimate to exclude gross errors; low counts are more accurately assessed by the hand (phase) technique.

Bleeding Time

Standardized Template Bleeding Time.[274] *Principle:* This test measures the overall hemostatic role of platelets in vivo by determining the duration of bleeding from a standard skin incision, 1 mm deep by 10 mm long, while maintaining increased venous pressure. It is also useful to assess platelet function in the presence of modest thrombocytopenia. A 5 mm by 0.5 mm incision has been used for neonates or young children.[275]

    Materials: Sterile Mielke template, blade holder, and gauge; Bard Parker No. 11 blade; blood pressure cuff; alcohol sponges; butterfly adhesives; filter paper; stop watches; hemostat.

    Procedure: Using a hemostat attach a sterile blade to the blade holder, hold the blade holder against the gauge and adjust knife blade so that the tip touches the base of the gauge. Tighten the set screw to maintain the blade in position.

    A site about midway on the volar surface of the forearm is cleaned with alcohol. A blood pressure cuff is applied to the upper arm and pressure of 40 mm Hg is maintained throughout the test. The template is placed on the arm and pressed firmly against the skin. Two longitudinal or horizontal incisions approximately 1 cm apart are made through the template slot. A stopwatch is started as each incision is made. At 30-second intervals, blot the blood with filter paper. Bring the filter paper close to the incision without touching the wound itself. When blood no longer stains the paper, the watch is stopped. The bleeding time reported is the average of the cuts. If duplicates do not agree within 2 to 3 minutes, the test should be repeated.

    Remove the blood pressure cuff and clean the incision of any residual clotted blood. Apply a tight bandage to hold the wound edges together in order to minimize scarring.

Interpretation. With platelet counts above 100,000 per μl, the normal bleeding time is 4.5 minutes ($\pm$ 1.5); borderline is 8 to 10 minutes; values greater than 10 minutes are associated with a significant hemostatic defect. In patients with platelet counts between 10,000 and 100,000 per μl, the expected bleeding time (BT) is approximated from the following formula (represented graphically in Fig. 22, Chapter 7):

$$\text{BT (min)} = 30 - \frac{\text{platelet count}}{4000}$$

Because drug-induced platelet dysfunction is so frequent (e.g., aspirin), specific questioning about medication is essential, and repeat testing may be necessary. A diagnosis should not depend on a single, unverified determination.

A more simple, spring-loaded device has become popular in recent years, and with careful attention to technique, comparable results were obtained in normal volunteers with the two methods.[276] Several patients with classical hemophilia, however, had prolonged bleeding times with the spring-loaded device,[277] so that it is more sensitive to other hemostatic defects and therefore less specific. Occasionally, otherwise normal subjects are encountered with significantly prolonged spring-loaded device times which are completely normal or repeat with the standardized template.

FACTOR SCREENING TESTS

Blood Sample

Anticoagulant. The standard anticoagulant used for screening tests and factor assays is 3.8 percent trisodium citrate (0.13 M). Nine volumes of blood are added to one volume citrate. The citrate complexes the calcium ion by lowering the free Ca^{++} concentration to the point where clotting is interrupted. There are a number of citrate anticoagulant preparations available in the commercially prepared vacuum tubes (usually blue-topped). Care should be taken to use the same anticoagulant as in the normal control plasma against which the screening tests are standardized. EDTA is too strong a Ca^{++} chelator for the clotting screening tests and causes spurious results. In some situations, heparin inadvertently contaminates the sample (see Chapter 7). Reliable results from coagulation tests may still be obtained, however, by using a simple column[220] or tablet[278] adsorption.

There is an optimal Ca^{++} concentration, and problems with excess or too little anticoagulant occur with polycythemia or more severe anemia, respectively. To correct for the variable plasma volumes, the normal 9:1 blood to citrate ratio should be modified by adding 25 percent more or less anticoagulant for each 15 percent points the hct is deviated from 45 (e.g., 1.25 or 1.5 ml citrate plus blood to 10 ml final volume for patients with hct of 30 or 15, respectively, or 0.75 ml for hct of 60).

Collection. Blood for coagulation studies must be collected with particular care, to avoid denaturation or activation, by drawing it gently into a plastic syringe from a clean venipuncture with minimal stasis. If there is difficulty with the venipuncture, blood flow, or improper mixing with the anticoagulant, the sample may be partially clotted, resulting in unreliable and misleading results. For vacuum collection tubes, the high flow-rate from filling may cause foaming and denaturation; blood should be transferred from a syringe to the tube by allowing the blood to run gently down the side of the tube. If the vacuum seal has leaked, the ratio of blood to anticoagulant can be altered.

Processing and Procedures. Citrated whole blood centrifuged at 3000 to 4000 rpm for 10 minutes will yield platelet-poor plasma. This plasma is satisfactory for coagulation studies run within four hours. A higher centrifugal force (e.g. 40,000 g for 30 minutes) is required to remove enough of the remaining platelets prior to freezing the plasma so that it can be stored at − 80°C before testing.

A variety of manual, semiautomated, and automated techniques are used to assess clot formation visually or by changes in electric conduction or optical density.[279] Commercial reagents vary considerably, especially for the prothrombin and partial thromboplastin times.

Thrombin Time

Thrombin Time Assay. *Principle:* Thrombin is added to plasma and cleaves the fibrinopeptides to produce fibrin monomer which polymerizes nonenzymatically to form a clot. The test bypasses all earlier steps in the coagulation sequence. Since a low concentration of thrombin is added, the enzymatic cleavage of fibrinopeptides is the rate-limiting step. The normal value should be as a measure of the overall fibrinogen clotting step, anything that interferes with either the enzymatic or polymerization steps prolongs the thrombin time.

Reagents: Bovine thrombin is diluted in 0.15 M NaCl to a concentration (determined by trial) to give a normal plasma clotting time of 18 to 20 seconds. The dilute thrombin solution is only stable 30 minutes.

Procedure: 0.2 ml of citrate plasma is incubated at 37°C for three minutes, 0.1 ml of dilute thrombin solution is added and the clotting time determined. Duplicate determinations are made on patient and normal control samples.

Interpretation. The normal value is 18 to 20 seconds; borderline prolongation is 22 to 24 seconds; abnormal, > 24 seconds. Prolonged thrombin time occurs with low fibrinogen (< 80 to 100 mg per dl), abnormal fibrinogen, inhibitors (traces of heparin, dysproteinemias, fibrin degradation products), uremia, hyperbilirubinemia, or incorrect anticoagulant (e.g., EDTA). It is used to monitor the effect of systemic fibrinolytic activity.[207] A shortened thrombin time is indicative of an activated sample. In order to distinguish between some of the features which give a long thrombin time, the results of the thrombin-fibrinogen clotting reaction run for a kinetic fibrinogen assay are compared.

Fibrinogen Assays

Kinetic (Clauss) Method.[280] *Principle:* The thrombin-fibrinogen clotting reaction is determined under conditions of excess thrombin with the rate-limiting step being polymerization of the fibrin monomer. The clotting time is proportional to fibrinogen concentration, provided there is normal polymerization. The kinetic test is most frequently used in routine hospital laboratories.

Reagents: Thrombin (60 NIH U per ml); barbital buffer (50 mM sodium barbital per 0.15 M NaCl); patient plasma; normal control plasma.

Procedure: Add 0.1 ml plasma to 0.9 ml barbital buffer to make a 1:10 dilution. Incubate 0.2 ml diluted plasma at 37°C for 3 minutes. Add 0.2 ml thrombin and determine clotting time. The fibrinogen concentration is determined from the clotting time by means of a calibrated standard curve made from dilutions of pooled normal plasma of known fibrinogen concentration by the total clottable fibrinogen method. Serial dilutions are made and a curve is constructed as in Figure 37.

Total Clottable Fibrinogen Protein Assay.[281,282] *Principle:* This is an equilibrium method in which an excess of thrombin is added to a measured volume of plasma which is allowed to clot completely. The formed clot is wound on a glass rod and the amount of clottable protein determined chemically.

Reagents: Stock solution of bovine topical thrombin-saline (200 NIH units per ml); 40 percent in 0.2 N NaOH; 0.15 M NaCl; patient plasma; normal control plasma.

Procedure: Add 10 ml 0.15 M NaCl, 0.5 ml plasma, and 0.25 ml thrombin solution to a 40-ml round-bottom tube. Set up patient and normal control plasma in duplicate. Gently swirl the tube. Insert a glass rod with a paddle end. Incubate 10 minutes at 37°C. Wind the clots onto the glass rod; wash each clot with 0.15 M NaCl. Place the glass rod with the adherent fibrin clot into a test tube containing 5 ml of 40 percent urea in 0.2 N NaOH. Let stand at room temperature for 30 minutes. Read the absorbance in a spectrophotometer at 282 nm against an alkaline urea blank.

$$\text{Calculation: fibrinogen (mg/100 ml)} = \text{absorbance} \times 618.4$$

Corrections for marked hyperlipidemia occasionally need to be made.

Interpretation. The normal value is 180 to 400 mg per dl by either method. Fibrinogen levels may increase two- to fourfold in inflammation. The total clottable determination is relatively insensitive to heparin, FDP, or variants of fibrinogen which polymerize slowly. It is the most reliable measurement of fibrinogen concentration, and is the best indicator for predicting bleeding due to hypofibrinogenemia. A greater fibrinogen level by total clottable than kinetic assay is often seen in severe, acute disseminated intravascular coagulation or dysfibrinogenemia. Other techniques, including a specific venom for Aα chain cleavage, and immunologic assays have been used or are being developed for clinical laboratory trials.[283]

Extrinsic System Screening

Prothrombin Time Assay.[284] *Principle:* The prothrombin time is performed by adding tissue thromboplastin and Ca^{++} to plasma. The tissue factor phospholipid combines with factor VII to activate factor X. The prothrombin time tests the overall integrity of the clotting system that involves factors VII, X, V, prothrombin, and fibrinogen. A variation, the Thrombo-test, uses a standardized thromboplastin and added factor V, and is commonly employed in Europe

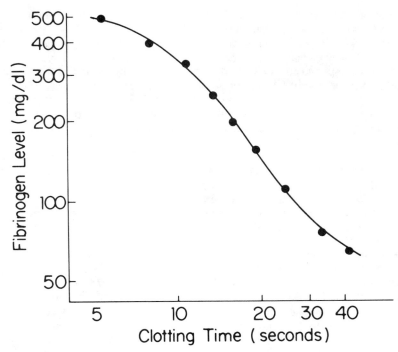

FIGURE 37. Standard curve for the kinetic fibrinogen assay. On log-log plots, the dilution curve is linear between 10 to 25 seconds. The clotting time of the sample must fall within the linear portion of the curve. Samples with clotting times outside the range must be repeated, with the appropriate dilution in the final concentration corrected accordingly (Henderson, RA, Counts, RB, with permission).

to monitor oral anticoagulant therapy.[285] A separate, two-stage assay uses the same reagents but allows assessment of prothrombin concentration.[286]

Reagents: Patient citrate plasma; normal control plasma; $CaCl_2$ (optimum concentration selected by trial; usually 0.02 to 0.03 M); and thromboplastin. The latter can be purchased from several commercial suppliers; the manufacturer's directions for reconstituting the dried material and performing the test should be strictly followed. Human brain thromboplastin is prepared and used by many reference coagulation laboratories as a more sensitive reagent.

Procedure: 0.1 ml plasma and 0.1 ml human brain thromboplastin are incubated at 37°C for three minutes. Add 0.1 ml calcium chloride and record clotting time. Duplicate determinations are made on patient and normal control plasma.

Calibration: Prothrombin time results are meaningful only when the test is calibrated. This applies whether human brain thromboplastin or one of the commercial preparations are used.

The commercial reagents vary considerably in their sensitivity to factor levels and nonspecific influences such as pH or free Ca^{++}. Consequently, there is no standard dose-response relationship for the prothrombin time. Because of this variability, each laboratory should calibrate the test system used. The dose-response curve can be determined readily by using mixtures containing known proportions of normal and prepared, deficient plasmas (Fig. 38). Alternatively, as commonly done in much of Europe, specific "reference" thromboplastins can be used or prepared patient plasmas (from several different individuals with various levels of anticoagulation) that have been carefully standardized.[287]

Interpretation. Normal values are usually 10 to 12 seconds for commercial and 13 to 15 seconds for human thromboplastins. As the calibration curve in Figure 38 indicates, the levels of the vitamin K-dependent factors must be less than 40 to 50 percent to prolong the prothrombin time. Prolongation of up to 3 seconds over normal control may occur because of nonspecific influences on the test. Generally, prothrombin times of 2 to 2.5 times the control value imply factor levels of 10 to 12 percent normal, and the therapeutic ranges for rabbit-brain thromboplastins commonly used in the United States are between 1.5 to 3.0 times prolonged, or 10 to 30 percent of standardized times.[287]

Since the test is sensitive to free Ca^{++}, variations in the ratio of blood or plasma to anticoagulants can lead to errors. The prothrombin time can be prolonged by low fibrinogen, fibrin split products, and changes caused by leaving the tubes standing unstoppered or by an incorrect anticoagulant (e.g., EDTA).

Usually, prothrombin times are most sensitive to low levels of factor VII. This should be kept in mind when treating vitamin K deficiency or coumarin anticoagulation with vitamin K. The prothrombin time may show a rapid return to normal consistent with the short doubling time of factor VII, but the patient may have a factor X or prothrombin deficiency severe enough to cause bleeding. Evaluating prothrombin levels more directly, as with chromogenic substrates or specific immunoassays, may be more helpful in monitoring oral anticoagulant therapy, as these may provide a stronger correlation with risks of bleeding or thrombosis.[213]

Intrinsic System Screening

Partial Thromboplastin Time (PTT). *Principle:* In the activated partial thromboplastin time (PTT), the intrinsic clotting sequence is contact-activated by the addition of a finely divided surface, usually kaolin,[288] silica, or ellagic acid. Ca^{++} and a phospholipid, necessary for several of the enzymatic reactions, are added and the clotting time measured. Preincubation times vary with reagents and, in general, manufacturer's directions must be adhered to for specific products. In the absence of abnormalities in the prothrombin time or fibrinogen step, a prolonged PTT implies a deficiency of factor(s) in the intrinsic pathway.

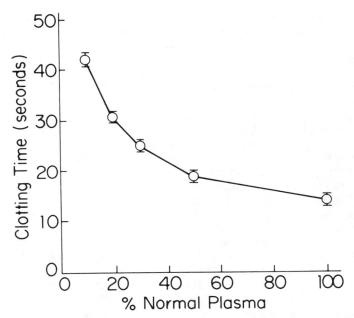

FIGURE 38. Calibration curve of the prothrombin time. Plasma deficient in factors II, VII and X, but not V and fibrinogen, is made by adsorbing pooled normal citrated plasma with ¹/₁₀ volume aluminum hydroxide suspension (Amphogel, unflavored). After 10 minutes at 37°C, the mixture is centrifuged at 3000 rpm for 20 minutes. Dilutions of normal and adsorbed plasma (10 to 100 percent) are then made. Prothrombin times are determined on each mixture and results plotted. Replicate determinations of the plasma mixture on different days will establish the sensitivity and statistical variability of the test. The curve in this figure represents a locally prepared human brain reagent as a source of tissue thromboplastin, diluted to give a 14-second normal control value (Henderson, RA, Counts, RB, with permission). Commercial thromboplastins are often less sensitive and variable in their dose-response curves.

Reagents: 0.5 percent kaolin in 20 mM imidazole buffer (pH 7.5); optimum CaCl₂, usually 30 to 35 mM; normal control plasma; phospholipid, prepared from human brain tissue[289] or may be purchased as a kit.

Procedure: 0.1 ml of plasma and 0.1 ml of phospholipid-kaolin are preincubated at 37°C for 6 minutes. 0.1 ml of CaCl₂ is added and the clotting time recorded. Perform the test in duplicate and run a normal control with each test plasma.

Calibration: Commercial phospholipid preparations vary even more than tissue thromboplastins. Calibration of the PTT should be done by each laboratory. Since factor VIII and IX deficiencies are the most common serious deficiencies in the intrinsic system, dose-response curves for the PTT should be determined by diluting pooled normal plasma with severe hemophilia A or B plasma to known levels of factor VIII or factor IX. This will define the normal, borderline, and abnormal (e.g., <30 percent factor VIII) ranges. Commercial controls often only define normal and grossly abnormal ranges, but even the shapes of dilution curves with the normal/deficient plasmas may vary with different reagents.

Interpretation. A normal value is usually 38 to 42 seconds, but can be as low as 25 seconds with some commercial reagents, especially those using ellagic acid as the activator. A more rapid time (e.g., 10 seconds shortened) may reflect partial activation (in vitro or in vivo) or simply elevated levels of factor VIII as seen in many patients with chronic inflammatory diseases. The PTT can be prolonged by a deficiency of any of the clotting factors except factors VII and XIII. The interpretation of PTT results requires clinical judgment, as the test is subject to considerable variability. Variable sensitivity to moderately low levels of factors VIII or IX limits the reliability of most commercial reagents as a screen for mild hemophilia or von Willebrand disease.[290] Influences other than clotting factor deficiencies may cause prolongations of a few to several sec. The test is affected by the kind of anticoagulant used, pH of the plasma, ratio of plasma to anticoagulant, low fibrinogen, fibrin split products, and traces of heparin. As shown in Figure 23 (Chapter 7), intrinsic clotting tests are less sensitive to heparin than the thrombin time; different commercial heparins vary, however, in their relative degree of prolongation of the PTT versus the thrombin time, and this effect is exaggerated by certain commercial PTT reagents.[279]

If an abnormally prolonged PTT persists after mixing equal volumes of normal and patient plasmas, one has presumptive evidence for inhibition. Again, sensitivity varies for the commonly use reagents. In the United States, for example, nearly half of lupus inhibitors would be missed.[291] Finally, hemophilic inhibitors may be time-dependent and may not manifest prolongations without a preincubation of up to two hours.

Recalcification Time. *Principle:* Citrated platelet-rich plasma is recalcified in a glass tube and the clotting time measured. The recalcification time is a variation of the whole blood clotting time that has been standardized to increase reproducibility. A whole blood modification is also used in some laboratories. Platelets provide the phospholipid and the glass tube provides the surface.[292]

Reagents: 30 mM $CaCl_2$; 50 mM barbital (pH 7.5); patient citrate plasma.

Procedure: Spin citrated blood at 100 g for 10 minutes for platelet-rich plasma and into a glass 10 × 75 mm test tube pipette 0.1 ml. Add 0.1 ml buffer. Incubate 1 minute at 37°C. Add 0.1 ml Ca^{++} and tip the tube in and out of a 37°C water bath to determine the time until clot formation.

Interpretation. The normal clotting time by this method is in the 100 to 150 seconds range. The test is primarily used to monitor heparin anticoagulation. It is less sensitive to low concentrations of the heparin than the PTT and can be prolonged by severe thrombocytopenia. On the other hand, it can adequately assess heparin effect and is considerably simpler and less time consuming than the PTT. One aims for a minimum heparin level which will give a recalcification time two times the patient pretreatment (baseline) recalcification time. The recalcification time is too insensitive to low clotting-factor levels to be used as a screening test for clotting-factor deficiencies. The relative sensitivities of clotting screening tests to heparin are shown in Figure 23 (Chapter 7).

Factor XIII Screening

Factor XIII Assay. *Principle:* Factor XIII forms covalent crosslinks between fibrin chains. In its absence, the fibrin clot can be dissolved by agents such as 5 M urea, which disrupts the hydrogen bonds. None of the other screening tests detect factor XIII deficiency.

Reagents: 5 M urea; bovine thrombin (200 NIH U per ml); 0.15 M NaCl; patient plasma; normal control plasma.

Procedure: 0.5 ml plasma and 0.1 ml thrombin solution are added to a 12 × 75 mm glass test tube. Incubate 30 minutes at 37°C. Remove clot with a glass rod; wash with cold saline. Place into a 12 × 755 mm tube containing 1 ml 5 M urea. The tube is left overnight at room temperature. The test is considered negative if the clot remains after 12 hours.

Interpretation. If the clot is insoluble in urea, it indicates a plasma factor XIII concentration of > 10 percent of normal. Since the minimum factor XIII level needed for normal hemostasis is around 5 percent, this simple test will reliably detect the rare individual with clinically significant factor XIII deficiency or an acquired inhibitor of normal crosslinking.[164] Specific kinetic crosslinking assays are also available, primarily for research.[56]

APPENDIX B
BLOOD COMPONENTS FOR HEMOSTASIS

The preparation of blood components for hemostasis depends upon efficient, maximal utilization of the community blood resources.[293] Increased demands on preparation of blood components have arisen with the advent of coronary bypass surgery, improved emergency care and trauma centers for severely injured patients, aggressive chemotherapy protocols for neoplasm and bone marrow transplantation, and more coordinated care, including surgeries for patients with hemophilia. One aspect of providing all of the blood component needs of a community from its volunteer blood donors is to fractionate and reconstitute blood, as summarized in Figure 39. In the Puget Sound region, for example, cryoprecipitate and platelet concentrates were made from nearly 54,000 and 66,000 units of blood, respectively, in 1981, with the total draw being 110,000 units in that year. A brief description of specific components, how they are prepared, and their general indications is provided in this appendix.

WHOLE BLOOD

Whole blood is drawn into a plastic bag containing one-tenth volume of an anticoagulant solution, citrate-phosphate-dextrose (CPD) with or without added adenine. It contains the oxygen-carrying capacity of red cells plus volume in the form of plasma. In essence, all platelets are aggregated or inactivated by the time the required hepatitis testing is completed. It can be stored up to 21 days at 4°C without loss of other clotting factor activities; up to 35 day storage

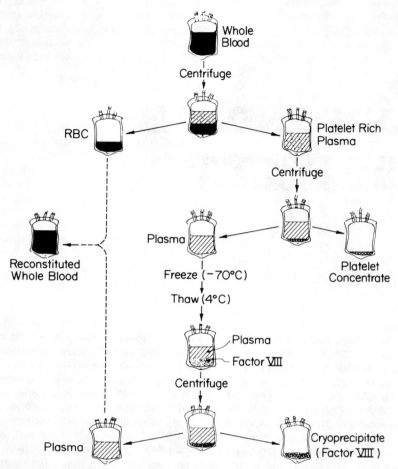

FIGURE 39. Preparation of components from whole blood. After drawing, fresh whole blood is stored at 4°C during processing and required hepatitis screening, and even if platelets are not removed during this period, whole blood becomes essentially platelet deficient as a transfusion product. Centrifugation can be used to prepare packed red blood cells with platelet-rich plasma being fractionated for other components. By centrifuging whole blood first at low speed, platelet-rich plasma can be transferred to a satellite bag and platelet concentrate prepared by subsequent higher speed centrifugation, leaving around 70 cc plasma for the platelets to be stored in. The platelet-poor plasma can be frozen and thawed to produce cryoprecipitate. The platelet-deficient, cryoprecipitate-poor plasma can then be used to reconstitute whole blood, as a separate plasma source, or as a source for concentrated factor IX, albumin, gammaglobulin, or other plasma protein fractions.

is allowed with adenine. After two to four days of storage, factors V and VIII levels fall to around 20 percent; other clotting factor activities are well maintained at three weeks. In practice, the amount of transfused factor VIII, in particular, is occasionally a concern in massively transfused patients who also have clinically significant DIC, as hemostatic levels are usually well maintained by the recipient despite "dilution."[177]

PACKED RED CELLS

This product is prepared by centrifuging whole blood after it has been drawn into a two-bag system and in a sterile manner transferring the plasma supernatant to the second bag. The red cell volume averages 200 ml with around 50 ml residual plasma and the hematocrits are near 72 percent. Packed red cells are the treatment of choice when oxygen carrying capacity is needed without a major blood volume or hemostatic factor requirement. For efficient utilization of blood components, transfusion to raise the red cell mass alone should be by packed red cells rather than by whole blood. Leukocyte-poor packed cells are indicated when patients develop routine fever or chills to packed cells; depending upon the preparative procedure, however, up to 40 percent of the volume may be lost.

PLATELET CONCENTRATES

Figure 39 summarizes the preparative steps in concentrating platelets. When the red cells are centrifuged at low speed, the smaller platelets remain in the plasma fraction and can be transferred as platelet-rich plasma to the second bag. Under a greater centrifugal force, the platelets can then be concentrated to the bottom of the second bag and the platelet-poor plasma so formed either transferred back to reconstitute whole blood or used for other purposes. In order to store platelet concentrates, 50 ml of plasma are left in the platelet bag and under special conditions (e.g., room temperature with agitation) they can remain functional for up to 48 to 72 hours after preparation.[128] They can thus be available at any time, including weekends and holidays. Because of the slight risk of isohemagglutinins which may be in high titer in a donor unit (anti-A in particular), it is preferable to use red cell type-specific preparations. For an average adult dose, 4 to 6 units are then pooled and should be kept at room temperature and transfused as soon as possible after pooling. To assess the effectiveness of transfusion, follow-up platelet counts at 1, 4, and 24 hours are important. In the absence of rapid immunologic destruction or splenomegaly, one can expect around a 10,000 per μl count increment per bag in an average adult. In the presence of significant DIC, the transfused platelets are often destroyed within the first 24 hours. Platelets are primarily indicated for bleeding in a thrombocytopenic patient (see Chapter 8). In idiopathic thrombocytopenic purpura, prophylactic support is precluded by the rapid destruction. Platelets are most often used in patients with massive transfusion[177] or marrow suppression.

CONCENTRATED FACTOR VIII

Cryoprecipitate. In 1964, Dr. Judith Pool at Stanford applied this simple concentration technique to develop a clinical concentrate of factor VIII[294] which has revolutionized the therapy of hemophilia. The procedure is summarized in Figure 39. Basically, plasma from the second bag (or third bag, if platelet concentrates have been made from the same donor unit) is rapidly frozen at − 70°C and then thawed at 4°C. Most of the plasma proteins enter solution during the thaw, but the cryoprecipitate remains as a whitish-gelatinous glob. The cryoprecipitate-poor plasma can then be returned to reconstitute whole blood or be processed further such as for albumin. The cryoprecipitate is then stored at − 20°C where it is stable for at least one year. It contains an average of 50 to 60 percent of the factor VIII and around one third of the fibrinogen which, after being dissolved in 20 ml saline per bag at 20 to 35°C, represents a four- to sixfold concentrated form. As there is little plasma in the saline-reconstituted system, the red cell type of the donor does not have to be considered. The pooled concentrate must be kept at room temperature and administered through a routine blood administration filter over 15 to 30 minutes. Longer infusions are helpful for patients with frequent allergic reactions. The usual adult dose is around 10 bags for a routine bleeding episode when each bag provides an average of 100 circulating factor VIII units. The latter number is derived from an observed yield from the process, which averages 125 units per bag and assumes an 80 percent recovery. Calculations of dosage are discussed in Chapter 10. The yield of the preparation must be known, as it can vary, and is occasionally as low as 50 units per bag in some communities. Cryoprecipitate is the treatment of choice for patients with von Willebrand disease,[155] and (when made from volunteer donor units) has the advantage of lower hepatitis risk to patients with mild factor VIII defects, in whom exposure to large numbers of donors can be limited.

Lyophilized Red Cross or Commercial Concentrates. These are more purified preparations in that they contain less fibrinogen, can be reconstituted in a smaller volume of dilutant and administered more rapidly with a syringe. They may also be stored at 4°C. As products from larger pools of donors,[155] they constitute a greater risk of hepatitis transmission, represent around one third as much preparative yield, and are frequently up to twice as expensive as cryoprecipitate. Lots have been preassayed and the number of units in each vial (e.g., 500) is printed on the label.[295]

FRESH FROZEN PLASMA

Plasma is prepared as individual units from whole blood containing an average of 250 ml, unless platelets have been taken from the same unit (in which the volume is 200 ml). Primarily for storage convenience, it is frozen either rapidly at − 70°C, which preserves the ability to make cryoprecipitate, or slowly at

−20°C. It is supplied as individual units and, once thawed, the clotting factors are stable at 4°C or room temperature for at least several hours. For thawing, room temperature and up to 37°C can be used. Each unit should be transfused over approximately one half to one hour, depending upon the previous exposure, history of allergic reactions, and cardiovascular status of the patient. Two to four units are used to treat bleeding episodes in factor IX deficiency. Plasma is also indicated for most of the other, albeit rare, congenital deficiency states and for mild factor VIII disorders when cryoprecipitate is not available. It is also indicated when immediate reversal of warfarin anticoagulation is needed. The large volumes that have to be transfused in order to significantly raise hemostatic levels of deficient factors constitute the major drawback of therapy with plasma. In massively transfused trauma or surgical patients, whole blood is certainly more convenient and essentially as effective as transfusing packed cells and plasma. The major hemostatic defect encountered in such patients is thrombocytopenia, often occurring with platelet dysfunction.[177]

COMMERCIAL FACTOR IX CONCENTRATES

Crude concentrates containing factor IX are prepared from large pools of plasma collected by plasmapheresis, usually from paid donors. In the United States, the Cohn-ethanol fractionation procedure provides the basic starting material. Two distinct techniques are used which include either (1) diethylaminoethyl (DEAE)-substituted cellulose or Sephadex, or (2) insoluble calcium salts. Prothrombin and factor X are likewise concentrated, although factor VII content is variable.[155] Because of the high risk of hepatitis transmission and an additional problem with thromboembolic complications, these concentrates should only be used for treatment of congenital deficiencies (primarily hemophilia B) when plasma will not suffice, or in investigational studies in hemophilia A patients with inhibitors.[155] For the latter indication, preparations that are partially "activated" are also being studied,[152] but the active factor(s) involved have not been identified or standardized.

ALBUMIN

Albumin comes as 5 or 25 percent solution and is used as a volume expander when saline is no longer sufficient. As a pasteurized, pooled, commercial product, there is no risk of hepatitis, but it contains no active clotting factors. The major indication is the acute need for volume expansion in the absence of bleeding, as with a sudden loss of plasma oncotic pressure. In patients with hypoalbuminemia, as in cirrhosis, nephrotic syndrome, or even the chronic stages of burn care, albumin levels are better maintained by attention to nutrition, as with hyperalimentation, than by transfusion of this expensive blood product. It can be used as a partial plasma substitute for plasmapheresis therapy, but has not proved helpful in acute management of the adult respiratory distress syndrome, or when a patient has continued active blood loss.

Whole blood, or red cells with plasma, can provide the needed oncotic pressure while supplying clotting factors, particularly in patients with massive bleeding. There has been growing awareness that the inordinate use of albumin over the past several years has largely been in clinical situations in which it is of no benefit. This has contributed to inflation of costs of health care while wasting a valuable natural resource.

REFERENCES

GENERAL REFERENCES

BLOOM, AL AND THOMAS, DP (EDS): *Haemostasis and Thrombosis.* Churchill Livingstone, Edinburgh, 1981.

COLEMAN, RW, ET AL (EDS): *Hemostasis and Thrombosis: Basic Principles and Clinical Practice.* JB Lippincott, Philadelphia, 1982.

REFERENCES CITED

1. MAJNO, G AND JORIS, I: *Endothelium: A review.* Adv Exp Med Biol, 104:169, 481, 1978.
2. SIMIONESCU, M, SIMIONESCU, N, AND PALADE, GE: *Segmental differentiations of cell junctions in the vascular endothelium.* J Cell Biol 67:863, 1975; 68:703, 1976; 79:27, 1978.
3. HARKER, LA, SCHWARTZ, SM, AND ROSS, R: *Endothelium and arteriosclerosis.* Clin Haematol 10:283, 1981.
4. HIRSCHBERG, H, BERGH, OJ, AND THORSBY, E: *Antigen presenting properties of human vascular endothelial cells.* J Exp Med 152:249, 1980.
5. WIGHT, TN: *Vessel proteoglycans and thrombogenesis.* Prog Hemostasis Thromb 5:1, 1980.

6. MONCADA, S AND VANE, JR: *Arachidonic acid metabolites and the interactions between platelets and blood-vessel walls.* N Engl J Med 300:1142, 1979.

7. LOSKUTOFF, DJ AND EDGINGTON, TS: *An inhibitor of plasminogen activator in rabbit endothelial cells.* J Biol Chem 256:4142, 1981.

8. LIEBERMAN, GE, LEWIS, GP AND PETERS, TJ: *A membrane-bound enzyme in rabbit aorta capable of inhibiting adenosine-diphosphate-induced platelet aggregation.* Lancet 2:330, 1977.

9. JOHNSON, AR AND ERDOS, EG: *Metabolism of vasoactive peptides by human endothelial cells in culture.* J Clin Invest 59:684, 1977.

10. LOLLAR, P AND OWEN, WG: *Clearance of thrombin from circulation in rabbits by high affinity binding sites on endothelium.* J Clin Invest 66:1222, 1980.

11. ESMON, CT AND OWEN, WG: *Identification of an endothelial cell cofactor for thrombin-catalyzed activation of protein C.* Proc Natl Acad Sci USA 78:2249, 1981.

12. COMP, PC AND ESMON, CT: *Generation of fibrinolytic activity by infusion of activated protein C into dogs.* J Clin Invest 68:1221, 1981.

13. HARLAN, JM AND HARKER, LA: *Hemostasis, thrombosis and thrombembolic disorders.* Med Clin North Am 65:855, 1981.

14. WHITE, JG, CLAWSON, CC, AND GERRARD, JM: *Platelet ultrastructure,* In BLOOM, AL AND THOMAS, DP (EDS): *Haemostasis and Thrombosis.* Churchill Livingstone, Edinburgh, 1981, p 22.

15. BAUMGARTNER, HR AND MUGGLI, R: *Adhesion and aggregation: Morphological demonstration and quantitation in vivo and in vitro.* In GORDON, JL (ED): *Platelets In Biology and Pathology.* Elsevier, New York, 1976, p 23.

16. ZUCKER, MB: *The functioning of blood platelets.* Sci Am 242:86, 1980.

17. BERNDT, MC AND PHILLIPS, DR: *Platelet membrane proteins: Composition and receptor function.* In GORDON, JL (ED): *Platelets in Biology and Pathology—2.* Elsevier, New York, 1981, p 43.

18. NURDEN, AT, CAEN, JP: *The different glycoprotein abnormalities in thrombasthenic and Bernard-Soulier platelets.* Sem Hematol 16:234, 1979.

19. BENNETT, JS AND VILAIRE, G: *Exposure of platelet fibrinogen receptors by ADP and epinephrine.* J Clin Invest 64:1393, 1979.

20. MARGUERIE, GA AND PLOW, EF: *Interaction of fibrinogen with its receptor: Kinetics and effect of pH and temperature.* Biochemistry 20:1074, 1981.

21. GERRARD, JM AND WHITE, JG: *Prostaglandins and thromboxanes: "middlemen" modulating platelet function in hemostasis and thrombosis.* Prog Hemostasis Thromb 4:87, 1978.

22. KAYWIN, P, ET AL: *Platelet function in essential thrombocythemia.* N Engl J Med 299:505, 1978.

23. PACKHAM, MA AND MUSTARD, JF: *Pharmacology of platelet-affecting drugs.* Circulation 62:V26, 1980.

24. LAPETINA, EG, BILLAH, MM, AND CUATRECASAS, P: *The initial action of thrombin on platelets.* J Biol Chem 256:5037, 1981.

25. NIEWIAROWSKI, S, ET AL: *Exposure of fibrinogen receptor on human platelets by proteolytic enzymes.* J Biol Chem 256:917, 1981.

26. KAPLAN, KL, ET AL: *Platelet alpha-granule proteins: Studies on release and subcellular localization.* Blood 53:604, 1979.

27. FILES, JC, ET AL: *Studies of human platelet alpha granule release in vivo.* Blood 58:607, 1981.

28. WEISS, HJ: *Congenital disorders of platelet function.* Sem Hematol 17:228, 1980.

29. HATHAWAY, DR, EATON, CR, AND ADELSTEIN, RS: *Regulation of human platelet myosin kinase by calcium-calmodulin and cyclic AMP.* In MANN, KG AND TAYLOR, FB, (EDS): *The Regulation of Coagulation.* Elsevier, New York, 1980, p 271.

30. BELL, RL AND MAJERUS, PW: *Thrombin-induced hydrolysis of phosphatidylinositol in human platelets.* J Biol Chem 255:1790, 1980.

31. GORMAN, RR, ET AL: *Analysis of biological activity of azoprostanoids in human platelets.* Fed Proc 40:1997, 1981.

32. MAJERUS, PW, ET AL: *The formation of thrombin on platelet surface.* In MANN, KG AND TAYLOR, FB (EDS): *The Regulation of Coagulation.* Elsevier, New York, 1980, p 215.

33. WALSH, PN AND, GRIFFIN, JH: *Contributions of human platelets to the proteolytic activation of blood coagulation factors XII and XI.* Blood 57:106, 1981.

34. PENINGTON, DG: *Thrombopoiesis.* In BLOOM, AL AND THOMAS, DP (EDS): *Haemostasis and Thrombosis* Churchill Livingstone, Edinburgh, 1981, p 1.

35. BURSTEIN, SA AND HARKER, LA: *Quantitative platelet disorders.* In BLOOM, AL AND THOMAS, DP (EDS): *Haemostasis and Thrombosis.* Churchill Livingstone, Edinburgh, 1981, p 279.

36. BURSTEIN, SA, ET AL: *Megakaryocytopoiesis in the mouse. Response to varying platelet demand.* J Cell Physiol 109:333, 1981.

37. HARKER, LA: *Platelet survival time: Its measurement and use.* Prog Hemostasis Thromb 4:321, 1978.

38. RITCHIE, JL, ET AL: *Indium-111 platelet imaging for detection of platelet deposition in abdominal aneurysms and prosthetic grafts.* Am J Cardiol 47:882, 1981.

39. JACKSON, CM AND NEMERSON, Y: *Blood coagulation.* Ann Rev Biochem 49:765, 1980.

40. DAVIE, EW, ET AL: *The role of serine proteases in the blood coagulation cascade.* Advan Enzymol 48:277, 1979.

41. COCHRANE, CG AND GRIFFIN, JH: *Molecular assembly in the contact phase of the Hageman factor system.* Am J Med 67:657, 1979.

42. KAPLAN, AP: *Initiation of the intrinsic coagulation and fibrinolytic pathways of man: The role of surfaces, Hageman factor, prekallikrein, high molecular weight kininogen, and factor XI.* Prog Hemostasis Thromb 4:127, 1978.

43. HEIMARK, RL, ET AL: *Surface activation of blood coagulation, fibrinolysis and kinin formation.* Nature 286:456, 1980.

44. STENFLO, J: *Vitamin K, prothrombin, and γ-carboxyglutamic acid.* Advan Enzymol 46:1, 1978.

45. HOYER, LW: *The factor VIII complex: Structure and function.* Blood 58:1, 1981.

46. BLOOM, AL: *The von Willebrand Syndrome.* Sem Hematol 17:215, 1980.

47. ZIMMERMAN, TS AND MEYER, D: *Structure and function of factor VIII/von Willebrand factor.* In BLOOM, AL, THOMAS, DP (EDS): *Haemostasis and Thrombosis.* Churchill Livingstone, Edinburgh, 1981, p 111.

48. COUNTS, RB, PASKELL, SL, AND ELGEE, SK: *Disulfide bonds and the quaternary structure of factor VIII/von Willebrand factor.* J Clin Invest 62:702, 1978.

49. SWITZER, MEP AND MCKEE, PA: *Reactions of thrombin with human factor VIII/von Willebrand factor protein.* J Biol Chem 255:10606, 1980.

50. BAJAJ, SP, RAPAPORT, SI, AND BROWN, SF: *Isolation and characterization of human factor VII.* J Biol Chem 256:253, 1981.

51. ZIMMERMAN, TS, FIERER, J, AND ROTHBERGER, H: *Blood coagulation and the inflammatory response.* Sem Hematol 14:391, 1977.

52. DAHLBACK, B: *Human coagulation factor V purification and thrombin-catalyzed activation.* J Clin Invest 66:583, 1980.

53. KATZMANN, JA, ET AL: *Isolation of functional human coagulation factor V by using a hybridoma antibody.* Proc Natl Acad Sci USA 78:162, 1981.

54. SHAPIRO, SS AND MCCORD, S: *Prothrombin.* Prog Hemostasis Thromb 4:177, 1978.

55. DOOLITTLE, RF: *Fibrinogen and fibrin.* Sci Am 245:126, 1981.

56. LORAND, L, LOSOWSKY, MS, AND MILOSZEWSKI, KJM: *Human factor XIII: Fibrin-stabilizing factor.* Prog Hemostasis Thromb 5:245-290, 1980.

57. SMITH, KJ AND THOMPSON, AR: *Labeled factor IX kinetics in patients with hemophilia-B.* Blood 58:625, 1981.

58. KISIEL, W: *Human plasma protein C: Isolation, characterization, and mechanism of activation by α-thrombin.* J Clin Invest 64:761, 1979.

59. HARPEL, P: *Blood proteolytic enzyme inhibitors: Their role in modulating blood coagulation and fibrinolytic pathways.* In COLEMAN, RW, ET AL (EDS): *Hemostasis and Thrombosis: Basic Principles and Clinical Practice.* JB Lippincott, Philadelphia, 1982, p 738.

60. ROSENBERG, RD: *Heparin-antithrombin system.* In COLEMAN, RW, ET AL (EDS): *Hemostasis and Thrombosis: Basic Principles and Clinical Practice.* JB Lippincott, Philadelphia, 1982, p 962.

61. AOKI, N: *Natural inhibitors of fibrinolysis.* Prog Cardiovasc Dis 21:267, 1979.

62. COLLEN, D: *On the regulation and control of fibrinolysis.* Thromb Haemostasis 43:77, 1980.

63. WIGGINS, RC, ET AL: *Activation of rabbit Hageman factor by homogenates of cultured rabbit endothelial cells.* J Clin Invest 65:197, 1980.

64. FRANCIS, CW, MARDER, VJ, AND BARLOW, GH: *Plasmic degradation of crosslinked fibrin: Characterization of new macromolecular soluble complexes and a model of their structure.* J Clin Invest 66:1033, 1980.

65. FOWLER, WE, ET AL: *Electron microscopy of plasmic fragments of human fibrinogen as related to trinodular structure of the intact molecule.* J Clin Invest 66:50, 1980.

66. MARCUS, AJ, ET AL: *Synthesis of prostacyclin from platelet-derived endoperoxides by cultured human endothelial cells.* J Clin Invest 66:979, 1980.

67. MOSHER, DF: *Fibronectin.* Prog Hemostasis Thromb 5:111, 1980.

68. MCEVER, RP, BAENZIGER, NL, AND MAJERUS, PW: *Isolation and quantitation of the platelet membrane glycoprotein deficient in thrombasthenia using a monoclonal hybridoma antibody.* J Clin Invest 66:1311, 1980.

69. BENNETT, JS, VILAIRE, G, AND BURCH, JW: *A role for prostaglandins and thromboxanes in the exposure of platelet fibrinogen receptors.* J Clin Invest 68:981, 1981.

70. JAFFE, EA, ET AL: *Thrombospondin is the endogenous lectin of human platelets.* Nature 295:246, 1982.

71. GINSBERG, MH, ET AL: *Thrombin increases expression of fibronectin antigen on platelet surface.* Proc Natl Acad Sci USA 77:1049, 1980.

72. DEUEL, TF, ET AL: *Platelet factor 4 is chemotactic for neutrophils and monocytes.* Proc Natl Acad Sci USA 78:4584, 1981.

73. GROTENDORST, GR, ET AL: *Attachment of smooth muscle cells to collagen and their migration toward platelet-derived growth factor.* Proc Natl Acad Sci USA 78:3669, 1981.

74. NESHEIM, ME, ET AL: *Participation of factor V_a in prothrombinase.* In MANN, KG AND TAYLOR, JR, FB, (EDS): *The Regulation of Coagulation.* Elsevier, New York, 1980, p 145.

75. SHUMAN, MA AND LEVINE, SP: *Relationship between secretion of platelet factor 4 and thrombin generation during in vitro blood clotting.* J Clin Invest 65:307, 1980.

76. KAPLAN, KL, DRILLINGS, M, AND LESZNIK, G: *Fibrinopeptide A cleavage and platelet release in whole blood in vitro.* J Clin Invest 67:1561, 1981.

77. RYBAK, ME, ET AL: *Relationship between platelet secretion and prothrombin cleavage in native whole blood.* J Clin Invest 68:405, 1981.

78. CARROLL, RC, GERRARD, JM, AND GILLIAM, JM: *Clot retraction facilitates clot lysis.* Blood 57:44, 1981.

79. GORDON, SG AND CROSS, BA: *A factor X-activating cysteine protease from malignant tissue.* J Clin Invest 67:1665, 1981.

80. EDGINGTON, TS, ET AL: *A unidirectional pathway of lymphocyte-instructed macrophage and monocyte function characterized by the generation of procoagulant monokines.* Adv Immunopathol 173, 1981.

81. SATOUCHI, K, ET AL: *Modification of the polar head group of acetyl glyceryl ether phosphorylcholine and subsequent effects upon platelet activation.* J Biol Chem 256:4425, 1981.

82. CLARK, RA, ET AL: *Myeloperoxidase-catalyzed inactivation of α_1-protease inhibitor by human neutrophils.* J Biol Chem 256:3348, 1981.

83. LONKY, SA AND WOHL, H: *Stimulation of human leukocyte elastase by platelet factor 4.* J Clin Invest 67:817, 1981.

84. NACHMAN, RL: *The platelet as an inflammatory cell.* In DE GAETANO, G AND GARATTINI, S (EDS): *Platelets.* Raven Press, New York, 1978, p 199.

85. ZIMMERMAN, TS AND KOLB, WP: *Human platelet initiated formation and uptake of the C5-9 complex of human complement.* J Clin Invest 57:203, 1976.

86. DAHLBACK, B AND STENFLO, J: *High molecular weight complex in human plasma between vitamin K-dependent protein S and complement component C4b-binding protein.* Proc Natl Acad Sci USA 78:2512, 1981.

87. MUSTARD, JF, PACKHAM, MA, AND KINLOUGH-RATHBONE, RL: *Mechanisms in thrombosis.* In BLOOM, AL AND THOMAS, DP (EDS): *Haemostasis and Thrombosis.* Churchill Livingstone, Edinburgh, 1981, p 503.

88. PRENTICE, CRM (ED): *Thrombosis.* Clin Haematol 10:259, 1981.

89. KARINO, T AND GOLDSMITH, HL: *Aggregation and adhesion of human platelets in an annular vortex distal to a tubular expansion.* Microvasc Res 17:217, 238, 1979.

90. FRY, DL: *Hemodynamic forces in atherosclerosis.* In SCHEINBERG, P (ED): *Cerebrovascular Diseases.* Raven Press, New York, 1976, p 77.

91. RATNOFF, OD: *The role of haemostatic mechanisms.* Clin Haematol 10:261, 1981.

92. SEVITT, S: *Organization of valve pocket thrombi and the anomalies of double thrombi and valve cusp involvement.* Br J Surg 61:641, 1974.

93. BECKER, CG, LEVI, R, AND ZAVECZ, J: *Induction of IgE antibodies to antigen isolated from tobacco leaves and from cigarette smoke condensate.* Am J Pathol 96:249, 1979.

94. BHAWAN, J, ET AL: *Effect of occlusion of large arteries.* Am J Pathol 88:355, 1977.

95. GINSBERG, MH AND HENSON, PM: *Enhancement of platelet response to immune complexes and IgG aggregates by lipid A-rich bacterial lipopolysaccharides.* J Exp Med 147:207, 1978.

96. MORRISON, DC AND COCHRANE, CG: *Direct evidence for Hageman factor (factor XII) activation by bacterial lipopolysaccharides (endotoxins).* J Exp Med 140:797, 1974.

97. HARKER, LA AND SLICHTER, SJ: *Platelet and fibrinogen consumption in man.* N Engl J Med 287:999, 1972.

98. ROSS, R: *Atherosclerosis: A problem of the biology of arterial wall cells and their interactions with blood components.* Arteriosclerosis 1:293, 1981.

99. HIRSH, J: *Blood tests for the diagnosis of venous and arterial thrombosis.* Blood 57:1, 1981.

100. NOSSEL, HL: *Reactive proteolysis of the fibrinogen B beta chain by thrombin and plasmin as a determinant of thrombosis.* Nature 291:165, 1981.

101. INGRAM, GIC: *Investigation of a long-standing bleeding tendency.* Br Med Bull 33:261, 1977.

102. THOMPSON, AR: *Bleeding disorders.* In EISENBERG, MS AND COPASS, MK (EDS): *Manual of Emergency Medical Therapeutics, ed 2.* WB Saunders, Philadelphia, 1982, p 77.

103. NYDEGGER, UE AND MIESCHER, PA: *Bleeding due to vascular disorders.* Sem Hematol 17:178, 1980.

104. KARPATKIN, M: *Screening tests in hemostasis.* Pediatr Clin North Am 27:831, 1980.

105. KITCHENS, CS: *The anatomic basis of purpura.* Prog Hemotasis Thromb 5:211, 1980.

106. RATNOFF, OD: *The psychogenic purpuras: A review of autoerythrocyte sensitization, autosensitization to DNA, "hysterical" and factitial bleeding, and the religious stigmata.* Sem Hematol 17:192, 1980.

107. FINCH, CA, HARKER, LA, AND COOK, JD: *Kinetics of the formed elements of human blood.* Blood 50:699, 1977.

108. SLICHTER, SJ AND HARKER, LA: *Thrombocytopenia: Mechanisms and management of defects in platelet production.* Clin Haematol 7:523, 1978.

109. APPELBAUM, FR AND FEFER, A: *The pathogenesis of aplastic anemia.* Sem Hematol 18:241, 1981.

110. OCHS, HD, ET AL: *The Wiskott-Aldrich syndrome: Studies of lymphocytes, granulocytes and platelets.* Blood 55:243, 1980.

111. THOMPSON, AR, WOOD, WG, AND STAMATOYANNOPOULOS, G: *X-linked syndrome of platelet dysfunction, thrombocytopenia and imbalanced globin chain synthesis with hemolysis.* Blood 50:303, 1977.

112. HARKER, LA, ET AL: *Mechanism of abnormal bleeding in patients undergoing cardiopulmonary bypass: Acquired transient platelet dysfunction associated with selective α-granule release.* Blood 56:824, 1980.

113. MURPHY, S AND GARDNER, FH: *Effect of storage temperature on maintenance of platelet viability—deleterious effect of refrigerated storage.* N Engl J Med 280:1094, 1969.

114. SHARP, AA: *Diagnosis and management of disseminated intravascular coagulation.* Br Med Bull 33:265, 1977.

115. RIDOLFI, RL AND BELL, WR: *Thrombotic thrombocytopenic purpura. Report of 25 cases and review of the literature.* Medicine 60:413, 1981.

116. THORSEN, CA, ET AL: *The treatment of the hemolytic-uremic syndrome with inhibitors of platelet function.* Am J Med 66:711, 1979.

117. KARPATKIN, S: *Autoimmune thrombocytopenic purpura.* Blood 56:329, 1980.

118. MCMILLAN, R: *Chronic idiopathic thrombocytopenic purpura.* N Engl J Med 304:1135, 1981.

119. NEAME, PB, AND HIRSH, J (EDS): *Disorders with increased platelet destruction.* Sem Hemosta. Thrombosis 8:75, 1982.

120. NOVAK, R AND WILIMAS, J: *Plasmapheresis in catastrophic complications of idiopathic thrombocytopenic purpura.* J Pediatr 92:434, 1978.

121. KARPATKIN, M, PORGES, RF, AND KARPATKIN, S: *Platelet counts in infants of women with autoimmune thrombocytopenia: Effects of steroid administration to the mother.* N Engl J Med 305:936, 1981.

122. VAIN, NE AND BEDROS, AA: *Treatment of isoimmune thrombocytopenia of the newborn with transfusion of maternal platelets.* Pediatrics 63:107, 1979.

123. SCHWARTZ, KA, SLICHTER, SJ, AND HARKER, LA: *Immune-mediated platelet destruction and thrombocytopenia in patients with solid tumors.* Br J Haematol 51:17, 1982.

124. MOSS, RA: *Drug-induced immune thrombocytopenia.* Am J Hematol 9:439, 1980.

125. PFUELLER, SL, HOSSEINZADEH, PK, AND FIRKIN, BG: *Quinine- and quinidine-dependent antiplatelet antibodies. Requirement of factor VIII-related antigen for platelet damage and for in vitro transformation of lymphocytes from patients with drug-induced thrombocytopenia.* J Clin Invest 67:907-910, 1981.

126. GERSTNER, JB, ET AL: *Posttransfusion purpura: Therapeutic failure of PI^{A1}-negative platelet transfusion.* Am J Hematol 6:71, 1979.

127. KELTON, JG, ET AL: *Elevated platelet-associated IgG in the thrombocytopenia of septicemia.* N Engl J Med 300:760, 1979.

128. SLICHTER, SJ AND HARKER, LA: *Preparation and storage of platelet concentrates.* Br J Haematol 34:395, 403, 1976.

129. BURSTEIN, SA, ET AL: *Immunologic stimulation of early murine hematopoiesis and its abrogation by cyclosporin A.* Blood 59:851, 1982.

130. ADAMSON, JW, ET AL: *Polycythemia vera: Stem-cell and probable clonal origin of the disease.* N Engl J Med 295:913, 1976.

131. BERK, PD, ET AL: *Increased incidence of acute leukemia in polycythemia vera associated with chlorambucil therapy.* N Engl J Med 304:441, 1981.

132. TARTAGLIA, AP, ET AL: *Aspirin and persantine do not prevent thrombotic complications in patients with polycythemia vera treated with phlebotomy.* Blood 53 (Suppl):872a, 1981.

133. SHATTIL, SJ AND BENNETT, JS: *Platelets and their membranes in hemostasis: Physiology and pathophysiology.* Ann Intern Med 94:108, 1981.

134. MALPASS, TW AND HARKER, LA: *Acquired disorders of platelet function.* Sem Hematol 17:242, 1980.

135. NURDEN, AT, ET AL: *Analysis of the glycoprotein and protein composition of Bernard-Soulier platelets by single and two-dimensional sodium dodecyl sulfate-polyacrylamide gel electrophoresis.* J Clin Invest 67:1431, 1981.

136. WEISS, HJ, ET AL: *Heterogeneity in storage pool deficiency: Studies on granule-bound substances in 18 patients including variants deficient in α-granules, platelet factor 4, β-thromboglobulin, and platelet-derived growth factor.* Blood 54:1296, 1979.

137. GERRARD, JM, ET AL: *Biochemical studies of two patients with the gray platelet syndrome. Selective deficiency of platelet alpha granules.* J Clin Invest 66:102, 1980.

138. PARETI, FI, ET AL: *Congenital deficiency of thromboxane and prostacyclin.* Lancet 1:898, 1980.

139. LAGARDE, M, ET AL: *Impairment of platelet thromboxane A_2 generation and of the platelet release reaction in two patients with congenital deficiency of platelet cyclo-oxygenase.* Br J Haematol 38:251, 1978.

140. WEISS, HJ, ET AL: *Isolated deficiency of platelet procoagulant activity.* Am J Med 67:206, 1979.

141. MILETICH, JP, ET AL: *Deficiency of factor X_a-factor V_a binding sites on the platelets of a patient with a bleeding disorder.* Blood 54:1015, 1979.

142. MEYER, D, ET AL: *Selective absence of large forms of factor VIII/von Willebrand factor in acquired von Willebrand's syndrome. Response to transfusion.* Blood 54:600, 1979.

143. SHATTIL, SJ, ET AL: *Carbenicillin and penicillin G inhibit platelet function in vitro by impairing the interaction of agonists with the platelet surface.* J Clin Invest 65:329, 1980.

144. ZAHAVI, J: EDITORIAL: *Acquired "storage pool disease" of platelets.* Thromb Hemostasis 35:501, 1976.

145. MOORE, A AND NACHMAN, RL: *Platelet Fc receptor. Increased expression in myeloproliferative disease.* J Clin Invest 67:1064, 1981.

146. COWAN, DH, GRAHAM, RC, AND BAUNACH, D: *The platelet defect in leukemia. Platelet ultrastructure, adenine nucleotide metabolism, and the release reaction.* J Clin Invest 56:188, 1975.

147. COWAN, DH: *Effect of alcoholism on hemostasis.* Sem Hematol 17:137, 1980.

148. SALZMAN, EW, ET AL: *Effect of heparin and heparin fractions on platelet aggregation.* J Clin Invest 65:64, 1980.

149. LEVINE, P: *The clinical manifestations and therapy of hemophilia A and B.* In COLEMAN, RW, ET AL (EDS): *Hemostasis and Thrombosis: Basic Principles and Clinical Practice.* JB Lippincott, Philadelphia, 1982, p 75.

150. PETTERSSON, H, ET AL: *Radiologic evaluation of prophylaxis in severe haemophilia.* Acta Paediatr Scand 70:565, 1981.

151. FEINSTEIN, DI: *Acquired inhibitors against factor VIII and other clotting proteins.* In COLEMAN, RW, ET AL (EDS): *Hemostasis and Thrombosis: Basic Principles and Clinical Practice.* JB Lippincott, Philadelphia, 1982, p 563.

152. BLOOM, AL: *Annotation: Factor VIII inhibitors revisited.* Br J Haematol 49:319, 1981.

153. HOLMBERG, L: *Prenatal diagnosis of congenital bleeding disorders.* Acta Paediatr Scand 69:809, 1980.

154. RUGGERI, ZM AND ZIMMERMAN, TS: *Variant von Willebrand's disease: Characterization of two subtypes by analysis of multimeric composition of factor VIII/von Willebrand factor in plasma and platelets.* J Clin Invest 65:1318, 1980.

155. ARONSON, DL: *Factor VIII (antihemophilic globulin); Factor IX complex.* Sem Thromb Hemostasis 6:12, 28, 1979.

156. BIGGS, R: *Recent advances in the management of haemophilia and Christmas disease.* Clin Haematol 8:95, 1979.

157. LUCAS, ON AND ALBERT, TW: *Epsilon aminocaproic acid in hemophiliacs undergoing dental extractions: A concise review.* Oral Surg 51:115, 1981.

158. HASIBA, U, ET AL: *Liver dysfunction in Pennsylvania's multitransfused hemophiliacs.* Digest Dis Sci 25:776, 1980.

159. SELIGSOHN, U: *High gene frequency of factor XI (PTA) deficiency in Ashkenazi Jews.* Blood 51:1223, 1978.

160. JACKSON, JM, MARSHALL, LR, AND HERRMANN, RP: *Passovoy factor deficiency in five Western Australian kindreds.* Pathology 13:517, 1981.

161. FAIR, DS, PLOW, EF, AND EDGINGTON, TS: *Combined functional and immunochemical analysis of normal and abnormal human factor X.* J Clin Invest 64:884, 1979.

162. SOFF, GA AND LEVIN, J: *Familial multiple coagulation factor deficiencies. I. Review of the literature: Differentiation of single hereditary disorders associated with multiple factor deficiencies from coincidental concurrence of single factor deficiency states.* Sem Thromb Hemostasis 7:112, 1981.

163. MÉNACHÉ, D: *Congenital abnormal fibrinogen.* In Ménaché, D, Surgenor, DM, Anderson, HD, (eds): *Hemophilia and Hemostasis,* Alan R Liss, New York, 1981, p 205.

164. KITCHENS, CS AND NEWCOMB, TF: *Factor XIII.* Medicine 58:413, 1979.

165. AOKI, N, ET AL: *Congenital deficiency of α-$_2$-plasmin inhibitor associated with severe hemorrhagic tendency.* J Clin Invest 63:877, 1979.

166. BLANCHARD, RA, ET AL: *Acquired vitamin K-dependent carboxylation deficiency in liver disease.* N Engl J Med 305:242, 1981.

167. GRALNICK, HR, GIVELBER, H, AND ABRAMS, E: *Dysfibrinogenemia associated with hepatoma: Increased carbohydrate content of the fibrinogen molecule.* N Engl J Med 299:221, 1978.

168. GALLOP, PM, LIAN, JB, AND HAUSCHKA, PV: *Carboxylated calcium-binding proteins and vitamin K.* N Engl J Med 302:1460, 1980.

169. HALL, HG, PAULI, RM, AND WILSON, KM: *Maternal and fetal sequelae of anticoagulation during pregnancy.* Am J Med 68:122, 1980.

170. HATHAWAY, WE AND BONNAR, J: *Perinatal Coagulation.* Grune & Stratton, New York, 1978, 235 pp.

171. HARPEL, PC: α_2-*Plasmin inhibitor and* α_2-*macroglobulin-plasmin complexes in plasma: Quantitation by an enzyme-linked differential antibody immunosorbent assay.* J Clin Invest 68:46, 1981.

172. MANT, MJ AND KING, EG: *Severe, acute disseminated intravascular coagulation: A reappraisal of its pathophysiology, clinical significance and therapy based on 47 patients.* Am J Med 67:557, 1979.

173. SAITO, H, ET AL: *Urinary excretion of Hageman factor (factor XII) and the presence of nonfunctional Hageman factor in the nephrotic syndrome.* Am J Med 70:531, 1981.

174. FURIE, B, ET AL: *Mechanism of factor X deficiency in systemic amyloidosis.* N Engl J Med 304:827, 1981.

175. THIAGARAJAN, P, SHAPIRO, SS, AND DEMARCO, L: *Monoclonal immunoglobulin M λ coagulation inhibitor with phospholipid specificity. Mechanism of a lupus anticoagulant.* J Clin Invest 66:397, 1980.

176. MUEH, JR, HERBST, KD, AND RAPAPORT, SI: *Thrombosis in patients with the lupus anticoagulant.* Ann Intern Med 92:156, 1980.

177. COUNTS, RB, ET AL: *Hemostasis in massively transfused trauma patients.* Ann Surg 190:91, 1979.

178. SILVERSTEIN, FE, FELD, AD, AND GILBERT, DA: *Upper gastrointestinal tract bleeding: Predisposing factors, diagnosis, and therapy.* Arch Interm Med 141:322, 1981.

179. BROWSE, N: *Diagnosis of deep-vein thrombosis.* Br Med Bull 34:163, 1978.

180. HULL, R, ET AL: *Clinical validity of a negative venogram in patients with clinically suspected venous thrombosis.* Circulation 64:622, 1981.

181. HANEL, KC, ET AL: *The role of two noninvasive tests in deep venous thrombosis.* Ann Surg 194:725, 1981.

182. HULL, R, ET AL: *Cost effectiveness of clinical diagnosis, venography, and noninvasive testing in patients with symptomatic deep-vein thrombosis.* N Engl J Med 304:1561, 1981.

183. WALSH, PN, STENGEL, JM, AND SHERRY, S, (EDS): *A national cooperative study: The urokinase pulmonary embolism trial.* Circulation 47 (Suppl II):7, 1973, *Urokinase-streptokinase embolism trial, phase 2.* JAMA 229:1606, 1974.

184. Sundquist, SB, et al: *Deep venous thrombosis of the arm: A study of coagulation and fibrinolysis.* Br Med J 283:265, 1981.

185. Llach, F, Papper, S, and Massry, SG: *The clinical spectrum of renal vein thrombosis: Acute and chronic.* Am J Med 69:819, 1980.

186. Grendell, JH and Ockner, RK: *Mesenteric Venous Thrombosis.* Gastroenterology 82:358, 1982.

187. Sack, GH, Levin, J, and Bell, WR: *Trousseau's syndrome and other manifestations of chronic disseminated coagulopathy in patients with neoplasms: Clinical, pathophysiologic, and therapeutic features.* Medicine 56:1, 1977.

188. Woodcock, JP: *Doppler ultrasound in clinical diagnosis.* Br Med Bull 36:243, 1980.

189. DeWood, MA, et al: *Prevalence of total coronary occlusion during the early hours of transmural myocardial infarction.* N Engl J Med 303:897, 1980.

190. Genton, E, et al: *Cerebral ischemia: The role of thrombosis and of antithrombotic therapy.* Stroke 8:150, 1977.

191. Weinfeld, FD (ed): *The national survey of stroke.* Stroke 12 (Suppl 1):1, 1981.

192. Garraway, WM, et al: *The declining incidence of stroke.* N Engl J Med 300:449, 1979.

193. Barnett, HJM: *Pathogenesis of transient ischemic attacks.* In Scheinberg, P (ed): *Cerebrovascular diseases.* Raven Press, New York, 1976.

194. Thompson, RL and Robinson, JS: *Stroke after acute myocardial infarction: Relation to infarct size.* Br Med J 2:457, 1978.

195. Salzman, EW and Merrill, EW: *Interaction of blood with artificial surfaces.* In Coleman, RW, et al (eds): *Hemostasis and Thrombosis: Basic Principles and Clinical Practice.* JB Lippincott, Philadelphia, 1982. p 931.

196. Williams, GM, et al: *Mural thrombus of the aorta. An important, frequently neglected cause of large peripheral emboli.* Ann Surg 194:737, 1981.

197. Adler, AJ, et al: *β-Thromboglobulin levels in the nephrotic syndrome.* Am J Med 69:551, 1980.

198. Vessey, MP and Mann, JI: *Female sex hormones and thrombosis. Epidemiological aspects.* Br Med Bull 34:157, 1978.

199. Bottiger, LE, et al: *Oral contraceptives and thromboembolic disease: Effects of lowering estrogen content.* Lancet 1:1097, 1980.

200. Thaler, E and Lechner, K: *Antithrombin III deficiency and Thromboembolism.* Clin Haematol 10:369, 1981.

201. Griffin, JH, et al: *Deficiency of protein C in congenital thrombotic disease.* J Clin Invest 68:1370, 1981.

202. Hedner, U and Nilsson, IM: *The role of fibrinolysis.* Clin Haematol 10:327, 1981.

203. SAKATA, Y AND AOKI, N: *Molecular abnormality of plasminogen.* J Biol Chem 255:5442, 1980.

204. KAPLAN, KL AND OWEN, J: *Plasma levels of β-thromboglobulin and platelet factor 4 as indices of platelet activation in vivo.* Blood 57:199, 1981.

205. GENTON, E: *Thrombolytic therapy of pulmonary thromboembolism.* Prog Cardiovasc Dis 21:333, 1979.

206. MARDER, VJ: *Guidelines for thrombolytic therapy of deep-vein thrombosis.* Prog Cardiovasc Dis 21:327, 1979.

207. BELL, WR AND MEEK, AG: *Guidelines for the use of thrombolytic agents.* N Engl J Med 301:1266, 1979.

208. RENTROP, P, ET AL: *Selective intracoronary thrombolysis in acute myocardial infarction and unstable angina pectoris.* Circulation 63:307, 1981.

209. SHARMA, GVRK, ET AL: *Thrombolytic therapy.* N Eng J Med 306:1268, 1982.

210. GRUNTZIG, AR, SENNING, A, AND SIEGENTHALER, WE: *Nonoperative dilatation of coronary-artery stenosis.* N Engl J Med 301:61, 1979.

211. SIMON, TL, ET AL: *Heparin pharmacokinetics: Increased requirements in pulmonary embolism.* Br J Haematol 39:111, 1978.

212. SALZMAN, EW, ET AL: *Management of heparin therapy. Controlled prospective trial.* N Engl J Med 292:1046, 1975.

213. BLANCHARD, RA, ET AL: *Plasma prothrombin and abnormal prothrombin antigen: Correlation with bleeding and thrombotic complications in patients treated with warfarin.* Blood 58 (Suppl I):231a, 1981.

214. O'REILLY, RA, ET AL: *Stereoselective interaction of phenylbutazone (with $^{12}C/^{13}C$) warfarin pseudoracemates in man.* J Clin Invest 65:746, 1980.

215. HULL, JH, ET AL: *Potential anticoagulant drug interactions in ambulatory patients.* Clin Pharmacol Ther 24:644, 1978.

216. KELTON, JG AND HIRSH, J: *Bleeding associated with antithrombotic therapy.* Sem Hematol 17:259, 1980.

217. FORFAR, JC: *A 7-year analysis of haemorrhage in patients on long-term anticoagulant treatment.* Br Heart J 42:128, 1979.

218. ANSELL, J, ET AL: *Heparin induced thrombocytopenia: A prospective study.* Thromb Haemostasis 43:61, 1980.

219. JONES, RR AND CUNNINGHAM, J: *Warfarin skin necrosis. The role of factor VII.* Br J Dermatol 100:561, 1979.

220. THOMPSON, AR AND COUNTS, RB: *Removal of heparin and protamine from plasma.* J Lab Clin Med 88:922, 1976.

221. HARTER, HR, ET AL: *Prevention of thrombosis in patients on hemodialysis by low-dose aspirin.* N Engl J Med 301:577, 1979.

222. STEELE, P, ET AL: *Effect of sulfinpyrazone on platelet survival time in patients with transient cerebral ischemic attacks.* Stroke 8:396, 1977.

223. SMITH, JB: *Dipyridamole may be more effective with sodium salicylate than with aspirin.* Am Heart J 101:686, 1981.

224. SULLIVAN, JM, HARKEN, DE, AND GORLIN, R: *Pharmacologic control of thromboembolic complications of cardiac-valve replacement.* N Engl J Med 284:1392, 1971.

225. RITCHIE, JL AND HARKER, LA: *Platelet and fibrinogen survival in coronary atherosclerosis: Response to medical and surgery therapy.* Am J Cardiol 39:595, 1977.

226. LEE, H, ET AL: *The in vitro effect of ticlopidine on fibrinogen and Factor VIII binding to human platelets.* Thromb Haemostasis 46:590, 1981.

227. GIMSON, AES, ET AL: *Prostacyclin to prevent platelet activation during charcoal haemoperfusion in fulminant hepatic failure.* Lancet 1:173, 1980.

228. MALPASS, TW, ET AL: *Prevention of acquired transient defect in platelet plug formation by infused prostacyclin.* Blood 57:736, 1981.

229. WOODS, HF, ET AL: *Prostacyclin can replace heparin in haemodialysis in dogs.* Lancet 2:1075, 1978.

230. SZCZEKLIK, A, ET AL: *Successful therapy of advanced arteriosclerosis obliterans with prostacyclin.* Lancet 1:1111, 1979.

231. MORRIS, GK AND MITCHELL, JRA: *Clinical management of venous thromboembolism.* Br Med Bull 34:169, 1978.

232. SHARMA, GVRK, BURLESON, VA, AND SASAHARA, AA: *Effect of thrombolytic therapy on pulmonary-capillary blood volume in patients with pulmonary embolism.* N Engl J Med 303:842, 1980.

233. BROWSE, NL, CLEMENSON, G, AND THOMAS, ML: *Is the postphlebitic leg always postphlebitic? Relation between phlebographic appearances of deep-vein thrombosis and late sequelae.* Br Med J 281:1167, 1980.

234. ALBRECHTSSON, U, ET AL: *Streptokinase treatment of deep venous thrombosis and the postthrombotic syndrome.* Arch Surg 116:33, 1981.

235. BARRITT, DW AND JORDAN, SC: *Anticoagulant drugs in the treatment of pulmonary embolism: A controlled trial.* Lancet 1:1309, 1960.

236. YUDELMAN, IM, AND GREENBERG, J: *Factors affecting fibrinopeptide A levels in patients with venous thromboembolism during anticoagulant therapy.* Blood 59:787, 1982.

237. HULL, R, ET AL: *Adjusted subcutaneous heparin versus warfarin sodium in the long-term treatment of venous thrombosis.* N Engl J Med 306:189, 1982.

238. HULL, R, ET AL: *Warfarin sodium versus low-dose heparin in the long-term treatment of venous thrombosis.* N Engl J Med 301:855, 1979.

239. SALZMAN, EW, ET AL: *Intraoperative external pneumatic calf compression to afford long-term prophylaxis against deep vein thrombosis in urological patients.* Surgery 87:239, 1980.

240. EDITORIAL. *Physical methods of prophylaxis against venous thrombosis.* Br Med J 282:1341, 1981.

241. KAKKAR, VV, CORRIGAN, TP, AND FOSSARD, DP: *Prevention of fatal postoperative pulmonary embolism by low doses of heparin.* Lancet 2:45, 1975.

242. BROZOVIC, M, STIRLING, Y, AND ABBOSH, J: *Plasma heparin levels after low dose subcutaneous heparin in patients undergoing hip replacement.* Br J Haematol 31:461, 1975.

243. SALZMAN, EW AND DAVIES, GC: *Prophylaxis of venous thromboembolism. Analysis of cost effectiveness.* Ann Surg 191:207, 1980.

244. HARKER, LA, THOMPSON, AR, AND HARLAN, JM: *Thrombosis: Its role and prevention in cardiovascular events—Part II. Anticoagulants and thrombolytic agents in cardiovascular disease; drugs that modify platelet function.* West J Med 134:315, 1981.

245. MITCHELL, JRA: *Anticoagulants in coronary heart disease—retrospect and prospect.* Lancet 1:257-262, 1981.

246. WINTZEN, AR, ET AL: *Risks of long-term oral anticoagulant therapy in elderly patients after myocardial infarction. Second report of the sixty-plus reinfarction study research group.* Lancet 1:64, 1982.

247. SULLIVAN, JM: EDITORIAL. *Streptokinase and myocardial infarction.* N Engl J Med 301:836, 1979.

248. ASPIRIN MYOCARDIAL INFARCTION STUDY RESEARCH GROUP: *A randomized, controlled trial of aspirin in persons recovered from myocardial infarction.* JAMA 243:661, 1980.

249. THE ANTURANE REINFARCTION TRIAL RESEARCH GROUP: *Sulfinpyrazone in the prevention of sudden death after myocardial infarction.* N Engl J Med 302:250, 1980.

250. THE PERSANTINE-ASPIRIN REINFARCTION STUDY RESEARCH GROUP: *Persantine and aspirin in coronary heart disease.* Circulation 62:449, 1980.

251. ELWOOD, PC AND SWEETNAM, PM: *Aspirin and secondary mortality after myocardial infarction.* Lancet 2:1314, 1979.

252. HINTON, RC, ET AL: *Influence of etiology of atrial fibrillation on incidence of systemic embolism.* Am J Cardiol 40:509, 1977.

253. HENRY, WL, ET AL: *Relation between echocardiographically determined left atrial size and atrial fibrillation.* Circulation 53:273, 1976.

254. FAIRFAX, AJ, LAMBERT, CD, AND LEATHAM, A: *Systemic embolism in chronic sinoatrial disorder.* N Engl J Med 295:190, 1976.

255. BROTT, WH, BOWEN, TE, AND GREEN, DC: *Dipyridamole-aspirin as thromboembolic prophylaxis in patients with aortic valve prosthesis. Prospective study with the model 2320 Starr-Edwards prosthesis.* J Thorac Cardiovasc Surg 81:632, 1981.

256. BJORK, VO AND HENZE, A: *Ten years' experience with the Bjork-Shiley tilting disc valve.* J Thorac Cardiovasc Surg 78:331, 1979.

257. OYER, PE, REITZ, BA, AND ROSSITER, SJ: *Long-term evaluation of the porcine xenograft bioprosthesis.* J Thorac Cardiovasc Surg 78:343, 1979.

258. JAMIESON, WRE, ET AL: *Embolic complications of porcine heterograft cardiac valves.* J Thorac Cardiovasc Surg 81:626, 1981.

259. DALE, ET AL: *Prevention of arterial thromboembolism with acetylsalicylic acid. A controlled clinical study in patients with aortic ball valves.* Am Heart J 94:101, 1977.

260. FELL, G, ET AL: *Ultrasonic duplex scanning for disease of the carotid artery.* Circulation 64:1191, 1981.

261. HUMPHREY, PRD AND MARSHALL, J: *Transient ischemic attacks and strokes with recovery prognosis and investigation.* Stroke 12:765, 1981.

262. UEDA, K, TOOLE, JF, AND MCHENRY, LC, JR: *Carotic and vertebrobasilar transient ischemic attacks: Clinical and angiographic correlation.* Neurology 29:1094, 1979.

263. MILLIKAN, CH AND MCDOWELL, FH: *Treatment of progressing stroke.* Stroke 12:397, 1981.

264. SANDOK, BA, ET AL: *Guidelines for the management of transient ischemic attacks.* Mayo Clin Proc 53:665, 1978.

265. FIELDS, WS, ET AL: *Controlled trial of aspirin in cerebral ischemia.* Stroke 8:308, 1977.

266. THE CANADIAN COOPERATIVE STUDY GROUP: *A randomized trial of aspirin and sulfinpyrazone in threatened stroke.* N Engl J Med 299:53, 1978.

267. SALZMAN, EW: *Surgical treatment of arterial thromboembolic disease.* In COLEMAN, RW, ET AL (EDS): *Hemostasis and Thrombosis: Basic Principles and Clinical Practice.* JB Lippincott, Philadelphia, 1982, p 1093.

268. CARUANA, JA, ET AL: *Factors that affect the outcome of peripheral arterial embolization.* Arch Surg 116:423, 1981.

269. MARTIN, M: *Thrombolytic therapy in arterial thromboembolism.* Prog Cardiovasc Dis 21:351, 1979.

270. GOHLKE, H ET AL: *Improved graft patency with anticoagulant therapy after aortocoronary bypass surgery: A prospective, randomized study.* Gohlke: *Circulation 64 (Suppl II):* 22, 1981.

271. SIBLEY, C: *Procedures used in the thrombosis and hemostasis laboratory.* In *Hematology Procedures Manual.* Bethesda: DHEW 78-8337, USPHS and CDC, 1977.

272. BULL, BS, SCHNEIDERMAN, MA, AND BRECHER, G: *Platelet counts with the Coulter counter.* Am J Clin Pathol 44:678, 1965.

273. WERTZ, RK AND TRIPLETT, D: *A review of platelet counting performance in the United States.* Am J Clin Pathol 74:575, 1980.

274. MIELKE, CH, JR, ET AL: *The standardized normal ivy bleeding time and its prolongation by aspirin.* Blood 34:204, 1969.

275. FEUSNER, JH: *Normal and abnormal bleeding times in neonates and young children utilizing a fully standardized template technic.* Am J Clin Pathol 74:73, 1980.

276. KUMAR, R, ET AL: *Clinical trial of a new bleeding-time device.* Am J Clin Pathol 70:642, 1978.

277. BUCHANAN, GR AND HOLTKAMP, CA: *Prolonged bleeding time in children and young adults with hemophilia.* Pediatrics 66:951, 1980.

278. COWAN, JF, ET AL: *An improved method for evaluation of blood coagulation in heparinized blood.* Am J Clin Pathol 75:60, 1981.

279. BRANDT, JT AND TRIPLETT, DA: *Laboratory monitoring of heparin. Effect of reagents and instruments on the activated partial thromboplastin time.* Am J Clin Pathol 76 (Suppl):530, 1981.

280. CLAUSS, A: *Gerinnungs physiologische schnell Methode zur Bestimmung des Fibrinogens.* Acta Haematol 17:237, 1957.

281. RATNOFF, OD AND MENZIE, C: *A new method for the determination of fibrinogen in small samples of plasma.* J Lab Clin Med 37:316, 1951.

282. JACOBSSON, K: *Studies on the determination of fibrinogen in human blood plasma.* Scand J Clin Lab Invest 7 (Suppl 14):3, 1955.

283. EXNER, T, ET AL: *An evaluation of currently available methods for plasma fibrinogen.* Am J Clin Pathol 71:521, 1979.

284. QUICK, AJ, STANLEY-BROWN, M, AND BANCROFT, FW: *A study of the coagulation defect in hemophilia and in jaundice.* Am J Med Sci 190:501, 1935.

285. WARE, AG AND SEEGERS, WH: *Two stage procedure for the quantitative determinant ion of prothrombin concentration.* Am J Clin Pathol 19:471, 1949.

286. OWREN, PA: *Thrombotest—A new method for controlling anticoagulant therapy.* Lancet 2:754, 1959.

287. LOELIGER, EA: *The optimal therapeutic range in oral anticoagulation history and proposal.* Thromb Haemostasis 42:1141, 1979.

288. PROCTOR, RR AND RAPAPORT, SI: *The partial thromboplastin time with kaolin—A simple screening test for first stage plasma clotting factor deficiencies.* Am J Clin Pathol 36:212, 1961.

289. BELL, WN AND ALTON, HG: *A brain extract as a substitute for platelet suspensions in thromboplastin generation test.* Nature 174:880, 1954.

290. O'BRIEN, PF, NORTH, WRS, AND INGRAM, GIC: *The diagnosis of mild haemophilia by the partial thromboplastin time test. WFH/ICTH study of the Manchester method.* Thromb Haemostasis 45:162, 1981.

291. MANNUCCI, PM, ET AL: *The varied sensitivity of partial thromboplastin and prothrombin time reagents in the demonstration of the lupus-like anticoagulant.* Scand J Haematol 22:423, 1979.

292. HUNTER, DT AND ALLENSWORTH, JL: *Improved coagulation screening by an activated recalcification test.* J Clin Pathol 20:244, 1967.

293. URBANIAK, SJ AND CASH, JD: *Blood replacement therapy.* Br Med Bull 33:273, 1977.

294. POOL, JG, HERSHGOLD, EJ, AND PAPPENHAGEN, AR: *High-potency anti-haemophilic factor concentrate prepared from cryoglobulin precipitate.* Nature 203:312, 1964.

295. ALEDORT, LM AND GOODNIGHT, SH: *Hemophilia treatment: Its relationships to blood products.* Prog Hematol 12:125, 1981.

296. HOAGLAND, HC: *Hematologic complications of cancer chemotherapy.* Sem Oncol 9:95, 1982.

297. HOUSER, OW ET AL: *Radiologic evaluation of ischemic cerebrovascular syndromes with emphasis on computed tomography.* Radiolog Clinics NA 20:123, 1982.

298. TEITEL, JM ET AL: *Studies of the prothrombin activation pathway utilizing radioimmunoassay for the F_2/F_{1+2} fragment and thrombin-antithrombin complex.* Blood 59:1086, 1982.

299. COWLEY, MJ AND GOLD, HK: *Use of intracoronary streptokinase.* Modern Concepts Cardiovas Dis 51:97, 1982.

INDEX

An *italic* number indicates a figure.
A "t" indicates a table.

Fibrinolysis—*Continued*
  plasmin and, 37-40
    plasminogen and, 35-37

GLA
  in coagulation, 25
Glycoprotein(s)
  biochemical properties of, 22-23, t
  Mechanisms of, 25, t, 26-28
  plasminogen, 35-37

HEART valve replacement
  anticoagulants and, 170
Hematoma(s)
  hemophilia and, 102-103
Hemolytic-uremic syndrome, 76
Hemophilia A and B
  arthropathy, 103, *28*
  carrier detection of, 104-105
    pregnancy and, 105
    testing for, 105, *29*
  clinical signs of, 101-104
    arthritis, 102-103, *28*
    dental problems, 103-104
    hemarthrosis, 102
    in adults, 102
    in infancy, 102
    intracranial bleeding, 103
  muscle hematomas
    nerve palsy and, 103
    treatment of, 103
    soft tissue hematomas, 103
  comparison of, 101
  degree of severity, 101-104
  inheritance of, 101, 102, *27*
  inhibitors and, 104
  prevalence of, 101
  social problems and, 104
  therapy for, 108, t
    factor IX deficiency and, 109-110
    complications of, 110
Hemorrhage
  cerebral, 139
  differential diagnosis of, 139
    CAT scan and, 139
Hemostasis
  interaction of components in, 42, *19*
  platelet count and, 80
  tests for, 175-185

Heparin
  acute arterial occlusions and, 172
  anticoagulant therapy and, 151-154
    administration of, 153
    complications associated with, 158
    dosage of, 153-154
    mechanisms of, 151, 152, *34*
    monitoring of, 153
    physiologic effect of, 151-152
    structure of, 152, *34*
    variability of response to, 153
  deep venous thrombosis and, 165
    standard dosage in, 165
  effect on screening tests, 63, *23*
  in preventive therapy, 167
    clinical studies, 167
  platelet disorders and, 97-98
  precautions in using, 167
  pulmonary embolism and, 164
Heparinization. *See* Heparin.
Hepatitis. *See* Liver disease.
Hermansky-Pudlak syndrome, 93
Homan sign, 132
Homocystinemia, 141
Hypofibrinogenemia, 113, 118

IMPEDANCE plethysmography
  accuracy of, 133
  limitations of, 133
Inhibitor(s)
  hemophilia A and, 104
Ischemic attack(s). *See also* Transient
      ischemic attack.
  aspirin and, 172
  stroke and, 171
  transient (TIA), 139
Isotopic venography
  accuracy of, 133

KALLIKREIN, 44

LEUKEMIA
  platelet disorders and, 96
Liver cells
  in coagulation, 28-29
Liver disease
  coagulation disorders and, 115-117
    bleeding management in, 117